lonely planet

Costa Rica

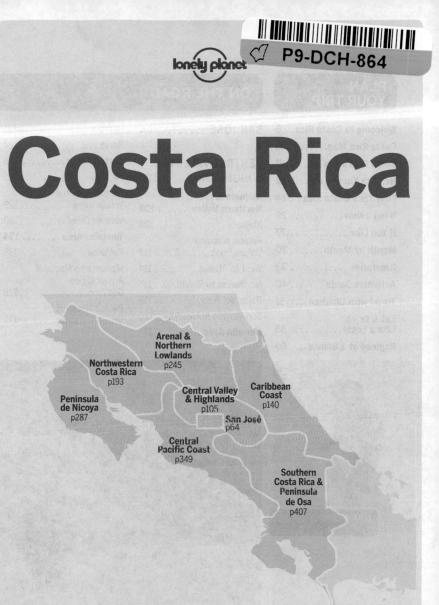

Arenal & Northern Lowlands p245

Northwestern Costa Rica p193

Península de Nicoya p287

Central Valley & Highlands p105

Caribbean Coast p140

San José p64

Central Pacific Coast p349

Southern Costa Rica & Península de Osa p407

THIS EDITION WRITTEN AND RESEARCHED BY

Wendy Yanagihara, Gregor Clark, Mara Vorhees

Contents

TANAGER P491

PLAYA AVELLANAS P312

Contents

TURRIALBA AREA P134

Contents

ON THE ROAD

CARRETAS P117

CATARATA DEL TORO P119

Contents

SPECIAL FEATURES

Welcome to Costa Rica

All trails seem to lead to waterfalls, misty crater lakes or deserted, jungle-fringed beaches. Explored by horseback, foot or kayak, Costa Rica is a tropical choose-your-own-adventure land.

The Peaceful Soul

As the eco- and adventure-tourism capital of Central America, Costa Rica has a worthy place in the cubicle daydreams of travelers around the world. With world-class infrastructure, visionary sustainability initiatives and no standing army, the country is a green, peaceful jewel of the region. Taking into account that more than a third of the land enjoys some form of environmental protection and there's greater biodiversity here than in the USA and Europe combined, it's a place that earns the superlatives.

Outdoor Adventures

Rainforest hikes and brisk high-altitude trails, rushing white-water rapids and world-class surfing: Costa Rica offers a dizzying suite of outdoor adventures. They come in every shape and size – from the squeal-inducing rush of a canopy zip line to a sun-dazed afternoon at the beach. National parks allow visitors to glimpse the seething life of the tropical rainforest; simmering volcanoes and cloud forests offer otherworldly vistas; and reliable surf breaks are suited to beginners and experts alike. Can't decide? Don't worry, you won't have to. Given the country's diminutive size, it's possible to plan a relatively short trip that includes all of the above.

The Wild Life

Such wildlife abounds in Costa Rica as to seem almost cartoonish: keel-billed toucans ogle you from treetops and scarlet macaws raucously announce their flight paths. A keen eye will discern a sloth on a branch or the eyes and snout of a caiman breaking the surface of a mangrove swamp, while alert ears will catch rustling leaves signaling a troop of white-faced capuchins or the haunting call of a howler monkey. Blue morpho butterflies flit amid orchid-festooned trees, while colorful tropical fish, sharks, rays, dolphins and whales thrive offshore – all as if in a conservationist's dream.

The Pure Life

And then there are the people. Costa Ricans, or Ticos as they prefer to call themselves, are proud of their little slice of paradise, welcoming guests to sink into the easygoing rhythms of *pura vida* (the pure life) – every bit as much a catchy motto as it is an enduring mantra. With the highest quality of life in Central America, Costa Rica's perfect waves, perfect sunsets and perfect beaches seem like the pure life indeed.

Why I Love Costa Rica

By Wendy Yanagihara, Author

Costa Rica seduced me as a young solo traveler in the mid-1990s with visions of tropical beaches, smoking volcanoes, abundant wildlife and friendly locals. I wasn't disappointed. In the intervening years, I've covered the country for Lonely Planet from Pacific to Caribbean, Nicaragua to Panama, and there's always something left to explore – the deep wilderness of Parque Internacional La Amistad, the far-flung diving paradise of Isla del Coco, the little nowhere village where I didn't have time to linger. What draws me back is not just Costa Rica's lyrical natural beauty but also the warmth of its people, who truly embody *pura vida*.

For more about our authors, see page 552

Above: Red-eyed tree frog

Costa Rica

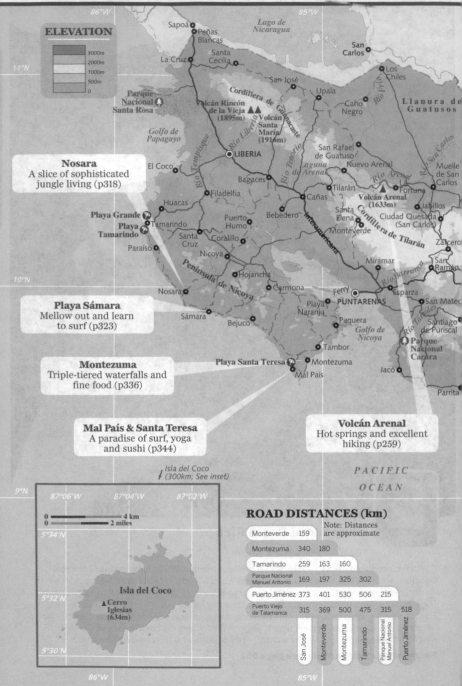

ELEVATION

3000m
2000m
1000m
500m
0

Nosara
A slice of sophisticated
jungle living (p318)

Playa Sámara
Mellow out and learn
to surf (p323)

Montezuma
Triple-tiered waterfalls and
fine food (p336)

Mal País & Santa Teresa
A paradise of surf, yoga
and sushi (p344)

Volcán Arenal
Hot springs and excellent
hiking (p259)

*Isla del Coco
(300km; See inset)*

PACIFIC

OCEAN

Isla del Coco

▲ Cerro
Iglesias
(634m)

ROAD DISTANCES (km)

Note: Distances
are approximate

	San José	Monteverde	Montezuma	Tamarindo	Parque Nacional Manuel Antonio	Puerto Jiménez
Monteverde	159					
Montezuma	340	180				
Tamarindo	259	163	160			
Parque Nacional Manuel Antonio	169	197	325	302		
Puerto Jiménez	373	401	530	506	215	
Puerto Viejo de Talamanca	315	369	500	475	315	518

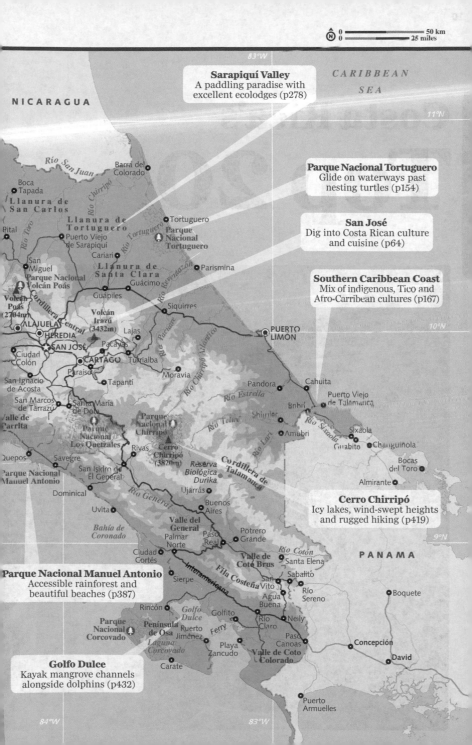

N
0
0
50 km
25 miles

CARIBBEAN
SEA

NICARAGUA

Sarapiquí Valley
A paddling paradise with
excellent ecolodges (p278)

Parque Nacional Tortuguero
Glide on waterways past
nesting turtles (p154)

San José
Dig into Costa Rican culture
and cuisine (p64)

Southern Caribbean Coast
Mix of indigenous, Tico and
Afro-Carribean cultures (p167)

Cerro Chirripó
Icy lakes, wind-swept heights
and rugged hiking (p419)

Parque Nacional Manuel Antonio
Accessible rainforest and
beautiful beaches (p387)

Golfo Dulce
Kayak mangrove channels
alongside dolphins (p432)

PANAMA

11°N

10°N

9°N

Río San Juan
Barra del
Colorado
Boca
Tapada
Llanura de
San Carlos
Pital
Río Tiro
San
Miguel
Parque Nacional
Volcán Poás
Volcán
Poás
(2704m)
Cordillera Central
ALAJUELA
HEREDIA
SAN JOSÉ
Ciudad
Colón
CARTAGO
Paraíso
San Ignacio
de Acosta
San Marcos
de Tarrazú
Santa María
de Dota
Valle de
Parrita
Quepos
Savegre
Parque Nacional
Manuel Antonio
San Isidro de
El General
Dominical
Uvita
Bahía de
Coronado
Ciudad
Cortés
Sierpe
Rincón
Parque
Nacional
Corcovado
Península
de Osa
Laguna
Corcovado
Carate
Puerto
Jiménez
Golfo
Dulce
Golfito
Ferry
Playa
Zancudo
Río
Claro
Neily
Paso
Canoas
Valle de Coto
Colorado
Puerto
Armuelles
David
Concepción
Boquete
Río Sereno
Agua
Buena
San
Vito
Sabalito
Santa Elena
Río Cotón
Valle de
Coto Brus
Potrero
Grande
Paso
Real
Palmar
Norte
Buenos
Aires
Ijarrás
Reserva
Biológica
Durika
Cerro
Chirripó
(3820m)
Parque
Nacional
Chirripó
Río General
Rivas
Parque
Nacional
Los Quetzales
Tapantí
Moravia
Turrialba
Pacayas
Lajas
Volcán
Irazú
(3432m)
Guápiles
Siquirres
Guácimo
Cariari
Puerto Viejo
de Sarapiquí
Llanura de
Santa Clara
Parismina
Río Reventazón
Río Tortuguero
Parque
Nacional
Tortuguero
Tortuguero
Llanura de
Tortuguero
Río Chirripó
Río Pacuare
Río Chirripó Atlántico
PUERTO
LIMÓN
Pandora
Cahuita
Puerto Viejo
de Talamanca
Bribrí
Shiroles
Amubri
Río Estrella
Río Telire
Río Lari
Río Sixaola
Río Yorkín
Cordillera de
Talamanca
Gnabito
Sixaola
Changuinola
Bocas
del Toro
Almirante
Fila Costeña
Interamericana
Llanura de
Tortuguero

Costa Rica's
Top 20

Bosque Nuboso Monteverde

1 A pristine expanse of virginal forest totaling 105 sq km, Monteverde Cloud Forest (p216) owes much of its impressive natural beauty to Quaker expats, who left the US in the 1950s to protest the Korean War and helped foster conservationist principles with Ticos of the region. But as fascinating as the history is, the real romance of Monteverde is in nature itself: a mysterious Neverland dripping with mist, dangling with mossy vines, sprouting with ferns and bromeliads, gushing with creeks, blooming with life and nurturing rivulets of evolution. Below left: Green-crowned brilliant hummingbird

Volcán Arenal & Hot Springs

2 While the molten night views are gone, this mighty, perfectly conical giant is still considered active and worthy of a pilgrimage. There are several beautiful trails to explore, especially the magnificent climb to Cerro Chato (p261). At its base, you are just a short drive away from the area's many hot springs. Some of these springs are free, and any local can point the way. Others are, shall we say, embellished, dressed up, luxuriated – dip your toes into the romantic Eco-Termales, for starters.

MINT IMAGES - FRANS LANTING / GETTY IMAGES ©

MACDUFF EVERTON / GETTY IMAGES ©

Montezuma

3 If you dig artsy-rootsy beach culture, enjoy rubbing shoulders with neo-Rastas and yoga freaks or have always wanted to fire twirl, study Spanish or lounge on sugar-white coves, find your way to Montezuma (p336). Strolling this intoxicating town and rugged coastline, you're never far from the rhythm of the sea. From here you'll have easy access to the famed Cabo Blanco reserve, and can take the tremendous hike to a triple-tiered waterfall. Oh, and when your stomach growls, the town has some of the best restaurants in the country.

White-Water Rafting

4 So many rivers, so little time. But the dedicated adrenaline junkie could easily cover some heart-pounding river miles in the span of a few days in this compact little country. For those without the drive to do them all, pick a river, any river: Pacuare, Reventazón, Sarapiquí. Any of the three are fun runs (though we're partial to the Pacuare, p136), with rapids ranging from Class II to Class V, and all have stretches of smooth water that allow rafters to take in the luscious jungle scenery surrounding these river gorges. Bottom: Río Sarapiquí

Parque Nacional Corcovado

5 Muddy, muggy and intense, the vast, largely untouched rainforest of Parque Nacional Corcovado (p458) is anything but a walk in the park. Here, travelers with a flexible agenda and a sturdy pair of rubber boots thrust themselves into the unknown and come out the other side with the story of a lifetime. And the further into the jungle you go, the better it gets: the country's best wildlife-watching, most desolate beaches and most vivid adventures lie down Corcovado's seldom-trodden trails. Above: Scarlet macaws

Zip Lining in the Rainforest Canopy

6 The wild-eyed, whoop-de-whoop happiness of a canopy tour is self-evident. Few things are more purely joyful than clipping into a high-speed cable that's laced above and through the teeming jungle. This is where kids become little daredevils and adults become kids. Invented in Monteverde, zip-lining outfits quickly multiplied, cropping up in all corners of Costa Rica. The best place to sample the lines is still Monteverde (p195), where the forest is alive, the mist fine and swirling, and the afterglow worth savoring. Top right: Zip line in Bosque Nuboso Monteverde

Parque Nacional Tortuguero

7 Canoeing the canals of Parque Nacional Tortuguero (p154) is a boat-borne safari, where thick jungle meets the water and you can get up close with shy caimans, river turtles, crowned night herons, monkeys and sloths. In the right season, under cover of darkness, watch the awesome, millenia-old ritual of turtles building nests and laying their eggs on the black-sand beaches. Sandwiched between extravagantly green wetlands and the wild Caribbean Sea, this is among the premier places in Costa Rica to watch wildlife.

8

9

Surfing

8 Costa Rica's best year-round surfing is on the Pacific side. It's home to a number of seaside villages where the day's agenda rarely gets more complicated than a scrupulous study of the surf report, a healthy application of sunblock and a few cold Imperials. With plenty of good breaks for beginners, and the country's most reliable rides (including what may be the world's second-longest left-hand break, in Pavones (p437), Costa Rica has inexhaustible potential for surfers. Top: Salsa Brava surf break (p176)

Mal País & Playa Santa Teresa

9 In the rugged little surf town of Mal País (p344), the sea is alive with marine wildlife and the waves are near-ideal shape, color and temperature. The hills are lush and the coastline long – both dotted with stylish boutique sleeps. And though the road in is still rutted, ending in an authentic Tico fishing hamlet where you can feel sort of like a castaway, you can still score a dinner worthy of royalty.

Wildlife-Watching

10 Monkeys, crocs, toucans and iguanas: Costa Rica's menagerie is a thrill for wildlife enthusiasts. With world-class parks, long-standing dedication to environmental protection, and mind-boggling biodiversity, the country is home to scores of rare and endangered species. Simply put, it's one of the globe's best wildlife-watching destinations. In fact, visitors hardly have to make an effort; no matter where you travel, the branches overhead are alive with critters, from lazy sloths and mischievous monkeys to a brilliant spectrum of tropical birds. Top: Emerald basilisk

Parque Nacional Manuel Antonio

11 Although droves of visitors pack Parque Nacional Manuel Antonio (p389) – the country's most popular (and smallest) national park – it remains an absolute gem. Capuchin monkeys scurry across idyllic beaches, brown pelicans dive-bomb clear waters and sloths watch over trails. It's a perfect place to introduce youngsters to the wonders of the rainforest, and splashing around in the waves you'll feel like a kid yourself. There's not much by way of privacy, but it's so lovely that you won't mind sharing.

Cerro Chirripó

12 The view of wind-swept rocks and icy lakes from the rugged peak of Cerro Chirripó (p419) – Costa Rica's highest summit – may not resemble the Costa Rica of the postcards, but the two-day hike above the clouds is one of the country's most satisfying excursions. A pre-dawn expedition rewards hardy hikers with the real prize: a chance to catch the fiery sunrise and see both the Caribbean Sea and the Pacific Ocean in a full and glorious panoramic view from 3820m high. Below: Parque Nacional Chirripó

San José

13 The heart of Tico culture lives in San José (p64), as do university students, intellectuals, artists and politicians. While not the most attractive capital in Central America, it does have some graceful neoclassical and Spanish-colonial architecture, leafy neighborhoods, museums housing pre-Columbian jade and gold, nightlife that goes on until dawn, and some of the most sophisticated restaurants in the country. Street art – of both officially sanctioned and guerrilla varieties – add unexpected pops of color and public discourse to the cityscape. Right: Barrio Amón, San José

13

14

Nosara

14 Nosara (p318) is a cocktail of international surf culture, jungled micro-climes and yoga bliss, where three stunning beaches are stitched together by a network of swerving, rutted earth roads that meander over coastal hills. Visitors can stay in the alluring surf enclave of Playa Guiones, where there are some fabulous restaurants and a drop-dead-gorgeous beach, or in Playa Pelada, which is as romantic as it is rugged and removed. One resident described the area as 'sophisticated jungle living', and who wouldn't want more of that in their life?
Left: Playa Guiones

Playa Sámara

15 Some expat residents call Playa Sámara (p323) the black hole of happiness, which has something to do with that crescent of sand spanning two rocky headlands, the opportunity to learn to surf, stand-up paddle board, surf cast or fly above migrating whales in an ultra-light, and the plethora of nearby all-natural beaches and coves. All of it is easy to access on foot or via public transportation, which is why it's becoming so popular with families, who come to enjoy Sámara's palpable ease and sense of tranquility.

Quetzal-Spotting

16 Once considered divine by pre-Columbian cultures of Central America, the strikingly beautiful resplendent quetzal was sought after for its long, iridescent-green tail feathers, which adorned the headdresses of royalty. This unusual, jewel-toned bird remains a coveted find in modern times, but now as a bucket-list sighting for bird-watchers. Fortunately, though the quetzal's conservation status is listed as near-threatened, it is commonly sighted in San Gerardo de Dota (p411) and at lodges such as Mirador de Quetzales (p414), especially during its breeding season in April and May.

Coffee Plantations of the Central Valley

17 Take a little country drive on the scenic, curvy back roads of the Central Valley, where the hillsides are a patchwork of varied agriculture and coffee shrubbery. If you're curious about that magical brew that for many makes life worth living, tour one of the coffee plantations and learn all about how Costa Rica's golden bean goes from plant to cup. A couple of the best places for a tour are Finca Cristina (p130) in the Orosi Valley and Café Britt Finca (p124) near Barva.

Paddling in the Golfo Dulce

18 Getting out in Golfo Dulce (the 'sweet gulf') brings kayakers and stand-up paddlers in contact with the abundant marine life in the bay – here dolphins play, whales breach and sparkling schools of tropical fish whiz by. You may even be graced with a visit from a surfacing sea turtle. Leaving the open water and navigating the maze of mangrove channels is another world completely, offering a chance to glide silently past herons and crested caracaras.

Sarapiquí Valley

19 Sarapiquí rose to fame as a principal port in the nefarious old days of United Fruit dominance, before it meandered into agricultural anonymity, only to be reborn as a paddler's mecca thanks to the frothing serpentine mocha magic of its namesake river. These days it's still a paddling paradise, and it's also dotted with fantastic ecolodges and private forest preserves that will educate you about pre-Columbian life, get you into that steaming, looming, muddy jungle, and get you up close to local wildlife.
Top right: Aracari

Southern Caribbean Coast

20 By day, lounge in a hammock, cruise by bike to snorkel off uncrowded beaches, hike to waterfall-fed pools and visit the remote indigenous territories of the Bribrí and Kèköldi. By night, dip into zesty Caribbean cooking and sway to reggaetón at open-air bars cooled by ocean breezes. The villages of Cahuita (p168), Puerto Viejo de Talamanca (p176) and Manzanillo (p188), all outposts of this unique mix of Afro-Caribbean, Tico and indigenous culture, are the perfect, laid-back home bases for such adventures.
Bottom right: Manzanillo

19

20

Need to Know

For more information, see Survival Guide (p505)

Currency
Costa Rican colón (₡)

Language
Spanish and English

Visas
Generally not required for stays of up to 90 days.

Money
ATMs are ubiquitous, typically dispensing colones or dollars. Credit and debit cards widely accepted, but it's sometimes cash only in more remote areas.

Cell Phones
GSM and 3G systems available, but those compatible with US plans require expensive international roaming; prepaid SIM cards are cheap and widely available.

Time
Central Standard Time (GMT/UTC minus six hours)

When to Go

Tamarindo
GO Nov–Apr

San José
GO Dec–Apr

Puerto Limón
GO Jan–Apr

Parque Nacional
Manuel Antonio
GO Dec–Feb

Puerto Jiménez
GO Feb, Mar, Sep & Oct

■ Tropical climate, rain year-round
■ Tropical climate, wet dry seasons

High Season
(Dec–Apr)

➡ 'Dry' season still sees some rain, but beach towns fill with domestic tourists.

➡ Accommodation should be booked well in advance; some places enforce two- or three-day minimum stays.

Shoulder
(May–Jul, Nov)

➡ Rain picks up and the stream of tourists starts to taper off.

➡ Roads are muddy, making off-the-beaten-track travel more challenging.

Low Season
(Aug–Oct)

➡ Rainfall is highest, but storms bring swells to the Pacific, and the best surfing conditions.

➡ Rural roads can be impassable due to river crossings.

➡ Accommodations prices lower significantly.

23

Useful Websites

Anywhere Costa Rica (www.anywherecostarica.com) Excellent overviews of local destinations; run by a tour agency that gets good reviews.

Essential Costa Rica (www.visitcostarica.com) The Costa Rica Tourism Board (ICT) website has general travel information as well as planning tips and destination details.

Tico Times (www.ticotimes.net) Costa Rica's English-language newspaper's website; its searchable archives can be helpful for trip planning around specific destinations.

Lonely Planet (www.lonelyplanet.com/costa-rica) Destination information, hotel bookings, traveller forum and more.

Important Numbers

Country code	✆506
International access code	✆011
International operator	✆00
Emergency	✆911
Costa Rica Board of Tourism	✆1-800-868-7476

Exchange Rates

Australia	A$1	₡492
Canada	C$1	₡496
Euro zone	€1	₡755
Japan	¥100	₡538
Mexico	MXN10	₡414
NZ	NZ$1	₡461
UK	£1	₡916
USA	US$1	₡550

For current exchange rates see www.xe.com.

Your Daily Costs

Budget:
Less than US$40

➡ Dorm bed: US$8–$15

➡ Eat at ubiquitous *sodas* (inexpensive eateries); shop at markets; self-cater: US$3–$7

➡ Go on DIY hikes without a guide

➡ Travel via local bus

Midrange:
US$40–$100

➡ Basic room with bathroom: US$20–$50 per day

➡ Eat at restaurants geared toward travelers for US$5–12

➡ Travel with an efficient 1st-class bus company such as Interbus

Top End:
Over US$100

➡ Luxurious beachside lodges and boutique hotels start at US$80

➡ Dine at international fusion restaurants: from US$15

➡ Hire guides for wildlife-watching excursions

➡ Take short flights; rent a 4WD for local travel

Opening Hours

Opening hours vary throughout the year. We've provided high-season opening hours; hours will generally decrease in the shoulder and low seasons.

Banks 9am to 4pm Monday to Friday, sometimes 9am to noon Saturday

Restaurants 7am to 9pm

Bars and clubs 8pm to 2am

Shops 8am to 6pm Monday to Saturday

Arriving in Costa Rica

Aeropuerto Internacional Juan Santamaria (San José; p100) Alajuela–San José buses (US$0.75) run frequently between 5am and 10pm and will drop you off anywhere along Paseo Colón. Taxis charge from US$20 to US$30 (depending on your destination in San José) and depart from the official stand; the trip takes 20 minutes to an hour. Many rental-car agencies have desks at the airport.

Getting Around

Bus Very reasonably priced, with extensive coverage of the country, though travel can be slow and some destinations have infrequent service.

Private bus For door-to-door service, private bus companies like Interbus (www.interbusonline.com) can save time by allowing you to schedule to your needs.

Car Renting a car allows you to access more remote destinations that are not served by buses, and frees you to cover as much ground as you like, within a limited time frame. Cars can be rented in most towns. Renting a 4WD vehicle is usually advantageous; avoid driving at night.

For much more on **getting around**, see p521

First Time Costa Rica

For more information, see Survival Guide (p505)

Checklist

➡ Check the validity of your passport

➡ Check visa situation and government travel advisories

➡ Organize travel insurance

➡ Check flight restrictions on luggage and camping or outdoors equipment

➡ Check your immunization history

➡ If you plan to rent a car, bring your driver's license and take note of the rules on insurance for tourists (p524)

What to Pack

➡ Swimsuit

➡ Camera

➡ Flip-flops and hiking boots

➡ Sunglasses

➡ Sunscreen – it's expensive in Costa Rica

➡ Refillable water bottle

➡ Bug repellent with DEET

➡ MP3 player

➡ Flashlight or headlamp

➡ Poncho

➡ Binoculars

➡ First-aid kit

Top Tips for Your Trip

➡ In Costa Rica, things have a way of taking longer than expected – Tico (Costa Rican) time is in effect. Make space for leisurely meals, learn to relax into delays and take these as opportunities to get to know the locals.

➡ Avoid driving at night – pedestrians, animals and huge potholes are difficult to see on Costa Rica's largely unlit roads. Also keep an eye out for impatient drivers passing slower traffic on two-lane roads.

➡ Although credit cards are widely accepted, it's often cash only in more remote areas. It's a good idea to have a stash of colones or dollars.

What to Wear

Although the coastal areas are hot and humid, calling for shorts and short sleeves, you'll want to pack a sweater and lightweight jacket for popular high-elevation destinations such as Volcán Irazú and Monteverde. If you plan to hike up Chirripó, bring lots of layers and a hat and gloves. Additionally, while hiking through the rainforest is often a hot and sweaty exercise, long sleeves and lightweight, quick-drying pants help keep the bugs away.

Sleeping

If you're visiting during high season, it's best to book ahead; this is especially important during the Christmas, New Year and Easter (Semana Santa) holidays. See p506 for more accommodations information.

➡ **Hotels** Hotels range from small, family-run affairs to boutique hotels to larger establishments, catering to all budgets and needs.

➡ **B&Bs** There's a great variety of B&Bs throughout the country, reflecting the diversity of the landscape as well as the individual proprietors.

➡ **Hostels** Costa Rica has a great bunch of hostels in the more popular locales, most providing dorms, wi-fi access, communal kitchens and excellent travel information.

Money

Both US dollars and Costa Rican colones are accepted everywhere and dispensed from ATMs across the country. You could spend US dollars only, if you're willing to accept an unfavorable, on-the-fly exchange rate; usually around ₡500 to the dollar. In US-dollar transactions the change will usually be given in colones. With the exception of the smallest towns and shops in rural areas, credit cards are accepted, as long as they have a Visa or MasterCard logo, but a processing fee of 3% to 5% is often added. Traveler's checks are difficult to exchange outside banks and big cities.

For more information, see p513.

Bargaining

In markets and in arranging informal tours or transport, it's common to haggle before settling on a price. Otherwise, expect to pay the stated price.

Tipping

Tips are uncommon and should only be given for exceptional service at top-end restaurants and hotels.

➡ **Restaurants** Your bill will usually include the 13% sales tax and a 10% service fee.

➡ **Taxis** It's optional, but many people round up to the nearest 100 colones or tip with a few coins.

➡ **Guides** It is customary to tip tour guides a few dollars per person for good service.

Language

Spanish is the national language of Costa Rica, and knowing some very basic phrases is not only courteous but also essential, particularly when navigating through rural areas. That said, a long history of North American tourists has made English the country's unofficial second language. With the exception of basic *sodas* (inexpensive eateries), local buses and shops catering exclusively to locals, travelers can expect bilingual menus, signs and brochures.

See Language (p527) for more information.

Etiquette

While Ticos are very laid-back as a people, they are also very conscientious about being *bien educado* (polite). A greeting when you make eye contact with someone, or more generally maintaining a respectful demeanor and a smile, will go a long way.

➡ **Asking for help** Say *disculpe* to get someone's attention, *perdón* to ask for an apology.

➡ **Visiting indigenous communities** Ask before taking photos, particularly of children, and dress more modestly than beachwear.

➡ **Surfing** Novices should learn the etiquette of the lineup, not drop in on other surfers and be aware of swimmers in their path.

➡ **Hitchhiking** Picking up hitchhikers in rural areas is common. If you get a ride from a local, offer a small tip.

➡ **Topless sunbathing** It isn't appropriate for women to sunbathe topless in public; respect local customs by resisting the urge.

BRIAN BAILEY / GETTY IMAGES ©

Exploring the Costa Rican forest

What's New

Costa Rica Craft Cerveza

Artisanal beers are gaining momentum in Costa Rica, a development that doubtless will thrill visiting beer aficionados. Over the last several years, craft breweries have popped up in various hot spots, bringing creative *birras* (beers) to palates thirsting for something more complex than the ubiquitous Imperial. Imagine sipping a locally brewed pineapple Hefeweizen, red ale or cacao stout at sunset – it brings a hoppy tear to our eye. (p58)

Río Perdido

A unique new resort on 600 acres of private reserve, Río Perdido is an out-of-the-way retreat, complete with canopy tour through unusual dwarf forest and thermal-spring-fed river. (p223)

Museo de Jade

Housing its spectacular collection of pre-Columbian jade and gold artifacts, this museum moved to new purpose-built digs across from the Museo Nacional in late 2014. (p67)

Big Forest Hike

Fit hikers can now do a two-day trek from Monteverde to Arenal through this iconic land of cloud forest and highland rivers. (p262)

Cinco Ceibas

This huge, new private reserve in the Valle de Sarapiquí features Costa Rica's longest boardwalk through the jungle and offers activities like horseback riding, kayaking and yoga. (p282)

Best Fest

Adding to the festival scene on the central Pacific coast, Best Fest brings international music to the Costa Ballena in early February. (p402)

Jungle Jam

This ever-growing Jacó music festival draws headliners like Slightly Stoopid and features live music that rocks the main jungle venue as well as local spots in town. (p363)

El Sótano

A fun, artsy nightspot in San José, this restored mansion has a very cool, intimate basement jazz club, plus a second stage upstairs where other live bands play. (p96)

Cartago Commuter Train

Weekday train service from San Jose's century-old Estación del Atlantico resumed in 2013. It's a convenient and fun way to travel between the two cities. (p129)

For more recommendations and reviews, see lonelyplanet.com/

If You Like...

Beaches

Playa Manuel Antonio With mischievous monkeys, perfect sand and idyllic turquoise water, this beach alone is worth the national park admission fee. (p392)

Playa Grande The nation's longest beach is good for endless strolling, and is a favorite of leatherback turtles and surfers alike. (p301)

Playa Guiones Backed by lush vegetation, these gentle waves are ideal for swimming, surfing or just frolicking. (p318)

Playa Negra This wild, pristine black-sand beach doesn't draw many surfers, making this Cahuita beach one of the best places in the country for swimming. (p168)

Parque Nacional Marino Ballena Dreaming of spending the day on an isolated desert island? The long, rugged, coconut-strewn beaches of Ballena are ideal. (p403)

White-Water Rafting & Kayaking

With Costa Rica's ample waterways and excellent operators, the opportunities for rushing down frothing white-water rapids and coasting through mangrove channels will satisfy even the greatest thirst for adventure.

Ríos Pacuare Take on exciting runs of Class II to IV rapids on the country's best white water, which is best between June and October. (p136)

Río Sarapiquí Finally making a comeback after losing its mojo due to the 2009 quake. It's a great place to learn how to kayak, as well. (p280)

Golfo Dulce Lucky kayakers can paddle out with dolphins and explore sea caves. (p432)

Canals of Tortuguero Excellent for kayaking through canals to get up close and personal with abundant birds and wildlife. (p154)

Surfing

Salsa Brava Near Puerto Viejo, this Caribbean break has the country's biggest surf and is aptly named – in December waves can get up to 7m. (p176)

Pavones One of the longest left-hand breaks on the planet draws the goofy-footed from near and far. (p437)

Dominical It's easy to see why so many foreigners show up to surf and can never can bring themselves to leave. (p396)

Playa Grande Costa Rica's most accessible, reliable break draws hordes – luckily it's so big that it never seems crowded. (p301)

Playa Hermosa Several beautiful beach breaks for the experienced, just a stone's throw from Jacó's beginner breaks and post-surf nightlife. (p370)

Playa Sámara The beach breaks here are some of the country's best for learning, but those with more experience can paddle out to reef breaks. (p323)

Bird- & Wildlife-Watching

Even for those who don't know their snowy-bellied emerald from their grey-breasted wood wren, Costa Rica's birds are a thrill.

IF YOU LIKE...VISITING INDIGENOUS COMMUNITIES

Book a homestay with Osa Wild, a tour organization that is deeply embedded in the communities of the Osa Peninsula and can arrange homestays in the rainforest. (p443)

Nearly 900 bird species – more than in the entire United States and Canada combined – fill Costa Rica's skies.

Wilson Botanical Garden About 1000m above sea level, this private reserve attracts many specialty birds of southern Costa Rica, including some very rare high-altitude species, as well as shy mammals like agoutis. (p425)

Península de Osa Although they're rare in the rest of the country, scarlet macaws frequently light up the skies around Puerto Jiménez and Parque Nacional Corcovado. (p458)

Parque Nacional Los Quetzales In a bucolic mountain setting, this park is named for its banner attraction, the flamboyantly colored ceremonial bird of the Aztecs and Maya. (p413)

Monteverde & Santa Elena Cloud Forest Reserves Keep your eyes peeled for the keel-billed toucan, three-wattled bellbirds and motmots. (p195)

Parque Nacional Tortuguero Herons, kites, ospreys, kingfishers, macaws: the bird list is a kilometer long at this wildlife-rich park. (p154)

Hiking

Rainforest trails and endless strolls down the beach, high-altitude mountains and cloud forest: the only way to see it all in Costa Rica is to don some boots and hit the trail.

Parque Nacional Chirripó Up and up and up: the trail to the very top of Costa Rica is a thrilling (chilly) adventure. (p419)

Parque Nacional Corcovado The challenging trails that go through the park are not to be trifled with, but they provide a supreme look

(Top) Bosque Nuboso Monteverde (p212)
(Bottom) White-water rafting, Río Pacuare (p136)

at the wonders of the rainforest, and offer a huge adventure. (p458)

Monteverde Cloud Forest Utterly fantastic for day hikes, a walk through cloud-forest gorges passes amazing plant and animal life. (p212)

Parque Nacional Volcán Tenorio The trails circumnavigate volcanoes and misty waterfalls. Add a few blue morpho butterflies for an ultimate sampler of Costa Rican scenery. (p221)

Volcán Barva A little tough to get to, but the trip is worth the reward: crater lakes and quiet cloud forest. (p144)

Luxury Spas & Resorts

Long gone are Costa Rica's rough-and-tumble days; nowadays travelers enjoy this country in the lap of luxury. These plush comforts are scattered throughout the country and many espouse standard-setting sustainability practices.

El Silencio Hanging at the edge of a canyon amid endless acres of rolling green, El Silencio is a sumptuous slice of Zen in the cloud forest. (p119)

La Paloma Lodge A posh delight in Costa Rica's wildest corner, this chic jungle lodge is far off the grid. (p454)

Hotel Villa Caletas Far out of the way atop a Pacific cliff, Caletas offers guests ultimate seclusion, personalized service and breathtaking Pacific sunsets. (p360)

Poás Volcano Lodge Surrounded by trails at the edge of the Poás volcano, this boutique hotel is bedecked in rough timbers and volcanic rock. (p114)

Ecolodges

Although Costa Rica's amazing natural resources are at risk of being loved to death, Costa Rica's wealth of top ecolodges give visitors an opportunity to make a minimal impact without sacrificing creature comforts.

Casa Corcovado Jungle Lodge Osa's only top-certified ecolodge is far removed from civilization, just a steamy hike from the wilds of Corcovado. (p457)

Villa Blanca Cloud Forest Hotel & Nature Reserve With the highest possible sustainability rating and a nightly movie screening, Villa Blanca offers plush, amenity-studded ecological digs. (p121)

Arenas del Mar The best ecolodge near Manuel Antonio, this architectural stunner has private Jacuzzis overlooking the coast. (p383)

San Luis Ecolodge By far the best ecolodge of the region, with the Monteverde Cloud Forest Reserve just outside the door. (p207)

Rancho Naturalista This bird-watching lodge earns lofty credits for sustainability. (p137)

Diving & Snorkeling

Although visibility varies greatly with the season and climate, Costa Rica's many small islands, caves and coastal rock formations are excellent for underwater exploration.

Isla del Coco The only truly world-class dive spot in Costa Rica, the crystal waters surrounding this offshore island are filled with marine life. A week-long liveaboard stint makes this an experts-only outing. (p439)

Isla del Caño Not ready to make the big trip out to Cocos? Caño has reliable visibility, sea turtles, barracudas and, if you're lucky, humpback whales. (p457)

Bahía Salinas These shallow waters make for fun, easy, entry-level diving and, when the weather is right, colorful snorkeling. (p242)

Playa Manzanillo In September and October this Caribbean beach has the best snorkeling in the entire country. (p344)

Fishing

Although a venture into the open sea can be a pricey proposition, Costa Rica's sportfishing is the stuff of legend.

Golfo Dulce Year after year boats leaving from little Puerto Jiménez and Golfito return with fish that challenge world records. The Pacific Gulf Stream and mineral-rich Golfo Dulce make ideal conditions. (p432)

Caño Negro An abundant population of tarpon and no-frills fishing ventures make this area a low-key option in the Caribbean. (p271)

Quepos Plenty of captains lead fishing ventures into the waters off Quepos, which offer a shot at marlin and sailfish between late December and May. (p373)

San Gerardo de Dota Trout-fishing in the clear upper regions of the Río Savegre is excellent. May and June is the time for fly-fishing in this unexpected alpine environment. (p411)

Playa Grande Epic surf casting brings in big fish from rocks that get thrashed with surf. (p301)

Month by Month

TOP EVENTS

Las Fiestas de Palmares, January

Día de los Muertos, November

Independence Day, September

Día de Juan Santamaría, April

Feria de la Mascarada, March

January

Every calendar year opens with a rush of visitors, as North American and domestic tourists flood beach towns to celebrate. January weather is ideal, with dry days and only occasional afternoon showers.

☆ Fiesta de la Santa Cruz

Held in Santa Cruz in the second week of January, this festival centers on a rodeo and bullfights. It also includes the requisite religious procession, music, dances and a beauty pageant.

☆ Jungle Jam

The biggest musical event to hit Jacó, the Jungle Jam stretches over several days and multiple venues outside of the main event, which is set in the lush tropical jungle just outside of town. Held in mid-January.

☆ Las Fiestas de Palmares

Ten days of beer drinking, horse shows and other carnival events take over the tiny town of Palmares in the second half of the month (www.fiestaspalmares.com). There's also a running of the bulls.

February

February is the perfect month to visit, with ideal weather and no holiday surcharges. The skies above the Nicoya are particularly clear, and it is the peak of turtle-nesting season.

☆ Best Fest

A young music festival that showcases up-and-coming Tico (Costa Rican) bands as well as others from elsewhere in Latin America and North America, Best Fest comes to Uvita in early February. (www.thebestfestival.com)

☆ Envision Festival

Held in Uvita in late February, this is a festival with a consciousness-raising, transformational bent, bringing together fire dancers and performance artists of all stripes, yoga, music and spiritual workshops (www.envisionfestival.com).

☆ Fiesta Cívica de Liberia

A beauty pageant and a carnival atmosphere enliven Liberia at the end of February.

March

Excellent weather continues through the early part of March, though prices shoot up at the end of the month if it corresponds with Semana Santa, the week leading up to Easter, and North American spring break.

☆ Día del Boyero

A colorful parade, held in Escazú on the second Sunday in March, honors oxcart drivers, and includes a blessing of the animals.

☆ Feria de la Mascarada

During the Feria de la Mascarada, people don massive colorful masks (some of which weigh up to 20kg) and gather to dance and parade around the town square of Barva; this event is usually held during the last week of March.

☆ Festival Imperial

A crowd of 30,000 music fans fills the La Guácima outdoor venue in Alajuela for the country's biggest rock festival. Performers recently included TV on the Radio, Skrillex, Björk, LMFAO and the Flaming Lips. Loosely scheduled every two years in March or April.

April

Easter and the preceding week, Semana Santa, can fall early in April, which makes beaches crowded and prices spike. Nicoya and Guanacaste are very dry and hot, with very little rain.

☆ Día de Juan Santamaría

Commemorating Costa Rica's national hero, who died in battle against American colonist William Walker's troops in 1856, this week-long celebration includes parades, concerts and dances. The most festive celebrations take place on April 11 in Alajuela, Santamaría's proud hometown.

✯ Festival Internacional de las Artes (FIA)

This multidisciplinary arts festival (www.festivalde lasartes.go.cr in Spanish) descends upon venues all across San José during the first half of April. The festival has been running since 1989.

May

Wetter weather patterns begin to sweep across the country in May, which begins the county's low season and discounted prices. Good bargains and reasonably good weather make it an excellent season for budget travel.

✗ Día de San Isidro Labrador

An opportunity to taste the bounty of the surrounding region (wherever you are in Costa Rica, but particularly in any town or village called San Isidro), this is one of the nation's largest agricultural fairs. It takes place on May 15.

June

The Pacific coast gets fairly wet during June, though this makes for good surfing swells. The beginning of the so-called green season, this time of year has lots of discounted rates.

✯ Día de San Pedro & San Pablo

Celebrations with religious processions are held in villages of the same name on June 29.

July

July is mostly wet, particularly on the Caribbean coast, but the month also occasionally enjoys a brief dry period that Ticos call *veranillo*, or summer. Expect rain, particularly late in the day.

✯ Fiesta de la Virgen del Mar

Held in Puntarenas and Playa del Coco, this party involves colorful, brightly lit regattas and boat parades. It's held on the Saturday closest to 16 July.

✯ Día de Guanacaste

Celebrates the annexation of Guanacaste from Nicaragua. There's also a rodeo in Santa Cruz. It takes place on July 25.

August

The middle of the rainy season doesn't mean that mornings aren't bright and sunny. Travelers who don't mind some rain will find great hotel and tour deals, and surfers will find storm-generated swells.

✯ La Virgen de los Ángeles

The patron saint of Costa Rica is celebrated with an important religious procession from San José to Cartago on August 2.

September

The Osa peninsula gets utterly soaked during September, which is in the heart of the rainy season and what Ticos refer to as *temporales del Pacífico* – the cheapest time of year to visit the Pacific side.

✯ Costa Rican Independence Day

Independence Day is a fun party throughout Costa

Rica. The center of the action is the relay race that passes a 'Freedom Torch' from Guatemala to Costa Rica. The torch arrives at Cartago on the evening of the 14th, when the nation breaks into the national anthem.

October

Many roads become impassable as rivers swell and rain continues to fall in one of the wettest months in Costa Rica. Many of the lodges and tour operators are closed until November.

✺ Día de la Raza

Columbus' historic landing on Isla Uvita has traditionally inspired a small carnival in Puerto Limón on October 12, with street parades, live music and dancing.

November

The weather can go either way in November. Access to Corcovado national park is very difficult after several continuous months of rain, though by the month's end the skies clear up.

✺ Día de los Muertos

On November 2 families visit graveyards and have religious parades in honor of the dead – a lovely and picturesque festival.

December

Although the beginning of the month is a great time to visit Costa Rica, with clearer skies and relatively uncrowded attractions, things really ramp up toward Christmas; travelers need to make reservations well in advance.

✺ Las Fiestas de Zapote

If you're around San José between Christmas and New Year's Eve, this week-long celebration of all things Costa Rican (namely, rodeos, cowboys, carnival rides, fried food and booze) annually draws tens of thousands of Ticos to the bullring in the suburb of Zapote.

✺ Fiesta de los Diablitos

Men wear carved wooden devil masks and burlap sacks and, after roaming from house to house for free booze, re-enact the fight between the indigenous people and the Spanish. Spoiler alert: in this one, the Spanish lose. The festival is held in Boruca from December 30 to January 2 and in Curré from February 5 to February 8.

Itineraries

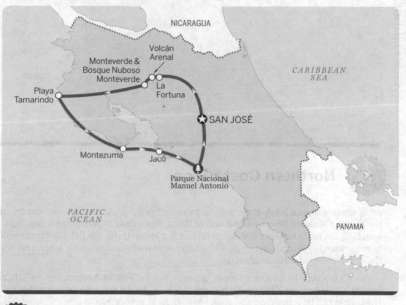

2 WEEKS Essential Costa Rica

This is the trip you've been dreaming about: a romp through paradise with seething volcanoes, tropical parks and ghostly cloud forests.

From **San José**, beeline north to **La Fortuna**. After hiking the forest on the flanks of **Volcán Arenal**, soak in the area's hot springs. Then catch a boat across Laguna de Arenal, and a bus to **Monteverde**, where you might encounter the elusive quetzal on a stroll through the **Bosque Nuboso Monteverde**.

Next: beach time. Head west to the biggest party town in Nicoya, **Playa Tamarindo**, and enjoy the ideal surf and rowdy nightlife.

Continuing south, linger a bit in chilled-out **Montezuma**, where you can connect via jet boat to **Jacó**, another town with equal affection for surfing and partying. Spend half a day busing to Quepos, the gateway to **Parque Nacional Manuel Antonio**. A full day in the park starts with some jungle hikes and wildlife-watching and ends with a picnic and a dip in the park's perfect waters.

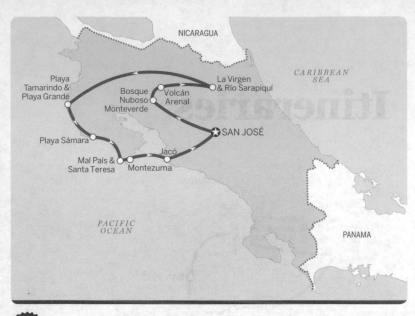

2 WEEKS Northern Costa Rica

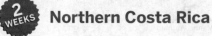

After landing in **San José**, make for the hanging bridges and breathtaking scenery of the **Bosque Nuboso Monteverde**, one of Costa Rica's most iconic destinations. Just watching the mists roll over the dense forests is a subtle thrill, but the add-ons around here sweeten the deal: dizzying zip lines and aerial walkways, excellent hikes and one of the country's best butterfly gardens.

After a few days in the cloud forest, hop on a bus for **Volcán Arenal**, the country's biggest active volcano. Though it's not spitting lava, Arenal remains an incredible sight. Hikes here can be complemented with soaks in local hot springs.

Now, leave the tourists behind and head into the real-life Costa Rica of the northern lowlands. Inviting ecolodges and homestays have sprung up in this historically farm-based economy. After a couple days of connecting with easygoing Ticos, make for **La Virgen** to raft the white water of **Río Sarapiquí**.

At least a few days in Costa Rica must be devoted to the beach. First stop: **Playa Tamarindo**, to party with other travelers, sample some of the country's best international cuisine and learn to surf. Visit during turtle season and **Playa Grande** will be hosting a horde of nesting leatherbacks; if not, the human action on the beach is an equally illuminating mating ritual.

Stay put or string together a series of southbound buses to visit one heavenly beach after the next: there's stunning sand and contemporary cuisine at **Playa Sámara** or legendary swells at **Mal País** and **Santa Teresa**. Any would be excellent places to swim in warm Pacific waters. Wind down your trip with some yoga in **Montezuma** and head back to San José via **Jacó** by jet boat and bus.

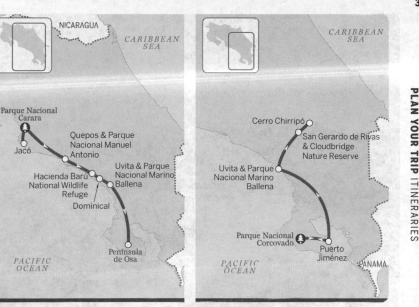

 ## Pacific Coast Explorer

2 WEEKS

Kick things off in **Jacó**, a scrappy, if relatively cosmopolitan, enclave of fine dining and raging nightlife. In case you need a reminder that you're still in Costa Rica, head north up the coast to **Parque Nacional Carara**, home to enchanting scarlet macaws.

Heading south along the coast, drop in on **Quepos**, a convenient base for the country's most popular national park, **Parque Nacional Manuel Antonio**. Here, the rainforest sweeps down to meet the sea, providing refuge for rare animals, including the endangered Central American squirrel monkey.

Continue on south, stopping to sample *ceviche* (seafood marinated in lemon or lime juice, garlic and seasonings) at roadside stands, and visit **Hacienda Barú National Wildlife Refuge** for sloth-spotting, or keep heading south to **Dominical** in search of more waves. For deserted beach wandering continue on to **Uvita**, where you can look for whales spouting offshore at **Parque Nacional Marino Ballena**.

From Uvita, you can move south to the far-flung **Península de Osa**.

Southern Costa Rica & Osa

2–3 WEEKS

Hands down the best itinerary for adventurers, this is the wilder side of Costa Rica. Either head down the Pacific coast or fly into **Puerto Jiménez**, gateway to Osa. Here, you can spend a day or so kayaking the mangroves and soaking up the charm.

The undisputed highlight of the Osa is **Parque Nacional Corcovado**, the crown jewel of the country's national parks. Spend a few days exploring jungle and beach trails with a local guide, whose expert eyes will spot tapirs and rare birds; trekkers willing to get down and dirty can tackle a through-hike of the park.

Return to Puerto Jiménez and travel up the Pacific Costanera Sur to **Uvita**, where you can wander empty beaches, surf and snorkel at **Parque Nacional Marino Ballena**.

Then it's off to the mountains. Link together buses for **San Gerardo de Rivas**, where you can spend a day acclimating to the altitude and hiking through the **Cloudbridge Nature Reserve**. End the trip with an exhilarating two-day adventure to the top of **Cerro Chirripó**, Costa Rica's highest peak.

AVENIDA 10

Above: Volcán Poás
(p112)

Left: San José (p64)

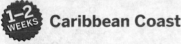 Caribbean Coast

1-2 WEEKS

Latin beats change to Caribbean rhythms as you explore the 'other Costa Rica.' Hop on the first eastbound bus out of **San José** for Cahuita, capital of Afro-Caribbean culture and gateway to **Parque Nacional Cahuita**. Decompress in this mellow village before moving on to **Puerto Viejo de Talamanca**, the Caribbean's center for nightlife, cuisine and all-round positive vibes.

From Puerto Viejo, rent a bicycle and ride to Manzanillo, jumping-off point for snorkeling, kayaking and hiking in **Refugio Nacional de Vida Silvestre Gandoca-Manzanillo**.

To fall further off the map, grab a boat from **Moín** to travel up the canal-ribboned coast to **Tortuguero**, where you can watch nesting green and leatherback turtles. But the real reason you're here is to canoe the mangrove-lined canals of **Parque Nacional Tortuguero**, Costa Rica's mini-Amazon.

After spotting your fill of wildlife, head back to San José via water taxi and bus through **Cariari** and **Guápiles**.

Central Valley

1 WEEK

The central valley circuit is about sleeping volcanoes, strong cups of coffee and the spiritual core of the country – all sans the madding crowds.

Begin the scenic route of volcanoes by hiking the volcanic lakes and trails surrounding **Volcán Poás**, one of Costa Rica's most accessible glimpses into an active crater. Move on to **Monumento Nacional Arqueológico Guayabo**, the country's only significant archaeological site, protecting ancient petroglyphs and aqueducts.

With the geological and archaeological wonders complete, raft the white water of the **Río Pacuare**, one of the country's best white-water runs and some of Central America's most scenic rafting.

Finally, swing south into the heart of the **Valle de Orosi**, Costa Rican coffee country, and take the caffeinated 32km loop passing the country's oldest church and endless green hills. End this short circuit on a spiritual note at the country's grandest colonial temple, the Basílica de Nuestra Señora de Los Ángeles in **Cartago**.

Off the Beaten Track: Costa Rica

BOCA TAPADA AREA

Travel through a Tico Costa Rican heartland of pineapple plantations to discover the pristine rainforest of Refugio Nacional de Vida Silvestre Mixto Maquenque. (p277)

LA ENSENADA LODGE & WILDLIFE REFUGE

A rustic getaway on a working ranch and national wildlife refuge. Explore mangroves by boat or tropical dry forest on horseback, or just relax and enjoy the scenery. (p219)

PLAYA PALO SECO

A dirt road through palm plantations winds up at a 6km finger of isolated black-sand beach, and nearby mangroves to explore by boat. (p376)

MATAPALO

Not far off the Costanera Sur, but surprisingly lightly trodden, Matapalo doesn't have much more than kilometers of gray-sand beach and wild waves for the more experienced surfing set. (p395)

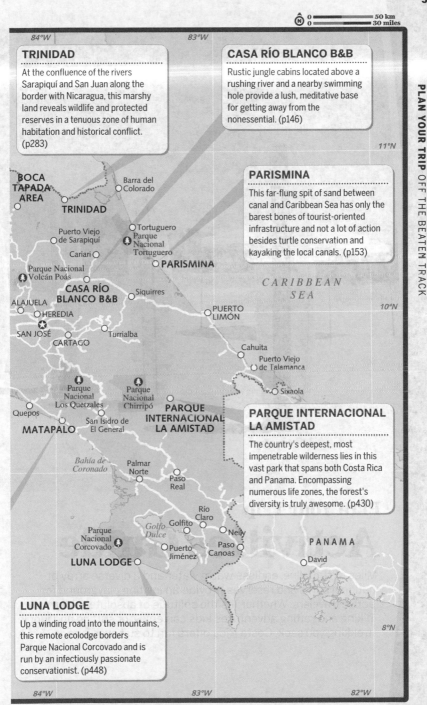

0 — 50 km
0 — 30 miles

TRINIDAD

At the confluence of the rivers Sarapiquí and San Juan along the border with Nicaragua, this marshy land reveals wildlife and protected reserves in a tenuous zone of human habitation and historical conflict. (p283)

CASA RÍO BLANCO B&B

Rustic jungle cabins located above a rushing river and a nearby swimming hole provide a lush, meditative base for getting away from the nonessential. (p146)

PARISMINA

This far-flung spit of sand between canal and Caribbean Sea has only the barest bones of tourist-oriented infrastructure and not a lot of action besides turtle conservation and kayaking the local canals. (p153)

PARQUE INTERNACIONAL LA AMISTAD

The country's deepest, most impenetrable wilderness lies in this vast park that spans both Costa Rica and Panama. Encompassing numerous life zones, the forest's diversity is truly awesome. (p430)

LUNA LODGE

Up a winding road into the mountains, this remote ecolodge borders Parque Nacional Corcovado and is run by an infectiously passionate conservationist. (p448)

Map labels:

84°W 83°W 82°W

11°N 10°N 8°N

BOCA TAPADA AREA
Barra del Colorado
TRINIDAD
Puerto Viejo de Sarapiquí
Tortuguero
Parque Nacional Tortuguero
Cariari
PARISMINA
Parque Nacional Volcán Poás
CASA RÍO BLANCO B&B
Siquirres
ALAJUELA
HEREDIA
PUERTO LIMÓN
SAN JOSÉ
CARTAGO
Turrialba
Cahuita
Puerto Viejo de Talamanca
Sixaola
Parque Nacional Los Quetzales
Parque Nacional Chirripó
Quepos
San Isidro de El General
MATAPALO
PARQUE INTERNACIONAL LA AMISTAD
Bahía de Coronado
Palmar Norte
Paso Real
Río Claro
Golfito
Neily
Golfo Dulce
Paso Canoas
Parque Nacional Corcovado
Puerto Jiménez
PANAMA
David
LUNA LODGE

CARIBBEAN SEA

Jacó (p360)

Plan Your Trip
Activities Guide

Miles of shoreline, endless warm water and a diverse array of national parks and reserves provide an inviting playground for active travelers. Whether it's the solitude of absolute wilderness, hiking and rafting adventures kids can enjoy, or surfing and jungle trekking you seek, Costa Rica offers fun to suit everyone.

Best Activities

Best Beginner Surf Beaches

➡ Playa Tamarindo (p303)

➡ Playa Jacó (p362)

➡ Playa Sámara (p323)

Best Epic Hikes

➡ Cerro Chirripó (p419)

➡ Corcovado Through-Hike (p458)

Best Dive Sites

➡ Isla del Coco (p439)

➡ Isla del Caño (p457)

Best Wildlife-Watching

➡ Parque Nacional Corcovado (p458)

Best Rainforest for Families

➡ Parque Nacional Manuel Antonio (p389)

Best White Water

➡ Río Pacuare (p136)

Hiking & Trekking

Hiking opportunities around Costa Rica are seemingly endless. With extensive mountains, canyons, dense jungles, cloud forests and two coastlines, this is one of Central America's best and most varied hiking destinations.

Hikes come in an enormous spectrum of difficulty. At tourist-packed destinations like Monteverde, trails are clearly marked and sometimes paved. This is fantastic if you're traveling with kids or aren't confident about route-finding. For long-distance trekking, there are lots more options in the remote corners of the country.

Opportunities for moderate hiking are typically plentiful in most parks and reserves. For the most part, you can rely on signs and maps for orientation, though it helps to have some navigational experience. Good hiking shoes, plenty of water and confidence in your abilities will enable you to combine several shorter day hikes into a lengthier expedition. Tourist-information centers at park entrances are great resources for planning your intended route.

If you're properly equipped with camping essentials, the country's longer and more arduous multiday treks are at your disposal. Costa Rica's top challenges are scaling Cerro Chirripó, traversing Corcovado and penetrating deep into the heart of La Amistad. While Chirripó can be undertaken independently, local guides are required for much of La Amistad and for all of Corcovado.

How to Make it Happen

If you're planning your trip around long-distance trekking, it's best to visit during the dry season (December to April). Outside this window, rivers become impassable and trails are prone to flooding. In the highlands, journeys become more taxing in the rain, and the bare landscape offers little protection.

Costa Rica is hot and humid: hiking in these tropical conditions, harassed by mosquitoes, can really take it out of you. Remember to wear light clothing that will dry quickly. Overheating and dehydration are the main sources of misery on the trails, so be sure to bring plenty of water and take rest stops. Make sure you have sturdy, comfortable footwear and a lightweight rain jacket.

Unfortunately, readers occasionally write in with horror stories of getting robbed while on some of the more remote hiking trails. Although this happens rarely, it is always advisable to hike in a group for added safety. Hiring a local guide is another excellent way to enhance your experience, avoid getting lost and learn an enormous amount about the flora and fauna around you.

Some of the local park offices have maps, but this is the exception rather than the rule. If you are planning to do

THESE BOOTS WERE MADE FOR WALKING

Some suggestions for sturdier tropical-hiking footwear, to supplement the flip-flops.

Rubber boots Pick these up at any hardware store (approximately US$6). They're indestructible, protect you from creepy-crawlies and can be hosed off at day's end. Downsides: not super-comfortable, and if they fill up with water or mud, your feet are wet for the rest of the day.

Sport sandals Chacos, Tevas or Crocs are great for rafting and river crossings. However, they offer minimal foot protection.

Waterproof hiking boots If you are planning a serious trek in the mountains, best to invest in a pair of solid, waterproof hiking boots.

Río Savegre

independent hiking on long-distance trails, be sure to purchase your maps in San José in advance.

A number of companies offer trekking tours in Costa Rica:

➜ **Osa Wild** (p443) Offers a huge variety of hikes in the Osa in partnership with a sustainability organization.

➜ **Costa Rica Trekking Adventures** (p421) Offers multiday treks in Chirripó, Corcovado and Tapanti.

➜ **Osa Aventura** (☑2735-5670; www.osaaventura.com) Specializes in treks through Corcovado.

Surfing

Point and beach breaks, lefts and rights, reefs and river mouths, warm water and year-round waves make Costa Rica a favorite surfing destination. For the most part, the Pacific coast has bigger swells and better waves during the latter part of the rainy season, but the Caribbean cooks from November to May. Basically, there is a wave waiting to be surfed at any time of the year.

For the uninitiated, lessons are available at almost all of the major surfing destina-

tions – especially popular towns include Jacó, Dominical and Tamarindo on the Pacific coast. Surfing definitely has a steep learning curve, and can be potentially dangerous if the currents are strong. With that said, the sport is accessible to children and novices, though it's advisable to start with a lesson and always inquire locally about conditions before you paddle out.

Throughout Costa Rica, waves are big (though not massive), and many offer hollow and fast rides that are perfect for intermediates. As a bonus, Costa Rica is one of the few places on the planet where you can surf two different oceans in the same day. Advanced surfers with plenty of experience can contend with some of the world's most famous waves. The top ones include Ollie's Point and Witch's Rock, off the coast of Parque Nacional Santa Rosa; Mal País and Santa Teresa, with a groovy scene to match the powerful waves; Playa Hermosa, whose bigger, faster curls attract a more determined (and experienced) crew of wavechasers; Pavones, a legendary long left across the sweet waters of the Golfo Dulce; and the infamous Salsa Brava in Puerto Viejo de Talamanca, for experts only.

Surfer's Map

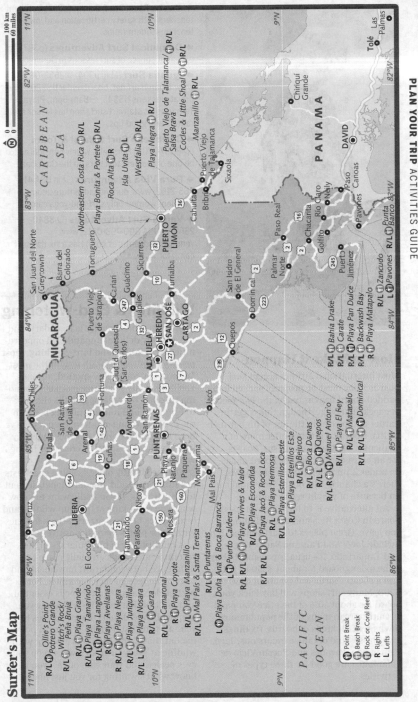

100 km
60 miles

CARIBBEAN SEA

Las Palmas
Tolé
Chiriquí Grande
PANAMA
DAVID
Paso Canoas
Nelly
Río Claro
Golfito
Puerto Jiménez
Punta Banco R/L
Pavones R/L
Zancudo R/L L

Northeastern Costa Rica R/L
Playa Bonita & Portete R/L
Roca Alta R
Isla Uvita L
Westfalia R/L
Playa Negra R/L
Puerto Viejo de Talamanca/ R/L
Salsa Brava
Cocles & Little Shoal R/L
Manzanillo R/L
Puerto Viejo de Talamanca
Bribrí
Sixaola

Cahuita
PUERTO LIMÓN
36
Sicuirres
32
Guácimo
10
Turrialba
CARTAGO
2
San Isidro de El General
Dominical 2
223
Palmar Norte
Paso Real
16
Chacarita
2
245

San Juan del Norte (Greytown)
Barra del Colorado
Tortuguero
Puerto Viejo de Sarapiquí
Cariari
247
Guápiles
4
HEREDIA
32
SAN JOSÉ
27
ALAJUELA
1
3
7
12
Quepos
235
235

NICARAGUA
Los Chiles
Upala
San Rafael de Guatuso
4
35
La Fortuna
6
19
Ciudad Quesada (San Carlos)
1
Arenal
142
Cañas
18
Monteverde
1
San Ramón
Jacó

La Cruz
164
1
LIBERIA
21
El Coco
Nicoya
160
Paraíso
21
150
Tamarindo
Nosara
Paquera
Montezuma
Mal País
PUNTARENAS
Playa Naranjo

R/L Bahía Drake
R/L Carate
R/L Playa Pan Dulce
R/L Backwash Bay
R Playa Matapalo

R/L Playa El Fey
R/L Matapalo
R/L Dominical

R Manuel Anton'o
R/L Quepos
R/L L
R/L Boca Damas
R/L Boca Damas

R/L Bejuco
R/L Playa Hermosa
R/L Playa Esterillos Oeste
R/L Playa Esterillos Este
R/L Playa Escondida
R/L Playa Jacó & Roca Loca
R/L Playa Tivives & Valor
L Puerto Caldera
L Playa Doña Ana & Boca Barranca
R/L Puntarenas
R/L Mal País & Santa Teresa
R/L Playa Manzanillo
R Playa Coyote
R/L Camaronal
R/L Garza
R/L Playa Nosara
R/L L Playa Junquillal
R Playa Negra
R Playa Avellanas
R R/L Playa Langosta
R/L Playa Tamarindo
R/L Playa Grande
R/L Witch's Rock/ Peña Bruja
R/L Potrero Grande
R/L Ollie's Point/

Point Break
Beach Break
Rock or Coral Reef
R Rights
L Lefts

PACIFIC OCEAN

11°N
10°N
9°N
86°W
85°W
84°W
83°W
82°W
11°N
10°N
9°N

GLENN BARTLEY / GETTY IMAGES ©

Pygmy owl

➡ **Costa Rica Surf Camp** (p397) Excellent teachers with safety certification and low teacher-student ratios.

➡ **Dominical Surf Adventures** (p397) An excellent source of surf lessons in Dominical.

➡ **Iguana Surf** (Map p304; ☑2653-0613; www.iguanasurf.net; board rental US$20, private lessons US$45; ⊙8am-6pm) Playa Tamarindo's stalwart surf shop has lessons, rentals and good tips.

➡ **Caribbean Surf School & Tours** (☑8357-7703) Hershel is widely considered to be one of the best teachers on the Caribbean.

➡ **Pura Vida Adventures** (☑in USA 415-465-2162; www.puravidaadventures.com) An excellent women-only surf-and-yoga camp.

➡ **Venus Surf Adventures** (☑8840-2365, in USA 800-793-0512; www.venussurfadventures.com) Has a six-day surf camp for women.

How to Make it Happen

Most international airlines accept surfboards (they must be properly packed in a padded board bag) as one of the two pieces of checked luggage, though this is getting harder and pricier in the age of higher fuel tariffs. Domestic airlines offer more of a challenge. They will accept surfboards for an extra charge, but the board must be under 2.1m in length. On full flights, there's a chance your board won't make it on because of weight restrictions.

An alternative is to buy a new or used board in Costa Rica and then sell it before you leave. Great places to start your search include Jacó, Mal País and Santa Teresa, and Tamarindo. It's usually possible to buy a cheap longboard for about $250 to $300, and a cheap shortboard for about $150 to $200. Many surf shops will buy back your board for about 50% of the price you paid.

Outfitters in many of the popular surf towns rent all kinds of boards, fix dings, give classes and organize excursions. Jacó, Tamarindo, Pavones and Puerto Viejo de Talamanca are good for these types of activities.

Wildlife- & Bird-Watching

Costa Rica's biodiversity is legendary, and the country delivers unparalleled opportunities for wildlife- and bird-watching. Most people are already familiar with the most famous, yet commonly spotted, animals. You'll instantly recognize monkeys bounding through the treetops, sloths clinging to branches and toucans gliding beneath the canopy. Young children, even if they've been to the zoo dozens of times, typically love the thrill of spotting creatures in the wild.

For the slightly older, keeping checklists is a fun way to add an educational element to your travels. If you really want to know what you're looking at, pick up wildlife and bird guides before your trip – look for ones with color plates for easy positive IDs.

A quality pair of binoculars is highly recommended and can really make the difference between far-off movement and a veritable face-to-face encounter. For expert birders, a spotting scope is essential, and multipark itineraries will allow you to quickly add dozens of new species to your all-time list. Finally, it's worth pointing out that Costa Rica is brimming with wildlife at every turn, so always keep your eyes peeled and your ears open – you never know what's waiting for you just ahead!

Above: Scarlet macaw

Right: Coppery-headed emerald hummingbird

MICHAEL MIKE L BAIRD / GETTY IMAGES ©

TOP FIVE SPOTS TO WATCH WILDLIFE

➡ **Parque Nacional Corcovado** (p458) At the heart of the Península de Osa, this is the country's richest wildlife area.

➡ **Área de Conservación Guanacaste, Santa Rosa sector** (p237) The tropical dry forest along the Pacific coast harbors a unique ecosystem.

➡ **Parque Nacional Tortuguero** (p154) Canals and waterways provide excellent bird-watching.

➡ **Refugio Nacional de Vida Silvestre Caño Negro** (p271) Expansive wetlands provide a refuge for reptiles and avians alike.

➡ **Monteverde** (p212) and **Santa Elena** (p203) These reserves provide unique insight into the cloud-forest ecosystem.

How to Make it Happen

➡ Aratinga Tours (p415) Some of the best bird tours in the country are led by Belgian ornithologist Pieter Westra.

➡ **Tropical Feathers** (www.costaricabirdingtours.com) Local owner and guide Noel Ureña has over 16 years' experience leading birding tours.

Windsurfing & Kitesurfing

Laguna de Arenal is the nation's undisputed windsurfing (and kitesurfing) center. From December to April winds are strong and steady, averaging 20 knots in the dry season, often with maximum winds of 30 knots, and windless days are a rarity. The lake has a year-round water temperature of 18°C (64°F) to 21°C (70°F) with 1m-high swells.

For warmer water (but more inconsistent winds), try Puerto Soley in the Bahía Salinas.

White-Water Rafting & Kayaking

White-water rafting has remained one of Costa Rica's top outdoor pursuits since the '80s. Ranging from family-friendly Class I riffles to nearly unnavigable Class V rapids, the country's rivers offer highly varied white-water experiences.

First-time runners are catered for year-round, while seasoned enthusiasts arrive en masse during the wildest months from June through to October. There is also much regional variation, with gentler rivers located near Manuel Antonio along the central Pacific coast, and world-class runs along the Río Pacuare in the Central Valley. Since all white-water rafting in Costa Rica requires the presence of a certified guide, you will need to book trips through a reputable tour agency.

River kayaking has its fair share of loyal fans. The tiny village of La Virgen in the northern lowlands is the unofficial kayaking capital of Costa Rica and the best spot to hook up with other paddlers. The Río Sarapiquí has an impressive variety of runs that cater to all ages and skill levels.

With 1228km of coastline, two gulfs and plentiful mangrove estuaries, Costa Rica is also an ideal destination for sea kayaking. This is a great way for paddlers to access remote areas and catch rare glimpses of birds and wildlife. Difficulty of access varies considerably, and is largely dependent on tides and currents.

How to Make it Happen

June to October are considered peak season for river rafting and kayaking, though some rivers offer good runs all year. Government regulation of outfitters is shoddy, so ask lots of questions about your guide's water-safety, emergency and medical training. If you suspect they're bluffing, move along. There are plenty of legit outfits.

River kayaking can be organized in conjunction with white-water rafting trips if you are experienced; sea kayaking is popular year-round.

➡ **Aguas Bravas** (☎2292-2072; www.costaricaraftingvacation.com) In La Virgen, this is the best outfitter on Costa Rica's best white water.

Canoeing, Parque Nacional Tortuguero (p154)

➡ **Exploradores Outdoors** (☎2222-0202; www.exploradoresoutdoors.com) This outfit offers one- and two-day trips on the Ríos Pacuare, Reventazón and Sarapiquí.

➡ **Pineapple Kayak Tours** (p307) Exciting half-day kayak trips go through caves and mangrove channels.

➡ **H2O Adventures** (☎2777-4092; www.h2ocr.com) Arranges two- and five-day adventures on the Río Savegre.

➡ **Ríos Tropicales** (☎2233-6455; www.riostropicales.com) Can set up multiday adventures on the Río Pacuare and two days of kayaking in Tortuguero.

➡ **Costa Rica Expeditions** (☎2521-6099; www.costaricaexpeditions.com) This outfitter handles small groups and offers rafting trips that cater to foodies.

➡ **Gulf Islands Kayaking** (☎in Canada 250-539-2442; www.seakayak.ca) Tours on offer with this company include five days of sea kayaking in Corcovado.

TOP FIVE SPOTS TO RAFT & KAYAK

➡ **Turrialba** (p135) Home to the country's most popular rafting rivers, the Pacuare and Reventazón.

➡ **La Virgen** (p279) The base town for rafting and kayaking on the Río Sarapiquí.

➡ **Parque Nacional Manuel Antonio** (p389) A tourist mecca that offers family-friendly rafting year-round.

➡ **Parque Nacional Tortuguero** (p154) Boasts 310 sq km of wildlife-rich and kayak-friendly lagoons and canals.

➡ **Bahía Drake** (p451) Extensive mangrove patches are optimally explored by kayak.

Canopy Tours

The most vibrant life in the rainforest takes place at canopy level, but with trees extending 30m to 60m in height, the average human has a hard time getting a look at what's going on up there. You will find canopy tours everywhere in Costa Rica, and many of them will also have a zip line or two to whiz along for a small additional charge. The most elaborate facilities also have Superman cables (which allow you to fly like the Man of Steel) and Tarzan swings.

Some companies have built elevated walkways through the trees. SkyTrek (p202) near Monteverde and Rainmaker (p372) near Quepos are two of the most established operations. A somewhat newer but equally popular operation is Actividades Arboreales near Santa María de Dota.

You can also take a ski-lift-style ride through the treetops, such as the Rainforest Aerial Tram (p146) near Braulio Carrillo or the smaller Monteverde Cloud Forest Train (p199) in Monteverde.

Cycling, Guanacaste province

Diving & Snorkeling

The good news is that Costa Rica offers body-temperature water with few humans and abundant marine life. The bad news is that visibility is low because of silt and plankton, and soft corals and sponges are dominant.

However, if you're looking for fine opportunities to see massive schools of fish, as well as larger marine animals such as turtles, sharks, dolphins and whales, then jump right in. It's also worth pointing out that there are few places in the world where you could feasibly dive in the Caribbean and the Pacific on the same day, though why not take your time?

The Caribbean Sea is better for novice divers and snorkelers, with the beach towns of Manzanillo and Cahuita particularly well suited to youngsters. Puerto Viejo lays claim to a few decent sites that can be explored on a discovery dive. Along the Pacific, Isla del Caño ups the ante for those with solid diving experience.

Isla del Coco is the exception to the rule – this remote island floating in the deep Pacific is regarded by veteran divers as one of the best spots on the planet. To dive the wonderland of Coco, you'll need to visit on a liveaboard and have logged some serious time underwater.

How to Make it Happen

Generally, visibility isn't great during the rainy months, when rivers swell and their outflow clouds the ocean. At this time, boats to offshore locations offer better viewing opportunities.

The water is warm: around 24°C (75°F) to 29°C (84°F) at the surface, with a thermocline at around 20m below the surface where it drops to 23°C (73°F). If you're keeping it shallow, you can skin-dive.

If you want to maximize your diving time, it's advisable to get diving certification beforehand. For more information, check out the **Professional Association of Diving Instructors** (PADI, ☑in Canada 800-565-813, in Switzerland 52-304-1414, in USA 800-729-7234; www.padi.com), a nonprofit or-

Rainforest Aerial Tram (p146)

ganization that provides diving insurance and emergency medical evacuation.

If you're interested in diving but aren't certified, you can usually do a one-day introductory course that will allow you to do one or two accompanied dives. If you love it, which most people do, certification courses take three to four days and cost around $350 to $500.

Horseback Riding

Though horseback-riding trips are ubiquitous throughout Costa Rica, quality and care for the horses vary. Rates range from $25 for an hour or two to more than $100 for a full day. Overnight trips with pack horses can also be arranged and are a popular way of accessing remote destinations in the national parks. Riders weighing more than 100kg (220lb) cannot be carried by small local horses.

Reliable outfitters with healthy horses include Discovery Horseback Tours (p362) and **Serendipity Adventures** (☏2556-2222, in North America 877-507-1358, 888 226 5050, in all other countries 2556-5852; www.serendipity-adventures.com).

Mountain Biking & Cycling

Although the winding, potholed roads and aggressive drivers can be a challenge, cycling is on the rise in Costa Rica. Numerous less-trafficked roads offer riders plenty of adventure – from rides along winding and scenic mountain paths with sweeping views to traveling down rugged trails that take riders through streams and past volcanoes.

The best of Costa Rica's long-distance rides are along the Pacific coast's Interamericana, which has a decent shoulder and is relatively flat, and on the road from Montezuma to the Reserva Natural Absoluta Cabo Blanco on the southern Península de Nicoya.

Mountain biking has taken off in recent years and there are good networks of trails around Corcovado and Arenal, as well as more rides in the central mountains. You can rent mountain bikes in almost any tourist town, but the condition of the equipment varies greatly.

For a monthly fee, **Trail Source** (www.trailsource.com) can provide you with information on trails all over Costa Rica and the world.

Most international airlines will fly your bike as a piece of checked baggage for an extra fee. Pad it well, because the box is liable to be roughly handled.

How to Make it Happen

Outfitters in Costa Rica and the USA can organize multiday mountain-biking trips. If you want to tour Costa Rica by bicycle, be forewarned that the country's cycling shops are decidedly more geared toward utilitarian concerns. Bring any specialized equipment (including a serious lock) from home.

Companies organizing bike tours in Costa Rica include **Backroads** (☎800-462-2848, in USA 510-527-1555; www.backroads.com), **Coast to Coast Adventures** (☎2280-8054; www.ctocadventures.com), Costa Rica Expeditions (p47), **Lava Tours** (☎2281-2458; www.lava-tours.com) and Serendipity Adventures (p49).

Exploring Costa Rica's forests

Plan Your Trip

Travel with Children

In a land of such dizzying adventure and close encounters with wildlife, waves, jungle zip lines and enticing mud puddles, it can be challenging to choose where to go. Fortunately, your options aren't limited by region, and kids will find epic fun in this accessible paradise (that parents will enjoy too).

Best Regions for Kids

Península de Nicoya

Excellent beaches and family-friendly resorts make this an ideal destination for families. This is a great place for kids (and their folks) to take surfing lessons.

Northwestern Costa Rica

The mysterious and ghostly cloud forests of Monteverde pique children's imaginations about the creatures that live there, while the area's specialty sanctuaries let them see bats, frogs, butterflies and reptiles up close.

Central Pacific Coast

Easy trails lead past spider monkeys and sloths to great swimming beaches at Parque Nacional Manuel Antonio, a busy but beautiful piece of coastal rainforest.

Caribbean Coast

The whole family can snorkel all day at the relatively tranquil waters of Manzanillo or Cahuita and set out on a night adventure to see nesting turtles.

Costa Rica for Kids

Mischievous monkeys and steaming volcanoes, mysterious rainforests and palm-lined beaches – Costa Rica sometimes seems like a comic-book reality. The perfect place for family travel, it is a safe, exhilarating tropical playland that will make a huge impression on younger travelers. The country's myriad adventure possibilities cover the spectrum of age-appropriate intensity levels. Plus, the warm, family-friendly culture is extremely welcoming of little ones.

In addition to amazing the kids, this small, peaceful country has all of the practicalities that rank high with parents, such as great country-wide transportation infrastructure, a low crime rate and an excellent health-care system. But the reason to bring the whole family is the opportunity to share unforgettable experiences like spotting a dolphin or a sloth, slowly paddling a kayak through mangrove channels or taking a night hike in search of tropical frogs.

Children's Highlights

Wildlife-Watching

You can't not spot wildlife in Costa Rica. Coatis cause regular traffic jams around Lake Arenal, and scarlet macaws loudly squawk in tropical-almond trees down the central Pacific coast. Stay a day or two at a jungle lodge, and the wildlife will come to you.

➡ **Parque Nacional Manuel Antonio** Tiny and easily accessible; a walk through this park usually yields sightings of squirrel monkeys, stripy iguanas and coatis. (p389)

➡ **Parque Nacional Cahuita** Seeing white-faced capuchins is practically assured along the beach trail; go with a guide and you'll probably also see sloths. (p175)

➡ **Parque Nacional Tortuguero** Boat tours through Tortuguero canals uncover wildlife all around, but staying in any jungle lodge outside the village will reveal the same. (p159)

➡ **Chilamate Rainforest Eco Retreat** In the steamy rainforest of the Sarapiquí valley, this family-friendly lodge has miles of trails for easy wildlife-spotting hikes. (p281)

➡ **Turtle-watching** An option on both the Pacific (p301) and the Caribbean coast (p159), one of Costa Rica's truly magical experiences is watching sea turtles lay their eggs under the cover of night.

Animal Sanctuaries

Not getting close enough to wildlife in the wild? Animal encounters are guaranteed at wildlife sanctuaries or animal refuges. Many of these organizations rescue and rehabilitate orphaned or injured animals for release or lifetime care.

➡ **Sloth Sanctuary of Costa Rica** With their slow-mo locomotion and Mona Lisa smiles, baby sloths might be the cutest creatures on the planet – and this sanctuary is the best place to meet some. (p169)

➡ **Fundacíon Santuario Silvestre de Osa** This boat-accessible sanctuary rehabilitates whatever injured and orphaned animals come their way. Friendly monkeys are allowed to roam freely and love to be petted. (p432)

➡ **Frog's Heaven** A frog-lover's heaven, this tropical garden is filled with all sorts of brightly colored (and transparent!) amphibians, including the iconic red-eyed tree frog. (p286)

➡ **Ecocentro Danaus** Walk the trails to look for monkeys and sloths, visit a pond full of caimans and turtles, delight in the butterfly garden and ogle frogs in the ranarium (frog pond). (p248)

➡ **Jaguar Centro de Rescate** No jaguars here, but you may get to hold a howler monkey or a baby sloth. You'll also see colorful snakes (in terrariums), raptors and frogs. (p185)

Beaches

➡ **Playa Ocotal** Placid, wooded gray-sand beach on the quiet northern end of Península de Nicoya. (p295)

➡ **Playa Pelada** In the Nosara area, this low-key beach has little wave action and big, intriguing boulders. (p318)

➡ **Playa Carrillo** South of family-friendly Sámara, this beach can be all yours during the week and convivially crowded with Tico (Costa Rican) families on the weekends. (p327)

➡ **Parque Nacional Manuel Antonio** Beach visits are usually enlivened by monkeys, coatis and iguanas. (p389)

➡ **Parque Nacional Marino Ballena** A yawning stretch of white-sand, jungle-fringed beach, a sand spit shaped like a whale's tail at low tide and the chance to see whales spouting offshore. (p403)

➡ **Playa Negra** This black-sand, blue-flag beach (meeting Costa Rica's highest ecological standards) has plenty of space to plant your own flag. (p168)

➡ **Playa Manzanillo** Beautiful, jungle-backed beach from here to Punta Mona (about as far south as you can go before you have to start bushwhacking). (p344)

Waterborne Adventures

➡ **Mangrove tours** Kayaking or canoeing through the still waters of mangrove canals can turn up waterbirds, caimans, sleeping bats and sloths. Try Parque Nacional Marino Ballena, around Puerto Jiménez and Tortuguero. (p403)

➡ **Surfing lessons** For surfing lessons specifically tailored to kids, check out One Love on the Caribbean coast; kids' lessons are also offered at beginner beaches in Jacó and Tamarindo. (p177)

Swimming near Volcán Miravalles (p223)

➡ **White-water rafting** Family-friendly rafting and 'safari trips' happen all year long on Ríos Sarapiquí (p283) and Pejibaye. (p136)

Other Family Fun

➡ **Parque Nacional Volcán Poás** Has a stroller-friendly walkway along the observation area, one of the few national parks accessible in this way. (p112)

➡ **Monteverde Cloud Forest Train** Kids with trains on the brain will love this scenic ride. (p199)

➡ **Beachside braids** Kids with long hair might like getting their hair braided and beaded by a beachside stylist in Puerto Viejo de Talamanca. (p176)

Planning

Although Costa Rica is in the heart of Central America, it's a relatively easy place for family travel, making the nature of pre-departure planning more similar to North America or Europe than, say, Honduras.

Wildlife-watching while swimming, Playa Ocotal (p295)

Throughout this book, we have marked particularly family-friendly accommodations with this symbol: 🏠.

Eating with Kids

Hydration is particularly crucial in this tropical climate, especially for children who aren't used to the heat and humidity; fortunately, Costa Rica's tap water is safe everywhere (we've noted the places that are rare exceptions).

➡ If you're traveling with an infant or small child, stock up on formula, baby food and snacks before heading to remote areas, where shops are few and far between.

➡ Kids love refreshing *batidos* (fresh fruit shakes), either *al agua* (made with water) or *con leche* (with milk); the variety of novel tropical fruits may appeal to older kids.

➡ Back at home, coconut water might be old news, but watching a smiling Tico hack open a *pipa fría* (cold young coconut) for you with a machete is another thing entirely.

Getting There & Around

➡ Children under the age of 12 receive a 25% discount on domestic-airline flights, while children under two fly free (provided they sit on a parent's lap).

➡ Children (except for those under the age of three) pay full fare on buses.

➡ Car seats for infants are not always available at car-rental agencies, so bring your own or make sure you double (or triple) check with the agency in advance.

Arroz con pollo (rice with chicken)

Eat & Drink Like a Local

Traditional Costa Rican fare, for the most part, is basic, mild comfort food. The diet consists largely of rice and beans or beans and rice – thatched country kitchens all over Costa Rica serve up hearty home-cooked specials known as *comida típica* (literally 'typical food').

Farmers Markets

Farmers markets (simply known as *ferias* in Costa Rica) take place daily throughout the country – often several times a week in different neighborhoods, in bigger cities.

Because the law mandates that only locally grown or produced fare can be sold at the *feria*, you can rest assured that not only are you buying fresh produce or handmade goods, but you're also supporting small-scale local farmers and makers.

Ask around locally for dates and times of the farmers markets and shop alongside area residents while you discover the specialties of your current locale – from sweet strawberries and soursop to fresh cheese and *chorreadas* (savory corn pancakes).

What to Eat & Drink

Breakfast for Ticos (Costa Ricans) is usually *gallo pinto* (literally 'spotted rooster'), a stir-fry of last night's rice and beans. When combined, the rice gets colored by the beans, and the mix obtains a speckled appearance. Served with eggs, cheese or *natilla* (sour cream), *gallo pinto* is generally cheap, filling and sometimes downright tasty. If you plan to spend the whole day surfing or hiking, you'll find that *gallo pinto* is great energy food. If you aren't keen on rice and beans, many hotels offer a tropical-style continental breakfast, usually consisting of toast with butter and jam, accompanied by fresh fruit. American-style breakfasts are also available in many eateries and are, needless to say, heavy on the fried foods and fatty meats.

Most restaurants offer a set meal at lunch and dinner called a *casado* (literally 'married'), a cheap, well-balanced plate of rice, beans, meat, salad and sometimes *plátanos maduros* (fried sweet plantains) or *patacones* (twice-fried plantains), which taste something like french fries.

Food is not heavily spiced, unless you're having traditional Caribbean-style cuisine. Most local restaurants will lay out a bottle of Tabasco-style sauce, homemade salsa and/or Salsa Lizano, the Tico version of Worcestershire sauce and the 'secret' ingredient of *gallo pinto*.

Specialties

Considering the extent of the coastline, it is no surprise that seafood is plentiful, and fish dishes are usually fresh and delicious. While not traditional Tico fare, *ceviche* (seafood marinated in lemon or lime juice, garlic and seasonings) is on most menus, usually made from *pargo* (red snapper), *dorado* (mahi-mahi), octopus or tilapia. Raw fish is marinated in lime juice with some combination of chilis, onions, tomatoes and herbs. Served chilled, it is a delectable way to enjoy fresh seafood. Emphasis is on 'fresh' here – it's raw fish, so if you have reason to believe it is not fresh, don't risk eating it.

Caribbean cuisine is the most distinctive in Costa Rica, having been steeped in indigenous, *criollo* (Creole) and Afro-Caribbean flavors. It's a welcome cultural change of pace after seemingly endless *casados*. Regional specialties include *rondón* (whose moniker comes from 'run-down', meaning whatever the chef can run down), a spicy seafood gumbo; Caribbean-style rice and beans, made with red beans, coconut milk and curry spices; and *patí*, the Caribbean version of an *empanada* (savory turnover), the best street food, bus-ride snack and picnic treat.

For a glossary of Costa Rican food terms, see p533.

Drinks

Coffee is probably the most popular beverage in the country and, wherever you go, someone is likely to offer you a *cafecito*. Traditionally, it is served strong and mixed with hot milk to taste, also known as *café con leche*. Purists can get *café negro* (black coffee); if you want a little milk, ask for *leche al lado* (milk on the side). Many trendier places serve espresso drinks.

For a refresher, nothing beats *batidos*. These fresh fruit shakes are made either *al agua* (with water) or *con leche* (with milk).

The array of available tropical fruit can be intoxicating and includes:

➡ mango
➡ papaya
➡ *piña* (pineapple)
➡ *sandía* (watermelon)
➡ *melón* (cantaloupe)
➡ *mora* (blackberry)
➡ *carambola* (starfruit)
➡ *cas* (a type of tart guava)
➡ *guanabana* (soursop or cherimoya)
➡ *tamarindo* (fruit of the tamarind tree)

If you are wary about the condition of the drinking water, ask that your *batido* be made with *agua enbotellada* (bottled water) and *sin hielo* (without ice), though water is generally safe to drink throughout the country.

Pipas are green coconuts that have had their tops hacked off with a machete and been spiked with a straw for drinking the coconut water inside – super-refreshing when you're wilting in the tropical heat. If you're lucky enough to find it, *agua dulce* is sugarcane water, a slightly grassy, sweet

GREG RODEN / GETTY IMAGES ©

Batido (fruit shake)

THE GALLO PINTO CONTROVERSY

No other dish in Costa Rica inspires Ticos (Costa Ricans) quite like their national dish of *gallo pinto*, that ubiquitous medley of rice, beans and spices. You might even hear Costa Ricans refer to themselves as *'más Tico que gallo pinto'* (literally, 'more Costa Rican than *gallo pinto*'). Exactly what type and amount of this holy trinity makes up authentic *gallo pinto* is the subject of intense debate, especially since it is also the national dish of neighboring Nicaragua.

Both countries claim that *gallo pinto* originated on their soil. Costa Rican lore holds that the dish and its iconic name were coined in 1930 in the neighborhood of San Sebastián, on the southern outskirts of San José. Nicaraguans claim that it was brought to the Caribbean coast of their country by Afro-Latinos long before it graced the palate of any Costa Rican.

The battle for the rights to this humble dish doesn't stop here, especially since the two countries can't even agree on the standard recipe. Nicaraguans traditionally prepare it with small red beans, whereas Costa Ricans swear by black beans. And let's not even get into the subtle complexities of balancing cilantro, salt and pepper.

Nicaragua officially holds the world record for making the biggest-ever pot of *gallo pinto*. On September 15, 2007, a seething vat of it fed 22,000 people, which firmly entrenched Nicaragua's name next to *gallo pinto* in the *Guinness Book of World Records*. Costa Rica responded in 2009 by cooking an even more massive avalanche of the stuff, feeding a small crowd of 50,000. Though the event was not officially recognized as setting any records, that day's vat of *gallo pinto* warmed the hearts and bellies of many a proud Tico.

Casado (set meal)

juice that's been pressed through a heavy-duty, hand-cranked mill.

On the Caribbean coast, look for *agua de sapo* (literally 'toad water'), a beautiful lemonade laced with fresh ginger juice and *tapa de dulce* (brown sugar; also known as *tapa dulce*).

Resbaladera, found mostly in the Guanacaste countryside, is a sweet milk drink (it's much like *horchata* – Mexican rice drink) made from rice, barley, milk and cinnamon.

Other local drinks you may encounter include *linaza,* a flaxseed drink said to aid digestion, and *chan,* a drink made from chia seed and lemon – this can be an acquired taste due to its slimy (yum!) texture.

The most popular alcoholic drink is *cerveza* (beer; aka *birra* locally), and there are several national brands. Imperial is the most popular – either for its smooth flavor or for the ubiquitous merchandise emblazoned with the eagle-crest logo. Pilsen, which has a higher alcohol content, is known for its saucy calendars featuring *las chicas Pilsen* (the Pilsen girls). Both are tasty pilsners. Bavaria produces a lager and Bavaria Negro, a delicious, full-bodied dark beer; this brand is harder to find. A most welcome burgeoning craft-beer scene is broadening the variety of Costa Rican beers and deepening the tastes of local palates.

After beer, the poison of choice is *guaro,* which is a colorless alcohol distilled from sugarcane and usually consumed by the shot, though you can order it as a sour. It goes down mighty easily but leaves one hell of a hangover.

As in most of Central America, the local rums are inexpensive and worthwhile, especially the Ron Centenario, which recently shot to international fame. And at the risk of alienating the most patriotic of Ticos, we would be remiss not to mention the arguably tastier Flor de Caña from Nicaragua (pause for rotten tomatoes). The most popular rum-based tipple is a *cuba libre* (rum and cola), which hits the spot on a hot, sticky day, especially when served with a fresh splash of lime. Premixed cans of *cuba libre* are also available in stores, but it'd be a lie to say the contents don't taste weirdly like aluminum.

Cuba libre (rum and cola)

How to Eat & Drink

Places to Eat

The most popular eating establishment in Costa Rica is the *soda*. These are small, informal lunch counters dishing up a few daily *casados*. Other popular cheapies include the omnipresent fried- and rotisserie-chicken stands.

A regular *restaurante* is usually higher on the price scale and has slightly more atmosphere. Many *restaurantes* serve *casados*, while the fancier places refer to the set lunch as the *almuerzo ejecutivo* (literally 'executive lunch').

For something smaller, *pastelerías* and *panaderías* are shops that sell pastries and bread, while many bars serve *bocas,* which are snack-sized portions of main meals.

Lunch is usually the day's main meal and is typically served around noon. Dinner tends to be a lighter version of lunch and is eaten around 7pm.

Vegetarians & Vegans

If you don't mind rice and beans, Costa Rica is a relatively comfortable place for vegetarians to travel.

Most restaurants will make veggie *casados* on request and many are now including them on the menu. They usually include rice and beans, cabbage salad and one or two selections of variously prepared vegetables or legumes.

With the high influx of tourism, there are also many specialty vegetarian restaurants or restaurants with a veggie menu in San José and tourist towns. Lodges in remote areas that offer all-inclusive meal plans can accommodate vegetarian diets with advance notice.

Vegans, macrobiotic and raw-food-only travelers will have a tougher time, as there are fewer outlets accommodating those diets, although this is slowly changing. If you intend to keep to your diet, it's best to choose a lodging where you can prepare food yourself. Many towns have *macrobióticas* (health-food stores) but selection varies. Fresh vegetables can be hard to come by in isolated areas and will often be quite expensive, although farmers markets are cropping up throughout the country.

Habits & Customs

When you sit down to eat in a restaurant, it is polite to say *buenos días* (good morning), *buenas tardes* (good afternoon) or *buenas noches* (good evening) to the waitstaff and any people you might be sharing a table with – and it's generally good form to acknowledge everyone in the room this way. It is also polite to say *buen provecho,* which is the equivalent of *bon appétit,* at the start of the meal.

Regions at a Glance

Where will your passion take you? Wildlife-watchers will be in heaven here, with several life zones supporting a multitude of colorful species, including the quetzal, the elusive jaguar and nesting sea turtles. Surfers will need no intro to the country, whose surf spots are open secrets, and novices will find plenty of beginner breaks. Hikers can traverse the thick, humid jungle of remote Corcovado, summit the country's highest peak, Chirripó, or just meander through cloud forests, around the rims of steaming volcanoes and along beachside trails on day hikes. We've summed up the regions of Costa Rica here, to help you pick your pleasure.

San José

Museums
Music
Food

Old Gold & Upstart Art

Gritty, no-nonsense San José doesn't offer much in the way of architectural beauty, but it's the innards that count. Visit a dense concentration of museums, exhibiting everything from pre-Columbian gold to the hottest multimedia installations.

Música en Vivo

As the country's cultural capital, this is where you come to catch chamber music, international touring bands and up-and-coming local talent. The venerable Jazz Café is a solid place to start.

Cuisine Scene

Argentinian, vegetarian, Asian-fusion and classic French cuisine shine in superb San José venues. Some of the country's finest restaurants reside here, bringing welcome diversity to *gallo pinto*–weary palates.

p64

Central Valley & Highlands

Volcanoes
Rapids
Highland Countryside

Volcanic Action

Volcanoes in this region range from the wild and moderately active (Turrialba) to the heavily trafficked (Poás), showing off ultramarine crater lakes and desolate, misty moonscapes.

White Water

World-class white water awaits on the Río Pacuare, which is well worth a run for its cascade of thrilling rapids through a stunningly beauteous jungle gorge.

Wind & Dine

The picturesque highland countryside of Costa Rica is often overlooked in favor of its beaches. But here cows nibble contentedly along twisting mountain roads, and villages boast organic farmers markets and parks with psychedelic topiaries.

p105

Caribbean Coast

Culture
Wildlife
Turtles

Afro-Caribbean Flavor

Set apart geographically and culturally from the rest of Costa Rica, the Caribbean coast has a distinct Afro-Caribbean flavor all of its own. Taste it in the coconut rice, hear it the local patois and live it in super-chill Cahuita.

Wildlife

The waterlogged coast along the Caribbean teems with sloths, three of Costa Rica's four monkey species, crocodiles, caimans, poison-dart frogs, manatees, tucuxi dolphins and over 375 species of bird.

Turtle Life

On this wild coast, turtle nesting is serious business. In Parismina and Tortuguero, the leatherback, green and hawksbill turtles return to their natal beaches to nest.

p140

Northwestern Costa Rica

Forests
Ecolodges
Water

Canopy Views

Studded with cathedral trees (which sprout dozens of species and shelter valuable watersheds), northwestern forests birthed the ubiquitous canopy tour. Experience forests on volcanic slopes, along the wild coast and leering over the continental divide.

Unique Sleeps

The sheer number of groovy, independently owned and operated ecolodges means you can choose from cute B&Bs, spectacular working farms or biological stations ensconced in forest.

Rafting, Surfing & More

Stare into the placid waters of a vast artificial lake, lose yourself in aquamarine rivers, ride perfect lefts that crash on wilderness beaches, or ride the wind on the most epic bay you've never heard of.

p193

Arenal & Northern Lowlands

Local Perspective
Birds
Water

Community Tourism

Discover real-life Costa Rica on working farm-stays, on tours through rainforest preserves, and on inky lagoons or mocha rivers with lifelong resident guides.

Birders Paradise

The humid swamps and, yes, hills of these lowlands are thick with forests and teeming with hundreds of species of bird, from storks and egrets to toucans and great green macaws.

Kayaking & Fishing

Whether you want to paddle frothing white water shadowed by forest, carve inland lakes by kayak, or just hop a motorboat to spot caimans or reel in tarpon, this is your Neverland.

p245

Península de Nicoya

Surfing
Diving
Food

Perfect Breaks

It's almost impossible to believe that there are so many waves on one spectacular, rugged peninsula. But, from the bottom to the top, there are countless perfect breaks to meet your needs.

Undersea Life

Don't expect Caribbean clarity or bathwater warmth, but if you do stride into the water you can expect mantas, bull sharks and schools of fish that will bend your brain.

Creative Local Eats

The creative kitchens that dot this intrepid coast source ingredients from local *fincas* (farms) and fishers, and the dishes are prepared with passion and skill.

p287

Central Pacific Coast

....

Surfing
National Park
Beaches

....

Surf for All

From the pros-only Playa Hermosa to the beginner-friendly Dominical, the famous breaks of the Pacific coast bring blissful swells and tons of variety.

Parque Nacional Manuel Antonio

Manuel Antonio, Costa Rica's smallest and most popular national park, is a kid-friendly, beach-lined delight. Sure, there are crowds of people, but at times they're outnumbered by monkeys, coatis and tropical birds.

Deserted Beaches

It's a bit of a hike to get to Parque Nacional Marino Ballena, but those lucky few who find themselves on its empty beaches can scan the sparkling horizon for migrating whales.

p349

Southern Costa Rica & Península de Osa

....

Mountain Peak
Hiking
Culture

....

Cerro Chirripó

Scaling the wind-swept peak of Chirripó is an exhilarating adventure into a wholly different Costa Rica from that of the postcards.

Corcovado

Jaguars, jungle trails and wild beaches galore: this is among the world's most biologically intense areas, representing a whopping 2.5% of the planet's biodiversity. Hiking Corcovado is a sublime trip into untamed tropical rainforest.

Indigenous Communities

Traveling deep into Costa Rica's mountains or the jungle of the Osa allows you to meet some of Costa Rica's diverse indigenous citizens who are keeping ancient traditions alive.

p407

On the Road

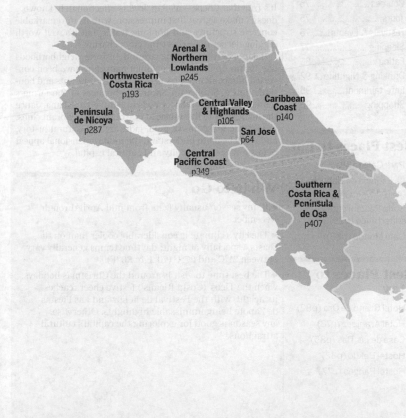

Northwestern Costa Rica
p193

Peninsula de Nicoya
p287

Arenal & Northern Lowlands
p245

Central Valley & Highlands
p105

San José
p64

Caribbean Coast
p140

Central Pacific Coast
p349

Southern Costa Rica & Peninsula de Osa
p407

San José

POP OVER 1.5 MILLION (GREATER METRO AREA) / ELEV 1170M / AREA 2366 SQ KM

Best Places to Eat

➡ Park Café (p88)

➡ La Esquina de Buenos Aires (p86)

➡ Sofía Restaurante Mediterráneo (p89)

➡ Café Mundo (p86)

Best Places to Stay

➡ Hotel Grano de Oro (p82)

➡ Hotel Aranjuez (p78)

➡ Casa de las Tías (p85)

➡ Hostel Bekuo (p82)

➡ Hostel Pangea (p77)

Why Go?

Chances are San José wasn't the top destination on your list when you started planning your Costa Rica trip, but give this city a chance and you just might be pleasantly surprised. It's true that Chepe – as San José is affectionately known – doesn't make a great first impression, with its unremarkable concrete structures and honking traffic, but it's well worth digging deeper to discover the city's charms.

Take your time poking around historic neighborhoods like Barrio Amón, where colonial mansions have been converted into contemporary art galleries, restaurants and boutique hotels. Stroll with Saturday shoppers at the farmers market, join the Sunday crowds in Parque La Sabana, dance the night away to live music at one of the city's vibrant clubs, or visit the museums of gold, jade, art and natural history, and you'll begin to understand the multidimensional appeal of Costa Rica's largest city and cultural capital.

When to Go

➡ Rainy season usually lasts from mid-April through December.

➡ The city's climate is considerably cooler than on the coasts, especially at night; daytime temps generally vary between 21°C and 27°C (70°F to 80°F).

➡ The best time to visit is around the Christmas holidays, when the Ticos' (Costa Ricans') festive cheer reaches its height, with the Festival de la Luz and Las Fiestas de Zapote being unmissable highlights. Otherwise, any season is good for exploring the capital's cultural attractions.

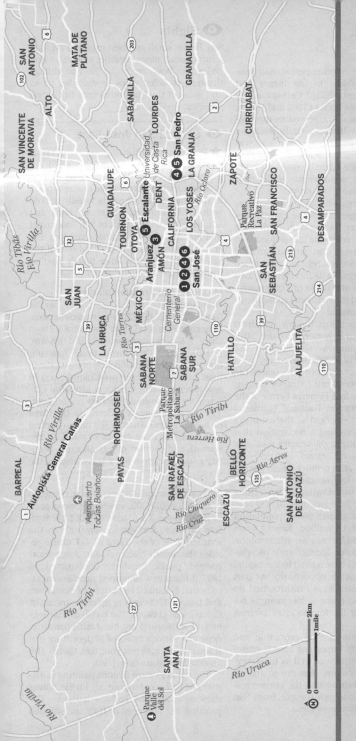

San José Highlights

❶ Admiring Costa Rica's artistic traditions past and present at the **Museo de Oro** (p66) and **Museo de Arte y Diseño Contemporáneo** (p70).

❷ Savoring classical music amid the beaux-arts interiors of the **Teatro Nacional** (p96).

❸ Poking around the lively **Feria Verde de Aranjuez** (p97) farmers market in search of locally grown and gourmet treats.

❹ Grooving to live bands at the storied **Jazz Café** (p96) in San Pedro or up-and-coming **El Sótano** (p96) downtown.

❺ Indulging your taste buds at the fun bars and fine eateries of **Barrio Escalante** (p85), or pub-crawling alongside hard-partying Tico students in **San Pedro** (p92).

❻ Exploring the vast universe of carved stone and ceramic treasures at the newly reopened **Museo de Jade** (p67).

SAN JOSÉ

History

For much of the colonial period, San José played second fiddle to the bigger and relatively more established Cartago, a city whose origins date back to 1563 and which, during the colonial era, served as the provincial capital. Villanueva de la Boca del Monte del Valle de Abra – as San José was first known – was not founded until 1737, when the Catholic Church issued an edict that forced the populace to settle near churches (attendance was down).

The city remained a backwater for decades, though it did experience some growth as a stop in the tobacco trading route during the late 18th century. Following independence in 1821, rival factions in Cartago and San José each attempted to assert regional supremacy. The struggle ended in 1823 when the two sides faced off at the Battle of Ochomongo. San José emerged the victor and subsequently declared itself capital.

Despite its new status, the city remained a quiet agricultural center into the 20th century. The calm was shattered in the 1940s, when parts of San José served as a battlefield in the civil war of 1948, one of the bloodiest conflicts in the country's history. Out of that clash, José Figueres Ferrer of the Partido de Liberación Nacional (National Liberation Party) emerged as the country's interim leader – signing a declaration that abolished the army at the armory that now serves as the Museo Nacional.

The rest of the 20th century would see the expansion of the city from diminutive coffee-trading outpost to sprawling urban center. In the 1940s San José had only 70,000 residents. Today, the greater metro population stands at almost 1.6 million. Recent years have been marked by massive urban migration as Ticos (Costa Ricans) and, increasingly, Nicaraguans have moved to the capital in search of economic opportunity. As part of this, shantytowns have mushroomed on the outskirts, and crime is increasingly becoming a part of life for the city's poorest inhabitants.

The city remains a vital economic and arts hub, home to important banks, museums and universities – as well as the everyday outposts of culture: live-music spaces, art centers, bookstores and the corner restaurants where *josefinos* (people from San José) gather to chew over ideas.

◉ Sights

San José is small and best explored on foot, joining locals along teeming sidewalks and pedestrian boulevards that lead to vintage theaters, crowded cafes, tree-shaded parks and some of the finest museums in Central America.

◉ Central San José East

★ Plaza de la Cultura   PLAZA
(Map p72; Avs Central & 2 btwn Calles 3 & 5) For many Ticos, Costa Rica begins here. This architecturally unremarkable concrete plaza in the heart of downtown is usually packed with locals slurping ice-cream cones and admiring the wide gamut of San José street life: juggling clowns, itinerant vendors and cruising teenagers. It is perhaps one of the safest spots in the city since there's a police tower stationed at one corner.

Museo de Oro Precolombino y Numismática   MUSEUM
(Map p72; ☑ 2243-4221; www.museosdelbanco-central.org; Plaza de la Cultura, Avs Central & 2 btwn Calles 3 & 5; adult/student/child US$11/8/free; ☻9:15am-5pm) This three-in-one museum houses an extensive collection of Costa Rica's most priceless pieces of pre-Columbian gold and other artifacts, including historical currency and some contemporary regional art. The museum, housed underneath the Plaza de la Cultura, is owned by the Banco Central and its architecture brings to mind all the warmth and comfort of a bank vault. Security is tight; visitors must leave bags at the door.

★ Teatro Nacional   NOTABLE BUILDING
(Map p72; ☑ 2010-1100; www.teatronacional.go.cr; Av 2 btwn Calles 3 & 5; admission US$7; ☻9am-6pm Jan-Apr, to 4pm Mon-Sat May-Dec) On the southern side of the Plaza de la Cultura resides the Teatro Nacional, San José's most revered public building. Constructed in 1897, it features a columned neoclassical facade that is flanked by statues of Beethoven and famous 17th-century Spanish dramatist Calderón de la Barca. The lavish marble lobby and auditorium are lined with paintings depicting various facets of 19th-century life. If you're looking to rest your feet, there's also an excellent onsite cafe (p86).

The theater's most famous painting is *Alegoría al café y el banano,* an idyllic canvas showing coffee and banana harvests. The painting was produced in Italy and shipped to Costa Rica for installation in the theater, and the image was reproduced on the old ₡5 note (now out of circulation). It seems clear that the painter never witnessed a banana harvest because of the way the man in the center is awkwardly grasping a bunch (actual banana workers hoist the stems onto their shoulders).

Across the street, also belonging to the national theater, is the Museo Homenaje Joaquín García Monge, which features temporary exhibitions by contemporary Costa Rican and Central American artists.

Museo Nacional de Costa Rica   MUSEUM
(Map p68; ✆2257-1433; www.museocostarica. go.cr; Calle 17 btwn Avs Central & 2; adult/child US$8/4; ◷8:30am-4:30pm Tue-Sat, 9am-4:30pm Sun) Entered via a beautiful glassed-in atrium housing an exotic butterfly garden, this museum provides a quick survey of Costa Rican history. Exhibits of pre-Columbian pieces from ongoing digs, as well as artifacts from the colony and the early republic are all housed inside the old Bellavista Fortress, which served historically as the army headquarters and saw fierce fighting (hence the pockmarks) in the 1948 civil war.

It was here that President José Figueres Ferrer announced, in 1949, that he was abolishing the country's military. Among the museum's many notable pieces is the fountain pen that Figueres used to sign the 1949 constitution. Don't miss the period galleries in the northeast corner, which feature turn-of-the-20th-century furnishings and decor from when these rooms served as the private residences of the fort's various commanders.

★ Museo de Jade   MUSEUM
(Map p72; ✆2287-6034; www.ins-cr.com; Plaza de la Democracia; adult/child US$9/free; ◷8:30am-3:30pm Mon-Fri, 10am-2pm Sat) Reopened in its brand-new home in mid-2014, this museum houses the world's largest collection of American jade (pronounced 'ha-day' in Spanish). The ample new exhibition space allows the public greater access to the museum's varied collection of nearly 7000 finely crafted, well-conserved pieces, from translucent jade carvings depicting fertility goddesses, shamans, frogs and snakes to incredible ceramics (some reflecting Mayan influences), including a highly unusual ceramic head displaying a row of serrated teeth.

Plaza de la Democracia   PLAZA
(Map p72; Avs Central & 2 btwn Calles 13 & 15) Between the national museum and the Museo de Jade is the stark Plaza de la Democracia, which was constructed by President Oscar Arias in 1989 to commemorate 100 years of Costa Rican democracy. The concrete

---

SAN JOSÉ IN...
....

One Day
Begin with a peek inside the city's most beautiful building, the 19th-century **Teatro Nacional** (p66). Enjoy an espresso at the theater's atmospheric cafe (p86) before heading into the nearby **Museo de Oro Precolombino y Numismática** (p66) to peruse its trove of the country's pre-Columbian gold treasures. From here, stroll northeast through Parque Morazán to the **Museo de Arte y Diseño Contemporáneo** (p70), Central America's most prominent contemporary-arts institution.

Take lunch on the terrace of **Café Mundo** (p86) or **Kalú** (p87). Afterwards, browse the shops of historic Barrio Amón, such as **Kiosco SJO** (p97), **Galería Namu** (p97) and **eÑe** (p97), then end your afternoon sampling Costa Rican microbrews at **Stiefel** (p93) or enjoying a happy-hour cocktail at **El Morazán** (p93).

Two Days
Start your second day in town with a primer on Costa Rican history at the **Museo Nacional** (p67), then cross Plaza de la Democracia to the newly relocated and expanded **Museo de Jade** (p67). After a stroll through the neighboring **Mercado Artesanal** (p98) for handicrafts, go west on Av Central to the **Catedral Metropolitana** (p72), where *josefinos* (people from San José) still pack the pews for daily mass. Afterward, head northwest to the **Mercado Central** (p72) to shop for Costa Rican coffee, cigars and cheap eats.

In the evening venture east to Los Yoses, Barrio Escalante and San Pedro, where you'll find some of San José's best neighborhood eateries and bars, and the city's most esteemed venue for live music, the **Jazz Café** (p96).

San José

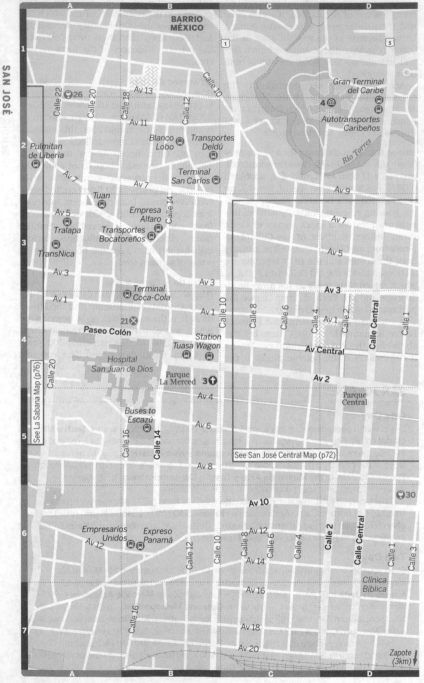

BARRIO
MÉXICO

Calle 10

Calle 22 26
Calle 20
Calle 18
Av 13
Calle 12
Av 11

Gran Terminal
del Caribe

4

Pulmitan
de Liberia

Blanco
Lobo
Transportes
Deldú

Autotransportes
Caribeños

Av 7

Terminal
San Carlos

Río Torres

Av 7

Av 9

Tuan

Calle 14

Empresa
Alfaro

Av 7

Av 5

Av 5

Tralapa

Transportes
Bocatoreños

Av 3

TransNica

Av 3

Av 1

Calle 10

Calle 8

Calle 6

Calle 4

Calle 2

Calle Central

Calle 1

Terminal
Coca-Cola

Av 3

Av 1

Av 1

21

Paseo Colón

Station
Wagon

Av Central

Tuasa

Hospital
San Juan de Dios

Av 2

Calle 20

Parque
La Merced

3

Parque
Central

Av 4

Buses to
Escazú

Av 6

Calle 16

Calle 14

Av 8

See San José Central Map (p72)

30

Av 10

Empresarios
Unidos

Av 12

Expreso
Panamá

Av 12

Calle 12

Calle 10

Calle 8

Calle 6

Calle 4

Av 14

Calle 2

Calle Central

Calle 1

Calle 3

Clínica
Bíblica

Av 16

Calle 16

Av 18

Av 20

Zapote
(3km)

See La Sabana Map (p76)

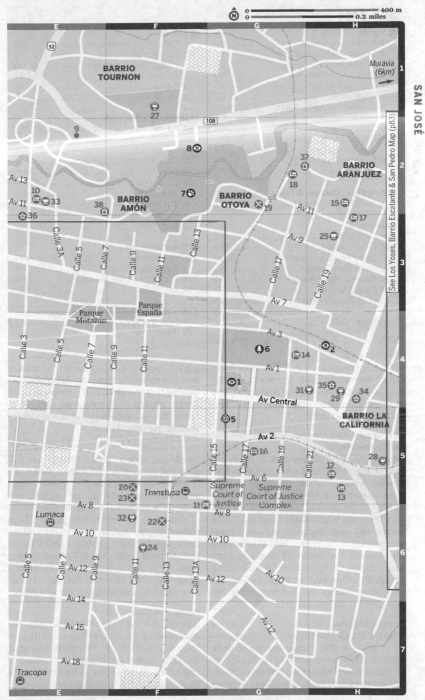

0 400 m
0 0.2 miles

Moravia
(6km)

BARRIO
TOURNON

27

108

9

8

Av 13

10 33

Av 11

36

38

BARRIO
AMÓN

7

BARRIO
OTOYA 19

37

18

BARRIO
ARANJUEZ

Av 11

15

17

Av 9

25

See Los Yoses, Barrio Escalante & San Pedro Map (p83)

Calle 3A

Calle 5

Calle 7

Calle 9

Calle 11

Calle 13

Calle 17

Calle 19

Av 7

Parque
España

Parque
Morazán

Calle 3

Calle 5

Calle 7

Calle 9

Calle 11

Av 3

6

2

14

Av 1

1

Av Central

31 35

29 34

BARRIO LA
CALIFORNIA

5

Calle 15

Av 2

Calle 17

16

Calle 19

Calle 21

12

28

13

20

23

Transtusa

Supreme
Court of
Justice

11

Av 6

Supreme
Court of Justice
Complex

Av 8

Lumaca

Av 8

32 22

Av 10

Av 10

24

Calle 5

Calle 7

Av 12

Calle 9

Calle 11

Calle 13

Calle 13A

Av 12

Av 10

Av 14

Av 16

Av 12

Av 18

Tracopa

San José

plaza is architecturally dull, but some of its elevated terraces provide decent views of the mountains surrounding San José (especially at sunset). On its western flank is an open-air crafts market (p98).

Museo de Arte y Diseño Contemporáneo MUSEUM
(Map p72; ☑ 2257-7202; www.madc.cr; cnr Av 3 & Calle 15; admission US$3, Mon free; ⊙ 9:30am-5pm Mon-Sat) Commonly referred to as MADC, the Contemporary Art & Design Museum is housed in the historic National Liquor Factory building, which dates from 1856. The largest and most important contemporary-art museum in the region, MADC is focused on showing the works of contemporary Costa Rican, Central American and South American artists and occasionally features temporary exhibits devoted to interior design, fashion and graphic art.

Parque España PARK
(Map p72; Avs 3 & 7 btwn Calles 9 & 11) Surrounded by heavy traffic, Parque España may be small, but it becomes a riot of birdsong every day at sunset when the local avian population comes in to roost. In addition to being a good spot for a shady break, the park is home to an ornate statue of Christopher Columbus that was given to the people of Costa Rica in 2002 by his descendants, commemorating the quincentennial of the explorer's landing in Puerto Limón.

Barrio Amón NEIGHBORHOOD
North and west of Plaza España lies this pleasant, historic neighborhood, home to a cluster of *cafetalero* (coffee grower) mansions constructed during the late 19th and early 20th centuries. In recent years many of the area's historic buildings have been converted into hotels, restaurants and offices, making this a popular district for an architectural stroll. You'll find everything from art deco concrete manses to brightly painted tropical Victorian structures in various states of upkeep. It is a key arts center.

Parque Morazán PARK
(Map p72; Avs 3 & 5 btwn Calles 5 & 9) To the southwest of the Parque España is Parque Morazán, named for Francisco Morazán, the 19th-century general who attempted to unite the Central American nations under a single flag. Once a notorious center of pros-

titution, the park is now beautifully illuminated in the evenings. At its center is the **Templo de Música** (Music Temple; Map p72), a concrete bandstand that serves as an unofficial symbol of San José.

Edificio Metálico
NOTABLE BUILDING

(Map p72; cnr Av 5 & Calle 9) One of downtown San José's most striking buildings, this century-old, two-story metal edifice on Parque España's western edge was prefabricated in Belgium, then shipped piece by piece to San José. Today it functions as a school and local landmark.

Casa Amarilla
NOTABLE BUILDING

(Map p72; Av 7 btwn Calles 11 & 13) On Parque España's northeast corner, this elegant colonial-style yellow mansion (closed to the public) houses the ministry of foreign affairs. The ceiba tree in front was planted by John F Kennedy during his 1963 visit to Costa Rica. If you walk around to the property's northeast corner, you can see a graffiti-covered slab of the Berlin Wall standing in the rear garden.

TEOR/éTica
GALLERY

(Map p72; ☎ 2221-1051; www.tcoretica.org; cnr Calle 7 & Av 11; ☺ 9am-5pm Mon-Fri, to 7pm Wed, 10am-4pm Sat) **FREE** This contemporary-art museum is the bricks-and-mortar gathering space for the TEOR/éTica Foundation, a nonprofit organization that supports Central American art and culture. Housed in a pair of vintage mansions across the street from one another, each of its elegant rooms exhibits cutting-edge works by established and emerging figures from Latin America and the world.

Parque Nacional
PARK

(Map p68; Avs 1 & 3 btwn Calles 15 & 19) One of San José's nicest green spaces, this shady spot lures retirees out to read newspapers and young couples to smooch coyly on concrete benches. At its center is the Monumento Nacional, a dramatic 1953 statue that depicts the Central American nations driving out American filibuster William Walker. The park is dotted with myriad monuments devoted to Latin American historical figures, including Cuban poet, essayist and revolutionary José Martí, Mexican independence figure Miguel Hidalgo and 18th-century Venezuelan humanist Andrés Bello.

Across the street, to the south, stands the **Asamblea Legislativa** (Legislative Assembly; Map p68), which also bears an important statue: this one a depiction of Juan Santamaría – the young man who helped kick the pesky Walker out of Costa Rica – in full flame-throwing action.

Estación del Ferrocarril de Costa Rica
NOTABLE BUILDING

(Map p68; cnr Av 3 & Calle 21) Less than a block to the east of the Parque Nacional is San José's historic train station to the Atlantic, which was built in 1908. Nowadays offering weekday train service to Heredia and Cartago, it's a remarkable example of tropical architecture, with swirling art nouveau-inspired beams and elaborate stonework all along the roofline.

SAN JOSÉ FOR CHILDREN

Chances are that if you're in Costa Rica on a short vacation you'll be headed out to the countryside fairly quickly. But if for some reason you're going to be hanging out in San José for a day – or two or three – with your kids, here are a few activities to keep them busy.

Near Parque La Sabana, the Museo de Ciencias Naturales (p74) will impress youngsters with its astounding array of skeletons and endless cases full of stuffed animals, while the Museo de los Niños (p73) is a sure hit for children who just can't keep their hands off the exhibits. Young nature lovers will enjoy getting up close and personal with butterflies at the Spirogyra Jardín de Mariposas (p73) or checking out the exotic animals at the **Parque Zoológico Nacional Simón Bolívar** (Map p68; ☎ 2233-6701; www.fundazoo.org; Av 11 btwn Calles 7 & 9; adult/child US$5/3.50; ☺ 8am-3:30pm Mon-Fri, 9am-4:30pm Sat & Sun; ⊕). Just a little further afield (an easy day trip from San José) is the wonderful zoo and wildlife-rescue center Zoo Ave (p115), where you can enjoy native birds and monkeys in a more naturalistic setting.

If you're spending more than a week in the city, note that many Spanish-language academies offer special custom-made lessons for teens.

Central San José

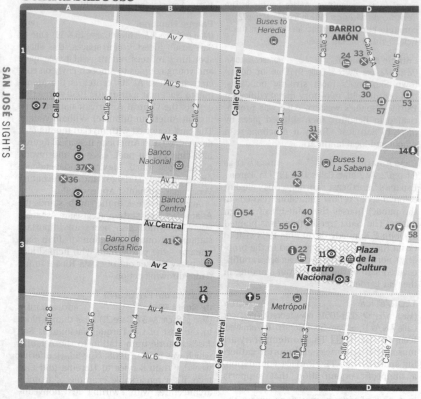

⊙ Central San José West

Parque Central
PARK

(Map p72; Avs 2 & 4 btwn Calles Central & 2) The city's central park is more of a run-down plaza than a park. At its center is a grandiose bandstand that looks as if it was designed by Mussolini: massive concrete arches support a florid roof capped with a ball-shaped decorative knob.

Catedral Metropolitana
CHURCH

(Map p72; Avs 2 & 4 btwn Calles Central & 1) East of Parque Central, the Renaissance-style Catedral Metropolitana was built in 1871 after the previous cathedral was destroyed in an earthquake. The graceful neoclassical interior has colorful Spanish-tile floors, stained-glass windows, and a Christ figure that was produced by a Guatemalan workshop in the late 17th century. On the north side of the

nave, a recumbent Christ that dates back to 1878 draws devout Ticos, who arrive here to pray and deposit pleas scribbled on small slips of paper.

Teatro Melico Salazar
HISTORIC BUILDING

(Map p72; ☎ 2295-6032; www.teatromelico.go.cr; Av 2 btwn Calles Central & 2) On the north side of Parque Central is this theater, which was built in 1928 in a beaux-arts style. It is named after the well-known Costa Rican tenor Melico Salazar (1887–1950), who performed internationally (among other places, he sang at the Metropolitan Opera in New York City). The theater was the site of the 2002 presidential inauguration, and regularly hosts fine-arts engagements.

Mercado Central
MARKET

(Map p72; Avs Central & 1 btwn Calles 6 & 8; ☉ 6am-6pm Mon-Sat) Though *josefinos* mainly do their shopping at chain supermarkets, San

◎ Central San José North

Museo de los Niños & Galería Nacional   MUSEUM

(Map p68; ☎ 2258-4929; www.museocr.org; Calle 4, north of Av 9; adult/child US$2.60/2; ☻8am-4:30pm Tue-Fri, 9:30am-5pm Sat & Sun; ⓦ) If you were wondering how to get your young kids interested in art and science, this unusual museum – actually two museums in one – is an excellent place to start. Housed in an old penitentiary built in 1909, it is part children's museum and part art gallery. Small children will love the hands-on exhibits related to science, geography and natural history, while grown-ups will enjoy the unusual juxtaposition of contemporary art in abandoned prison cells.

Spirogyra Jardín de Mariposas   GARDENS

(Map p68; ☎ 2222-2937; www.butterflygardencr. com; Barrio Amón; adult/child US$7/5; ☻8am-4pm; ⓦ; ⬛to El Pueblo) Housing more than 30 species of butterfly – including the luminescent blue morpho – in plant-filled enclosures, this small butterfly garden is a great spot for kids. Visit in the morning to see plenty of fluttering. The garden is 150m east and 150m south of Centro Comercial El Pueblo, which can be reached on foot (about a 20- to 30-minute walk from downtown), by taxi or by bus.

◎ La Sabana

West of downtown, the bustle of the city's congested center gives way to private homes, condo towers and shopping areas chock-full of Ticos. At the heart of this district lies the sprawling Parque Metropolitano La Sabana, a popular recreation center and a welcome patch of green amid the concrete.

Parque Metropolitano La Sabana   PARK

(Map p76) Once the site of San José's main airport, this 72-hectare green space at the west end of Paseo Colón is home to a museum, a lagoon and various sports facilities – most notably Costa Rica's national soccer stadium. During the day, the park's paths make a relaxing place for a stroll, a jog or a picnic.

Museo de Arte Costarricense   MUSEUM

(Map p76; ☎ 2256-1281; www.musarco.go.cr; ☻9am-4pm Tue-Sun; ⓦ) **FREE** At the eastern entrance to the Parque La Sabana is the Museo de Arte Costarricense, in a Spanish-style structure that served as San José's main

José's crowded indoor markets retain an old-world feel. This is the main market, lined with vendors hawking everything from spices and coffee beans to *pura vida* (pure life) souvenir T-shirts

Mercado Central Annex   MARKET

(Map p72; Avs 1 & 3 btwn Calles 6 & 8) The Mercado Central Annex is less touristy than Mercado Central, and is crowded with butchers, fishmongers and informal counters dishing out typical Costa Rican *casados* (a set meal of rice, beans and cabbage slaw served with chicken, fish or meat).

Mercado Borbón   MARKET

(Map p72; cnr Av 3 & Calle 8) The Mercado Borbón is more focused on produce, though it sells a bit of everything. (Be aware: the streets get sketchy around the Borbón.)

Central San José

airport terminal until 1955. The newly re-modeled museum features regional art and other exhibits.

Museo de Ciencias Naturales La Salle
MUSEUM
(☏ 2232-1306; lasalle.ed.cr/museo.php; adult/child US$2/1.60; ⊘8am-4pm Mon-Sat, 9am-5pm Sun; ⊕) Ever want to see a spider-monkey skeleton (they're cool!) or a herd of taxidermied tapirs? This natural-history museum near Parque La Sabana's southwest corner has an extensive collection of stuffed animals and birds from Costa Rica and far beyond, alongside animal skeletons, minerals and specimens preserved in formaldehyde. Kids in particular will appreciate this place.

◉ Los Yoses, Barrio Escalante & San Pedro

Museo de Insectos
MUSEUM
(Insect Museum; ☏ 2511-5318; www.miucr.ucr.ac.cr; admission US$2; ⊘1-4:45pm Mon-Fri) Reputedly Central America's largest insect museum, this place has an extensive collection assembled by the Facultad de Agronomía at the Universidad de Costa Rica. Curiously, it is housed in the basement of the music building (Facultad de Artes Musicales), a brutalist structure painted an incongruous shade of Barbie pink. The museum is signposted from the Iglesia de San Pedro.

🏃 Activities

Golfers can reserve tee times at **Parque Valle del Sol** (✆ ext 3 2282-9222; www.vallesol. com; 1.7km west of HSBC Bank; 18 holes US$67, incl golf cart US$95; ◷ 6:30am-6pm Tue-Sun, 8am-6pm Mon), outside Escazú.

If you want to swim with the kiddies and your hotel doesn't have a pool, head to the Ojo de Agua Springs (p109) in San Antonio de Belén, a popular swimming spot for Tico families.

Parque Metropolitano La Sabana (Map p76; ✆ 2284-8700) has a variety of sporting facilities, including tennis courts, volleyball, basketball and baseball areas, jogging paths and soccer pitches. Pickup soccer games can be had on most days, though you'd better be good: Ticos can sink a drop shot by age seven. There is also an Olympic-size swimming pool for serious lap swimmers.

🤸 Courses

You can improve your dance moves at Merecumbé, a chain of studios that will get you grooving to everything from salsa to waltz. Most courses are for locals, but some sessions are geared to foreign travelers. Schedules vary; call ahead. The company has various studios, including one in **Escazú** (Map p79; ✆ 2289-4774, 8884-7553; cnr Av 26 & Calle Cortés) and another in **San Pedro** (✆ 2224-3531; 100m south & 25m west of the Banco Popular), though, unfortunately, nothing downtown.

☞ Tours

The city is small and easily navigable, but if you're looking for a walking tour that will guide you to key sites, there are plenty on offer.

ChepeCletas   TOUR
(✆ 8849-8316, 2222-7548; www.chepecletas.com) This dynamic Tico-run company offers cultural walking and cycling tours of San José, including a free (tips accepted) Thursday-morning city tour, a foodie-oriented exploration of the Mercado Central, a bar-hopping tour focused on traditional downtown *cantinas* (canteens) and a guided visit to San José's parks and green spaces.

Barrio Bird Walking Tours   WALKING TOUR
(✆ 6050-1952; www.toursanjosecostarica.com; tours from US$28) The knowledgeable and engaging Stacey Corrales shows visitors San José's famous and not-so-famous sights, providing history and insights on the city's architecture, murals and urban art. Specialized tours also cater to gourmands, photographers and bar-crawlers.

Carpe Chepe   TOUR
(✆ 8326-6142; www.carpechepe.com; guided pub crawl US$20; ◷ 7pm Thu & Sat) For an insider's look at Chepe's nightlife, join one of these lively Thursday- and Saturday-evening guided pub crawls, led by an enthusiastic group of young locals. A free welcome shot is included at each of the five bars visited. Online bookings receive a 20% discount.

TALK LIKE A TICO

San José is loaded with schools that offer Spanish lessons (either privately or in groups) and provide long-term visitors to the country with everything from dance lessons to volunteer opportunities. A few well-established options are listed below.

Already speak Spanish? To truly talk like a Tico (Costa Rican), check out the **Costa Rica Idioms** app, available for iPod, iPad and Android. It's quite basic but defines local lingo and uses each term in a sentence. *Tuanis, mae!* (Cool, dude!)

Amerispan Study Abroad (✆ in USA & Canada 800-511-0179, worldwide 215-531-7917; www.amerispan.com; from US$380/225) Offers a variety of educational programs, as well as volunteer placements and medical Spanish.

Costa Rican Language Academy (✆ 2280-5834, in USA 866-230-6361; www.crlang. co.cr; Calle Ronda, Barrio Dent) In addition to Spanish, it offers cooking and dance classes.

Institute for Central American Development Studies (ICADS; ✆ 2225-0508; www. icads.org; Montes de Oca, San Pedro) Month-long programs with or without homestays are combined with lectures and activities focused on environmental and political issues.

Personalized Spanish (✆ 2278-3254, in USA 786-245-4124; www.personalizedspanish. com; Tres Ríos) As the name implies, private classes that cater to your needs.

La Sabana

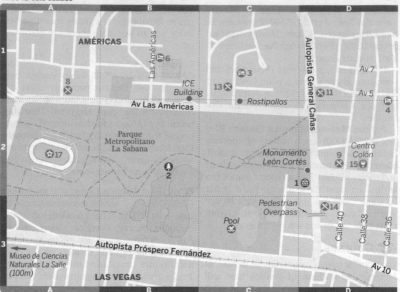

La Sabana

◎ Sights
1	Museo de Arte Costarricense	D2
2	Parque Metropolitano La Sabana	B2

● Activities, Courses & Tours
	Parque Metropolitano La Sabana	(see 2)

⊜ Sleeping
3	Apartotel La Sabana	C1
4	Gaudy's	D2
5	Hotel Grano de Oro	E3
6	Mi Casa Hostel	B1
7	Rosa del Paseo	E2

✖ Eating
8	El Chicote	A1

9	Las Mañanitas	D2
10	Machu Picchu	E2
11	Más X Menos	D1
12	Pali	F2
13	Park Café	C1
	Restaurante Grano de Oro	(see 5)
14	Soda Tapia	D3

◉ Drinking & Nightlife
15	Club Vertigo	D2
16	Energy Club	F2
	Rapsodia	(see 9)

✪ Entertainment
17	Estadio Nacional de Costa Rica	A2
18	Sala Garbo	E3

Costa Rica Art Tour TOUR
(☎ 2288-0896, 8359-5571; www.costaricaarttour.com; per person US$150) This small outfit run by Molly Keeler organizes a recommended day tour that visits five artists studios, where you can view (and buy) the work of local painters, sculptors, printmakers, ceramicists and jewelers. Lunch and hotel pickup is included in the price. Reserve at least a week in advance.

Swiss Travel Service WALKING TOUR
(Map p68; ☎ 2282-4898; www.swisstravelcr.com) ✈ This long-standing agency offers a four-hour city tour of San José that hits all the key sites.

✷✸ Festivals & Events

Día de San José RELIGIOUS
(St Joseph's Day) On March 19, San José marks the day of its patron saint with Mass in some churches.

Map

```
0        400 m
0      0.2 miles
```

RINCÓN DE CUBILLOS

See San José Map (p68)

Av 3   Tica Bus

Calle 24

⊗10   Av 1

Edificio Torre Mercedes Benz

Paseo Colón   Pedestrian Overpass   16   12 ⊗

7   ✿18

5   Av 2

Central San José (1km)

Calle 34   Calle 32   Calle 30   Av 4   Calle 28   Calle 26   Calle 24   Calle 22

Av 6

Día del Boyero   CULTURAL

On the second Sunday of March, Escazú holds this popular event honoring Costa Rica's *boyeros* (oxcart drivers). Dozens of attendees from all over the country decorate traditional, brightly painted carts and form a colorful (if slow) parade.

Festival de las Artes   ARTS

(www.festivaldelasartes.go.cr) Every even year, San José becomes host to the biennial citywide arts showcase that features theater, music, dance and film. It's held for two weeks in March or April. Keep an eye out for information in the daily newspapers.

Desfile de los Boyeros   CULTURAL

(Oxcart Parade) This parade of oxcarts down Paseo Colón takes place every November and is a celebration of the country's agricultural heritage.

Festival de la Luz   RELIGIOUS

(Festival of Light; www.festivaldelaluz.cr) December brings San José's big Christmas parade, marked by elaborate costumes and floats, and an absurd amount of plastic 'snow.'

Las Fiestas de Zapote   CULTURAL

(www.fiestaszapote.com; ⊘ Dec 25 to Jan 5) Every year, tens of thousands of Ticos head to the bullring in the suburb of Zapote, just south-

east of San José, for this week-long festival. Expect plenty of entertainment, including rodeos, cowboys and carnival rides, as well as fried food and booze.

🛏 Sleeping

Accommodations in San José run the gamut from simple but homey hostels to luxurious boutique retreats. You'll find the cheapest sleeps in the city center, with nicer midrange and top-end spots clustered in more well-to-do districts such as Barrio Amón and La Sabana. Also worthwhile for their charm, safety and serenity are the adjacent neighborhoods of Los Yoses and San Pedro, which lie within walking distance of downtown.

For tonier options, the upscale suburb of Escazú – a 20-minute bus ride away – is a good choice. If you're flying into or out of Costa Rica from here, it may be more convenient to stay in Alajuela, as the town is minutes from the international airport.

Reservations are recommended in the high season (December through April), in particular the two weeks around Christmas and Semana Santa (Holy Week, the week preceding Easter).

🛏 Central San José East

Most of downtown's better sleeping options are located east of Calle Central, many of them in historic Victorian and art deco mansions. Many of the top-end hotels accept credit cards.

★ **Hostel Pangea**   HOSTEL $

(Map p72; ☑ 2221-1992; www.hostelpangea.com; Av 7 btwn Calles 3 & 3A, Barrio Amón; dm US$14, d with/without bathroom US$45/34, ste from US$55; ℗@🛜🐕) This industrial-strength, Tico-owned hostel – 25 dorms and 25 private rooms – has been a popular 20-something backpacker hangout for years. It's not difficult to see why: it's smack in the middle of the city and comes stocked with a pool, a rooftop restaurant-lounge with stellar views, and a combination bar–movie theater. Needless to say, it's a party spot.

Rooms are tidy, mattresses firm and the shared bathrooms enormous and clean. The hostel's five suites have king-size beds and flat-screen TVs. Other perks include free internet, free phone calls to North America, luggage storage and 24-hour airport shuttles (from US$12).

★**Hostel Casa del Parque** HOSTEL **$**
(Map p68; ☑2233-3437; www.hostelcasadelparque.
com; Calle 19 btwn Avs 1 & 3; dm US$13, d with/
without bathroom US$45/35; ☜) A vintage art
deco manse from 1936 houses this cozy and
welcoming spot on the northeastern edge
of Parque Nacional. Five large, basic private
rooms (one with private bathroom) and
a 10-bed dormitory upstairs have parquet
floors and simple furnishings. Take some
sun on the plant-festooned outdoor patio,
lounge in the funkily furnished living room
and take advantage of the shared kitchen.

The bilingual young owner, Federico
Echeverría, is a good source of local dining
information.

Costa Rica Backpackers HOSTEL **$**
(Map p68; ☑2221-6191, 2223-2406; www.cos-
taricabackpackers.com; Av 6 near Calle 21; dm
US$13, d without bathroom US$32; ℗@☜⛱)
This extremely popular hostel has 15 basic
but clean dormitories and 13 doubles with
shared bathrooms surrounding a spacious
hammock-filled garden and a free-form
pool. Two bars, a restaurant and ambient
chill-out music enhance the inviting, laid-
back atmosphere. Other benefits include
a communal kitchen and TV lounge, free
luggage storage, internet access, an onsite
travel agency and low-cost airport transfers.

Casa Ridgway GUESTHOUSE **$**
(Map p68; ☑2233-6168, 2233-2693; www.
casaridgwayhostel.com; cnr Calle 15 & Av 6A; incl
breakfast dm US$15, s/d US$25/38, without bathroom US$22/34; ℗☻☜) This small, peaceful
guesthouse on a quiet side street is run by
the adjacent Friends' Peace Center, a Quaker
organization promoting social justice and
human rights. There is a small lounge, a
communal kitchen and a lending library
filled with books about Central American
politics and society. No smoking or alcohol
is allowed, with quiet hours from 10pm to
6am.

Costa Rica Guesthouse GUESTHOUSE **$**
(Map p68; ☑2223-7034; www.costa-rica-guest-
house.com; Av 6 btwn Calles 21 & 25; incl breakfast
d with/without bathroom US$50/39; ℗@☜)
This 1904 guesthouse has simple, graceful
rooms with spacious bathrooms and hall-
ways lined with Spanish tile. Furnishings
are basic (creaky beds), but it's a tranquil,
couple-friendly spot. There's a small internet lounge, an outdoor patio adorned with
epiphytes and an enclosed parking area out
back. Laundry service (per kilo US$2) is
available.

Casa Hilda GUESTHOUSE **$**
(Map p68; ☑2221-0037; c1hilda@racsa.co.cr; Av
11 btwn Calles 3 & 3A; s/d US$26/36) Run by
the charming Quesada family, this simple
peach-colored guesthouse has five basic,
clean rooms with private bathrooms surrounding a peaceful courtyard. Check out
the natural spring in the center of the house
that has been bubbling potable water for
more than 90 years (even during dry season). Credit cards accepted.

★**Hotel Aranjuez** HOTEL **$$**
(Map p68; ☑2256-1825; www.hotelaranjuez.com;
Calle 19 btwn Avs 11 & 13; incl breakfast s US$37-
52, d US$52-67, s/d without bathroom US$27/36;
℗@☜) This rambling hotel in Barrio Aran-
juez consists of five nicely maintained vin-
tage homes that have been strung together
with a labyrinth of gardens and connecting
walkways. The 36 spotless rooms come in

VOLUNTEERING IN SAN JOSÉ

For travelers who want an experience beyond vacation, there are dozens of not-for-profit organizations in San José that gladly accept volunteers.

Central American Service Expeditions (☑8839-0515; www.serviceexpeditions.com) A Costa Rican nonprofit that creates custom volunteer expeditions for families and teens, focused on sustainability.

GeoVisions (☑1-203-453-5838, in USA 1-855-875-6837; www.geovisions.org) An interna-tional nonprofit that places volunteers in Costa Rican schools and medical facilities.

Sustainable Horizon (☑1-732-410-5677, in USA & Canada 1-866-273-2500; www.sustaina-blehorizon.com) Arranges a wide variety of volunteer trips, including opportunities to help out at children's shelters.

United Planet (☑1-617-267-7763, in USA & Canada 1-800-292-2316; www.unitedplanet.org) Places volunteers in orphanages, day-care centers and health-care positions.

Escazú

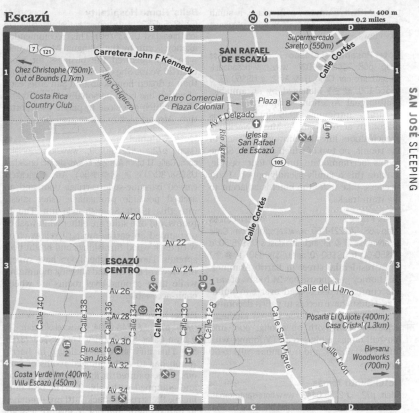

various configurations, all with lockboxes and cable TV. The hotel's best attribute, however, is the lush garden patio, where a legendary breakfast buffet is served every morning.

Though the architecture can be a bit creaky and the walls thin, the service is efficient and the hotel is a solid, family-friendly option. Rooms in the new apartment-building annex half a block away lack the charm and sense of community of the main hotel, but annex guests still have access to the bounteous breakfast and pleasant common areas across the street.

Raya Vida Villa   GUESTHOUSE **$$**
(Map p68; ☎2223-4168; www.rayavida.com; Calle 15, off Av 11; s/d incl breakfast US$85/95, extra person US$20; [P][🛜]) This long-running B&B, housed in an elegant hilltop villa originally designed as the Spanish ambassador's residence, reflects owner Michael Long's interest in art and antiques. Four well-appointed rooms have polished-wood floors, bright floral linens and expansive bathrooms. Aesthetically pleasing touches include a

patio with a fountain, a fireplace, a small garden, and an upstairs deck with pleasant city views.

Hotel Posada del Museo GUESTHOUSE **$$**
(Map p68; ☎2258-1027; www.hotelposadadelmuseo.com; cnr Calle 17 & Av 2; s US$50-73, d US$68-100; @ 📶) Managed by an amiable, multilingual Argentine couple, this architecturally intriguing, 1928-vintage inn is diagonally across from the Museo Nacional. French doors line the entrances to each of the rooms, no two of which are alike. Some rooms accommodate up to four people, making this a family-friendly option. Light sleepers, take note: the hotel is adjacent to the train tracks.

Kaps Place GUESTHOUSE **$$**
(Map p68; ☎2221-1169; www.kapsplace.com; Calle 19 btwn Avs 11 & 13; incl breakfast s US$25-50, d US$50-60, tr US$60-70, apt US$90-130; P @ 📶) On a residential street in Barrio Aranjuez, this homey guesthouse has 24 rooms of various configurations spread over two buildings. Guests have access to patios decorated in colorful mosaics, three shared kitchens, a games room with ping-pong, pool and foosball tables, a big-screen TV lounge with huge DVD library, and free phone calls to 60 countries.

Hotel Santo Tomás HOTEL **$$**
(Map p72; ☎2255-0448; www.hotelsantotomas.com; Av 7 btwn Calles 3 & 5; r incl breakfast US$64-88; P ⊖ @ 📶 ≋) A Barrio Amón landmark that once belonged to the Salazar family of *cafetaleros,* this stately early-20th-century colonial-style mansion oozes history. Slightly frayed rooms with high ceilings and period furnishings occupy the mansion itself, while a back annex offers more modern amenities. The garden courtyard contains a swimming pool with tiled water slide, Jacuzzi and small open-air gym.

Hemingway Inn HOTEL **$$**
(Map p72; ☎2257-8630, 2221-1804; www.hemingwayinn.com; cnr Calle 9 & Av 9; incl breakfast s US$40-68, d US$57-85; 📶) This funky little spot in Barrio Amón offers 17 simple, comfortable and unique rooms in a rambling *cafetalero* house dating to the 1920s. The garden, shared kitchen and wall murals lend the inn a relaxed and friendly ambience, and room prices include a full made-to-order breakfast. As a rare perk, pets can be accommodated with prior notice.

Bells' Home Hospitality HOMESTAY **$$**
(☎2225-4752; www.homestay-thebells.com; s/d incl breakfast US$35/60) This recommended agency is run by the bilingual Marcela Bell, who has operated the business for more than 20 years. She can arrange stays in more than a dozen homes around San José, each of which has been personally inspected and all of which are close to public transportation. Airport pickup is also available.

Hotel Colonial HOTEL **$$**
(Map p72; ☎2223-0109; www.hotelcolonialcr.com; Calle 11 btwn Avs 2 & 6; s/d/ste incl breakfast US$68/80/113; P ❄ @ 📶 ≋) An intricately carved baroque-style carriage door and an arched poolside promenade usher guests into this 1940s Spanish-style inn. The 16 rooms and one suite are either whitewashed or painted an earthy mustard yellow color, with dark wood furnishings and bright bedspreads. Those on higher floors have sweeping views of the city and outlying mountains, while three ground-level rooms are wheelchair-accessible.

Hotel Kekoldi HOTEL **$$**
(Map p72; ☎2248-0804; www.kekoldi.com; Av 9 btwn Calles 5 & 7; s/d/tr from US$62/73/85; 📶) This airy art-deco building in Barrio Amón has 10 high-ceilinged rooms of various sizes, painted in light shades of pastel and equipped with cable TV. The best ones facing the street or back yard are drenched in natural light; interior rooms are less appealing. Common spaces include a cheerful breakfast room and a garden for lounging.

Hotel Rincón de San José HOTEL **$$**
(Map p72; ☎2221-9702; www.hotelrincondesanjose.com; cnr Av 9 & Calle 15; s/d/tr/q incl breakfast from US$62/65/85/113; @ 📶) Comprising four houses of varying ages in Barrio Otoya, this tidy spot has 42 guest rooms – ranging from rather faded older units to modern ones with bright linens and ceramic tile. Breakfast is served in an attractive interior garden courtyard, and there's a small sun terrace with nice views of surrounding houses and distant mountains.

Casa Alfi HOTEL **$$**
(Map p72; ☎2221-2102; www.casaalfihotel.com; Calle 3 btwn Avs 4 & 6; s/d/tr incl breakfast US$43/62/77; @ 📶) Steps from the Teatro Nacional, this simple two-story structure comprises nine guest rooms – each with TV, telephone, private bathroom and lockbox – surrounding a covered courtyard. Friendly

AWAY FROM SAN JOSÉ

For many visitors to Costa Rica, a night in San José is practically obligatory at the beginning or end of every trip. But if you have a car, you can instead arrange to stay at one of the following country inns. All lie within an hour's drive of the international airport – and most have incredible mountain scenery.

➡ Just outside Alajuela, Trapp Family Lodge (p110), Tacacori Ecolodge (p111) and Xandari Resort Hotel & Spa (p111) have verdant settings and are five to 15 minutes from the airport.

➡ A 30-minute cruise along the Interamericana is Vista del Valle Plantation Inn (p115).

➡ The dreamy Finca Rosa Blanca (p124) is less than half an hour from the airport check-in.

➡ Vista Atenas B&B (p115), only 30 minutes west of the terminal, is perched so spectacularly high above the valley, you'll think you're flying again.

➡ To the north, Poás Volcano Lodge (p114) and Poás Lodge (p113) are about 45 minutes to one hour from the airport.

and well-traveled owner Alfi offers guests three breakfast choices: continental, tropical or traditional Costa Rican.

Hotel Fleur de Lys   HOTEL $$

(Map p72; ☎ 2223-1206; www.hotelfleurdelys.com; Calle 13 btwn Avs 2 & 6; incl breakfast s US$78-98, d US$86-106, ste junior/master US$126/156; P ⊜ @ ☎) Pristinely maintained, this century-old, bright-pink Victorian mansion houses 31 spotless wood-paneled rooms with firm beds, ceiling fans and wicker furnishings. A small onsite bar hosts a daily happy hour and, on special occasions, live music. The staff are attentive and the location central (note the proximity of the train tracks). German, French and English are spoken; credit cards accepted.

Gran Hotel Costa Rica   HOTEL $$$

(Map p72; ☎ 2221-4000; www.granhotelcostarica.com; Calle 3 btwn Avs Central & 2; incl breakfast d standard/superior/deluxe $96/119/141, ste master/presidential $198/299; ⊜ ✳ @ ☎) Constructed in 1930, the city's first prominent hotel is recognized as a national landmark (John F Kennedy and soccer legend Pelé both stayed here). Frequent renovations keep the 107 rooms modern and comfortable, though they retain period touches such as brass bed frames and wood furnishings. The popular terrace bar-restaurant out front features live piano music on weekday evenings.

Some rooms have wonderful views of the Teatro Nacional, and here and there are subtle architectural reminders of the hotel's history: exposed beams, molded ceilings and the dramatic entrance hall – lined with vintage photographs of San José.

Hotel Don Carlos   HOTEL $$$

(Map p72; ☎ 2221-6707; www.doncarloshotel.com; Calle 9 btwn Avs 7 & 9; incl breakfast s US$85-96, d $96-107; P @ ☎ ✳) Built around an early-20th-century house that once belonged to President Tomás Guardia, this welcoming Barrio Amón inn exudes a slightly campy colonial-era vibe. Thirty-three rooms are nestled around a faux-pre-Columbian sculpture garden with a sundeck, jacuzzi and small kiddie-depth pool. All rooms have cable TV, lockbox and hair dryer; upstairs units are generally nicer than the mustier ones downstairs.

Don't miss the Spanish-tile mural, just outside the onsite restaurant, which beautifully depicts central San José in the 1930s. Credit cards accepted.

🏨 La Sabana & Surrounds

You'll find everything from hostels to vintage B&Bs in the neighborhoods that surround Parque Metropolitano La Sabana.

Gaudy's   HOSTEL $

(Map p76; ☎ 2248-0086; www.backpacker.co.cr; Av 5 btwn Calles 36 & 38; dm US$13-17, s/d without bathroom US$22/34, r with bathroom US$38-39; P @ ☎) Popular among shoestring travelers for years, this homey hostel inside a sprawling modernist house northeast of Parque La Sabana has 13 private rooms and two dormitories. The Colombian owners keep the design scheme minimalist and the vibe mellow, with professional service and well-maintained rooms. There's a communal kitchen, a TV lounge, a pool table and a courtyard strung with hammocks.

Mi Casa Hostel
HOSTEL $

(Map p76; ☑2231-4700; www.micasahostel.com; incl breakfast dm US$13, r with/without bathroom from US$34/30; P@⊛) This converted modernist home in La Sabana has polished-wood floors, vintage furnishings and 15 eclectic guest rooms to choose from, including one 10-person dorm and another room that's wheelchair-accessible. Mellow communal areas are comfortably furnished, and the shared kitchen is clean and roomy. There is a pleasant garden, a pool table, free internet, and laundry service.

Rosa del Paseo
HOTEL $$

(Map p76; ☑2257-3225, 2257-3258; www.rosadelpaseo.com; Paseo Colón btwn Calles 28 & 30; s/d/ste from $75/85/90; P@⊛) ✿ Don't let the Paseo Colón location and the small facade fool you: this sprawling Victorian-Caribbean mansion (built in 1910 by the Montealegre family of coffee exporters) has 18 rooms reaching way back into an interior courtyard far from the city noise. The hotel still maintains the original tile floors and other historic details, including antique oil paintings and sculptures.

Rooms are simple, with polished-wood floors and period-style furnishings. There's a wonderful front sitting room where guests can listen to vintage vinyl discs on the phonograph, and the garden, where breakfast is served each morning, is filled with heliconias and bougainvilleas. Credit cards accepted.

Colours Oasis Resort
HOTEL $$

(☑2296-1880, in USA & Canada 866-517-4390; www.coloursoasis.com; cnr Triángulo de Pavas & Blvr Rohrmoser; s/d/ste from US$78/89/157; ⊛✉) This longtime LGBT-friendly hotel occupies a sprawling Spanish-colonial-style complex in the elegant Rohrmoser district (northwest of La Sabana). Rooms and mini-apartments have modern furnishings and impeccable bathrooms. Facilities include TV lounge, mini-gym, pool, sundeck and Jacuzzi, as well as an onsite bar-restaurant, ideal for evening cocktails. The bilingual owners offer helpful insights on gay travel in Costa Rica.

Apartotel La Sabana
HOTEL $$

(Map p76; ☑2220-2422; www.apartotel-lasabana.com; d/apt/f incl breakfast from US$78/93/137; P⊛@⊛✉) This lovely, well-maintained apartment complex 150m north of Rostipollos has 32 units in various configurations that draw long-term business travelers as well as families. Apartments (with and without kitchen) are accented with wood furnishings and folk art. The interior courtyard has a nice pool, and free shuttle service is offered both from and to the airport. Special rates are available for weekly stays.

★ Hotel Grano de Oro
BOUTIQUE HOTEL $$$

(Map p76; ☑2255-3322; www.hotelgranodeoro.com; Calle 30 btwn Avs 2 & 4; d US$170-289, f/garden/vista-del-oro ste US$300/345/515; P⊛@⊛) It's easy to see why honeymooners love it here. Built around a sprawling early-20th-century Victorian mansion, this elegant inn has 39 demure 'Tropical Victorian' rooms furnished with wrought-iron beds and rich brocade linens. A few rooms even boast private courtyards with gurgling fountains, while the public areas sparkle with fresh tropical flowers and polished-wood accents.

If you want to experience the Costa Rica of a gilded age, this would be the place to do it.

🛏 Los Yoses, Barrio Escalante & San Pedro

Locals use several prominent landmarks when giving directions, including Spoon restaurant, the Fuente de la Hispanidad fountain and Más x Menos supermarket.

★ Hostel Bekuo
HOSTEL $

(☑1-813-343-8877, 2234-1091; www.hostelbekuo.com; dm US$11, d from US$29; ⊛) For pure positive energy, you won't find a nicer hostel anywhere in San José. This restful spot, 100m south of Av Central and 325m west of Spoon, feels extremely homey, thanks to frequent backyard barbecues, spontaneous pitchers of free sangria, a living room with piano and guitar and a kitchen equipped with good knives, appliances and an inviting central workspace.

The airy modernist structure has nine unique and colorful rooms with high-quality beds and mattresses (including four dormitories, one reserved especially for women), along with large tiled bathrooms, an expansive TV lounge dotted with bean bags, and an interior courtyard slung with hammocks. Well-traveled owner Brian Van Fleet and his staff go the extra mile for guests, with colorful and well-conceived information displays and evening outings designed to show visitors the best of San José's nightlife. Yet this remains a place where you can get a good night's sleep; silent time is respected from 11pm onwards.

Los Yoses, Barrio Escalante & San Pedro

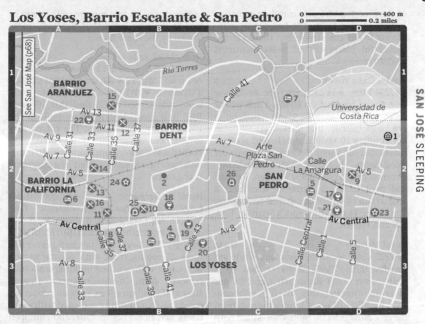

SAN JOSÉ SLEEPING

Los Yoses, Barrio Escalante & San Pedro

Hostel Urbano   HOSTEL **$**
(📞 2281-0707; www.hostelurbano.com; dm US$13, d with/without bathroom US$38/32) Within easy walking distance of the university and its associated nightlife, yet right on the bus line into downtown San José, this immaculate new hostel in a 1950s home opposite Parque

Kennedy in San Pedro makes guests feel instantly welcome with its open floor plan, spacious back yard, pool table, modern internet facilities and a kitchen-dining area that's nice enough to host a dinner party.

Smaller rooms, which are often rented out as private doubles, are also ideal for groups of three or four friends traveling together. Even the larger 12- and 16-bed dorms manage not to feel claustrophobic, thanks to the thoughtful placement of well-constructed modern bunks.

Hostel Casa Yoses
HOSTEL $

(☑2234-5486; www.casayoses.com; Av 8 near Calle 41; incl breakfast dm US$13, d with/without bathroom US$38/32; ℗@☎) Perched on a Los Yoses hillside, this mellow HI-affiliated hostel offers 10 stylish, simple and spotless rooms (six of them dorms) with parquet wood floors. Shared amenities include big-screen computers, a guest kitchen, foosball and pool tables, a barbecue area and a Jacuzzi tub in one of the shared bathrooms. The young Tico owners speak Spanish, English and French.

Hotel Milvia
B&B $$

(☑2225-4543; www.hotelmilvia.com; s/d/tr incl breakfast US$67/78/85; @☎) Owned by a well-known Costa Rican artist and former museum director, this lovely Caribbean-style building offers a homey retreat from the city. Nine eclectic rooms, all dotted with bright artwork, surround a pleasant courtyard with trickling fountain. An upstairs terrace provides views of the mountains. Hotel Milvia is located in San Pedro, 250m east, 100m north and 100m east of Más x Menos.

Hotel Ave del Paraíso
HOTEL $$

(☑2283-6017; hotelavedelparaiso.com; s/d incl breakfast US$68/79; @☎) Decorated with beautiful mosaic tiles (right down to the backyard recycling area), this hotel run by an artsy Polish-Tico family is set back from the busy street just far enough to permit a good night's sleep. It's very convenient to the

university (just a two-minute walk north) as well as the wonderful Café Kracovia (p88), owned by the same family.

Hotel 1492 Jade y Oro
B&B $$

(☑2225-3752, 2256-5913; www.hotel1492.com; Av 1 btwn Calles 29 & 33; incl breakfast s US$57, d US$68-79; ℗☎) On a quiet Barrio Escalante side street you'll find this 10-room B&B in a Spanish-style house built in the 1940s by the Volio family. The rooms vary in size, but all are nicely accented, with Portuguese tilework and some original furnishings. Breakfast is served in a charming rear garden.

Hotel Le Bergerac
BOUTIQUE HOTEL $$$

(☑2234-7850; www.bergerachotel.com; Calle 35 btwn Avs Central & 8; d standard/superior/deluxe/grande incl breakfast US$110/132/160/177; ℗@☎) This Los Yoses standard-bearer features 25 rooms, most with private garden patio, in a whitewashed building tranquilly removed from the main street. Though sizes and configurations vary, all rooms are comfortable and sunny, accented with wood floors and floral bedspreads, and equipped with immaculate bathroom, cable TV, telephone and safe. There is an onsite restaurant with a full bar.

🛏 Escazú

Escazú is a stylish area with accommodations ranging from sleek boutique inns to homey B&Bs – but there's not much for the budget traveler. Street addresses aren't always given; call directly or check hotel websites for directions (which are invariably complicated).

Three kilometers west of Escazú is the affluent expat suburb of Santa Ana. On the road between the two, you'll find a few out-of-the-way spots to stay.

Costa Verde Inn
INN $$

(☑2228-4080, in USA 1-800-773-5013; www.costaverdeinn.com; s/d/tr incl breakfast $60/70/80, d apt from $90; ℗@☎⊠) This homey stone inn is surrounded by gardens that contain a hot tub, a mosaic-tile swimming pool, a BBQ area and a sundeck with wi-fi. Fourteen rooms of various sizes have king-size beds, comfy rocking chairs and folk-art accents. Five apartments come with fully equipped kitchen. A generous Tico breakfast is served on the outdoor terrace. Weekly rates are available.

A COSTA RICAN ART COLONY

If you work in the arts and want to spend some time in Costa Rica, the **Julia and David White Artists' Colony** (☑2249-1414; www.forjuliaanddavid.org; studio apt for 2 weeks from US$575; ⊠) offers the perfect refuge. Located 16km west of Escazú, the 5-hectare compound in the hills surrounding Ciudad Colón comes equipped with a swimming pool, hiking trails and comfortable studios.

Posada El Quijote
B&B $$

(✆2289-8401; www.quijote.cr; Calle del Llano; d standard/superior/deluxe/studio incl breakfast US$85/95/105/115; P➔❄🐾) This Spanish-style hillside *posada* in Bello Horizonte rates as one of the area's top B&Bs. Homey standard rooms have wood floors, throw rugs, cable TV and hot-water bathrooms; superior and deluxe units have a patio or a private terrace. Guests are invited to take a nip at the honor bar, then soak up sweeping Central Valley views on the patio.

Villa Escazú
B&B $$

(✆2289-7971; www.hotels.co.cr/villaescazu; d incl breakfast US$49-65; P🐾) This wooden chalet with wraparound veranda is surrounded by gardens and fruit trees. The two quaint, wood-paneled rooms feature local artwork, comfy couches and a shared bathroom. Breakfast is served on the outdoor balcony. A fully equipped studio and apartment are also available (from US$250 per week). Two-night minimum stay; reserve well in advance. It's 900m west of Banco Nacional.

★ Casa de las Tías
B&B $$$

(Map p79; ✆2289-5517; www.casadelastias.com; s/d/tr incl breakfast US$102/113/124, junior ste US$124-135; P➔🐾) In a quiet area of San Rafael, this yellow-and-turquoise Cape Cod–style house (complete with picket fence) has five immaculate, individually decorated rooms, all with private bathrooms. The house is adorned with crafts that friendly, helpful owners Xavier and Pilar have picked up on their travels in Latin America, lending the place a cozy, intimate feel.

Out of Bounds
B&B $$$

(✆2288-6762; www.bedandbreakfastcr.com; Carretera John F Kennedy; d standard/junior/deluxe/ste incl breakfast US$102/108/130/141; P❄🐾) This friendly, contemporary inn 1km west of Costa Rica Country Club has five simple rooms with blond-wood floors; large, comfortable beds; painted sinks with folk-art motifs; mini-refrigerators and in-room coffeemakers. Two units come with air-con and two are wheelchair-accessible. A broad outdoor deck with pleasant views is stocked with rocking chairs for lounging.

Casa Cristal
INN $$$

(✆2289-2530, in USA 786-206-1506; www.casacristalcr.com; d standard/master/superior incl breakfast US$112/158/202; P➔❄🐾) This chic, whitewashed Bello Horizonte hotel boasts an incomparable setting: at the end of a winding mountain road, on a hillside overlooking several dozen hectares of uninhabited parkland, with San José's twinkling lights in the distance. Most of the eight individually decorated contemporary guest rooms (some with Jacuzzi tubs) have floor-to-ceiling windows affording uninterrupted Central Valley views. No children under 12.

Beacon Boutique Hotel
BOUTIQUE HOTEL $$$

(Map p79; ✆2228-3110, in USA 1-866-978-6168; www.beaconescazucostarica.com; Av 30 btwn Calles 138 & 140; d incl breakfast US$179-299; P❄@🐾) This stylish 27-room inn at the heart of Escazú Centro comes stocked with all manner of luxury goodies: high-thread-count linens, down comforters, king-size beds, plush robes, in-room coffeemakers and even a pillow menu. Room decor is contemporary Spanish Mediterranean, with amenities such as an onsite gym, spa, wine bar and courtyard with a pool. Check the website for substantial online discounts.

✖ Eating

From humble corner stands dishing out gut-filling *casados* to contemporary bistros serving fusion everything, in cosmopolitan San José you will find the country's best restaurant scene. Dedicated eaters should also check out the dining options in Los Yoses and San Pedro, as well as Escazú.

Top-end restaurants tend to get busy on weekend evenings; make a reservation.

✖ Central San José East

Long-standing neighborhood *sodas* (lunch counters) mix effortlessly with contemporary cafes and Asian-fusion eateries on San José's eclectic east side.

Supermarkets include **Automercado** (Map p72; ✆2233-5511; www.automercado.co.cr; cnr Calle 3 & Av 3; ⊙7am-9pm Mon-Sat, 8am-4pm Sun), with a good selection of cheeses, produce, liquor, coffee and chocolate, and economical **Perimercado** (Map p72; ✆2222-2252; Calle 3 btwn Avs Central & 1; ⊙7am-9pm Mon-Sat, 8am-3pm Sun), conveniently located downtown.

★ Café de los Deseos
CAFE $

(Map p68; ✆2222-0496; www.facebook.com/ Cafedelosdeseos; Calle 15 btwn Avs 9 & 11; mains US$5-12; ⊙2-10pm Tue-Sat) Abuzz with artsy young bohemians, this cozy, colorful Barrio Otoya cafe makes a romantic spot for drinks (from wine to cocktails to smoothies), *bocas* (handmade tortillas with Turrialba cheese, salads, teriyaki chicken, individual pizzas), and tempting desserts. Walls are hung with the work of local artists and rooms are adorned with hand-painted tables, beaded curtains and branches entwined with fairy lights.

Alma de Café   CAFE $

(Map p72; ☑ 2010-1119; www.almadecafe.net; Teatro Nacional; mains US$5-10; ⊗ 9am-7pm Mon-Sat, to 7pm Sun) One of the most beautiful cafes in the city, this atmospheric spot evokes early-20th-century Vienna. In other words, a perfect place to sip cappuccino, enjoy a crêpe or quiche and take in the lovely ceiling frescoes.

Delicias del Perú   PERUVIAN, COSTA RICAN $

(Map p72; Calle 3A btwn Avs 7 & 9; mains US$7-12; ⊗ 11am-4pm) Service with a smile and tasty seafood are the specialties at this friendly neighborhood *soda* near the heart of town. Lighter appetites can indulge in steaming bowls of *parihuela* (Peruvian-style seafood soup) made with *corvina* (sea bass) or *mariscos* (mixed seafood), while bigger eaters will appreciate the delicious garlic shrimp and the reasonably priced *casados* (US$6.50).

Restaurante La Criollita   COSTA RICAN $

(Map p72; ☑ 2256-6511; Av 7 btwn Calles 7 & 9; breakfast from US$5, casados US$8-10; ⊗ 6:30am-9pm Mon-Fri, 7am-4pm Sat) This homey local spot, popular with office types, dishes out a changing menu of simple Costa Rican specialties, such as stewed chicken or grilled fish. The setting is pleasant and the service efficient, and you can accompany your meal with a glass of Chilean or Spanish wine (US$3).

Restaurante Shakti   VEGETARIAN $

(Map p68; ☑ 2222-4475; cnr Av 8 & Calle 13; mains US$5-10; ⊗ 7:30am-7pm Mon-Fri, 8am-6pm Sat; ☑) This informal neighborhood health-food outpost has simple, organic-focused cooking as well as freshly baked goods. Favorites include veggie burgers, along with various fish and chicken dishes, but most people come for the vegetarian *plato del día* – only US$6 for soup, salad, main course and fruit drink (US$8 with coffee and dessert thrown in)!

Vishnu   VEGETARIAN $

(Map p72; ☑ 2256-6063; www.vishnucr.com; Av 1 btwn Calles 1 & 3; mains US$4-9; ⊗ 9am-7pm Mon-Sat, to 7pm Sun; ☑) You'll find a rainbow of fresh local produce, vegetable stews and well-rendered soy burgers at this informal chain of vegetarian cheapies. Most folks pile in for the reasonably priced lunch specials (US$7), which generally include salad, fresh juice and dessert. There are a few vegan specialties as well. Vishnu has several branches dotted around downtown.

★Café Mundo   ITALIAN $$

(Map p72; ☑ 2222-6190; cnr Av 9 & Calle 15; mains US$8-36; ⊗ 11am-10:30pm Mon-Thu, 11am-11:30pm Fri, 5pm-midnight Sat; ☑) Location. Location. Location. This longtime Italian cafe and expat favorite has it. Set on a sprawling terrace in a vintage Barrio Otoya mansion, it's a perfect spot to enjoy a glass of wine and good (if not earth-shattering) pizzas and pastas within sight of a splashing outdoor fountain. At lunchtime on weekdays, don't miss the good-value *plato del día* (US$8).

Nuestra Tierra   COSTA RICAN $$

(Map p72; ☑ 2258-6500; cnr Av 2 & Calle 15; mains US$6-22; ⊗ 6am-midnight; ☑) Touristy but fun, this bustling eatery maintains a calculatedly rustic atmosphere, with picnic-style tables, taxidermied bull's heads and strings of metal cups dangling from the rafters. Cheery waiters deliver well-prepared if sometimes overpriced Tico food, from tasty pork tamales to wooden platters piled with heaping *casados*. A fine spot for lunch and sangria after a visit to the nearby museums.

Don Wang   CHINESE $$

(Map p68; ☑ 2233-6484, 2223-5925; www.don-wangrestaurant.com; Calle 11 btwn Avs 6 & 8; mains US$8-18; ⊗ 11am-3:30pm & 5:30-10pm Sun-Thu, to 11pm Fri & Sat; ☑ ☑) This hopping Cantonese eatery is an ideal place for dim sum – served all day every day – as well as a long list of Chinese specialties, from stir-fried shrimp with cashews to *mu shu* vegetables (there are more than a dozen veggie dishes to choose from). Parents will love the children's play area in the corner – ideal for restless toddlers.

★La Esquina de Buenos Aires   ARGENTINE $$$

(Map p72; ☑ 2223-1909; laesquinadebuenos-saires.com; cnr Calle 11 & Av 4; mains US$15-29; ⊗ 11:30am-3pm & 6-10:30pm Mon-Thu, 12:30-11pm Fri & Sat, noon-10pm Sun; ☑) Spanish-tile floors, white linens and the sound of old tangos evoke the atmospheric bistros of San Telmo, as does the menu, featuring grilled

Argentine cuts of steak, house-made *empanadas* (turnovers stuffed with meat or cheese) and an extensive selection of fresh pastas in exquisite sauces. The excellent South American–centric wine list, attentive service and flickering candlelight make this an ideal place for a date. Reservations recommended.

★**Kalú Café & Food Shop** INTERNATIONAL $$$
(Map p68; ☎2221-2081; www.kalu.co.cr; cnr Calle 7 & Av 11; mains US$15-21; ۩ noon-7pm Mon & Tue, noon-10pm Wed-Fri, 8am-10pm Sat; ☛) Sharing a sleek space with Kiosco SJO (p97) in Barrio Amón, chef Camille Ratton's exceptional back-patio cafe serves a global fusion menu of soups, salads, sandwiches, pastas and unconventional delights such as the fish taco trio filled with mango-glazed salmon, red curry prawns and macadamia-crusted tuna. Don't miss the mind-meltingly delicious cheesecake, served with fresh strawberries stewed in balsamic.

Restaurante Tin-Jo ASIAN $$$
(Map p68; ☎2221-7605; www.tinjo.com; Calle 11 btwn Avs 6 & 8; mains US$11-19; ۩ 11:30am-2:30pm & 6-10pm Mon-Thu, noon-2:30pm & 6-11pm Fri & Sat, noon-9pm Sun; ☛) The interiors of this popular Asian standard-bearer are a riot of pan-Asian everything, just like the menu. Expect a wide range of fare from various regions – from *kung pao* shrimp to spicy tuna *maki* to *pad thai* – as well as an extensive vegetarian menu.

Otoya 1155 ITALIAN $$$
(Map p72; ☎2222-3636; Av 9 btwn Calles 11 & 13; mains US$14-20; ۩ 6pm-midnight Tue-Sun) At this intimate Italian restaurant in a 19th-century Barrio Otoya mansion behind Casa Amarilla, a series of elegant rooms, including an open-air 2nd-floor terrace, create a casual, romantic backdrop for cocktails, Italian wines and a short but sweet chalkboard menu that includes homemade pasta and gelato. On the downside, portions run small, and the food is less spectacular than the setting.

✖ **Central San José West**

The city's hectic commercial heart has some of the cheapest eats in town. One of the best places for a budget-priced lunch is the Mercado Central, where you'll find a variety of *sodas* serving *casados*, tamales, seafood and everything in between.

Mariscos Poseidon SEAFOOD $
(Map p72; Mercado Central Annex; mains US$5-12; ۩ 9am-6pm Mon-Sat) The congenial Doris runs this narrow, blue-and-yellow seafood joint in the central market's northern annex. The *ceviche mixto* appetizer (fish, shrimp and octopus marinated in lime juice) is tasty and cheap, as are the generous portions of seafood-studded rice.

La Sorbetera de Lolo Mora DESSERTS $
(Map p72; ☎2256-5000; Mercado Central; desserts US$2-5; ۩ 9:30am-5:45pm Mon-Sat) Head to the main market for dessert at this century-old local favorite that serves up fresh sorbet and cinnamon-laced frozen custard. Do as the locals do and order *barquillos* (cylindrical sugar cookies that are perfect for dipping).

Pastelería Merayo BAKERY $
(Map p68; ☎2223-5758; Calle 16 btwn Paseo Colón & Av 1; pastries US$1-2; ۩ 7am-6:30pm Mon-Sat) This informal pastry shop has a wide variety of freshly baked, cavity-inducing goodies. The coffee is strong and it's a sweet way to pass the time if you're waiting for a bus at the Coca-Cola terminal.

Q Café CAFE $$
(Map p72; ☎2221-0707; 2nd fl, cnr Av Central & Calle 2; mains US$8-17; ۩ 8am-9pm Mon-Sat, 10am-8pm Sun) A sleek, monochromatic cafe with excellent views of the ornate Correo Central building, this modern 2nd-story spot near the heart of San José's pedestrian zone is perfect for coffee drinks (including delicious iced mocha) and pastries. Try the *empanadas*, which go well with the cafe's homemade hot sauce.

✖ **La Sabana & Surrounds**

Supermarkets include **Más X Menos** (Map p76; ☎2248-0968; www.masxmenos.co.cr; cnr Autopista General Cañas & Av 5; ۩ 7am-midnight Mon-Sat, to 9pm Sun; ℗), which means 'more for less', in case you were wondering, and **Palí** (Map p76; ☎2256-5887; www.pali.co.cr; Paseo Colón btwn Calles 24 & 26; ۩ 8:30am-7pm Mon-Thu, to 8pm Fri & Sat, to 6pm Sun; ℗).

Soda Tapia FAST FOOD $
(Map p76; ☎2222-6734; www.sodatapia.com; cnr Av 2 & Calle 42; mains US$4-10, desserts US$2-7; ۩ 6am-2am Mon-Thu, 24hr Fri & Sat, 6am-1am Sun; ℗ ♿) An unpretentious '50s-style diner with garish red-and-white decor, this place is perpetually filled with couples and families noshing on grilled sandwiches and gener-

ous *casados*. If you have the nerve, try the monstrous 'El Gordo,' a pile of steak, onions, cheese, lettuce and tomato served on Spanish bread. Save room for dessert: ice-cream and fruit sundaes are a specialty here.

Machu Picchu   PERUVIAN $$
(Map p76; ☑ 2255-1717; www.restaurantemachupic-chu.com; Calle 32 btwn Avs 1 & 3; mains US$9-22; ☺ 11am-10pm Mon-Sat, to 6pm Sun; ☐ ☎ ☻) This locally renowned Peruvian restaurant will do you right if you have a hankering for all things Andean. A popular spot for a leisurely Sunday lunch, it has an encyclopedic menu featuring Peruvian classics such as *pulpo al olivo* (octopus in olive sauce), *ají de gallina* (a nutty chicken stew) and *causa* (chilled potato terrines stuffed with shrimp and avocado).

Las Mañanitas   MEXICAN $$
(Map p76; ☑ 2256-5737; Calle 40 btwn Paseo Colón & Av 3; mains US$6-17; ☺ 11:30am-10pm Mon-Sat) At this authentic Mexican place near the park, well-rendered specialties include tacos in sets of four – corn tortillas accompanied by chicken, steak, sea bass or *carne al pastor* (spiced pork). Fans of *mole poblano* (central Mexico's famous chili and chocolate sauce) will also want to try it here, as the restaurant's owner hails from Puebla.

★ Park Café   EUROPEAN $$$
(Map p76; ☑ 2290-6324; parkcafecostarica.blogspot.com; tapas US$6-15; ☺ 5:30-9:30pm Tue-Sat) At this felicitous fusion of antique shop and French restaurant, Michelin-starred chef Richard Neat offers an exquisite degustation menu featuring smaller sampling plates (Spanish-tapas style) and a carefully curated wine list. The romantic, candle-lit courtyard is eclectically decorated with Asian antiques imported by Neat's partner, Louise French. It's near Parque La Sabana's northeast corner (100m north of Rostipollos restaurant).

The tantalizing menu includes classic flavor combinations – carpaccio of beef with mustard dressing – alongside innovative offerings such as crab ravioli with asparagus and ginger cappuccino, crispy leg of duck with cucumber-mint salad or gorgonzola gnocchi with prune-stuffed pork fillet, all prepared with passion and flair by Neat himself. An eight-table limit enhances the intimate atmosphere.

Restaurante Grano de Oro   FUSION $$$
(Map p76; ☑ 2255-3322; www.hotelgranodeoro.com; Calle 30 btwn Avs 2 & 4; lunch mains US$15-29, dinner mains US$19-42; ☺ 7am-10pm) Known for its Costa Rican–fusion cuisine, this stately, flower-filled restaurant is one of San José's top dining destinations. The menu is laced with unique specialties such as sea bass breaded with toasted macadamia nuts or seared duck crowned with caramelized figs, and there's an encyclopedic international wine list. For dessert, don't miss the coffee cream pie. Reservations recommended for dinner.

El Chicote   STEAKHOUSE $$$
(Map p76; ☑ 2232-0936; www.elchicote.com; Av Las Américas; mains US$15-30; ☺ 11am-3pm & 6-10pm Mon-Fri, 11am-10pm Sat & Sun) A pleasant family spot in Sabana Norte that draws carnivores for long Sunday lunches, El Chicote grills up beefy sirloins and serves them with black beans, fried bananas and steamy baked potatoes. If you don't do red meat, there are plenty of chicken and seafood options as well. The six-page wine list is strong on Mediterranean and South American vintages.

✄ Los Yoses, Barrio Escalante & San Pedro

Succulent Turkish sandwiches, Caribbean-style *rondón* (seafood gumbo), wood-fired pizzas – you can find every type of cuisine imaginable in this corner of the city. Just north of Los Yoses, Calles 33 and 35 in Barrio Escalante are prime foodie destinations, boasting several fine restaurants within a few city blocks.

Self-caterers can visit San Pedro's large, modern supermarket **Más X Menos** (☑ 2225-0636; Av Central; ☺ 7am-midnight Mon-Sat, to 9pm Sun) or Los Yoses' **Automercado** (☑ 2225-0361; Av Central btwn Calles 39 & 41; ☺ 7am-9pm Mon-Sat, 8am-8pm Sun), with a good selection of healthy items, including veggie burgers.

Café Kracovia   CAFE $
(☑ 2253-9093; www.cafekracovia.com; snacks US$5-9, mains US$8-14; ☺ 10:30am-8pm Mon, to 11pm Tue-Sat; ☎) With several distinct spaces, from a lower-lit, intimate downstairs to an outdoor garden courtyard, this hip cafe has something for everyone. Contemporary artwork and a distinct university vibe create an appealing ambience for lunching on crepes,

wraps, pastries, salads and daily specials. It's 500m north of the Fuente de la Hispanidad traffic circle where San Pedro and Los Yoses converge.

Giacomin
BAKERY $

(☎2224-3463; www.pasteleriagiacomin.com; Av Central; pastries from US$1.50; ⊗8am-noon & 2-7pm Mon-Sat) Obscured by the Automercadeo parking lot in Los Yoses is this 1960s pastry shop that some *josefinos* swear is the best in town. Here you'll find delicious mushroom mini-pizzas, flaky croissants, cream puffs, truffles, petits-fours and what has to be Central America's best *arrollado de canela* (cinnamon roll). The upstairs lounge and balcony make a tranquil spot for a cappuccino break.

★Sofía Restaurante Mediterráneo
MEDITERRANEAN $$

(☎2224-5050; www.sofiamediterraneo.com; cnr Calle 33 & Av 1; mains US$8-22; ⊗noon-11pm Tue-Sat, to 5pm Sun; ☑) This hidden Barrio Escalante gem serves a superb mix of authentic Mediterranean specialties, including house-made hummus, dolmas, tortellini, grilled lamb and a rotating selection of daily specials, accompanied by sweet, delicate baklava for dessert. The restaurant doubles as a community cultural center where Turkish owner Mehmet Onuralp hosts occasional theme dinners featuring musicians, chefs and speakers from around the Mediterranean.

★Rávi Gastropub
PUB $$

(☎2253-3771; www.facebook.com/ravicostarica; cnr Calle 33 & Av 5; mains US$9-18; ⊗11:30am-noon Tue-Sat) New in 2013, this cool corner pub in Barrio Escalante is awash in bright murals, with seating in funky red booths, intimate back rooms or at the convivial bar stools up front. A menu of *bocas*, sandwiches, pizzas and more is served with craft brew on tap or homemade tropical-fruit sodas served in cute little Bell jars.

At lunchtime, pick from the rotating menu of nine appetizers and nine main dishes and throw in a homemade soda, all for US$10.

★Olio
MEDITERRANEAN $$

(☎2281-0541; www.facebook.com/Restaurante. olio; cnr Calle 33 & Av 3; tapas from US$5, dishes US$10-20; ⊗noon-midnight Mon-Fri, from 6pm Sat; ☑) This cozy, Mediterranean-flavored gastropub in a century-old brick building

in Barrio Escalante serves a long list of tempting tapas, including divine *hongos madrileños* (stuffed mushrooms), goat-cheese croquettes, house-made pastas and garlic shrimp. The enticing drinks list includes homemade sangria and a decent selection of beers and wines. It's a romantic spot for a date, with imaginative, conversation-worthy quirks of decor and beautiful patrons.

Lolo's
PIZZERIA $$

(☎2283-9627; pizzas US$12-22; ⊗6pm-midnight Mon-Sat) Fans of bohemian chic will appreciate this quirky pizzeria, hidden in a mustard yellow house (No 3396) along the railroad tracks north of Av Central in Barrio Escalante. The vibrantly colorful, low-lit interior, hung with an eclectic collection of plates and other knick-knacks, creates an artsy, romantic setting for sangria and pizzas fired up in the bright red oven out back.

Mantras
VEGETARIAN $$

(☎2253-6715; www.facebook.com/mantrasveggiecafe; Calle 35 btwn Avs 11 & 13; mains US$8-15; ⊗9am-5pm Mon-Sat) Widely recognized as the best vegetarian restaurant in San José (if not all of Costa Rica), Mantras draws rave reviews from across the foodie spectrum for meatless main dishes, salads and desserts so delicious that it's easy to forget you're eating healthy. It's in Barrio Escalante.

Restaurant Whapin
CARIBBEAN $$

(☎2283-1480; cnr Calle 35 & Av 13; mains US$12-28; ⊗8am-10pm Mon-Fri, 11am-10pm Sat) For a taste of the Caribbean without leaving San José, try this corner spot in Barrio Escalante painted Rasta red, yellow and green. Steamy bowls of *rondón* (seafood gumbo), rice and red beans, and fish simmered in spicy coconut sauce go well with *agua de sapo,* a zesty sweet ginger drink. Don't forget the fried plantains and, in season, the crisp breadfruit.

El Buho
VEGETARIAN $$

(☎2224-6293; www.facebook.com/ElBuhoVegetariano; Av 5, 25m east of Calle 3; mains US$10-18; ⊗11:30am-8pm Mon-Fri) Drawing health-food devotees from the nearby university and much further afield, this buzzing San Pedro eatery just off Calle de la Amargura serves a variety of vegan, vegetarian and gluten-free treats, from eggplant croquettes to stir-fries, mushroom casseroles to passionfruit tarts.

1. Museo Nacional de Costa Rica (p67)
This former fortress houses pre-Columbian artifacts and colonial relics.

2. Teatro Nacional (p66)
The theater's most famous painting depicts coffee and banana harvests.

3. Outdoor markets (p96)
San José's many markets offer everything from fresh fruit and vegetables to hammocks and souvenirs.

4. Basílica de Nuestra Señora de Los Ángeles (p128)
Costa Rica's most venerated religious shrine is located in Cartago, which was the country's original capital.

✗ Escazú

On Saturday, head down to the farmers market that's held along Av 2, just south of the park in Escazú Centro. There's also an organic farmers market on Wednesday, featuring produce as well as delectables such as cheese, honey and fish. Find it 1km south of Paco, across from the Red Cross building.

Self-caterers will find plenty of choice in Escazú's supermarkets. The best is the gigantic **Automercado** (Map p79; ☑2588-1812; Atlantis Plaza, Calle Cortés, San Rafael; ⊗7am-10pm Mon-Sat, 8am-9pm Sun), but there's also **Más X Menos** (Map p79; ☑2228-0954; Centro Comercial Escazú, Carretera John F Kennedy, San Rafael; ⊗6:30am-midnight Mon-Sat, to 10pm Sun) and **Supermercado Saretto.** (☑2228-0247; San Rafael; ⊗8am-8pm Mon-Sat, 9am-2pm Sun)

La Esquina Argentina   ARGENTINE $

(Map p79; ☑2288-2811; cnr Av 30 & Calle 128; empanadas US$1.60, casados US$7; ⊗7am-3pm) This popular corner eatery sells piping-hot *empanadas,* breakfasts, *casados,* smoked meats and tasty mashed potatoes. The outdoor patio is a good spot to linger over a cup of coffee.

Chez Christophe   BAKERY $

(☑2228-2512; ⊗7am-7pm Tue-Sat, 8am-6pm Sun) If you have a hankering for a coffee éclair, croque monsieur or a plain (but transcendent) croissant, linger here awhile. Waffles are reserved for Sunday, but every other day this authentic French bakery offers freshly baked breads and pastries, as well as espresso and a full breakfast and lunch menu. It's just south of Centro Comerical El Paco in San Rafael.

Soda Río de Janeiro   COSTA RICAN $

(Map p79; ☑8811-5263; cnr Calle 132 & Av 32; mains US$6-10; ⊗6am-6pm Mon-Sat) Located southeast of the Iglesia Escazú, this charismatic little *soda* decked out with bright-red tablecloths is frequently full. Typical Tico fare includes pork chops, chicken or fish accompanied by big jars of spicy pickled vegetables. There's a tiny aquarium of angelfish that you can watch while you wait for a seat.

Buena Tierra   ORGANIC $

(Map p79; ☑2288-0342; www.facebook.com/CafeOrganicoBuenaTierra; cnr Calle 134 & Av 34; mains US$6-8; ⊗9am-5:30pm Mon-Fri, to 2pm Sat; ☑) With tree-trunk tabletops and huge windows letting in fresh breezes, this cute, friendly cafe in Escazú Centro is a good place to detox. Only organic fruits, vegetables, rice and beans are used, while *batidos* (fruit shakes) are made with your choice of water, milk, goat's milk, yogurt or almond milk. The cafe also organizes a Wednesday-morning organic farmers market.

La Casona de Laly   COSTA RICAN $

(Map p79; ☑2288-5807; cnr Av 26 & Calle 132; bocas $2-5, mains $6-15; ⊗11am-midnight Mon-Sat, to 6pm Sun) At the heart of Escazú Centro, this much-loved restaurant-tavern specializes in country-style Tico fare. Locals and expats alike pack the joint for cheap, lip-smacking *bocas,* ice-cold beers and a soundtrack of merengue accompanied by the cackling of the owner's pet birds, who inhabit the cages along the restaurant's west wall. Don't miss the delicious *dados de queso* (fried cheese cubes).

Tiquicia   COSTA RICAN $$

(☑8828-1280, 2289-5839; www.miradortiquicia.com; bocas US$5-17, mains US$13-23; ⊗noon-midnight Tue-Thu, to 2am Fri & Sat, to 9pm Sun) This long-running hilltop restaurant 5km south of Escazú Centro serves up bounteous platters, along with live folk music on weekends. Yes, the food is only so-so, but you're not here to eat, you're here to admire the extravagant views of the Central Valley. It's tricky to find; call for directions or check the website for a map.

🍷 Drinking & Nightlife

Whatever your poison, San José has plenty of venues to keep you lubricated.

Good spots for people-watching over a beer or a coffee include Café 1930 at the Gran Hotel Costa Rica (p81) with unbeatable views of Teatro Nacional; the upstairs terrace at **El Patio del Balmoral** (Map p72; ☑2221-1700; www.elpatiodelbalmoral.com; Av Central btwn Calles 7 & 9; mains US$9-27; ⊗6am-10pm, terrace bar 4-10pm), overlooking the pedestrian walkway on Av Central; and Café de los Deseos (p85) in Barrio Otoya.

Chepe's artsiest, most sophisticated drinking venues are concentrated north and east of the center, in places like Barrio Amón and Barrio Escalante. For a rowdier, younger scene, head to Barrio La California (between downtown and Los Yoses) or the UCR university district. Calle 3 north of Av Central in San Pedro – locally known as Calle La Amargura (Sorrow St) – has the highest concentration of bars of any single street in the city, many of them packed with students even during daylight hours. Places come and go, but **Terra U** (☑ 2283-7728; www. terrau.com; Calle La Amargura; ⊙ 10am-2:30am Mon-Sat, 3pm-2:30am Sun) and **Caccio's** (www. caccios.com; Calle de la Amargura) are longtime party spots here. The area gets rowdy in the wee hours.

San José also has a thriving club scene. From thumping electronica to hip-hop to salsa, merengue and reggaetón, Chepe's clubs offer a galaxy of musical styles to help you get your groove on. Most spots open at around 10pm, but don't truly get going until after midnight. Admission charges vary (generally US$5 to US$10) depending on the location, the DJ and the night. Places come and go with alarming regularity, so ask around before heading out.

Be safe. Enterprising thieves sometimes lurk around popular nightspots, waiting to relieve drunken party people of their wallets. When leaving a bar late at night, keep your wits about you and take a taxi.

💡 Central San José East

Jungle Fruit
JUICE BAR

(Map p72; ☑ 8835-9222; Calle 7 btwn Calles Central & 1; juices US$1.50-3.50; ⊙ 7am-6pm Mon-Fri, 9am-6pm Sat) A juice fiend's dream come true, this centrally located hole-in-the-wall serves up satisfying 16oz and 24oz juices and smoothies at prices that just might help you kick your Coca-Cola habit.

Café del Barista
CAFE

(Map p68; www.cafedelbarista.com; Calle 19 btwn Avs 9 & 11; ⊙ 7am-7pm Mon-Fri, 8am-5pm Sat) This corrugated-roofed, warehouse-like space in Barrio Aranjuez brews up a great cup of gourmet coffee (and makes a halfway-decent cinnamon roll too).

Talentum
CAFE

(Map p68; ☑ 2256-6346; www.galeriatalentum. com; Av 11 btwn Calles 3 & 3A; ⊙ 11:30am-6:30pm Mon-Fri, 9am-4pm Sat) This vibrant, quirky new cultural space in a renovated mansion runs the gamut from cafe to art gallery. Sporting local artwork inside and out, with cozy seating on vintage couches and an outdoor deck, it's a fun place for a midday break. The ever-changing cultural agenda includes book signings, film and anatomical drawing classes and occasional live music.

★ Stiefel
PUB

(Map p72; www.facebook.com/StiefelPub; ⊙ 6pm-1am Mon-Sat) A dozen-plus Costa Rican microbrews on tap and an appealing setting in a historical building create a convivial buzz at this recently opened pub half a block from Plaza España. Grab a pint of Pelona or Maldita Vida, Praying Nun or Japi Ending; better yet, order a flight of four miniature sampler glasses and try 'em all!

Chelle's
BAR

(Map p72; ☑ 2221-1369; cnr Av Central & Calle 9; ⊙ 24hr) If you're drinking the night away with Ticos, you might find yourself here at 4am, clutching a cold one and professing your love for recent acquaintances. This venerable 24-hour *soda* doubles as one of Chepe's most atmospheric spots for a nightcap, with surly service and big buses careening around the corner outside, looking perilously close to crashing through the window.

El Morazán
BAR

(Map p72; ☑ 2256-5110; www.facebook.com/barmorazan; cnr Calle 9 & Av 3, cocktails US$5-7; ⊙ 5pm-2am Mon-Sat) Facing Parque Morazán, this exposed-brick, Spanish-tile-clad space dates back to 1904. Throughout its long life it has hosted all manner of historical figures (including Che Guevara, according to one account). It is a popular hangout among Chepe's young artsy set. In addition to beer, there is a full menu of classic cocktails and snacks. On some nights, there is live music.

Bar Morazán
BAR

(Map p72; ☑ 2222-4622; 2nd fl, Calle 7 btwn Avs 1 & 3; ⊙ 11am-2am) Decidedly local, in the heart of the San José tourist belt, this humble little bar has reasonably priced drinks, a sports-betting window, a stack of TVs displaying the games and a supersized mural of dogs playing poker. Awesome.

La Concha de la Lora
BAR

(Map p68; ☑ 2222-0130; www.facebook.com/laconchalora; Calle 21 btwn Avs Central & 1; ⊙ 8:30pm-2:30am Thu-Sat) An enthusiastic young crowd packs in here nightly for foosball, ping pong, good bar snacks, DJs spinning everything from Latin music to Jimi Hendrix, and occasional live bands. Low cover charges (free to US$6) help maintain the upbeat mood.

Hoxton Pub PUB
(⛿7168-1083; www.hoxtoncr.com; ⊘6pm-2am Tue-Sat, 3pm-midnight Sun) Tasty fish and chips, good cocktails, great music and a lively dance floor in a cool old Los Yoses mansion just east of Subaru.

El Observatorio CLUB
(Map p68; ⛿2223-0725; www.elobservatorio.tv; Calle 23 btwn Avs Central & 1; ⊘6pm-2am Mon-Sat) This popular Barrio La California club stands out for its unusual mix of salsa, rock and stand-up comedy nights.

Craic Irish Pub PUB
(Map p68; cnr Av 2 & Calle 25A; ⊘6pm-2am) This popular pub in Barrio La California serves a wide variety of beers accompanied by burgers, fries and other bar snacks.

Centro Comercial El Pueblo BAR, CLUB
(Map p68; ⛿2221-9434; ⊘hours vary) This Mediterranean-style outdoor mall in Barrio Tournon is a warren of bars, clubs and music venues. The proximity of one place to the next makes it ideal for a pub crawl and there's stringent security (though wee hours can get a bit unruly). Things get going around 9pm and can go as late as 7am. Best of all, there's no cover charge midweek.

🍸 Central San José West

Castro's DJ
(Map p68; ⛿2256-8789; cnr Av 13 & Calle 22) Chepe's oldest dance club, this classic Latin American disco in Barrio México draws crowds of locals and tourists to its large dance floor with a dependable mix of salsa, cumbia and merengue.

🍸 La Sabana

Rapsodia LOUNGE
(Map p76; ⛿2248-1720; www.rapsodiacr.com; cnr Paseo Colón & Calle 40; ⊘10pm-6am Fri & Sat) This hyper-chic, see-and-be-seen club clad in white and gold has an extensive list of cocktails and a menu of Mediterranean-inspired dishes and snacks. Guest DJs set the mood with a mix of electronica and other sounds every Friday and Saturday.

Club Vertigo CLUB
(Map p76; ⛿2257-8424; www.vertigocr.com; Paseo Colón btwn Calles 38 & 40; cover US$6-15; ⊘10pm-dawn) Located on the ground floor of the nondescript Centro Colón office tower, the city's premier club packs

in Chepe's beautiful people with a mix of house, trance and electronica. Downstairs is an 850-person-capacity sweat-box of a dance floor; upstairs is a chill-out lounge lined with red sofas. Dress to the nines and expect admission charges to skyrocket on guest-DJ nights.

🍸 Los Yoses, Barrio Escalante & San Pedro

Roots Reggae Bar BAR
(⛿2253-1953; www.facebook.com/rootscoolandcalm; Av 8; ⊘7pm-midnight Tue-Sun) The dreadlocked set crowds this cool Los Yoses lounge bar that brings in DJs from as far afield as Puerto Viejo on the Caribbean coast. It's a sweet spot to get a beer and hang with reggae-loving locals. Find it between Calle 43 and Spoon.

Río Bar BAR
(⛿2225-8371; Av Central; ⊘noon-midnight Sun-Tue, to 2am Wed-Sat) Just west of Calle 43 and the Fuente de la Hispanidad (the official boundary between Los Yoses and San Pedro), this large, popular bar with an upstairs lounge has live bands on some nights and flat-screen TVs showing the current game. It's a good spot to watch the rush-hour traffic crawl by in the company of an after-work crowd.

Un Lugar Resto-bar BAR
(⛿2225-3979; www.facebook.com/barunlugar; Calle 33 btwn Avs 11 & 13; ⊘11am-2am Mon-Sat) This small wood-lined bar in Barrio Escalante serves as a neighborhood hangout that draws artsy types and young professionals for cold beer and *bocas*.

🍸 Escazú

If you're looking to sip fine vintages, visit the stylish ground-floor wine bar at the Beacon Boutique Hotel (p85), open 7pm to midnight.

Taberna Arenas BAR
(Map p79; ⛿2289-8256; cnr Av 30 & Calle 130; ⊘from 4pm) This delightful, old-fashioned Tico bar is an Escazú institution. Arenas has good *bocas* and a wide selection of domestic and imported beers. Owner Don Israel has his photo with various heads of state on the walls, along with the agricultural implements that are de rigueur in any country bar.

GAY & LESBIAN VENUES

The city is home to Central America's most thriving gay and lesbian scene. As with other spots, admission charges vary depending on the night and location (from US$5 to US$10). Some clubs close on various nights of the week (usually Sunday to Tuesday) and others host women- or men-only nights; inquire ahead or check individual club websites for listings.

Many clubs are on the south side of town, which can get rough after dark. Take a taxi.

La Avispa (Map p68; ☑2223-5343; www.laavispa.com; Calle 1 btwn Avs 8 & 10; ⊗8pm-1am Thu, 8pm-3am Fri & Sat, 5pm-3am Sun) A gay establishment that has been in operation for more than three decades, La Avispa (the Wasp) has a bar, pool tables and a boisterous dance floor that's been recommended by travelers. There are lesbian nights once or twice a month (including the last Friday of every month).

Bochinche (Map p68; ☑2221-0500; cnr Calle 11 & Av 10; ⊗8pm-5am Wed-Sat) A club that features everything from classic disco to electronica, as well as special themed nights. As this club is on the south side of town, it can get rough after dark.

Energy Club (Map p76; www.facebook.com/EnergyClubCR; cnr Paseo Colón & Calle 28; ⊗Thu-Sun) A recent arrival on Chepe's gay club scene, this place features Thursday singles nights, Friday drag shows, Saturday disco nights and Sunday-night strippers.

Pucho's Nightclub (Map p68; ☑2256-1147; www.puchosnightclub.com; cnr Calle 11 & Av 8; ⊗Mon-Sat) This gay male outpost is more low rent (and significantly raunchier) than some; it features scantily-clad go-go boys and over-the-top drag shows.

Pub BAR
(Map p79; ☑2288-3062; Av 26 btwn Calles 128 & 130; ⊗from 11am) This small, friendly American-owned pub has a list of more than two dozen international beers, a dozen local brews and a selection of shots with scary-sounding names like 'Test Tube Baby' and 'Anti-Freeze'. Well-priced happy-hour drinks specials keep things hopping 6pm to 8pm every night except Friday, and a greasy bar menu is available to soak up the damage.

☆ Entertainment

Pick up *La Nación* on Thursday for listings (in Spanish) of the coming week's attractions. The *Tico Times* 'Weekend' section (in English) has a calendar of theater, music and museum events. The free publication **GAM Cultural** (www.gamcultural.com) and the website **San José Volando** (www.sanjosevolando.com) are also helpful guides to nightlife and cultural events.

Cinemas

Many cinemas show recent Hollywood films with Spanish subtitles and an English soundtrack. Occasionally, films are dubbed over in Spanish (*doblado* or *hablado en español*) rather than subtitled; ask before buying a ticket. Movie tickets cost about US$4 to US$5, and generally Wednesday is cheaper. Check newspaper listings or individual theater websites for schedules.

There are bigger multiplexes in Los Yoses and San Pedro, while the most modern theaters are in Escazú.

Sala Garbo CINEMA
(Map p76; ☑2222-1034; www.salagarbocr.com; cnr Av 2 & Calle 28) Art-house and classic films.

Centro de Cine CINEMA
(Map p72; ☑2223-0610, 2223-2127; www.centrodecine.go.cr; cnr Calle 11 & Av 9) This rambling Victorian mansion houses the government-run film center, but festivals, lectures and events are held in outside venues; check the site for current events.

Cine Magaly CINEMA
(Map p68; ☑2223-0085; www.facebook.com/CineMagaly; Calle 23 btwn Avs Central & 1) Screens the latest releases in a large theater.

Multicines San Pedro CINEMA
(☑2283-5715, 2283-5716; www.ccmcinemas.com; 2nd fl, Mall San Pedro) This popular multiplex has 10 screens showing the latest Hollywood flicks.

Cinemark CINEMA
(☑2201-5050; www.cinemarkca.com/multiplaza-escazu; Multiplaza Escazú) This multi-screen complex in Escazú shows first-run movies.

Live Music

Centro Comercial El Pueblo (p94) has a number of spots that feature live Latin combos and rock bands – and everything in between.

★ **Jazz Café**   LIVE MUSIC
(☏2253-8933; www.jazzcafecostarica.com; Av Central; cover US$6-10; ⊙6pm-2am Mon-Sat) This San Pedro venue is *the* destination in San José for live music, with a different band every night. Countless performers have taken to the stage here, including legendary Cuban bandleader Chucho Valdés and Colombian pop star Juanes. Its sister club in **Escazú** (☏2288-4740; north side of Autopista Próspero Fernández; ⊙from 7pm) features a similar mix of local and international bands. Variable cover charges start around US$5.

★ **El Sótano**   LIVE MUSIC
(Map p68; ☏2221-2302; www.facebook.com/sotanocr; cnr Calle 3 & Av 11; ⊙8pm-2am) One of Chepe's most atmospheric new nightspots, Sótano is named for its cellar jazz club, where people crowd in for frequent performances including intimate Tuesday jam sessions; upstairs, a cluster of elegant high-ceilinged rooms in the same mansion have been converted to a gallery space, stage and dance floor where an eclectic mix of groups play regular live gigs.

El Cuartel de la Boca del Monte   LIVE MUSIC
(Map p68; ☏2221-0327; www.facebook.com/elcuartelcr; Av 1 btwn Calles 21 & 23; ⊙11:30am-2pm Mon-Fri, 6pm-midnight daily) This atmospheric old Barrio La California bar has long drawn cheek-by-jowl crowds for live bands. Friday is a good night to visit, as is Monday, when women get free admission and the band cranks out a crazy mix of calypso, salsa, reggae and rock. It's popular with university students, who arrive to flirt and drink and various combinations thereof.

Theater

There is a wide variety of theatrical options in San José, including some in English. Local newspapers, including the *Tico Times*, list current shows. Most theaters are not very large, so performances tend to sell out; get tickets as early as possible.

Teatro Nacional   THEATER
(Map p72; ☏2010-1111; www.teatronacional.go.cr; Calles 3 & 5 btwn Avs Central & 2) Costa Rica's most important theater stages plays, dance, opera, symphony, Latin American music and other major events. The main season runs from March to November, but there are performances throughout the year.

Teatro Melico Salazar   THEATER
(Map p72; ☏2295-6032; www.teatromelico.go.cr; Av 2 btwn Calles Central & 2) The restored 1920s theater has regular fine-arts performances, including music, theater, ballet and other dance.

Auditorio Nacional   CONCERT VENUE
(Map p68; ☏2222-7647; www.museocr.com; Museo de los Niños, Calle 4) A grand stage for concerts, dance, theater and plays, affiliated with the Centro Costarricense de Ciencia y Cultura. It's north of Av 9.

Teatro Universitario   THEATER
(Teatro de Bellas Artes; ☏2511-6733; www.teatro.ucr.ac.cr) On the southeast side of the UCR campus in San Pedro is the Teatro Universitario, which has a wide variety of programming, including works produced by the university's fine-arts department.

Teatro Eugene O'Neill   THEATER
(☏2207-7554; www.centrocultural.cr; Calle 37) Has performances sponsored by the Centro Cultural Costarricense Norteamericano, a cultural center that promotes ties between Costa Rica and the United States. It's north of Av Central, in San Pedro.

Little Theatre Group   THEATER
(☏8858-1446; www.littletheatregroup.org) This English-language performance troupe has been around since the 1950s and presents several plays a year; call or go online to find out when and where the works will be shown.

Casinos

Gamblers will find casinos in several of the larger hotels. Most of these are fairly casual, but in the nicer spots it's advisable to ditch the T-shirts in favor of a button-down shirt as there may be a dress code. Gents: be advised that casinos are frequented by prostitutes, so be wary if you're suddenly the most desirable person in the room.

Casino Club Colonial   CASINO
(Map p72; ☏2258-2807; www.casinoclubcolonial.com; Av 1 btwn Calles 9 & 11; ⊙24hr) San José's most elegant casino.

Casino del Rey
CASINO

(Map p72; ☎ 2257-7800; www.delreyhotel.com; Hotel del Rey, cnr Calle 9 & Av 1; ⊗24hr) A jam-packed shocking-pink building offering everything from roulette to slot machines and what has to be the highest density of prostitutes in the city.

Sports

Bullfighting is popular and fights are held seasonally in the southern suburb of Za-pote over the Christmas period. Members of the public (usually drunk) are encour-aged to participate in the action (the bull isn't killed in the Costa Rican version of the sport).

Estadio Nacional de Costa Rica
STADIUM

(Map p76; Parque Metropolitano La Sabana) Costa Rica's graceful, modernist 35,000-seat na-tional soccer stadium, constructed with funding from the Chinese government and opened to the public in 2011, is the venue for international and national Division-1 *fútbol* (soccer) games. Its predecessor, dat-ing to 1924 and located in the same spot in Parque Metropolitano La Sabana, hosted everyone from Pope John Paul II to soccer legend Pelé to Bruce Springsteen over its 84-year history.

🛍 Shopping

Whether you're looking for indigenous carvings, high-end furnishings or a plastic howler monkey, San José has no shortage of shops, running the gamut from artsy bou-tiques to tourist traps stocked full of tropi-cal everything. Haggling is not tolerated in stores and shops (markets are the excep-tion). In touristy shops, keep an eye peeled for 'authentic' woodworks that have 'Made in Indonesia' stamped on the bottom.

For the country's finest woodcrafts, it is absolutely worth the trip to visit the Biesanz Woodworks workshop in Escazú.

★ Feria Verde de Aranjuez
MARKET

(Map p68; www.feriaverde.org; ⊗7am-noon Sat) For a foodie-friendly cultural experience, don't miss this fabulous Saturday farmers market, a weekly meeting place for San José's artists and organic growers since 2010. You'll find organic coffee, artisanal chocolate, tropical-fruit popsicles, fresh produce, baked goods, leather, jewelry and more at the long rows of booths set up in the park at the north end of Barrio Aranjuez.

Galería Namu
HANDICRAFTS

(Map p72; ☎ 2256-3412, in USA 800-616-4322; www.galerianamu.com; Av 7 btwn Calles 5 & 7; ⊗9am-6:30pm Mon-Sat year-round, plus 1-4pm Sun Dec-Apr) This fair-trade gallery brings together artwork and cultural objects from a diverse population of regional ethnici-ties, including Boruca masks, finely woven Wounaan baskets, Guaymí dolls, Bribrí canoes, Chorotega ceramics, traditional Huetar reed mats, and contemporary urban and Afro-Caribbean crafts. It can also help arrange visits to remote indigenous territo-ries in different parts of Costa Rica.

Kiosco SJO
ARTS & CRAFTS

(Map p68; ☎ 2258-1829; www.kioscosjo.com; cnr Av 11 & Calle 7; ⊗noon-7pm Mon & Tue, noon-8pm Wed-Fri, 10am-8pm Sat) With a focus on sus-tainable design by Latin American artisans, this sleek shop in Barrio Amón stocks hand-made jewelry, hand-tooled leather boots and bags, original photography, artisanal choco-lates, fashion and contemporary home decor by established regional designers. It's pricey, but rest assured that everything you find here will be of exceptional quality.

eÑe
ARTS & CRAFTS

(Map p72; ☎ 2222-7681; laesquina13y7@gmail.com; cnr Av 7 & Calle 13; ⊗10am-6:30pm Mon-Sat) This hip little design shop across from Casa Am-arilla sells all manner of pieces crafted by

---

THE FINE WOODCRAFTS OF BARRY BIESANZ

Located in the hills of Bello Horizonte in Escazú, the workshop of **Biesanz Wood-works** (☎2289-4337; www.biesanz.com; ⊗8am-5pm Mon-Fri, 9am-3pm Sat) is one of the finest woodcrafting studios in the nation, run by celebrated artisan Barry Biesanz. His bowls and other decorative containers are exquisite and take their inspiration from pre-Columbian techniques, in which the natural lines and forms of the wood determine the shape and size of the bowl. The pieces are expensive (from US$135 for a palm-size bowl), but they are unique – and so delicately crafted that they wouldn't be out of place in a museum.

Costa Rican designers and artists, including clothing, jewelry, handbags, picture frames, zines and works of graphic art.

Librería Lehmann BOOKS

(Map p72; ☑2522-4848; www.librerialehmann. com; Av Central btwn Calles 1 & 3; ◷8am-6:30pm Mon-Fri, 9am-5pm Sat, 11am-4pm Sun) Good selection of English-language books, maps and guidebooks (including Lonely Planet).

Mora Books BOOKS

(Map p72; ☑8383-8385; www.morabooks.com; Calle 5 btwn Avs 5 & 7; ◷11am-7pm) Dog-eared paperbacks in English, Spanish, French and German teeter in precarious towers atop crammed shelves at this chaotic jumble of a used bookstore. The best place in town for stocking up on reading material for the road. Hours are hit and miss.

La Casona MARKET

(Map p72; Calle Central btwn Avs Central & 1; ◷9:30am-6:30pm Mon-Sat) Step right up to the number-one tourist trap in Chepe! What you give up in authenticity you'll make up for in convenience. Various stalls spread out over two floors stock T-shirts, banana-leaf paper journals and tree-frog stickers. Shop around, as some quality crafts can be found.

Mercado Central MARKET

(Map p72; Avs Central & 1 btwn Calles 6 & 8; ◷6am-6pm Mon-Sat) This is the best and cheapest place in the city to buy just about anything, from hammocks (*Hecho en Nicaragua*) to *pura vida* T-shirts (made in China) to a vast assortment of forgettable knickknacks. For something decidedly more Costa Rican, export-quality coffee beans and cigars can be bought here at a fraction of the price you'll pay in tourist shops.

Mercado Artesanal MARKET

(Crafts Market; Map p72; Plaza de la Democracia, Avs Central & 2 btwn Calles 13 & 15; ◷9am-6pm) A touristy open-air market that sells everything from handcrafted jewelry and Bob Marley T-shirts to elaborate woodwork and Guatemalan sarongs.

Rincón del Habano CIGARS

(Map p72; Calle 7 btwn Avs Central & 1; ◷9am-6:30pm Mon-Sat, 9:30am-5:30pm Sun) You'll find a wide selection of cigars in this tiny shop. The international array of stogies includes brands from Costa Rica, the Dominican Republic, Nicaragua and Cuba.

🔒 Los Yoses, Barrio Escalante & San Pedro

Mall San Pedro MALL

(☑2283-7516; http://tumallsanpedro.com) This busy four-story mall (often used as a landmark) houses a multi-screen cinema, a food court, a video arcade and the usual mix of clothing, phone and other retailers. It's northwest of Fuente de la Hispanidad.

🔒 Escazú

Multiplaza Escazú MALL

(◷10am-8pm Mon-Sat, to 7pm Sun) Costa Rica's most stylish and massive shopping mall has everything you need (or don't). If you're coming from San José, the mall can be reached by taking any bus marked 'Escazú Multiplaza'.

❶ Orientation

San José's center is arranged in a grid with *avenidas* (avenues) running east to west and *calles* (streets) running north to south. Av Central is the nucleus of the downtown area and is a pedestrian mall between Calles 6 and 9. The downtown has several loosely defined *barrios* (neighborhoods); those of greatest interest to tourists are north and east of Plaza de la Cultura, including Barrio Amón, Barrio Otoya, Barrio Aranjuez and Barrio La California. The central area is home to innumerable businesses, hotels and cultural sites, while the area immediately west of downtown is home to San José's central market and many of its bus terminals.

Slightly further west of downtown is La Sabana, named for its huge and popular park where many *josefinos* spend their weekends jogging, swimming, picnicking or attending soccer matches.

A few kilometers southwest is the affluent outer suburb of Escazú, really three neighborhoods in one: Escazú Centro with its peaceful central plaza and unhurried Tico ambience; the USA expatriate enclave of San Rafael, dotted with strip malls, top-end car dealerships, tract housing and chain restaurants; and San Antonio, a hillside mix of humble rural homes, sprawling estates and spectacular views.

East (and within walking distance) of the center are the contiguous neighborhoods of Los Yoses and San Pedro, the former a low-key residential area with some nice accommodations, the latter home to the tree-lined campus of the UCR, the country's most prestigious university. Marking the dividing line between Los Yoses and San Pedro is a traffic roundabout graced by a large fountain known as the Fuente de la Hispanidad (a frequently referenced local landmark). North of Los Yoses is Barrio Escalante, home to some of San José's trendiest bars and restaurants.

You can pick up a free map of the city at the tourist office.

ℹ️ Information

DANGERS & ANNOYANCES

Though Costa Rica has the lowest crime rate of any Central American country, crime in urban centers such as San José is a problem. The most common offense is opportunistic theft (eg pickpocketing and mugging). Keep a streetwise attitude and follow the tips below.

➡ Do not wear flashy jewelry.

➡ Keep your camera in your bag when you are not using it.

➡ Carry only as much cash as you'll need for the day.

➡ Unless you think you'll need it for official business, leave your passport in the hotel safe; a photocopy will do for most purposes.

➡ Be wary of pickpockets at crowded events and the areas around bus stops.

➡ Never put your bag in the overhead racks on a bus.

➡ Do not walk around alone at night, and stick to licensed taxis.

➡ If you are renting a car, always park it in a secure, guarded lot, and never leave anything in it.

➡ Men should be aware that prostitutes are known for their sleight-of-hand abilities, and that they often work in pairs.

Neighborhoods reviewed in this book are generally safe during the day, though you should be especially careful around the Coca-Cola bus terminal and the red-light district south of Parque Central, particularly at night. Be advised that adjacent neighborhoods can vary greatly in terms of safety; inquire locally before setting out.

Gridlocked traffic, gigantic potholes, noise and smog are unavoidable components of the San José experience. Most central hotels are subject to street noise, no matter how nice they are. Be skeptical of touts and taxi drivers who try to sell you tours or tell you that the hotel you've booked is a crime-infested bordello. Many of these folks will say anything to steer you to the places that pay them commissions.

EMERGENCY

Fire (☎ 118)

Red Cross (Cruz Roja Costariccense; ☎ 128, in San José 2542-5000; www.cruzroja.or.cr; Av 8 btwn Calles 14 & 16)

Traffic Police (Policía de Tránsito; ☎ 2222-9245, 2222-9330; www.transito.go.cr)

SAN JOSÉ INFORMATION

ℹ️ TOURIST POLICE

The establishment of a *policía turística* (tourist police) in 2007 has alleviated petty crimes against foreigners (you'll see them patrolling in pairs around San José, on foot, bicycle and even on horseback). These officers can be helpful in the event of an emergency since most of them speak at least some English. But if you find yourself the victim of a crime, you'll have to file a report in person at the **Organismo de Investigación Judicial** (☎ 2221-5337, 2222-1365; Calle 17 btwn Avs 6 & 8; ⊙ 9am-5pm Mon-Fri) in the Supreme Court of Justice building on the south side of downtown.

MEDICAL SERVICES

For serious medical emergencies, head to **Hospital CIMA** (☎ 2208-1000; www.hospitalcima.com; Los Laureles) in San Rafael de Escazú, whose facilities are the most modern in the greater San José area.

Clínica Bíblica (☎ 2522-1000, emergency 2522-1030; www.clinicabiblica.com; Av 14 btwn Calles Central & 1) The top private clinic downtown has a 24-hour emergency room; doctors speak English, French and German.

Hospital La Católica (☎ 2246-3000; www.hospitallacatolica.com; Guadalupe) Pricey private clinic geared toward medical-tourism patients from abroad.

Hospital San Juan de Dios (☎ 2547-8000; cnr Paseo Colón & Calle 14) Free public hospital open 24 hours; expect long waits.

POST

Correo Central (Central Post Office; Map p72; ☎ 2223-9766; www.correos.go.cr; Calle 2 btwn Avs 1 & 3; ⊙ 7:30am-5:30pm Mon-Fri, to noon Sat) In a gorgeous historic building near the center of town. Express and overnight services.

TOURIST INFORMATION

Canatur (Cámara Nacional de Turismo; ☎ 2234-6222, 2440-1676; www.canatur.org; Aeropuerto Internacional Juan Santamaría; ⊙ 7am-10pm) The Costa Rican National Chamber of Tourism provides information on member services from a small stand next to international baggage claim.

Instituto Costarricense de Turismo (ICT; Map p72; ☎ 2222-1090, in USA & Canada 866-267-8274; www.visitcostarica.com; Edificio de las Academias, Av Central btwn Calles 1 & 3; ⊙ 9am-5pm Mon-Fri) The government tourism office provides handy intercity bus schedules, as well as free maps of San José and Costa Rica.

ℹ Getting There & Away

San José is the country's transportation hub, and it's likely that you'll pass through the capital a number of times throughout your travels (whether you want to or not).

AIR

All international flights leave from Juan Santamaría (SJO) airport outside Alajuela. For airlines serving San José, see p519.

Aeropuerto Internacional Juan Santamaría (☎2437-2400; http://fly2sanjose.com) Handles all international flights and NatureAir domestic flights in its main terminal. Domestic flights on Sansa depart from the Sansa terminal.

Aeropuerto Tobías Bolaños (☎2232-2820) In the San José suburb of Pavas; services private charter flights.

BUS

Bus transportation in San José can be bewildering. There is no public bus system and no central terminal. Instead, dozens of private companies operate out of stops scattered throughout the city. Many bus companies have no more than a stop (in this case pay the driver directly); some have a tiny office with a window on the street, while some operate from bigger terminals serv-

DOMESTIC BUSES FROM SAN JOSÉ

See p102 for information about each bus company.

DESTINATION	BUS COMPANY	FARE (US$)	DURATION (HR)	FREQUENCY
Cahuita	Autotransportes Mepe	9.35	4	6am, 10am, noon, 2pm, 4pm
Cañas	Pulmitan de Liberia	5.75	3½	2 to 3 daily
Cariari	Autotransportes Caribeños	3.30	2	6:30am, 9am, 10:30am, 1pm, 3pm, 4:30pm, 6pm, 7pm
Cartago	Lumaca	1.15	1	every 15min
Ciudad Neily	Tracopa	14.70	8	5am, 10am, 1pm, 4:30pm, 6:30pm
Ciudad Quesada	Autotransportes San Carlos	3.60	3	hourly
Dominical & Uvita	Tracopa	8.70-11.50	4½-5½	6am, 6:30am, 3pm
Golfito	Tracopa	14.70	8	7am, 3:30pm
Grecia	Tuan	2.15	1	half-hourly
Guápiles	Autotransportes Caribeños	2.75	1¼	half-hourly
Jacó	Transportes Jacó	4.75	2½	every 2hr 7am-7pm
La Fortuna	Autotransportes San Carlos	5	4½	6:15am, 8:40am, 11:30am
Liberia	Pulmitan de Liberia	7	4	hourly
Los Chiles	Autotransportes San Carlos	5.85	5	5:30am, 3pm
Manzanillo	Autotransportes Mepe	12.10	5	noon
Monteverde/ Santa Elena	Transmonteverde	5.65	4½	6:30am, 2:30pm
Montezuma/ Mal País	Transportes Cobano	15.10	5½-6	6am, 2pm
Nicoya	Empresa Alfaro	7.85	5	7:30am, 10am, 1pm, 3pm, 5pm
Palmar Norte	Tracopa	11.50	5	5am, 7am, 10am, 1pm, 6:30pm
Paso Canoas	Tracopa	15.40	6	5am, 11am, 1pm, 6:30pm
Peñas Blancas	Transportes Deldú	9.25	6	11 daily

icing entire regions. See below for a summary of the major terminals, a list of bus companies with their contact info, and a table showing prices and times for major destinations.

Note that bus schedules and prices change regularly. Pick up a copy of the free (but not always up-to-date) booklet *Itinerario de Buses* from San José's downtown tourist office, or download a PDF version from www.visitcostarica.com (most easily located in your search engine by typing 'Costa Rica Itinerario de Buses'). Buses are crowded on Friday evening and Saturday morning and packed to the gills at Christmas and Easter.

For buses that run infrequently, it is advisable to buy tickets in advance. For a hassle-free start to your trip, consider contacting **A Safe Passage** (☎ 8365-9678, in USA 970-439-5446; www.costaricabustickets.com), which can purchase bus tickets in advance for a small fee. It also arranges airport transfers.

Bus Terminals

Collectively, the following four San José terminals serve Costa Rica's most popular destinations. Chances are you'll be passing through one or more of them during your trip. Be aware that thefts are common in many bus terminals. Stay alert, keep your valuables close to you and don't

DESTINATION	BUS COMPANY	FARE (US$)	DURATION (HR)	FREQUENCY
Playa del Coco	Pulmitan de Liberia	8.30	5	8am, 2pm, 4pm
Playa Flamingo	Tralapa	12.60	6	8am, 10:30am, 3pm
Playa Hermosa	Tralapa	10.90	5	3:30pm
Playa Nosara	Empresa Alfaro	9.60	6	5:30am
Playa Sámara	Empresa Alfaro	8.95	5	noon
Playa Tamarindo	Empresa Alfaro	11.30	5	11:30am, 3:30pm
Playa Tamarindo	Tralapa	11.50	5	7:15am, 4pm
Puerto Jiménez	Blanco Lobo	15	8	8am, noon
Puerto Limón	Autotransportes Caribeños	6.30	3	hourly
Puerto Viejo de Sarapiquí	Autotransportes Caribeños	5	2	13 daily
Puerto Viejo de Talamanca	Autotransportes Mepe	10.85	4½	6am, 10am, noon, 2pm, 4pm
Puntarenas	Empresarios Unidos	5.10	2½	hourly
Quepos/Manuel Antonio	Tracopa	9.05	4	every 1-2hr
San Isidro del General	Tracopa	7.10	3	hourly
San Vito	Tracopa	13.45	7	6am, 8:15am, noon, 4pm
Santa Cruz	Empresa Alfaro	10.85	5	7 daily
Santa Cruz	Tralapa	11	5	9am, noon, 2pm, 6pm
Sarchí	Tuan	2.15	1½	12:15pm, 5:30pm, 6pm Mon-Fri
Siquirres	Autotransportes Caribeños	3.20	2	hourly
Sixaola	Autotransportes Mepe	13.30	5½	6am, 10am, 2pm, 4pm
Tilarán	Pulmitan de Liberia	7.90	4	7:30am, 9:30am, 12:45pm, 3:45pm, 6:30pm
Turrialba	Transtusa	2.80	2	hourly
Volcán Irazú	Metrópoli	9, round trip	2	8am

stow anything important (such as passports and money) in the overhead racks or luggage compartment of a bus.

Gran Terminal del Caribe (Map p68; Calle Central) A roomy station north of Av 13; serves destinations on the Caribbean slope, with connections to Tortuguero.

Terminal Coca-Cola (Map p68; Av 1 btwn Calles 16 & 18) A well-known, labyrinthine landmark; buses leave from the terminal and the four-block radius around it to points all over Costa Rica, including the Central Valley and the Pacific coast.

Terminal San Carlos (Terminal del Atlántico Norte; Map p68; cnr Av 9 & Calle 12) A small, rather decrepit terminal serving Monteverde, La Fortuna and southern Caribbean coastal destinations.

Terminal Tracopa (p102) On the south end of town; serves southern and southwestern destinations including Golfito, Quepos/Manuel Antonio and Paso Canoas on the Panama border.

Domestic Bus Companies

Autotransportes Caribeños (Map p68; 2221-7990, 2222-0610; www.grupocaribenos.com; Gran Terminal del Caribe, Calle Central) Buses to northeastern destinations including Puerto Limón, Guápiles, Cariari, Siquirres and Puerto Viejo de Sarapiquí. The Caribeños group encompasses several smaller companies (Empresarios Guapileños, Líneas del Atlántico etc), all of which share the same terminal and customer-service phone number.

Autotransportes Mepe (2257-8129; www.mepecr.com; Terminal San Carlos) Buses to southern Caribbean destinations including Cahuita, Puerto Viejo de Talamanca, Manzanillo, Bribrí and Sixaola.

Autotransportes San Carlos (2255-0567, 2255-4300; Terminal San Carlos) Buses to La Fortuna, Ciudad Quesada and Los Chiles.

Blanco Lobo (Map p68; 2257-4121; Calle 12 btwn Avs 9 & 11) Buses to Puerto Jiménez.

Coopetrans Atenas (2446-5767; www.coopetransatenas.com; Terminal Coca-Cola) Buses to Atenas.

Empresa Alfaro (Map p68; 2222-2666; www.empresaalfaro.com; Av 5 btwn Calles 14 & 16) Buses to Nicoya, Nosara, Sámara, Santa Cruz and Tamarindo.

Empresarios Unidos (Map p68; 2222-8231; cnr Av 12 & Calle 16) Buses to San Ramón and Puntarenas.

Lumaca (Map p68; 2552-5280, 2537-2320; Av 10 btwn Calles 5 & 7) Buses to Cartago.

Metrópoli (Map p72; 2530-1064; Av 2 btwn Calles 1 & 3) Buses to Volcán Irazú.

Pulmitan de Liberia (Map p68; 2222-1650; Calle 24 btwn Avs 5 & 7) Buses to northwestern destinations including Cañas, Liberia, Playa del Coco and Tilarán. The Pulmitan group encompasses the smaller companies of Empresa La Cañera and Autotransportes Tilarán, both of which use Pulmitan's terminal.

Station Wagon (Map p68; 2441-1181; Av 2 btwn Calles 10 & 12) Buses to Alajuela and the airport.

Tracopa (Map p68; 2221-4214; www.tracopacr.com; Calle 5 btwn Avs 18 & 20) Buses to southwestern destinations including Ciudad Neily, Dominical, Golfito, Manuel Antonio, Palmar Norte, Paso Canoas, Quepos, San Isidro del General, San Vito and Uvita. Tracopa encompasses the smaller companies Delio

INTERNATIONAL BUSES FROM SAN JOSÉ

DESTINATION	BUS COMPANY	FARE (US$)	DURATION (HR)	FREQUENCY
Changuinola (Panama)	Transportes Bocatoreños	14	7	9am
David (Panama)	Tracopa	21	9	7:30am, noon
Guatemala City	Tica Bus	99	48	3am
Managua (Nicaragua)	Tica Bus	28-40	9	3am, 6am, 7:30am, 12:30pm
Managua (Nicaragua)	TransNica	27-38	8-9	4am, 5am, 9am, noon
Panama City	Expreso Panamá	40	14	noon
Panama City	Tica Bus	42-58	15	noon, 11pm
San Salvador (El Salvador)	Tica Bus	80	19-20	3am
Tegucigalpa (Honduras)	TransNica	50	18	4am

Morales and Unidos La Costanera, which now share Tracopa's terminal.

Tralapa (Map p68; ☑ 2221-7202; Av 5 btwn Calles 20 & 22) Buses to several Península de Nicoya destinations, including Playa Flamingo, Playa Hermosa, Playa Tamarindo and Santa Cruz.

Transmonteverde (☑ 2256-7710; www. facebook.com/Transmonteverde; Terminal San Carlos, cnr Av 9 & Calle 12) Buses to Monteverde.

Transportes Cobano (☑ 2221-7479; trans-portescobano@gmail.com; Terminal San Carlos, cnr Av 9 & Calle 12) Buses to Montezuma and Mal País.

Transportes Deldú (Map p68; ☑ 2256-9072; www.transportesdeldu.com; Av 9 btwn Calles 10 & 12) Buses to Peñas Blancas (Nicaraguan border).

Transportes Jacó (☑ 2290-7920, 2290-2922; www.transportesjacoruta655.com; Terminal Coca-Cola, Av 1 btwn Calles 16 & 18) Buses to Jacó.

Transtusa (Map p68; ☑ 2222-4464; www. transtusacr.com; Calle 13A btwn Avs 6 & 8) Buses to Cartago and Turrialba.

Tuan (Map p68; ☑ 2494-2139, 2258-2004; cnr Av 5 & Calle 18A) Buses to Grecia.

Tuasa (Map p68; ☑ 2442-6900; Av 2 btwn Calles 12 & 14) Buses to Alajuela and the airport.

International Bus Companies

International buses get booked up fast. Buy your tickets in advance – and take your passport.

Expreso Panama (Map p68; ☑ 2221-7694; www.expresopanama.com; Terminal Empresarios Unidos, cnr Av 12 & Calle 16) Buses to Panama City.

Tica Bus (Map p76; ☑ 2221-0006; www. ticabus.com; cnr Transversal 26 & Av 3) Buses to Nicaragua, Panama, El Salvador and Guatemala.

TransNica (Map p68; ☑ 2223-4123; www. transnica.com; Calle 22 btwn Avs 3 & 5) Buses to Nicaragua and Honduras.

Transportes Bocatoreños (Map p68; ☑ 2223-7011, 2227-9523; cnr Av 5 & Calle 16) Buses (departing opposite Hotel Cocori) to Changuinola, Panama (for Bocas del Toro).

Shuttle Buses

Grayline (☑ 2220-2126; www.graylinecostarica. com; $33-89) and **Interbus** (☑ 2283-5573; www. interbusonline.com; US$37-57) shuttle passengers in air-conditioned minivans from San José to a long list of popular destinations around Costa Rica. They are more expensive than the standard bus service, but they offer door-to-door service and can get you there faster.

ⓘ SCAMS

Note that many taxi drivers in San José are commissioned by hotels to bring them customers, and the hotel scene is so competitive that drivers will say just about anything to steer you to the places they represent. Among other things, they will 'call' your hotel and a voice on the other end will tell you that they're fully booked. Be skeptical. Tell drivers firmly where it is you would like to go. And if you have concerns about where you have chosen to stay, ask to see a room before settling in for the night.

ⓘ Getting Around

Central San José frequently resembles a parking lot – narrow streets, heavy traffic and a complicated one-way system mean that it is often quicker to walk than to take the bus. The same applies to driving: if you rent a car, try to avoid downtown. If you're in a real hurry to get somewhere that's more than 1km away, take a taxi.

If traveling by bus, you'll arrive at one of several international bus terminals sprinkled around the western and southern parts of downtown. Some of this area is walkable provided you aren't hauling a lot of luggage and are staying nearby. But, if you're arriving at night, take a taxi, since most terminals are in dodgy areas.

TO & FROM THE AIRPORTS

International flights arrive at Aeropuerto Internacional Juan Santamaría in nearby Alajuela.

In normal traffic, an official taxi from the airport to downtown San José should cost between US$25 and US$30, as measured on the meter. You can reserve a pickup with **Taxi Aeropuerto** (☑ 2221-6865). Plan on spending extra for wait time during periods of heavy traffic.

Interbus (p103) runs shuttles in both directions between the airport and San José hotels (US$15 per adult, US$7.50 per child under 12), good value if you're traveling alone.

Even cheaper are the public buses (US$1.10) operated by Tuasa (p103) and Station Wagon (p102), which pick up passengers at a stop on the main road in front of the airport. Make sure to verify the destination before boarding, as some buses from this stop go to Alajuela, others to San José. On the return trip, board at the Tuasa or Station Wagon terminal in downtown San José (both opposite Iglesia de La Merced near the corner of Av 2 and Calle 12) and be sure to tell the driver that you are getting off at the airport (*Voy al aeropuerto, por favor*). Most hotels can also arrange for private airport pickup at reasonable rates.

From downtown, the drive to the airport can take anywhere from 20 minutes to an hour (more if you take the bus) – and vice versa. Plan accordingly.

BUS

Local buses are useful to get you into the suburbs and surrounding villages, or to the airport. Most buses run between 5am and 10pm and cost between US$0.40 and US$1.10.

For buses to **Alajuela** and **Heredia**, see p112 and p124

La Sabana

To catch a bus heading west from San José towards La Sabana (US$0.40), head for the convenient downtown stop at the southeast corner of Av 3 and Calle 3. Buses returning from Parque La Sabana to downtown follow Paseo Colón, then go over to Av 2 at the San Juan de Dios hospital. They then go three different ways through town before eventually heading back to La Sabana. Buses are marked Sabana–Estadio, Sabana–Cementerio or Cementerio–Estadio. These buses are a good bet for a cheap city tour.

Los Yoses and San Pedro

Catch eastbound buses to Los Yoses and San Pedro (US$0.50) from the northeast corner of Calle Central and Av 9. These buses run east along Av 2 and then switch over to Av Central at Calle 29. (Many are easily identifiable by the big sign that says 'Mall San Pedro' on the front window.)

Escazú

Buses southwest to Escazú (US$0.65 to US$0.80, 15 to 25 minutes) leave from two different locations: Av 6 between Calles 14 and 16 (south of the Hospital San Juan de Dios), and Calle 16 between Avs 1 and 3 (near the Coca-Cola terminal). Buses labeled 'San Antonio de Escazú' climb the hill south of Escazú and end near the Iglesia San Antonio de Escazú; those labeled 'Escazú Centro' end in Escazú's main plaza; others, labeled 'Guachipelín' go west on the Carretera John F Kennedy and pass the Costa Rica Country Club. All go through San Rafael.

CAR

It is not advisable to rent a car just to drive around San José. The traffic is heavy, the streets are narrow and the meter-deep curbside gutters make parking nerve-wracking. In addition, break-ins are frequent, and leaving a car – even in a guarded lot – might result in a smashed window and stolen belongings.

If you are renting a car to travel throughout Costa Rica, there are more than 50 car-rental agencies – including many of the global brands – in and around San José. Travel agencies and upmarket hotels can arrange rentals; you can also arrange rentals online and at the airport.

One excellent local option is **Wild Rider** (☎ 2258-4604; www.wild-rider.com; Paseo Colón btwn Calles 30 & 32; ☺ 8am-6pm), run by a charming pair of Germans. They have a fleet of over 60 very reasonably priced 4WD vehicles (from US$380 per week in high season, including all mandatory insurance coverage). Reserve well in advance.

MOTORCYCLE

Wild Rider rents sports bikes like the Honda XR-250 or the Suzuki DRZ-400S. Prices start at US$420 per week in high season (including insurance, taxes and helmets). It organizes on- and off-road guided tours as well.

TAXI

Red taxis can be hailed on the street day or night, or you can have your hotel call one for you.

Marías (meters) are generally used, though a few drivers will tell you they're broken and try to charge you more – especially if you don't speak Spanish. Not using a meter is illegal. The rate for the first kilometer should automatically appear when the meter starts up (at the time of writing, the correct starting amount was 610 colones). Make sure the *maría* is operating when you get in, or negotiate the fare up front. Short rides downtown cost US$2 to US$4. There's a 20% surcharge after 10pm that may not appear on the *maría*.

You can hire a taxi and a driver for half a day or longer if you want to do some touring around the area; for such trips, it is best to negotiate a flat fee in advance.

Central Valley & Highlands

Best Places to Eat

➡ Xandari (p112)

➡ Finca Rosa Blanca (p124)

➡ La Casona del Maíz (p115)

➡ Jalapeños Central (p111)

➡ Colbert Restaurant (p114)

Best Places to Stay

➡ Poás Volcano Lodge (p114)

➡ Vista del Valle Plantation Inn (p115)

➡ Casa de Lis Hostel (p136)

➡ Vista Atenas B&B (p115)

Why Go?

It is on the coffee-cultivated hillsides of the Central Valley that you'll find Costa Rica's heart and soul. This is not only the geographical center of the country, but also its cultural and spiritual core. It is here that the Spanish first settled, here that coffee built a prosperous nation, here that picturesque highland villages still gather for centuries-old fiestas. It is also here that you'll get to fully appreciate Costa Rica's country cooking: artisanal cheeses, steamy corn cakes and freshly caught river trout.

Curvy mountain roads force travelers to slow their roll. Quaint and quirky agricultural towns invite leisurely detours to farmers markets and church processions, a refreshing break from the tourist-industrial complex on the coasts. But it's not all cows and coffee – world-class rapids, resplendent quetzals and close encounters with active volcanoes all show off the rich landscape in which Costa Rica's character is rooted.

When to Go

➡ An elevated altitude and landlocked location mean that the Central Valley and highlands are far more temperate than the coasts.

➡ Temps hover around 25°C (77°F) year-round, making the region a popular retreat for weekending *josefinos* (inhabitants of San José) seeking to escape the heat.

➡ During 'green' season, from June to December, afternoon showers are not uncommon, but the sun usually shines through after an hour or so of rain. This is also the high season for rafting, June through October being the best months.

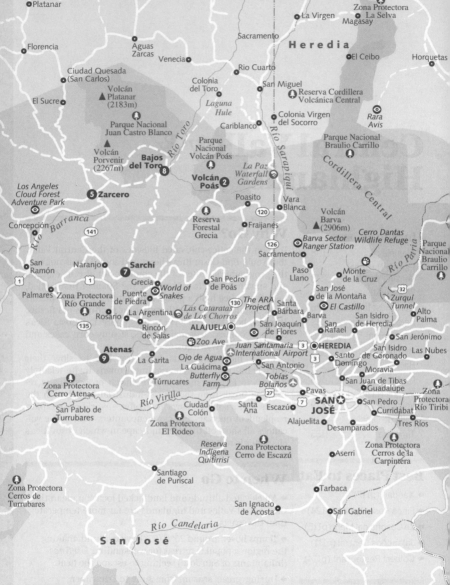

Platanar

Central Valley & Highlands Highlights

❶ Paddling for your life down the cascading rapids of the **Río Pacuare** (p136) near Turrialba.

❷ Peering into mammoth craters and volcanic lakes at **Volcán Irazú** (p129) and **Volcán Poás** (p112) national parks.

❸ Contemplating the aqueducts and petroglyphs at Costa Rica's largest archaeological site, **Monumento Nacional Arqueológico Guayabo** (p138).

❹ Exploring the wilderness, culture and coffee *fincas* of **Valle de Orosi** (p130).

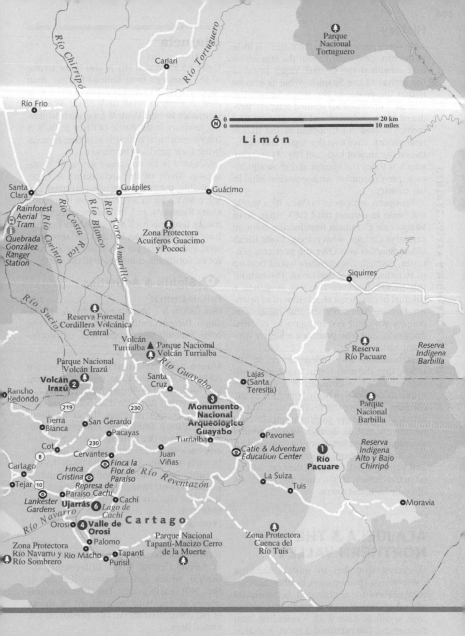

History

As in other parts of the country, there is little in the historical record about the ethnicities that inhabited the Central Valley prior to the arrival of the Spanish. What is known is that the people of the area – largely the Huetar – practiced an animist religion, produced stone sculpture and clay pottery, and communicated in a Chibchan dialect that is now extinct. They also developed and maintained the ancient highland city of Guayabo, which is today the biggest and most significant pre-Columbian archaeological site in the country.

European settlement in Costa Rica would not begin in earnest until 1563, when Juan Vásquez de Coronado founded the colonial capital of Cartago, what is today Costa Rica's oldest Spanish city. Over the next two centuries, Spanish communities would pop up in Heredia, San José and Orosi. Throughout this period, however, the area remained a colonial backwater, a checkerboard of Spanish farming communities and indigenous peoples who had not come under colonial dominion, and who practiced a largely itinerant agriculture.

It was only after independence, in the 1830s, that the area began to prosper with the expanded cultivation of coffee. The *grano de oro* (golden bean) transformed the country, providing the revenue to invest in urban infrastructure such as electricity and pavements, not to mention many baronial mansions. Coffee has since been overtaken as a key agricultural export by pineapples and bananas. But its legacy lives on, reflected in the culture, architecture and traditions of many highland towns.

ALAJUELA & THE NORTHERN VALLEY

Volcanoes shrouded in mist, undulating coffee *fincas* (plantations), bustling agricultural centers: the area around the provincial capital of Alajuela, 18km northwest of San José, seems to have it all – including Juan Santamaría International Airport, just 3km outside the city. The proximity to the airport makes this area a highly convenient transit point if you are entering or leaving the country here. For travelers seeking to avoid San José, it offers a good selection of local restaurants and accommodations.

Alajuela

POP 43,000

Costa Rica's second city is also home to one of the country's most famous figures: Juan Santamaría, the humble drummer boy who died putting an end to William Walker's campaign to turn Central America into slaving territory in the Battle of Rivas in 1856. A busy agricultural hub, it is here that farmers bring their products to market.

Alajuela is by no means a tourist 'destination.' Much of the architecture is unremarkable, the streets are often jammed and there isn't a lot to see. But it's an inherently Costa Rican city, and, in its more relaxed moments, it reveals itself as such, where families have leisurely Sunday lunches and teenagers steal kisses in the park. It's also a good base for exploring the countryside to the north.

◉ Sights & Activities

Parque Central   PARK
(Avs Central & 1 btwn Calles Central & 2) The shady Parque Central is a pleasant place to relax beneath the mango trees, or people-watch in the evenings.

Museo Juan Santamaría   MUSEUM
(☑2441-4775; Av 1 btwn Calles Central & 2; ◉10am-5pm Tue-Sun) FREE Situated in a century-old structure that has served as both a jail and an armory, this museum chronicles Costa Rican history from early European settlement through the 19th century, with special emphasis on the life and history of Juan Santamaría and the pivotal mid-1850s battles of Santa Rosa, Sardinal and Rivas. Exhibits include videos, vintage maps, paintings and historical artifacts related to the conflict that ultimately safeguarded Costa Rica's independence.

Cathedral   CHURCH
(Calle Central btwn Avs Central & 1) To the east of Parque Central is the 19th-century cathedral, which suffered severe damage in the 1991 earthquake. The hemispherical cupola is unusually constructed of sheets of red corrugated metal. Two presidents are buried here.

Parque Juan Santamaría   PLAZA
(Calle 2 btwn Avs 2 & 4) Two blocks south of Parque Central, this plaza features a statue of the hero in action, flanked by cannons. Across the way, the **Parque de los Niños** has a more parklike scene going, complete

with playground equipment, chattering toddlers and canoodling teenagers.

Ojo de Agua Springs
SWIMMING

(☎2441-0655; www.incop.go.cr; San Antonio de Belén; admission US$3, under 6yr free; ☉7:30am-4:30pm; ⚅) About 6km south of Alajuela, this picturesque working-class water park gets packed with local families on weekends. Approximately 20,000L of water gushes from the spring each minute, powering a small waterfall and filling various pools (including an Olympic-size lap pool complete with diving tower) and an artificial boating lake. Half-hourly buses to the springs depart from the main terminal area on Alajuela's southwestern edge. From San José, drivers can take the San Antonio de Belén exit off the Interamericana.

✸ Festivals & Events

In the town that gave birth to Juan Santamaría, it would be expected that the anniversary of the **Battle of Rivas**, on April 11, would be particularly well celebrated. This momentous event is commemorated with civic events, including a parade and lots of firecrackers.

🛏 Sleeping

Since Alajuela is so close to the international airport, most hotels and B&Bs can arrange airport transfers for a small fee (or for free, as noted in individual listings below). If you are driving your own car, note that many places in the city center don't have dedicated parking, but there are many guarded lots available. Also, expect street noise to be a fact of life.

As in other spots, taxi drivers will try to steer you to places that pay them a commission. Remember: be skeptical, don't believe everything you hear and if you're unsure about where you've chosen to stay, ask to see a room.

A few of the budget hotels also offer dorm rooms. All top-end hotels accept credit cards, as do most midrange spots.

Hostel Maleku
HOSTEL $

(☎2430-4304; www.malekuhostel.com; incl breakfast dm US$15, s/d without bathroom US$25/38; @🖳) This super-friendly, family-run backpackers' abode has five spick-and-span rooms tucked into a vintage home between the airport and downtown Alajuela (opposite Hospital San Rafael). There's a communal kitchen, plus free storage for items

brought from home that you don't need while in Costa Rica (winter coats, bike boxes). Free airport drop-off service is available hourly between 5am and 5pm.

Alajuela Backpackers Boutique Hostel
HOTEL $

(☎2441-7149; www.alajuelabackpackers.com; cnr Av 4 & Calle 4; dm/r/ste US$17/55/70; ❄@🖳) This four-story place with cookie-cutter rooms may feel a tad institutional at first glance, but dig deeper and you'll discover some big pluses: free shuttles to and from the airport, air-conditioned dorms and doubles with en-suite bathrooms and a super cool 4th-floor bar terrace where you can sip beers while watching planes take off in the distance.

Hotel Pacandé
B&B $

(☎2443-8481; www.hotelpacande.com; Av 5 btwn Calles 2 & 4; incl breakfast r US$50-60, without bathroom US$35; P@🖳) This popular, locally run option is spotlessly clean throughout, offering 10 large rooms with wood furnishings, folk-art touches and cable TV. Less expensive rooms share bathrooms. The bright and sunny breakfast nook is a great spot for a morning brew.

Hotel Trotamundos
HOTEL $

(☎2430-5832; www.hoteltrotamundos.com; Av 5 btwn Calles 2 & 4; incl breakfast dm US$12, d with/without bathroom US$35/30; @🖳) This basic place in the heart of town has clean rooms and friendly service. One dorm and nine private rooms with cable TV (four with private bathroom) are nestled into a two-story house surrounding a small courtyard. Other perks include a shared kitchen and free shuttle service to the airport.

Alajuela

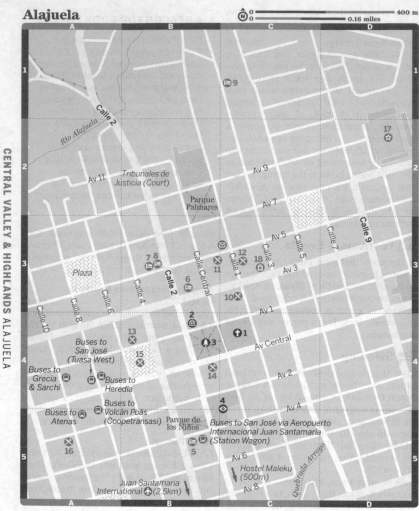

Trapp Family Lodge
INN $$

(☑ 2431-0776; www.trappfam.com; incl breakfast r US$99, additional person US$20, child 3-11yr US$15; P@🛜🏊) The most attractive option you'll find so close to the airport landing strip, this hacienda-style country inn houses eight terra-cotta-tiled rooms with comfortable beds. The best units come with balconies overlooking the inviting turquoise pool and verdant garden laced with bougainvillea and fig trees. Despite the accommodation's rural feel, it's only 2km from the international airport; free airport transfers are provided.

Hotel Los Volcanes
GUESTHOUSE $$

(☑ 2441-0525; www.hotellosvolcanes.com; Av 3 btwn Calles Central & 2; incl breakfast s/d without bathroom US$35/46, with bathroom US$46/60, with air-con US$64/74; P🔌❄@🛜) Tranquil and centrally located, this welcoming place in a refurbished 1920s home has 15 rooms, from vintage units with period-style furniture and clean, shared bathrooms, to contemporary rooms with flat-screen TV, air-con and safe. There's an enjoyable courtyard in the back, complete with gurgling fountain. The helpful Tico owners arrange free airport drop-off at the end of your stay.

Alajuela

Vida Tropical B&B B&B $$
(☑2443-9576; www.vidatropical.com; Calle 3; incl breakfast s/d US$45/65, without bathroom US$35/50; P@🌐🐾) In a quiet residential neighborhood a five-minute walk north of downtown Alajuela, this friendly Colombian-American-run house has seven snug, simple guest rooms awash in bright murals; two share a bathroom. The well-tended backyard is perfect for catching some sun in a hammock, and laundry service is available. Owners can help arrange airport pickup (US$8) at any hour.

Tacacori Ecolodge BUNGALOW $$$
(☑2430-5846; www.tacacori.com; d incl breakfast US$110, extra person US$15) French owners Nadine and Patrick and their two sheepdogs run this peaceful retreat high above Alajuela. Four spacious bungalows with ultramodern fixtures and abundant ecofriendly touches (solar hot water, LED lighting, dual-flush toilets) sit astride a verdant hillside. Attractively priced 'Hello-Goodbye' packages and 15-minute airport transfers (US$15 uphill, US$10 downhill) provide incentive to begin and end your travels here.

★Xandari Resort Hotel & Spa HOTEL $$$
(☑2443-2020, in USA 1866-363-3212; www.xandari.com; d villa US$299-418, q villa US$622; P🅿✳🌐🏊) ⊘ With spectacular bird's-eye views of the Central Valley, this romantic spot is the fanciful creation of a Californian architect-designer couple. Spacious individual villas, tastefully but playfully decorated in vibrant tropical colors and hand-woven textiles, include garden-view shower and sitting area. The grounds offer

4km of trails, five waterfalls, three pools, two Jacuzzis, a spa and an organic-foods restaurant.

Hotel Buena Vista HOTEL $$$
(☑2442-8595, in USA 1800-506-2304; www.hotelbuenavistacr.com; incl breakfast d standard/deluxe/junior ste/villa US$157/169/189/236; P🅿@🌐🏊) ⊘ About 5km north of Alajuela, this whitewashed Mediterranean-style hotel, perched on a mountaintop, has panoramic views of the nearby volcanoes. The best of the tastefully decorated rooms have private balconies with valley views; five villas offer privacy along with wood-beamed ceilings, minibar and private balcony. A small trail leads down through a coffee *finca* to the main road.

✕ Eating

For the cheapest meals, head to the enclosed **Mercado Central** (Calles 4 & 6 btwn Avs 1 & Central; ⊙7am-6pm Mon-Sat). Self-caterers can stock up on groceries at the **Palí** (cnr Av 2 & Calle 10; ⊙8am-8pm), **MegaSuper** (Av Central btwn Calles Central & 2; ⊙8am-9pm) or **Más X Menos** (Av 1 btwn Calles 4 & 6; ⊙7am-9pm Mon-Sat, to 8pm Sun).

★Jalapeños Central MEXICAN $
(☑2430-4027; Calle 1 btwn Avs 3 & 5; mains US$4-8; ⊙11:30am-9pm Mon-Sat, to 8pm Sun) Run by an animated Colombian-American from New York City, this popular Tex-Mex spot will introduce some much-needed spice into your diet. You'll also find Tico specialties, spit-roasted chicken and New York-style cheesecake.

El Chante Vegano VEGETARIAN, VEGAN $
(☑8911-4787; www.elchantevegano.com; mains US$7-10; ☑) A young Tico chef and his friendly mom have teamed up to open this new eatery specializing in healthy, organic food. Vegan treats are served on an open-air, street-facing patio, including garbanzo (chickpea) and portobello-mushroom burgers, falafel, textured-soy-protein nachos, pasta, pizza and sandwiches like the Veggie Lú (grilled veggies, avocado and sprouts on homemade bread).

Coffee Dreams Café CAFE $
(☑2430-3970; cnr Calle 1 & Av 3; mains US$5-9; ☺7:30am-9pm Mon-Sat, 9am-7pm Sun; ☑) For breakfast, *bocas* (appetizers) and a variety of *típico* (traditional Costa Rican) dishes, this centrally located cafe is a reliably good place to dine or enjoy a coffee accompanied by one of its rich desserts.

Puntalitos de Manuela CAFE $
(☑8855-8650; Museo Juan Santamaría; daily specials US$6; ☺11am-5:30pm Tue-Sat) Tranquilly tucked into the courtyard of Alajuela's historic museum, this simple cafe with comfy booths and cushioned chairs makes a good spot to relax over sweet and savory snacks or the well-priced *plato del día* (daily special).

★**Xandari** INTERNATIONAL $$$
(☑2443-2020; www.xandari.com; Xandari Resort Hotel & Spa; mains US$9-24; ☺7am-10pm; ☑) ❤
If you want to impress a date, you can't go wrong at this elegant restaurant with incredible views. The menu is a mix of Costa Rican and international, with plenty of vegetarian options. The restaurant utilizes the resort's homegrown organic produce, supplemented by locally grown organic produce whenever possible – making for tasty *and* feel-good gourmet meals.

☆ **Entertainment**

The perennial Costa Rican soccer champions, Alajuela's own La Liga, play at the Estadio Morera Soto at the northeast end of town on Sunday during *fútbol* (soccer) season.

For beer and *bocas,* the relaxed 4th-floor terrace bar at Alajuela Backpackers Boutique Hostel (p109) is the airiest spot in town. Otherwise, there's no shortage of dive bars and karaoke, if that's more your style.

ℹ **Information**

Citibank (cnr Calle 2 & Av 6; ☺9am-5pm Mon-Fri, to noon Sat) Near the bus terminals; has ATMs dispensing dollars and colones.
Hospital San Rafael (☑2436-1000; www.hospitalsanrafael.sa.cr; Calle 4) Alajuela's new hospital, housed in a three-story complex 300m south of Av 10.

ℹ **Getting There & Around**

Taxis charge between US$5 and US$8 (depending on destination) for the five- to 10-minute drive from Juan Santamaría International Airport into Alajuela.

There is no central bus terminal; instead, a number of small terminals and bus stops dot the southwestern part of the city. Note that there are two Tuasa terminals (east and west) right across the street from each other.
Atenas (Coopetransatenas) US$1.40, 45 minutes, departs every 30 to 90 minutes from 7am to 10:30pm Monday to Saturday, less frequently on Sunday.
Grecia (Transportes Tuan) US$1.40, 45 minutes, departs half-hourly from 6am to 10pm (hourly from 8am to 10pm on weekends).
Heredia (Tuasa East) US$1.05, 30 minutes, departs every 15 minutes from 4am to 10pm.
San José (Tuasa West) US$1.10, 45 minutes, departs every 10 minutes from 5am to 11pm.
San José via Juan Santamaría International Airport (Station Wagon) US$1.10, 45 minutes, departs every 10 minutes from 4am to 11:30pm.
Sarchí (Transportes Tuan) US$1.65, 1¼ hours, departs half-hourly from 6am to 10pm (hourly from 8am to 10pm on weekends).
Volcán Poás (Coopetransasi) round-trip US$4.60, 1½ hours each way, departs 9am, returns at 2:30pm.

Parque Nacional Volcán Poás

Just 37km north of Alajuela by a winding and scenic road is the most heavily trafficked **national park** (☑2482-1226; admission US$10; ☺8am-3:30pm) in Costa Rica, ideal for those who want to peer into an active volcano without the hardship of hiking one. Volcán Poás (2704m) had its last blowout in 1953, which formed the enormous crater, measuring 1.3km across and 300m deep.

Poás offers the wonderful opportunity to watch the bubbling, steaming cauldron belch sulfurous mud and water hundreds of meters into the air. There are two other craters, as

LA PAZ WATERFALL GARDENS

This touristy garden complex just east of Volcán Poás is host to 3.5km of hiking trails and five scenic waterfalls, including the largest, **La Catarata de la Paz** (Peace Waterfall). Visitors can also tour a butterfly conservatory, a hummingbird garden, an aviary, an orchid display, a serpentarium, a ranarium (frog garden), and wildlife areas that host native cats and monkeys of Costa Rica. It's an ideal spot for active seniors and small children, since many of the trails are smooth and well maintained.

You can stay onsite at the **Peace Lodge** (☎2482-2720; www.waterfallgardens.com; d standard/deluxe/villa US$375/445/575, additional adult/child US$40/20; ℗ ☎ ⛱), whose over-the-top rooms boast gorgeous valley views, private deck with Jacuzzi, fireplace and huge bathroom with another Jacuzzi tub. There's also a heated outdoor infinity pool complete with heated waterfall.

well, one of which contains a sapphire-blue lake ringed by high-altitude forest.

The main crater at Poás continues to be active to varying degrees. In fact, the park was briefly closed in May 1989 after a minor eruption sent volcanic ash spouting more than 1km into the air, and lesser activity closed the park intermittently in 1995. In recent years, Poás has posed no imminent threat, though scientists still monitor it closely.

🏃 Activities

From the visitors center there is a paved, wheelchair-accessible 600m path that leads to a crater lookout. Because of the toxic sulfuric-acid fumes that are emitted from the cauldron, visitors are prohibited from descending into the crater.

Upon leaving the lookout, you can simply retrace your steps to the parking lot, or continue touring the park on a series of trails that collectively make a 3.6km loop back to the main path. For the longer loop, head east from the crater lookout onto **Sendero Botos**, a 1.4km, 30-minute trail that takes you through dwarf cloud forest, which is the product of acidic air and freezing temperatures. Here you can wander about looking at bromeliads, lichens and mosses clinging to the curiously shaped and twisted trees growing in the volcanic soil. Birds abound, especially the magnificent fiery-throated hummingbird, a high-altitude specialty of Costa Rica. The trail ends at **Laguna Botos**, a peculiar cold-water lake that has filled in one of the extinct craters.

From here, continue south on **Sendero Canto de Aves**, a 1.8km, 45-minute trail through taller forest, which gets significantly less traffic than the other parts of the park and is ideal for bird-watching.

Species to look for include the sooty robin, black guan, screech owl and even the odd quetzal (especially from February to April). Although mammals are infrequently sighted in the park, coyotes and the endemic montane squirrel are present.

Return to the main path via the 400m, 10 minute **Sendero Escalonia**, which will drop you at the restrooms just north of the visitors center.

🛏 Sleeping & Eating

There is no camping or other accommodations inside the park itself.

🛏 On the Road to Poás

The road up to the park is lined with stands selling fruit (especially local strawberries), cheese and snacks – as well as countless touristy spots serving typical Tico fare – so you won't go hungry. Bring your own bottled water, though, as the tap water is undrinkable.

Lagunillas Lodge LODGE $
(☎8959-0119, 2448-5837; www.lagunillaslodge.com; d US$30-35, cabinas US$50) Run by a charming Tica family, this rustic lodge and farm 3km below the park entrance is the closest accommodation to Poás. Hillside log *cabinas* offer stellar views; basic lodge rooms cost less. Amenities include trails, horseback rides (from US$15), breakfast (US$6) and dinners (US$10 to US$12) featuring fresh-caught trout. Four-wheel drive is indispensable for navigating the treacherously steep 1km dirt driveway.

Poás Lodge B&B $$
(☎2482-1091; www.poaslodge.com; d incl breakfast US$85-95; ℗ ☎) Texan brothers Stephan and

Jimmie, new owners since 2013, have amped up the cozy, welcoming vibe at this roadside hotel perched high on Poás' slopes 4km south of the park entrance. The upstairs restaurant's wraparound picture windows offer gorgeous sunset perspectives, while a roaring fireplace invites convivial pre- and post-dinner conversation. Downstairs, four comfortable, contemporary rooms have satellite TV, excellent wi-fi and stunning views.

East of Poás

About 10km before the entrance to the national park, a winding, paved road heads east through Poasito, crossing bucolic high pastureland en route to the village of Vara Blanca, where it turns north towards the famed La Paz Waterfall Gardens. This is scenic, uncluttered countryside – the ideal place for a pleasant drive or to spend the night.

★ **Poás Volcano Lodge**   LODGE **$$$**
(📋 2482-2194; www.poasvolcanolodge.com; Vara Blanca; incl breakfast junior ste US$145, master ste US$195-295; P@🕾) For contemporary class in an idyllic rural setting, visit this high-altitude dairy farm, whose dozen suites combine rusticity and elegance; the best have balcony and private garden and/or fireplace. Spacious, inviting common areas include a games room and a library. More than 3km of hiking trails offer views of the volcano (and all the way to Nicaragua!) on clear days.

★ **Colbert Restaurant**   FRENCH **$$**
(📋 2482-2776; www.colbert.co.cr; Vara Blanca; mains US$7-24; ⊙noon-8pm) At this charming restaurant with lovely views, 6km east of Poasito, the toque-clad, amply mustachioed French chef Joël Suire looks like he's straight out of Central Casting. Naturally, the menu is loaded with traditional French items such as onion soup and house-made paté. A good wine list (bottles from US$16) is strong on vintages from South America and France.

ℹ Information

Some 250,000 people visit the park annually, making Poás the most packed national park in the country; weekends get especially jammed. The best time to go is on a weekday in the dry season. In particular, arrive early in the morning before the clouds obscure the view. If the summit is cloudy, hike to the other craters and return to the cauldron later – winds shift and sometimes the cloud cover is blown away.

Near the entrance there's a visitors center with a souvenir shop, a cafe, a small museum and informative videos that play hourly between 9am and 3pm.

Be advised that overnight temperatures can drop below freezing, and it may be windy and cold during the day. Also, Poás receives almost 4000mm of rainfall each year. Dress accordingly.

ℹ Getting There & Away

Numerous local companies offer daily tours to the volcano (US$40 to US$100). However, it's much cheaper and nearly as easy to visit the volcano on the daily bus from Alajuela. The downside to both of these options is that they typically reach the summit at around 10am – right when the clouds start rolling in.

To beat the clouds and crowds, your best bet is to hire a car (per day from US$40) or a taxi (around US$30 from Alajuela, US$50 from San José) and arrive up top near the park's 8am opening time. If you're driving, the road from Alajuela to the volcano is well signed.

Coopetransasi (📋 2449-5141) runs a daily bus to the summit (round trip US$4.60, 1½ hours each way), leaving Alajuela at 9am and returning from the mountaintop at 2:30pm. If you're coming from San José, catch a local Tuasa bus (US$1.10, 45 minutes) no later than 8:15am from Tuasa's terminal on Av 2 between Calles 12 and 14, then upon arrival in Alajuela walk one block south to the Volcán Poás bus stop.

West to Atenas

From Alajuela, a narrow, paved highway leads 25km west to the lovely mountain town of Atenas. It's a nice day trip, with a perfect climate and a charming rural atmosphere.

La Garita

In an area that attracts scientists who research maize, it is not surprising that this town – spread out along the road that connects Alajuela to Atenas – is lined with restaurants whose specialty is corn: corn soup, cornbread, tamales and *chorreadas* (savory corn pancakes) to be exact. It's located 11km west of Alajuela and worth the pilgrimage if you are looking for good country eats. The road is dotted with little family-run establishments where you can sample these regional treats.

About 10km west of Alajuela, you'll find **Zoo Ave** (☑2433-8989; www.zooavecostarica. org; La Garita; adult/child US$11/5; ☉9am-5pm; ☐☑), a well-designed animal park sheltering more than 115 species of birds on colorful, squawking display in a relaxing 14-hectare setting. The zoo houses all four species of Costa Rican monkey, wild cats, reptiles and other native critters, many of which are rescues. Though technically a zoo, it is also an important animal-breeding center that aims to reintroduce native species into the wild; admission fees fund wildlife rescue, rehabilitation, release and conservation programs.

Continue west and the road slides over the Interamericana. Just north of the intersection, **La Casona del Maíz** (☑2433-5363; mains US$4-16; ☉7am-9pm) is usually jam-packed with families enjoying the spectacular Tico country cooking. The menu is heavy on grilled meats and corn dishes, though there are veggie *casados* (set meals) as well. The *chorreadas* are excellent, but don't leave without sampling the tasty corn soup, studded with sweet, fresh kernels, or the falling-off-the-bone *costillas de cerdo* (pork ribs).

Buses (US$1, 30 minutes) run between Alajuela and La Garita, via Zoo Ave, every half-hour.

Atenas

This small village, on the historic *camino de carretas* (oxcart trail) that once carried coffee beans as far as Puntarenas, is best known as having the most pleasant climate in the world, at least according to a 1994 issue of *National Geographic*. It's not too heavy on sights, but springtime is always in the air, and the sizable expatriate community gives the town a cosmopolitan feel.

About 1km before the center of town, you'll see the **Monumento al Boyero** (Monument to the Oxcart Driver) on the north side of the road.

Atenas' social hub is its appealing, shady central plaza, just a couple blocks up from the main road through town. On the plaza's west side, the astroturf-carpeted gelatería-cafe **Gelly's** (☑2455-0044; www.facebook.com/gellyscr; gelato US$1.50-3, snacks US$3-6; ☉noon-8pm Tue-Sun; ☜☑) is a great spot for Italian-style gelato, sweet and savory crepes, burritos, salads and – if you're lucky – a touch of magic;

Mexican owner and professional magician Alex Solis sometimes regales guests with improvised shows.

On the eastern end of town you'll find the typical **Restaurant La Trocha del Boyero** (☑2446-0533; casados US$9, mains US$9-15; ☉11:30am-8:30pm Thu-Tue; ☜☑). Tico families and local expats pour onto the pleasant outdoor deck on weekends for beef (the house specialty), sea bass, snapper, shrimp and heaping bowls of *chifrijo* (rice and beans with fried pork, corn chips and fresh tomato salsa). It's located just off the main road to Alajuela, 300m east of the gas station, and 100m to the south. Look for a sign at the turnoff.

Only five minutes west of town (and straight up!), **Vista Atenas B&B** (☑2446-4272, in USA & Canada 209-257-4908; www.vistaatenas.com; r incl breakfast US$65-85, cabina/casita without breakfast US$75/95; ☜☒) is a bright and peaceful hillside oasis whose mix of comfy rooms and self-catering cabins is enhanced by spectacular valley views from the swimming-pool terrace. Belgian owner Vera has lovingly enhanced the property with ecofriendly touches including solar-pumped and -heated spring water. Multilingual Tico manager Jonathan goes out of his way to make guests feel welcome.

Half-hourly buses run to Atenas from Alajuela (US$1.40, 45 minutes) and San José (US$1.95, 1¼ hours) throughout the day. The area is quite spread out, however, and best navigated by car.

Northwest to Sarchí

To the northwest of Alajuela, the carefully cultivated hills are home to the picturesque agricultural towns of Grecia (22km), Sarchí (29km), Naranjo (35km) and Zarcero (52km) – among others – many of which are popular weekend getaways for *josefinos* in search of fresh mountain air.

Rosario Area

Along the Interamericana, about 2km west of the Grecia turnoff, watch for the well-signed exit for the **Vista del Valle Plantation Inn** (☑2451-1165, 2450-0900; www.vistadelvalle.com; d incl breakfast US$100-170; ☐☉@ ☜☒) ✦. This peaceful retreat features 14 individually designed villas with gorgeous wood and stone details, a verdant hilltop setting and magnificent views of distant mountains across the forested gorge below. Private trails lead to a 90m-high waterfall in the adjoining Zona Protectora Río Grande reserve, and the staff can arrange massages and horseback tours. There is also an open-air **restaurant** (mains US$8–20) serving fine Costa Rican fusion cuisine.

At the same exit off the Interamericana, you'll find the offices of **Tropical Bungee** (🔧 bridge 2450-3434, cell 8980-5757, office 2248-2212; www.bungee.co.cr; 1st/2nd jump US$75/45), where you can arrange to hurl yourself off the 80m-high bridge over the Río Colorado, rappel down a 60m waterfall or both. It's easiest to make a reservation online.

Grecia

POP 14,900

The village of Grecia – once named the 'Cleanest Little Town in Latin America' – is centered on pleasant **Parque Central** (Central Plaza), which is anchored by one of the most charming churches in Costa Rica.

◉ Sights

Catedral de la Mercedes   CHURCH
At the heart of town you'll find the incredibly quaint Catedral de la Mercedes, a red metal structure that was prefabricated in Belgium and shipped to Costa Rica in 1897 – and resembles a gingerbread church. It has an airy nave, bright Spanish-tile floors and a Gothic-style altar covered in marble.

World of Snakes   ZOO
(🔧 2494-3700; www.theworldofsnakes.com; adult/child US$11/6; ⊙ 8am-4pm) Grecia's premier attraction lies 1.5km south of the bus station, along the old road to Alajuela. It is a well-run breeding center focused on supporting endangered snake populations. More than 150 snakes (representing more than 50 species) are displayed in large cages labeled in English and Spanish.

Rock Bridge   BRIDGE
About 5km south of Grecia, a bend in the road leads to an 18th-century rock bridge, which connects the hamlets of Puente de Piedra and Rincón de Salas. Locals say that the only other rock bridge like this is in China, and some tales have it that it was built by the devil. In 1994 it was declared a National Site of Historic Interest. With all

that hype, don't be surprised that it's small. Ask for directions, as it's hard to find.

Las Cataratas de Los Chorros   WATERFALL
(admission US$5; ⊙ 8am-5pm Tue-Sun) About 7km southeast of Grecia, toward Flores and Tacares, are two gorgeous waterfalls and a swimming hole surrounded by picnic tables. It's a popular spot for weekending couples. Get detailed directions before setting out.

🛏 Sleeping & Eating

A **Palí** (🔧 2444-6696; ⊙ 8am-7pm Mon-Thu, to 8pm Fri & Sat, to 6pm Sun) supermarket sits to the southeast of the church. Cheap eats can be found at the lunch counters and shops in the bus station, and a farmers market takes place north of town on Friday afternoon and Saturday morning.

Mangífera Hostel   HOSTEL $
(🔧 2494-6065; www.mangiferahostel.com; incl breakfast dm/s/d US$12/32/38, s without bathroom US$17; 🅿 🛜) This cozy hostel on the north side of Parque Central feels instantly welcoming, with its wood floors and friendly ambience. It has only five rooms, two of which are dorms. There's a shared kitchen and small garden in the back. Laundry service is available.

B&B Grecia   B&B $$
(🔧 2444-5326; www.bandbgrecia.com; incl breakfast d US$61, s/d without bathroom US$40/51; 🛜) Guests love the relaxed, homey environment at this tiny B&B 150m south of Parque Central. A sweet breakfast area and inviting garden space out back complement the four spotless rooms, the best of which comes with a large Jacuzzi tub. There's also one family-friendly unit sleeping up to five. The lovely innkeeper, Grettel, can help arrange area tours.

Café Delicias   CAFE $
(🔧 2494-2093; sandwiches US$4-7, dishes US$7-15; ⊙ 7am-9pm; 🛜) For rich coffee drinks, cinnamon rolls, sandwiches and light meals, as well as free wi-fi, hit this enjoyable spot near the southwest corner of Parque Central.

❶ Information

Banco de Costa Rica (⊙ 9am-4pm Mon-Fri) Directly across from the cathedral entrance; has a 24-hour ATM.

Getting There & Away

Buses for San José and Sarchí stop at the TUAN bus terminal, 150m north of Grecia's central plaza.

San José US$2.15, one hour, departs at least half-hourly from 5:30am to 8:30pm.

Sarchí, connecting to Naranjo US$1, 20 minutes, departs half-hourly from 5am to 8:30pm.

Sarchí

POP 12,300

Welcome to Costa Rica's most famous crafts center, where artisans produce the ornately painted oxcarts and leather-and-wood furnishings for which the Central Valley is known. You'll know you've arrived because just about everything is covered in the signature geometric designs – even city hall. Yes, it's a tourist trap, but it's a pretty one. The town is stretched out along a road that weaves through hilly countryside.

Most people come in for an afternoon of shopping and call it a day, but if you have time on your hands, it is possible to meet different artisans and custom order a creation.

Sarchí is divided by the Río Trojas into Sarchí Norte and Sarchí Sur, and is rather spread out, straggling for several kilometers along the main road from Grecia to Naranjo. It's easiest to explore by private car.

In Sarchí Norte, you'll find the heart of the village, including a twin-towered **church**, some restaurants and *pulperías* (corner stores), and what is purported to be the **world's largest oxcart** (photo op!).

Sights

Jardín Botánico Else Kientzler GARDENS

(☎2454-2070; www.elsegarden.com; Sarchí Norte; adult/child US$13/7; ⌚8am-4pm; 👪) This well-tended botanical garden 1.4km north of Sarchí Norte's soccer field has 2km of trails winding through more than 2000 types of clearly labeled plants, including succulents, fruit trees, palms, heliconias and orchids. There's also a picnic area and an excellent playground, outfitted with sturdy multi-level climbing structures and three zip lines.

Sleeping & Eating

If you're using public transit, Sarchí works best as a day trip; the few budget hotels downtown are not attractive.

A great farmers market is held on Friday behind Fábrica de Carretas Eloy Alfaro, where you can grab homemade snacks, *queso palmito* (a local cheese) and lots of produce.

Hotel Paraíso Río Verde BUNGALOW $$

(☎2454-3003; www.hotelparaisorioverde.com; San Pedro de Sarchí; r US$30-40, bungalows from US$60; P 📶 🏊) A worthwhile 3.4km detour northeast of Sarchí, this German-Tica–run spot in the highland village of

SHOPPING SARCHÍ

Most travelers come to Sarchí for one thing only: *carretas*, the elaborate, colorfully painted oxcarts that are the unofficial souvenir of Costa Rica – and official symbol of the Costa Rican worker. In Sarchí, these come ready for the road (oxen sold separately) or in scaled-down versions. But the area produces plenty of other curios as well: leather-and-wood furniture (including those incredible rocking chairs that collapse for shipping), wood tableware and trinkets emblazoned with the colorful mandala-design popularized by *carretas*.

There are more than 200 vendors, and prices and quality vary, so it pays to shop around. Workshops are usually open from 8am to 4pm daily; they accept credit cards and US dollars, and they can arrange international shipping for you. Listed below are two of the most respected and popular spots.

Fábrica de Carretas Eloy Alfaro (☎2454-4131; Sarchí Norte) Just west of the town center (100m north of the Palí supermarket); produced the massive oxcart in Sarchí's main plaza.

Fábrica de Carretas Joaquín Chaverri (☎2454-4411; Sarchí Sur) Sarchí's oldest and best-known factory, 1.5km southeast of the plaza; watch artisans doing their meticulous work in the small studio in the back.

San Pedro enjoys spectacular panoramic vistas of coffee plantations and volcanoes Poás, Barva and Irazú. Two inexpensive doubles (including one with prime morning perspectives on the valley) are complemented by a pair of spacious four-person bungalows with kitchenette. Optional breakfast is on offer and costs US$8 per person.

Finding the place can be tricky. With advance notice, owners can provide GPS coordinates or meet you beside the giant oxcart in Sarchí's plaza. Credit cards are not accepted, and wi-fi only works in the outdoor common areas.

Don Felipe COSTA RICAN **$$**
(☎2454-4374, 8816-8212; Sarchí Sur; mains US$8-18; ⏲9am-5pm Tue-Sun) One of the most popular spots for a lunch break is this family restaurant adjacent to the Fábrica de Carretas Joaquín Chaverri. Steak is the specialty here, but it also serves up a full range of *típico* cuisine.

Super Mariscos SEAFOOD **$$**
(☎2454-4330; mains US$9-24; ⏲11am-10pm; Ⓟ📶) At a low-lying bend in the road in Sarchí Sur, 1km southeast of the plaza, Super Mariscos serves up good *ceviche* (seafood marinated in lemon or lime juice, garlic and seasonings), rice dishes and seafood galore, as well as pasta and a few beef dishes. Everything comes with a side of fries and a smidgen of salad.

ℹ Information

Banco Nacional (⏲8:30am-3:45pm Mon-Fri) On the soccer field, about 200m west of the church; changes money.

ℹ Getting There & Around

If you're driving from San José, from the Interamericana take the signed exit to Grecia and from there follow the road north to Sarchí. If you're coming from the west, take the turnoff north to Naranjo, then head east to Sarchí.

Buses arrive and depart from Sarchí Norte.

Alajuela US$1.65, 1¼ hours, departs half-hourly from 5am to 10pm.

Grecia US$1, 20 minutes, departs half-hourly from 5am to 8:30pm.

San José US$2.25, 1½ hours, three direct buses daily; otherwise make connections in Grecia.

Zarcero

POP 4000

North of Naranjo, the road winds for 20km until it reaches Zarcero's 1736m perch at the western end of the Cordillera Central. This is a gorgeous location: the mountains look as if they've been lifted from landscape paintings and the climate is famously fresh. But the real reason you're here is to see the country's most surreal shrubbery.

Parque Francisco Alvarado, in front of the blue Iglesia de San Rafael (built 1895), was just a normal plaza until the 1960s, when a gardener named Evangelisto Blanco suddenly became inspired to shave the ordinary, mild-mannered topiary into a bizarre series of drippy, abstract shapes. Over the years, these have morphed into fanciful chimeras, blobby dancing creatures and a double tunnel of melting arches. In other words, bring your camera.

Zarcero is also a center for Costa Rica's organic-farming movement. You can find unusual varieties of pesticide-free goodies all over town, and the surrounding mountains are just perfect for an afternoon picnic. If there was ever a place where the roadside stands are worth it, this is it. Winding country lanes in the area are all lined with stands selling fresh cashews, honey, sweets and *queso palmito,* a locally made cheese with a delicate taste (it goes well with fresh tomatoes and basil).

🛏 Sleeping

Hotel Don Beto HOTEL
(☎2463-3137, in USA & Canada 240-415-1179; www.hoteldonbeto.com; d with/without bathroom US$35/25, tr US$45; Ⓟ📶) Located just across from the church, Hotel Don Beto is a friendly, comfortable spot housing eight tidy rooms with hardwood floors – many come with private balcony.

ℹ Getting There & Away

Transportes Zarcero (☎2451-4080) runs direct buses to San José (US$2.40, 1¾ hours) five times daily. Hourly buses traveling between San José and Ciudad Quesada also stop at Zarcero, but may be full by the time they reach Zarcero, particularly on weekends. There are also buses to/from Alajuela, San Ramón and Grecia. All buses stop along the main street below the square.

Bajos del Toro

POP 275

A gorgeous road snakes northeast out of Zarcero, climbing steeply through hillsides dotted with family dairy farms, then plunging abruptly into the stunning valley of the Río Toro, surrounded by the lower reaches of the area's cloud-forest ecosystem. If you were looking for a little piece of Costa Rica where everybody knows everybody, then look no further. This 250-person town (full name: Bajos del Toro Amarillo) is rural idyll at its finest.

There are no banks and only one tiny internet cafe. Bring all the cash you need.

🛏 Sleeping & Eating

Catarata del Toro   CABINA $$
(☑2476-0800; www.catarata-del-toro.com; r US$50-60) At this roadside spot 6km north of Bajos del Toro, three rustic wood-paneled rooms are tucked under A-frame-style eaves. However, the real attraction is the adjacent waterfall, a 100m-tall beauty that cascades dramatically into an ancient

volcanic crater, reached by a steep but well-maintained trail (admission US$10). There's also a restaurant where humming-birds flock to feed alongside the humans.

Bosque de Paz Rain/Cloud Forest Lodge & Biological Reserve   LODGE $$$
(☑2234-6676; www.bosquedepaz.com; s/d incl 3 meals from US$163/246; 🅿🏠) ✎ A bird-watcher's paradise, this 10-sq-km reserve straddles an important wilderness corridor between Parque Nacional Volcán Poás and Parque Nacional Juan Castro Blanco, with more than 22km of trails in tropical old-growth forest. The dozen spacious, terra-cotta-tiled rooms, within earshot of a rushing river, feature large windows with forest views.

Vegetarian and vegan diets can be accommodated. Advance reservations are recommended.

El Silencio   LODGE $$$
(☑2476-0303, reservations 2231-6122; www.elsilenciolodge.com; ste/villa incl breakfast & guided hike US$325/688; 🅿♿🏠) ✎ Secluded above town, this upscale lodge comprises

---

OFF THE BEATEN TRACK

PARQUE NACIONAL JUAN CASTRO BLANCO

This 143-sq-km **national park** (admission by donation) was created in 1992 to protect the slopes of Volcán Platanar (2183m) and Volcán Porvenir (2267m) from logging and mining. The headwaters for five major rivers originate here as well, making this one of the most important watersheds in the country.

While federally protected, much of the park is still privately owned by various plantation families – only those parts that have already been purchased by the government are technically open to travelers. Park info is available at the brand-new **visitors center** (☑8815-7094; apanajuca@gmail.com), opened in late 2012, at the end of a rough 10km road from El Sucre, 20km north of Zarcero. The road is passable for 2WD vehicles until the final descent; if you don't have 4WD, park on the hilltop 300m before the visitors center.

From the visitors center a broad 1.5km trail climbs through reclaimed pasture-land, then descends steeply to **Pozo Verde**, a sparkling green lake surrounded by mountains. A much rougher trail continues 3.5km to **Las Minas**, an abandoned mine site.

The park is popular among anglers as each of the five rivers is brimming with trout. The limited infrastructure and tourist traffic means that your chances of spotting rare wildlife (such as quetzals, black guans and curassow) are higher than average. Guides can be arranged through tour agencies and hotels in the area.

Tucked into a pretty valley about 1km below park headquarters, **Restaurante El Congo** (☑8872-9808; mains US$11; ⊙9am-5pm Sat & Sun) serves up fresh-caught trout, while the adjacent **Albergue Ecológico Pozo Verde** (☑8872-9808, 2460-8452; www.alberguepozoverde.com; d incl breakfast US$50-70) offers accommodation in six rustic cabins. Both keep irregular hours, so call ahead to make sure they're open. Resplendent quetzals can often be seen in the area between March and April.

16 luxuriously designed *cabina* suites with private deck, rocking chairs, Jacuzzi and fine mountain views, plus two six-person villas with gas fireplaces and full kitchens. Additional amenities include a spa and 8km worth of trails (one leading to a stunning waterfall).

Another bonus is a health-conscious restaurant whose meals (US$30 to US$35) feature organic produce grown onsite.

Soda Restaurante Nené COSTA RICAN $
(☑ 2476-0130; mains US$6-10; ☺ 8am-5pm) Just south of town, tucked slightly back from the main road, this simple green shack of a restaurant is flanked by well-stocked trout ponds. Catch your own fish, then enjoy it fried or grilled with garlic at the rustic picnic-bench-style tables.

❶ Getting There & Away

Driving north from the Interamericana through Zarcero, take a right immediately after the church and continue northeast about 15km. Alternatively, take the road due north from Sarchí's central plaza. Both roads are almost entirely paved but involve steep climbs and hairpin turns; 4WD is helpful but not obligatory. There are a couple of daily buses from Sarchí (US$2, one hour).

San Ramón & Around

POP 8700

The colonial town of San Ramón is no wallflower in the pageant of Costa Rican history. The 'City of Presidents and Poets' has sent five men to the country's highest office, including ex-president Rodrigo Carazo, who built a tourist lodge a few kilometers to the north at the entrance to the Los Ángeles Cloud Forest.

◉ Sights

Parque Central PLAZA
The twin spires of the ash-gray Iglesia de San Ramón tower over this square at the center of town. The best time to visit is on Saturday during the farmers market, when cheeses and chorizo are on display and the locals can be found shopping and gossiping.

🛏 Sleeping & Eating

🛏 San Ramón

Hotel La Posada INN $$
(☑ 2445-7359, in USA 407-374-6032; www.posada-hotel.net; s/d US$44/60, incl breakfast US$50/70; ▣✱@☎) Well-maintained rooms surround a lush, plant-filled courtyard at this pleasant inn, 400m north of the church. Rooms are somewhat baroque-looking, outfitted with massive, handcrafted beds that lie somewhere on the design continuum between Louis XIV and African safari. All have mini-fridge and cable TV; more expensive units come with Jacuzzis. Some are wheelchair-accessible, and a few have air-conditioning.

El Rincón Poeta COSTA RICAN $$
(☑ 2447-3942; Calle 1; mains US$7-18; ☺ 11am-10pm) Hidden away off the main street and decorated with historic black-and-white photos of San Ramón, this spot is popular with locals and serves up large platters of *típico* meat, seafood and rice dishes. Diners can choose between eating in the dining room filled with sturdy tree-trunk tables or the pleasant vine-shaded gravel patio up front. You'll find the restaurant 150m southeast of the church.

WORTH A TRIP

LAS FIESTAS DE PALMARES

If you're around in mid-January, be sure to detour through Palmares for the rowdy annual **Fiestas de Palmares** (www.fiestaspalmares.com). The 13-day, beer-soaked extravaganza features carnival rides, a *tope* (horse parade), fireworks, big-name bands, small-name bands, exotic dancers, fried food, *guaro* (local firewater) tents and the densest population of merry Ticos you've ever seen. It is one of the biggest events in the country – crowds can reach upwards of 10,000 people. For the other 352 days of the year, Palmares is a tumbleweed town, where life is centered on the ornate stained-glass church in the attractive, palm-fringed main plaza.

🛏 North of San Ramón

Casa Amanecer
B&B $$

(📞2445-2100; www.casa-amanecer-cr.com; s/d incl breakfast US$65/75; 🅿🛜) A 10-minute drive northeast of San Ramón, this sleekly designed B&B, owned and managed by former Habitat for Humanity volunteers, offers five graceful contemporary rooms with polished-concrete floors and orthopedic beds. Tasty veggie breakfasts are served on the breezy shared terrace. Additional meals and airport transfers (US$75 for up to four people) can be arranged with advance reservation.

★ Villa Blanca Cloud Forest Hotel & Nature Reserve
LODGE $$$

(📞2461-0300, in USA & Canada 1877-256-8399; www.villablanca-costarica.com; d superior/deluxe/honeymoon US$205/230/255, additional person US$50, child under 6yr free; 🅿@🛜) 🌿 Occupying a cloud-forest aerie, this private reserve, 18km north of San Ramón, is centered on a lodge and dairy ranch once owned by ex-president Rodrigo Carazo. Its 35 free-standing *casitas* (little houses) come with wi-fi, private terraces and minibar but deliberately eschew TVs. Additional facilities include a restaurant, a spa, a yoga center and a movie theater screening films nightly.

The surrounding 800 hectares of primary and secondary cloud forest offer excellent wildlife-spotting opportunities. Bilingual naturalist guides are available to lead horseback-riding trips (per hour US$25), morning and evening cloud-forest walks (US$26), and bird-watching (US$26) and quetzal-spotting (US$72) tours. Certified at the highest level of sustainability, the lodge practices composting, recycling and energy-efficient practices. The turnoff is well signposted from the Interamericana. A taxi from San Ramón costs about US$20.

Tierras Enamoradas
LODGE $$$

(Lands in Love; 📞2447-9331, in USA 1408-215-1000; www.landsinlove.com; Hwy 702; d incl breakfast US$132, additional person US$27; 🅿🛜♿🏊) 🌿 Midway between San Ramón and La Fortuna, this well-signposted, Israeli-run vegetarian lodge has eclectic rooms with bright floral motifs, a lounge, an outdoor swimming pool, a pet hotel (US$20 per night) and a plethora of adventure activities, from a canopy tour to canyoning to horseback riding. The restaurant serves an international mix of (rather pricey) vegetarian and vegan dishes.

ℹ Information

Banco de Costa Rica (🕐9am-4pm) Has an ATM; 300m west of Parque Central.

Banco Nacional (🕐8:30am-3:45pm Mon-Fri, 9am-1pm Sat) Has an ATM that also dispenses US dollars; 100m south of southwest corner of church.

ℹ Getting There & Away

San Ramón is served by hourly buses (US$2.70, 1¼ hours) from San José's Empresarios Unidos terminal (p102). Frequent buses also head north to Ciudad Quesada via Zarcero. Bus stops are just northwest of Parque Central.

HEREDIA AREA

Though microchips produced in Heredia have become one of Costa Rica's most important exports, the region also remains a vital coffee producer and a gateway to one of Costa Rica's largest swaths of highland forest, Parque Nacional Braulio Carrillo.

Heredia

POP 123,600

During the 19th century, La Ciudad de las Flores (the City of the Flowers) was home to a *cafetalero* (coffee grower) aristocracy that made its fortune exporting Costa Rica's premium blend. Today the historic center retains some of this well-bred air, with a leafy main square, and low-lying buildings reflecting Spanish-colonial architectural style.

Although only 11km from San José, Heredia is – in personality – removed from the grit and grime of the capital. Yet it still maintains a cosmopolitan vibe – largely due to the high-tech corporations that have settled amid the area's coffee *fincas*. In addition, the Universidad Nacional (National University) keeps things a touch bohemian, and on any afternoon you're bound to find local bars and cafes abuzz with young folk idling away their time.

Heredia is also the most convenient base from which to explore the little-visited Volcán Barva, within the Parque Nacional Braulio Carrillo.

Heredia

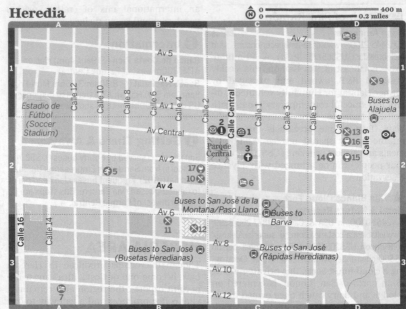

Heredia

◉ Sights
1 Casa de la Cultura..................................C2
2 El Fortín...C2
3 Iglesia de la Inmaculada
  Concepción..C2
4 Universidad Nacional.............................D2

◉ Activities, Courses & Tours
5 Intercultura...A2

◉ Sleeping
6 Hotel América..C2
7 Hotel Las Flores.....................................A3
8 Hotel Valladolid......................................D1

◉ Eating
9 Cowboy Steakhouse...............................D1
10 Espigas...B2
11 Más X Menos...B3
12 Mercado Municipal.................................B3
13 Vishnu...D2

◉ Drinking & Nightlife
14 El Bulevar Relax.....................................D2
15 El Rancho de Fofo..................................D2
16 La Choza...D2
17 Miraflores Disco Club............................B2

◉ Sights

Iglesia de la Inmaculada
Concepción   CHURCH
Built in 1797, this striking white church facing wide, pleasant **Parque Central** is still in use. The church's thick-walled, squat construction is attractive in a Volkswagen Beetle sort of way. The solid shape has withstood the earthquakes that have damaged or destroyed almost all the other buildings in Costa Rica that date from this time.

El Fortín   TOWER
This tower, constructed in 1876 by order of Heredia's provincial governor, is the official symbol of Heredia. It was declared a national historic monument in 1974, but because of its fragile state, it remains closed to the public.

Casa de la Cultura   MUSEUM
(☎2261-4485; cnr Calle Central & Av Central; ⊙hours vary) **FREE** Occupying a privileged position on the corner of the plaza just above the church, this low-lying Spanish structure dates back to the late 18th century. It served at one point as the residence of President Al-

fredo González Flores, who governed from 1913 to 1917. It is beautifully maintained and now houses permanent historical displays as well as rotating art exhibits.

INBioparque GARDENS

(📞 2507-8107; www.inbioparque.com/en; Santo Domingo; adult/student/child US$25/19/15, separate serpentarium admission adult/child US$3/2; ⊗ 9am-3pm Fri, 9am-4pm Sat & Sun; 🚼) 🏊 At this excellent, wheelchair-accessible botanical garden, run by the non-profit National Biodiversity Institute (INBio), visitors can admire native plants and animals in miniature versions of the country's various life zones. Other attractions include farm animals, a butterfly garden, a serpentarium and a model sustainable home. Children's theater and multimedia shows run throughout the day. It's 4km south of Heredia; see the website for directions.

🛌 Sleeping

Hotel Las Flores HOTEL $

(📞 2261 8147; www.hotel-lasflores.com; Av 12 btwn Calles 12 & 14; s/d/tr US$18/34/44; 🅿🛜) A bit of a walk from the action, but worth it for its friendly, homey feel, this spotless family-run place has 29 basic, brightly painted rooms with hot-water shower and TV. The attached *soda* (cheap lunch counter) serves breakfast and lunch.

Hotel Valladolid HOTEL $$

(📞 2260-2905; www.hotelvalladolid.net; cnr Calle 7 & Av 7; s/d incl breakfast US$75/87; 🅿✳@🛜) This business hotel on a quiet street has 12 bright, clean and business-like tiled rooms with microwave, mini-fridge, cable TV and private bathroom with hot water.

Hotel América HOTEL $$

(📞 2260-9292; www.hotelamericacr.com; Calle Central btwn Avs 2 & 4; s/d/tr incl breakfast US$66/77/88; @🛜) Of the four hotels in this local chain, this is the best deal. It is centrally located just south of the church, and though unspectacular in design, it's clean and comfortable. Tile-floor rooms come equipped with solar hot water, cable TV, safe and fan.

Hotel Chalet Tirol INN $$$

(📞 2267-6222; www.hotelchaleteltirol.com; d/ste US$98/138; 🅿🛜) Northeast of Heredia (3km north of Castillo Country Club), this charming hotel channels the gingerbread quaintness of the Alps. (It once served as a backdrop for a German beer advert.) The 25 suites and chalets have cable TV, room service and a gorgeous mountain setting; some also have Jacuzzis, fireplaces or wheelchair accessible facilities. The in-house restaurant hosts live music on weekends.

Hotel Bougainvillea HOTEL $$$

(📞 2244-1414; www.hb.co.cr; Santo Domingo; d incl breakfast US$123-152; 🅿🐕@🛜🏊) Set on 4 hectares about 6km outside of town, this efficient hotel is surrounded by an expansive, well-manicured garden dotted with old-growth trees, stunning flowers and plenty of statuary. Eighty-two crisp, whitewashed rooms have balconies with views of mountains or city, and several private trails wind by the swimming pool and tennis courts, through forest and orchards. Credit cards accepted.

🍴 Eating

In the grand tradition of university towns worldwide, Heredia offers plenty of spots for pizza slices and cheap vegetarian grub, not to mention one branch of every fast-food outlet imaginable.

You can fill up for a couple of thousand colones at the **Mercado Municipal** (Calle 2 btwn Avs 6 & 8; ⊗ 6am-6pm), which has *sodas* to spare and plenty of very fresh groceries. **Más X Menos** (Av 6 btwn Calles 4 & 6; ⊗ 8:30am-9pm) is a supermarket with everything else.

Espigas COSTA RICAN $

(📞 2237-3270; cnr Av 2 & Calle 2; meals US$7-8; ⊗ 7am-9pm) One of the only eateries open on Sunday, Espigas is the go-to cafe for traditional *casados* and breakfasts, with views of the main plaza diagonally across the street. Order sit-down meals at the counter, stop by the front window to pick up fresh *batidos* (fruit shakes) or pop in for a look at the tantalizing pastry case.

Vishnu VEGETARIAN $

(📞 2237-2526; Calle 7 btwn Avs Central & 1; dishes US$4-8; ⊗ 8am-7pm Mon-Sat; 🖊) This branch of the famous San José chain is the top spot in town for vegetarian fare, including a wide array of colorful salads and cheap, gut-filling *casados*.

Cowboy Steakhouse STEAKHOUSE $$

(📞 2237-8719; Calle 9 btwn Avs 3 & 5; dishes US$7-18; ⊗ 5-11pm Mon-Sat) This yellow-and-red joint with two bars has patio seating and the best beef cuts in town. As the title suggests, steak is the focal point, making it a meat lover's must. But the hearty salads and extensive list of *bocas* are worth a nibble as well.

🍸 Drinking & Nightlife

With a thriving student body, there's no shortage of live music, cultural events and the odd happening. Stay aware: downtown Heredia can get a bit dodgy at nighttime.

The university district is hopping most nights of the week. **La Choza** (Av Central btwn Calles 7 & 9), **El Bulevar Relax** (cnr Calle 7 & Av Central; ⊙ 11am-1am) and **El Rancho de Fofo** (www.ranchofofo.com; Av Central btwn Calles 7 & 9; ⊙ 11am-1:30am) are three long-running watering holes clustered together one block west of the university.

After a few rounds of beers, the party really kicks off at the **Miraflores Discotheque** (cnr Av 2 & Calle 2; ⊙ 8pm-6am Thu-Sun), where locals groove to a mix of international beats.

❶ Information

Hospital San Vicente de Paul (☑ 2562-8100; Calle 12) Modern hospital south of Av 14.

Scotiabank (Av 4 btwn Calles Central & 2; ⊙ 8:30am-5pm Mon-Fri, 9am-1pm Sat) Has a 24-hour ATM dispensing US dollars.

❶ Getting There & Away

There is no central bus terminal; buses leave from stops scattered between the university and the Mercado Central.

Alajuela US$1.05, 45 minutes, departs every 15 minutes from 5am to 10pm.

Barva US$0.55, 15 minutes, departs half-hourly from 5:15am to 11:30pm.

San José (Busetas Heredianas) US$1.05, 20 minutes, departs every 10 minutes from 5am to 11pm.

San José (Rápidas Heredianas) US$0.85, 20 minutes, departs every 15 minutes from 4:40am to 11pm. Best option if you're transferring to a Caribbean-bound bus, as it drops you near San José's Terminal Caribeña.

San José de la Montaña/Paso Llano for Volcán Barva (Transportes del Norte; ☑ 2266-0019; www.transportesdelnorteltda.com); US$1.40, one hour, departs at 5:25am and 6:25am Monday to Friday, 6:40am Saturday, 6:45am Sunday.

Barva

POP 5000

Surrounded by picturesque mountains only 2.5km north of Heredia is the historic town of Barva, a settlement that dates back to 1561 and has been declared a national monument. The town center is dotted with low-lying 19th-century buildings and is centered on the towering **Iglesia San Bartolomé**, which was constructed in 1893. The surrounding area was once popular with the Costa Rican elite: Cleto González Víquez (1858–1937), twice president of Costa Rica (he built the original National Library), was born and raised here. It's a perfect spot for a lazy afternoon stroll.

◉ Sights & Activities

Museo de Cultura Popular   MUSEUM
(☑ 2260-1619; Santa Lucía; ⊙ 8am-4pm Mon-Fri, 10am-5pm Sun) **FREE** Housed in a restored 19th-century farmhouse 1.5km southeast of Barva and 3km north of Heredia, this tiny museum surrounded by well-labeled gardens is run by the Universidad Nacional. Visitors can tour rooms full of antique furniture, textiles, ceramics and other period pieces. On Sunday the onsite restaurant La Fonda serves *casados* (US$8) on its pleasant open-air terrace.

Café Britt Finca   GUIDED TOUR
(☑ 2277-1600; www.coffeetour.com; with/without lunch adult US$37/22, student US$32/17; ⊙ tours 11am year-round, plus 3pm seasonally; 🚗) Costa Rica's most famous coffee roaster offers a 90-minute bilingual tour of its plantation that includes coffee tasting, a video presentation and a hokey stage play about the history of coffee (small kids will likely dig it). More in-depth tours are available, as are packages including transport from San José; reserve ahead. Drivers won't be able to miss the *many* signs between Heredia and Barva.

✦ Festivals & Events

Every March the town is home to the famous **Feria de la Mascarada**, a tradition with roots in the colonial era, in which people don massive colorful masks (some of which weigh up to 20kg), and gather to dance and parade around the town square. Demons and devils are frequent subjects, but celebrities and politicians also figure in the mix (you haven't lived until you've seen a 6m-tall Celia Cruz). The festival is usually held during the last week of the month, but dates vary from one year to the next; inquire locally.

🛏 Sleeping

★ **Finca Rosa Blanca**   INN $$$
(☑ 2269-9392, in USA 305-395-3042; www.fincarosablanca.com; Santa Bárbara; d incl breakfast US$305-540; 🅿@🛜🏊) 🍃 Set amid a stunning hillside coffee plantation 6km northwest of Barva, this honeymoon-ready,

SPANISH SCHOOLS IN THE CENTRAL VALLEY

Unless otherwise noted, prices are given for five four-hour days of instruction, with/without a week's homestay. Prices include two meals a day.

Adventure Education Center (☑2556-4609; www.adventurespanishschool.com; US$475/325)

Amerispan Study Abroad (☑ in USA & Canada 800-511-0179, worldwide 1-215-531-7917; www.amerispan.com; from US$380/225)

Centro Panamericano de Idiomas (CPI; ☑2265-6306, in USA 877-373-3116; www.cpi-edu.com; US$550/390)

Finca la Flor de Paraíso (☑2534-8003; www.la-flor.org; per week incl full board US$450) See p128 for details.

Intensa (☑2442-3843, in USA & Canada 866-277-1352; www.intensa.com; US$437/307)

Intercultura (☑2260-8480, in USA & Canada 866-978-6668; www.interculturacostarica.com; US$483/315)

Montaña Linda (☑2533-3640; www.montanalinda.com) See p131 for details.

Spanish by the River (☑2556-7380, in USA 1-877-268-3730; www.spanishatlocations.com; US$305/195)

Gaudí-esque confection of suites and villas is cloaked in fruit trees that shade private trails. Thirteen sparkling white adobe rooms with wood-beam ceilings and private balconies are lavishly appointed; one tops a tower with 360-degree views, reached by a winding staircase made from a tree trunk.

Shower in an artificial waterfall, take a moonlit dip in the pool, have an organic citrus-coffee bath soak at the spa – or, better yet, dip into a very romantic dinner at the hotel's recommended restaurant, which serves locally focused dishes, such as mountain trout with sweet-corn ragout. Credit cards accepted.

❶ Getting There & Away
Half-hourly buses travel between Heredia and Barva (US$0.55, 15 minutes), picking up and dropping off in front of Barva's church.

CARTAGO AREA

The riverbank setting of the city of Cartago was handpicked by Spanish governor Juan Vásquez de Coronado, who said that he had 'never seen a more beautiful valley.' Cartago was founded as Costa Rica's first capital in 1563, and Coronado's successors endowed the city with fine colonial architecture. However, as things tend to happen in Costa Rica, the city was destroyed during a 1723 eruption of Volcán Irazú. Any remaining landmarks were toppled by earthquakes in 1841 and 1910.

Although the city was relegated to backwater status when the seat of government moved to San José in 1823, the surrounding area, particularly the Valle de Orosi, flourished during the days of the coffee trade. Today much of the region continues to be devoted to the production of coffee, among other agricultural products. And though Cartago no longer has the prestige of being a national capital, it nonetheless remains a vital commercial hub – not to mention the site of the most important religious monument in the country.

Cartago
POP 147,900

After the rubble was cleared, in the early 20th century, nobody bothered to rebuild Cartago to its former quaint specifications. As in other commercial towns, expect plenty of functional concrete structures. One exception is the bright white Basílica de Nuestra Señora de los Ángeles, which is visible from many parts of the city, standing out like a snowcapped mountain above a plain of one-story edifices.

The city is thrown briefly into the spotlight every August, when pilgrims from every corner of the country descend on the basilica to say their most serious prayers. The remainder of the year, Cartago exists mainly as

OG PHOTO / GETTY IMAGES ©

1. Volcán Poás (p112)
Although it last erupted in 1953, the volcano's main crater is still active.

2. Coffee plantation, Valle de Orosi (p130)
This river valley is famous for its mountain vistas, hot springs and coffee.

3. Oxcart, Sarchí (p117)
The *carretas* (elaborate and colorfully painted oxcarts) are a Costa Rican icon and the official symbol of the country's workers.

JOHN COLETTI / GETTY IMAGES ©

a commercial and residential center, though the beauty of the surrounding mountains helps take the edge off modern life.

◎ Sights

Basílica de Nuestra Señora de Los Ángeles
CHURCH

(Calle 15 btwn Avs 0 & 1) Cartago's most important site, and Costa Rica's most venerated religious shrine, this basilica exudes airy Byzantine grace, with fine stained-glass windows, hand-painted interiors and ornate side chapels featuring carved wood altars. Though the structure has changed many times since 1635, when it was first built, its central relic remains unharmed: La Negrita (the Black Virgin), a small (less than 1m tall), probably indigenous, representation of the Virgin Mary, found on this spot on August 2, 1635.

As the story goes, when the woman who discovered the statuette tried to take it with her, it miraculously reappeared back where she'd found it. Twice. So the townspeople built a shrine around her. In 1824, she was declared Costa Rica's patron Virgin. She now resides on a gold, jewel-studded platform at the main altar. Each August 2, on the anniversary of the statuette's miraculous discovery, pilgrims from every corner of the country (and beyond) walk the 22km from San José to the basilica. Many of the penitent complete the last few hundred meters of the pilgrimage on their knees.

Las Ruinas de la Parroquia
RUIN

(Iglesia del Convento; Calle 0 btwn Avs 0 & 2) This now-ruined church was built in 1575 as a shrine to St James the Apostle (Santiago, in Spanish), destroyed by the 1841 earthquake, rebuilt a few years later and then destroyed again in the 1910 earthquake. Today only the outer walls remain, but 'the Ruins' are a pleasant spot for hanging out and people-watching – though legend has it that the ghost of a headless priest wanders the ground on foggy nights.

Mercado Central
MARKET

(Av 1 btwn Calles 2 & 4; ☺ 6am-5pm Mon-Sat, to noon Sun) This wonderful old-school covered market is conveniently located right around the corner from the bus and train stations that serve San José. It's fun just to wander the labyrinth of aisles, where you'll find fresh produce and food items of every description.

🛏 Sleeping & Eating

Cartago works well as a day trip from San José or Orosi, as attractive lodging options here are limited. For an atmospheric, authentically local eating experience, pull up a seat at one of the *sodas* inside the Mercado Central, or browse the aisles for fresh produce. You'll also find plenty of bakeries and other eateries along Avs 0 and 1 in the heart of town.

Los Ángeles Lodge
B&B $$

(☑2591-4169, 2551-0957; hotel.los.angeles@hotmail.com; Av 1 btwn Calles 13 & 15; incl breakfast s US$35-40, d US$50-65; 🅿 🛜) With its balconies overlooking the Plaza de la Basílica, this decent B&B stands out with spacious and comfortable rooms, hot showers and breakfast made to order.

La Puerta del Sol
COSTA RICAN $$

(☑2551-0615; Av 1 btwn Calles 13 & 15; mains US$8-13; ☺ 8am-10pm) Located downstairs from Los Ángeles Lodge and decorated with vintage photos of Cartago, this pleasant restaurant has been around since 1957 and serves myriad Tico specialties along with burgers and sandwiches.

❶ Information

Banco Nacional (cnr Calle 4 & Av 0) Has a 24-hour ATM.

A NATURAL EDUCATION

Immerse yourself in the Central Valley's rural culture with a stay at **Finca La Flor de Paraíso** (☑2534-8003; www.la-flor.org; 🅿) 🌿 outside Cartago. This not-for-profit organic farm operated by the Association for the Development of Environmental and Human Consciousness (Asodecah) has a recommended volunteer-work program that will allow you to get your hands dirty on projects related to agriculture, reforestation, animal husbandry and medicinal-herb cultivation. There is also an onsite Spanish school.

The cost of the volunteer-work programs, including room and board (in simple wood *cabinas* and dormitories), is US$28 daily. Vacationers can arrange guided visits (per person US$10) or overnight stays (per person with breakfast US$35, with three meals US$50). Family rates are available; advance reservations necessary.

Hospital Max Peralta (☑ 2550-1999; www.
hmp.sa.cr; Av 6 btwn Calles 2 & 4) Emergency
and medical services.

❶ Getting There & Away

Bus stops are scattered around town.

Orosi (Autotransportes Mata Irola) US$0.95,
40 minutes, departs every 20 minutes between
5:30am and 10pm Monday to Saturday, from
Calle 3 between Avs 2 and 4.

San José (Lumaca) US$1.15, 55 minutes,
departs every 15 minutes between 5am and
midnight, from the terminal on Calle 6 between
Avs 3 and 5.

Turrialba (Transtusa) US$1.65, 1½ hours,
departs every 45 minutes from 6am to 10pm
weekdays, less frequently on weekends, from
Av 4 between Calles 5 and 7.

Train service was reinstated in late 2013 between San José's Estación del Pacífico and Cartago's downtown **station** (Av 3 btwn Calles 4 &
6). The 40-minute trip costs US$1.10. Trains run
Monday to Friday only, with a schedule weighted
towards morning and afternoon commute hours.

Parque Nacional Volcán Irazú

Looming on the horizon 19km (as the crow
flies) northeast of Cartago, Irazú, which derives its name from the indigenous word *ara-
tzu* (thunder-point), is the largest and highest (3432m) active volcano in Costa Rica. In
1723 the Spanish governor of the area, Diego
de la Haya Fernández, watched helplessly as
the volcano unleashed its destruction on the
city of Cartago (one of the craters is named in
his honor). Since the 18th century, 15 major
eruptions have been recorded.

One of the most memorable occurred in
March 1963, welcoming visiting US president John F Kennedy with a rain of volcanic
ash that blanketed most of the Central Valley
(it piled up to a depth of more than 500mm).
During two years' worth of subsequent activity, agricultural lands northeast of the
volcano were devastated, while clogged
waterways flooded the region intermittently.
In 1994 Irazú unexpectedly belched a cloud
of sulfurous gas, though it quickly quietened
down. At the time of research, the volcano
was slumbering peacefully, aside from a few
hissing fumaroles.

The national park was established in 1955
to protect 23 sq km around the base of the
volcano. The summit is a bare landscape of
volcanic-ash craters. The principal crater
is 1050m in diameter and 300m deep; the
adjacent Diego de la Haya Crater is 690m
in diameter and 80m deep; and the shallowest, Playa Hermosa Crater, is slowly being
colonized by sparse vegetation. There is also
a pyroclastic cone, which consists of rocks
that were fragmented by volcanic activity.

☞ Tours

Tours are arranged by a variety of San José
operators and cost US$40 to US$60 for a
half-day, and up to US$100 for a full day
combined with lunch and visits to sights
such as the Lankester Gardens (p130) or the
Orosi Valley.

Tours from hotels in Orosi (US$25 to
US$40) can also be arranged – these may
include lunch and visits to the basilica in
Cartago or sights around the Orosi Valley.

✕ Eating

Restaurant 1910　　　　　COSTA RICAN $$
(☑ 2536-6063; www.restaurant1910.com; mains
US$9-22; ⊙ 11:30am-9pm Mon-Thu, to 10pm Fri &
Sat, to 6:30pm Sun; ℗ 🐾) On the road to Irazú,
300m north of the Christ statue marking
the Guayabo turnoff, this homey spot with
a glass-walled front deck is worth a stop just
to see its collection of old photographs docu-
menting the 1910 earthquake that completed
the destruction of colonial Cartago. Expect a
long list of Tico specialties, and a sumptuous
Sunday buffet (adult/child US$22/10).

❶ Information

Pay admission and parking fees at the **ranger
station** (☑ 2200-5025, in Cartago 2551-9398;
pnvolcanirazu@accvc.org; admission US$10,
parking US$2.20; ⊙ 8am-3:30pm) at the park's
entrance, 1.5km before the summit. There's a
basic cafe and gift shop inside the park. Note
that cloud cover starts thickening, even under
the best conditions, by about 10am, about
the same time the bus rolls in. If you're on one
of those buses, do yourself a favor and head
straight for the craters. If you have a car, make
an effort to arrive early and you'll likely be
rewarded with the best possible views and an
uncrowded observation area. The park is busiest
on Sunday and holidays, when a line of cars up to
1km long queues at the entrance.

At the summit it's theoretically possible to see
both the Pacific Ocean and the Caribbean Sea,

but it is rarely clear enough. The best chance for a clear view is in the very early morning during the dry season (January to April). It tends to be cold and windy up here and there's an annual rainfall of 2160mm – come prepared with warm, rainproof clothes.

From the parking lot, a 200m trail leads to a viewpoint over the main crater. Wooden railings prevent visitors from getting too close to the edge, but you're welcome to leave the paved trail and wander the volcanic sands of the adjacent Playa Hermosa Crater. About 300m above the main parking lot, a rutted 1km side road allows walkers and intrepid drivers to climb to Irazú's summit. While hiking, be on the lookout for high-altitude bird species, such as the volcano junco.

ⓘ Getting There & Away

A daily bus to Irazú (US$9) departs from San José at 8am and arrives at the summit around 10am. The bus departs from Irazú at 12:20pm.

A round-trip taxi from Cartago to the summit will cost about US$45; drivers usually allow you one hour to explore up top.

If you're in a group, renting a car is the best deal, as you can get to the park early before the skies cloud over and the crowds arrive. Take Hwy 8 from Cartago, which begins at the northeast corner of the plaza and continues 31km to the summit. The road is well signed.

Valle de Orosi

This straight-out-of-a-storybook river valley is famous for its mountain vistas, hot springs, a lake formed by a hydroelectric facility, a truly wild national park and coffee – lots and lots of coffee. A well-paved 32km scenic loop winds through a landscape of rolling hills terraced with shade-grown coffee plantations and expansive valleys dotted with pastoral villages, all set against the backdrop of the region's two volcanoes, Irazú and Turrialba. If you're lucky enough to have a rental car (or a good bicycle), you're in for a treat, though it's still possible to navigate most of the loop via public buses.

The loop road starts 8km southeast of Cartago in Paraíso, heads south to Orosi, then doubles back northeast and west around the artificial Lago de Cachí, passing the historic church at Ujarrás en route back to Paraíso. Alternatively, from Orosi you can branch south into Parque Nacional Tapantí-Macizo Cerro de la Muerte, an end-of-the-road national park with superb river and mountain scenery.

Paraíso Area

Though the village of Paraíso isn't all that its name implies, it does lead to the wonderful Valle de Orosi beyond.

About 3km west of Paraíso, the University of Costa Rica runs the tranquil 11-hectare **Lankester Gardens** (☑ 2511-7939; www.jbl.ucr.ac.cr; adult/student US$7.50/5; ☉ 8:30am-4:30pm); take the main road west towards Cartago and look for a pink monolith marking the turnoff. Founded as a private botanical garden by British orchid enthusiast Charles Lankester in 1917, it was turned over to the university for public administration in 1973. Orchids are the big draw here, with more than 1000 species at their showiest from March to May. Other attractions along the meandering loop trail include a Japanese garden, a bamboo tunnel and sections dedicated to palms, ferns, cacti and bromeliads. This is one of the few places in the country where foreigners can legally purchase orchids to take home. Guided tours in English and Spanish can be arranged with prior reservation; the garden is wheelchair-accessible.

From downtown Paraíso, the road north to Turrialba meanders 3km before branching right to **Finca Cristina** (☑ 2574-6426, in USA 203-549-1945; www.cafecristina.com; guided tour per person US$15; ☉ by appointment only), an organic coffee farm (look for the white sign up in a tree at the intersection, then keep an eagle eye for its driveway on your left). Linda and Ernie have been farming in Costa Rica since 1977, and a two-hour tour of their *microbeneficio* (miniprocessing plant) is a fantastic introduction to the processes of organic-coffee growing, harvesting and roasting.

Heading south from Paraíso towards Orosi, you'll hit **Mirador Orosi** (☉ 6am-5pm) **FREE**, a scenic overlook complete with toilets, secure parking lot, and ample photo and picnic opportunities.

About 2km south of Paraíso, and 1km off the main road, **Sanchirí Mirador & Lodge** (☑ 2574-5454; www.sanchiri.com; s/d incl breakfast US$67/82; P ☎ ☜) ⌀ is a delightful, family-run B&B whose dozen ceramic-tiled rooms come with comfortable wood furnishings and staggering vistas of the Río Reventazón valley below; five rustic two-level *cabinas* offer a cozier atmosphere but less dramatic views. Green touches include an organic garden, a bio-digestor for recycling food waste into cooking fuel, and a small collection of farm animals that kids will find irresistible. If you only need a lunch stop, the onsite **restaurant** (mains US$7-25; ⏰7am-9pm) is a great choice for generous portions and even more extravagant views.

Orosi

POP 4500

Named for a Huetar chief who lived here at the time of the Conquest, Orosi charmed Spanish colonists in the 18th century with its perfect climate, rich soil and wealth of water, from lazy hot springs to bracing waterfalls. So, in the typical fashion of the day, they decided to take the property off Orosi's hands. Today the area remains picturesque – and is a good spot to revel in beautiful scenery and a small-town atmosphere.

⊙ Sights

Iglesia de San José Orosi　　　CHURCH

Orosi is one of the few colonial-era towns to survive Costa Rica's frequent earthquakes, which have thankfully spared the photogenic village church. Built in 1743, it is the oldest religious site still in use in Costa Rica. The roof of the church is a combination of thatched cane and ceramic tiling, while the carved-wood altar is adorned with religious paintings of Mexican origin.

Museo de San José Orosi　　　MUSEUM

(☎2533-3051; admission US$1; ⏰1-5pm Tue-Sat, 9am-5pm Sun) Adjacent to Orosi's church, this small museum displays interesting examples of Spanish-colonial religious art and artifacts, some of which date back to the 17th century.

☆ Activities

Being in a volcanic region means that Orosi has the perks of thermal springs. Though not on the scale of the steaming-hot waters found near Fortuna, Orosi does offer a pair of warm-water-pool complexes. **Balneario de Águas Termales Orosi** (☎2533-2156; www.balnearioaguastermalesorosi.com; admission US$4; ⏰7:30am-4pm Wed-Mon) is the nicer and more centrally located of the two, with four pools of varying sizes flanked by grassy expanses and a shaded bar-restaurant terrace. **Los Patios** (☎2533-3009; www.facebook.com/BalnearioDeAguasTermalesLosPatios; admission US$5; ⏰8am-4pm Tue-Sun) is a larger complex 1.5km south of town, whose waters include a 43°C (109.4°F) therapeutic pool suitable for adults only.

The town is also a perfect base from which to explore Parque Nacional Tapantí-Macizo Cerro de la Muerte, which offers excellent bird-watching and some lovely hikes, or to rock climb in nearby Cachí.

Aventuras Orosi　　　RAFTING

(☎2533-4000; www.aventurasorosicr.com; ⏰9am-4pm) Operated by the charming Luis, who served as a guide for the venerable Ríos Tropicales rafting company for years, this small outfit organizes canopy tours and rafting expeditions (US$75 each, $115 for both), as well as custom itineraries.

Xplore Orosi　　　ADVENTURE SPORTS

(☎2574-3504; www.xplore-orosi.com; ⏰8am-4pm Tue-Sun) On the road to Paraíso, about 4km south of Orosi, this new outfit specializes in adrenaline sports, including a canopy tour, a Tarzan swing, rappeling and bungee jumping.

Monte Sky　　　HIKING

(☎2228-0010, 8382-7502; www.facebook.com/MonteSkyME; day use US$8) About 5km south of Orosi, high in the hills off the road to Tapantí, this 536-hectare private reserve teems with 290 bird species and offers hiking trails with jaw-dropping vistas. Call for directions; the folks at OTIAC (p132) in Orosi can also help arrange a visit.

Panadería Suiza　　　BICYCLE RENTAL

(half-/full day US$8/16; ⏰6am-5pm Tue-Sat, to 3pm Sun) On the main street, Orosi's Swiss bakery rents out bikes.

☘ Courses

Montaña Linda　　　LANGUAGE COURSE

(☎2533-3640; www.montanalinda.com; 1-week course incl hostel/homestay accommodation US$195/300) One of the most affordable Spanish-language schools in the country; check the website for current prices and schedule. Located 300m south of Orosi's plaza.

⌂ Sleeping & Eating

★**Montaña Linda**　　　HOSTEL $

(☎2533-3640; www.montanalinda.com; dm US$9, s/d/tr without bathroom US$15/22/30, guesthouse s/d/tw US$30/30/35; P@) A short walk southwest of the bus stop, this welcoming, chilled-out budget option has 11 tidy dorms and private rooms surrounding a homey terrace with flowers, hammocks and a wood-heated hot tub. All share a guest kitchen and

THE CENTRAL VALLEY FOR CHILDREN

Family-friendly attractions abound in the Central Valley. Here are a few spots guaranteed to please kids and adults alike.

Topiary gardens, Zarcero (p118) Kids will love zigzagging through rows of bushes sculpted into stegosauruses and other fantastic shapes.

Río Pejibaye (p136) Turrialba outfitters lead rafting trips on this Class I–II river that's plenty scenic but not too rough.

Zoo Ave (p115) Stroll the grounds alongside peacocks and giant lizards, visit with monkeys or take the canopy tour at this zoo and animal-rescue center.

Parque Nacional Tapantí-Macizo Cerro de la Muerte Easy hiking trails lead down to sandy beaches where kids can splash in a boulder-strewn river.

Volcán Turrialba Lodge (p139) Cuddle with lambs and ride horses at the foot of Costa Rica's most active volcano.

four bathrooms with hot showers. Owners provide an exceptional information packet highlighting local attractions, including hot springs, waterfalls and more.

Two blocks up the hill, a more upmarket (but still budget-priced) sister facility offers rooms with private bathrooms.

★**Orosi Lodge** INN $$
(☎2533-3578; www.orosilodge.com; d/tr US$66/77, d/tr/q chalet US$107/124/141; P🐾) This quiet haven, run by a friendly German couple, has six bright rooms with wood-beam ceilings, tile floors, minibar, coffeemaker and free organic coffee. Most face a lovely garden courtyard with a fountain, and one is wheelchair-accessible. Delicious, wholesome breakfasts cost US$8 at the colorfully decorated onsite cafe with scenic balcony seating.

Next door is a two-story, three-bedroom chalet that sleeps up to five, with its own parking spot and private entrance, a kitchen and comfy sitting area downstairs, and a master suite and deck upstairs offering incredible views of volcanoes Irazú and Turrialba. Across the street there's also a *casita* sleeping up to four.

Panadería Suiza BAKERY $
(☎8706-6777; www.costarica-moto.com/caf-y-panaderia-suiza; pastries from US$1, breakfast US$6-7; ☺6am-5pm Tue-Sat, to 3pm Sun) Starting at the crack of dawn, ebullient Swiss expat Franzisca serves healthy breakfasts and snacks at her main-street bakery, 100m south of Banco Nacional, including sweet and savory pastries, wholegrain breads and lunch packets for outdoors enthusiasts.

Restaurante Coto COSTA RICAN $$
(☎2533-3032; mains US$7-15; ☺8am-9pm) Established in 1952, this eatery on the north side of the park dishes out good *típico* food in a wood-beamed dining room with open-air seating. It's a great place to enjoy mountain views and the goings-on about town.

Batidos La Uchuva JUICE BAR
(☎8802-9925; batidos US$2-3.50; ☺9am-5pm Tue-Sun) At this simple stall 100m south of Banco Nacional, Tico owner André whips up flavorful *batidos* made with milk, water or yogurt. Choose from his long list of creative combinations, or invent your own.

🅘 Information

Find more information about the area on the village website (www.orosivalley.com). Banco Nacional, 300m south of the park, has an ATM and changes money.

OTIAC (Orosi Tourist Information & Arts Café; ☎2533-3640; ☺8am-6pm Mon-Fri, 10:30am-5pm Sun; 🐾) Run by multilingual long-term residents Toine and Sara, this exceptionally helpful organization functions as an information center, cafe, cultural hall and book exchange. They can help arrange tours and are a good source of information about volunteer and teaching opportunities. Find it 200m south of the park and one block west of the main road.

🅘 Getting There & Away

Autotransportes Mata Irola (☎2533-1916) runs buses (US$0.95) every 15 to 30 minutes to Paraíso (20 minutes) and Cartago (40 minutes) from multiple stops along Orosi's main street. Transfer in Paraíso for buses to Ujarrás and Cachí (US$1.15).

Parque Nacional Tapantí-Macizo Cerro de la Muerte

Protecting the lush northern slopes of the Cordillera de Talamanca, this 580-sq-km **national park** (adult/child 6-12yr US$10/1; ☯8am-4pm; 🖮) is the wettest in Costa Rica, receiving an average of 7000mm of precipitation per year. Known simply as Tapantí, the park protects wild and mossy country that's fed by literally hundreds of rivers. Waterfalls abound, vegetation is thick and the wildlife is prolific, though not always easy to see because of the rugged terrain. In 2000 the park was expanded to include the infamous Cerro de la Muerte (Mountain of Death), a precipitous peak that marks the highest point on the Interamericana and the northernmost extent of *páramo*, a highland shrub and tussock-grass habitat – most commonly found in the Andes – that shelters a variety of rare bird species.

🏃 Activities

Wildlife-Watching

More than 300 bird species have been recorded in the park, including hummingbirds, parrots, toucans, trogons and eagles. The bird-watching opportunities here are legendary, as it's possible to spot a large variety in a small area. Though rarely sighted due to the thick vegetation, monkeys, coatis, pacas, tayras and even pumas, ocelots and oncillas are present.

Hiking

A well-graded dirt road, popular with mountain bikers, runs 4km into the park from the information center, dead-ending at a *mirador* (lookout point) that affords broad views across the valley. Three signed trails branch off from this road: the 1.2km **Sendero Oropéndola** heads downhill to a picnic area, then follows the banks of the Río Grande de Orosi for a few hundred meters before looping back uphill; **Sendero La Pava** (0.4km) and **Sendero La Catarata** (0.9km) both descend from a common trailhead to boulder-strewn river beaches, the latter affording excellent views of a dramatic waterfall across the valley; the 2km **Sendero Natural Árboles Caídos** climbs steeply uphill from the main road before descending to rejoin it further west. Tapantí is not open to backcountry hiking.

🛏 Sleeping & Eating

Kiri Mountain Lodge　　　　　LODGE **$**
(📋8488-4085, 2533-2272; www.kirilodge.net; s/d incl breakfast US$35/45; 🄿🛜) About 2km before the park entrance, Kiri has six rustic *cabinas* with intermittent wi-fi and hot water, surrounded by 50 mossy hectares of land. Trails wind into the nearby Reserva Forestal Río Macho, and the lodge's **restaurant** (casados US$8-12; ☯7am-8pm) specializes in trout, which can be caught in several well-stocked ponds and served however you like.

ℹ Information

Visitors receive a simple trail map upon paying fees at the park entrance. Fishing is allowed in season (April to October; permit required), but the 'dry' season (January to April) is generally considered the best time to visit. Rain gear is advisable year-round.

ℹ Getting There & Away

With your own car, you can drive the 11km from Orosi to the park entrance; about halfway along, near the town of Purisil, the route becomes a bumpy gravel road (4WD recommended but not required).

Renting a bike in Orosi is another good option; the ride to the park takes about an hour. Buses only make it as far as Purisil, 5km from the entrance. Taxis charge about US$18 one way from Orosi to the park.

Orosi to Paraíso

From Orosi, a scenic loop circles the artificial **Lago de Cachí**. The lake was created following the construction of the **Represa de Cachí** (Cachí Dam), which supplies San José and the majority of the Central Valley with electricity. Buses run from Orosi to the dam and nearby ruins, though this stretch is best explored by car or bicycle – and it's worth exploring as this is beautiful countryside.

Sights here are all listed traveling counterclockwise around the lake, from Orosi to Ujarrás. After Ujarrás, the road continues west for a few kilometers back to Paraíso, where you can catch the main road south to Orosi.

Near the town of Cachí, on the left-hand side of the road about 2km southeast of the dam, the charming lakeside **La Casona del Cafetal** (📋2577-1414, 2577-1515; www.lacasonadelcafetal.com; mains US$8-29; ☯11am-5pm; 🖮) is situated in the middle of a coffee plantation and is especially popular with local families on buffet Sundays. Specialties include fresh river trout and coffee-laced desserts. There's a small playground, short trails and a lagoon with paddle boats for rent (in high season).

Across the main road from La Casona is the turnoff for two peaceful mountaintop retreats (private transportation is a must here). Follow the signs through the town of Cachí, then continue up the steep hill 3km to **Cabañas de Montaña Piedras Albas** (☑ 8883-6449, 2577-1462; www.cabinas.co.cr; cabinas US$60; P), an ideal place to really slow down. Simple wood *cabinas* come with kitchen, cable TV, and private deck with lake and mountain views, and access to private hiking trails.

For a more upscale experience, continue 1km beyond Piedras Albas' driveway till the steep, unpaved road dead-ends at beautiful **Hotel Quelitales** (☑ 2577-2222; www.hotelquelitales.com; d US$160-185; ☎). This idyllically sited collection of six contemporary-chic bungalows features spacious rooms with wood floors, ultra-comfy mattresses, indoor and outdoor showers, private decks (some with waterfall views) and large canvases depicting the hummingbirds, ladybugs, toucans and other critters for whom the cabins are named. The onsite restaurant (open to non-guests on weekends only) serves trout and other Tico specialties.

Back down on the main road, 300m east of Casona del Cafetal and 1.5km south of the dam, is **Casa del Soñador** (Dreamer's House; ☑ 2577-1186; ☽ 8am-6pm) FREE, an artisanal woodworking studio run by Hermes and Miguel Quesada, sons of renowned Tico carver Macedonio Quesada. The brothers maintain the *campesino* (peasant farmer) tradition of whittling gnarled coffee-wood branches into ornate religious figures and whimsical characters. Their workshop displays sculptures of all sizes, with pieces available for purchase.

Just south of the dam, a side road forks off the main lake loop towards Tucurrique. Follow this 2.2km to reach **Escalada Cachí** (☑ 8867-8259, 2577-1974; rockclimbingcachi@hotmail.com; ☽ 8am-4pm Sat-Sun, by appointment only Mon-Fri), a sport-climbing spot with routes of varying difficulty. The US$20 fee includes equipment rental, as much climbing as you can crank out, and a soak in its lovely river-diverted pool afterwards. Heed the roadside sign that recommends 4WD – if you don't think you or your rental can negotiate a super-steep track covered in marbles, park and hike down (and don't leave anything in your car). Call ahead.

About 3km past the dam, you'll find the town of **Ujarrás** at the foot of a long, steep hill. To reach the old village, which was damaged by an 1833 flood and abandoned, turn left off the main road at the 'Ujarrás' sign and wind about 1km gently downhill, passing the well-signposted Restaurant La Pipiola en route.

Only the crumbling walls remain of **Iglesia de Nuestra Señora de la Limpia Concepción** (☽ 8am-4:30pm; ♿), a 1693 colonial stone church once home to a miraculous painting of the Virgin, discovered by a local fisherman. According to lore, the relic refused to be moved, forcing clerics to build the church around it. In return the Virgin helped locals defeat a group of marauding British pirates in 1666. After floods and a few earthquakes, however, the painting conceded to move to Paraíso, leaving the ruins to deteriorate photogenically in a rambling park. (Kids can let off some steam at the playground here.) Every year, usually on the Sunday closest to April 14, there's a procession from Paraíso to the ruins, where Mass, food and music help celebrate the day of La Virgin de Ujarrás. The church's grassy grounds are a popular picnicking spot on Sunday afternoons – but go in the middle of the week and chances are that you'll have them all to yourself.

After Ujarrás, the route continues west for a few more kilometers to rejoin the main road at Paraíso.

TURRIALBA AREA

In the vicinity of Turrialba, at an elevation of 650m above sea level, the Río Reventazón gouges a mountain pass through the Cordillera Central. In the 1880s this geological quirk allowed the 'Jungle Train' between San José and Puerto Limón to roll through, and the mountain village of Turrialba grew prosperous from the coffee trade. Later, the first highway linking the capital to the coast exploited this same quirk. Turrialba thrived.

However, things changed by the early 1990s when the straighter, smoother Hwy

DAMNING THE RIVERS?

Considered one of the most beautiful white-water-rafting rivers in the world, the wild Río Pacuare became the first federally protected river in Central America in 1985. Within two years, however, Costa Rica's national power company, the Instituto Costarricense de Electricidad (ICE), unveiled plans to build a 200m gravity dam at the conveniently narrow and screamingly scenic ravine of Dos Montañas.

The dam would be the cornerstone of the massive Siquirres Hydroelectric Project, which would include four dams in total, linked by a 10km-long tunnel. If built, rising waters on the lower Pacuare would not only flood 12km of rapids up to the Tres Equis put-in, but also parts of the Reserva Indígena Awari and a huge swath of primary rainforest where some 800 animal species have been recorded.

The project was intended to help ICE keep up with the country's rapidly increasing power demands. But as the proposal moved from speculation to construction, a coalition of local landowners, indigenous leaders, conservation groups and, yep, white-water-rafting outfits organized against it. (Rafael Gallo, of the Fundación Ríos Tropicales, the charitable arm of the venerable rafting company, was a key figure in this fight.)

The group filed for the first Environmental Impact Assessment (EIA) in the region's history – and won. The move required ICE to seek an independent study of the dam's environmental impact and economic feasibility, effectively stalling its construction. In the meantime, organizers were able to draw international attention to the situation. In 2005 residents of the Turrialba area held a plebiscite on the issue of the dam. Of the 10,000 residents polled, 97% gave the project a thumbs down – a resounding 'No.'

As a result of these efforts, the project has been shelved until 2016, and the lower part of the river is now protected as a forest reserve. But there is still talk of installing a dam further up the river. Meanwhile, the neighboring Río Reventazón has already lost a third of its Class-V rapids due to the Siquirres Project. If you were thinking of going rafting in Costa Rica, the time to do it is now.

32 through Guápiles was completed and an earthquake shut down the railway for good. Suddenly, Turrialba found itself off the beaten path. Even so, the area remains a key agricultural center, renowned for its mountain air, strong coffee and Central America's best white-water rafting. To the north, the area is home to two important sites: the majestic Volcán Turrialba and the archaeological site of Guayabo.

Turrialba

POP 31,100

When the railway shut down in 1991, commerce slowed down, but Turrialba nonetheless remained a regional agricultural center, where local coffee planters could bring their crops to market. And with tourism on the rise in the 1990s, this modest mountain town soon became known as the gateway to some of the best white-water rafting on the planet. By the early 2000s, Turrialba was a hotbed of international rafters looking for Class-V thrills. For now, the Río Pacuare runs on, but its future is uncertain.

◉ Sights

Catie GARDENS
(Centro Agronómico Tropical de Investigación, Center for Tropical Agronomy Research & Education; ☑ 2556-2700; www.catie.ac.cr; adult/student/youth US$10/8/6, guided tours US$25-50; ⊙ 7am-4pm Mon-Fri, 8am-4pm Sat & Sun) Catie's sprawling grounds, 2km east of Turrialba, encompass 10-sq-km dedicated to tropical agricultural research and education. Agronomists from all over the world recognize this as one of the most important centers in the tropics. You need to make reservations for one of several guided tours through laboratories, greenhouses, a seed bank, experimental plots and one of the most extensive libraries of tropical-agriculture literature in the world. Alternatively, pick up a map and take a self-guided walk.

WHITE-WATER RAFTING IN THE CENTRAL VALLEY

The Turrialba area is a major center for white-water rafting. Traditionally the two most popular rafting rivers have been the **Río Reventazón** and the **Río Pacuare**, but the former has been dramatically impacted by a series of hydroelectric projects, including a huge 305MW dam currently under construction.

As a result, most organized expeditions from Turrialba now head for the Río Pacuare, which arguably offers the most scenic rafting in Central America. The river plunges down the Caribbean slope through a series of spectacular canyons clothed in virgin rainforest, through runs named for their fury and separated by calm stretches that enable you to stare at near-vertical green walls towering hundreds of meters above.

➡ **Lower Pacuare** With Class II–IV rapids, this is the more accessible run: 28km through rocky gorges, past an indigenous village and untamed jungle.

➡ **Upper Pacuare** Classified as Class III–IV, but a few sections can go to Class V, depending on conditions. It's about a two-hour drive to the put-in, after which you'll have the prettiest jungle cruise on earth all to yourself.

The Pacuare can be run year-round, though June to October are considered the best months. The highest water is from October to December, when the river runs fast with huge waves. March and April are when the river is at its lowest, though it is still challenging.

Trips & Prices

Rafting trips are offered by several Turrialba-based agencies as well as reputable national companies such as **Exploradores Outdoors** (www.exploradoresoutdoors.com) and **Ríos Tropicales** (www.riostropicales.com).

Day trips usually raft the Class II–IV Lower Pacuare, thanks to its relative ease of access. A tamer alternative for beginners and families is the Class I–II Río Pejibaye. Other runs – such as the Upper Pacuare and/or remaining navigable segments of Río Reventazón – require more time spent in a van and tend to be more expensive.

For day trips (many of which originate in San José), expect to pay anywhere from US$99 to US$125 depending on transportation, accessibility and amenities. It is generally less expensive to leave from Turrialba (day trips from US$80). Multiday excursions with camping or lodge accommodations are also offered by numerous companies. For two-day trips, prices vary widely depending on accommodations, but expect to pay US$200 to US$300 per person. Children must be at least nine years old for most trips, and older for tougher runs.

⌖ Tours

Plenty of local operators offer either kayaking or rafting in the area.

Costa Rica Ríos (☎2556-8664, in USA & Canada 888-434-0776; www.costaricarios.com) Offers week-long rafting and kayak trips that must be booked in advance.

Locos (☎2556-6035, in USA 707-703-5935; www.whiteh2o.com)

Explornatura (☎2556-0111, in USA & Canada 866-571-2443; www.explornatura.com; Av 4 btwn Calles 2 & 4)

Tico's River Adventures (☎2556-1231; www.ticoriver.com)

🛏 Sleeping

🛏 Turrialba

★**Casa de Lis Hostel** HOSTEL $
(☎2556-4933; www.hostelcasadelis.com; Av Central near Calle 2; dm US$10, s/d/tr/q US$36/40/45/50, without bathroom US$20/25/35/40; 🛜) Hands down Turrialba's best value option, this sweet, centrally located six-room place (which was expanding to 10 rooms at research time) is a traveler's dream come true. Spotless dorms and doubles with comfy mattresses and individual reading lamps are complemented by a fully equipped kitchen, volcano-view roof terrace, pretty back gar-

den, fantastic information displays and a distinctly friendly atmosphere. Breakfasts (US$6) and laundry service (per load US$8) are available.

Hotel Interamericano
HOTEL $

(2556-0142; www.hotelinteramericano.com; Av 1 near Calle 1; s/d/tr/q US$27/37/50/65, without bathroom US$12/22/33/44; P ♠) On the south side of the old train tracks is this basic 21-room hotel, traditionally regarded by rafters as *the* meeting place in Turrialba. The eclectic collection of rather tired-looking rooms includes some with private bathrooms, some without and many that combine bunks with regular beds. Upstairs units are brighter and more welcoming; it's worth comparing before committing.

🛏 Around Turrialba

There are some stellar hotels around the Turrialba area. All can arrange tours and rafting trips.

Turrialtico Lodge
LODGE $$

(2538-1111; www.turrialtico.com; d incl breakfast US$58-75; P ♠) Commanding dramatic, sweeping views of the Río Reventazón valley, this Tico-run lodge in an old farmhouse 9km east of Turrialba (off the highway to Siquirres) offers 19 attractive, polished-wood-panel rooms decorated with local artwork. Rooms in the reception building share a large terrace and sitting area, and a pleasant open-air restaurant (mains US$4 to US$18) serves up country cooking.

Rancho Naturalista
LODGE $$$

(2554-8101; www.ranchonaturalista.net; per person incl 3 meals US$170; P @) About 1.3km south of Tuis and 900m above sea level, this small lodge on 50 hectares of land attracts dedicated bird-watchers, who have recorded 433 species in the area (more than 250 from the lodge balcony alone). Fourteen simple lodge rooms are complemented by a cluster of private *casitas,* surrounded by pretty landscaped grounds. Meals include organic produce grown onsite.

Casa Turire
LUXURY HOTEL $$$

(2531-1111; www.hotelcasaturire.com; d standard/ste/master ste incl breakfast US$160/250/400, additional person US$25-35, child under 6yr free; P ✳ @ ♠ ≋) ✐ This elegant three-story plantation inn has 16 graceful, well-appointed rooms with high ceilings, wood floors and wrought-iron beds; a massive master suite comes with a Jacuzzi and excellent views of the coffee and macadamia-nut plantations in the distance. Adding icing to the cake are spa services, a restaurant and bar, horseback riding, bird-watching and kayaking on the onsite lake.

Take the La Suiza/Tuis turnoff from Hwy 10, head south for 2.3km, then follow signs an additional 1.4km down a dirt road to the hotel.

🍽 Eating

For cheap eats, stroll along Calle 1, where you'll find *sodas,* pizzerias and roast-chicken places galore. Self-caterers can find supplies at the well-stocked **MegaSuper** (cnr Calle 3 & Av 2).

Restaurant Betico Mata
BARBECUE $

(2556-8640; Hwy 10; gallos US$1.80, mains US$5-9; ⊙11am-midnight, until later Sat & Sun) This carnivore's paradise at the south end of town specializes in *gallos* (open-face tacos on corn tortillas) piled with succulent, fresh-grilled meats including beef, chicken, sausage or pork, all soaked in the special house marinade. All go smashingly well with an ice-cold beer. A street-facing counter makes it easy to park and grab a snack if you're driving through town.

Wok & Roll
ASIAN $

(2556-6756; Calle 1; mains US$7-11; ⊙11.30am-10pm Wed-Mon) Pan-Asian cuisine, from Singapore-style noodles to Chinese steamed buns, fills the menu at this new eatery near Turrialba's main square. OK, perhaps they're overdoing the fusion thing with the Turri Volcano Roll (made with avocado, cucumber and, yes, Turrialba cheese!), but nobody can argue with tempura ice cream for dessert. Don't miss the homemade mint lemonade and honey-sweetened jasmine tea.

La Feria
COSTA RICAN $

(2556-5550; Calle 6 north of Av 4; mains US$6-15; ⊙11am-10pm Wed-Mon, to 2:30pm Tue; ✐) This unremarkable-looking eatery has friendly service and excellent, reasonably priced home cooking.

ℹ Information

There's no official tourist office, but most hotels and rafting outfits can organize tours, accommodations and transportation throughout the region.

Banco de Costa Rica (cnr Av Central & Calle 3; ⊙9am-4pm Mon-Fri) One of two banks on this corner with 24-hour ATMs.

Cafe Internet (☑2556-4575; cnr Av 2 & Calle 4; per hour US$0.80; ⊙8am-9pm Mon-Sat, to noon Sun)

ⓘ Getting There & Away

A modern bus terminal is located on the western edge of town off Hwy 10.

San José via Paraíso and Cartago US$2.80, 1¾ hours, departs hourly from 5am to 6:30pm.

Siquirres, for transfer to Puerto Limón US$2.30, 1½ hours, departs every 60 to 90 minutes from 6am to 6pm.

Monumento Nacional Arqueológico Guayabo

Nestled into a patch of stunning hillside forest 19km northeast of Turrialba is the largest and most important archaeological site in the country. Guayabo (☑2559-1220; adult/child 6-12yr US$6/1; ⊙8am-3:30pm) is composed of the remains of a pre-Columbian city that was thought to have peaked at some point in AD 800, when it was inhabited by as many as 20,000 people. Today visitors can examine the remains of petroglyphs, residential mounds, an old roadway and an impressive aqueduct system – built with rocks that were hauled in from the Río Reventazón along a cobbled, 8km road. Amazingly, the cisterns still work, and (theoretically) potable water remains available onsite.

The settlement, which may have been occupied as early as 1000 BC, was mysteriously abandoned by AD 1400 and Spanish explorers left no record of ever having found the ruins. For centuries, the city lay largely untouched under the cover of the area's thick highland forest. But in 1968, archaeologist Carlos Aguilar Piedra of the University of Costa Rica began systematic excavations of Guayabo, finding polychromatic pottery and gold artifacts that are now exhibited at San José's Museo Nacional.

In 1973, as the site's importance became evident, Guayabo was declared a national monument, with further protections set forth in 1980. The site occupies 232 hectares, most of which remains unexcavated. It's a small place, so don't go expecting Mayan pyramids.

🏃 Activities

The site currently protects the last remaining premontane forest in the province of Cartago, and although mammals are limited to squirrels, armadillos and coatis, there are good bird-watching opportunities here. Particularly noteworthy among the avifauna are the oropendolas, which colonize the monument by building sacklike nests in the trees. Other birds include toucans and brown jays – the latter are unique among jays in that they have a small, inflatable sac in their chest, which causes the popping sound that is heard at the beginning of their loud and raucous calls.

ⓘ Information

Across the road from the ticket office there's a small information and exhibit center that provides an overview of what the city may have once looked like. Bilingual interpretive signs are placed at regular intervals along the well-maintained loop trail that runs through the ruins and surrounding forest; featured stops include the central mound where the city's largest dwelling once stood, the remains of an acqueduct and retaining pool, a viewpoint overlooking the entire site and a two-sided petroglyph depicting a jaguar and a lizard. (The best archaeological pieces can be found at the Museo Nacional in San José.) Guided tours are available from **Asociación de Guías U-Suré** (☑8534-1063; guided tour for 1-3 people US$15, for 4-9 people US$30), whose office is directly adjacent to the ticket window.

Camping (per person US$2) is permitted; services include flush toilets and running water. Average annual rainfall is about 3500mm, making dry season (January to April) the best time to visit – though it might still rain. Bring insect repellent; it gets mighty buggy.

ⓘ Getting There & Away

By car, head north out of Turrialba and make a right after the metal bridge. The road is well signed from there, and all but the last 3km is paved; 4WD is recommended, though not required, for the final rough section.

Buses from Turrialba (US$0.95, one hour) depart at 6:20am, 11:15am, 3:10pm and 5:30pm Monday through Saturday and at 9am and 3pm on Sunday. Buses return from Guayabo to Turrialba at 7am, 12:30pm and 4pm daily. You can also take a taxi from Turrialba (about US$25 round trip, with one hour to explore the park).

Parque Nacional Volcán Turrialba

This rarely visited active volcano (3328m) was named Torre Alba (White Tower) by early Spanish settlers, who observed plumes of smoke pouring from its summit.

Turrialba was declared a national park in 1955, and protects a 2km radius around the volcano. Below the summit, the park consists of mountain rainforest and cloud forest, dripping with moisture and mosses, full of ferns, bromeliads and even stands of bamboo. Although small, these protected habitats shelter 84 species of bird and 11 species of mammal.

Turrialba's last major eruption was in 1866, but a century and a half later, the slumbering giant has begun showing sustained signs of life. Since 2010 it has regularly been belching forth quantities of sulfuric gas and ash, damaging the road to the summit, killing off trees and other vegetation and displacing small farming communities from the volcano's western slopes.

At the time of research visitors were only being allowed to climb as far as the park entrance gate, 3km below the summit; the park itself remained closed, pending completion of road repairs and construction of a protective bunker at the summit. For up-to-the-minute details on the volcano's status, contact **park headquarters** (☑ 8704-2432, 2557-6262; pnvolcanturrialba@gmail.com; ☺ 8am-3:30pm). At research time it was anticipated that, when the park does reopen, entrance fees will be higher than at other national parks, as all visitors will need to be accompanied by an official guide.

In the meantime, a good way to experience some of Turrialba's magic up close is via a guided horseback excursion along the volcano's western flanks, offered by Volcán Turrialba Lodge.

🛏 Sleeping

Volcán Turrialba Lodge LODGE $
(☑ 2273-4335; www.volcanturrialbalodge.com; per person incl breakfast US$45; ℗ 🛜) Reached by a tortuous, rugged road (4WD recommended), this working sheep and cattle ranch 14km northwest of Santa Cruz truly gets you away from it all. Tidy, lemon-yellow *cabinas* come with wood stoves and full kitchens, and many offer fantastic views of Volcán Turrialba. The staff can also organize hikes and horseback rides.

Meals (US$15 to US$19) feature typical country cooking and are served in front of a blazing stove at the restaurant-lounge, where there is a TV, board games and a small bar. It gets chilly up here, so bring warm clothes.

ℹ Information

Because of the recent volcanic activity, it's imperative to inquire locally about conditions in the national park before attempting a visit. If and when the summit reopens, bear in mind that the average temperature is only about 15°C (59°F), so dress accordingly.

ℹ Getting There & Away

The volcano is only about 15km northwest of Turrialba as the crow flies, but more than twice that far by car. From the village of Santa Cruz (13km from Turrialba and connected via public buses), an 18km road climbs to the top of the volcano. At the time of research, it was only possible to drive as far as Volcán Turrialba Lodge, about 6km shy of the summit.

Caribbean Coast

Best Places to Eat

➡ Sobre las Olas (p174)

➡ Selvin's Restaurant (p188)

➡ Stashu's con Fusion (p182)

➡ La Pecora Nera (p186)

➡ Taylor's Place (p162)

Best Off the Beaten Track

➡ Selva Bananito (p173)

➡ La Danta Salvaje (p145)

➡ Punta Mona (p191)

➡ Turtle Beach Lodge (p161)

➡ Aiko-logi (p177)

Why Go

While the sunny climate and easy accessibility of the Pacific have paved the way (literally) for development on that rich coast, the Caribbean side has languished in comparison. The same rain-drenched malarial wildness that thwarted the first 16th-century Spaniards from settling here also isolated this region for centuries afterward. Thus, its culture – influenced by indigenous peoples and West Indian immigrants – blended slowly and organically and is distinctly different from that of the rest of Costa Rica. It still takes a little more effort to travel here to see the nesting turtles of Tortuguero, raft the Río Pacuare or dive the reefs of Manzanillo. Life is more rugged and rustic on this coast, allowing wildlife to thrive. And it's well worth tasting its unique flavors: the *rondón* (spicy seafood gumbo), the lilt of patois, and the uncrowded stretches of black-sand beaches.

When to Go

➡ As evidenced by the spectacularly lush greenery in this region, there's no traditional 'dry season.' It rains throughout the year, though less in February and March and September and October – this latter period conveniently coinciding with when the rest of the country is getting soaked.

➡ Surfers, note: the biggest swells hit the southern Caribbean from December to March.

➡ Turtle-nesting season runs from March to October.

➡ January to June and September to December are best for sportfishing, although fishing is good year-round in the northern Caribbean.

History

In 1502 Christopher Columbus spent a total of 17 days anchored off the coast of Puerto Limón on what would be his fourth and final voyage to the New World. He dropped anchor at an isle he baptized La Huerta (today known as Isla Uvita), loaded up on fresh water, and never returned.

For Costa Rica's Caribbean coast, this small encounter foreshadowed the colonization that was to come. But it would be centuries before Europeans would fully dominate the area. Because of the difficult nature of the terrain (croc-filled swamps and steep mountain slopes) and the malaria delivered by relentless fleets of mosquitoes, the Spanish steadfastly avoided it. For hundreds of years, in fact, the area remained the province of indigenous ethnicities – the Miskito in the north and the Cabécar, Bribrí and Kèköldi in the south – along with a mix of itinerant Afro-Caribbean turtle hunters from Panama and Colombia.

It was the building of the railroad, beginning in 1871, that would solidify the area's West Indian accent, with the arrival of thousands of former Jamaican slaves in search of employment. The plan was to build a port at the site of a grand old lemon tree (hence the name, Puerto Limón) on the Caribbean Sea, so that coffee barons in the Central Valley could more easily export their crops to Europe. The railway was intended to unify the country, but it was a source of segregation as well. Blacks were not allowed to vote or travel freely around Costa Rica until 1949. Out of isolation, however, sprung an independent culture, with its own musical and gastronomic traditions, and even its own unique language, a creole called Mekatelyu – which is still spoken today.

Parks & Reserves

Many refuges and parks line the Caribbean coast. These are some of the most popular.

Parque Nacional Cahuita (p175) A patch of coastal jungle is home to armadillos, monkeys and sloths, and the protected reef is one of the most important on the coast.

Parque Nacional Tortuguero (p154) Jungle canals obscure snoozing caimans, while howler, spider and capuchin monkeys traipse overhead. The star attraction, however, are the sea turtles, which nest here from March to October.

Refugio Nacional de Vida Silvestre Barra del Colorado (p166) A remote park that draws fishing enthusiasts who come to hook species such as snook, tarpon and gar.

Refugio Nacional de Vida Silvestre Gandoca-Manzanillo (p190) A rich rainforest and wetland tucked away along the country's southeastern border, with rivers full of manatee, caiman and crocodile.

ℹ Dangers & Annoyances

The Caribbean coast region has had a bad reputation over the years for being more dangerous than other parts of Costa Rica. In reality, crime levels against tourists are no higher here than in any other part of the country. As anywhere else, exercise common sense.

A bigger problem is the sea: riptides get ferocious (even in shallow water) and in the north, sharks are a regular presence. Swim in safe areas – if unsure, ask a local.

ℹ Getting There & Around

When traveling to Puerto Limón and the southern Caribbean, it's easy enough to hop on any of the regular buses from San José. Buses also connect most towns along the coast, from Sixaola, on the Panamanian border, to Puerto Limón. The roads are in good condition, so driving is also an option.

The north is a little trickier. Much of the area is only linked up by waterways, making boats the sole means of transport. Puerto Limón, Tortuguero, Parismina and Barra del Colorado all have landing strips, but only Tortuguero has daily commercial flights.

THE ATLANTIC SLOPE

The idea was simple: build a port on the Caribbean coast and connect it to the Central Valley by railroad, thereby opening up important shipping routes for the country's soaring coffee production. Construction began in 1871, through 150km of dense jungles and muddy mountainsides along the Atlantic slope. It took almost two decades to build the railroad, and the first 30km reportedly cost 4000 men their lives. But when the last piece of track was laid down in 1890, the economic forces it unleashed permanently changed Costa Rica (and the rest of Central America, for that matter). It was the dawn of the banana boom, an industry that would

Caribbean Coast Highlights

① Sliding silently through jungle canals in search of wildlife or volunteer to protect endangered sea turtles in **Tortuguero** (p154).

② Surfing, sampling the culinary scene, lazing on the beach and partying in **Puerto Viejo de Talamanca** (p176).

③ Visiting cacao farms and indigenous villages around **Bribrí** (p191).

④ Chilling out in rustic bliss in **Cahuita** (p168) and soaking up its Caribbean creole culture.

⑤ Overdosing on the cuteness of monkeys, sloths and other convalescing critters at Jaguar Centro de Rescate in **Playa Chiquita** (p177).

⑥ Snorkeling the teeming reefs off of end-of-the-road **Manzanillo** (p188).

⑦ Witnessing the dramatic meeting of the murky Río Sucio and the crystal-clear Río Hondura in **Parque Nacional Braulio Carrillo** (p144).

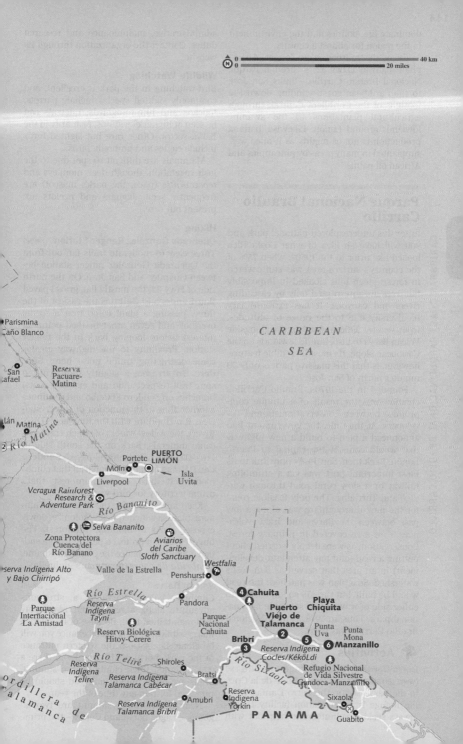

dominate life, politics and the environment in the region for almost a century.

Today, the railroad is no longer. An asphalt highway (Hwy 32) – through Parque Nacional Braulio Carrillo – links San José to the Caribbean coast, winding down the foothills of the Cordillera Central, through agricultural plantations to the swampy lowlands around Limón. Likewise, banana production is not as mighty as it once was, supplanted in many areas by pineapples and African oil palms.

Parque Nacional Braulio Carrillo

Enter this underexplored national park and you will have an idea of what Costa Rica looked like prior to the 1950s, when 75% of the country's surface area was still covered in forest: steep hills cloaked in impossibly tall trees are interrupted only by cascading rivers and canyons. It has extraordinary biodiversity due to the range of altitudes, from steamy 2906m cloud forest alongside Volcán Barva to lush, humid lowlands on the Caribbean slope. Its most incredible feature, however, is that this massive park is only 30 minutes north of San José.

Founded in the 1970s, Braulio Carrillo's creation was the result of a unique compromise between conservationists and developers. At the time, the government had announced a plan to build a new highway that would connect the capital to Puerto Limón. Back then, San José's only link to its most important port was via a crumbling railway or a slow rural road through Cartago and Turrialba. The only feasible route for the new thoroughfare was along a low pass between the Barva and Irazú volcanoes – an area covered in primary forest. Conservationists were deeply worried about putting a road (and any attendant development) in an area that served as San José's watershed. So a plan was hatched: the road would be built, but the 475 sq km of land to either side of it would be set aside as a national park. Thus, in 1978, Parque Nacional Braulio Carrillo was born.

🏃 Activities

Cerro Dantas Wildlife Refuge VOLUNTEERING
(www.cerrodantas.com) Near Monte de la Cruz, in the Barva sector, the Cerro Dantas Wildlife Refuge is an education facility that is always seeking volunteers to help out with administrative, maintenance and research duties. Contact the organization through its website.

Wildlife-Watching

Bird-watching in the park is excellent, and commonly sighted species include parrots, toucans and hummingbirds; quetzals can be seen at higher elevations, primarily in the Barva sector. Other rare but sighted birds include eagles and umbrella birds.

Mammals are difficult to spot due to the lush vegetation, though deer, monkeys and *tepezcuintle* (paca, the park's mascot) are frequently seen. Jaguars and ocelots are present but rare.

Hiking

Quebrada González Ranger Station HIKING
Three easy to moderate trails fan out from the Quebrada González ranger station between Guápiles and San José. On the north side of Hwy 32, the mostly flat, gravel-paved 1km **Sendero El Ceibo** is the easiest of the three, passing a giant ceibo tree, a scenic overlook and seven other marked points of interest before looping back to the ranger station. Proximity to the highway creates some distracting traffic noise here. **Sendero Botarrama**, a slightly more rugged spur trail (expect mud and exposed roots) branches off Sendero El Ceibo and continues another 1km to the junction of the crystal-clear Río Hondura with the Río Sucio (Dirty River), the yellow waters of which carry volcanic minerals. Back on the south side of Hwy 32, the 1.6km, gravel-paved **Sendero Las Palmas** is another loop trail that climbs moderately into dense rainforest that's prime territory for bird-watching.

Keep an eye out for the distinctive Gunnera plants, which quickly colonize newly exposed parts of montane rainforest. The huge leaves can protect a person from a sudden downpour – hence the plant's nickname, *sombrilla de pobre* (poor man's umbrella).

Volcán Barva HIKING
Climbing Volcán Barva is a strenuous adventure along a remote but reasonably well-maintained trail. Because of its relative inaccessibility, there is a good chance you will be alone. Begin from the western entrance of the park, north of Heredia. From there a 2.5km signed track climbs to the summit. Trails are often muddy, and you should be prepared for rain any time of the year.

Near the volcano's summit are two lagoons – Lagos Barva and Copey – the prime

A JUNGLE RETREAT ON THE NATIONAL PARK'S EDGE

If your dream vacation involves slowing down and getting totally immersed in nature, make a beeline for **La Danta Salvaje** (☎2750-0012; www.ladantasalvaje.com; 3-night package incl meals per person US$250) ✎, a remote, off-the-grid ecolodge right on the border of Parque Nacional Braulio Carrillo.

Getting here involves a 45-minute 4WD trip into the hills above Guápiles, followed by a strenuous three-hour hike into a fabulous 410-hectare private rainforest reserve (altitude 800m) in a critical buffer zone adjoining the national park. Small groups spend four days and three nights hiking in the jungle, spotting wildlife, splashing around in idyllic swimming holes and returning to delicious home-cooked meals followed by evening card games and hot chocolate beside the wood stove. It all adds up to unparalleled fun for adventurous-spirited individuals, couples and families. Prices include guided hikes and three meals daily. Reserve ahead.

destinations on a network of four trails that also leads to waterfalls and other scenic spots along the way.

Camping is allowed at basic campsites near the ranger station; bring your own drinking water.

ℹ Information

The park's three most accessible hiking trails originate at **Quebrada González station** (☎2206-5500; admission US$8; ☉8am-4pm) in the park's northeast corner, 21km past the Zurquí tunnel on the south side of the San José–Guápiles highway. Here, you'll find safe parking, toilets, drinking water and a ranger-staffed info booth. For security reasons, don't leave your car parked anywhere along the main highway.

People who want to climb Volcán Barva on a day trip or camp overnight can stop by the **Barva Sector ranger station** (☎2266-1883, 2266-1892; admission US$8; ☉8am-4pm), in the southwest of the park, 3km north of Sacramento.

Temperatures fluctuate drastically, and annual rainfall can be as high as 6000mm. The best time to go is the 'dry' season (January to April), but it is liable to rain then, too. Bring warm clothing, wet-weather gear and sturdy footwear.

ℹ Getting There & Away

Frequent buses between San José and Guápiles can drop you off at the Quebrada González station, but the return trip is more challenging. While it's possible to flag a bus down on busy Hwy 32, your luck will depend on the driver's discretion and how full the bus is.

Drivers can reach the Barva station by following the decent paved road north from Heredia through Barva village to San José de la Montaña, Paso Llano and Sacramento. From Sacramento, a signed, 4WD-only trail leads 3km north to the entrance. It is not advisable to drive this stretch

in rainy season as the road is a mess of car-swallowing potholes. Public buses from Heredia can only get you as far as Paso Llano, 7km from the park entrance. For a day trip without your own vehicle, you'll need to take an early bus; see the Heredia section (p124) for schedule details. Make sure you're catching a bus that goes all the way to Paso Llano, or you'll be left more than 15km from the park's entrance.

Guápiles & Around

POP 36,500

A pleasant and decidedly nontouristy (if not terribly scenic) lowland agricultural town, Guápiles lies at the base of the northern foothills of the Cordillera Central. It serves as a transportation center for the Río Frío banana-growing region and also makes a convenient base from which to explore Parque Nacional Braulio Carrillo – a 20-minute drive away – or to organize excursions to Tortuguero.

The center of town is about 1km north of Hwy 32, reached by a pair of well-marked turnoffs on either side of the impossible-to-miss Burger King restaurant. Guápiles' two major streets are one way, running parallel to each other east and west. Most of the services are on the loop that these streets make through the busy downtown.

🛌 Sleeping

🛌 Guápiles

Cabinas Irdama CABIN $
(☎2710-7034; hotel.cabinas.irdama@gmail.com; s/d with fan US$23/29, r with air-con US$32) This well-tended motel-like structure near the center of town offers 22 clean rooms and

WORTH A TRIP

RAINFOREST AERIAL TRAM

The brainchild of biologist Don Perry, a pioneer of rainforest-canopy research, the **Rainforest Aerial Tram** (☎2257-5961, in USA 1-866-759-8726; www.rainforestadventure.com; adult/student & child tram US$60/30, zip line US$50/35; ⬛) carries visitors to the heights of the forest canopy in a gondola. The 2.6km ride takes 40 minutes each way, affording unusual plant-spotting and bird-watching opportunities. The fee includes a knowledgeable guide, which is helpful since the dense vegetation can make observing animals difficult. A variety of other organized adventures, including a 14-platform, 10-cable zip-lining tour and the new 2000m AdrenaLine (longest zip line on Costa Rica's Caribbean slope), are also available. Book online or in the San José **office** (Map p72; ☎2257-5961; Av 7 btwn Calles 5 & 7; ◷9am-5pm Mon-Fri).

a small attached **restaurant** (meals US$6; ◷6am-8pm) serving breakfast and *casados* (set meals). Look for it 50m north of the Más x Menos supermarket (about 1km northeast of the bus terminal).

Hotel Country Club Suerre　　　HOTEL $$$
(☎2713-3000; www.suerre.com; s/d US$90/124, each additional person US$20; P◷✳☎🐕) On the road to Cariari, 1.5km north of the Servicentro Santa Clara, this Holiday Inn–like business resort has 98 spacious, tidy rooms and two restaurants. The meticulous grounds house a casino, a large pool, a gym, shaded tennis courts and a children's play area.

🛏 Around Guápiles

★ Casa Río Blanco B&B　　　B&B $$
(☎2710-4124; www.casarioblanco.com; s/d/tr/q incl breakfast US$53/77/93/107; P🐕) ⚲ One of Costa Rica's original ecolodges, this welcoming place offers four cabins on a 2-hectare hillside above the Río Blanco. Devoid of cable TV and air-con, it's a throwback to earlier days when ecotourism was all about unplugging. Croaking frogs and flickering lightning bugs provide late-night entertainment, while daytime diversions include visits to the spectacular nearby swimming hole.

Helpful owners Annette and Herbie organize rafting tours on the Río Pacuare and off-the-beaten-path day excursions through the Tortuguero canals. The lodge offers 20%-discount vouchers for the Rainforest Aerial Tram and zip line in the adjacent Parque Nacional Braulio Carrillo. Additional organic meals (including vegetarian options) can be arranged, and there's free wi-fi in the open lounge. To get here, travel 1km south of the Río Blanco bridge on Hwy 32 (7km west of Guápiles near La Marina). Call ahead or email for reservations.

🍴 Eating

🍴 Guápiles

El Rubio　　　COSTA RICAN $
(☎2710-2323; Guápiles; mains US$5-12) The clutter of pick-up trucks out front is a clue that you've stumbled onto this popular family eatery serving grilled fish, roasted meats and *bocas* (savory bar snacks). Our favorite is *chifrijo*, rice and beans studded with fried pork, tomato salsa and chips. Head north 250m on the paved road just east of Burger King, then turn east another 250m.

Soda Buenos Aires　　　COSTA RICAN $
(☎2710-1768; Hwy 32; casados US$5; ◷6am-7pm Mon-Sat) Situated 600m west of Burger King on the south side of the main highway, this popular *soda* (cheap, informal lunch counter) is a good bet for early-morning breakfasts and affordable *casados*.

Más X Menos　　　SUPERMARKET $
(◷7am-9pm Mon-Sat, to 8pm Sun) This huge supermarket is 800m northeast of the bus terminal, along Guápiles' eastbound main street.

🍴 Around Guápiles

★ Restaurante El Yugo　　　COSTA RICAN $
(☎2711-0090; mains US$3-10; ◷24hr) If there's a Costa Rican truck-stop heaven, it must look something like this. Strategically placed just below Hwy 32's tortuous climb into Parque Nacional Braulio Carrillo (13km west of Guápiles), it's the perfect spot to brace yourself for the road ahead or recuperate from the harrowing descent. A fabulous array of tasty, affordable cafeteria-style food is available 24/7.

ℹ Getting There & Away

Guapiles' modern bus terminal, complete with eateries and **internet cafe** (⏰9am-5pm), is 800m north of the main highway from the western Burger King turnoff.

Cariari (Coopetraca) US$1; 20 minutes; departs every 15 minutes from 6am to 10pm.

Puerto Limón via Guácimo & Siquirres (Tracasa) US$4.30; two hours; departs hourly from 6am to 7pm.

Puerto Viejo de Sarapiquí (Guapileños) US$2.40; one hour; departs at 5:30am, 8am, 9am, 10:30am, noon, 1:15pm, 2:30pm, 4pm, 5pm and 6:30pm.

San José (Guapileños) US$2.75; 1¼ hours; departs every 30 minutes from 6:30am to 7pm.

La Pavona for boat transfer to Tortuguero (estación vieja) US$2.20, one hour, departs at 6am, 9am, 11:30am and 3pm.

Puerto Lindo for boat transfer to Barra del Colorado (estación vieja) US$5, 2½ hours, departs at 4am and 2pm.

San José (estación nueva) US$3.35, two hours, departs daily at 7:30am, 9am, 11:30am, 1pm, 3pm and 5:30pm.

If driving, the turnoff for the paved road to Cariari is about 1km east of Guápiles, at the Servicentro Santa Clara. Drivers heading to Tortuguero can leave cars at the guarded parking by the boat dock on the Río Suerte in La Pavona (about 30km north of Cariari). Casa Marbella in Tortuguero has posted a very helpful map of the exact route from Guápiles to La Pavona (see casamarbella.tripod.com/id10.html)

Cariari

POP 34,200

Due north of Guápiles, Cariari is a blue-collar, rough-around-the-edges banana town. Most travelers make their way quickly through here, en route to Tortuguero. If that's you, Cariari is your last opportunity to get cash.

If you get stranded, spend the night at **Hotel El Trópico** (☎2767-7070; www.hoteleltropico.com; s/d with fan US$25/31, with air-con US$29/33; 🅿❄🛜) on the main road 600m north of Terminal Caribeño, which has 17 tidy rooms (angle for one of the three with front-porch hammocks) and an onsite restaurant (open 7am to 10pm).

There's a gas station and a branch of **Banco de Costa Rica** (opposite San José bus terminal; ⏰9am-4pm Mon-Fri) with a 24-hour ATM on the Cirrus system.

ℹ Getting There & Away

Cariari has two bus terminals. Buses from San José arrive at the *estación nueva* (new station) at the southern end of town. Those serving Guápiles and the northern Caribbean use the *estación vieja* (old station, also known as Terminal Caribeño), about 500m north, on the west side of main street.

To reach Tortuguero, take a bus from the *estación vieja* to the dock at La Pavona, then transfer to one of the several boat services that make multiple daily trips to Tortuguero.

When returning from Tortuguero, if headed to the southern Caribbean coast, take a bus to Guápiles and then transfer to one of the regular hourly buses to Puerto Limón.

Guápiles (estación vieja) US$1; 20 minutes; departs every 15 minutes from 5:30am to 7pm.

Siquirres

POP 31,600

The steamy lowland town of Siquirres has long served as an important transportation hub. It sits at the intersection of Hwy 32 (the main road that crosses the Atlantic slope to Puerto Limón) and Hwy 10, the old road that connects San José with Puerto Limón via Turrialba.

Even before the roads were built, it was a significant location – for it was in Siquirres in the early 20th century that the lines of segregation were drawn. At the time, blacks were barred from traveling west of here without special permission. So any train making its way from Limón to San José was required to stop here and change its crew: black conductors and engineers would change places with their Spanish counterparts and the train would continue on its route to the capital. This ended in 1949, when a new constitution outlawed racial discrimination.

Today Siquirres still marks the place where Costa Rica takes a dip into the Caribbean – and not just geographically. This is where Costa Rican *casados* give way to West Indian *rondón*, where Spanish guitar is replaced with the strains of calypso, and where Costa Rica's inherently *mestizo* (mixed ancestry) race gives way to Afro-Caribbean features.

There is little reason to stop in Siquirres, unless you're heading to Parismina – in which case this is a good spot to find banking, internet and telephone services. (Tip: buy phone cards here; they aren't sold in

Parismina.) For purposes of orientation, the Siquirres church – a highly recognizable, round, red-domed building – is located to the west side of the soccer field.

If you need somewhere to crash for the night, head 1km northeast of the park to **Centro Turístico Las Tilapias** (☎2768-9293; d with fan/air-con US$45/50; P✳︎🛜🖥️), where you'll find 17 clean-but-basic rooms perched above an artificial lagoon, as well as a restaurant and bar. Take a taxi, as it's tricky to find.

Sodas and bakeries are plentiful in town.

Banco de Costa Rica (⊘9am-4pm), 100m north of the park, has a 24-hour ATM on the Cirrus network.

ⓘ Getting There & Away

Siquirres has two main bus terminals. The one on the southeast corner of the park serves the first three destinations listed on the next page. Buses for Turrialba leave from a separate terminal on the north side of the park.

THE TROUBLED LEGACY OF BANANAS

The banana. Nothing embodies the tumultuous history of Latin America – and its complicated relationship with the United States – quite like this common yellow fruit. It is the crop that has determined the path of current affairs in more than one Central American nation. It is the sobriquet used to describe corrupt, dictatorial regimes – 'the banana republic.' Bananas are a symbol of frivolity, the raw material for Carmen Miranda hats and Busby Berkeley dance numbers. (Want to blow your mind? Look up 'The Lady with the Tutti Frutti Hat' from the 1942 musical flick *The Gang's All Here* – it's a hallucinogenic panorama of dancing bananas.)

It was in Costa Rica, interestingly, where the idea of bananas as an industry was born. Imported from the Canary Islands by sailors during the colonial period, the fruit had long been a basic foodstuff in the Caribbean islands. But it was 19th-century railroad baron Minor Keith who turned it into a booming international business. After building the railroad between San José and Limón, Keith proceeded to carpet vast swaths of Central America in bananas. Over the course of the 20th century, the company he founded – United Fruit – would become an integral part of the region's economies and a behind-the-scenes puppet master in its political systems. (For a highly readable history on this topic, pick up *Bananas: How the United Fruit Company Shaped the World,* by journalist Peter Chapman.)

Part of the reason bananas became a continent-wide crop boils down to profit and biology. Bananas – a fruit afflicted with a high rate of spoilage – require a vast economy of scale (and cheap labor) to be profitable. It's also an inordinately delicate fruit to cultivate, partly because bananas are clones. The fruit doesn't grow from seeds; its propagation requires that a cutting be taken from an existing plant and put into the ground. This makes them incredibly vulnerable to illness – what kills one banana kills all bananas. Entire networks of plantations can be devastated by fungus, such as the diseases that swept through Costa Rica's southern Caribbean coast in the 1910s and '20s.

Over the years, this weakness has led growers to turn to a veritable arsenal of chemicals to protect their crops. This, in turn, has taken a toll on both the environment and the workers who spray them, some of whom have been rendered sterile by powerful fungicides such as DBCP (now banned). Groups of workers in various countries have filed numerous lawsuits against fruit companies and chemical manufacturers – and won – but these victories are generally short-lived. Even when Central American courts rule in workers' favor, it is practically impossible for plaintiffs to secure payouts.

There have been some attempts at growing bananas organically, but according to some experts, those efforts will never be enough to replace the intense agribusiness that currently supplies the world with its fourth major foodstuff, after rice, wheat and milk. Costa Rica is sometimes thought of as a country of coffee producers, a nation built on the work of humble, independent farmers. But the fact is that bananas remain the country's number-one agricultural export – as they have been for decades. They are an inextricable part of the country's DNA. And, unless everyone suddenly starts putting sliced apples into their cereal, that likely won't change any time soon.

Guápiles US$1.75, 45 minutes, hourly 7am to 7pm.

Limón US$2.30, one hour, almost hourly 5:50am to 7:50pm.

San José US$3.20, two hours, almost hourly 4:30am to 7pm.

Turrialba US$2.35, 1½ hours, almost hourly 5:30am to 7pm.

TO PARISMINA

At the terminal on the park's northern edge, you'll find buses to Caño Blanco, for transfer by boat to Parismina. **Caño-Aguilar** (☎ 2768-8172) operates the route to Caño Blanco (US$2.20, two hours, weekday departures at 4:10am, noon and 3:15pm, weekend departures at 7:15am, noon and 3:15pm). At Caño Blanco you'll transfer to a water taxi (US$2) that makes the 10-minute trip to Parismina. (Take small change to pay the boatman.) There's a small restaurant with bathrooms by the Caño Blanco dock.

Note: the Caño Blanco bus can get crowded. Get to the station early to buy your ticket and join the queue at least 15 minutes before the scheduled departure time.

Puerto Limón

POP 61,100

The biggest city on Costa Rica's Caribbean coast, the birthplace of United Fruit and capital of Limón Province, this hardworking port city sits removed from the rest of the country. Cruise ships deposit dazed-looking passengers between October and May. Around here, business is measured by truckloads of fruit, not busloads of tourists, so don't expect any pampering.

A general lack of political and financial support from the federal government means that Limón is not a city that has aged gracefully. It is a grid of dilapidated buildings, overgrown parks and sidewalks choked with street vendors. Crime is a problem: the city, distressingly, has as many homicides annually as San José – even though San José has five times the population. It's worth noting, however, that most of this violence is related to organized crime and does not affect travelers. Despite its shortcomings, Limón can be a compelling destination for adventurous urban explorers.

History

Until the 1850s, the most frequent visitors to Limón were pirates, who used the area's natural deep-water bays as hideouts. At the time, the country's main port was in Puntarenas, on the Pacific, but when the railroad arrived in the late 19th century, Limón blossomed into a full-blown trade hub. The city ultimately served as the key export point for the country's newest agribusiness: bananas.

Beginning in 1913, a series of blights shut down many Caribbean *fincas* (farms) and a large portion of the area's banana production moved to the southern Pacific coast. Afro-Caribbean workers, however, couldn't follow the jobs, as they were forbidden to leave the province. Stranded in the least-developed part of Costa Rica, many turned to subsistence farming, fishing or managing small scale cacao plantations. Others organized and staged bloody strikes against United Fruit. Fed up with the status quo, Limón provided key support to José Figueres (a Costa Rican revolutionary) during the 1948 civil war. This act was rewarded the following year when the new president enacted a constitution that granted blacks full citizenship and the right to work and travel freely throughout Costa Rica.

Even though segregation was officially dismantled, Limón continues to live with its legacy. The province was the last to get paved roads and the last to get electricity (areas to the south of the city weren't on the grid until the late 1970s), and the region has chronically higher crime and unemployment rates than the rest of the country.

While two major new infrastructure developments have been announced in recent years (the construction of a $1 billion container port in Moín by the multinational corporation APM and a Chinese-financed US$221 million initiative to widen Hwy 32 to four lanes), it is unclear whether the economic benefits of these projects will be shared by the local population. Indeed, plans for the container port have sparked massive protests by dockworkers' union members in Limón and Moín who fear that privatization of the port will undermine, rather than improve, their standard of living.

◉ Sights & Activities

Limón itself has no beach; for a swim, you'll need to head out of town to Playa Bonita.

Parque Vargas PARK

The city's waterfront centerpiece won't ever win best in show, but its decrepit bandstand, paths and greenery are surprisingly appealing, all shaded by palms and facing the docks.

Puerto Limón

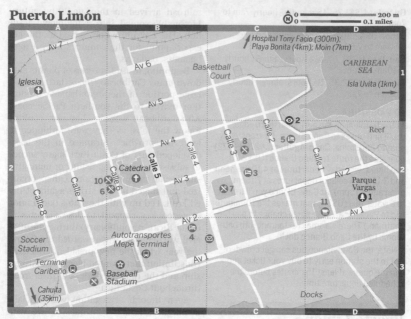

Puerto Limón

◎ Sights
1 Parque Vargas	D2
2 Sea Wall	C1

🛏 Sleeping
3 Hotel Acon	C2
4 Hotel Miami	B3
5 Park Hotel	C2

✕ Eating
6 Caribbean Kalisi Coffee Shop	B2
7 Central Market	C2
8 Más X Menos	C2
9 Palí	A3
10 Restaurant Bionatura	B2

🍷 Drinking & Nightlife
11 El Crucero	D2

Playa Bonita   BEACH

While not the Caribbean's finest beach, Playa Bonita, 4km northwest of town on the Limón–Moín bus route, offers sandy stretches of seashore and good swimming. Surfers come for Bonita's point/reef break, which makes for a powerful (and sometimes dangerous) left. Experienced surfers might also want to hit the punishing reef break at Isla Uvita, the wild green rock 1km offshore.

✦ Festivals & Events

Festival Flores de la Diáspora Africana   CULTURE
(www.festivaldiasporacr.org; ⊙ late Aug) A celebration of Afro-Caribbean culture. While it is centered on Puerto Limón, the festival sponsors events showcasing African heritage throughout the province and San José.

Día de la Raza   CULTURE
(Columbus Day; ⊙ Oct 12) Puerto Limón celebrates Día de la Raza with a boisterous week of Carnaval festivities, including live music, dancing and a big Saturday parade. During this time, book hotels in advance.

⌂ Sleeping

Limón offers nothing remotely upscale; for something nicer, head to nearby Playa Bonita.

Hotel Miami   HOTEL $
(✆ 2758-0490; hmiamilimon@yahoo.com; Av 2 btwn Calles 4 & 5; s/d US$27/35, with air-con US$39/52; P ❋ @) For its location on the main drag, this clean, mint green place feels surprisingly serene, especially in the rooms in back. All 34 tidy rooms are equipped with cable TV and fan. Rooms with air-con have hot water. Welcoming staff, common balco-

nies overlooking the street and secure setup add up to the best value in town.

Hotel Playa Bonita   HOTEL $$
(☑2795-1010; www.hotelplayabonita.com; incl breakfast s/d standard US$52/80, executive US$66/86; P❋☎☎) This seaside hotel has simple whitewashed rooms and a breezy ocean-view restaurant that serves everything from burgers to jumbo shrimp. It's about 5km from downtown Puerto Limón and 2.5km from the entrance to the docks at Moín.

Park Hotel   HOTEL $$
(☑2798-0555; www.parkhotellimon.com; Av 3 btwn Calles 1 & 2; s/d standard US$55/74, superior US$64/90, deluxe US$77/103; P❋@☎) Downtown Limón's most attractive hotel has 32 rooms in a faded yellow building that faces the ocean. Tiled rooms are tidy and sport clean bathrooms with hot water; superior and deluxe units come with ocean views and balconies. The hotel also houses the swankiest restaurant in the town center.

Hotel Acon   HOTEL $$
(☑2758-1010; cnr Av 3 & Calle 3; s/d US$44/64; ❋☎) The '60s-style modernist building is in a ramshackle state, but the place is generally clean. The 39 rooms are basic: bare linoleum floors and aged wood furnishings, all with creaky air-con units and hot-water bathrooms.

✗ Eating & Drinking

Find cheap eats at the *sodas* in the **central market** (Av 2 btwn Calles 3 & 4; ☺6am-8pm Mon-Sat). You can get groceries at the large **Más X Menos** (cnr Av 3 & Calle 3; ☺8am-9pm), or at the **Palí** (cnr Calle 7 & Av 1; ☺8am-7pm Mon-Thu, 8am-7:30pm Fri & Sat, 8:30am-6pm Sun) next to the Terminal Caribeño.

Bars by Parque Vargas and a few blocks west are popular hangouts for coastal characters: banana workers, sailors, ladies of the night, entrepreneurs, boozers, losers and everyone else. The standard warnings for solo women travelers go double here. (If you feel like having a beer, hit a restaurant.) This is a lousy town for getting drunk – keep your wits about you.

Caribbean Kalisi Coffee Shop   CARIBBEAN $
(☑2758-3249; Calle 6 btwn Avs 3 & 4; mains from US$5; ☺7am-8pm Mon-Fri, 8am-7:30pm Sat, 8am-5pm Sun) Belly up to the cafeteria-style counter at this friendly family spot and cobble together a plate of coconut rice, red beans and whatever Caribbean meat and veggie dishes are cooking today. Also recommended in the mornings for its affordable à la carte breakfasts and excellent *café con leche* (coffee with milk).

Restaurant Bionatura   VEGETARIAN $
(☑2798-7474; Calle 6 btwn Avs 3 & 4; mains US$5-8; ☺8:30am-6pm Mon-Sat; ✍) This restaurant shines for its focus on healthy vegetarian cuisine, including fresh fruit salads, veggie burgers, *bistek de soya* (soy steak) *casados* and a US$6 *plato del día* (daily special).

Reina's   SEAFOOD $$
(☑2795-0879; mains US$9-15; ☺10am-10pm) On the beach at Playa Bonita, Reina's has loud music, good vibes and plenty of *mariscos* (seafood) and *cerveza* (beer) on the menu.

El Crucero   CAFE
(☑2758-7003; cnr Calle 1 & Av 1; ☺6:30am-6pm Mon-Sat) Kick back with a smoothie, an empanada or an iced espresso and let the cross-breeze cool you at this corner cafe facing Parque Vargas and the docks.

ℹ Information

Though police presence has ramped up noticeably, pickpockets can be a problem, particularly in the market and along the sea wall. In addition, people do get mugged here, so stick to well-lit main streets at night, avoiding the sea wall and Parque Vargas. If driving, park in a guarded lot and remove everything from the car.

If you're traveling onward to Parismina or Tortuguero, Limón will be your last opportunity to get cash (and phone cards, for the Parismina-bound).

There's an Internet cafe in the Autotransportes Mepe Terminal.

Hospital Tony Facio (☑2758-2222) Serves the entire province. It's northeast of the center.

Scotiabank (cnr Av 3 & Calle 2; ☺9am-5pm Mon-Fri, to 1pm Sat) Exchanges cash and has a 24-hour ATM that dispenses US dollars.

ℹ Getting There & Away

Puerto Limón is the transportation hub of the Caribbean coast.

BOAT
Cruise ships dock in Limón, but smaller passenger boats bound for Parismina and Tortuguero use the port at Moín, about 7km west of town.

BUS
Buses from all points west arrive at **Terminal Caribeño** (Av 2 btwn Calles 7 & 8), just west of the baseball stadium.

WORTH A TRIP

VERAGUA RAINFOREST RESEARCH & ADVENTURE PARK

Nestled into the foothills of the Cordillera de Talamanca, this sprawling **rainforest adventure park** (☑2296-5056; www.veraguarainforest.com; adult with/without zip-line tour US$99/66, child with/without zip-line tour US$75/55; ⌗) has guided tours of the forest along elevated walkways and maintained trails, as well as an aerial tram, a reptile vivarium, an insectarium, and hummingbird and butterfly gardens. And what would it be without a zip-line canopy tour? Many of the attractions are wheelchair-accessible – a good way of exploring nature if traveling with an elderly person or small children. To get here, take the signed turnoff south from Hwy 32 at Liverpool, 12km west of Puerto Limón.

San José (Autotransportes Caribeños) US$6.30, three hours, departs almost hourly 5am to 7pm.

Siquirres/Guápiles (Tracasa) US$2.30/4.30, one hour/two hours, departs hourly 6am to 6pm.

Buses to points south all depart from **Autotransportes Mepe Terminal** (☑2758-1572; Calle 6 btwn Avs 1 & 2), on the east side of the stadium.

Bribrí/Sixaola US$4.40/6.35, two hours/three hours, departs hourly between 5am and 7pm.

Cahuita/Puerto Viejo de Talamanca US$2.40/3.60, one hour/1½ hours, departs almost hourly 5:30am to 7pm.

Manzanillo US$4.90, two hours, departs every one to two hours between 5:30am and 6:30pm.

Moín

Just 8km northwest of Puerto Limón, this is the town's main transportation dock, where you can catch a boat to Parismina or Tortuguero.

❶ Getting There & Away

BOAT

The journey by boat from Moín to Tortuguero can take anywhere from three to five hours, depending on how often the boat stops to observe wildlife (many tours also stop for lunch). Indeed, it is worth taking your time. As you wind through these jungle canals, you're likely to spot howler monkeys, crocodiles, two- and three-toed sloths and an amazing array of wading birds, including roseate spoonbills.

Tourist boat schedules exist in theory only and change frequently depending on demand. If you're feeling lucky, you can just show up in Moín in the morning and try to get on one of the outgoing tour boats (there's often at least one departure at 10am). But you're better off reserving in advance, particularly during slower seasons when boats don't travel the route on a daily

basis. If the canal becomes blocked by water hyacinths or logjams, the route might be closed altogether. Call ahead for departure times and reservations.

One-way fares generally run between US$30 and US$40 to Tortuguero, or between US$25 and US$30 to Parismina. Two recommended agencies are **Tortuguero Wildlife Tour** (William Guerrero (TUCA); ☑8371-2323, 2798-7027; www.tortuguero-wildlife.com), run by master sloth-spotter William Guerrero and his wife, Martha, and **All Rankin's Tours** (☑8815-5175, 2709-8101; www.greencoast.com/allrankin), run by longtime local resident Willis Rankin. Both are ideal for leisurely rides to Tortuguero; Rankin also offers package deals including accommodations in his rustic lodge near Tortuguero's airstrip. Another outfit that arranges transport on various boats is **ABACAT** (Asociación de Boteros de los Canales de Tortuguero; ☑8360-7325). For additional operators, see the Tortuguero section (p163).

BUS

Tracasa buses to Moín from Puerto Limón (US$0.60, 20 minutes) depart from Terminal Caribeño hourly from 5:30am to 6:30pm (less frequently on Saturday and Sunday). Get off the bus before it goes over the bridge. If driving, leave your car in a guarded lot in Limón.

NORTHERN CARIBBEAN

Running north–south along the country's waterlogged eastern shore, the Canales de Tortuguero (Tortuguero Canal) serves as the liquid highway that connects Puerto Limón to the lush lowland settlements to the north: Parismina, Tortuguero and Barra del Colorado. This is the wettest region in Costa Rica, a network of rivers and canals that are home to diminutive fishing villages and slick sportfishing camps, raw rainforest and all-inclusive resorts – not to mention plenty of wading birds and sleepy sloths.

Most significantly, the area's long, wild beaches serve as the protected nesting grounds for three kinds of sea turtle. In fact, more green turtles are born here than anywhere else in the world. Much of the region lies only a 30-minute flight from San José – but it nonetheless can feel like the end of the earth.

Parismina

For a sense of what Costa Rica's Caribbean coast was like prior to the arrival of mass tourism, jump ship in this sleepy coastal fishing village, wedged between the Canales de Tortuguero and the Caribbean Sea. Bereft of zip lines and 4WD adventure tours, it's the sort of spot where old men play dominoes on front porches and kids splash in muddy puddles in the road.

For those intrepid enough to make the journey and stick around a while, Parismina is also a great place to view turtles and aid in their conservation, without the crowds you'll find at Tortuguero. Leatherbacks nest on the beach between late February and early October, with the peak season in April and May. Green turtles begin nesting in June, with a peak in August and September. Hawksbills are not as common, but they are sometimes seen between February and September.

Sportfishing is the other traditional tourist draw. The top tarpon season is from January to mid-May, while snook are caught from September to November.

Every year around July 16, fishers and local boat captains have a small waterborne procession in honor of the Virgen del Carmen, the patron saint of sailors.

🏃 Activities

You can rent kayaks for US$10 per day at Carefree Ranch (p153) or **Iguana Verde** (☑2758-6400, 8765-1280) to explore the canals and their denizens.

Asociación Salvemos Las Tortugas de Parismina   VOLUNTEERING
(ASTOP, Save the Turtles of Parismina; ☑2798-2220; www.parisminaturtles.org; ☺by arrangement Mar-Sep) ✐ Directed by 35-year resident and former Peace Corps volunteer Vicky Taylor, this grassroots turtle-protection organization with strong community support employs former poachers as 'turtle guides' and maintains a guarded turtle hatchery. Travelers can volunteer as guards to patrol the beaches alongside local turtle guides. Volunteers (five-night minimum commitment) pay a one-time US$35 registration fee, plus a daily US$10 training fee.

ASTOP also organizes homestays (per night with three meals US$17), offers internet access (per hour US$2), and can arrange horseback-riding trips, bike rentals, turtle-watching tours (per person US$20), wildlife-viewing excursions by boat, and farm and heliconia-garden tours in Caño Blanco.

Barrita   SWIMMING
A 15-minute walk south of town brings you to the jungle-fringed freshwater lagoon called Barrita. From the Catholic church, head toward the beach and hang a right at the airstrip, then follow the path until it opens out onto the beach and (croc-free!) lagoon.

👉 Tours

Río Parismina Lodge (☑2229-7597, in USA 210-824-4442, in USA 800-338-5688; www.riop. com; rates by arrangement; ☺☒) organizes package sportfishing expeditions from the USA.

🛏 Sleeping & Eating

Don Alex at the hardware store, about 300m north of the dock, has camping and basic huts (US$7; high season only), with access to showers, bathrooms and a shared kitchen.

Carefree Ranch   CABINA $
(☑8744-6483; r per person US$10) Opposite the Catholic church on the southern end of town, this clapboard house – bright yellow with green trim – has nine tidy rooms and an inviting, broad front porch. In Parismina, it's about as quaint as things get. Tasty home-cooked *casados* (US$6) are also available.

Parismina Gamefish Lodge   CABINA $
(☑2758-0724, 8971-1756; r per person with fan/air-con US$15/20; ☒) At this basic place in the center of town, six simple, tiled rooms (two with air-con, four with fan) surround a garden lined with hammocks.

Green Gold Ecolodge   LODGE $$
(☑8697-2322, 8647-0691; greengoldeco-lodge. webs.com; dm adult/child incl 3 meals US$50/30) About 3km south of the dock, this simple solar- and generator-powered retreat, steps from the beach and surrounded by 36 hectares of jungle, is an authentic rainforest hideaway. Run by the charming (and

bilingual) Jason and Juliana, its rustic but comfortable facilities include dorm beds in screened-in upstairs rooms, a shared open-air kitchen and shared bathrooms.

Jason leads tours of all kinds, and the area is rife with as much wildlife as in Tortuguero, but hardly any people. Walk in from the village, or arrange for a truck ride from town (US$10 one way); advance reservations recommended.

Soda Rancho La Palma COSTA RICAN $
(casados US$7; ⊙6am-7pm Mon-Sat) Right next to the dock, no-nonsense doña Amelia serves up fresh and tasty *casados*. She also keeps the small plaster statue of the Virgin that is paraded during the annual boat procession in July.

❶ Information

There are no banks or post offices in Parismina, and credit cards are not accepted, so make sure you bring enough cash. While the village has a couple of pay phones, no one in town sells phone cards – bring your own. You can find internet access (per hour US$2) at ASTOP.

❶ Getting There & Away

Parismina is only accessible by boat or chartered flight.

The only scheduled boat service is to Caño Blanco (for transfer to Siquirres). Water taxis (US$2, 10 minutes) leave from the Parismina dock at 5:30am, 1:30pm and 4:30pm on weekdays, and at 9am, 1:30pm and 4:30pm on weekends. A bus will be waiting at Caño Blanco's dock to continue the journey to Siquirres (US$2.20, two hours), where you can find onward transport.

For travel to Tortuguero or Puerto Limón (via Moín), it's possible to reserve a seat on one of the tourist boats that travel between the two destinations, but advance planning is essential. Note that it may take 24 to 48 hours to secure transportation (around US$25 to either destination), as Parismina is not a regular stop. Call one of the boat companies in Moín or Tortuguero directly, or ask doña Amelia at Soda Rancho La Palma to help you book.

Parque Nacional Tortuguero

'Humid' is the driest word that could truthfully be used to describe Tortuguero, a 311-sq-km coastal park that serves as the most important breeding ground of the green sea turtle. With annual rainfall of up to 6000mm in the northern part of the park, it is one of the wettest areas in the country. In addition, the protected area extends into the Caribbean Sea, covering about 5200 sq km of marine habitat. In other words, plan on spending quality time in a boat.

The famed **Canales de Tortuguero** are the introduction to this park. Created to connect a series of lagoons and meandering rivers in 1974, this engineering marvel allowed inland navigation between Limón and coastal villages in something sturdier than a dugout canoe. Regular flights service the village of Tortuguero – but if you fly, you'll be missing half the fun. The leisurely taxi-boat ride, through banana plantations and wild jungle, is equal parts recreation and transportation.

Most visitors come to watch sea turtles lay eggs on the wild beaches. The area attracts four of the world's eight species of sea turtle, making it a crucial habitat for these massive reptiles. It will come as little

TURTLE BEACH TRAGEDY

The Caribbean's turtle-conservation community suffered a devastating blow on the night of May 30, 2013, when 26-year-old Costa Rican environmentalist Jairo Mora Sandoval was murdered while patrolling a stretch of Moín beach near Puerto Limón. The tragedy shines a light on the challenges facing turtle conservationists. While many communities along the coast have successfully engaged the participation of former poachers in guide and conservation work, turtle eggs continue to be prized on the black market for their supposed aphrodisiac qualities. The remote section of beach where Mora was working, near Costa Rica's biggest Caribbean port, is also frequented by drug-runners, some armed with semiautomatic weapons. Mora's death sparked strong international and domestic protest, with calls for beefed-up police presence and stronger conservation measures. While six suspects were taken into custody two months after the murder, the ultimate outcome of Mora's case remains to be seen. Meanwhile, turtle-conservation efforts up and down the Caribbean coast continue.

surprise, then, that these hatching grounds gave birth to the sea-turtle-conservation movement. The Caribbean Conservation Corporation, the first program of its kind in the world, has continuously monitored turtle populations here since 1955. Today green sea turtles are increasing in numbers along this coast, but the leatherback, hawksbill and loggerhead are in decline.

The area, however, is more than just turtles: Tortuguero teems with wildlife. You'll find sloths and howler monkeys in the treetops, tiny frogs and green iguanas scurrying among buttress roots, and mighty tarpons and endangered manatees swimming in the waters.

Activities

Turtle-Watching

Most female turtles share a nesting instinct that drives them to return to the beach of their birth, or natal beach, in order to lay their eggs. (Only the leatherback returns to a more general region, instead of a specific beach.) During their lifetimes, they will usually nest every two to three years and, depending on the species, may come ashore to lay eggs 10 times in one season. Often, a turtle's ability to successfully reproduce depends on the ecological health of this original habitat.

The female turtle digs a perfect cylindrical cavity in the sand using her flippers, and then lays 80 to 120 eggs. She diligently covers the nest with sand to protect the eggs, and she may even create a false nest in another location in an attempt to confuse predators. She then makes her way back to sea – after which the eggs are on their own. Incubation ranges from 45 to 70 days, after which hatchlings – no bigger than the size of your palm – break out of their shells using a caruncle, a temporary tooth. They crawl to the ocean in small groups, moving as quickly as possible to avoid dehydration and predators. Once they reach the surf, they must swim for at least 24 hours to get to deeper water, away from land-based predators.

Because of the sensitive nature of the habitat and the critically endangered status of some species, tours to see this activity are highly regulated. So as to not alarm turtles as they come to shore (a frightened turtle will return to the ocean and dump her eggs), tour groups gather in shelter sites close to the beach and a spotter relays a turtle's location via radio once she has safely crossed

the high-tide mark and built her nest. At this time, visitors can then go to the beach and watch the turtle lay her eggs, cover her nest and return to the ocean. Seeing a turtle is not guaranteed, but licensed guides will still make your tour worthwhile with the wealth

Around Tortuguero

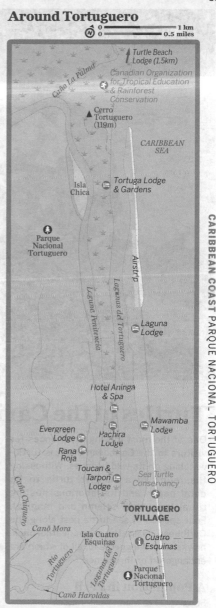

Turtles of the Caribbean

One of the most moving experiences for visitors to the Caribbean coast is turtle-watching on its wild beaches. Witnessing the return of a massive turtle to its natal beach and its laborious nesting ritual feels both solemn and magical. Four species of sea turtle nest along the Caribbean coast: the green, leatherback, hawksbill and loggerhead, all of which are endangered or threatened.

A Population in Peril

Since it takes many years for sea turtles to mature and reproduce, their populations are quite vulnerable to environmental hazards such as pollution and poaching. Thus, conservation efforts are crucial to their survival – these efforts include guarding hatchlings from predators and providing incentives for local communities to protect turtles and their eggs. Volunteer opportunities are plentiful along the Caribbean coast, with tasks ranging from beach patrols, data collection and tagging to removing eggs to hatcheries and hatchling release.

Planning a Tour

Because of the sensitive habitat and critically endangered status of some species, turtle-nesting tours are highly regulated. Groups must be accompanied by licensed guides, who ensure that the turtles are able to lay their eggs in peace and that other nests are left undisturbed. Nesting season runs from March to October, with July and August being the most active period for green turtles. April is another good month, when leatherback turtles arrive.

1. Studying turtle eggs
2. Olive ridley turtles
3. Green turtle hatchlings

Depending on when you visit, you may find yourself watching a newly arrived mother hauling herself onto the beach, laboriously digging a nest with her flippers and hatching dozens of ping-pong-ball-sized eggs. At another time, you might see a parade of new hatchlings on their slow, determined and endearingly clumsy crawl back to the sea.

Turtle-watching tours can be arranged through **ATEC** (p178) in Puerto Viejo, the **Asociación Salvemos Las Tortugas de Parismina** (ASTOP; p153) in Parismina, and by licensed guides in Tortuguero village.

Doing Time for the Turtles

There are many opportunities for volunteers to help protect sea turtles and the many other creatures that inhabit the Caribbean coast. In most cases, organizations require a minimum commitment of a week. A few options:

ASTOP Small, locally run organization in Parismina.

Asociación Widecast (p176) Grass-roots NGO that has volunteer opportunities in Cahuita and north of the mouth of the Río Pacuare.

Canadian Organization for Tropical Education & Rainforest Conservation (p159) Canadian not-for-profit with a research station in Tortuguero.

Sea Turtle Conservancy (p159) Long-time organization with a research station in Tortuguero.

of turtle information they'll share. By law, tours can only take place between 8am and midnight. Some guides will offer tours after midnight; these are illegal.

Visitors should wear closed-toe shoes and rain gear. Tours cost US$20 (a flat rate established by the village; at the time of writing, there was talk of raising this to US$25). This rate includes the purchase of a US$4 sticker that pays for the patrols that help protect the nesting sites from scavengers and looters. Nesting season runs from March to October, with July and August being prime time. The next best time is April, when leatherback turtles nest in small numbers. Flashlights and cameras are not allowed on the beach.

Other Wildlife-Watching

More than 300 bird species, both resident and migratory, have been recorded in Tortuguero – a bird-watchers' paradise. Due to the wet habitat, the park is especially rich in waders, including egrets, jacanas, 14 different types of heron, as well as species such as kingfishers, toucans and the great curassow (a type of jungle peacock known locally as the *pavón*). The great green macaw is a highlight, most common from December to April, when the almond trees are fruiting. In September and October, look for flocks of migratory species such as eastern kingbird, barn swallows and purple martins. The Sea Turtle Conservancy conducts a biannual monitoring program, in which volunteers can help scientists take inventory of local and migratory species.

Certain species of mammal are particularly evident in Tortuguero, especially mantled howler monkeys, the Central American spider monkey and white-faced capuchin. If you've got a good pair of binoculars and a good guide, you can usually see both two- and three-toed sloths. In addition, normally shy neotropical river otters are reasonably

habituated to boats. Harder to spot are timid West Indian manatees. The park is also home to big cats such as jaguars and ocelots – but these are savvy, nocturnal animals and sightings are very rare.

Most wildlife-watching tours are done by boat. To get the best from Tortuguero, be on the water early or go out following a heavy rain, when all the wildlife comes out to sunbathe. It is also highly recommended to take tours by canoe or kayak – since these smaller, silent craft will allow you to get into the park's less trafficked nooks and crannies.

Boating

Four aquatic trails wind their way through Parque Nacional Tortuguero, inviting waterborne exploration. **Río Tortuguero** acts as the entranceway to the network of trails. This wide, beautiful river is often covered with water lilies and frequented by aquatic birds such as herons, kingfishers and anhingas – the latter of which is known as the snakebird for the way its slim, winding neck pokes out of the water when it swims.

Caño Chiquero and **Cañŏ Mora** are two narrower waterways with good wildlife-spotting opportunities. According to park regulation, only kayaks, canoes and silent electric boats are allowed in these areas (a rule that is constantly violated by many area tour companies and lodges). Caño Chiquero is thick with vegetation, especially red guácimo trees and epiphytes. Black turtles and green iguanas like to hang out here. Caño Mora is about 3km long but only 10m wide, so it feels as if it's straight out of *The Jungle Book*. **Caño Harold** is actually an artificially constructed canal, but that doesn't stop the creatures – such as Jesus Christ lizards and caimans – from inhabiting its tranquil waters.

Canoe rental and boat tours are available in Tortuguero village.

Hiking

Behind Cuatro Esquinas station, **El Gavilán Land Trail** is the only public trail through the park that is on solid ground. Visitors can hike the muddy, 2km out-and-back trail that traverses the tropical humid forest and parallels a stretch of beach. Green parrots and several species of monkey are commonly sighted here. The short trail is well marked. Rubber boots are required (for rent at hotels and near the park entrance).

ℹ PARK ADMISSION FEES

A separate park admission fee is charged for each day you visit the national park. If you're planning multiple activities within the park, you can save a few colones by concentrating them in a single day; for example, if you go out on a boat tour in the early morning, then hike the El Gavilán Land Trail that same afternoon, you'll only pay the park admission fee once.

ℹ Information

Park headquarters is at **Cuatro Esquinas** (☎2709-8086; park admission US$10; ⊙6-7am, 7:30am-noon & 1-4pm), just south of Tortuguero village. This is a helpful ranger station, with maps and info.

Jalova Station (⊙6am-6pm) is on the canal at the south entrance to the national park, accessible from Parismina by boat. Tour boats from Moín often stop here for a picnic; you will find a short nature trail, bathroom, drinking water and rudimentary camping facilities that may or may not be open (and may or may not be flooded).

ℹ Getting There & Away

The park is a short walk south of the village of Tortuguero (the most common entry point) and also accessible by boat from Parismina.

Tortuguero Village

Located within the confines of Parque Nacional Tortuguero, accessible only by air or water, this bustling little village with strong Afro-Caribbean roots is best known for attracting hordes of sea turtles (the name Tortuguero means 'turtle place') – and the hordes of tourists who want to see them. While the peak turtle season is in July and August, the park and village have begun to attract travelers year-round. Even in October, when the turtles have pretty much returned to the sea, caravans of families and adventure travelers arrive to go on jungle hikes and to canoe the area's lush canals.

🏃 Activities

Volunteering

Sea Turtle Conservancy   VOLUNTEERING (formerly Caribbean Conservation Corporation; ☎2709-8091, in USA 352-373-6441; www.conserveturtles.org; museum admission US$2) About 200m north of the village, Tortuguero's original turtle-conservation organization operates a research station, visitor center and museum. Exhibits focus on all things turtle-related, including a 20-minute video about the history of local turtle conservation.

STC also runs a highly reputable environmental volunteer program. During nesting season, volunteers can assist with turtle tagging and egg counts, and during bird-migration seasons, help with mist-netting and point-counts. Volunteer fees (starting at US$1524) include accommodations, meals and transport to and from San José.

Canadian Organization for Tropical Education & Rainforest Conservation   VOLUNTEERING (COTERC; ☎2709-8052; www.coterc.org) This not-for-profit organization operates the Estación Biológica Caño Palma, 7km north of Tortuguero village. This small biological research station runs a volunteer program in which visitors can assist with upkeep of the station and ongoing research projects, including sea-turtle and bird monitoring and plant-diversity inventories. Volunteer fees start at US$250 per week and include accommodations in dormitory buildings and three meals per day. A two-week minimum commitment is required. Call ahead to arrange a visit.

Boating & Canoeing

Nonmotorized boat transport obviously offers the best chance of spotting wildlife while exploring the surrounding waterways. Numerous area businesses rent kayaks and canoes and offer boat tours.

Hiking

Hikers can follow the self-guided El Gavilán Land Trail (adjacent to Cuatro Esquinas ranger station); parallel the beach on the well-worn coastal trail north from the village to the airport; or walk the beach during daylight hours. Other hiking opportunities exist in and around the park but require the services of a guide. Inquire at the agencies listed under Tours. Note: night hiking in the national park is not allowed.

👉 Tours

Guides have posted signs all over town advertising their services for canal tours and turtle walks. The two most dependable and convenient places to arrange tours are at local hotels and at the official **Asociación de Guías de Tortuguero** (☎2767-0836; www.asoprotur.com) kiosk by the boat landing. Rates at the time of writing were US$20 per person for a two-hour turtle tour (possibly increasing to US$25), and US$20 to US$35 for a two- to three-hour boat tour. Other options include walking (US$20 to US$25), bird-watching (US$35) and fishing (US$65) tours. For more specialized guides, see the list below.

Tinamon Tours   TOUR (☎8842-6561, 2709-8004; www.tinamontours.de) Trained zoologist and 20-year Tortuguero resident Barbara Hartung offers hiking, canoe, cultural and turtle tours in German, English, French or Spanish.

Castor Hunter Thomas TOUR
(☎ 8870-8634; http://castorhunter.blogspot.com; Soda Doña María) Excellent local guide and 40-year Tortuguero resident who has led hikes, turtle tours and canoe tours for over 20 years. Contact Castor at Soda Doña María.

Ballard Excursions TOUR
(www.tortugerovillage.com/ballardexcursions) Ross Ballard, a Canadian with deep local roots, leads 3½-hour walking tours focusing on the biology and ecology of the species-rich rainforest at the foot of Cerro Tortuguero, the region's tallest hill.

Don Chico Tours TOUR
(☎ 2709-8033) Longtime local guide Chico offers both hiking and canoe tours; look for his sign just beyond Miss Miriam's restaurant (towards the beach on the north side of the soccer field).

🛏 Sleeping

🛏 Tortuguero Village

In addition to places listed below, the village has a number of basic *cabinas* (cabins) charging US$18 and up for a double room.

★ Casa Marbella B&B $$
(☎ 2709-8011, 8833-0827; http://casamarbella.tripod.com; incl breakfast s US$35-60, d US$40-65, extra person US$10; @ 🛜) In the heart of the village, with a spacious and delightful canalside deck, this B&B owned by naturalist Daryl Loth is easily Tortuguero's most appealing in-town option. Ten simple, well-lit rooms come with ceiling fans, superclean bathrooms and hearty breakfasts served overlooking the water.

Streetside rooms pick up some noise from Tortuguero's village bustle during daylight hours; reserve ahead for the three popular upstairs rooms (one facing the river). It's a two-minute walk north (left) from the village boat landing.

Princesa del Mar CABINA $
(☎ 2709-8131; albertovr2206@hotmail.com; r per person US$10, incl breakfast US$15; 🛜 🖾) This oceanfront spot offers excellent value for budget travelers. A clapboard structure with 22 basic wood-and-concrete rooms faces an open garden with two pools (one for children), and there's an onsite restaurant with

ocean views serving Caribbean-Tico cuisine. It's 50m east of the Guardia Rural post on main street, or about 100m up the beach from the soccer field.

Cabinas Miss Miriam II CABINA $
(☎ 8873-2671, 2709-8107; rojasmauricio45@yahoo.com; s/d with fan US$20/25, d with ocean-view terrace US$35, d with air-con US$40; 🛜) This beachside branch of Miss Miriam's budget *cabinas* has clean tiled rooms surrounding a small garden courtyard. All have firm mattresses and hot water, and a couple offer air-con. Best is the fan-and-breeze-cooled front room with its own ocean-view terrace. Breakfast costs US$5 extra per person. It's south of the soccer field, 25m east of the Adventist church.

La Casona CABINA $
(☎ 2709-8092, 2709-8047; lacasonadetortuguero@yahoo.com; s/d US$18/25, d with kitchenette US$35; 🛜) Ten cute cement rooms with rustic touches surround a garden at this family-run spot. Three units have kitchenettes with hot plates. It has a pleasant restaurant that serves Caribbean and Italian meals, and the managers can help arrange tours. It's on the north side of the soccer field.

Hotel Miss Junie CABINA $$
(☎ 2709-8102; www.iguanaverdetours.com; incl breakfast s/d standard US$45/50, superior US$55/65; 🛜) Tortuguero's longest-established lodging, Miss Junie's place is set on spacious palm-shaded grounds strewn with hammocks and wooden armchairs. Spotless wood-paneled rooms in a nicely kept tropical-plantation-style building are tastefully decorated with wood accents and bright bedspreads. Upstairs rooms share a breezy balcony overlooking the canal. It's at the northern end of the town's main street.

🛏 North of the Village

Most of the lodges north and west of the village cater to high-end travelers on package deals, though most will accept walk-ins (er, boat-ins) if they aren't full. Multinight packages typically include accommodations, three meals daily, boat and walking tours and transport to/from San José. Note that Mawamba Lodge and Laguna Lodge are on the same peninsula as Tortuguero Village, so you can walk or boat into town. Other lodges lie across the canal and are only accessible by boat or water taxi.

Toucan & Tarpon Lodge
CABINA $

(☑ 8524-1804; www.toucanandtarpon.com; s/d/tr/q incl breakfast US$30/40/45/50) Just across the river from Tortuguero village, this place was opened in late 2013 by Canadian expatriates Jeff and Sue. Three simple *cabinas* with solar electricity and Guatemalan textiles sleep between two and four. Other amenities include delicious homemade breakfasts, a communal kitchen with well-stocked spice cabinet, free canoe use and excellent wildlife-spotting (monkeys, sloths, toucans) in the surrounding trees.

★ Rana Roja
LODGE $$

(☑ 2223-1926, 2709-8260; www.tortugueroranaroja.com; r/cabins per person incl breakfast US$40/45, r or cabins per person incl 3 meals US$60; @ 🛜 ⊠) This Tico-run spot is one of Tortuguero's best value places, especially for solo travelers. Twelve immaculate rooms and five cabins with private terraces and rockers are connected by elevated walkways; all have tile floors, hot showers and awesome jungle views. Free kayaks are available onsite and guests can make use of the pool at the adjacent Evergreen Lodge.

Turtle Beach Lodge
LODGE $$$

(☑ 2248-0707, after hours 8837-6969; www.turtlebeachlodge.com; 2-night package per adult/child US$299/90; @ ⊠) 🌿 Surrounded by 70 hectares of tropical gardens and rainforest, Tortuguero's northernmost lodge (8km outside the village) is flanked by beach and river. Spacious wood cabins have tile floors, hardwood furniture and huge screened windows. Guests can explore the onsite network of jungle trails, kayak the adjacent canal, or lounge around the turtle-shaped pool or thatch-roofed hammock hut.

Tortuga Lodge & Gardens
LODGE $$$

(☑ 2521-6099, 2257-0766; www.tortugalodge.com; r US$138-238, 2-night package per adult/child US$548/348; 🛜 ⊠) This elegant lodge, operated by Costa Rica Expeditions, is set amid 20 serene hectares of private gardens, directly across the canal from Tortuguero's airstrip. The 27 demure rooms channel a 19th-century safari vibe, with creamy linens, handmade textiles, vintage photos and broad terraces that invite lounging. The grounds come equipped with private trails and a riverside pool, bar and restaurant.

Evergreen Lodge
LODGE $$$

(☑ 2222-6841; evergreentortuguero.com; 2-night package per adult/child US$258/129; 🛜 ⊠) One of three hotels operated by the Pachira group, this pleasant place has a more rustic, less resorty feel than its counterparts, with 60 newly remodeled rooms and private bungalows surrounded by jungle greenery. Guests have access to a sunny pool area, Tortuguero's only canopy tour (US$30), free use of kayaks and an upstairs bar overlooking the river.

Laguna Lodge
LODGE $$$

(☑ 2272-4943, in USA 888-259-5615; www.lagunatortuguero.com; 2-night package per adult/child US$299/150; 🛜 ⊠) This expansive lodge, liberally decorated with gorgeous mosaic art and trim, has 110 graceful rooms with high ceilings and wide decks lined with Sarchí-made leather rocking chairs. It also has a restaurant, two bars (canalside and poolside), a massage room, a soccer pitch and a Gaudí-esque reception area.

Pachira Lodge
LODGE $$$

(☑ 2257-2242, 2256-6340; www.pachiralodge.com; 2-night package per adult/child US$299/150; 🛜 ⊠) A sprawling compound set on 5 landscaped hectares of land, this 88-room hotel with turtle-shaped pool is a popular family spot. Pristine, brightly painted clapboard bungalows with shared terraces house blocks of rooms that sleep up to four. Cribs and children's beds are available.

Mawamba Lodge
LODGE $$$

(☑ 2293-8181, 2709-8181; www.mawamba.com; 2-night package per adult/child US$299/150; 🛜 ⊠) With pool tables, foosball, a mosaic swimming pool, and butterfly and frog gardens, this lodge sits between the canal and Tortuguero's main turtle-nesting beach, within walking distance of town. Simple wood-paneled rooms have firm beds, good fans and spacious bathrooms with hot water. All are fronted by wide verandas with hammocks and rocking chairs.

Hotel Aninga & Spa
LODGE $$$

(☑ 2222-6840, 2222-6841; www.aningalodgetortuguero.com; 2-night package per adult/child US$299/150; 🛜 ⊠) One of the trio of lodges run by the Pachira Group, this place 1km north of the village has similar grounds and facilities to the adjacent Pachira Lodge, along with Tortuguero's only spa. Non-guests can make appointments for massages (US$40 to US$80) and other treatments here.

✖ Eating

★ Taylor's Place   CARIBBEAN $

(mains US$7-10; ⏰ 6-8:30pm) Low-key atmosphere and high-quality cooking come together beautifully at this backstreet eatery southwest of the soccer field. The inviting garden setting, with chirping insects, and picnic benches spread under colorful paper lanterns, is rivaled only by friendly chef Ray Taylor's culinary artistry. House specialties include beef in tamarind sauce, grilled fish in garlic sauce, and fruit drinks both alcoholic and otherwise.

Sunrise Restaurant   CARIBBEAN $

(mains US$4-8; ⏰ 9:30am-9pm Wed-Mon) Between the boat dock and the national park, this cozy log-cabin-like place will lure you in with the delicious smoky aroma of its grilled chicken and pork ribs, but it also serves breakfast and a full Caribbean menu at lunch and dinnertime, at some of the best prices in town.

Miss Miriam's   CARIBBEAN $

(mains US$9.50; ⏰ 8am-9pm) This little place on the north side of the soccer field dishes out flavorful local food, including pork chops, fish and well-spiced Caribbean chicken.

Soda Doña María   COSTA RICAN $

(☑ 8870-8634; dishes US$5-8; ⏰ 7:30am-8pm) Recover from a hike in the park at this riverside soda, serving jugos (juices), burgers and casados. It's about 200m north of the park entrance.

Miss Junie's   CARIBBEAN $$

(☑ 2709-8029; mains US$13-20; ⏰ 7-9am, noon-2pm & 6-9pm) Over the years, Tortuguero's best-known eatery has grown from a personal kitchen to a full-blown restaurant. Prices have climbed accordingly, but the menu remains true to its roots: chicken, fish and whole lobster cooked in flavorful Caribbean sauces, with coconut rice and beans. It's at the northern end of the main street.

Wild Ginger   FUSION $$

(☑ 2709-8240; www.wildgingercr.com; mains US$8-26; ⏰ noon-9pm) Run by a Tico-Californian couple, this low-lit spot near the beach north of town specializes in fusion cuisine incorporating fresh local ingredients, such as lobster mango ceviche (seafood marinated in lemon or lime juice, garlic and seasonings), Caribbean beef stew and passionfruit crème brûlée. It's 150m north of the elementary school.

Budda Cafe   EUROPEAN $$

(mains US$7-10, pizzas US$9-20; ⏰ noon-8:30pm; ☑) Ambient club music and stenciled 'om' symbols impart a hipster vibe to this cafe between the main road and the river. It's a pleasant setting for pizzas, cocktails and crepes (savory and sweet). Grab a table outside for a prime view of the yellow-bellied flycatchers zipping across the water.

☕ Drinking & Nightlife

La Culebra   BAR

(⏰ 8pm-close) Next to the public dock in the center of town, this bright-purple nightclub (Tortuguero's one and only) plays thumping music and serves beer and bocas right on the canal.

La Taberna Punto de Encuentro   BAR

(⏰ 11am-11pm) Adjacent to the Super Bambú pulpería (corner store), this popular tavern is mellow in the afternoons but draws the party people after dark with cold beer and blaring reggaetón. The highlight, however, is the life-size statue of Jar Jar Binks.

ℹ Information

The community's website, **Tortuguero Village** (www.tortuguerovillage.com), is a solid source of information, listing local businesses and providing comprehensive directions on how to get to Tortuguero.

There are no banks or ATMs in town and only a few businesses accept credit cards, so bring all the cash you'll need. Several local accommodations have internet connections, but these can be iffy, especially during heavy rains.

Centro de Información Turístico PNT (⏰ 6am-6:30pm) Immediately to the left of the boat landing; staffed by members of the local tour guides' association.

ℹ Getting There & Away

If you're coming from San José, the two most convenient ways to get to Tortuguero are by air or all-inclusive bus-boat shuttles – though budget travelers can save money by taking public transit.

If coming from the southern Caribbean, your best bets are the private boat operators from Moín (just outside Puerto Limón) or shuttle deals from Cahuita and Puerto Viejo.

AIR

The small airstrip is 4km north of Tortuguero village. **Nature Air** (☑ 2299-6000; www.natureair.com) has early-morning flights daily to/from San José and twice weekly to La Fortuna. Charter flights land regularly here as well.

BUS & BOAT

The classic public-transit route to Tortuguero is by bus from San José to Cariari to La Pavona, then by boat from La Pavona to Tortuguero. Alternatively, Tortuguero is accessible by private boat from Moín, near Puerto Limón on the Caribbean coast.

From San José/Cariari

From San José, take the 6:10am, 9am or 10:30am bus to Cariari (three hours) from Gran Terminal del Caribe. In Cariari, you will arrive at a bus station at the south end of town (known as the *estación nueva*). From here, walk or take a taxi 500m north to the *estación vieja* (old station), otherwise referred to as the Terminal Caribeño. Here you can catch a local Coopetraca bus (US$2.20, 6am, 9am, 11:30am and 3pm) to La Pavona, where you'll transfer onto the boat (US$3.20 to US$4) to Tortuguero.

On the return trip, boats leave Tortuguero for La Pavona daily at 5:30am, 9am, 11am and 2:45pm, connecting with Cariari-bound buses at the La Pavona dock.

From Moín

Moín–Tortuguero is primarily a tourist route. While there isn't a scheduled service, boats do ply these canals frequently. When running, boats typically depart at 10am in either direction, charging US$30 to US$40 for the three- to five-hour trip. With advance notice, these same boats can stop in Parismina (one way from either Tortuguero or Moín US$25). Bear in mind that it may take 24 to 48 hours to secure transportation – especially in the low season. For onward transportation beyond Moín, catch a local bus (US$0.60, 20 minutes) to Puerto Limón's bus terminal.

Tropical Wind (☎8327-0317, 2798-6059) and **Viajes Bananoro** (☎2709-8005; per person 1 way US$35) are two Tortuguero-based agencies that make the run regularly. Alternatively, you can make arrangements with companies operating out of Puerto Limón.

SHUTTLE SERVICES

If you prefer to leave the planning to someone else, convenient shuttle services can whisk you to Tortuguero from San José, Arenal-La Fortuna or the southern Caribbean coast in just a few hours. Shuttle companies typically offer minivan service to La Pavona or Moín, where waiting boats take you the rest of the way to Tortuguero. This is a relatively inexpensive, hassle-free option, as you only have to buy a single ticket, and guides help you negotiate the van-to-boat transfer.

Jungle Tom Safaris (☎2221-7878; www.jungle-tomsafaris.com) Offers one-way shuttles between Tortuguero and San José (US$17), Cahuita (US$39), Puerto Viejo (US$39) and Arenal-La Fortuna (US$55), as well as all-inclusive day trips (US$99), overnight packages (from US$120) and two-night packages (from US$152).

Caribe Shuttle (☎8849-7600, 2750-0626; http://caribeshuttle.com/from-tortuguero) Shuttles from Puerto Viejo (US$65) and Arenal-La Fortuna (US$55).

Willie's Tours (p169) Shuttles from Cahuita (US$65).

Terraventuras (p179) Shuttles from Puerto Viejo (US$65).

Gecko Trail (p179) Shuttles from Puerto Viejo and Cahuita (US$70 each).

Ride CR (☎2479-9833; www.ridecr.com) Shuttles from Arenal-La Fortuna (US$55).

Riverboat Francesca Nature Tours (☎2226-0986; www.tortuguerocanals.com) Shuttles from San José to Tortuguero via Moín (US$75, including lunch) as well as package deals including accommodation.

Exploradores Outdoors (☎2222-6262, www.exploradoresoutdoors.com) More expensive package deals that include transport from San José, Puerto Viejo or Arenal-La Fortuna, a mid-journey Río Pacuare rafting trip, and accommodations in Tortuguero.

ⓘ GETTING TO SAN JUAN DE NICARAGUA

If you're planning to head further into Nicaragua, you can make arrangements with your lodge for a water taxi to take you to the border town of San Juan del Norte – now called San Juan de Nicaragua (or Greytown). It's a tranquil village, with few services but an interesting history. At various times over the centuries, it has been under the control of Miskito people, Spanish colonists, British troops and even US Marines. Much of it was destroyed during the Contra-Sandinista conflict of the 1980s.

This is a little-used border crossing, however, so don't make the trip without first checking in with **Costa Rican immigration officials** (☎in Puerto Limón 2798-2097, in San José 2299-8100). Barra del Colorado does not have an immigration office of its own, so you may need to secure an exit stamp prior to arriving there.

In San Juan de Nicaragua, **Río Indio Ecolodge** (☎2231-4299, 2220-3594; www.therio-indiolodge.com; s/d incl meals US$200/336; @☒) has 34 spacious polished-wood rooms, a restaurant and bar. Fishing is the thing to do, but you can also go hiking or kayaking.

San Juan is linked to the rest of Nicaragua by irregular passenger boats sailing up the Río San Juan to San Carlos, on the Lago de Nicaragua.

JONATHAN GREGSON / LONELY PLANET ©

KRYSSIA CAMPOS / GETTY IMAGES ©

OLIVER JONES / GETTY IMAGES ©

MATTHEW MICAH WRIGHT / GETTY IMAGES ©

1. Pargo (red snapper) dish
Seafood is plentiful in Costa Rica, and snapper appears in many dishes.

2. Refugio Nacional de Vida Silvestre Gandoca-Manzanillo (p190)
A highlight of this reserve, which protects nearly 70% of Costa Rica's southern Caribbean coast, is its pristine jungle-backed beaches.

3. Cricket, Parque Nacional Tortuguero (p154)
Most visitors come to see the green sea turtles, but Tortuguero teems with all kinds of wildlife.

4. Puerto Viejo de Talamanca (p176)
There are plenty of beautiful beaches on this stretch of coast.

Refugio Nacional de Vida Silvestre Barra del Colorado

At 904 sq km, including the frontier zone with Nicaragua, Refugio Nacional de Vida Silvestre Barra del Colorado, or 'Barra' for short, is the biggest national wildlife refuge in Costa Rica. It is also one of the most remote – more so since Costa Rica's commercial airlines suspended service to the area in 2009. This means that the only way to get to Barra is via local bus-boat transportation from Cariari, charter boat from Tortuguero or charter flight from San José.

The area has long been a favorite of sportfishers, who arrive to hook gar, tarpon and snook. But those who aren't into fishing will be rewarded with the incredible landscape. The Ríos San Juan, Colorado and Chirripó all wind through the refuge and out to the Caribbean Sea – through a soggy wetland habitat made up of marshes, mangroves and lagoons. Here, you'll find West Indian manatees, caimans, monkeys, tapirs and three-toed sloths, plus a riotous bird population that includes everything from keel-billed toucans to white hawks. There are countless species of water bird.

The northern border of the refuge is the Río San Juan, the border with Nicaragua (many local residents are Nicaraguan nationals). This area was politically sensitive during the 1980s, due to the Nicaraguan conflict. Today, however, it's possible to journey north along the Río Sarapiquí and east along the Río San Juan, technically entering Nicaragua. While Costa Ricans have right of use, foreign travelers should carry a passport and the official US$25 permit fee when out fishing.

The village of Barra del Colorado lies near the mouth of the Río Colorado and is divided by the river into Barra del Norte and Barra del Sur. The airstrip is on the south side, but more people live along the north side. The area outside the village is swampy and there are no roads; travel is almost exclusively by boat.

☂ Activities

Fishing is the bread and butter of area lodges, and anglers go for tarpon from January to June and snook from September to December. Fishing is good year-round, however, and other catches include barracuda, mackerel and jack crevalle, all inshore; or bluegill, *guapote* (rainbow bass) and mach-

aca in the rivers. There is also deep-sea fishing for marlin, sailfish and tuna, though this is probably better on the Pacific. Dozens of fish can be hooked on a good day, so 'catch and release' is an important conservation policy of all the lodges.

All of the lodges can also organize custom wildlife-watching excursions along mangroves, lagoons and canals (from US$40).

🛏 Sleeping & Eating

Places listed below are all west of the airstrip, on the south side of the river. Tarpon Land Lodge is accessible on foot. Other lodges will have a boat waiting when you arrive with prior reservation. There are also a few basic family-run *cabinas* between the airstrip and the beach, charging US$25 to US$40 per night.

Tarpon Land Lodge   CABINA $
(☎ 8818-9921;   tarponlandlodge@hotmail.com; s/d US$20/24, with sportfishing & full board US$350/550; ☒) Situated right next to the airstrip, this is Barra's most dependable budget option. The 16 worn wood rooms have hot showers, while the attached restaurant-bar is a local gathering spot and a good place for fish *casados* (mains from US$6).

Río Colorado Lodge   LODGE $$$
(☎ 2232-4063, in USA 800-243-9777; www.riocoloradolodge.com; r per person incl 3 meals US$175, incl 3 meals, 8hr fishing trip & happy hour US$550; ☀☎) Owned by a retired Mississippi lawyer, this 18-room lodge is housed in a rambling tropical-style building with breezy rooms connected by covered walkways, a pool table and an outdoor deck with satellite TV. Its bar, within walking distance of the landing strip, attracts a local crowd, and regular afternoon happy hours have reinforced its reputation as a 'party lodge.'

Silver King Lodge   LODGE $$$
(☎ 2794-0139, in USA 877-335-0755; www.silverkinglodge.com; 3-day package per person US$2750-3960; ☀@☒) This excellent sportfishing lodge caters to couples and families. Huge hardwood rooms have cane ceilings and lots of amenities. Outside, covered walkways lead to a large swimming pool and jacuzzi. Bounteous meals are served buffet-style and an open-air bar whips up tropical drinks. Rates include equipment, fishing license and air transport to and from San José.

ℹ Information

A couple of *pulperías* and a souvenir shop alongside the landing strip sell basic food supplies and dry goods. There is a public phone and patchy internet access. The Servicio de Parques Nacionales (SPN) maintains a small **ranger station** (refuge admission US$10, 60-day freshwater fishing license US$30; ⊘ 6am-6pm) west of the village, in Barra del Sur. However, there are no facilities here. Bring exact change to pay for your entry fee, as the rangers rarely have change.

ℹ Getting There & Away

Public bus-boat transportation from Cariari is the cheapest transport option. Take the 4am or 2pm bus from Cariari to Puerto Lindo (US$5, 2½ hours), then transfer to the boat for Barra del Colorado (US$6, 45 minutes). Return boats from Barra del Colorado to Puerto Lindo leave at 5am and 3pm.

An alternative, more scenic way to reach Barra del Colorado is by chartering a boat from Tortuguero. The 90-minute trip costs upwards of US$100 (price varies depending on gas prices, season and number of passengers). A recommended guide is **Roberto Abram** (☑ 8818-8749), who can be contacted through Casa Marbella in Tortuguero village; he also leads local river trips originating in Barra del Colorado.

Otherwise, most folks get here on air charters from San José arranged by the individual lodges.

SOUTHERN CARIBBEAN

The southern coast is the heart and soul of Costa Rica's Afro-Caribbean community. Jamaican workers arrived in the middle of the 19th century to build the railroad and then stayed on to serve as labor for United Fruit. After the banana industry began its decline in the 1920s, government-mandated segregation kept the black community here. For more than eight decades, they existed independently of the rest of Costa Rica, managing subsistence farms, speaking English and Mekatelyu, eating spicy Caribbean gumbos and swaying to the beat of calypso. Although the racial borders fell in 1949, the local culture retains its unique traditions.

Also in this area, to the interior, are some of the country's most prominent indigenous groups – cultures that have managed to remain intact despite several centuries' worth of incursions, first from the Spanish, later from the fruit industry and currently from the globalizing effects of tourism. They principally inhabit the Cocles/Kèköldi, Talamanca Cabécar and Bribrí indigenous territories.

Naturally, this fascinating cultural bubble wouldn't remain isolated forever. Since the 1980s the southern coast has seen the arrival of surfers, backpackers and adventurous families on holiday – many of whom have stayed, adding Italian, German and North American inflections to the cultural stew. For the traveler, it is a rich and rewarding experience – with lovely beaches to boot.

Reserva Biológica Hitoy-Cerere

One of Costa Rica's most rugged and rarely visited reserves, Hitoy-Cerere (☑ 2795-3170; admission US$6; ⊘ 8am-4pm) is only about 60km south of Puerto Limón. The 99-sq-km reserve sits on the edge of the Cordillera de Talamanca, characterized by varying altitudes, evergreen forests and rushing rivers. This may be one of the wettest reserves in the parks system, inundated with 4000mm to 6000mm of rain annually.

Naturally, wildlife is abundant. The most commonly sighted mammals include gray four-eyed opossums, tayras (a type of weasel), and howler and capuchin monkeys. There are plenty of ornithological delights as well (with more than 230 avian species), including keel-billed toucans, spectacled owls, green kingfishers and the ubiquitous Montezuma oropendola, whose massive nests dangle from the trees like twiggy pendulums. The moisture, in the meantime, keeps the place hopping with various species of poison-dart frog.

The reserve is surrounded by some of the country's most remote indigenous reserves, which you can visit with a local guide.

Although there is a ranger station with bathrooms at the reserve entrance, there are no other facilities nearby. A 9km trail leads south to a waterfall, but it is steep, slippery and poorly maintained. Jungle boots are recommended.

ℹ Getting There & Away

By car (4WD recommended) from Puerto Limón, head south to Penshurst. Just south of the Río Estrella bridge, head west on the signed road to Valle de la Estrella. Another sign at the bus stop sends you down a dirt road about 15km to the reserve.

Cahuita

POP 8300

Even as tourism has mushroomed on Costa Rica's southern coast, Cahuita has managed to hold onto its laid-back Caribbean vibe. The roads are made of dirt, many of the older houses rest on stilts and chatty neighbors still converse in Mekatelyu. A graceful black-sand beach and a chilled-out demeanor hint at a not-so-distant past, when the area was little more than a string of cacao farms.

Cahuita proudly claims the area's first permanent Afro-Caribbean settler: a turtle fisherman named William Smith, who moved his family to Punta Cahuita in 1828. Now his descendants, along with those of so many other West Indian immigrants, run the backyard eateries and brightly painted bungalows that hug this idyllic stretch of coast.

Situated on a pleasant point, the town itself has a waterfront but no beach. For that, most folks make the five-minute jaunt up the coast to Playa Negra or southeast into neighboring Parque Nacional Cahuita.

◉ Sights & Activities

★ Playa Negra   BEACH

At the northwest end of Cahuita, Playa Negra is a long, black-sand beach flying the *bandera azul ecológica*, a flag that indicates the beach is kept to the highest ecological standards. This is undoubtedly Cahuita's top spot for swimming and is never crowded. When the swells are big, this place also has an excellent beach break for beginners.

Playa Blanca   BEACH

At the entrance to the national park. A good option for swimming.

Tree of Life   GARDENS

(☏ 2755-0014, 8610-0490; www.treeoflifecostarica.com; adult/child US$12/6, guided tour US$15-20; ⊙ 9am-3pm Tue-Sun Nov–mid-Apr, daily tour 11am

Cahuita

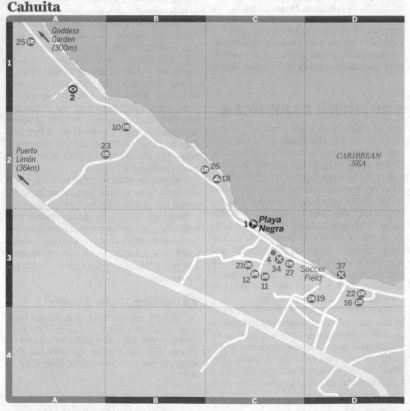

Jul & Aug, closed mid-Apr–Jun & Sep-Oct) This lovingly maintained wildlife center and botanical garden 3km northwest of town on the Playa Negra road rescues and rehabilitates animals while also promoting conservation through education. The rotating cast of residents typically includes kinkajous, peccaries, sloths, monkeys and toucans. There's excellent English-language signage throughout. It's also possible to volunteer here; see the website for information.

Sloth Sanctuary of Costa Rica
WILDLIFE RESERVE

(formerly Aviarios del Caribe; ☑2750-0775; www.slothsanctuary.com; 2hr group tour adult/child 5-11yr US$25/15, private half-day tour per person US$150; ☺8am-2pm Tue-Sun) About 10km northwest of Cahuita, bordering the Río Estrella, the Arroyo family runs this private 88-hectare wildlife sanctuary dedicated to caring for injured and orphaned sloths. Visitors can observe these unique animals

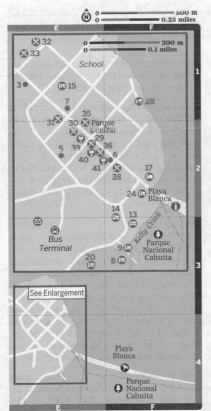

up close on group or private tours. (Irrefutable fact: there is nothing cuter than a baby sloth.) Though many of the reserve's rehabilitated sloths lack the skills to return to the wild, the Arroyos have successfully released more than 100 of them back into area forests.

Tours

Snorkeling, horseback riding, chocolate tours and visits to nearby indigenous territories are standard offerings.

Willie's Tours
TOUR

(☑8917-6982, 2755-1024; www.williestourscostarica.com; ☺8am-noon & 2-7pm Mon-Sat, 5-7pm Sun) A full-service tour agency that can also arrange further-flung tours and transport.

Centro Turístico Brigitte
HORSE RIDING

(☑2755-0053; www.brigittecahuita.com; Playa Negra) Does it all, but specializes in horseback tours (90 minutes to six hours, US$40 to US$85) and surf lessons (US$30 including use of board); check website or stop by in person for full details.

Cahuita Tours
TOUR

(☑2755-0101; www.cahuitatours.com) One of the most established agencies in town.

Mister Big J's
TOUR

(☑2755-0060, 8887-4695; ☺8am-7:30pm) Offers the usual range of tours.

Roberto's Tours
FISHING

(☑2755-0117; aventurasrobertocr@yahoo.com) Specializes in sportfishing tours *and* has a restaurant for cooking up your catch.

Sleeping

There are two general areas to stay in Cahuita: the town center (which can be a little noisy) or north of town along Playa Negra. If walking between Playa Negra and the center at night, don't carry valuables; better yet, bike or take a taxi, especially if traveling alone.

Center

Cabinas Secret Garden
CABINA $

(☑2755-0581; koosiecosta@live.nl; dm/s/d US$10/18/25; 🅿🛜) This tiny Dutch-run place with a lush garden has five tiled units with fans, mosquito nets and hot-water showers in cubicle-style bathrooms, plus one five-bed dorm with cold showers. There's also a nice shared kitchen with free coffee.

Cahuita

Cabinas Riverside   CABINA $
(☑ 8893-2252; d with/without kitchen US$27/23; ℗) Managed by friendly Cahuita local Peck Ferguson and family, this tidy budget place just around the corner from Kelly Creek ranger station offers nine simple rooms with mosquito nets and hot showers; five units also come with kitchens. The grassy yard abuts a swampy area perfect for spotting caimans, monkeys and sloths.

Cahuita National Park Hotel   HOTEL $
(☑ 2755-0244; hotelnationalpark03@gmail.com; s or d US$45, tr or q US$60; ℗❄️🛜) The hotel-style rooms here are large and bare, with dowdy brown curtains and industrial tile floors, but you still might be tempted by the prime location right at the national-park entrance. Beach and ocean views from the upstairs terrace (and several rooms) are spectacular.

Cabinas Smith 1 & 2   CABINA $
(☑ 2755-0068; s/d/tr with fan US$12/16/21, s/d/tr/q with air-con US$25/31/36/46; ℗❄️🛜) These clean rooms spanning two properties between the main drag and the waterfront are run by a friendly older couple with deep local roots. Eight newer units adjacent to the owners' home have TV, air-con and wi-fi; five

older fan-cooled units around the corner are primarily of interest to the seriously budget-minded. All share a guest kitchen.

Spencer Seaside Lodging   CABINA $
(☑ 2755-0027; s/d downstairs US$16/26, upstairs US$20/30; ℗) Rooms at this longtime, locally owned spot are rough around the edges but big – and nothing at this price level can match the seaside setting within two blocks of the town center. Upstairs units have better views, as well as a shared terrace strung with hammocks.

★**Alby Lodge**   BUNGALOW $$
(☑ 2755-0031; www.albylodge.com; d/tr/q US$60/65/70; ℗🛜) This fine German-run lodge on the edge of the park has spacious landscaped grounds that attract howler monkeys and birds. Four raised bungalows (two sleeping three people, two sleeping four) are spread out, allowing for plenty of privacy. High ceilings, mosquito nets and driftwood details make for pleasant jungle decor. A common *rancho* (thatched gazebo) has excellent communal kitchen facilities.

Kelly Creek Hotel   CABINA $$
(☑ 2755-0007; www.hotelkellycreek.com; s/d US$50/60, extra person US$10; ℗🛜) At this

place just outside the national-park entrance, you may be serenaded by the dulcet squawks of the resident parrot; draw closer and find four graceful natural-wood *cabinas* with high ceilings, cream-colored linens and mosquito nets. Local artwork adorns the reception area, and the onsite restaurant (open from 6pm) serves paella with advance notice (US$16 per person, minimum two people).

Bungalows Aché
BUNGALOW **$$**
(2755-0119; www.bungalowsache.com; bungalows s US$45, d US$50-55; P🐾) In Nigeria, Aché means 'Amen,' and you'll likely say the same thing when you see these three spotless polished-wood bungalows nestled into a grassy yard bordering the national park. Each octagonal unit comes with a lockbox, minifridge, kettle and small private deck with hammock. A three-bedroom vacation house (doubles US$70, up to seven people US$120) is available 1km inland.

Ciudad Perdida
BUNGALOW **$$$**
(2755-0303; www.ciudadperdidaecolodge.com; d standard/superior incl breakfast US$106/127, q US$212, P🐾) In a shady, peaceful spot bordering the national park but only a five-minute walk from Cahuita's town center, this eco-conscious lodge offers cute one- and two-room, candy-colored wood bungalows surrounded by landscaped gardens. All include hammocks, ceiling fans, refrigerators and safe boxes. One house has a Jacuzzi, three have kitchens and all have cable TV.

🛏 Playa Negra

Cabinas Tito
BUNGALOW **$**
(8880-1904, 2755-0286; www.cahuita-cabinas-tito.com; d with/without hot water US$30/25, additional person US$10, 4-person houses US$70; P🐾) Only 200m northwest of Cahuita, yet surrounded by extensive tropical gardens and banana plants, this quiet family-run oasis offers seven brightly painted, clean and simple *casitas* (one with kitchen) plus a family-friendly Caribbean-style house. Tito, the kind and charming young Tico (Costa Rican) host, is a recent university graduate who's actively seeking to create habitat for birds, frogs and other wildlife.

Cabinas Algebra
BUNGALOW **$**
(2755-0057; www.cabinasalgebra.com; bungalows US$20-35; P🐾) This long-time German-Swiss-run place has three rustic cabins, with hammocks, tucked into a peaceful backyard garden at Playa Negra's northern end. The

spacious, inviting front deck doubles as a restaurant and common area, with wood floors, books, games and wi-fi. It's 2km northwest of Cahuita, but the owners offer free bus-station pickup with advance notice.

Centro Turístico Brigitte
CABINA **$**
(2755-0053; www.brigittecahuita.com; cabinas US$30-50, s without bathroom US$15; P@🐾) Behind Reggae Restaurant in the heart of Playa Negra, this well-signed backstreet spot offers a couple of basic wood *cabinas* and two private single rooms. However, the big draw here is the bevy of services offered by Swiss expatriate owner Brigitte (a 30-year Cahuita resident): surf classes, bike rentals, horseback rides, tours, laundry service and a good onsite restaurant.

Camping María
CAMPGROUND **$**
(2755-0091; mmizell12@hotmail.com; campsites per person US$6, incl tent rental US$7; 🐾) Seven sweet and well-spaced campsites share a gorgeous section of waterfront near the northern end of Playa Negra, shaded by coconut palms and a variety of fruit trees. Campers have access to rudimentary cooking facilities, two bathrooms with cold-water showers and an upstairs library and recreation room with guitar and pool table. María brews free morning coffee for everyone.

Cabinas Iguana
CABINA **$$**
(2755-0005; http://cabinas-iguana.com/en; d bungalow US$45-55, d without bathroom US$25; P🐾) Set back from the beach on the road marked by the Reggae Restaurant, this Tico-family-run spot features rather faded but nicely shaded simple wood cabins of various sizes, all nestled into forested grounds with abundant wildlife.

★ Playa Negra Guesthouse
BUNGALOW **$$**
(2755-0127; www.playanegra.cr; s/d US$70/85, cottages US$110-160; P🐾) Managed by a delightful Québecois couple, this meticulously maintained place offers three charming rooms in a Caribbean-style plantation house, complemented by three kitchen-equipped storybook cottages. Tropical accents include colorful mosaics in the bathrooms and cozy wicker lounge furniture on the private verandas. A lovely pool, honor bar and barbecue area are tucked into the well-manicured garden dotted with fan palms.

Every unit has thoughtful touches, including a minifridge and coffeemaker, and the staff go out of their way to help guests explore the area. A winner all around.

La Piscina Natural CABINA $$
(☑2755-0146; piscinanatural@cahuita.cr; d/tr US$45/60; P❋⚅) Run by Cahuita native Walter and former Colorado schooteacher Patty, this chilled-out gem of a spot near Playa Negra's northern end is a self-proclaimed 'Caribbean Paradise'. The rooms, which share access to a huge kitchen and open-air lounge, are comfortable enough, but what really make this place special are the lush grounds, gorgeous waterfront and stunning, rock-fringed natural ocean-water pool.

Cabinas Nirvana CABINA $$
(☑2755-0110; www.cabinasnirvana.com; d US$30, cottages US$45-85; ❋❋⚅) Eight *cabinas* come in a variety of configurations at this tranquil garden spot surrounding a pool, just inland from the Reggae Restaurant. Five units have kitchens, one has air-con and all have pleasant sitting areas on private front porches. There's also one cheaper room for budget travelers. Friendly Portuguese-German owners Yolanda and Sepp rent bikes for easy access to town.

Casa Marcellino CABINA $$
(☑2755-0390; http://casamarcellino.com; d US$85-96, q US$102-113; ❋) In a peaceful garden setting, just inland down a side road between Cahuita and Playa Negra, you'll find this Italian-run cluster of spotless wood cabins with fully equipped kitchens. More expensive units have large bathtubs, plus spacious porches with hammocks and retractable awnings.

El Encanto B&B B&B $$
(☑2755-0113; www.elencantocahuita.com; incl breakfast s/d US$75/85, d studio/ste US$105/200, extra person US$25; P❋⚅) This pleasant French-and-Spanish-owned B&B, only about 200m northwest of downtown Cahuita, is set in landscaped grounds dotted with easy chairs and hammocks. Demure bungalows have high ceilings, tile floors and firm beds draped in colorful textiles. The studio and a brand-new upstairs apartment both have fully equipped kitchens.

Hotel Suizo Loco Lodge BUNGALOW $$$
(☑2755-0349; www.suizolocolodge.com; incl breakfast s/d/tr US$85/115/165, ste d/tr US$140/203; P❋⚅) Ten immaculate, whitewashed bungalows have king-size beds and folk-art decor at this serene family-friendly lodge (cribs available). All units have safe, mini-fridge, solar-heated showers and small, private terraces. The perfectly landscaped grounds contain an impressive mosaic-tile pool with a swim-up bar. It's along the road forking off the main Playa Negra road about 2km northwest of Cahuita.

Coral Hill Bungalows BUNGALOW $$$
(☑2755-0479, 2755-0554; www.coralhillbungalows.com; d incl breakfast US$136; ❋) Popular with honeymooners, these three immaculate private bungalows in a wildlife-friendly garden setting are done up with tropical decor: polished-wood floors, bamboo furniture, mosquito nets, hand-painted ceramic sinks and porches with hammocks and leather rocking chairs. Luxuries include pillow-top mattresses, high-thread-count sheets, fresh flowers and full breakfasts served by the gracious American hosts. Follow signs from Reggae Restaurant.

Goddess Garden LODGE $$$
(☑2755-0055, in USA & Canada 800-854-7761; www.thegoddessgarden.com; d 5-night packages incl lodging & 3 meals daily US$1320-1450; P❋⚅) Surrounded by old-growth jungle (including an awe-inspiring 'Goddess Tree'), this place at the end of the Playa Negra road is geared toward larger groups and yoga retreats, but independent travelers looking for a peaceful, meditative five- to seven-day immersion experience are also welcome.

Kenaki Lodge BUNGALOW $$$
(☑2755-0485; www.kenakilodge.com; d incl breakfast US$102, d/tr/q bungalows US$124/124/237; P❋) Directly opposite Playa Grande (the next beach north of Playa Negra), this appealing new place is the creation of Parisian expatriate Isabelle and Costa Rican tae kwon do master Roberto. Three bright, high-ceilinged modern rooms, an older triple bungalow and two brand-new bungalows with satellite TV and modern kitchen fixtures surround a spacious landscaped yard and a wooden breakfast deck.

✗ Eating

✗ Center

Soda Kawe COSTA RICAN $
(☑2755-0233; casados US$6; ⊙5:30am-7pm) This humble spot on Cahuita's main street serves delicious, reasonably priced *casados* cooked over a wood fire. Breakfasts here include free coffee; other meals come with your choice of fruit drink.

OFF THE BEATEN TRACK

A STAY IN THE FOREST: SELVA BANANITO

One of the Caribbean's most inspiring and appealing ecotourism ventures is this rustic but comfortable family-run **farm and lodge** (☎2253-8118, 8375-4419; www.selvabananito. com; s/d incl breakfast from US$85/100, incl full board from US$130/200, incl transport from Bananito, meals & daily activities from US$180/320, 2-night package incl transport from San José, meals & daily activities US$475/860; ℙ) ✍. Gorgeously situated on the edge of Parque Internacional La Amistad, the 1700-hectare private reserve occupies a transitional zone between farmland and primary growth forest, transected by the headwaters of the Río Bananito and teeming with wildlife.

Above all, this is an environmentally conscious spot: the Stein family has owned this property for over 40 years, and has dedicated the last three decades to developing sustainable ecotourism and wise land-management practices. Major projects funded by tourism dollars include education of the local community about ecological issues, protection of the Río Banano and Bananito watersheds (which provide 100% of Puerto Limón's drinking water), reforestation with native species, and efforts to establish a wildlife corridor that will eventually allow jaguars to move freely between Parque Internacional La Amistad and the Caribbean coast.

The onsite lodge employs solar energy and uses biodegradable soaps and cleaning products. Comfortable cabins are all crafted from recycled hardwoods and constructed Caribbean-style, on stilts, for optimum ventilation, and three delicious home-cooked meals are included in the daily rates. Packages include transfers from San José, as well as your choice of activities, including bird-watching, waterfall tours, horseback riding, rappeling and tree-climbing.

If you are driving yourself, note that the last 4km of the route requires river crossings and is 4WD only. Selva Bananito staff can meet you at the first big river if you call ahead. Detailed driving directions are posted online.

Smoothie Bar & Crêpe Café JUICE BAR, CREPERIE **$**
(juices US$1.60-4, crepes US$4-6; ⊗8am-6:30pm)
At this friendly main-street spot, Sherilyn and Eddy whip up fresh fruit crepes and juices mixed with water, milk, yogurt or ice cream. There's always an attractively priced juice of the day (US$1.60), but even better is the *agua de sapo,* a delicious, sinus-clearing Caribbean concoction made with lemon juice, water, brown sugar and *loads* of fresh ginger.

Cafe Chocolatte 100% Natural BAKERY, INTERNATIONAL **$**
(dishes US$4-9; ⊗6:30am-3pm) Greet the morning with a cup o' joe and a warm cinnamon roll, or unwind in the afternoon with a refreshing *jugo*. Breakfast offerings include French toast and waffles, while the lunch menu revolves around salad, spaghetti, baked potatoes and rice dishes. Hearty sandwiches on homemade wholegrain bread are perfect for beach picnics at the national park.

Pizzeria CahuITA PIZZERIA **$$**
(☎2755-0179; pizzas US$5-12; ⊗4-10pm Mon-Wed, noon-10pm Fri-Sun) As the red-white-and-green color scheme implies, the ITA here stands for Italy, motherland of the two expatriate families who opened this excellent, unpretentious pizzeria in 2013. Grab a seat at the aluminum tables on the cement back patio and enjoy a surf and insect serenade while you wait for your thin-crusted beauty to emerge from the wood-fired oven.

Luisa Steak House STEAKHOUSE **$$**
(☎7039-9689; mains US$6-16; ⊗6am-10pm Mon-Sat) In the corner veranda of an old house, this cozy spot specializes in filet mignon, tenderloin and T-bone steaks, but you'll also find plenty of other savory treats, including chicken in jalapeño or coconut sauce, pork chops, grilled seafood skewers and *ceviche.*

Restaurant La Fé SEAFOOD **$$**
(dishes US$7-16; ⊗7am-11pm) Chef and owner Walter, a Cahuita native, serves up tall tales and tasty meals at this reasonably priced spot. There's a laundry list of Tico and Caribbean items, but the main draw is anything doused in the restaurant's spicy-delicious coconut sauce.

Miss Edith's   CARIBBEAN $$
(☑ 2755-0248; mains US$6-24; ⊘ 7am-8pm; 🖍) This longtime local restaurant serves a slew of Caribbean specialties – including jerk chicken and potatoes stewed in garlic – and a number of vegetarian options.

Cocoricó   ITALIAN $
(mains US$7-14; ⊘ 4-10pm Mon-Thu, noon-10pm Sat & Sun) The menu here revolves around pizza, pasta and other Italian-themed mains, but the place is better known for its regular movie screenings.

✖ Playa Negra

Near Playa Negra, you can also head to the restaurants at Cabinas Algebra or Centro Turístico Brigitte for good breakfasts.

Reggae Restaurant   CARIBBEAN $
(mains US$6-10; ⊘ noon-10pm) Exuding a friendly, laid-back vibe, this *soda* serves sandwiches and Caribbean-style *casados* on a wooden deck hung with green, red and yellow lampshades in the heart of Playa Negra. Reggae music and waves crashing on the beach across the street enhance the chilled-out atmosphere.

★ Sobre Las Olas   SEAFOOD $$
(☑ 2755-0109; pastas US$12-15, mains US$12-25; ⊘ noon-10pm Wed-Mon; 🖍) Garlic shrimp, seafood pasta, or fresh grilled fish of the day come accompanied by crashing waves and sparkling blue Caribbean vistas at this sweet spot owned by a lively Tico-Italian couple. Cahuita's top option for romantic waterfront dining, it's only a 400m walk northwest of Cahuita, on the road to Playa Negra. Save room for the delicious *tiramisù*.

🍷 Drinking & Nightlife

Low-key Cahuita is home to one insanely loud drinking hole: **Coco's Bar** (⊘ noon-last man standing). You can't miss it at the main intersection, painted Rasta red, gold and green and cranking the reggaetón up to 11. On some nights (usually on weekends) there's also live music. Across the street you'll find a couple more bars, including **Riki's** and **Splash**, the latter with its own swimming pool.

ℹ Information

The town's helpful website, www.cahuita.cr, has lodging and restaurant information, including pictures of many of the spots listed here. It also has a 'Cahuita Cam' showing live shots of Playa Blanca.

Banco de Costa Rica (⊘ 9am-4pm Mon-Fri) At the bus terminal; has an ATM.

Internet Palmer (per hour US$2; ⊘ 7am-7:30pm) Internet access in the heart of town.

ℹ Getting There & Away

Autotransportes Mepe buses arrive and depart at the bus terminal about 200m southwest of Parque Central.

Sixaola US$3.95; two hours; departs hourly from 6am to 7pm, passing through Bribrí en route.

Puerto Limón US$2.40; 1½ hours; departs half-hourly from 6am to 9pm.

Puerto Viejo de Talamanca/Manzanillo US$1.50/2.40; 30 minutes/one hour; departs roughly every two hours between 7:15am and 7:15pm.

San José US$9.35; four hours; departs 7am, 8am, 9:30am, 11:30am and 4:30pm.

ℹ Getting Around

The best way to get around Cahuita – especially if you're staying out along Playa Negra – is by bicycle. Several places around town rent bikes, including Mister Big J's in Cahuita and Centro Turístico Brigitte in Playa Negra. Most places charge between US$7 and US$10 per day.

CACAO TRAILS

Halfway between Cahuita and Puerto Viejo de Talamanca in Hone Creek, this **botanical garden and chocolate museum** (☑ 2756-8186; www.cacaotrails.com; Hone Creek; guided tour US$25, incl canoe trip & lunch US$47; ⊘ 7am-4pm; 🖍) has a couple of small museums devoted to indigenous and Afro-Caribbean culture, a lush garden bursting with bromeliads and heliconias, as well as an onsite chocolate factory where cacao is processed in traditional ways. Two-hour tours include a visit to all of these spots, plus a hike to a nearby organic farm. Additional expeditions allow for further exploration by canoe on the adjacent Río Carbón. Any bus between Cahuita and Puerto Viejo can drop you at the entrance. This is a great outing for kids.

Parque Nacional Cahuita

This small but beautiful park – just 10 sq km – is one of the more frequently visited national parks in Costa Rica. The reasons are simple: the nearby town of Cahuita provides attractive accommodations and easy access; more importantly, the white-sand beaches, coral reef and coastal rainforest are bursting with wildlife.

Declared a national park in 1978, Cahuita is meteorologically typical of the entire coast (very humid), which results in dense tropical foliage, as well as coconut palms and sea grapes. The area includes the swampy **Punta Cahuita**, which juts into the sea between two stretches of sandy beach. Often flooded, the point is covered with cativo and mango trees and is a popular hangout for birds such as green ibis, yellow-crowned night heron, boat-billed heron and the rare green-and-rufous kingfisher.

Red land and fiddler crab live along the beaches, attracting mammals such as crab-eating raccoon and white-nosed coati. White-faced capuchin, southern opossum and three-toed sloth also live in these parts. The mammal you are most likely to see (and hear) is the mantled howler monkey, which makes its bellowing presence known. The coral reef represents another rich ecosystem that abounds with life.

🏃 Activities

Hiking

An easily navigable 8km **coastal trail** leads through the jungle from Kelly Creek to Puerto Vargas. At times the trail follows the beach; at other times hikers are 100m or so away from the sand. At the end of the first beach, Playa Blanca, hikers must ford the dark Río Perezoso, or 'Sloth River,' which bisects Punta Cahuita. Inquire about conditions before you set out: under normal conditions, this river is easy enough to wade across, but during periods of heavy rain it can become impassable since it serves as the discharge for the swamp that covers the point.

The trail continues around Punta Cahuita to the long stretch of Playa Vargas. It ends at the southern tip of the reef, where it meets up with a road leading to the Puerto Vargas ranger station. Once you reach the ranger station, it's another 1.5km along a gravel road to the park entrance. From here, you can hike the 3.5km back to Ca-

Parque Nacional Cahuita

huita along the coastal highway or catch a ride going in either direction.

Swimming

Almost immediately upon entering the park, you'll see the 2km-long **Playa Blanca** stretching along a gently curving bay to the east. The first 500m of beach may be unsafe for swimming, but beyond that, waves are generally gentle. (Look for green flags marking safe swimming spots.) The rocky Punta Cahuita headland separates this beach from the next one, **Playa Vargas**. It is unwise to leave clothing or other belongings unattended when you swim.

Snorkeling

Parque Nacional Cahuita contains one of the last living coral reefs in Costa Rica. While the reef represents some of the area's best snorkeling, it has incurred damage over the years from earthquakes and tourism-related activities. In an attempt to protect the reef from further damage, snorkeling is only permitted with a licensed guide. The going rate for one person is about US$25.

You'll find that conditions vary greatly, depending on the weather and other factors. In general, the drier months in the highlands (from February to April) are best for snorkeling on the coast, as less runoff results in less silt in the sea. Conditions are often cloudy at other times.

Volunteering

Though not renowned as a sea-turtle destination, Cahuita's beaches are nonetheless an important habitat for several breeds. Asociación Widecast (☑2236-0947; www.widecast. org) has volunteering opportunities for those interested in assisting on in-water research projects and various conservation-related activities. Reserve in advance.

It's also possible to volunteer at Tree of Life (p168) wildlife-rescue center, on the road to Playa Negra.

✖ Eating

Boca Chica　　　ITALIAN, COSTA RICAN $
(☑2755-0415; meals US$8-10; ◷9am-6pm) After a long, hot jungle hike, you may think you're hallucinating when you see this small, whitewashed place at the end of the road. It's not a mirage, just a well-placed bar-restaurant, run by charming Italian expatriate Rodolfo and his Tica wife, Karen. The menu features cold *jugos,* Caribbean specialties, homemade pastas and delicious *platos del día* from noon onwards.

❶ Information

The **Kelly Creek ranger station** (☑2755-0461; admission by donation; ◷6am-5pm) is convenient to the town of Cahuita, while 3.5km down Hwy 36 is the well-signed **Puerto Vargas ranger station** (☑2755-0302; admission US$10; ◷8am-4pm Mon-Fri, 7am-5pm Sat & Sun).

Visitors who enter the park at Kelly Creek are not required to pay the official US$10 entrance fee; however, donations are accepted and encouraged. The park service is habitually underfunded, and tourist dollars provide important support for education, conservation and maintenance programs.

Puerto Viejo de Talamanca

There was a time when the only travelers to the little seaside settlement once known as Old Harbor were intrepid surfers who padded around the quiet, dusty streets, board under arm, on their way to surf Salsa Brava. That, certainly, is no longer the case. This burgeoning party town is bustling with tourist activity: street vendors ply Rasta trinkets and Bob Marley T-shirts, stylish eateries serve global-fusion everything and intentionally rustic bamboo bars pump dancehall and reggaetón. The scene can get downright hedonistic, attracting dedicated revelers who arrive to marinate in ganja and *guaro* (a local firewater made with sugarcane).

Despite its reputation, Puerto Viejo manages to hold on to an easy charm. Stray a couple of blocks off the main commercial strip and you might find yourself on a sleepy dirt road, savoring a spicy Caribbean stew in the company of locals. Nearby, you'll find rainforest fruit farms set to a soundtrack of cackling birds and croaking frogs, and wide-open beaches where the daily itinerary revolves around surfing and snoozing. So, chill a little. Party a little. Eat a little. You've come to just the right place.

SALSA BRAVA
....

One of the biggest breaks in Costa Rica, Salsa Brava is named for the heaping helping of 'spicy sauce' it serves up on the sharp, shallow reef, continually collecting its debt of fun in broken skin, boards and bones. The wave makes its regular, dramatic appearance when the swells pull in from the east, pushing a wall of water against the reef, in the process generating a thick and powerful curl. There's no gradual build-up here: the water is transformed from swell to wave in a matter of seconds. Ride it out and you're golden. Wipe out and you'll rocket headfirst into the reef. In his memoir, *In Search of Captain Zero,* surfer and screenwriter Allen Weisbecker describes it as 'vicious.' Some mordant locals have baptized it 'the cheese-grater.'

Interestingly, this storied wave helped turn Puerto Viejo into a destination. More than 30 years ago the town was barely accessible. But that didn't dissuade dogged surfers from the bumpy bus rides and rickety canoes that hauled them and their boards on the week-long trip from San José. They camped on the beach and shacked up with locals, carbo-loading at cheap *sodas.* Other intrepid explorers – biologists, Peace Corps volunteers, disaffected US veterans looking to escape the fallout of the Vietnam War – also materialized during this time, helping spread the word about the area's luminous sunsets, lush rainforests and monster curls. Today Puerto Viejo has a fine paved road, global eateries and wi-fi. The fierceness of Salsa Brava, however, remains unchanged.

◉ Sights

Finca La Isla
GARDENS

(☎ 8886-8530, 2750-0046; self-guided/guided tour US$6/12; ⏰ 10am-4pm Fri-Mon) West of town, this farm and botanical garden has been producing organic pepper, cacao, tropical fruits and ornamental plants for over a decade. Birds and wildlife abound, including sloths, poison-dart frogs and toucans. Informative guided tours (minimum three people) include admission, fruit tasting and a glass of fresh juice; alternatively, buy a booklet (US$1) and take a self-guided tour.

Aiko-logi
WILDLIFE RESERVE

(☎ 2750-2084, 8997-6869; http://aiko.peppendale. com; day tour incl transport & lunch US$60, overnight stay per person incl meals US$99; P) Nestled into the Cordillera de Talamanca, 15km outside Puerto Viejo, this private 135-hectare reserve is centered on a former *finca,* on land fringed with dense primary rainforest. It's ideal for bird-watching, hiking and splashing around in swimming holes. Day tours from Puerto Viejo (or Cahuita) can be arranged, as can overnight tent platform stays. Reserve ahead.

🏃 Activities

ATEC (p178) is an excellent source of general information on local activities.

Surfing

Breaking on the reef that hugs the village is the famed **Salsa Brava**, a shallow break that is also one of the country's most infamous waves. It's a tricky ride – if you lose it, the waves will plow you straight into the reef – and definitely not for beginners. Salsa Brava offers both rights and lefts, although the right is usually faster. Conditions are best with an easterly swell.

For a softer landing, try the beach break at **Playa Cocles** – where the waves are almost as impressive and the landing far less damaging. Cocles is about 2km east of town. Conditions are usually best early in the day, before the wind picks up.

Waves in the area generally peak from November to March, and there is a surfing miniseason from June to July. From late March to May, and in September and October, the sea is at its calmest.

Several surf schools around town charge US$40 to US$50 for two hours of lessons. Stands around town rent boards from about US$20 per day.

Caribbean Surf School
SURFING

(☎ 8357-7703) Lessons by super-smiley surf instructor Hershel Lewis, widely considered the best teacher in the town.

One Love Surf School
SURFING

(☎ 8719-4654; jewell420@hotmail.com) Julie Hickey and her surfing sons Cedric and Solomon specialize in surf lessons for women and children.

Swimming

The entire southern Caribbean coast – from Cahuita all the way south to Punta Mona – is lined with unbelievably beautiful beaches. Just northwest of town, **Playa Negra** offers the area's safest swimming.

Southeast of town you will find some gems – stretches of smooth white sand, fringed by jungle and ideal for surfing, body surfing and, when the swell is low, swimming. Playa Cocles (2km east of town), **Playa Chiquita** (4km east), Punta Uva (7km east) and Manzanillo all offer postcard-perfect beach paradises. Swimming conditions vary greatly, however, and the surf can get dangerous. Riptides and powerful undertows can be deadly. Inquire at your hotel or with local tour operators about conditions before setting out.

Snorkeling

The waters from Cahuita to Manzanillo are sheltered by Costa Rica's only two living reef systems, which form a naturally protected sanctuary, home to some 35 species of coral and 400 species of fish, not to mention dolphins, sharks and, occasionally, whales. Generally, underwater visibility is best when the sea is calm.

Just south of **Punta Uva**, in front of the Punta Uva Dive Center, is a decent spot for snorkeling, when conditions are calm. The reef is very close to the shore and features include stunning examples of reindeer coral, sheet coral and lettuce coral. The reef at **Manzanillo** is also easily accessible. Local operators offer snorkeling trips for about US$40 to US$60 per person.

Diving

Divers in the southern Caribbean will discover upward of 20 dive sites, from the coral gardens in shallow waters to deeper sites with amazing underwater vertical walls. Literally hundreds of species of fish swim around here, including angelfish, parrotfish, triggerfish, shark and different species of jack and snapper.

Puerto Viejo de Talamanca

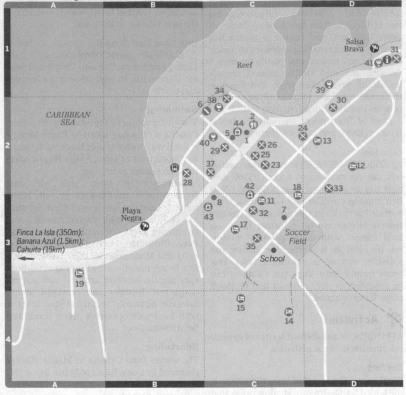

CARIBBEAN COAST PUERTO VIEJO DE TALAMANCA

Reef Runner Divers   DIVING
(☎ 2750-0480; www.reefrunnerdivers.net; 1-/2-tank dive US$65/100; ⏰ 8am-6pm) If you are not certified, you can use a temporary license for US$55 or spring for the full PADI (Professional Association of Diving Instructors) certification for US$335.

Hiking

There are superb coastal hiking opportunities within 15km of Puerto Viejo in Parque Nacional Cahuita and the Refugio Nacional de Vida Silvestre Gandoca-Manzanillo.

White-Water Rafting

Exploradores Outdoors   RAFTING
(☎ 2750-2020; www.exploradoresoutdoors.com; 1-day trip incl 2 meals & transportation from US$99) This outfit offers one- and two-day trips on Ríos Pacuare and Reventazón. Staff can pick you up and drop you off in Cahuita, Puerto Viejo, San José or Arenal. It has an office in the center of town.

📖 Courses

Spanish School Pura Vida   LANGUAGE COURSE
(☎ 2750-0029; www.spanishschool-puravida.com) Located at the Hotel Pura Vida, this school offers everything from private hourly tutoring to intensive five-hours-a-day, multi-week classes.

🧭 Tours

Tour operators generally require a minimum of two people on any excursion. Rates may be discounted for larger groups.

ATEC   TOUR
(Asociación Talamanqueña de Ecoturismo y Conservación; ☎ 2750-0398; www.ateccr.org; ⏰ 8am-8pm) 🖉 This highly reputable not-for-profit organization promotes sustainable tourism by working with local guides and supporting local communities. Activities include hiking, horseback riding, snorkeling, fishing, dolphin-watching, rafting, kayaking,

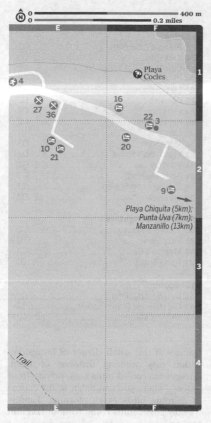

Playa Cocles

Playa Chiquita (5km); Punta Uva (7km); Manzanillo (13km)

Trail

surfing, bird-watching, courses in Caribbean dance, cooking and hair braiding, and trips to indigenous territories and local farms. Note that 24-hour notice is required for some tours. Visit the office or the website for a complete price list.

Gecko Trail Adventures TOUR
(☑2756-8412, in USA & Canada 415-230-0298; www.geckotrail.com) This full-service agency arranges local tours as well as transportation, accommodations and tours throughout Costa Rica. It has offices downtown and at Banana Azul resort west of town.

Terraventuras TOUR
(☑2750-0750; www.terraventuras.com; ⊘7am-7pm) Offers overnights in Tortuguero (US$95 to US$199), along with the usual local tours. Also has its very own 23-platform, 2.1km-long canopy tour (US$55), complete with Tarzan swing.

Caribe Shuttle TOUR
(☑2750-0626; http://caribeshuttle.com/puerto-viejo-tours) Based at Rocking J's Hostel, this company offers a wide variety of tours in the Puerto Viejo area and also specializes in excursions to Bocas del Toro, Panama.

🛏 Sleeping

Puerto Viejo has a little bit of everything. All budget spots have private hot-water bathrooms unless otherwise stated. Note that rates are generally discounted slightly when paid in cash.

Hotel Pura Vida HOTEL $
(☑2750-0002; www.hotel-puravida.com; s/d/tr US$34/38/48, without bathroom US$28/32/42; P🛜) Despite the budget prices, this Chilean-German-run inn opposite the soccer field offers solidly midrange amenities. Ten breezy, immaculate rooms come clad in polished wood, bright linens and ceramic-tile floors; No 6 is especially nice, with views of town from its solar-heated shower. There's a lounge with easy chairs and hammocks, and breakfasts, snacks and chilled beers are available.

Rocking J's HOSTEL $
(☑2750-0657; www.rockingjs.com; camping per person US$6-8, hammock US$7, dm/d/tr US$11/26/39, ste US$60-70; P🛜) Puerto Viejo's grooviest hostel and 'hammock hotel' is owned by the charismatic, mischievous 'J,' who organizes full-moon parties and drinking games. Good times, good vibes and new friends await here. The accommodations are basic: tight rows of tents and hammocks, snug dorms and private doubles share rickety showers in an environment brightened by a veritable explosion of psychedelic mosaics.

Surfboards, snorkels and bikes are available for rent, and in addition to an onsite restaurant and bar, there's also a music studio–survival bunker made from reclaimed shipping containers.

Jacaranda Hotel & Jungle Garden CABINA $
(☑2750-0069; www.cabinasjacaranda.net; s/d/tr/q from US$30/45/50/55; P🛜) In a blooming garden intersected by mosaic walkways, this place near the soccer field has 15 simple wood *cabinas* with spotless ceramic-tile floors and murals of flowers, along with a small shared kitchen and patio. Yoga classes are offered, the onsite One Love Spa offers massage and bodywork, and there's an organic 'supermarket' (new in 2014) right next door.

Puerto Viejo de Talamanca

Cabinas Guaraná CABINA $

(☎2750-0244; www.hotelguarana.com; s/d/tr/q US$35/43/53/60; P@🛜) Amid a riotous tropical garden in town, 10 brightly painted concrete *cabinas* are decorated with wooden furniture and colorful folk tapestries, and each one comes with a small private terrace with hammock. There is a spacious shared kitchen and a vertigo-inducing tree house that offers spectacular sea views.

Hostel Pagalú HOSTEL $

(☎2750-1930; www.pagalu.com; dm US$12, s/d US$27/32, s/d without bathroom US$23/26; P🛜) This peaceful, contemporary hostel offers a break from Puerto Viejo's party scene. Clean, airy dorms and doubles abound in niceties, including large lockers, charging stations for MP3 players and bunkside reading lamps. There's a shared open-air kitchen and a quiet lounge with tables and hammocks, plus a supply of spring water for refilling your own reusable plastic bottle.

Bungalows Calalú BUNGALOW $

(☎2750-0042; www.bungalowscalalu.com; s/d/tr US$35/45/50, d/tr/q with kitchen & air-con US$60/70/80; P❄🛜🏊) A lovely tropical-garden setting, swimming pool and convenient parking are among the appealing features at this small cluster of bungalows within easy walking distance of town. Cheaper fan-cooled units have private front porches where you can listen to the chorus of chirping birds every morning. Family-friendly larger units come with air-con and kitchen.

Cabinas Tropical CABINA $

(☎2750-0283; www.cabinastropical.com; s/d/tr US$40/45/55; P😊❄🛜) Ten spacious rooms, decorated with varnished wood and shiny tiles, surround a primly landscaped garden on the eastern end of town. The comfortable quarters are just part of the appeal: biologist owner Rolf Blancke leads excellent bird-watching hikes at dawn (per person US$65, minimum three people, breakfast provided).

Monte Sol CABINA $

(☎2750-0098; www.montesol.net; r US$38, without bathroom US$30, d/q bungalows with kitchen US$52/72; P@🛜) Clean, basic *cabinas* in a quiet locale east of town have tile floors, mosquito nets and hammocks.

La Ruka Hostel HOSTEL $

(☎2750-0617; www.facebook.com/laruka.hostel; dm/r without bathroom US$10/25; 🛜) If the cute painting of the surfing dog doesn't lure you in, the friendly welcome from owners Dannie and Dave will. Just east of town, this relative newcomer has spacious common areas up front, a brand-new kitchen out back, dorm space and a couple of private rooms upstairs with shared bath.

Kaya's Place
GUESTHOUSE $

(☑2750-0690; www.kayasplace.com; s/d without bathroom US$19/27, d US$35-55, ste US$70; P🛜) Across the road from the beach at Puerto Viejo's western edge, this funky guesthouse has 17 snug, basic rooms, ranging from dim units with shared cool-water showers to more spacious garden rooms with air-con and private bathroom. A 2nd-floor lounge is filled with hammocks and offers prime ocean views. Bikes are available for rent.

Escape Caribeño
BUNGALOW $$

(☑2750-0103; www.escapecaribeno.com; s/d/tr garden view US$/0//5/85, ocean view US$90/95/105; P❄@🛜) Charming Italian owners keep these 14 spick-and-span bungalows with spotless bathrooms, some on the beach side and others in the garden across the road, 500m east of town toward Playa Cocles. More expensive units are in lovely Caribbean-style structures with stained-glass shower stalls, but all have stocked minifridges, cable TV, fans and hammocks. Breakfast (US$5 to US$9 extra) is also available.

Coco Loco Lodge
BUNGALOW $$

(☑2750-0281; www.cocolocolodge.com; d US$55-69, d bungalow US$75-87; P@🛜) You'll find various accommodations at this quiet, Austrian-run hotel. The most charming are the palm-thatched bungalows, equipped with shining wood floors, minifridge and coffeemaker. All of these have private terrace with hammock, offering views of the expansive garden. Credit cards accepted.

Casa Verde
CABINA $$

(☑2750-0015; www.cabinascasaverde.com; s/d/tr/q US$62/78/95/109, s/d without bathroom from US$40/46; P🛜🏊) Tiled walkways wind through gardens with 17 tidy rooms, each with high ceilings, stained-wood furniture, folk-art touches and private terraces with hammocks. Cheaper rooms are more basic, but the shared bathrooms shine. A pool and hot tub – encrusted with rock formations – are straight out of *Fantasy Island*. Credit cards accepted.

Blue Conga Hotel
B&B $$

(☑2750-0681; www.hotelblueconga.com; incl breakfast d/tr/q upstairs US$85/100/115, downstairs US$75/90/105; P🛜🏊) This backstreet B&B 1km east of town has 14 simple rooms in a two-story, tropical-style building. Best value are the six airy upstairs units, with high ceilings, clerestory windows, canopy beds with mosquito nets, handcrafted lamps, private terraces, coffeemakers and microwaves. Rooms downstairs are less inspiring. Breakfast is served on a lovely open-air garden deck, beside the brand-new pool.

Cashew Hill Jungle Cottages
BUNGALOW $$$

(☑2750-0001, 2750-0256; www.cashewhilllodge.co.cr; cottages US$90-150; P🛜🏊) Perched on a lush hillside five minutes above town are seven bright, colorful and comfortable three- to eight-person cottages with full kitchens, loft-style sleeping areas and charming rustic touches. All have private decks or patios stocked with comfy chairs and hammocks, while the two-bedroom Playa Negra cabin offers exquisite ocean views. A brand-new yoga platform hosts classes twice daily.

Banana Azul
LODGE $$$

(☑2750-2035; www.bananaazul.com; incl breakfast d US$104 129, d ste US$164; P🛜🏊) Removed from town, this wonderful hotel sits astride a blissfully tranquil black-sand beach. Jungle-chic decor (white linens, mosquito nets, bromeliads in the showers) is complemented by fine ocean vistas from upstairs terraces. Best is the Howler Suite, a corner room with multidirectional views. There's also an onsite restaurant-bar, plus bike and boogie-board rentals. No children under 16.

✗ Eating

With the most diverse restaurant scene on the Caribbean coast, Puerto Viejo has the cure for *casado* overkill.

Find groceries at the local **Old Harbour Supermarket** (☉6:30am-8:30pm) or the incongruous chain-store **MegaSuper** (☉8am-7pm). Don't miss the Saturday **organic market** (☉6am-6pm Sat), when area vendors and growers sell snacks typical of the region.

★ Bread & Chocolate
BREAKFAST $

(☑2750-0723; cakes US$3, meals US$5-8; ☉6:30am-6:30pm Wed-Sat, to 2:30pm Sun; ☑) Ever had a completely homemade PB&J

(ie bread, peanut butter *and* jelly all made from scratch)? That and more can be yours at this dream of a gluten-lover's cafe. Coffees are served in individual French presses; mochas come unconstructed so you have the pleasure of mixing your own homemade chocolate, steamed milk and coffee; and everything else – from the gazpacho to the granola to the bagels – is lovingly and skilfully made in-house.

Flip Flop INTERNATIONAL $
(🖅2750-2031; mains US$5-16; ⊘noon-10pm; 🍴) Atmospherically lit with colorful paper globe lanterns, this place has something for everyone: Thai, Indian and Indonesian curries, tacos, sushi, pasta, seafood, burgers and steaks. Throw in a wide-ranging, reasonably priced drinks list (sangria, mojitos, caipirinhas and every kind of *colada* imaginable), and desserts like warm chocolate brownies and banana splits, and you've got one very popular eatery.

Soda Shekiná CARIBBEAN $
(🖅2750-0549; mains US$7-12; ⊘11:30am-9pm Wed-Mon) Some of Puerto Viejo's best traditional Caribbean home cooking can be found at this backstreet eatery with wooden slab tables on an open-air terrace, just northwest of the soccer field. Everything is served with coconut rice and beans, salad and delicious caramelized fried bananas.

De Gustibus BAKERY $
(baked goods from US$1; ⊘7am-6pm) This Italian-owned bakery on Puerto Viejo's main drag draws a devoted multitude with its fabulous focaccia (US$2 a slice), along with apple strudel, profiteroles and all sorts of other sweet and savory goodies. Eat in, or grab a snack for the beach.

Veronica's Place VEGETARIAN $
(🖅2750-0263; www.veronicasplacepv.com; dishes US$4-8; ⊘8:30am-8pm; 🍴) This delightful vegetarian cafe with breezy upstairs seating offers delicious juices and smoothies along with fresh, healthy interpretations of Caribbean food, using fresh fruits and vegetables. Raw food and vegan options are available. Veronica rents *cabinas,* has a macrobiotic health-food store onsite, offers Caribbean cooking classes and runs a volunteer work exchange on her organic farm.

Pan Pay BAKERY $
(🖅2750-0081; dishes US$3-6; ⊘7am-5pm) This popular corner spot on the beachside road in town is excellent for strong coffee, fresh baked goods and hearty wedges of fluffy Spanish omelet served with crisp tomatobread. There are sandwiches and other light meals, but it's the flaky chocolate croissants that make us want to jump out of bed in the morning.

Café Rico CAFE $
(🖅2750-0510; caferico.puertoviejo@yahoo.com; breakfast US$3-7; ⊘5:30am-1pm; 🍴) Home to some of Puerto Viejo's best coffee, this cozy garden cafe serves breakfast accompanied by a plethora of other services: free wi-fi, laundry, a book exchange, and rentals of bikes and snorkeling gear.

Dee-Lite ICE CREAM $
(gelato US$2-3; ⊘12:30am-8pm) Directly across from the bus stop, this authentic *gelateria* is the perfect place to cool off after a long, hot bus ride.

★ Laszlo's SEAFOOD $$
(mains US$14; ⊘6-9:30pm) Whaddya get when you take a champion sportfisher, born and raised in Transylvania, and transplant him to Puerto Viejo by way of New Jersey? Answer: an amazing, eclectic eatery with no sign and no menu that only opens whenever owner Laszlo catches enough fish. The day's catch comes with garlic and parsley, homemade French fries and grilled veggies. Yum!!!

★ Stashu's con Fusion FUSION $$
(🖅2750-0530; mains US$10-18; ⊘5-10pm Thu-Tue; 🍴) Stroll 250m out of town toward Playa Cocles to this romantic candlelit patio cafe serving up creative fusion cuisine that combines elements of Caribbean, Indian, Mexican and Thai cooking. Steamed spicy mussels in red-curry sauce and tandoori chicken in coconut are just a couple of standouts. Excellent vegetarian and vegan items round out the menu. Owner and chef Stash Golas is an artist inside the kitchen and out. Do not miss.

Miss Lidia's Place CARIBBEAN $$
(🖅2750-0598; dishes US$6-20; ⊘9am-9pm) A long-standing favorite for classic Caribbean flavors, Miss Lidia's has been around for years, pleasing the palates and satisfying the stomachs of locals and tourists alike. Fruit-and-veggie lovers will appreciate the ice-cold *batidos* (fresh fruit drinks) and the delicious assortment of broccoli, green

beans, cauliflower, corn-on-the-cob, carrots and mushrooms accompanying most dishes.

Chile Rojo ASIAN $$
(☑2750-0025; mains US$6-15; ☺11:30am-10pm Thu-Tue; 🖉) Monday nights at this Asian fusion spot mean the US$13 all-you-can-eat (and quite decent) sushi and Asian buffet. Any other night of the week, this trendy 2nd-story spot offers excellent views of the main drag, and the sushi bar opens around 7:30pm. The cuisine is truly pan-Asian, running the gamut from tabbouleh to tikkas to Thai curries.

Café Viejo ITALIAN $$$
(☑2750-0817; www.cafeviejo.net; mains US$9-28; ☺6pm-1am Wed-Mon) This pricey, sceney Mediterranean lounge and restaurant stands out for its fresh pastas, tasty pizzas, fancy cocktails and upscale, romantic ambience. Its main-street location makes for excellent people-watching.

Koki Beach LATIN AMERICAN $$$
(☑2275-0902; www.kokibeach.com; mains US$11-24; ☺2pm-midnight Wed-Sun; 🕾) A high-end favorite for drinks and dinner, this sleek eatery cranks reggae-lite and sports colorful Adirondack chairs that face the ocean from an elevated wooden platform on the east end of town. There's a decent selection of Peruvian-inflected *ceviches*, meat and seafood dishes, but slim pickings for vegetarians.

INDIGENOUS COMMUNITIES IN THE SOUTHERN CARIBBEAN

The area is home to a number of thriving indigenous communities, many of which can be visited by travelers. Brush up on a little local knowledge first:

Bribrí & Cabécar

At least two indigenous groups occupied the territory on the Caribbean side of the country from pre-Columbian times. The Bribrí tended to inhabit lowland areas, while the Cabécar made their home high in the Cordillera de Talamanca. Over the last century, members of both ethnic groups have migrated to the Pacific side. But many have stayed on the coast, intermarrying with Jamaican immigrants and even working in the banana industry. Today the Bribrí tend to be more acculturated, while the Cabécar are more isolated.

The groups have distinct languages (which are preserved to some degree), though they share similar architecture, weapons and canoe style. They also share the spiritual belief that the planet – and the flora and fauna contained within it – are gifts from Sibö (God). *Taking Care of Sibö's Gifts*, by Juanita Sánchez, Gloria Mayorga and Paula Palmer, is a remarkable record of Bribrí oral history.

Visiting Indigenous Communities

There are several reserves on the Caribbean slopes of the Cordillera de Talamanca, including the Talamanca Cabécar territory (which is more difficult to visit) and the Bribrí territory, where locals are more equipped to handle visitors. ATEC (p178) organizes trips out of Puerto Viejo.

The most interesting destination is **Yorkín**, in the Reserva Indígena Yorkín. While you are there, you can meet with a local women's artisan group, **Mujeres Artesanas Stibrawpa**, who offer demonstrations in roof thatching, cooking and basket-weaving. It's a rewarding trip, well worth the time and effort to get there (day trips US$70, overnights US$90).

Alternatively you can visit the larger, modern village of **Shiroles**, about 20km west of Bribrí, where you can observe and participate in local chocolate production (half-day trip US$35). Half-day trips (US$25) also visit an iguana farm on the **Kèköldi territory** (this is a tiny ethnicity related to the Bribrí).

Note: it is not recommended to visit these territories independently. Not only are many spots difficult to reach, but in most cases villages do not have the infrastructure to accommodate streams of tourists. Of course, remember to be respectful – these are people's private homes and work spaces, not tourist attractions.

☕ Drinking & Nightlife

Lazy Mon CLUB
Puerto Viejo's most dependable spot for live music, Lazy Mon draws big crowds with reggae at happy hour (5pm to 7pm), then keeps things hopping with more of the same throughout the evening.

Salsa Brava BAR
(☏2750-0241; ⊗noon-10pm) Specializing in fresh seafood and open-grill cooking, this popular spot is the perfect end-of-day cocktail stop – hit happy hour between 5pm and 7pm and you'll also catch two-for-one mojitos for sunset overlooking the Salsa Brava surf break. On Friday and Sunday it brings in DJs for the popular reggae nights.

Johnny's Place CLUB
(⊗1pm-3am) At this central beachside institution, Saturday is the big night, with DJs spinning reggaetón, dance hall, hip-hop and salsa. A mix of locals and travelers take up the dance floor and surround the late-night beach bonfires outside.

Maritza's Bar BAR
(☏2750-0003) This nonfancy local spot down by the beach has regular karaoke nights and DJs playing salsa and merengue.

🛍 Shopping

Makeshift stalls clutter the main road, selling knick-knacks and Rasta-colored accoutrements aplenty.

Lulu Berlu Gallery ARTS & CRAFTS
(☏2750-0394; ⊗9am-9pm) On a backstreet parallel to the main road, this gallery carries folk art, clothing, jewelry, ceramics, embroidered purses and mosaic mirrors, among many other one-of-a-kind, locally made items.

ℹ Information

Be aware that though the use of marijuana (and harder stuff) is common in Puerto Viejo, it is nonetheless illegal.

As in other popular tourist centers, theft can be an issue. Stay aware, use your hotel safe, and if staying outside of town avoid walking alone late at night.

ATEC (p178) Has internet access and reliable information on local tours and activites.

Banco de Costa Rica (⊗9am-4pm Mon-Fri) Two ATMs work on Plus and Visa systems, dispensing both colones and dollars. Sometimes they run out of cash on weekends, and can be finicky; if one machine won't let you withdraw cash, try the other.

Banco Nacional Just off main street near the bridge into town. Dispenses colones only.

Costa Rica Way (☏2750-3031; www.costaricaway.net; ⊗8am-6pm) Operates a tourist-information center near the waterfront east of town and lists hotel and restaurant info on its website.

Puerto Viejo Satellite (www.puertoviejosatellite.com) Another website with information on local lodgings, eating and activities.

ℹ Getting There & Away

BUS

All public buses arrive and depart from the bus stop along the beach road in central Puerto Viejo. The ticket office is diagonally across the street.

Bribri/Sixaola US$1.50/3.35; 30/90 minutes; departs roughly every hour from 6:30am to 7:30pm.

Cahuita/Puerto Limón US$1.50/3.60; 30/90 minutes; departs roughly every hour from 5:30am to 7:30pm.

Manzanillo US$1.20; 30 minutes; departs every two hours between 6:45am and 6:45pm (less frequently on weekends).

San José US$10.90; five hours; departs 7:30am, 9am, 11am and 4pm daily, plus 1pm Sunday.

VAN SHUTTLE

An ever-growing number of companies offer convenient van shuttles from Puerto Viejo to other tourist hot spots around Costa Rica and down the coast to Bocas del Toro, Panama. For an exhaustive list, see Gecko Trail's very helpful website geckotrail.com/shuttle.htm. The following companies operate out of Puerto Viejo.

Caribe Shuttle (☏2750-0626; http://caribe-shuttle.com/from-puerto-viejo) Serves Bocas del Toro (Panama), San José and Tortuguero.

Gecko Trail (p179) Standard shuttle service to San José and Tortuguero; also offers good-value Adventure Connection packages that provide transport to San José or Arenal, with a half-day, 30km Río Pacuare rafting trip included in the price.

Interbus (☏4100-0888; www.interbusonline.com) Serves Arenal-La Fortuna, San José, Siquirres and Puerto Viejo de Sarapiquí.

ℹ Getting Around

A bicycle is a fine way to get around town, and pedaling out to beaches east of Puerto Viejo is one of the highlights of this corner of Costa Rica. You'll find rentals all over town for about US$5 per day.

Puerto Viejo to Punta Uva

A 13km road winds east from Puerto Viejo, through rows of coconut palms, alongside coastal lodges and through lush lowland rainforest before coming to a dead end at the sleepy town of Manzanillo. The road was paved for the first time in 2003, dramatically shortening the amount of time it took to travel this route. The roadway is narrow, however, so if you're driving, take your time and be alert for cyclists and one-lane bridges.

If you want to stay close to Puerto Viejo while having access to a nice beach, Playa Cocles has a good mix of isolation and amenities, offering a wide variety of places to stay and eat. After that, the pickings get thin until you get closer to Punta Uva, where you'll find a cluster of lodges and restaurants – as well as one of the prettiest beaches in the region.

Buses heading from Puerto Viejo to Manzanillo will drop you at any of these places along the way.

Sights

Jaguar Centro de Rescate WILDLIFE REFUGE
(2750-0710; www.jaguarrescue.com; adult/child under 10yr US$15/free; ⊙tours 9:30am & 11:30am Mon-Sat; ⊕) Named in honor of its original resident, this well-run wildlife-rescue center in Playa Chiquita now focuses mostly on other animals, including raptors, sloths and monkeys. Founded by Spanish zoologist Encar and her partner Sandro (an Italian herpetologist), the center rehabilitates orphaned, injured and rescued animals for reintroduction into the wild whenever possible. Volunteer opportunities are available with a two-week minimum commitment.

Activities

The region's biggest draws involve surf, sand, wildlife-watching and attempts to get a decent tan between downpours. **Playa Cocles** is known for its great surfing and organized lifeguard system, which helps offset the dangers of the frequent riptides, while **Punta Uva** features the best and safest beaches for swimming.

Punta Uva Dive Center DIVING
(2759-9191; www.puntauvadivecenter.com; 1-/2-tank dives from US$65/80) Clearly signposted off the main road in Punta Uva. Offers diving, PADI courses and snorkeling.

Tours

Chocolate Forest Experience TOUR
(8836-8930; http://caribeanscr.com/chocolate-tour.html; Playa Cocles; guided tour US$26; ⊙tours 10am Mon, 10am & 2pm Tue & Thu, 2pm Fri & Sat) Playa Cocles–based chocolate producer Caribeans leads tours of its sustainably managed cacao forest and chocolate-creation lab, accompanied by gourmet chocolate tastings.

Crazy Monkey Canopy Tour ADVENTURE TOUR
(www.almondsandcorals.com/tours/crazy-monkey-canopy-ride; per person US$45; ⊙8am-2pm) The region's only canopy tour, operated by Almonds & Corals Lodge between Punta Uva and Manzanillo.

Sleeping & Eating

All of the following places are listed from west (Puerto Viejo) to east (Punta Uva).

Playa Cocles

A broad stretch of white-sand beach lies just 1.5km east of Puerto Viejo, offering proximity to the village and its many restaurants, but plenty of peace and quiet, too.

Cabinas El Tesoro CABINA $
(2750-0128; www.cabinaseltesoro.com; dm US$10, d/tr/q with fan US$35/45/55, with air-con US$60/70/80;) Directly opposite the Playa Cocles beach break are these 12 clean, simple *cabinas* with tile floors and queen beds, some with air-con and cable TV. The attached Mi Casa Hostel sleeps 16 in four-bed dorms. Bikes can be rented onsite, and surfboard rentals and lessons are available across the road. The bar next door hosts live music on Tuesday.

Finca Chica BUNGALOW $$
(2750-1919; www.fincachica.com; bungalows US$65-130, per week US$370-750;) Surrounded by lush tropical greenery, these four stand-alone wooden houses range from a two-person bungalow to an amazing three-story structure known as 'La Casita del Río' that sleeps up to six people. All have fully equipped kitchens, and three have spacious living and dining areas. It's tucked down a dead-end dirt driveway, a few hundred meters off the main road.

El Tucán Jungle Lodge CABINA $$
(2750-0026; www.eltucanjunglelodge.com; s/d/tr/q US$38/50/60/70;) Only 1km off the road, this jungle retreat feels miles from

anywhere, making it ideal for bird-watchers. Four clean wooden *cabinas* on the banks of the Caño Negro share a broad patio with hammocks from which you can observe sloths, toucans and more. Upon request, the welcoming German owners serve breakfast (per person US$5) and organize walks in the area.

La Isla Inn
CABINA $$
(☑2750-0109; www.laislainn.com; s/d with fan US$62/79, with air-con US$73/102; P✳️🛜❄️) Opposite the lifeguard tower at the main hub of the beach lies this efficient wooden lodge with 12 expansive rooms, all of which are equipped with safe, cable TV and handmade wood furnishings crafted from the slightly curved outer boards that are discarded during lumber processing.

Azánia Bungalows
BUNGALOW $$$
(☑2750-0540; www.azania-costarica.com; d incl breakfast US$107, additional person US$25; P@❄️) Ten spacious but dark thatch-roofed bungalows are brightened up by colorful linens at this charming inn set on landscaped jungle grounds. Nice details include woven bedspreads, well-designed bathrooms and wide-plank hardwood floors. A free-form pool and a Jacuzzi nestle into the greenery, and there's an Argentine restaurant and bar.

La Costa de Papito
BUNGALOW $$$
(☑2750-0080; www.lacostadepapito.com; d incl breakfast US$107, additional adult/child US$17/7; P🛜) Relax in rustic comfort in the sculpture-studded grounds at this popular Cocles outpost, which has wood and bamboo bungalows decked out with hand-carved furniture, stone bathrooms straight out of *The Flintstones* and roomy porches draped with hammocks. The onsite restaurant serves Italian-influenced specialties, while the rustic, palm-thatched Indulgence Spa (☑2750-0536; www.indulgencespa-salon. com; ☉11am-6pm Mon-Sat) offers massage and spa treatments.

Physis
B&B $$$
(☑8866-4405, 2750-0941; www.physiscaribbean. net; incl breakfast d US$100-125, tr US$135) Creature comforts abound at this four-bedroom B&B, tucked down a Playa Cocles side road and managed by expatriate Californians Jeremy and Emily. There are free Netflix movies in the smaller downstairs units, satellite TV in the honeymoon suite, and superstrong wi-fi, sound systems, dehumidifiers, air-con and mini-fridges throughout. An up-

stairs deck with well-stocked bar doubles as the breakfast area.

★ La Pecora Nera
ITALIAN $$$
(☑2750-0490; mains US$12-30; ☉5pm-late Tue-Sun; 🍴) If you splurge for a single fancy meal during your trip, do it at this romantic eatery run by Tuscan-born Ilario Giannoni. On a lovely candlelit patio, deftly prepared Italian seafood and pasta dishes are served alongside unusual offerings such as the delicate *carpaccio di carambola:* transparent slices of starfruit topped with shrimp, tomatoes and balsamic vinaigrette.

There is an extensive wine list (from US$32 a bottle), but you can't go wrong with the well-chosen and relatively inexpensive house wines. The restaurant has also branched out to a more casual spot next door, Gatta Ci Cova (☑2750-0730; sandwiches US$7-11, mains US$10-14; ☉noon-10pm Tue-Sun; 🍴), where you can grab panini and drinks.

🛏 Playa Chiquita

It isn't exactly clear where Playa Cocles ends and Playa Chiquita begins, but conventional wisdom applies the name to a series of beaches 4km to 6km east of Puerto Viejo.

Villas del Caribe
HOTEL $$
(☑2750-0202, 2233-2200; www.villasdelcaribe. com; incl breakfast d standard/junior US$80/110, junior villa/villa US$120/150; P✳️❄️) With a prime location near the beach, this resort offers lovely, brightly painted rooms, comfortable beds, sitting areas and roomy bathrooms with Spanish tile. Junior suites also come with kitchenettes, while the two-story villas have ocean views, king-size beds, kitchens and BBQ. All have private decks with hammocks.

Aguas Claras
BUNGALOW $$
(☑2750-0131; www.aguasclaras-cr.com; 1-/2-/3-room cottages US$70/130/220; P@) Five tropical Victorian cottages painted in bright candy colors and edged in lacy woodwork sit tucked amid the trees on the beach side of the road. All come with fully equipped kitchens.

Tierra de Sueños
BUNGALOW $$$
(☑2750-0378; www.tierradesuenoslodge.com; bungalows incl breakfast US$95-165; P🛜) 🍴 True to its name ('land of dreams'), this blissful garden retreat comprises several adorable wood bungalows with mosquito nets and private decks.

The quiet, tropical atmosphere is complemented by regular yoga classes on an open-air platform. Bike rentals (US$5 per day), snorkeling gear (free) and laundry (US$10 per load) are available, as is wi-fi (in common areas only).

La Kukula
BUNGALOW $$$

(☑2750-0653; www.lakukulalodge.com; incl breakfast d/tr US$130/147, 2-/3-bedroom houses US$260/300) Three tastefully spaced 'tropical contemporary' bungalows bring guests close to nature with natural ventilation (super-high ceilings and screen walls), and open jungle views from the rainfall showers. The wood-decked pool is great for bird- and frog-watching. For larger groups, a brand-new three-bedroom house sleeps up to nine, with private kitchen and pool. Delicious included breakfasts feature homemade bread and marmalade.

Shawandha Lodge
BUNGALOW $$$

(☑2750-0018; www.shawandhalodge.com; d incl breakfast US$147, additional person US$25; P✳@🛜🏊) Immersed in greenery, with frogs, agoutis and other tropical critters close at hand, this upscale lodge has 13 private, spacious nature-themed bungalows painted in earth tones and equipped with large mosaic-tiled bathrooms. A meticulously maintained thatched *rancho* serves as an open-air lounge, and there's a French-Caribbean restaurant. A private path across the road leads to the beach.

La Botánica Orgánica
VEGETARIAN, VEGAN $

(www.labotanicaorganica.com; mains US$4-8; ⊘8am-3pm Tue-Sun; ☑) 🌿 Sporting massive wood chairs and tables on a breezy open-air terrace, this friendly roadside spot specializes in vegetarian and vegan breakfasts and lunches, from banana pancakes and breakfast burritos to lentil-veggie burgers and avocado and cheese sandwiches on homemade wholewheat bread. Everything comes adorned with hibiscus flowers and served with a smile. The attached gift shop sells earth-friendly souvenirs.

Chocorart
CAFE $

(☑8866-7493; snacks from US$2; ⊘10am-sunset) This Swiss-run roadside cafe makes a perfect place to break your bike ride and get a quick chocolate fix. *Batidos*, coffee and ice cream are all available, but the real stars here are the brownies, hot chocolate and other delectables made from cocoa grown

on the adjacent farm; excellent chocolate tours are also available here.

Jungle Love Garden Café
CAFE $$

(☑2750-0162; www.junglelovecafe.com; mains US$9-20; ⊘5-9:30pm Tue-Sun; ☑) American bohemian meets the Caribbean at this popular porch-front cafe that serves amazing flash-cooked tuna, pizzas, pasta, tropical-themed salads and chicken dishes, and an eponymous Jungle Love Milkshake, a very grown-up blend of Baileys, *guaro* and local ice cream. The menu has veggie options and vegan items can be prepared on request. There are only eight tables; reserve ahead.

Pura Gula
INTERNATIONAL $$

(☑8634-6404; mains US$13-20; ⊘6-10pm) The short but solid menu at this casually elegant Catalan-owned eatery includes steak with gorgonzola sauce, fried calamari, spinach-cheese ravioli in pesto sauce, and shrimp accompanied by sauteed veggies and sesame mashed potatoes. Everything's served on a pleasant open-air deck, just off the main road between Playa Chiquita and Punta Uva.

🛏 Punta Uva

Punta Uva is known for the region's most swimmable beaches, each lovelier than the next. To find the turnoff to the point (about 7km east of Puerto Viejo), look for the Punta Uva Dive Center sign.

Walaba Hostel
HOSTEL $

(☑2750-0147; www.walabahostel.com; dm/s/d/tr/q without bathroom US$13/25/35/50/60, s/d cabinas with bathroom US$35/45) Funky, colorful and amazingly cheap for Punta Uva, this ramshackle collection of open-air dorms, private rooms (including an 'attic' double reached by a ladder) and small cabins is surrounded by a flowery garden and managed by a friendly Dutch couple. Guests share ample kitchen facilities, hot and cold showers and a creaky-floored communal area with games, books and DVDs.

★ Cabinas Punta Uva
CABINA $$

(☑2759-9180; www.cabinaspuntauva.com; cabinas US$60, with private kitchen US$90) Only steps from idyllic Playa Punta Uva, this Catalan-owned cluster of three cabinas with tiled bathrooms, polished-wood verandas, hammocks and a shared open-air kitchen is dreamily hidden down a dead-end street in a verdant garden setting. Fall asleep to the sound of crashing waves and chirping insects and wake up to the roar of the resident howler monkeys.

Casa Viva
BUNGALOW $$$

(☑ 2750-0089; www.puntauva.net; 1-bedroom houses US$100, 2-bedroom houses d/tr/q US$130/160/190; P ❄ 🛜) Beautifully handcrafted by a master carpenter, these enormous, fully furnished hardwood houses, each with tiled shower, kitchen and wraparound veranda, are set on a property that fronts the beach – an ideal spot in which to chill out in a hammock and observe the local wildlife. Weekly and monthly rates are also available.

Costa Rica Tree House Lodge
BUNGALOW $$$

(☑ 2750-0706; www.costaricatreehouse.com; d US$200-390, extra person US$50; P) 🍃 Adventurers who like their lodgings rustic and whimsical will appreciate these four open-air casitas of various sizes, including a literal 'tree house', a two-story cabin built around the base of a living sangrillo tree. All have kitchens, BBQs, spacious decks with easy chairs and hammocks, and private paths leading to a small white-sand beach. Proceeds support an iguana-breeding program.

Korrigan Lodge
BUNGALOW $$$

(☑ 2759-9103; www.korriganlodge.com; d incl breakfast US$105; P) Nestled into a patch of jungle near the main road, these four thatch-roofed wood and concrete bungalows come with minibar, safe, modern bathroom and private terrace with hammock. All guests have access to free bikes. Breakfast is served in an open-air rancho surrounded by gardens.

Almonds & Corals Lodge
BUNGALOW $$$

(☑ 2271-3000, in USA 1-888-373-9042; www.almondsandcorals.com; incl breakfast & dinner s/d US$196/250, s/d master ste US$276/350, additional child/adult from US$40/65; P @ 🍽) 🍃 Buried deep in the jungle, this longtime luxury spot popular with honeymooners has 24 palm-roofed suites connected by wooden boardwalks, with four-poster beds, Jacuzzi tubs and private patios with hammocks. Rooms are screened in, making them comfortable, but you'll still be able to enjoy the nightly serenade of insects and frogs. Meals are served family-style in an open-air dining room.

★ Selvin's Restaurant
CARIBBEAN $$

(☑ 2750-0664; mains US$10-18; ⊘ 8am-8pm Wed-Sun) Selvin is a member of the extensive Brown family, noted for their charm, and his place is considered one of the region's best, specializing in shrimp, lobster, a terrific rondón and a succulent chicken caribeño (chicken stewed in a spicy Caribbean sauce).

El Refugio
ARGENTINE, INTERNATIONAL $$$

(☑ 2759-9007; mains US$15-25; ⊘ 5-9pm Thu-Tue) This tony Argentine-owned restaurant with only five tables is renowned for its rotating menu of three appetizers, five main dishes and three desserts. New offerings get chalked up on the board daily, anchored by perennial favorites such as red tuna in garlic, bife de entraña with chimichurri (a marinade of parsley, garlic and spices) and dulce de leche crepes. Reserve ahead.

Manzanillo

The chill village of Manzanillo has long been off the beaten track, even since the paved road arrived in 2003. This little town remains a vibrant outpost of Afro-Caribbean culture and has also remained pristine, thanks to the 1985 establishment of the Refugio Nacional de Vida Silvestre Gandoca-Manzanillo, which includes the village and imposes strict regulations on regional development.

Activities are of a simple nature, in nature: hiking, snorkeling and kayaking are king. (As elsewhere, ask about riptides before heading out.) Other than that, you may find the occasional party at the locally renowned Maxi's bar and restaurant at the end of the road (where buses arrive).

🏃 Activities

Aquamor Talamanca Adventures
SNORKELING

(☑ 2759-9012; www.greencoast.com/aquamor.htm) Near the bus stop in Manzanillo, this outfit rents snorkel gear and kayaks. Hours vary; call ahead.

🛏 Sleeping & Eating

Cabinas Bucus
CABINA $

(☑ 2759-9143; www.costa-rica-manzanillo.com; s/d/tr US$25/35/45, s/d/tr/q apt US$40/45/60/70; P 🛜) Four tidy, brightly painted tiled rooms in a two-story mustard yellow structure have mosquito nets and private bathrooms, all sharing a small kitchen. There are also two kitchen-equipped apartments sleeping up to four people each. Omar, one of the co-owners, is one of Manzanillo's top guides.

Cabinas Manzanillo
CABINA $$

(☑2759-9033; s/d US$40/50; [P][?]) Run by the ever-helpful Sandra Castillo and Pablo Bustamante, these eight *cabinas* on Manzanillo's western edge are so clean you could eat off the tile floors. Cheery rooms have big beds, industrial-strength ceiling fans and spacious bathrooms. There's also a shared kitchen. From Maxi's, travel 300m west toward Punta Uva, then make a left onto the signposted dirt road.

Congo Bongo
BUNGALOW $$$

(☑2759-9016; www.congo-bongo.com; d/tr/q US$165/185/205, per week US$990/1110/1230; [P][?]) About 1km outside Manzanillo towards Punta Uva, these six charming Dutch-owned cottages surrounded by dense forest (formerly a cacao plantation) offer fully equipped kitchens and plenty of living space, including open-air terraces and stra-tegically placed hammocks that are perfect for wildlife-watching. A network of trails leads through the 6 hectares of grounds to the beautiful beach.

Cool & Calm Cafe
CARIBBEAN $$

(☑8843-7460; www.coolandcalmcafe.com; mains US$9-18; ⊙4-9pm Mon, 11am-9pm Wed-Sun) Directly across from Manzanillo's western beachfront, this front-porch eatery regales visitors with fine Caribbean cooking, from snapper to shrimp, and chicken to lobster, with a few extras including guacamole, ta-cos and veggie curry thrown in for good measure. Owners Andy and Molly offer Caribbean cooking classes and a 'reef-to-plate' tour where you dive for your own lobster or fish.

Maxi's Restaurant
CARIBBEAN $$

(mains US$9-21, lobster US$23-67; ⊙noon-9pm; [☑]) Manzanillo's most famous restaurant draws a tourist crowd with large platters of grilled seafood, *pargo rojo* (whole red snappers), steaks and Caribbean-style lobsters (expensive and not necessarily worth it).

ⓘ GETTING TO GUABITO & BOCAS DEL TORO, PANAMA

Welcome to Costa Rica's most entertaining border crossing! An old railroad bridge that spans the churning waters of the Río Sixaola connects Costa Rica with Panama amid a sea of agricultural plantations. Until recently, oversized buses and trucks also plied this route – making for a surreal scene whenever one of these vehicles came clattering along the wood planks, forcing pedestrians to scatter to the edges. Today there's a parallel bridge for motor-vehicle traffic, inaugurated in mid-2012, but pedestrians still get the fun of walking across the old bridge.

From here, most travelers make for Bocas del Toro in Panama, a picturesque archipelago of jungle islands that is home to lovely beaches and endangered red frogs, and is easily accessible by regular water taxis from the docks at Almirante.

The border is open 7am to 5pm (8am to 6pm in Guabito, Panama, which is an hour ahead of Costa Rica), though one or both sides may close for lunch at around 1pm. At the entrance to the bridge, on the right-hand side, pay the US$7 Costa Rica departure tax and get your exit stamp at the **Costa Rica immigration office** (☑2754-2044). Once over the bridge, stop at Panama immigration to get your passport stamped and pay the US$3 entry tax. Note that Panama no longer requires tourist cards for foreigners entering from Costa Rica, but you will be required to show proof of onward travel out of Panama, such as a copy of your plane ticket home. Personal cars (not rentals) can cross here.

Guabito has no hotels or banks, but in a pinch you can exchange colones at the market across the street. From the border, half-hourly buses (US$1.25, one hour) run to Terminal Piquera in Changuinola, where you can transfer to one of the frequent buses to Almirante (US$1.75, 45 minutes) for the water taxi. Alternatively, from Guabito you can take a collective taxi (per person US$10, one hour) straight to Almirante. From this point, hourly water taxis (per person US$6, 25 minutes) make the trip to Bocas del Toro between 6:30am and 7pm.

For a more streamlined, if slightly more expensive, trip to Bocas del Toro, take one of the daily shuttles from Cahuita or Puerto Viejo de Talamanca.

Despite the somewhat lackadaisical service, the open-air upstairs dining area is a wonderful seaside setting for a meal and a beer with views of the beach and the street below.

❶ Getting There & Away

Buses from Puerto Viejo to Manzanillo (US$1.20, 30 minutes) depart at 6:45am, 7:45am, 9:45am, 11:45am, 1:45pm, 4:45pm and 6:45pm, returning to Puerto Viejo at 7am, 8am, 10am, noon, 2pm, 4pm and 6pm. These buses all continue to Puerto Limón (US$4.90, two hours) for onward transfers. Transportes Mepe also runs one direct bus daily between Manzanillo and San José (US$12, five hours), leaving Manzanillo at 7am and returning from San José at noon.

Refugio Nacional de Vida Silvestre Gandoca-Manzanillo

This little-explored refuge – called Regama for short – protects nearly 70% of the southern Caribbean coast, extending from Manzanillo all the way to the Panamanian border. It encompasses 50 sq km of land plus 44 sq km of marine environment. The peaceful, pristine stretch of sandy white beach is one of the area's main attractions. It's the center of village life in Manzanillo, and stretches for miles in either direction – from Punta Uva in the west to Punta Mona in the east. Offshore, a 5-sq-km coral reef is a teeming habitat for lobsters, sea fans and long-spined urchins.

Other than the village itself, and the surrounding farmland areas (grandfathered when the park was created in 1985), the wildlife refuge is composed largely of rainforest. Cativo trees form the canopy, while there are many heliconia in the undergrowth. A huge 400-hectare swamp – known as Pantano Punta Mona – provides a haven for waterfowl, as well as the country's most extensive collection of holillo palms and sajo trees. Beyond Punta Mona, protecting a natural oyster bank, is the only red-mangrove swamp in Caribbean Costa Rica. In the nearby Río Gandoca estuary there is a spawning ground for Atlantic tarpon, and caimans and manatees have been sighted.

The variety of vegetation and the remote location of the refuge attract many tropical birds; sightings of the rare harpy eagle have been recorded here. Other birds to look out for include the red-lored parrot, the red-capped manikin and the chestnut-mandibled toucan, among hundreds of others. The area is also known for incredible raptor migrations, with more than a million birds flying overhead during autumn.

Despite the idyllic nature of the environment, there has been some political squabbling between Minae (the government agency that administers the national parks in Costa Rica) and some local businesses over the management of the refuge. Some local operators are trying to get the village excluded from the confines of the refuge – which would open the door to increased development in the area. (In fact, unapproved constructions have already materialized – some within 50m of the high-tide line, a zone in which construction is prohibited by national law.) Others oppose it. It will likely take years – and armies of lawyers – to sort the mess out.

🏃 Activities

Hiking

A coastal trail heads 5.5km east out of Manzanillo to Punta Mona. The first part of this path, which leads from Manzanillo to Tom Bay (about a 40-minute walk), is well trammeled, clearly marked and doesn't require a guide. Once you pass Tom Bay, however, the path gets murky and it's easy to get lost, so ask about conditions before you set out, or hire a guide. It's a rewarding walk – with amazing scenery, as well as excellent (and safe) swimming and snorkeling at the end.

Another, more difficult, 9km trail leaves from just west of Manzanillo and skirts the southern edges of the Pantano Punta Mona, continuing to the small community of Gandoca. This trail is not commonly walked, as most people access Punta Mona and Gandoca from the park entrance at the northern edge of the refuge, which is located on the road to Sixaola. If you want to try to hike this, be sure to hire a guide.

Snorkeling & Diving

The undersea portion of the park cradles one of the two living coral reefs in the country. Comprising five types of coral, the reefs begin in about 1m of water and extend 5km offshore to a barrier reef that local fishers have long relied on and researchers have only recently discovered. This colorful undersea world is home to some 400 species of fish and crustaceans. Punta Mona is a popular destination for snorkeling, though it's a trek so you may wish to hire a boat.

CARIBBEAN COAST REFUGIO NACIONAL DE VIDA SILVESTRE GANDOCA-MANZANILLO

Otherwise, you can snorkel offshore at Manzanillo at the eastern end of the beach (the riptide can be dangerous here; inquire about conditions before setting out). Also check out the Coral Reef Information Center at Aquamor Talamanca Adventures (p188) in Manzanillo.

Conditions vary widely, and clarity can be adversely affected by weather changes.

Kayaking

You can explore some of the area's waterways by kayak, available from Aquamor Talamanca Adventures (per hour/day US$6/25). Paddle out to the reef, or head up the Quebrada Home Wark, in the west of the village, or the tiny Simeon Creek, at the east end of the village. These are short paddles – ideal if you've got kids.

Dolphin-Watching

In 1997 a group of local guides in Manzanillo identified tucuxi dolphins, a little-known species previously not found in Costa Rica, and began to observe their interactions with bottlenose dolphins. A third species – the Atlantic spotted dolphin – is also common in this area. This unprecedented activity has attracted the attention of marine biologists and conservationists, who are following these animals with great interest.

For dolphin watching tours in the reserve (from US$55), contact ATEC (p178) in Puerto Viejo.

Turtle-Watching

Marine turtles – especially leatherback but also green, hawksbill and loggerhead – all nest on the beaches between Punta Mona and the Río Sixaola. Leatherbacks nest from March to July, with a peak in April and May. Local conservation efforts are underway to protect these nesting grounds since the growth of the area's human population has led to increased theft of turtle eggs.

During turtle season, no flashlights, beach fires or camping are allowed on the beach. All tourists must be accompanied by a local guide to minimize disturbance of the nesting turtles.

☞ Tours

You could explore the refuge on your own, but without a guide you'll likely miss out on the incredible diversity of medicinal plants, exotic birds and earthbound animals. Most guides charge US$35 per person for a four- to five-hour trek, depending on the size of the group. Ask around at Maxi's or at Casa de Guías (☏ 2759-9064).

Recommended local guides include Florentino Grenald (☏ 8841-2732, 2759-9043), who used to serve as the reserve's administrator, Omar (☏ 2759-9143; Cabinas Bucus) and Abel Bustamante (☏ 2759-9043).

ATEC (p178), Aquamor Talamanca Adventures (p188) and Casa de Guías offer tours of the area.

🛌 Sleeping & Eating

★ Punta Mona   CABINA $$

(www.puntamona.org; incl 3 organic meals campsites/r per person US$35/65; @) Accessible only by foot or boat, this 40-hectare organic farm and retreat 5km southeast of Manzanillo is a thriving experiment in permaculture design and sustainable living. It grows over 200 varieties of fruit and nut trees and hundreds of edible greens, roots, veggies and medicinal plants, which comprise 90% of the huge vegetarian meals included in the daily rate.

Check the website for myriad educational and volunteer opportunities here. To arrange accommodations and transportation, email contact@puntamona.org ahead of your visit.

ℹ Information

An excellent photo book on the area, with commentary in Spanish and English, is *Refugio Nacional de Vida Silvestre Gandoca-Manzanillo* by Juan José Pucci, available locally.

Minae (☏ 2759-9100; ⊗ 8am-noon & 1-4pm) is located in the green wooden house as you enter Manzanillo, and generally has trail maps of the refuge.

Aquamor Talamanca Adventures (p188) and Casa de Guías (p191) are also good sources of information on what to do in the park.

Bribrí

This bustling, no-stoplight town in the foothills of the Cordillera de Talamanca lies at a bend in the paved road that connects Cahuita to Sixaola and the Panama border. The village is primarily an agricultural center and a spot for nearby indigenous communities to take care of errands; most travelers just pass through on their way to the border or on local tours.

From Bribrí, a 34km paved road takes the traveler to the border at Sixaola.

◉ Sights & Activities

For information about tours to local indigenous villages, drive 2km west of town to Rancho Grande and ask for Catato (his house is just opposite Rancho Grande's football field).

Studio of Fran Vázquez   GALLERY
(☑2751-0205) On the road to Bribrí, 350m north of the Sixaola turnoff, find the studio of this self-taught folk painter whose colorful acrylic landscapes are well known in Puerto Viejo and San José. Look for the brightly painted sign outside a small one-story house. Call ahead to visit, as hours vary.

🛏 Sleeping & Eating

There are a few basic lodging options, a supermarket and the requisite Musmanni bakery. Accommodations tend to fill up on market days (Monday and Tuesday).

Cabinas El Piculino   CABINA $
(☑2751-0130; d with fan/air-con US$30/40; P❋🛰) Connected to the great soda (casados US$5; ☺Mon-Sat) run by the same family, this spotless place has 22 clean, simple, brightly painted rooms with private hot showers; all have TV and most have air-con.

Restaurante Bribrí   COSTA RICAN $
(☑2751-0044; breakfast US$3, casados US$5; ☺5am-5pm Mon-Sat) Run by the helpful Carlos and Miriam, this busy restaurant adjacent to the bus stop serves breakfast, *casados,* chicken with rice, fried plantains and tamales.

Restaurante Kaya Chökök
Mlàs Mlàs   CARIBBEAN $
(casados US$5-7, mains US$5-9; ☺7am-4pm) A pleasant 2nd-story terrace restaurant located near the Banco Nacional, this place serves up superdelicious cooking, including the delectably carnivorous 'Arroz Kaya' (US$6), a steaming pile of fried rice studded with bacon, ham, chicken and steak, and served with salad and fried plantains.

ℹ Information

Banco Nacional (☺8:30am-3:45pm) Has an ATM and changes US dollars. It's 100m north of the bus stop.

ℹ Getting There & Away

Buses arrive and depart hourly from in front of Restaurante Bribrí.
Puerto Limón, via Cahuita US$4.40; three hours; departs hourly from 6am to 7pm.
San José US$11.80; 5½ hours; departs 6:30am, 8:30am, 10:30am and 3:30pm.
Sixaola US$1.95; 30 minutes; departs hourly from 6am to 8pm.

Sixaola

POP 8900
This is the end of the road – literally. Bumpy tarmac leads to an old railroad bridge over the Río Sixaola that serves as the border crossing into Panama. Like most border towns, Sixaola is hardly scenic: it's an extravaganza of dingy bars and roadside stalls selling rubber boots.

Sixaola is centered on the optimistically named Mercado Internacional de Sixaola, a gravelly square where you can find taxis and a handful of *sodas.* The market is about two blocks from the border crossing.

There's no good reason to stay in Sixaola, but if you get stuck, head for safe, clean **Cabinas Sanchez** (☑2754-2105; r US$16). From the border, head north along the lower road and walk about 100m to the tunnel on the left. After exiting the underpass, walk west another 100m to find the *cabinas.*

The bus station is just north of the border crossing, one block east of the main drag. Buses to either San José (US$13.30, six hours, 6am, 8am, 10am and 3pm) or Puerto Limón (US$6.35, three hours, hourly from 5am to 6pm) all stop at Bribrí and Cahuita. There are also regular buses to Puerto Viejo de Talamanca (US$3.35, one hour, hourly between 5:30am and 5:30pm Monday through Saturday, every two hours on Sunday).

Northwestern Costa Rica

Best Places to Eat

➡ Café Caburé (p209)

➡ Trio (p209)

➡ Bar-B-Q Tres Hermanas (p220)

➡ Café Liberia (p229)

➡ Plaza Copal (p244)

Best Places to Sleep

➡ Casa Tranquilo (p204)

➡ Los Pinos Cabañas y Jardines (p206)

➡ Celeste Mountain Lodge (p221)

➡ Rio Perdido (p223)

Why Go

What did you come to Costa Rica for? To lounge on pristine beaches and ride glorious waves? To hike up volcanoes and soak in geothermal springs? To spy on birds and monkeys and get lost among ancient trees? The northwestern corner of Costa Rica packs in all this and more. Unlike any other part of Costa Rica, Guanacaste – in the far northwest – is a wide, flat expanse of grasslands and dry tropical forest, where savanna vistas are broken only by windblown trees. Further east, the Cordillera de Guanacaste rises majestically out of the plains in a line of sputtering, steaming volcanic peaks that beg exploration. Further south, higher altitudes create a misty, mystical cloud forest, teeming with life. What did you come to Costa Rica for? Here it is...

When to Go

➡ Guanacaste is Costa Rica's driest province, getting very little rain from November to April, when the winds bless (and blast) Bahía Salinas.

➡ By contrast, the 'green' season is very, very green in the cloud forest.

➡ Humpback whales migrate up the coast in September and October.

➡ Other seasonal events to watch out for are the blooming of the yellow cortezes in March and the *fiestas Guanacastecas* that occur throughout the year.

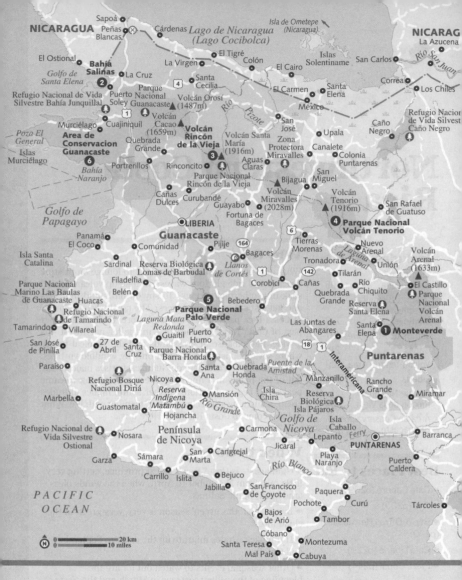

Northwestern Costa Rica Highlights

1 Spotting the resplendent quetzal through the mist at one of the reserves near **Monteverde** (p195).

2 Satisfying your need for speed with a kitesurfing course on windy **Bahía Salinas** (p242).

3 Trekking the circuit of waterfalls, thermal pools and volcanic vents at **Volcán Rincón de la Vieja** (p234).

4 Hiking along the raging Río Celeste at the **Parque Nacional Volcán Tenorio** (p221) and marvelling at her cerulean blue waters.

5 Watching wildlife at Costa Rica's largest wetland sanctuary, **Parque Nacional Palo Verde** (p224).

6 Exploring the Santa Rosa Sector of the **Área de Conservación Guanacaste** (p237) to discover the flora and fauna of the dry tropical forest.

Parks & Reserves

Northwestern Costa Rica has a wealth of parks and reserves, ranging from little-visited national parks to the highlight on many visitors' itineraries, Monteverde.

Área de Conservación Guanacaste (p237) Access legendary surf, hike through Central America's largest stand of tropical dry forest and visit a historical battle site.

Parque Nacional Guanacaste (p239) One of the least-visited parks in Costa Rica. The land transitions between dry tropical forest and humid cloud forest.

Parque Nacional Palo Verde (p224) Stay at the research station and take a guided tour to see some of the 300-plus bird species recorded in this rich wetland.

Parque Nacional Rincón de la Vieja (p234) Peaceful, muddy isolation can be found just outside of Liberia, where bubbling thermal activity abounds.

Refugio Nacional de Vida Silvestre Bahía Junquillal (p240) Another small, peaceful protected site, this refuge has a beach backed by mangrove swamp and tropical dry forest.

Reserva Biológica Bosque Nuboso Monteverde (p212) Costa Rica's most famous cloud forest, Monteverde receives a steady stream of visitors without having lost its magic.

Reserva Biológica Lomas de Barbudal (p226) If you're here in March, you might be lucky enough to catch the yellow blooms of the *corteza amarilla* tree in this tropical dry forest reserve.

Reserva Santa Elena (p203) Slightly less crowded and at a higher elevation than Monteverde, this is also a good place to spot a quetzal.

MONTEVERDE & AROUND

Monteverde & Santa Elena

POP 6750

Strung between two lovingly preserved cloud forests, this slim corridor of civilization consists of the Tico (Costa Rican) village of Santa Elena and the Quaker settlement of Monteverde, each with an eponymous cloud-forest reserve. A 1983 feature article in *National Geographic* described this unique landscape and subsequently billed the area as the place to view one of Central America's most famous birds, the resplendent quetzal. Suddenly, hordes of tourists armed with tripods and telephoto lenses started braving Monteverde's notoriously awful roads, which came as a huge shock to the then-established Quaker community. In an effort to stem the tourist flow, local communities lobbied to stop developers from paving the roads.

It worked – for a while. But the towns grew anyway, attracting tourists as well as new European and North American residents. Eventually, the lobby to spur development bested the lobby to limit development. With the paving of the main access road, this precious experiment in sustainable ecotourism will undergo a new set of trials.

The cloud forests around Monteverde and Santa Elena are among Costa Rica's premier destinations for everyone from budget backpackers to well-heeled retirees. On a good day, Monteverde is a place where you can be inspired about the possibility of a world in which organic farming and alternative energy sources are the norm. On a bad day, Monteverde can feel like Disneyland in Birkenstocks. Take heart in the fact that the local community continues to fight the good fight to maintain the fragile balance of nature and commerce.

◉ Sights

Butterfly Garden   ZOO
(Jardín de Mariposas; ☑2645-5512; www.monteverdebutterflygarden.com; adult/student/child US$15/10/5; ⊙8:30am-4pm) Everything you ever wanted to know about butterflies, with four gardens representing different habitats and home to more than 40 species. Up-close observation cases allow you to witness the butterflies as they emerge from the chrysalis (if your timing is right). Other exhibits feature the industrious leafcutter ant. Explore on your own or take advantage of the knowledgeable naturalist guides.

Monteverde Theme Park   ZOO
(Monteverde Frog Pond; ☑2645-6320; per attraction $13-17, canopy $35; ⊙9am-8pm) Formerly known as the Ranario, or Frog Pond, this place has recently added a butterfly garden and canopy tour – hence, it's now a theme park. The frogs are still the highlight: about 25 species reside in transparent enclosures lining the winding indoor jungle paths.

Monteverde & Santa Elena

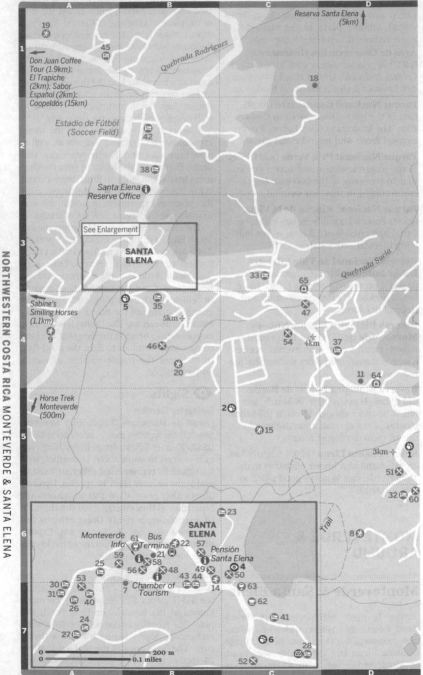

Reserva Santa Elena (5km)

Quebrada Rodríguez

19

45

Don Juan Coffee
Tour (1.9km);
El Trapiche
(2km); Sabor
Español (2km);
Coopeldós (15km)

18

Estadio de Fútbol
(Soccer Field)

42

38

Santa Elena
Reserve Office

See Enlargement

**SANTA
ELENA**

Quebrada Sucia

33

65

5

35

47

Sabine's
Smiling Horses
(1.1km)

5km

54

4km

37

9

46

20

11

64

Horse Trek
Monteverde
(500m)

2

15

3km

1

51

32

60

**SANTA
ELENA**

23

Monteverde
Info

Bus
Terminal

61

22

57

Pensión
Santa Elena

59

21

58

4

25

56

48

49

50

43

44

63

30

53

14

62

31

7

Chamber of
Tourism

Trail

8

26

40

41

24

6

27

28

52

0 _____ 200 m
0 _____ 0.1 miles

Sharp-eyed guides lead informative tours in English or Spanish, pointing out frogs, eggs and tadpoles with flashlights. Your ticket entitles you to two visits, so come back in the evening to see the nocturnal species. Combined tickets are available.

Bat Jungle
ZOO

(☎ 2645-7701; www.batjungle.com; adult/child US$12/10; ☺ 9am-7:30pm) Learn about echolocation, bat-wing aerodynamics and other amazing flying-mammal facts. The so-called Bat Jungle is small but informative, with good bilingual educational displays and a free-flying bat habitat housing almost 100 bats.

Serpentarium
ZOO

(Herpentario; ☎ 2645-6002; adult/student/child US$13/11/8; ☺ 9am-8pm) A guide will show you around and introduce you to some 40 species of slithery snakes, plus a fair number of frogs, lizards, turtles and other coldblooded critters.

Jardín de Orquídeas
GARDENS

(Orchid Garden; ☎ 2645-5308; www.monteverdeorchidgarden.net; adult/child US$10/free; ☺ 8am-5pm) This sweet-smelling garden has shady trails winding past more than 400 types of orchid organized into taxonomic groups. On your guided tour, you'll see such rarities as *Platystele jungermannioides*, the world's smallest orchid. If you have orchids at home, here's your chance to get tips from the experts on how to keep them beautiful and blooming.

🏃 Activities

Bosque Eterno de los Niños
HIKING

(Children's Eternal Forest, BEN; ☎ 2645-5003; www.acmcr.org; adult/student US$12/6, guided night hike US$20/17, Estación Biológica San Gerardo all-inclusive US$52; ☺ 7:30am-5:30pm, night hike 5:30pm) What became of the efforts of a group of schoolchildren to save the rainforest? Only this enormous 220-sq-km reserve – the largest private reserve in the country. It is mostly inaccessible to tourists, with the exception of the well-marked 3.5km **Sendero Bajo del Tigre** (Jaguar Canyon Trail), which is actually a series of shorter trails. At the entrance there's an education center for children and a fabulous vista over the reserve.

Make reservations in advance for the popular two-hour night hikes. The Estación Biológica San Gerardo, reachable from a rather gnarly 2½-hour trail from Reserva

Monteverde & Santa Elena

Santa Elena, is managed by BEN and has dorm beds for researchers and students, but you may be able to stay overnight with prior arrangements.

Curi-Cancha Reserve
HIKING

(www.curi-cancha.com; admission US$12, guided hike US$15; ⊙ 7am-3:30pm, guided hike 7:30am & 5:30pm) Bordering Monteverde but without the crowds, this lovely private reserve on the banks of the Cuecha River is popular among birders. There are about 10km of well-marked trails, a hummingbird garden and a view of the Continental Divide.

Santuario Ecológico
HIKING

(Ecological Sanctuary; ☏ 2645-5869; www.santuarioecologico.com; adult/student/child US$10/8/6, guided night tour US$15/12/10; ⊙ 7am-5:30pm, guided night tours 5:30-7:30pm) Offering hikes of varying lengths, Santuario Ecológico has four loop trails through private property comprising premontane and secondary forest, coffee and banana plantations, and past a couple of waterfalls and lookout points. Coatis, agoutis and sloths are commonly sighted, as are monkeys, porcupines and other animals. Birders have a good chance of spotting hummingbirds, hawks and toucans as well as high-profile species like the resplendent quetzal and wattled bellbird.

Hidden Valley   HIKING
(Valle Escondido; ☑2645-6601; www.monteverdenighttour.com; day use US$8, guided hike incl lunch US$40, night tour adult/child US$25/15; ⊙7am-4pm, night walk 5:30pm) This trail begins behind Pensión Monteverde Inn and slowly winds its way through a deep canyon into an 11-hectare reserve. During the day, Valle Escondido is quiet and relatively undertouristed, so it's a good trail for birding and wildlife-watching. The two-hour guided night tour is popular, so reserve in advance.

Cerro Amigos   HIKING
FREE Take a hike up to the highest peak in the area (1842m) for good views of the surrounding rainforest and, on a clear day, Volcán Arenal, 20km away to the northeast. The trail begins behind Hotel Belmar and ascends roughly 300m in 3km. From the hotel, take the dirt road going downhill, then the next left. Note that this trail does not connect to the trails in the Monteverde reserve.

Santa Maria Night Walk   WALKING
(☑2645-6548; www.nightwalksantamarias.com; per person US$22; ⊙tour 5:30pm) Night walks have become super popular, perhaps because 80% of the cloud-forest creatures are nocturnal. Expert guides point out all kinds of wildlife that are active in the evening, ranging from snakes and spiders to sloths and kinkajous. Flashlights are provided.

Sabine's Smiling Horses   HORSE RIDING
(☑8385-2424, 2645-6894, www.smilinghorses. com; per person US$45-65) Conversant in four languages (in addition to equine), Sabine will make sure you are comfortable on your horse, whether you're a novice rider or an experienced cowboy. Her long-standing operation in Monteverde offers a variety of treks including a popular waterfall tour (three hours). And yes, the horses really really do smile.

Horse Trek Monteverde   HORSE RIDING
(☑8359-3485; www.horsetrekmonteverde.com; per person US$45-85) Owner and guide Marvin Anchia is a Santa Elena native, a professional horse trainer and an amateur naturalist who offers an excellent, intimate horse-riding experience. Tours range from scenic half-day rides in the cloud forest to all-day cowboy experiences to multiday treks. The horses are well cared for, well trained and a joy to ride.

Caballeriza El Rodeo   HORSE RIDING
(☑2645-5764, 2645-6306; elrodeo02@gmail.com; per person $40-60) Based at a *finca* (farm), this outfit offers tours on private trails through field and forest. The specialty is a sunset tour to a spot overlooking the Golfo de Nicoya.

SkyTram   SCENIC RIDE
(☑2645-5238; www.skyadventures.travel; adult/child US$44/28) Owned by SkyTrek, SkyTram is a wheelchair-accessible cable car that floats gently over the cloud forest. On a clear day you can see from the volcanoes in the east to the Pacific in the west. Packages are available if you're also interested in the SkyTrek (canopy tour) and SkyWalk (hanging bridges).

Monteverde Cloud Forest Train   SCENIC RIDE
(☑2645-5700; adult/child US$50/free; ♿) This charming narrow-gauge train system travels 6.4km through the forest, penetrating one tunnel and crossing four bridges. The scenic railroad offers amazing views of Monteverde and Arenal lake and volcano. This is a great option for families with young children who are loco for locos. It's located 5km north of downtown Santa Elena; take the road toward Reserva Santa Elena and follow the signs.

Finca Modelo Ecologica   OUTDOORS
(☑2645-5581; www.familiabrenestours.com; canyoning US$50, farm tours US$15-25; ⊙tours 8am, 11am & 2pm) This 3000-acre family *finca* offers a number of diversions, including two-hour dairy tours and a similar perusal of its organic vegetable garden, but its raison d'être is a two-hour canyoning tour, which descends six glorious waterfalls, the largest of which is 40m. No experience necessary – just an adventurous spirit! Located 2km north of Santa Elena in the village of La Cruz.

🎓 Courses

Centro Panamericano
de Idiomas   LANGUAGE COURSE
(CPI; ☑2265-6306; www.cpi-edu.com; week-long classes US$390; ⊙8am-5pm) Specializes in Spanish-language education, with courses geared toward families, teenagers, medical professionals and retirees. For fun: optional dance and cooking classes are included with your tuition.

1. Three-toed sloth, Sloth Sanctuary of Costa Rica (p169)
Orphaned and injured sloths are cared for in this private wildlife sanctuary.

2. SkyTram (p199)
The cable car glides over the Monteverde cloud forest, offering views of the canopy below, volcanoes and the Pacific.

3. Volcán Arenal (p259)
This active volcano is surrounded by an area of high biodiversity that is home to hundreds of species of birds and animals.

Monteverde Institute　　　LANGUAGE COURSE

(☑2645-5053; www.monteverde-institute.org; week-long courses US$360, homestay incl meals per day US$22) This nonprofit educational institute offers interdisciplinary courses in Spanish, as well as more specialized programs in tropical biology, conservation and sustainable development, among other topics. Courses are occasionally open to the public, as are volunteer opportunities in education and reforestation.

👉 Tours

Wonder where the whole canopy-tour craze was born? Santa Elena is the site of Costa Rica's first zip lines, today eclipsed in adrenaline by the nearly 100 imitators who have followed, some of which are right here in town. You won't be spotting any quetzals or coatis as you whoosh your way over the canopy, but if you came to Costa Rica to fly, this is the absolute best place to do it. If you want to explore the treetops without the adrenaline rush, several of these outifts also have systems of hanging bridges. Transportation from your lodging is included in the price.

Keep in mind that Monteverde works on a commission-based system, so take all unsolicited advice with a degree of skepticism. When in doubt, it's good to talk to the friendly, unbiased staff at Pensión Santa Elena if you want the full scoop.

Aventura　　　CANOPY TOUR

(☑2645-6388; www.monteverdeadventure.com; canopy adult/child US$45/35, bridges US$35/25; ☉7am-4pm) Aventura has 19 platforms that are spiced up with a Tarzan swing, a 15m rappel and a Superman zip line that makes you feel as if you really are flying. Aventura's cables and bridges are laced through secondary forest only. It's about 3km north of Santa Elena on the road to the reserve, but there's a booking office in town.

Extremo Canopy　　　CANOPY TOUR

(☑2645-6058; www.monteverdeextremo.com; canopy US$40, super cable US$30, bungee US$60, tarzan swing $35; ☉8am-4pm) This outfit doesn't bother with extraneous attractions if all you really want to do is fly down the zip lines. Located in secondary forest, there's a canopy ride, allowing you to fly Superman-style through the air; the highest and most adrenaline-addled Tarzan swing in the area; and a bungee jump. One way or another, you will scream.

Original Canopy Tour　　　CANOPY TOUR

(☑2291-4465; www.canopytour.com; adult/student/child US$45/35/25; ☉7:30am-4pm) On the grounds of Cloud Forest Lodge, this is the fabled zip-line route that started this adventure/theme park trend. These lines aren't as elaborate as the others, but with 14 platforms, a rappel through the center of an old fig tree and 5km of private trails worth a wander afterward, you can enjoy a piece of history that's far more entertaining than most museums. It's 1km north of town, on the way to Reserva Santa Elena.

Selvatura　　　CANOPY TOUR

(☑2645-5929; www.selvatura.com; canopy US$45, walkways US$30, each exhibit US$15; ☉7:30am-4pm) One of the bigger games in town, Selvatura has 3km of cables, 18 platforms and one Tarzan swing over a stretch of incredibly beautiful primary cloud forest. In addition to the cables it has 3km of 'Treetops Walkways', as well as a hummingbird garden, a butterfly garden and an amphibian and reptile exhibition. Selvatura is 6km north of Santa Elena, near the reserve, but there's a booking office in town.

SkyTrek　　　CANOPY TOUR

(☑2645-5238; www.skyadventures.travel; adult/child SkyWalk US$35/22, SkyTrek US$71/45; ☉7:30am-5pm) This seriously fast canopy tour consists of 11 platforms attached to steel towers that are spread out along a road and zoom over swatches of primary forest. We're talking serious speeds of up to 64km/h, which is probably why SkyTrek was the first canopy tour with a real brake system. The SkyWalk is a 2km guided tour over five suspended bridges; a night tour is also available.

Café Monteverde　　　COFFEE TOUR

(☑2645-5901; www.cafemonteverde.com; per person US$15; ☉7:30am-6pm) 🍃 Run by the small-scale Cooperative Santa Elena, this highly recommended tour takes visitors to organic *fincas* that are also implementing sustainable growing techniques like composting and biodiesel. Help to pick perfect coffee beans, then head to the *beneficio* (coffee mill) to watch the beans get washed and dried, roasted and packed. The tour includes a taste of the final product.

Coopeldós RL　　　COFFEE TOUR

(☑2693-8441; www.coopeldos.com) Coopeldós is a cooperative of 450 small and medium-sized organic coffee growers from the area.

DON'T MISS

RESERVA SANTA ELENA

Though Monteverde gets all the attention, the misty **Reserva Santa Elena** (☑2645-7107, 2645-5390; www.reservasantaelena.org; adult/student US$14/7, guided hike US$15; ⊙7am-4pm) has plenty to recommend it. You can practically hear the epiphyte-draped canopy breathing out humid exhales as water drops onto the leaf litter and mud underfoot. The odd call of the three-wattled bellbird and the low crescendo of a howler monkey punctuate the higher-pitched bird chatter. While Monteverde Crowd...er...Cloud Forest entertains almost 200,000 visitors annually, Santa Elena sees fewer than 20,000 tourists each year, which means its dewy trails through mysteriously veiled forest are usually far quieter.

This cloud forest is slightly higher in elevation than Monteverde's, and as some of the forest is secondary growth, there are sunnier places for spotting birds and other animals throughout. There's a stable population of monkey and sloth, many of which can be seen on the road to the reserve. Unless you're a trained ecologist, the old-growth forest in Santa Elena will seem fairly similar in appearance to Monteverde.

At 310 hectares, the community-run Santa Elena is much smaller than the other forest. More than 12km of trails are open for hiking, including four circular trails of varying difficulty and length. Guided hikes depart from the visitors center four times a day (reservations recommended).

The reserve is about 6km northeast of the village of Santa Elena, but the **reserve office** (☑2645-5693; ⊙8am-4pm Wed-Fri) is located at the high school. To reach the reserve itself, catch the bus (US$2, 30 minutes, four daily) from the Banco Nacional in town.

You might drink Coopeldós blends back home, as this Fairtrade certified organization sells to Starbucks, among other clients. Tours include a visit to the industrial facility, followed up by some hands-on (mouth-on) quality control. The co-op is located in the village of El Dós, about halfway between Tilarán and Monteverde. Make special arrangements if you want to visit a nearby organic coffee plantation.

Don Juan Coffee Tour　COFFEE TOUR
(☑2645-7100; www.donjuancoffeetour.com; adult/child US$30/12; ⊙7am-4:30pm) Don Juan is a more commercial operation offering a three-in-one tour, where you can learn about all of your favorite vices – coffee, chocolate and sugar (OK, maybe not *all* of your favorites, but three of the good ones). See how sugarcane is harvested and processed. Learn how cacao beans are transformed into that dark, decadent dessert. And witness the whole coffee process, from plant to bean to cup.

El Trapiche　COFFEE TOUR
(☑2645-7650; www.eltrapichetour.com; adult/child US$32/12; ⊙10am & 3pm Mon-Sat, 3pm Sun) Visit this family *finca*, where they grow not only coffee but also sugarcane, bananas and plantains. The tour covers the entire coffee process and includes a ride in a traditional oxcart. Finish with a cup of coffee or a sample of the area's other famous beverage, *saca de guaro* (sugarcane liquor).

Caburé Chocolate Tour　CHOCOLATE TOUR
(☑2645-5020; www.cabure.net) Bob, the owner of Caburé chocolate shop, shares his secrets about the magical cacao pod and how to transform it into the food of the gods. There are plenty of opportunities for taste testing along the way, and you'll try your hand at making truffles.

Monteverde Cheese Factory　CHEESE FACTORY
(La Lechería; ☑2645-7090; www.monteverdecheesefactory.com; tours adult/child US$12/10; ⊙tours 9am & 2pm Mon-Sat, store 7:30am-5pm Mon-Sat, to 4pm Sun) Learn about the history of the Quakers in Costa Rica and their methods for producing and pasteurizing cheese. The Monteverde Cheese Factory is now the second-largest cheese producer in the country. Don't miss the chance to sample Monte Rico, a Monteverde original.

🛏 Sleeping

Budget travelers have loads of options in Santa Elena, while midrange and high-end travelers might want to take a look in nearby Cerro Plano, Monteverde and the forested hills around town.

Reservations are practically required during holiday weeks, and recommended throughout the high season. We have listed high-season rates, which drop 30% to 40% during the low season.

🛏 Santa Elena

★ Casa Tranquilo
B&B $

(📞 2645-6782; www.casatranquilohostel.com; dm/r per person incl breakfast US$10/15; 🅿@🛜) At Casa Tranquilo, the wonderful Tico hospitality starts first thing in the morning with homemade banana bread. In addition to the excellent breakfast, staff lead free guided hikes, sharing their in-depth local expertise. The rooms are simple and spotless, some featuring skylights and gulf views. Colorful murals adorn the outside, so you'll know you are in the right place.

Pensión Santa Elena
HOSTEL $

(📞 2645-5051; www.pensionsantaelena.com; incl breakfast dm US$12, s/d/tr without bathroom from US$16/24/36, standard s/d/tr US$19/29/36, plus s/d US$25/37; 🅿@🛜) This full-service hostel right in central Santa Elena is a perennial favorite, offering budget travelers top-notch service and *pura vida* (pure life) hospitality. Each room is different, with something to suit every budget. The 'plus' rooms in the annex feature perks like superior beds, stone showers and iPod docks.

Cabinas Eddy
CABINA $

(📞 2645-6635; www.cabinas-eddy.com; d US$40-60, without bathroom US$35; 🅿@🛜) This reader-recommended budget spot contin-ues to get raves for its amazing breakfasts, attentive service and delightful manager Freddy (son of Eddy, by the way). The rooms are spotless, as is the fully equipped communal kitchen. The balcony is a great place to relax with a cup of free coffee and take in the view.

Monteverde Hostel Lodge
HOSTEL $

(📞 2645-5989; www.monteverdehostellodge.com; dm US$16, s/d/tr/q from US$37/44/57/68; 🅿🛜) Think of a classy mountain lodge with lots of amenities, where you meet cool people and share adventures. That's the concept behind the hostel-lodge. Rooms range from stylish six-bed dorm rooms to private, semi-luxurious treetop cabins. All guests are invited to the huge common area to listen to some tunes, access free wi-fi and sip happy-hour cocktails.

Prices include a guided hike on the woodsy grounds, home to friendly white-faced capuchin monkeys. Movie nights, barbecue dinners and other events mean that you will have something to do after sunset.

Camino Verde B&B
B&B $

(📞 2645-5641; www.hotelcaminoverde.com; incl breakfast s/d US$30/40, s/d without bathroom $25/30; 🅿🛜) This well-loved travelers' nest offers an assortment of spacious, bright rooms with wood ceilings and tile floors. There's a sweet little restaurant and a rambling garden. Rocking chairs are scattered about the porch, offering a perfect spot to soak up the scenic view.

QUAKERS IN MONTEVERDE

In 1949 four members of the Society of Friends, or Quakers, were jailed in Alabama for their refusal to be drafted into the Korean War. Since Quakers are obligated by their religion to be pacifists, the four men were eventually released from prison. However, in response to the incarceration, 44 Quakers from 11 Alabama families left the USA and headed for greener pastures, literally. The Quakers chose Monteverde (Green Mountain) for two reasons: a few years prior, the Costa Rican government had abolished its military, and the cool mountain climate was ideal for grazing cattle. Ensconced in their isolated refuge they adopted a simple, trouble-free life of dairy farming and cheese production. In an effort to protect the watershed above its 15-sq-km plot in Monteverde, the Quaker community agreed to preserve the mountaintop cloud forests.

The Quaker community is still active in Monteverde, both in preservation of the land and in production of the cheese. Visit them at the **Friends Meeting House** (⊘ meetings 10:30am Sun, 9am Wed) or the Monteverde Cheese Factory (p203). If you're willing to give at least a six-week commitment, there are numerous volunteer opportunities. For more information, contact the **Monteverde Friends School** (www.mfschool.org).

Cabinas El Pueblo
CABINA $

(☎2645-6192; www.cabinaselpueblo.com; d incl breakfast with/without bathroom US$40/24; P@☎) On a quiet road steps from the town, this pleasant hostel is run by an attentive Tico couple, Marlenne and Freddy. Well-furnished rooms are bright and clean, if cramped. You'll also find a communal kitchen, hammocks, and – most importantly – an exceedingly warm welcome. All guests are gifted a treat from the family coffee plantation.

Sloth Backpackers
HOSTEL $

(☎2645-5793; www.hotelslothbackpackers.com; dm/r per person incl breakfast US$8/15; P☎) This colorful corrugated-tin and cinderblock hostel comes with super-friendly management and excellent hammock swings. The rooms are simple, but they all have wooden beds covered with quilts and frilly homemade toilet-seat covers, featuring (of course) an adorable sloth.

Sleepers
HOSTEL $

(☎8305-0113; www.sleeperssleepcheaperhostels.com; incl breakfast dm US$9, d US$25-30, apt US$30-45) You can't miss this lime green and aqua blue building in central Santa Elena. Downstairs it looks like a friendly restaurant, but it's actually a communal kitchen, where happy travelers prepare and share meals. Upstairs it looks like a modern motel, but it's actually a hostel, where happy travelers surf the web and catch a breeze on the balcony.

Rooms are spotless, with en suite bathrooms. The 3rd-floor efficiency apartment is a steal.

Monteverde Backpackers
HOSTEL $

(☎2645-5844; www.monteverdebackpackers.com; incl breakfast dm US$10-12, d/tr/q US$30/45/56; P@☎) Small and friendly, Monteverde Backpackers is part of the Costa Rica Hostel Network. The wood-paneled rooms are clean and comfy enough, the showers are hot, the location is quiet, the management is helpful. Breakfast is DIY, so you can make 'em how you like 'em (eggs, that is).

Arco Iris Ecolodge
LODGE $$

(☎2645-5067; www.arcoirislodge.com; s/d/tr budget from US$32/42/52, standard US$67/88/98, superior US$105/115/130; P@☎) This clutch of pretty cabins is on a little hill overlooking Santa Elena and the surrounding forests. Rooms vary in size and style, but all are quite lovely, with lots of stained wood, rainforest showers and private terraces. A system of private trails winds through the property, including one that leads to a lookout with views to the Pacific.

Monteverde Rustic Lodge
HOTEL $$

(☎2645-6256; www.monteverderusticlodge.com; d/tr/q incl breakfast US$70/85/105; P) Funny thing about the Rustic Lodge: it's not that rustic. The tree-trunk posts and furnishings play along with the theme, but the remodeled rooms are spotless, comfortable and even upscale. Decorated in subtle earth tones, the rooms have lots of stained wood, tile floors and floral curtains. The shared balcony or terrace overlooks a blooming garden.

Mar Inn B&B
B&B $$

(☎2645-5279; www.monteverdemarinn.com; d incl breakfast without/with view US$62/79; P@☎) This humble, homey B&B is a family-run place that makes all guests feel warm and welcome. Rooms are rustic but reasonably comfortable. There's a communal kitchen and a shared balcony where rocking chairs are oriented toward those lovely sunset views of Santa Elena and the Golfo de Nicoya.

Hotel El Atardecer
HOTEL $$

(☎2645-5485; www.atardecerhotel.com; s/d/tr/q incl breakfast US$40/65/85/98; P☎) This attractive two story wooden lodge is located away from the main drag, guaranteeing a good night's rest (as long as your neighbors aren't too noisy). Surrounding a spacious courtyard restaurant, the tiled rooms have high, beamed ceilings, good mattresses and new bathroom tile. All in all, it's not a bad place to come home to.

Hotel Claro de Luna
B&B $$

(☎2645-5269; www.clarodelunahotel.com; d incl breakfast US$72-93; P☎) This graceful old mahogany gingerbread-style house is surrounded by lush gardens bursting with heliconias, orchids and other tropical blooms. The rooms are also cheerful, with brightly painted interiors and floral quilts. Unfortunately, sound travels easily in this old house: get a room in the downstairs annex if you can.

Swiss Hotel Miramontes
HOTEL $$

(☎2645-5297; www.swisshotelmiramontes.com; s/d/chalets incl breakfast US$45/57/90; P☎) About 500m north of the soccer field on the road to Juntas, this charming Euro-inspired retreat is well situated in a grove of pine trees and tropical flowers. Expansive grounds are landscaped with trails winding through the gorgeous orchid gardens. The eight wood-paneled rooms are a little stuffy but satisfactory, while the chalets offer porches and more privacy.

Hotel Poco a Poco
HOTEL $$$

(☑2645-6000; www.hotelpocoapoco.com; d incl breakfast from US$151; P🐾@🛜🏊) There's a lot to love about Poco a Poco. The spa, of course. The restaurant is also excellent, and the contemporary architecture is striking. The whole place is family friendly, with a small playground, a kiddie pool, and ceramic critters peeking out in unexpected places. Rooms show off a sophisticated style, with soothing earth tones and wooden accents.

Pay more for the views from the upper floors.

Ficus Sunset Suites
HOTEL $$$

(☑2645-6200, 2645-5157; d incl breakfast US$149; P❄@🛜) Just south of Santa Elena, these brand-new rooms are spacious and stylish, with private terraces and sweet views of the town and forest beyond. Unfortunately, the landscaping is nonexistent and the design is more 'suburban condo' than 'cloud-forest lodge'. Nonetheless, after a day trekking through the mist and the mud, you'll appreciate that hot shower and comfy bed.

🛏 Around Santa Elena

★Los Pinos Cabañas y Jardines
LODGE $$

(☑2645-5252; www.lospinos.net; cabaña d/ste/d US$70/85/140, superior d US$115; P🅿🛜) 🌿 Fourteen freestanding *cabañas* (cabins) are scattered around the peaceful, forested gardens of this 9-hectare property, which once formed part of the family *finca*. With plenty of space between them, each *cabaña* affords plenty of privacy, plus a fully equipped kitchen and small terrace. It's a superb setting for those seeking a little solitude, with some great options for families.

If you're looking for a bit of luxury, there is that too, with new 'superior' rooms that are fitted with fireplaces and balconies.

Hotel El Bosque
HOTEL $$

(☑2645-5221; www.bosquelodgecr.com; s/d/tr/q incl breakfast US$62/73/85/96; P❄🛜) On the edge of the Bosque Eterno de los Niños, this place is a pleasant surprise. Stand-alone

wood cabins are surrounded by tropical gardens and primary forest, with many kilometers of trails to get lost on. Wildlife abounds – keep your eyes open for agoutis, coatis, cappuchin monkeys and amazing birds. Walking distance to pastries and pizza.

Finca Terra Viva
LODGE $$

(☑2645-5454; www.terravivacr.com; d/q incl breakfast US$50/80; P🅿@🛜) 🌿 A 300-acre working dairy *finca* surrounded by lush forest, this is a unique sleep that offer guests a typically Costa Rican rural experience. Try your hand at milking cows and making cheese at the organic dairy, or go horse riding around farm and forest. Kids love this place. It's about 3.5km out on the road toward Reserva Santa Elena.

Mariposa B&B
B&B $$

(☑2645-5013; www.mariposabb.com; s/d/tr incl breakfast US$40/60/72; P🛜) Just 1.5km from the Monteverde reserve, this friendly family-run place has quite nice rooms with stained-wood walls, terra-cotta floors and beamed ceilings, not to mention a sweet Tico family looking after guests. It's nestled in the forest, with a sunny terrace for observing wildlife or just savoring a cup of local joe. There's not much in the vicinity, so you'll want wheels.

La Colina Lodge
LODGE $$

(☑2645-5009; www.lacolinalodge.com; d incl breakfast without/with bathroom US$35/55; P) Unpretentious and inviting, this peaceful property is aflutter with feathered friends and other farmyard animals. Slightly ragged rooms are hand-painted in cheery colors with unique furniture and decor. The sunny grounds include a communal kitchen and plenty of places to relax. The place is looking a bit worse for wear, but it's charming.

Formerly the Flor Mar, this hotel was first opened in 1977 by Marvin Rockwell, one of the area's original Quakers, who was jailed for refusing to sign up for the draft in 1949 in Alabama.

Hotel El Viandante
HOTEL $$

(☑2645-6475; www.hotelelviandante.com; s/d/tr/q incl breakfast US$68/80/96/113; P🅿@🛜) Perched on a small but steep hill in Cerro Plano with views of the gulf, this stone lodge is a solid choice. The rooms are pretty standard, with plain furniture, pinewood interiors and high ceilings, but the service is outstanding. Italian-American couple Renzo

WORTH A TRIP

SAN LUIS ECOLODGE & RESEARCH STATION

Formerly a tropical biology research station, this drop-dead-gorgeous facility is Monteverde's best-kept secret. Administered by the University of Georgia, it integrates academia with high-quality ecotourism and education. The 62-hectare campus is set on a cinematic jade plateau with cloud-forested mountains jackknifing on three sides and keyhole sea views to the west. Adjoining the southern reach of the Monteverde reserve, much of the campus overlooks the boiling waters of the RÍO San Luis. Its average elevation of 1100m makes it a tad lower and warmer than Monteverde, and bird-watchers have recorded some 230 species attracted by the slightly nicer weather. There's a working farm with tropical-fruit orchards and a coffee harvest from November to March, and a number of trails into primary and secondary forest.

Comfortable accommodations at the **lodge** (☑ 2643-7363; www.ecolodgesanluis.com; dm/s/d incl meals US$49/102/192, 🅿 @ 🛜) are available for anyone interested in learning about the cloud-forest environment and experiencing a bit of rural Costa Rican life. Rooms are built into a long house with soaring beamed ceilings and a common balcony overlooking a forest teeming with monkeys and migratory birds. Rates include meals, guided hikes, and a variety of slideshows and seminars about natural history. Discounts can be arranged for students, researchers, large groups and long stays.

The ecolodge also runs a resident naturalist volunteer program, though there is a preference for University of Georgia students and graduates, and a six-month commitment is required. The position entails leading a number of workshops and guided walks, as well as participating in development projects on the station and in the community. Training, room and board are provided. Yes, this is a special place to spend a few days/weeks/months/years.

From the main road between Santa Elena and Monteverde, it's a steep 3km walk from the signed road where the bus will drop you off. A 4WD taxi from Santa Elena costs about US$15 each way, and the lodge can also arrange transportation from San José in advance.

and Grace are your charming hosts. Enjoy an American breakfast with a view from the top-floor lounge.

It's about 1.5km south of Santa Elena.

★ **Hotel Belmar** HOTEL $$$
(☑ 2645-5201; www.hotelbelmar.net; peninsula r US$150-160, deluxe chalets US$178-308; 🅿 @ 🛜 🏊) 🏄 Every room at the Belmar boasts a spectacular view of forest or gulf. (Indeed, you can see both from the 270 degrees of windows in some of the deluxe chalets.) The gorgeous light-filled rooms are decked out with hand-crafted furniture, high-thread-count linens and spectacular sunsets from the private balconies – and the higher you go, the more spectacular they are.

The chalets are truly splurge worthy, with floor-to-ceiling windows, huge balconies and hot tubs. Other perks (for everybody) include yoga classes, spa services and a fabulous restaurant with those same jaw-dropping views. Incidentally, this place is a *real* eco-resort, boasting five leaves from the Certificate of Sustainable Tourism program.

Solar-heated water, biodigested energy and rainwater harvesting are just a few of the sustainable practices at the Belmar.

Hidden Canopy Treehouses BOUTIQUE HOTEL $$$
(☑ 2645-5447; www.hiddencanopy.com; incl breakfast d US$254, tree houses US$322-390; 🅿 ⊖ 🛜) Hidden within 13 acres of private rainforest are five stunning stilted tree houses, built of wood and windows. Guests relish the private treetop balconies, luxurious bedding, waterfall showers, custom-made furniture and local artwork. There are two less expensive, less spacious, but equally attractive rooms in the main house. Prices include sunset drinks, featuring an amazing light show in the sky.

Hidden Canopy is 3km north of Santa Elena on the road to the reserve. No kids; two-night minimum.

Hotel Fonda Vela LODGE $$$
(☑ 2645-5125; www.fondavela.com; d/ste US$135/180; 🅿 ⊖ @ 🛜 🏊) With unique architectural styling, 14 hectares of trail-laced

grounds and a private stable, this classy retreat is a sophisticated base for enjoying nature. Standard rooms are spacious and light, with wood accents and large windows; and the suites are among the nicest rooms in town, featuring wood ceilings, bathtub, balcony and sitting room. Located about 2km from the Monteverde reserve.

Cloud Forest Lodge   LODGE $$$
(☎2645-5058; www.cloudforestlodge.com; s/d/tr/q US$102/113/124/135; ⓟ@☎) Sleep in the clouds: this hilltop lodge is up there, surrounded by 28 hectares of primary and secondary forest. There are trails to walk, species to check off your bird list and gulf views to marvel at. The rooms are rather basic for the price, but they are clean and comfortable and – frankly – you won't be spending much time there.

The Original Canopy Tour is right here at the lodge, which is about 1km from Santa Elena. It's a pleasant walk into town, but you'll get your exercise on the way back.

Vista Verde Lodge   LODGE $$$
(☎2200-5259; www.info-monteverde.com; d standard/superior US$108/116; ⓟ) Wanna get away? Drive your 4WD 7km north of town to this remote, weather-beaten lodge, where you'll fall asleep to the sounds of the rainforest. Wood-paneled rooms with picture windows take in views of Volcán Arenal and beyond. If it feels a little damp (as it does), head to the cozy common area to warm your feet beside the fire.

Some 4km of trails run through 64 hectares of primary and secondary forest. Hike to the waterfall, which provides the hydroelectric energy that this place runs on.

Trapp Family Lodge   HOTEL $$$
(☎2645-5858; www.trappfam.com; d from US$113; ⓟ☺@☎) You can't get much closer to the Monteverde reserve than here (less than 1km

from the entrance). The trade-off, of course, is that it's far away from everything else. The 20 spacious rooms have high wooden ceilings, big bathrooms and fabulous views from picture windows (which overlook gardens or cloud forest). The restaurant is elegant but overpriced.

✗ Eating

Santa Elena has most of the budget kitchens in the area, but there's good eating throughout the Monteverde swirl.

The giant **SuperCompro** (☎2758-7351; ☺7am-9pm) grocery store in Santa Elena has everything you could possibly need, including organic produce. The tiny **Whole Foods Market** (☺7:30am-5:30pm) – no relation to the corporate-organic global dominatrix – in Cerro Plano has a smaller selection, but profits are reinvested in the community (it's part of the Casem cooperative).

✗ Santa Elena

Taco Taco   MEXICAN $
(mains US$5-8; ☺noon-8pm; ☎) Quick and convenient, this *taquería* (taco stall) offers tasty Tex-Mex tacos, burritos and quesadillas filled with shredded chicken, slow-roasted short rib, pork *al pastor* (cooked on a spit), roasted veggies and battered mahi mahi. The only difficulty is deciding (but you really can't go wrong).

Orchid Cafe   BAKERY $
(☎2645-6850; mains US$2-12; ☺7am-7pm; ☎) 🍴 If you have a hankering for something sweet, go straight to this lovely little cafe. Take a seat on the front porch and take a bite of heaven. Aside from pastries and pies, crepes and cookies, there's a full menu of savories, such as ciabatta sandwiches, interesting and unusual salads and delicious quiche. Breakfast also gets an A+.

MONTEVERDE CHEESE FACTORY

Until the upswing in ecotourism, Monteverde's number-one employer was the Monteverde Cheese Factory (p203). Started in 1953 by Monteverde's original Quaker settlers, the factory produces everything from a creamy Gouda to a very nice sharp, white cheddar, sold all over the country, as well as other dairy products such as yogurt and, most importantly, ice cream. Reservations are required for the two-hour tour of the factory, but you can pop in any time to sample the creamy goodness. Bonus: now there's a Santa Elena **outlet** (ice creams $US2-4; ☺10am-8pm), right next door to the Catholic church.

Sabor Tico　　　　　　　　SODA **$**
(☑2645-5847; http://restaurantesabortico.com; mains US$5-8; ☺9am-9pm) 🍴 Ticos and travelers alike rave about this local joint. Look for some tasty twists on the standard fare, such as *chalupas* (boat-shaped tostadas filled with meat or cheese), tamales and delicious rice dishes. *Casados* (set meals) are served with delicious homemade corn tortillas. If you have room for dessert, go for fried plaintains in cinnamon syrup.

The original location is opposite the soccer field, and there's a newer outlet in the Centro Comercial.

Soda La Amistad　　　　　SODA **$**
(☑2645-6108; mains US$3-6; ☺9am-10pm) 🍴 Friendly and family run, this is a well-loved *soda* that's a bit off the beaten track. You'll find the typical, tasty *casados*, burgers, pasta and breakfast on the menu. Herbivores will appreciate the options, including veggie burgers and veggie *casados*. These ladies know their stuff (and it's cheap).

Tree House Restaurant & Café　CAFE **$$**
(☑2645-5751; www.treehouse.cr; mains US$7-18; ☺11am-10pm; 🛜) Built around a half-century-old *higuerón* (fig) tree, this hip cafe serves up decent (if overpriced) food in a unique setting. It's a lively space to have a bite, linger over wine and occasionally catch live music.

★**Trio**　　　　　　　　　　FUSION **$$$**
(☑2645-7254; mains US$7-17; ☺11:30am-9:30pm; 🛜) In a funny location behind the Super-Compro, Trio has a classy, contemporary open-air dining room perched in the trees. The menu is all about blending unexpected elements into a delightful surprise for the taste buds, such as sea-bass *ceviche* (seafood marinated in lemon or lime juice, garlic and seasonings) in coconut milk, barbecue ribs with guava sauce, and a highly touted burger with figs. The dessert menu does amazing things with tropical fruits.

El Jardín　　　　　INTERNATIONAL **$$$**
(☑2257-0766; www.monteverde.com; mains US$16-23; ☺7am-10pm; 🛜) 🍴 Arguably the 'finest' dining in the area. The menu is wide ranging, always highlighting the local flavors. But these are not your typical *tipica*: beef tenderloin is served on a sugarcane kebab, pan-fried trout is topped with orange sauce. The setting – with windows to the trees – is lovely and service is superb. Romantics can opt for a private table in the

garden. Located on the grounds of the Monteverde Lodge.

Morpho's Restaurant　INTERNATIONAL **$$$**
(☑2645-7373; www.morphosrestaurant.com; mains US$8-20; ☺11am-9pm; 🅿🍴) Dine among gushing waterfalls and pretty butterflies at this romantic downtown restaurant. The sophisticated menu combines local ingredients with gourmet flair – the results are sure to please any palate.

✖ Around Santa Elena

Stella's Bakery　　　　　BAKERY **$**
(☑2645-5560; mains US$4-8; ☺6am-10pm; 🛜♿) A bakery for birders. Come in the morning for strong coffee and sweet pastries, or come later for sandwiches on homemade bread and rich, warming soup. Whenever you come, keep on eye on the bird feeder, which attracts tanagers, mot-mots and an emerald green toucanet.

★**Café Caburé**　　　　　　CAFE **$$**
(☑2645-5020; www.cabure.net; mains US$10-12; ☺9am-8pm Mon-Sat; 🅿🛜) The Argentine cafe above the Bat Jungle specializes in creative and delicious everything, from sandwiches on homemade bread and fresh salads, to more elaborate fare like tortillas stuffed with chicken mole, chipotle-rubbed steak, curried potatoes, and lemon shrimp. Save room for dessert because the chocolate treats are high art.

Sabor Español　　　　　　SPANISH **$$**
(☑2645-5387; saborespanola@hotmail.com; mains US$8-18; ☺noon-9pm Tue-Sun) One word: sangria. But that's just the beginning – the food here is creative and crazy good. The specialty is Spanish fare – seafood paella and *patatas bravas* (fried potatoes with sauce) – but there are dishes that you've never heard of before, such as bacon-wrapped chicken and banana kebabs or whisky shrimp flambé. The ambience is rustic, intimate and *tranquilo* – well worth the trip 2km west of downtown.

Sofia　　　　　　　　　　FUSION **$$**
(☑2645-7017; mains US$12-16; ☺11:30am-9:30pm; 🛜) Sofia has established itself as one of the best places in town with its Nuevo Latino cuisine – a modern fusion of traditional Latin American cooking styles. Think sweet-and-sour fig roasted pork loin, plantain-crusted sea bass, and shrimp with green-mango curry. The ambience is enhanced by groovy

music, picture windows, romantic candle lighting and potent cocktails.

Pizzería Tramonti
ITALIAN $$

(☑2645-6120; www.tramonticr.com; mains US$10-16; ☺11:30am-9:30pm Mon-Sat; 🖫) Tramonti offers authentic Italian, specializing in fresh seafood, hearty pastas and wood-fired pizzas. There's a decent selection of wines from Italy and Argentina. With a greenery-filled dining room twinkling with lights, the ambience is relaxed yet romantic.

Johnny's Pizzería
PIZZERIA $$

(☑2645-5066; www.pizzeriadejohnny.com; mains US$11-24; ☺11:30am-10pm; 🛜🖫) Johnny's has been serving up wood-fired, thin-crust pizzas since 1993. Keep it simple with a margherita or let Johnny impress you with one of his creative combos (like the Monteverde, with prosciutto, green olives and home-grown organic leeks).

🍸 Drinking & Entertainment

Nightlife in these parts generally involves a guided hike and nocturnal critters, but since this misty green mountain draws artists and dreamers, there's a smattering of regular cultural offerings. When there's anything going on you'll see it heavily advertised around town with flyers.

Bar Amigos
BAR

(☑2645-5071; www.baramigos.com; ☺noon-3am) With picture windows overlooking the mountainside, this Santa Elena mainstay evokes the atmosphere of a ski lodge. But no, there are DJs, karaoke, billiards, and sports on the screens. This is the one consistent place in the area to let loose, so there's usually a good mix of Ticos and tourists. Also, the food is surprisingly good.

La Taberna
BAR

(☑2645-5883; ☺variable) Known by many names in recent years, this drinking establishment will always be remembered as La Taberna. No matter what you call it, you'll find a friendly outdoor bar, drink specials, pub fare and live music.

Common Cup
CAFE

(☑2645-6247; coffee from US$2; ☺7am-6pm; 🛜) A cute yet sophisticated coffee shop with its own roastery. The name belies the fact that the gentleman barista crafts quite an uncommon cup of joe. The coffee beans are locally grown, the brew is fabulous and the milky foam is a medium for art.

🛍 Shopping

★Luna Azul
JEWELRY

(☑2645-6638; lunaazulmonteverde@gmail.com; ☺9am-6pm) This super-cute gallery and gift shop is packed to the gills with jewelry, clothing, soaps, sculpture and macramé, among other things. The jewelry in particular is stylish and stunning, crafted from silver, shell, crystals and turquoise.

Monteverde Art House
HANDICRAFTS

(Casa de Arte; ☑2645-5275; www.monteverdearthouse.com; ☺9am-6:30pm) You'll find several rooms stuffed with colorful Costa Rican artistry. The goods run the gamut, including jewelry, ceramic work, Boruca textiles and traditional handicrafts. There's a big variety, including some paintings and more contemporary work, but it's mostly at the the the crafts end of the artsy-craftsy spectrum. Great for souvenirs.

Casem
HANDICRAFTS

(Cooperativa de Artesanía Santa Elena Monteverde; ☑2645-5190; www.casemcoop.blogspot.com; ☺8am-5pm Mon-Sat year-round, plus 10am-4pm Sun Dec-Apr) Begun in 1982 as a women's cooperative representing eight female artists, today Casem has expanded to reportedly include almost 150 local artisans (eight of whom are men). Honestly, it's an underwhelming selection, featuring embroidered clothing and painted handbags, polished wooden tableware, and some painted bookmarks and greeting cards. There are more interesting paintings and woodwork in the Sky Gallery upstairs.

ℹ Information

EMERGENCY
Police (☑2645-6248)

INTERNET ACCESS
There is an abundance of internet cafes (per hour US$1 to US$2) in and around Santa Elena. Nearly all hotels and hostels are wired with wi-fi.

MEDICAL SERVICES
Consultorio Médico (☑2645-7778; ☺24hr) Across the intersection from Hotel Heliconia.
Red Cross (☑2645-6128; www.cruzroja.or.cr; ☺24hr) A hospital located just north of Santa Elena.

MONEY
Banco de Costa Rica (☺8am-4pm Mon-Fri, to noon Sat) Has a 24-hour ATM.

Banco Nacional (⊘8:30am-3:45pm) A 24-hour ATM in the new building behind the parking lot.

Banco Popular A 24-hour ATM.

POST

Correos de Costa Rica (⊘8am-4:30pm Mon-Fri, to noon Sat) Across from the shopping mall.

TOURIST INFORMATION

Chamber of Tourism (☑2645-6565; www.visitmonteverde.com; ⊘8am-8pm) Operated by the local chamber of commerce, this office promotes its member hotels and tour companies, so it's not necessarily an unbiased source.

Monteverde Info (☑2479-8811; www.monteverdeinfo.com) Located inside the Tree House (p209), this organization maintains a comprehensive travel website and can also help book tours.

Pensión Santa Elena (www.pensionsantaelena.com) A more objective option than the tourist office, even if you're not staying here. Talk to friendly hostel staff, who can also book tours, or better yet check out its comprehensive website.

ⓘ Getting There & Away

After resident protesters took to the streets in 2013, the transportation ministry announced that it would invest the necessary US$16 million to pave the 18km road from Guacimal to Santa Elena, which is the main access route to Monteverde. There was no sign of asphalt at the time of writing, but this plan is moving forward and may be completed by the time you read this. Enjoy the smooth ride. Travel times will obviously be reduced, but that's not the only change that road will bring.

BUS

All buses stop at the **bus terminal** (☑2645-5159; ⊘5:45-11am & 1:30-5pm Mon-Fri, to 3pm Sat & Sun) in downtown Santa Elena, where most of the budget digs are, and do not continue into Monteverde. You'll have to walk or take a taxi if that's where you plan to stay. On the trip in, keep an eye on your luggage, particularly on the San José–Puntarenas leg, as well as on the Monteverde–Tilarán run. Keep all bags at your feet and not in the overhead bin. Stories of theft and loss are legion.

Cañas There's no direct bus. Most people take a bus to Juntas, then transfer from there to frequent Interamericana-route buses for Cañas, Liberia and beyond.

Las Juntas (TransMonteverde) US$2; 1½ hours; departs from the bus station at 4:30am, 6am and 3pm. Buses to Puntarenas and San José can drop you off in Las Juntas.

> ⓘ **SCENIC ROUTE**
>
> If you're coming from Arenal, consider taking the lakeside route through Tronadora and Rio Chiquito, instead of going through Tilarán. The roads are rougher, but the panoramas of the lake, volcano and surrounding countryside are magnificent.

Managua (Nicaragua) (Tica Bus) US$28; eight hours; a small shuttle bus (US$2) departs from the bus station at 6am and brings you to the Interamericana in Lagartos. The local agent for Tica Bus is **Monteverde Experts** (☑2645-7263; www.monteverdeexperts.com).

Puntarenas (TransMonteverde) US$3; three hours; departs from in front of Banco Nacional at 4:20am, 6am and 3pm.

Reserva Monteverde US$1.20; 30 minutes; departs from in front of Banco Nacional at 6:15am, 7:30am, 9:30am, 1:30pm and 3pm; returns at 6:40am, 8:30am, 11am, 2pm and 4pm.

Reserva Santa Elena US$2; 30 minutes; departs from in front of Banco Nacional at 6:30am, 8:30am, 10:30am and 12:30pm; returns at 11am, 1pm and 4pm.

San José (Tilarán Transportes) US$5; five hours; departs the Santa Elena bus station at 6:30am and 2:30pm.

Tilarán, with connection to La Fortuna US$3; 2½ hours to Tilarán, seven hours in total; departs from the bus station at 4am and 12:30pm. This is a long ride, as you will need to hang around for two hours in Tilarán. If you have a few extra dollars, the jeep-boat-jeep option to La Fortuna is recommended.

CAR

While most Costa Rican communities regularly request paved roads in their region, preservationists in Monteverde have done the opposite. All roads around here are shockingly rough. Even if you arrive on a newly paved road via Guacimal, you'll still want a 4WD to get around to the more remote lodges and reserves.

There are three roads from the Interamericana: coming from the south, the first well-signed turnoff is at Rancho Grande (18km north of the Puntarenas exit). The first stretch of this route (from Sardinal to Guacimal) is newly paved, as of 2011. The remaining 18km (from Guacimal to Santa Elena) is scheduled to be paved in 2014. At the time of writing it took about three hours to drive to San José, but that time will be reduced with the road improvements.

A second, shorter road goes via Juntas, but it's not paved except for the first few kilometers. Finally, if coming from the north, drivers could take the paved road from Cañas via Tilarán and then take the rough road from Tilarán to Santa Elena.

There are now two gas stations open for business in the area.

HORSEBACK

A number of outfitters offer transportation on horseback (per person US$65 to US$185, five to six hours) to La Fortuna, usually in combination with a boat ride. There are three main trails used: the Lake Trail (safe year-round), the Chiquito Trail (safe most of the year) and the gorgeous but infamous Castillo Trail (passable only in dry season by experienced riders).

Sabine's Smiling Horses (p199) and Horse Trek Monteverde (p199) both offer versions of this journey. **Desafío Adventure** (📞 2645-5874; www.monteverdetours.com) is a reliable, reputable agency that can also make arrangements. Ask lots of questions and confirm the route before setting out.

JEEP-BOAT-JEEP

The fastest route between Monteverde–Santa Elena and La Fortuna is a jeep-boat-jeep combo (US$22 to US$32, three hours), which can be arranged through almost any hotel or tour operator in either town. A 4WD minivan takes you to Río Chiquito, meeting a boat that crosses Laguna de Arenal, where a van on the other side continues to La Fortuna. This is increasingly becoming the primary transportation between La Fortuna and Monteverde as it's incredibly scenic, reasonably priced and saves half a day of rough travel. In case you're wondering: no, absolutely no jeeps whatsoever are involved in the process.

Reserva Biólogica Bosque Nuboso Monteverde

Here is a virginal forest dripping with mist, dangling with mossy vines, sprouting with ferns and bromeliads, gushing with creeks, blooming with life and nurturing rivulets of evolution. It is so moving that when Quaker settlers first arrived in the area, they agreed to preserve about a third of their property in order to protect this watershed. By 1972, however, encroaching squatters threatened its sustainability. The community joined forces with environmental organizations to purchase 328 hectares adjacent to the already preserved area. This was called the **Reserva Biológica Bosque Nuboso**

Monteverde (Monteverde Cloud Forest Wildlife Biological Reserve; 📞 2645-5122; www.reservamonteverde.com; adult/concession US$18/9; ⏱ 7am-4pm), which the Centro Científico Tropical (Tropical Science Center) began administering in 1975. Nowadays the reserve totals 105 sq km.

Monteverde Cloud Forest Reserve is the result of private citizens working for change, rather than waiting around for a national park administered by the government. And yes, the reserve still relies partly on donations from the public. As the underfunded Minae struggles to protect the national-park system, enterprises like this are more important than ever for maintaining cohesive wildlife corridors.

Visitors should note that the walking trails can be muddy, even during the dry season. You're essentially walking around in a cloud, so quit complaining and bring rain gear, suitable boots and a smile. Many of the trails have been stabilized with concrete blocks or wooden boards, but unpaved trails deeper in the preserve turn sloppy during the rainy season.

Because of the fragile environment, the reserve allows a maximum of 160 people at any time. During the dry season this limit is usually reached by 10am, so arrive early (before the gates open). Alternatively, head across town to the Reserva Santa Elena (p203), which gets about 10% of the number of visitors as Monteverde.

🏃 Activities

Hiking

There are 13km of marked and maintained trails – a free map is provided with your entrance fee. The most popular of the nine trails, suitable for day hikes, make a rough triangle (El Triángulo) to the east of the reserve entrance. The triangle's sides are made up of the popular **Sendero Bosque Nuboso** (1.9km), an interpretive walk through the cloud forest that begins at the ranger station, paralleled by the more open, 2km **El Camino**, a favorite of bird-watchers. The **Sendero Pantanoso** (1.6km) forms the far side of El Triángulo, traversing swamps, pine forests and the continental divide. Returning to the entrance, **Sendero Río** (2km) follows the Quebrada Cuecha past a few photogenic waterfalls.

Bisecting the triangle, the gorgeous **Chomogo Trail** (1.8km) lifts hikers to 1680m,

LAS FIESTAS DE GUANACASTE

Guanacastecos love their horses almost as much as they love their fiestas. And what better way to get the best of both worlds than with a *tope* (horse parade), a mix of Western rodeo and country fair, complete with cattle auction, food stalls, music, dancing, drinking and, of course, bull riding. In Costa Rica the bulls are never killed, so watching the insane, helmetless, bareback bucking-bronco action is usually gore free. Even better than watching the bull riding is the aftermath, when the local drunks and young machos jump into the ring to act as volunteer rodeo clowns.

Though the bull riding usually draws the biggest crowds, the main event is the *tope* itself, where you can see the high-stepping gait of the horse of the *sabanero* (cowboy), which demands endurance and skill from both horse and rider.

Topes are also a great place to catch the region's traditional dance, known as the *punto guanacasteco*. The women wear long, flowing skirts meant to resemble an oxcart wheel, which is a traditional Costa Rican craft. The old-fashioned courtship dance is frequently interrupted by young men, who shout rhyming verses to try to win over a love interest. The dance and accompanying music are fast paced, full of passion, and fun to watch.

Topes usually occur on Costa Rican civic holidays, though you can bet on finding big parties during Semana Santa (the week before Easter), the week between Christmas and New Year, and on July 25, the anniversary of Guanacaste's annexation.

the highest point in the triangle. Other little trails crisscross the region, including the worthwhile **Sendero Brillante** (300m), with bird's-eye views of a miniature forest. However, keep in mind that despite valiant efforts to contain crowd sizes, these shorter trails are among the most trafficked in the country.

The trail to the **Mirador La Ventana** (elevation 1550m) is moderately steep and leads further afield to a wooden deck overlooking the continental divide. To the west, on clear days you can see the Golfo de Nicoya and the Pacific. To the east you can see the Peñas Blancas valley and the San Carlos plain. Even on wet, cloudy days it's magical, especially when the winds are howling and fine swirling mist washes over you in waves. All over these woods, in hidden pockets and secluded gullies, that mist collects into rivulets that gather into threads that stream into a foaming *cascada,* visible from **Sendero Cascada.** From here the water pools, then forms into a gushing river, best glimpsed from **Sendero Río** or **Sendero Chuecha.** There's a 100m suspension bridge about 1km from the ranger station on **Sendero Wilford Guindon.** A mini Golden Gate suspended in the canopy, you can feel it rock and sway with each step.

There are also trails to three backcountry shelters that begin at the far corners of the triangle. Even longer trails, many of them less developed, stretch out east across the reserve and down the Peñas Blancas river valley to the lowlands north of the Cordillera de Tilarán and into the Bosque Eterno de los Niños. If you have the time to spare, these hikes are highly recommended, as few tourists venture beyond the triangle. It's important to first talk to the park service, as you will be dealing with rugged terrain; a guide is highly recommended. Also, backcountry camping and sleeping in these shelters is normally no longer allowed.

Wildlife Watching

Monteverde is a bird-watching paradise, with the list of recorded species topping out at more than 400. The resplendent quetzal is most often spotted during the March and April nesting season, though you may get lucky any time of year. Keep your ears open for the three-wattled bellbird, a kind of cotinga that is famous for its distinctive call. If you're keen on birds, a specialized bird tour is highly recommended.

For those interested in spotting mammals, the cloud forest's limited visibility and abundance of higher primates (namely human beings) can make wildlife-watching quite difficult, though commonly sighted species (especially in the backcountry) include coatis, howler monkeys, capuchins, sloths, agoutis and squirrels (as in 'real' squirrel, not the squirrel monkey). Most animals avoid the main trails, so get off the beaten track.

Life in the Cloud Forest

To explore the Monteverde cloud forest is to arrive at the pinnacle of Costa Rica's continental divide. A blast of swirling, misty euphoria surrounds you, where lichen-draped trees soar, exotic birds gossip, and orchids and bromeliads bloom. Life is abundant, throbbing and palpable.

Two Forests, Two Ecosystems

Warm, humid trade winds from the Caribbean sweep up forested slopes to the Reserva Biológica Bosque Nuboso Monteverde (p212), where they cool and condense into clouds that congregate over the nearby Reserva Santa Elena (p203). The two forests are rich in diversity and oxygen, but the slight temperature and topographical differences mean that each has its own unique ecosystem.

Cloud Flora

The most abundant life form in the cloud forest, epiphytes seem to take over the trees they are growing on, yet they are not parasites and they do not harm their hosts. These clever plants get their nutrients from the floating mist, which explains their exposed roots. Look closely, and you'll see that one tree might be covered in dozens of epiphytes. This is one of the major reasons that cloud forests can claim such biodiversity: in Monteverde it's estimated that epiphytes represent almost 30% of the flora species.

The biggest family of epiphytes is the orchids, with nearly 500 species (the greatest diversity of orchids on the planet). Most amazingly, this figure includes some 34 endemic species – those that do not exist anywhere else.

Cloud Birds

Playing an important role in the pollination of orchids and other blooming plants, hummingbirds are among the most visible of the cloud-forest creatures. Their unique ability to fly in place, backwards and upside down allows them to drink on the fly, as it were. There are some 30 species buzzing around; check them out at Cafe Colibri (p216), just outside the Monteverde reserve.

You'll hear the three-wattled bellbird long before you see him, as his distinctive song is supposedly one of the loudest birdcalls on earth. As you might guess, he has three long wattles hanging from his beak.

The most famous cloud-forest resident is the resplendent quetzal. With long plumes of jade green and electric blue, this exotic beauty lives up to its name. The quetzals move seasonally between elevations, but if you're in the right place at the right time, a good bird guide should be able to find one.

Quaker Connection

The Quakers were the original conservationists here. In the early 1950s, about a dozen pacifist farming families decided to leave the United States so that they would not be drafted to fight in the Korean War. They settled in this remote perch and called it Monteverde (literally 'Green Mountain'). The Quakers have been actively involved in protecting this unique environment ever since.

1. Hiking in the cloud forest 2. Orchid 3. Violet sabrewing hummingbird

MINT IMAGES - FRANS LANTING / GETTY IMAGES ©

JONATHAN GREGSON / LONELY PLANET ©

PAUL SOUDERS / GETTY IMAGES ©

☞ Tours

Although you can (and should) hike around the reserve on your own, a guide will provide an informative overview and enhance your experience. Make reservations at least a day in advance for park-run tours. The English-speaking guides are trained naturalists; proceeds benefit environmental-education programs in local schools.

The reserve can also recommend excellent guides for private tours. Costs vary depending on the season, the guide and where you want to go, but they average about US$60 to US$100 for a half-day; reserve-admission fees are sometimes extra.

Bird-Watching Tours   TOUR
(per person excluding entry fee US$60; ☉ departs 6am) Guided bird-watching tours begin at Stella's Bakery near Santa Elena and set out on a five-hour quest. They usually see more than 40 species. There's a two-person minimum and six-person maximum. Longer tours go on request for a higher fee, resulting in a higher number of species checked off the list.

Natural History Tours   TOUR
(☑ 2645-5122, reservations 2645-5112; excluding entry fee US$17; ☉ departs 7:30am, 11:30am & 1:30pm) Guided natural-history tours start with an informative 10-minute orientation, followed by a 2½- to three-hour walk in the woods. You'll learn all about the characteristics of a cloud forest and identify some of its most unique flora. Your ticket is valid for the entire day, so you can continue to explore on your own after the tour is over.

Night Tours   TOUR
(with/without transportation US$20/17; ☉ departs 5:45) Two-hour night tours offer the opportunity to observe the 70% of regional wildlife that has nocturnal habits. Frogs, bats and other night critters are increasingly active as the sun sets. Tours are by flashlight (bring your own for the best visibility).

🛏 Sleeping & Eating

If you can carry everything you need, you might inquire about staying at the three backcountry shelters, though they are normally used only by researchers.

La Casona   LODGE $$$
(☑ 2645-5122; www.reservamonteverde.org; incl 3 meals per adult/child private r US$73/37, shared r US$62/37) Near the Reserva Biológica Bosque Nuboso Monteverde park entrance is this mountain lodge with capacity for 47 people. It's usually used by researchers and student groups but is often available to tourists – make reservations.

Restaurant   SANDWICHES $
(plates US$3-9; ☉ 7am-4pm) There's a small restaurant at the entrance to the reserve, which has a good variety of sandwiches, salads and typical dishes.

Cafe Colibri   CAFE $
(☑ 2645-7768; www.cafesantamarta.com; sandwiches $3-5, coffee drinks US$2; ☉ 8am-5pm) Just outside the reserve gates, the 'hummingbird cafe' is a top-notch choice for coffee and cakes. The gourmet coffee comes from beans sourced from the family's *finca*, Santa Marta. The drinks will warm your body, but the humming of dozens of hummingbirds in the garden will delight your heart. An identification board shows the nine species that you're likely to see. Great photo ops.

ℹ Information

The **visitors center** (☑ 2645-5122; www.cct.or.cr; park entry adult/student & child/child under 6yr US$17/9/free; ☉ 7am-4pm) is adjacent to the reserve gift shop, where you can get information and buy trail guides, bird and mammal lists and maps, as well as souvenirs and postcards. Leave your passport to rent a pair of binoculars (US$10).

The annual rainfall here is about 3000mm, though parts of the reserve reportedly get twice as much. It's usually cool, with high temperatures around 18°C (65°F), so wear appropriate clothing. It's important to remember that the cloud forest is often cloudy (!). The reserve is managed by the Centro Científico Tropical and supported by donations through the **Friends of Monteverde Cloud Forest** (www.friendsofmonteverde.org).

ℹ Getting There & Away

Public buses (US$1.20, 30 minutes) depart the Banco Nacional in Santa Elena at 6:15am, 7:30am, 9:30am, 1:30pm and 3pm. Buses return from the reserve at 6:40am, 8:30am, 11am, 2pm and 4pm. You can flag down the buses from anywhere on the road between Santa Elena and the reserve – inquire at your hotel about what time they will pass by. Taxis are also available for around US$10.

The 6km walk from Santa Elena is uphill but offers lovely views – look for paths that run parallel to the road. The bird-watching is magnificent, especially in the last 2km.

THE TALE OF THE GOLDEN TOAD

Once upon a time, in the cloud forests of Monteverde, there lived the golden toad (*Bufo periglenes*), also known as the *sapo dorado*. Because this bright-orange, exotic little toad was often seen scrambling amid the Monteverde leaf litter – the only place in the world where it appeared – it became something of a Monteverde mascot. Sadly, the golden toad has not been seen since 1989 and is now believed to be extinct.

In the late 1980s, unexplained rapid declines in frog and toad populations all over the world spurred an international conference of herpetologists to address these alarming developments. Amphibians once common were becoming rare or had already disappeared, and the scientists were unable to agree upon a reason for the sudden demise of so many amphibian species in so many different habitats.

Several factors may be to blame for these declines, including the fact that amphibians breathe both with primitive lungs and through their perpetually moist skin, which makes them susceptible to airborne toxins. Their skin also provides little protection against UV light, which studies have shown can result in higher mortality rates to amphibian embryos and damaged DNA that in turn causes deformities. Pesticides also have been proven to cause deformities and hermaphroditism. And then there's the global issue of habitat loss. If all that didn't tell a bleak enough story, scientists have since discovered that the worldwide spread of chytridiomycosis disease (caused by the fungus *Batrachochytrium dendrobatidis*, in case you were wondering) has decimated amphibian populations everywhere.

According to the Global Amphibian Assessment, 30% of New World amphibians (1187 species) are currently threatened with extinction. In response to this dire statistic, an international coalition of zoos and wildlife-conservation organizations have jointly established **Amphibian Ark** (www.amphibianark.org), an attempt to 'bank' as many species as possible in the event of further die-offs. We may never know what happened to the golden toad, but as one of the first warning signs that the ecosystem is off balance, its mysterious disappearance might have given a chance for survival – and a happy never-ending? – to other amphibian species.

Juntas de Abangares

POP 5300

Las Juntas de Abangares is a small town on the Río Abangares that was the center of the gold-mining industry in the late 19th and early 20th centuries. Today it's a pleasant mountain market town, set in a verdant bowl, blessed with ample sunshine, and peopled with ranchers and farmers. Most travelers don't hang long, but it's a mildly interesting stop en route to Monteverde.

The town is centered on the stained-glass Catholic church. The small but bustling downtown is about 300m north of the church, with a Banco Nacional, several *sodas* and small markets.

◉ Sights

Ecomuseo de las Minas de Abangares　　　　　MUSEUM
(☑2662-0310; adult/child US$4/2; ☺8am-5pm Tue-Fri) It's not often that you see the terms 'eco' and 'mining' so close together. Set on 38 hectares, this little museum has exhibits of photographs and models depicting the old mining practices of the area. There are a picnic area and children's play area on the grounds. A good system of trails skirts mining artifacts, offering opportunities for birding, with occasional appearances by monkeys.

☞ Tours

Mina Tours　　　　　TOUR
(☑2662-0753; www.minatours.com; day trips from US$30; ☺8am-5pm Mon-Fri) Behind the church, Mina Tours is a family-run tour outfit that can arrange transportation and offers several gold-themed tours, including of the Ecomuseo and abandoned mines.

⛏ Sleeping & Eating

Cabinas y Restaurante Heliconias　　CABINA $
(☑2662-2260; www.cabinasheliconias.com; s/d US$28/40; P❄) Set along the river, this leafy property has 12 freestanding cabins with high, beamed ceilings, rustic wood

furnishings and ceiling fans. It's the best sleep within walking distance of the town center (it's set about 1km west of town). The attached restaurant serves a tasty, smoky barbecue pork.

Pueblo Antiguo Lodge & Spa LODGE $$
(✆2662-1913; www.puebloantiguo.com; s/d US$52/65; P❇☷) This rustic getaway rests on the lip of a wooded ravine next to the Ecomuseo. Its 10 wooden lodge rooms aren't fancy but are very comfy, and there's a good chance wildlife will appear on your doorstep. There's plenty of recreation and relaxation onsite, including hot springs, spring-fed swimming pool, spa and nature trails. Staff arrange tours to the museum and gold mines.

❶ Getting There & Away

The bus terminal is two blocks east of the main road, parallel to Parque Central. There are no buses to the Ecomuseo, but a taxi will cost about US$8 one way.

Cañas/Liberia US$1/3, 45 minutes/two hours, departs 5:30am

San José US$3, three hours, departs at 6:30am and 10:45am

Drivers should take the turnoff from the Interamericana, 27km south of Cañas (at the gas station). Monteverde is 30km northeast of Las Juntas on a partially paved road; the last 12km are rough, though normally passable for regular cars in the dry season. From Juntas, take your first left after the plaza, cross the one-lane bridge, turn right and follow the signs to Monteverde.

INTERAMERICANA NORTE

Despite Tico speed demons and lumbering big rigs, the Interamericana, which bisects the travel hub of Liberia, offers a wide-angle view of the region. The main artery connecting San José with Managua runs through kilometers of tropical dry forest and neat roadside villages to the open Guanacaste grasslands, where savanna vistas are broken only by windblown trees. Along the way, thin, (mostly) earthen roads branch off and wander up the slopes of hulking volcanoes shrouded in cloud forest, skirt hidden waterfalls and meander into vast estuaries that kiss pristine bays.

Cañas
POP 25,900

If you're cruising north on the Interamericana, Cañas is the first town of any size in Costa Rica's driest province, Guanacaste. *Sabanero* (cowboy) culture is evident on the sweltering streets, where full-custom pick-up trucks share the road with swaggering cowboys on horseback. It's a dusty, typically Latin American town, where almost everyone struts slowly and businesses shut down for lunch. It's all centered on the Parque Central and the decidedly atypical Catholic church.

Although you're better off basing yourself in livelier Liberia, Cañas is a good place to organize rafting trips on the nearby Río Corobicí or for exploring Parque Nacional Palo Verde. And if you need to stop for gas, it's worth a stroll; just make sure you lock your car.

◉ Sights & Activities

Iglesia de Cañas CHURCH
You might not expect an architectural landmark in this otherwise innocuous town, so don't miss the local Catholic church, designed by famed local painter Otto Apuy. From top to bottom (including a 30m belfry) it's covered in psychedelic mosaics, taking the form of sinewy vines and colorful starbursts. The theme of the artwork ranges from religious stories to jungle scenes. The church is striking from afar, but up close the intricacy and artistry are amazing.

Las Pumas ZOO
(✆2669-6044; www.centrorescatelaspumas.org; adult/child US$10/5; ⏱8am-4:30pm) This wild-animal shelter was started in the 1960s by the late Lilly Hagnauer, a Swiss environmentalist. It's the largest shelter of its kind in Latin America, housing big cats including pumas, jaguars, ocelots, jaguarundis and margays – plus a few deer, foxes, monkeys, peccaries, toucans, parakeets and other birds that were either orphaned or injured. It's located about 5km north of Cañas on the Interamericana.

The shelter is still operated by the Swiss Family Hagnauer, a local Cañas institution. This is a labor of love. The shelter does not receive any government funding and relies on visitor admission and donations to survive. Volunteers are always welcomed, but you must make arrangements beforehand.

LA ENSENADA LODGE & WILDLIFE REFUGE

Is the 'beaten track' getting you down? Stop the tourist madness and experience something really special at **La Ensenada Lodge & Wildlife Refuge** (✆2289-6655; www. laensenada.net; s/d/tr/q US$60/74/94/100, meals US$8-16; 🛜🏊) 🐾. This is a wonderfully remote 800-acre *finca* (farm) and working cattle ranch, salt farm and papaya orchard. Thanks to an ongoing reforestation effort, some 30% of the property is now covered by trees. Containing primary and secondary forest (a rarity in this part of the country), as well as mangrove swamps at the mouth of Río Abangares, this property has been declared a national wildlife refuge. It's an incredible setting for birding, horseback riding and good old-fashioned rest and relaxation.

Rustic but comfortable wooden bungalows face out onto the Golfo de Nicoya, and have private solar-heated bathrooms and private patios with hammocks – perfect for watching sunsets (or birds). There's also a pool, restaurant, tennis courts, a romantically rickety jetty and a terrific trail network. The place offers boat tours to the mangroves (per person US$82), where you can glimpse dozens of bird species, caimans and crocs, as well as horseback tours (US$27) through the tropical dry forest.

Safaris Corobicí   RAFTING
(✆2669-6191; Interamericana Km 193; 2hr tour US$52, 3hr bird-watching tour US$60, white-water trip US$95; ⊙departures 7am 3pm; 🚗) These gentle rafting trips down the Río Corobicí emphasize wildlife observation rather than exciting white-water rafting. The river is Class I–II (in other words, pretty flat), but families and birders will love it. Swimming holes are found along the river. The company also offers one Class III–IV white-water trip per day. Discounts for kids under 14.

Ríos Tropicales   RAFTING
(✆2233-6455; www.rinconcorobici.com; adult/child US$50/35, white-water rafting US$90; ⊙departures 7am-3pm; 🚗) The popular Ríos Tropicales offers Class I–II family 'float tours' for flora and fauna viewing. For the more adventurous, there are Class III–V white-water rafting trips on Río Tenorio that feature a death-defying 3.6m drop. Ríos Tropicales operates out of the Rincón Corobicí restaurant.

🛏 Sleeping & Eating

Many of the restaurants in town shut down on Sunday, but luckily there's an enormous **SuperCompro** (⊙8am-8pm) right on the Interamericana and a **Palí** (Av 5 btwn Calles 4 & 2; ⊙8am-8pm) just around the corner.

Hotel Cañas   HOTEL $
(✆2669-0039; www.hotelcanascr.com; cnr Calle 2 & Av 3; s/d US$24/32; 🅿🏊🛜) Here is a professionally run collection of decent tiled rooms with wooden beds, air-con and hot water, off the main drag. It's quiet and super clean.

Portions in the popular restaurant (mains US$4 to US$10) are quite generous.

Caña Brava Inn   HOTEL $$
(✆2669-1294; www.hotelcanabrava.com; cnr Interamericana & Av 5; s/d US$45/60; 🅿🏊🛜🏊) The newest and most upscale hotel in town has all the modern amenities, including well-insulated rooms with flat-screen TV, comfy bedding and contemporary dark-wood furnishings.

Hotel La Pacífica   HOTEL $$
(✆2669-6050; www.pacificacr.com; d/apt US$76/114; 🅿🏊@🛜🏊) A nature reserve with a working hacienda and an elegant restaurant, this property is 4.5km north of Cañas on the Interamericana. Set on 9 hectares of dry tropical forest, the grounds are superb for birds and wildlife. Wooden furniture and hand-painted tilework adorn the spacious suites, which are decked with hammock-strung terraces.

The restaurant is also recommended, with many of the ingredients grown right here on experimental organic plots. The result is *típica* meals (mains US$8 to US$24), prepared and presented with taste and grace.

Rincón Corobicí   COSTA RICAN $$
(✆2669-1234; www.rinconcorobici.com; mains US$6-12; ⊙8am-6pm) A great lunch stop, this attractive Swiss-run restaurant is 4km north of Cañas on the banks of the Río Corobicí. A terrace provides river and garden views, and a short trail follows the riverbank, where you can take a cool dip.

ℹ️ Information

You can find public phones, a post office, a library, a Banco Nacional and a Banco Popular with ATMs on the streets surrounding the Parque Central.

Emergency Clinic (📞2669-0092; cnr Av Central & Hwy 1; ⏰7am-4pm Mon-Fri) Has 24-hour on-call service.

Minae/ACT Office (📞2669-2200; Av 9 btwn Calles Central & 1; ⏰8am-4pm Mon-Fri) Has limited information about nearby national parks and reserves.

ℹ️ Getting There & Away

All buses arrive at and depart from **Terminal Cañas** (⏰8am-1pm & 2:30-5:30pm) at the northern end of town. There are a few *sodas* and snack bars, and you can store your bags (US$0.50) at the desk. There's also a taxi stand in front.

Juntas US$2; two hours; departs about 4:30pm.

Liberia US$3; 1½ hours; departs hourly from 4:30am to 6:30pm.

San José US$5; 3½ hours; departs daily at 4am, 4:50am, 6:15am, 8:50am and 12:10pm.

Tilarán US$1; 30 minutes; departs nine times from 6am to 5:30pm.

Upala US$3; two hours; departs 4:30am, 6am, 8:30am, 11:15am, 1pm, 3:30pm and 5:30pm.

Volcán Tenorio Area

Parque Nacional Volcán Tenorio, part of the Área de Conservación Arenal (ACA), is one of the highlights of northwestern Costa Rica. It's a cool, misty, magical place highlighted by cloud forests and the icy blue Río Celeste, the region's namesake. The park entrance is located just north of Bijagua (pronounced 'bee-hag-gwa'). If you have your own wheels, the park is a fairly long but certainly doable day trip from Liberia or Cañas, but there are some fabulous mountain lodges in the area, so spend the night if you have the time.

Bijagua

Bijagua is the only sizable town in the Tenorio sphere. It has a few hotels, a Banco Nacional ATM and several small *sodas* and bars, but no gasoline; the nearest gas pumps are in Upala or Cañas.

Most of the accommodations and a few restaurants are along the main highway.

🛏️ Sleeping & Eating

Hotel Cacao HOTEL **$**
(📞2466-8052; www.hotelcacaocr.com; dm/s/d/q US$14/30/40/80; 🅿️✳️📶) The best budget option in town is located 300m northwest of the main highway. Set in a yellow concrete building, spacious rooms have new tiles and wooden beds. There is plenty of deck seating with lovely views of Volcán Miravalles. Follow the trail along the river to cool off in the local swimming hole.

Cataratas Bijagua Lodge BUNGALOW **$$**
(📞8937-4687; www.cataratasbijagua.com; d/tr/q incl breakfast US$70/85/100; 🅿️📶) 🍴 Owners Warner and Carla turned their family's dairy farm into a beautiful ecolodge. Now, five rustic cabins are set on gorgeous jungle grounds, with views of both Tenorio and Miravalles. The grounds – filled with wildlife – are ripe for exploring, with a river trail leading to a private waterfall. The place operates on power from a hydroelectric generator.

It's located 2km west of Bijagua: look for the turnoff near the Casita del Maiz. Warner and Carla don't speak much English, so brush up on your Spanish.

Casitas Tenorio BUNGALOW **$$**
(📞8312-1248; www.casitastenorio.com; d incl breakfast US$65; 🅿️📶) 🍴 This is a sweet family-run farm with a few *casitas* and room for camping. The *casitas* are simple, spacious and clean, and surrounded by wild-

---

WORTH A TRIP

BAR-B-Q TRES HERMANAS

Long before you get here, you'll notice signs on the Interamericana advertising the best steakhouse in Guanacaste – **Bar-B-Q Tres Hermanas** (📞2232-6850; www.bbqtresher-manas.com; cnr Interamericana & Rte 18; mains US$7-18; ⏰7am-9pm; 🅿️📶♿). Believe the hype. This local landmark's specialty is barbecue beef and pork ribs, marinated and slow cooked for eight hours. It's located about 20km south of Cañas. Look for the giant bull.

This is a perfect pit stop if you're making the long drive to or from the Península de Nicoya. Kids will love the playground and everyone else will appreciate the spotless, almost swanky restrooms.

life. Owners Donald and Pip are committed to community rural tourism, and the charm of this place is experiencing life on the farm, visiting the animals and exploring the fruit-tree-laden grounds. Your breakfast comes straight from the chickens!

Drive about 2km southeast from Bijagua on the road to Heliconia Lodge.

Sueño Celeste   B&B $$
(☑2466-8221; www.sueno-celeste.com; d/tr/q US$86/109/132; P🛜🖺) This cute, funky B&B has a collection of stylish bungalows with polished-concrete floors, frilly bed linens, molded-concrete rain showers and beamed ceilings, scattered around a garden plot with Tenorio views. The fastidious French owners Daniel and Dominique will make sure you are oriented and informed during your stay.

★Celeste Mountain Lodge   LODGE $$$
(☑2278-6628; www.celestemountainlodge.com; s/d/tr/q incl all meals US$150/190/225/260; P🛜) 🌿 Innovative and sustainable, this contemporary open-air hilltop lodge in the shadow of Volcán Tenorio is absolutely stunning. The 18 rooms are small but stylish, with wooden shutters that open onto immobilizing vistas. Winding through labyrinthine gardens, a trail is laid with geotextile (no more muddy shoes!), which makes for soundless hiking and prime bird-watching. The price includes meals at the excellent gourmet restaurant.

Hot water comes from solar power, and cooking gas is partially produced by kitchen waste. There's even an ingenious 'tropical hot bath' heated by burning salvaged wood. The lodge is located at the end of a 3.5km-long, rough (4WD required) access road that begins at the northern end of Bijagua.

Tenorio Lodge   LODGE $$$
(☑2466-8282; www.tenoriolodge.com; s/d/tr/q incl breakfast US$130/140/170/190; P🖲🛜) Located on a lush hilltop with amazing views of Volcán Tenorio, this lodge has 12 romantic and roomy bungalows, featuring orthopedic beds, stone or wood floors and floor-to-ceiling windows with volcano views. On the 17-acre property you'll find a restaurant, two ponds, a heliconia garden and two hot tubs to enjoy after a long day of hiking. Located 1km south of Bijagua.

Hummingbird Cafe   INTERNATIONAL $$
(☑8416-4731; www.fincaagroecologica.com; mains US$8-12, guided farm tour US$12; ⊙noon-11pm Tue-Sun; 🖲🖶) 🌿 On the grounds of the Finca Verde Lodge, this family restaurant is a surprising change of pace from the Tico fare in town. Look for innovative preparations like red-chili enchiladas, rolled tilapia and shrimp salad with avocado and bacon. The menu also includes plenty of basics like burgers and pizzas.

Come early and take a tour of the family's **organic farm** (guided tour US$12; P🖶) to see where your ingredients come from. There are also four comfortable cabins (doubles/triples/quads including breakfast US$65/85/95) on the grounds.

❶ Getting There & Away

About 6km northwest of Cañas, a paved road branches off the Interamericana and heads north to Upala, passing between Volcán Miravalles to the west and Volcán Tenorio (1916m) to the east. Smack-dab in the middle of these two mighty volcanoes sits the little town of Bijagua. It's about 40km north of Cañas and 27km south of Upala.

Buses between San José and Upala stop in Bijagua (US$8, four daily). There are also six daily buses that run between Upala (US$1) and Cañas (US$1.25) via Bijagua.

Parque Nacional Volcán Tenorio

It is said that when God finished painting the sky blue, he washed his paintbrushes in the Río Celeste. The heavenly blue river, waterfalls and lagoons of Parque Nacional Volcán Tenorio are among the most spectacular natural phenomena in Costa Rica, which is probably why the park is known to locals simply as Río Celeste.

Established in 1976, this magical 184-sq-km national park remains a blissfully pristine rainforest abundant with wildlife. Soaring 1916m above the cloud rainforest is the park's namesake, Volcán Tenorio, which actually consists of three peaked craters: Montezuma, Tenorio I (the tallest) and Tenorio II.

Your first stop will be the **Puesto El Pilón ranger station** (☑2200-0135; www.acarenaltempisque.org; adult/child US$10/free; ⊙8am-4pm, last entry 2:30pm), which houses a small exhibit of photographs and dead animals. Pick up a free English or Spanish hiking map.

DON'T MISS

THE BACK ROAD BETWEEN TENORIO & MIRAVALLES

An epic back road, 4WD track links Tenorio to Miravalles. This is useful for road trippers who wish to base themselves in Tenorio and visit Miravalles for the day (an itinerary that we recommend highly). About 12km south of Bijagua make a right where you see a sign toward the *pueblo* (small town or village) of Rio Chiquito. It's a rather small sign, and once you make the turn you'll be in the even smaller *pueblo*. The road narrows immediately and severely. Don't worry, there is no dead end. After fording a stream it goes crazy vertical. Shift into 4-low and grind up the 200m hill. At the top are marvelous vistas of the two mountains, acres of rangeland and the vast valley below. Then you'll go down again, ford another stream, navigate a steeper incline and be rewarded with massive views once more. By now you'll be in old Tico (Costa Rican) cattle country. Enjoy it. Within an hour you'll be dipping into hot springs. From Miravalles, detour down the slope on paved roads toward the Interamericana, take in the Llano de Cortes Waterfall near Bagaces and return to the Río Celeste area via Hwy 6.

🏃 Activities

A well-signed trail begins at the ranger-station parking lot and winds 1.5km through the rainforest until you reach an intersection. Turn left and climb down a very steep but sturdy staircase to the Catarata de Río Celeste, a milky blue waterfall that cascades 30m down the rocks into a fantastically aquamarine pool.

It's 400m further to the Mirador, where you'll have gorgeous views of Tenorio from the double-decker wooden platform. Further on is the Technicolor Pozo Azul (Blue Lagoon). The trail loops around the lagoon 400m until you arrive at the confluence of rivers known as Los Teñidores (The Stainers). Here, two small rivers – one whitish blue and one brownish yellow – mix together to create the blueberry milk of Río Celeste.

Note that swimming is strictly prohibited everywhere along this trail. The nearby hot springs have also been closed, after some tourists were burned in 2011. Hiking to the volcano crater is also strictly prohibited.

Plans for a circuit trail are afoot, but for now the trail ends at Los Teñidores. Retrace your steps to return to the ranger station.

Allow three to four hours to complete the entire hike. It's about a 7km round trip, but parts of the trail are steep and rocky. And because this is a rainforest, the trail can be wet and muddy almost year-round. Good hiking shoes or boots are a must. After your hike, you'll find an area to wash your footwear near the trailhead.

🛏 Sleeping & Eating

Posada Río Celeste CABINA $
(☑ 8356-0285, for English 8978-2676; www.posadarioceleste.com; r incl meals per person US$40; 🅿) Formerly called Posada La Amistad, this homey property offers clean, rustic rooms and hearty, home-cooked meals, all on a family farm in a rural ranching community 1km northeast of the park entrance. Two talkative parrots inhabit the blooming gardens. Staff can organize hiking and swimming in and out of the park.

Even if you're not staying here, this is a perfect pit stop for lunch (US$5) after hiking in the park. There's no menu: Wilber and his wife will serve up whatever they have cooking on their stove. Portions are huge, prices are reasonable.

Cabinas Piuri HOTEL $$
(☑ 8324-3064; aspiuri@hotmail.com; s/d incl breakfast US$35/50, planetarium r US$55, ste US$80; 🅿) About 1km past the national-park gates, a massive fountain erupts against a cloud-forest backdrop at the entrance to this unusual property. It's perched on a gorgeous slice of the milky-blue Río Celeste. Soak in an inviting stone dipping pool on the riverbanks or take this unique opportunity to swim in the magnificent river itself.

The accommodations are varied, ranging from colorful *cabinas* with king-size beds to an egg-shaped, animal-sculpted 'planetarium'. There's also a spacious restaurant with windows overlooking the river and forest.

Catarata Río Celeste Hotel HOTEL $$
(☑ 8938-9927, 8876-4382; www.cataratarioceleste.com; r/bungalows incl breakfast US$60/68; 🅿 🤶)

Located about 1km from the park entrance, this family-run resort is spread out over nice landscaped grounds. There are six simple tiled rooms that share a hammock-strung terrace, as well as five more luxurious bungalows with Jacuzzis, outdoor showers and volcano views. There are many different tours on offer, as well as a pleasant open-air restaurant that attracts the tour groups passing through.

La Carolina Lodge LODGE $$
(2466-6393; www.lacarolinalodge.com; per person incl meals US$70-90; P) Flanked by a roaring river and tucked into the trees on the volcano slope, this isolated lodge is also a working cattle ranch. Amazing organic meals – featuring poultry and meat from the farm – are cooked over an outdoor wood-burning stove. Cabins are rustic and romantic. The river is delicious for swimming, and a wood-fired hot tub is luxurious for soaking.

Room rates include meals, guided hikes and horse rides in the surrounding countryside. The lodge is about 1.3km west of the charming ranching hamlet of San Miguel; turn off the highway 5km north of Bijagua and follow the signs.

Rio Celeste Hideaway HOTEL $$$
(2206-5114; www.riocelestehideaway.com; d incl breakfast US$216-292; P🤟) This elegant address is just 550m from the park gate. Sprinkled among lush landscaped grounds, the spectacular property has huge, 90-sq-meter thatched *casitas* with wooden floors, pastel paint jobs and antique furnishings. Beds are covered with canopies and draped in 300-thread-count sheets. Even the bathrooms are luxurious here, with soaking tubs, outdoor showers, and 'his' and 'hers' basin sinks.

ℹ Getting There & Away

There's no bus to the national park. The closest you can get is Bijagua, from where you can book a tour at almost any hotel.

A 30km road now connects Bijagua (Hwy 6) and Guatuso (Hwy 4), passing the national park (and most of these lodgings) along the way. The entrance to the national park is about 9km from Bijagua and 21km from Guatuso. This road is very rough in places (4WD required), so it's easier to approach from the west. But if you're coming from the La Fortuna area, and you have the appropriate vehicle, it's faster to brave the road from Guatuso.

Five kilometers north of Bijagua is the gravel road to San Miguel. Turning left at the San Miguel intersection will bring you to La Carolina Lodge (1.3km). The rough dirt road (4WD required) continues another 13km until it meets up with Hwy 4, the main Upala–Fortuna thoroughfare. Turning right will take you 4km down an even rougher road to the national-park gate.

Volcán Miravalles Area

Volcán Miravalles (2028m) is the highest volcano in the Cordillera de Guanacaste, and although the main crater is dormant, the geothermal activity beneath the ground has led to its rapid development as a hot-springs destination. Miravalles isn't a national park or refuge, but the volcano itself is afforded a modicum of protection by being within the Zona Protectora Miravalles.

North of Fortuna, the government-run Proyecto Geotérmico Miravalles is an ambitious project that uses geothermal energy to produce electricity, primarily for export to Nicaragua and Panama. It also produces about 18% of Costa Rica's electricity. A few bright steel tubes from the plant snake along the flanks of the volcano, adding an eerie, alien feel to the remote landscape.

But the geothermal energy most people come here to soak up comes in liquid form. The hot springs are north of the tiny village of Fortuna de Bagaces (not to be confused with La Fortuna de Arenal or Bagaces). Most of the facilities also have sleeping accommodations, but they are pretty mediocre (with one noteworthy exception). If your budget does not accommodate top-end lodging, consider basing yourself in Tenorio.

🏃 Activities

Rio Perdido HOT SPRINGS
(2673-3600; www.rioperdido.com; thermal canyon & river adult/child US$40/30) This fabulous new facility – set amid an otherworldly volcanic landscape – is a wonderful way to soak in the soothing waters of Miravalles. The 'thermal canyon experience' includes a guided hike along the river, with plenty of opportunities to swim in the luscious coolness, before arriving at the thermal river, where termperatures range from 32°C to 46°C. There's a swim-up bar, hanging bridges and glorious views all around.

If you care to spend the night (or several) at Rio Perdido, eco-chic bungalows (singles/doubles US$204/250) are contemporary and cool, with polished-concrete floors, bold patterns, lots of windows and raised terraces facing the forest.

Thermo Manía
HOT SPRING

(☑2673-0233; www.thermomania.net; adult/child US$12/10; ⊙8am-10pm; 🖟) The biggest complex in the area has some Disney–Flintstone *queso* (cheese) to it, but there are 11 thermal pools, which range from lukewarm to warm. The upper pool complex has a swim-up bar and waterslide. Much more tasteful are the five stone pools and sauna in the leafy lower sector. There's also a full spa (with private mud baths), playground, museum, soccer field and picnic tables. Families love it here.

Guests who stay in the 26 log-cabin rooms (per adult/child from US$44/30) have free access to the pools during their stay, with TV and cold-water bathroom (neatly counter-balancing the lack of cold-water pools).

El Guayacán
HOT SPRING

(☑2673-0349; www.termaleselguayacan.com; adult/child US$10/8; ⊙8am-10pm; 🖟) Just behind Thermo Manía, this is a family *finca* that's hissing and smoking with vents and mud pots. There are eight thermal pools and one cold pool with a water slide. You can also take a guided tour of the fumaroles (stay on the trail!). If you wish to spend the night, bed down in one of the clean cold-water *cabinas* (singles/doubles from US$30/60) brushed in bright colors, or in a spacious villa with kitchenette.

Yökö Termales
HOT SPRING

(☑2673-0410; www.yokotermales.com; adult/child US$10/8; ⊙7am-10pm; 🖟) Yökö has four hot springs and a larger pool with a small waterslide and waterfall, set in an attractive meadow at the foot of Miravalles. The views are magnificent, but there's still little shade around the pools. The 12 canary-tinted rooms (singles/doubles/triples/quads including breakfast US$40/75/100/125) are comfy, with beamed and plywood ceilings that look unfinished. It's a decent, but not magical, sleeping option.

Termales Miravalles
HOT SPRING

(☑2673-0606, 8305-4072; adult/child US$5/3; ⊙7:30am-10pm; 🖟) For some local flavor, Termales Miravalles has four pools and a super waterslide, all lying along a thermal stream. There's a small restaurant and space for camping. It's usually open on weekends year-round, and daily during high season.

The access road is directly across from Yökö hot springs.

Las Hornillas
HIKING

(☑2100-1233, 8839-9769; www.lashornillas.com; tours US$35-55; ⊙9am-5pm) On the southern slopes of Miravalles, Las Hornillas has a unique lunar landscape, with bubbling pools and fumaroles on the property. Hike to explore a small volcanic crater and bathe in the mud pools. Or traverse a hanging bridge and discover a spectacular waterfall.

Miravalles Volcano Adventure Center
CANOPY TOUR

(☑2673-0469; www.volcanoadventuretour.com; canopy tour adult/child US$40/30, tours US$30-70) There's something for everybody at this adventure center near the base of the volcano. The centerpiece of the complex is the canopy tour, which has 12 cables and hanging bridges through fields and forest. There's a camping area and a swimming pool that's fed by mountain-spring water. The place also organizes hiking and horseback-riding tours, including one all-day expedition to the Miravalles crater.

❶ Getting There & Away

Volcán Miravalles is 27km northeast of Bagaces and can be approached by a paved road that leads north of Bagaces through the communities of Salitral and Torno, where the road splits. From the left-hand fork, you'll reach Guayabo, with a few *sodas* and basic *cabinas*; to the right, you'll find Fortuna de Bagaces, with easier access to the hot springs. Both towns are small population centers, and are not of much interest to travelers. The road reconnects north of the two towns and continues toward Upala.

By bus, you can connect through Bagaces, which has hourly buses to and from Guayabo and Fortuna (US$1, 45 minutes).

Parque Nacional Palo Verde

The 184-sq-km **Parque Nacional Palo Verde** (☑2524-0628; www.ots.ac.cr; adult/child US$10/1; ⊙8am-4pm) is a wetland sanctuary in Costa Rica's driest province. It lies on the northeastern bank of the mouth of the Río Tempisque and at the head of the Golfo de Nicoya. All the major rivers in the region drain into this ancient intersection of two basins, which creates a mosaic of habitats, including mangrove swamps, marshes, grassy savannas and evergreen forests. A number of low limestone hills provide lookouts over the park, and the park's shallow, permanent lagoons are focal points for wildlife. The park derives its name from its abundant *palo verde* (green tree), a small shrub that's green year-round.

Palo Verde has the greatest concentrations of waterfowl and shorebirds in Central America, and over 300 bird species have been recorded in the park. Bird-watchers come to see the large flocks of heron (including the rare black-crowned night heron), stork (including the endangered jabirú), spoonbill, egret, ibis, grebe and duck; and forest birds, including scarlet macaws, great curassows, keel-billed toucans and parrots, are also common. Frequently sighted mammals include deer, coati, armadillo, monkey and peccary, as well as the largest population of jaguarundi in Costa Rica. There are also numerous reptiles in the wetlands, including crocodiles that are reportedly up to 5m in length.

The dry season (December to March) is the best time to visit, as flocks of birds tend to congregate in the remaining lakes and marshes. Plus, the trees lose their leaves, allowing for clearer viewing. There are also far fewer insects in the dry season, and mammals are occasionally seen around the watering holes. Take binoculars or a spotting scope if possible. That said, the entire basin swelters during the dry season, so bring adequate sun protection. During the wet months, large portions of the area are flooded, and access may be limited.

The park is also contiguous in the north with the 73-sq-km Refugio de Vida Silvestre Dr Rafael Lucas Rodríguez Caballero and the Reserva Biológica Lomas de Barbudal.

🏃 Activities & Tours

To fully appreciate the size and topography of the park, it's worth organizing a boat trip (US$45 to US$57) down the Río Tempisque, a wide, brown, brackish river contained on either side by mangroves. Arrangements can be made through the Organization of Tropical Studies (OTS) Palo Verde Biological Station. Travelers also recommend the guided bird-watching tours (US$28 to US$30) that can be arranged there. Tour operators in San José and La Fortuna run package tours to Palo Verde, but you'll save money by arranging everything yourself.

You can also explore the park's four maintained trails on your own. La Venda (2.1km) is the longest and runs adjacent to the lagoon. The best vegetation is visible from El Querque (650m), and La Jacana is a short (200m) trail elevated above the lagoon that birders love. No matter which trail you choose, know that it gets fiercely hot in the dry season, so carry ample water and a sun hat and avoid hiking during midday.

WORTH A TRIP

LLANOS DE CORTÉS WATERFALL

If you have time to visit only one waterfall in Costa Rica, make it **Llanos de Cortés** (admission by donation; ⊙8am-5pm). This beautiful hidden waterfall is located about 3km north of Bagaces; head north on the Interamericana, turn left on the dirt road after the Río Piedras bridge, then follow the bumpy road (4WD required) for about 1km, and turn right at the guarded gate, where you'll make a donation (US$2 will do the job) in exchange for your admission. Proceeds help fund the local primary school.

Continue down the dirt road about 300m to the parking area, then scramble down the short, steep trail to reach this spectacular 12m-high, 15m-wide waterfall, which you'll be able to hear from the parking lot. The falls drops into a tranquil pond with a white sandy beach that's perfect for swimming and sunbathing. Go 'backstage' and relax on the rocks behind the waterfall curtain, or shower beneath the lukewarm waters. On weekends this is a popular Tico (Costa Rican) picnic spot, but on weekdays you'll often have the waterfall to yourself.

There are no services here except for the occasional vendor selling fruit in the parking area. As always, don't leave valuables exposed in your car. If you don't have a car, any bus trawling this part of the Interamericana can drop you at the turnoff, but you'll have to hike from there to the falls.

🛏 Sleeping & Eating

Overnight visitors should make reservations and must also pay the US$10 entry fee.

OTS Palo Verde Research Station LODGE $$$
(📞2524-0607; www.ots.ac.cr; r incl meals per person US$98; 🅿🛜) Run by the OTS, Hacienda Palo Verde Research Station conducts tropical research and teaches university graduate-level classes. But it also has rustic cabins with bunk beds and fans, which are rented out to ecotourists. A few basic two- and four-bed rooms with shared bathrooms are also available, but they are often occupied by researchers and students working onsite.

The research station is on a well-signed road 8km from the park entrance. Camping is also permitted here.

❶ Getting There & Away

The main road to the entrance, usually passable to ordinary cars year-round, begins from a signed turnoff from the Interamericana, opposite Bagaces. The 28km gravel road has tiny brown signs that usually direct you when the road forks, but if in doubt, take the fork that looks more used. Another 8km brings you to the limestone hill, Cerro Guayacán (and the OTS Palo Verde Research Station), from where there are great views; 2km further are the Palo Verde park headquarters and ranger station. You can drive through a swampy maze of roads to the Reserva Biológica Lomas de Barbudal without returning to the Interamericana, but be sure to inquire with rangers about road conditions.

Buses connecting Cañas and Liberia can drop you in Bagaces, opposite the turnoff to the park. If you're staying at the Palo Verde Research Station, the staff may be able to pick you up, but be sure to make advance arrangements.

Liberia
POP 63,000

The sunny rural capital of Guanacaste has long served as a transportation hub connecting Costa Rica with Nicaragua, as well as being the standard-bearer of Costa Rica's *sabanero* culture. Even today, a large part of the greater Liberia area is involved in ranching operations, but tourism is fast becoming a significant contributor to the economy. With an expanding international airport, Liberia is a safer and more chilled-out alternative Costa Rican gateway to San José, which means more travelers are spending a night or two in this small but sweet college town, knitted together by corrugated-tin fencing, mango trees and magnolias.

Most of the historic buildings in the town center are a little rough around the edges

---

WORTH A TRIP

RESERVA BIOLÓGICA LOMAS DE BARBUDAL

Forming a cohesive unit with Parque Nacional Palo Verde, the 26-sq-km Lomas de Barbudal is an option for more off-the-beaten-track, independent hiking.

This is tropical dry forest, with a prolonged dry season that sometimes feels like a drought. Nearly 70% of the trees in the reserve are deciduous, and during the dry season they shed their leaves just like fall in a temperate forest. This allows the trees to conserve water and enables sunlight to filter through to facilitate the growth of thick underbrush.

The reserve protects several species of endangered trees, such as mahogany and rosewood, as well as the common and quite spectacular *corteza amarilla*. This tree is what biologists call a 'big-bang reproducer' – all the yellow cortezes in the forest burst into bloom on the same day, and for about four days the forest is an incredible mass of yellow-flowered trees. This usually occurs in March, about four days after an unseasonal rain shower.

Lomas de Barbudal is also known for its insects. There are about 250 species of bee in this fairly small reserve – representing about a quarter of the world's bee species. There are also more than 200 bird species, including endangered species such as the great curassow, king vulture, scarlet macaw and jabirú stork.

A small visitors center, **Casa Patrimonio**, has exhibits about the park's flora and fauna, as well as maps and other information. Several hiking trails radiate from here.

The turnoff to Lomas de Barbudal from the Interamericana is 14km southeast of Liberia or 12km northwest of Bagaces. From here it's 7km to the entrance of the reserve on a rough unpaved road. Some steep sections may require 4WD in the rainy season.

and in desperate need of a paint job. That said, the 'white city' is a pleasant one, with a good range of accommodations and services for travelers on all budgets. The streets in downtown Liberia are surprisingly well signed, a rarity in Costa Rica. Still, it's largely a launch pad for exploring Rincón de la Vieja National Park and the beaches of the Península de Nicoya.

⊙ Sights

Near the entrance of town, a **statue** of a steely-eyed *sabanero*, complete with an evocative poem by Rodolfo Salazar Solórzano, stands watch over Av 25 de Julio, the main street into town. The blocks around the intersection of Av Central and Calle Real contain several of Liberia's oldest houses, many dating back about 150 years. There is a long-term plan to pedestrianize Calle Real south of the park; it was the historic thoroughfare into and out of the city.

Parque Central   PARK
The somewhat shady but not particularly picturesque Parque Central frames Iglesia Inmaculada Concepción de María. The park is also the seasonal hangout of the Nicaraguan grackle, a tone-deaf bird that enjoys eating parrot eggs and annoying passers-by with its grating calls.

Museo de Guanacaste   HISTORIC BUILDING
(☑ 2665-7114; cnr Av 1 & Calle 2; ⊙ 8am-4pm)
FREE It's not much of a museum, but Liberia's old city jail is definitely interesting. Depressing dorms and cells surround a barren concrete courtyard, and it has occasional student concerts and exhibits. The place lacks resources, but there are plans to stage an actual museum here...at some point.

La Agonía   CHURCH
(La Iglesia de la Ermita de la Resurección; Av Central)
Six blocks northeast of the park you'll find the oldest church in town, popularly called La Agonía. It's a gloriously decrepit mud-and-brick relic, locked and closed to the public. The adjacent park has become the de facto skate park – complete with poured-concrete ramps and charming local skate punks. A stroll through the surrounding, somewhat seedy blocks is an interesting way to spend an hour.

Africa Mía   WILDLIFE RESERVE
(☑ 2666-1111; www.africamiacr.com; adult/child US$18/12, van tour US$30/24, safari tour US$65/55; ⊙ tours 9:30am, 11am, 1pm & 2pm)

About 10km south of Liberia is a private wildlife reserve with free-roaming elephants, zebras, giraffes, ostriches and other animals. Splurge for the deluxe African Safari Wildlife Tour in an open-top Hummer, which allows you to get up close and personal with the giraffes.

⏾ Sleeping

Liberia is at its busiest during the dry season – reservations are strongly recommended over Christmas, Easter and Día de Guanacaste (July 25) and on weekends. During the wet season, however, most of the midrange and top-end hotels give discounts.

Hospedaje Dodero   HOSTEL $
(☑ 8729-7524; www.hospedajedodero.yolasite.com; Av 11 btw Calles 12 & 14; per person US$11-19; ❋ ☎)
Three things: super clean, super service and close to the bus station. Small dorms and private rooms share bathrooms. There's a communal outdoor kitchen, overlooking a yard lit with Christmas lights and hung with a hammock. Also home to one dog, one cat and two parrots. It's nothing fancy, but it's very friendly.

Hotel Liberia   HOTEL $
(☑ 2666-0161; www.hotelliberiacr.com; Calle Real btwn Avs Central & 2; dm US$13, torre s/d US$28/35, casona s/d US$35/40; ₱ ☎) It's hard to resist the glorious shady courtyard at this historic guesthouse, which is one of Liberia's best budget options. The most appealing '*casona*' rooms are set in the old building, where the high ceilings, tile floors and wooden furniture contribute to an old-fashioned ambience. Less atmospheric '*torre*' rooms and dorms are in the newer concrete building at the back of the courtyard.

La Posada del Tope   GUESTHOUSE $
(☑ 2666-3876;   www.laposadadeltope.com; Calle Real btwn Avs 2 & 4; s/d from US$20/30; ₱ ⊙ @ ☎) Rooms are in the '*casa real*' across the street from the wooden lobby. Set around an awesome garden and furnished with an eclectic collection of art and antiques, this place has a lot of personality for a budget hotel. Rooms are decidedly basic with mostly shared bathrooms, but the price is right. The bilingual Tico owner, Denis, is a wealth of information.

★ Casa del Papel   B&B $$
(☑ 2666-0626; posadadelacallereal@gmail.com; cnr Calle Real & Av 4; r incl breakfast US$50-70; ₱ ❋ ☎ ☲) This historic house has been

Liberia

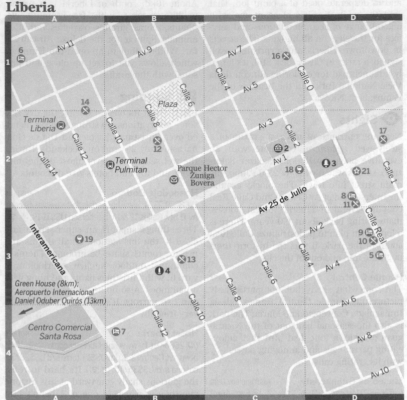

artfully converted into an exquisite guesthouse, easily recognizable by its newsprint facade. The rooms are simply and tastefully decorated with wooden floors, soaring ceilings and antique furniture. The common lounge is hung with original art and vintage furnishings, while gorgeous gardens, swimming pool with Jacuzzi and hammocks are at your disposal.

All of the art (including the exterior) is the work of national artist and owner Karen Clachar.

Hotel Javy
HOTEL **$$**

(📞2666-9253; www.hoteljavy.com; cnr Av 19 & Calle 21; d incl breakfast US$50; P❄🛜) Clara and Isabella are your hostesses with the *mostestes*. These charming ladies go out of their way to make sure their guests are happy, not least preparing an enormous, delicious breakfast to send you off feeling satisfied. The rooms are not going to win any style awards, but they are comfortable, with firm beds, incongruously formal furnishings and spotless new bathrooms.

The location, about 2km northeast of Parque Central, is not convenient.

Hotel Boyeros
HOTEL **$$**

(📞2666-0722; www.hotelboyeros.com; cnr Interamericana & Av 2; s/d incl breakfast US$60/70; P❄❄@🛜🏊) The largest hotel in Liberia feels like a cross between a dude ranch and the Holiday Inn. Once-proud rooms, arced around the pool on two floors, all have comfortable furnishings, tile floors and cable TV, but they are aging quite conspicuously. There's also a 24-hour restaurant, pool with waterslide, kiddie pool and a shaded sitting area.

Look for the sculpture of the *boyero* (oxcart driver) out front.

Liberia

◎ Sights

🛏 Sleeping

✕ Eating

🍷 Drinking & Nightlife

🎭 Entertainment

✕ Eating

Before you board that long bus ride, pick up cheap eats and fresh fruit and veggies at the traditional covered **market** (Ave 7 btwn Calles 10 & 12; ⊙6am-7pm Mon-Sat, 6am-noon Sun) conveniently located next to Terminal Liberia.

Donde Pipe　　　　　　　　　　CAFE $
(☑2665-4343; www.dondepipe.com; cnr Calle 8 & Av 5; mains US$6-8; ⊙7am-6pm Mon-Sat; 🛜🍴👶) Perhaps the only proper cafe in Liberia, where you can sit for long hours inside or out, drinking strong coffee, munching home-made brownies and taking advantage of the free wi-fi. In addition to burgers, sandwiches and breakfast items, the menu features local specialties like *chifrijos* (rice and pinto beans with fried pork, topped with tomato salsa and corn chips) and tamales, and of course refreshing fresh fruit juices. This place is a local favorite.

Restaurante El Pilon　　　RESTAURANT $
(☑2665-5869; Calle Central btwn Avs 5 & 7; casados US$6; ⊙7am-3pm) A great little find for fans of *casados*. This local diner serves seven daily, featuring fresh *pescado* (fish), *pollo* (chicken), steak, lamb and more. Relax around wooden tables in the cool, dark-tiled dining room.

★ Café Liberia　　　　　ORGANIC $$
(☑2665-1660; Calle Real btwn Avs 2 & 4; mains US$8-15; ⊙7am-10pm Mon-Sat; ❄🍴🛜) This beautifully restored colonial building has heavy wooden furniture and frescoed ceilings, creating a romantic ambience for rich coffee and gourmet fare. Simple food is taken to new levels: *ceviche* (seafood marinated in lemon or lime juice, garlic and seasonings) is served with irresistible, warm, fresh-baked tortilla chips. It's also an atmospheric setting for live music and other occasional performances.

Pizza Pronto　　　　　　　PIZZERIA $$
(☑2666-2098; cnr Av 4 & Calle 1; mains US$8-17; ⊙11am-11pm) This very cute, old-world

pizzeria, where the wood is stacked next to the smoking courtyard oven, keeps it romantic and simple – just pizza, pasta and salads. The pizzas are delish, ranging from the recommended vegetarian option to the not-so-recommended taco pizza. Don't worry, you can choose from a long list of toppings and create your own.

Green House   VEGETARIAN $$
(Casa Verde; ☑ 2665-5037, 2665-8901; Hwy 21; mains US$6-12; ⊙ 11am-9pm; ☜☑☷) When they say 'green house' they mean it, as in a glass building filled with plants. Plus, there are green panels on the windows and – yes – many veggie options on the menu. Come into the light-filled dining room for a delightful fusion of flavors, such as grilled chicken with mango salsa and excellent fish tacos.

Located on the road to the airport, about 8km west of town.

Copa de Oro   RESTAURANT $$
(☑ 2666-0532; cnr Calle Central & Av 2; mains US$5-16; ⊙ 11am-10pm Wed-Mon; ☜☷) This congenial family restaurant is popular with locals and gringos alike. There's an extensive food and drink menu. Try the rice and seafood house specialty, *arroz copa de oro*. The *casados* are excellent and there's a nice *ceviche* menu too. With high quality and large portions, this place is excellent value.

Jauja   RESTAURANT $$$
(☑ 2665-2061; www.restaurantejaujacr.com; cnr Av 25 de Julio & Calle 10; mains US$8-18; ⊙ 11am-11pm; ℗☜) This stylish, indoor-outdoor bar and cafe on the main drag is unique in Liberia for its upscale ambience and classy cuisine. Service is also excellent. Look for wood-fired pizza, tender grass-fed steaks, and burgers on home-baked buns. The place is popular among Liberia's local professional set, as well as tourists and expats.

Toro Negro Steakhouse   STEAKHOUSE $$$
(☑ 2666-2456; cnr Ave Central & Calle 1; mains US$12-18; ⊙ noon-10pm; ℗☜☷) Located in a beautiful colonial building, this family-friendly restaurant has an extensive international menu specializing in meat including New York strip, filet mignon and burgers. The rustic interior is inviting, but you can't beat the outdoor balcony for people-watching and enjoying the evening breeze.

☳ Drinking & Entertainment

Live music and dance performances are often held at the Parque Central gazebo and at the nearby La Gobernación (cnr Av Central & Calle Central), an old municipal building.

★ Palermo Lounge   COCKTAIL BAR
(www.palermolounge.com; cnr Av Central & Calle 3) The city's most pleasant place for a drink is this tropical garden, lush with greenery and waterfalls. There are also sports and music videos on the big screen, but the volume is turned down so patrons can enjoy the tranquil atmosphere. The menu offers very tasty pub grub and Tico fare.

Ciro's   BAR
(☑ 2665-3022; http://cirosbar.com; Calle 2 btwn Avs Central & 1; ⊙ 4pm-2am) The liveliest bar in Liberia belongs to this branch of the San José favorite. It's not much, just a handful of tables, a simple bar and doors that roll open onto the sidewalk. But the sound system rocks and the locals bring the party.

Morales House   BAR
(☑ 2665-2490; cnr Av 1 & Calle 14; ⊙ 3pm-2am) A real Guanacaste *sabanero* hangout, this barnlike bar with cowboy motif has bulls' heads on the walls, blaring *ranchera* music and American sports on TV. Bonus: thick, juicy steaks for hungry buckaroos.

❶ Information

MEDICAL SERVICES
Hospital Dr Enrique Baltodano Briceño (☑ 2666-0011, emergencies 2666-0318) Behind the stadium on the northeastern outskirts of town.

MONEY
Most hotels will accept US dollars and may be able to change small amounts. Liberia probably has more banks per square meter than any other town in Costa Rica.

BAC San José (☑ 2666-2020; Centro Comercial Santa Rosa; ⊙ 9am-6pm Mon-Fri, to 1pm Sat) Changes travelers checks; try this 24-hour ATM if others won't accept your card.

Banco de Costa Rica (☑ 2666-2582; cnr Calle Central & Av 1) A 24-hour ATM.

Banco Nacional (☑ 2666-0191; Av 25 de Julio btwn Calles 6 & 8; ⊙ 8am-3:45pm Mon-Fri, 9am-1pm Sat) Has a 24-hour ATM.

Citibank (cnr Interamericana & Av 25 de Julio; ⊙ 9am-6pm Mon-Fri, to 12:30pm Sat) Has a 24-hour ATM and changes money.

ℹ Getting There & Away

AIR

Since 1993 **Aeropuerto Internacional Daniel Oduber Quirós** (LIR; www.liberiacostaricaairport.net), 12km west of Liberia, has served as the country's second international airport, providing easy access to all those beautiful beaches without the hassle of San José. In January 2012 it unveiled its sleek, mod new US$35-million terminal.

The majority of international flights still go to the USA and Canada, in addition to some regional flights on Copa Air (to Panama) and Taca (to Guatemala). Domestic flights mainly go to San José.

NatureAir (☑International Airport Daniel Oduber Quirós 2668-1106, reservations 2299-6000; www.natureair.com) To/from San José.

Sansa (☑International Airport Daniel Oduber Quiros 2668-1017, reservations 2290-4100; www.flysansa.com) To/from San José.

To/From the Airport

There are no car-rental desks at the airport; make reservations in advance, and your company will meet you at the airport with a car. Taxis from Liberia to the airport are about US$20. Or you can catch a bus in front of the Mercado Municipal (30 minutes, hourly) which runs from 5:30am to 6:30pm, Monday through Friday only.

BUS

Buses arrive at and depart from **Terminal Liberia** (Av 7 btwn Calles 12 & 14) and **Terminal Pulmitan** (Av 5 btwn Calles 10 & 12). Routes, fares, journey times and departures are as follows:

Cañas US$2; 1½ hours; departs Terminal Liberia every 30 minutes from 5am to 9:30pm. It's quicker to jump off the San José–bound bus in Cañas.

Curubandé US$2, 40 minutes, departs Terminal Liberia at 6:40am, noon and 5pm.

Juntas de Abangares US$3.50, two hours, departs Terminal Liberia at 3:50pm.

La Cruz/Peñas Blancas US$2.50; 1½ to two hours; departs Terminal Liberia hourly from 5am to 6pm.

Nicoya, via Filadelfia and Santa Cruz US$2.25; 1½ hours; departs Terminal Liberia every 30 minutes from 3:30am to 9pm.

Playa Flamingo US$3; 1½ hours; departs Terminal Liberia at 4:30am, 6am, 8am, 11am and 6pm.

Playa del Coco US$1.20; one hour; departs Terminal Pulmitan every hour from 5am to 7pm.

Playa Hermosa, Playa Panamá US$1.60; 1¼ hours; departs Terminal Liberia eight times from 4:50am to 5:30pm.

Playa Tamarindo US$2.75; 1½ to two hours; departs the Mercado Municipal hourly between 3:50am and 6pm. Some buses take a longer route via Playa Flamingo.

Puntarenas US$3; three hours; nine buses from in front of Terminal Liberia from 5am to 3:30pm. It's quicker to jump off the San José–bound bus in Puntarenas.

San José US$6; four hours; 12 departures from Terminal Pulmitan from 4am to 8pm.

CAR

Liberia lies on the Interamericana, 234km north of San José and 77km south of the Nicaraguan border post of Peñas Blancas. Hwy 21, the main artery of the Península de Nicoya, begins in Liberia and heads southwest. A dirt road leads 25km from Barrio La Victoria to the Santa María entrance of Parque Nacional Rincón de la Vieja; the partially paved road to the Las Pailas entrance begins from the Interamericana, 5km north of Liberia.

There are more than a dozen rental-car agencies in Liberia (none of which have desks at the airport itself); rates can vary and you'll get steep discounts for rentals of a month or more. Most companies can arrange pickup in Liberia and drop-off in San José, though they'll charge you extra. Some companies will drop off your car in town upon request.

Adobe (☑2667-0608, in USA 866-767-8651; www.adobecar.com; ☺8am-5pm) One of the cheapest companies in Costa Rica.

Avis (☑2668-1196; www.avis.co.cr; ☺6am-10pm)

Budget (☑2668-1024, 2436-2000; www.budget.com; ☺6am-11:30pm)

Europcar (☑2668-0125; www.europcar.co.cr; ☺8am-5pm)

Hola (☑2667-4040; www.hola.net)

Mapache (☑2586-6363; www.mapache.com) Green car rental. Mapache is 100% carbon neutral and has been awarded four green leaves by OTS.

Toyota Rent a Car (☑2258-1213, 2668-1212; www.toyotarent.com) Just 800m north of the airport.

VIP Car Rental (☑2666-0052; www.vipcarrentaltours.com) Expect discount prices on well-maintained vehicles. It's not a kinder, gentler option, just the best value, and staff will meet you at your Liberia-area hotel for drop-offs and pickups, although you may have to call and remind them.

OOPHOTO / GETTY IMAGES ©

1. Llanos de Cortés (p225)
This beautiful waterfall spills into a tranquil pond, perfect for swimming in.

2. Área de Conservación Guanacaste (p237)
The grasslands of Guanacaste, dotted with bromeliads and cacti, make up the largest remaining area of tropical dry forest in Central America.

3. Bosque Nuboso Monteverde (p212)
Suspended in the canopy is a 100m suspension bridge that rocks and sways with each step.

JOHN COLETTI / GETTY IMAGES ©

Parque Nacional Rincón de la Vieja

Given its proximity to Liberia – really just a hop, a skip and a few bumps away – this 141-sq-km national park feels refreshingly uncrowded and remote. The name means 'old lady's nook' and it's named after the active Volcán Rincón de la Vieja (1895m), the steamy main attraction. The park also covers several other peaks in the same volcanic range, including the highest, Volcán Santa María (1916m). The park exhales geothermal energy. It bubbles with multi-hued fumaroles, tepid springs and steaming flatulent mud pots, as well as a young and feisty *volcancito* (small volcano). All of these can be visited on foot and horseback on well-maintained but sometimes steep trails.

The park was created in 1973 to protect a vital watershed that feeds 32 rivers and streams. Its relatively remote location means that wildlife, rare elsewhere, is out in force here, with the major volcanic crater a rather dramatic backdrop to the scene. Volcanic activity has occurred many times since the late 1960s, with the most recent eruption of steam and ash in 2012. At the moment, however, the volcano is gently active and does not present any danger – ask locally for the latest, as volcanoes do act up. (The crater itself is off-limits since the 2012 eruptions have made it unsafe.)

Elevations in the park range from less than 600m to 1916m, so visitors pass through a variety of habitats as they ascend the volcanoes, though the majority of the trees in the park are typical of those found in dry tropical forests throughout Guanacaste. The park is home to the country's highest density of Costa Rica's national flower, the increasingly rare purple orchid *(Cattleya skinneri),* locally known as *guaria morada.*

Most visitors to the park are here for the hot springs, where you can soak to the sound of howler monkeys overhead. Many of the springs are reported to have therapeutic properties, which is always a good thing if you've been hitting the *cacique guaro* a little too hard. Several lodges, just outside the park, provide access and arrange tours. You can also book transportation and tours from Liberia. Note that the park is closed on Monday.

🏃 Activities

Hiking

A circular trail east of Las Pailas ranger station – about 3km in total – takes you past boiling *las pailas* (mud pools), sulfurous fumaroles and a *volcancito.*

About 350m west of the ranger station is the well-signed trail to Pozo Azul, which offers a marvelous river view and a stunning aquamarine swimming hole. Further away along the same trail are several waterfalls – the largest, Catarata La Cangreja, 5.1km west, is a classic, dropping 50m straight from a cliff into a small lagoon where you can swim. Dissolved copper salts give the falls a deep-blue color. This trail winds through forest, past truly massive strangler figs, then on to open savannah spiked with yucca on the volcano's flanks, where you can enjoy views as far as the Palo Verde wetlands and the Pacific beyond.

The slightly smaller Cataratas Escondidas (Hidden Waterfalls) are 4.3km west on a different trail and a bit higher on the slope.

Since the 2012 eruptions the trek to the summit of Rincón de la Vieja is no longer open to the public.

From the Santa María ranger station a trail leads 2.8km west through the 'enchanted forest' and past a waterfall to sulfurous hot springs with supposedly therapeutic properties. Don't soak in them for more than about half an hour (some people suggest much less) without taking a dip in the nearby cold springs, 2km away, to cool off. There's also a lovely 1.1km trail to the Catarata Bosque Encatnado, Santa María's best waterfall. If you cobble all the Santa María trails together you'll have a gorgeous 12km day hike.

Hot Springs & Spas

Hot Springs Rio Negro   HOT SPRING
(www.guachipelin.com; per person US$10; ⊙9am-5pm) Set in the dry forest along the Rio Negro, this magical place is managed by the Hacienda Guachipelín. Six natural, stone-crafted hot pools are accessible by a lovely wooded trail. Those closest to the hanging bridge, on either side of the river, are the hottest, topping out at 40°C. Admission comes with a short tour through the woods describing indigenous medicinal flora.

About 1km from the Las Pailas ranger station, turn toward Rincon de la Vieja Lodge and the Santa María sector. The hot springs will be on your right.

HOTTEST SPOTS FOR THERMAL POOLS & MUD POTS

Costa Rica's volcano-powered thermal pools and mud pots provide plenty of good, clean fun for beauty queens and would-be mud wrestlers alike.

Hot Springs Rio Negro On the slopes of Volcán Rincón de la Vieja, this spot has several pools in a transporting jungle setting.

Eco Thermales Hot Springs (p251) While some hot spots around Arenal charge outrageous fees to soak in sparkly surrounds, here a sense of elegance is maintained by limiting guest numbers.

Rio Perdido (p223) Thermal pools, hanging bridges and low-key luxury characterize this thermal canyon experience near Volcán Miravalles.

Borinquen Mountain Resort & Spa (p236) The pinnacle of indulgent dirt exists in the remote heights of Rincón de la Vieja where, if mineral mud is not your thing, you can opt instead for a wine or chocolate skin treatment.

Canyon de la Vieja Adventure Lodge HOT SPRINGS
(☎ 2665-5912; www.thecanyonlodge.com; spa US$15, tours US$30-40) On the bank of the crystal blue Río Colorado, this sprawling lodge operates a full-service spa, complete with warm pools, mud baths and a Tarzan swing dropping into the inviting river. The current is strong, but the swimming hole is glorious for cooling off on a hot, sunny day (unfortunately, there's not much shade here). In addition to the spa, the adventure lodge offers tours including horse tours, tubing, rafting and canopy tours.

Accommodation (singles/doubles including breakfast US$80/100) is also available.

☞ Tours

All lodges can arrange a number of tours, including horseback riding (US$25 to US$35), mountain biking (US$10 to US$30), guided waterfall and hot-spring hikes (US$15 to US$25), rappelling (US$20 to US$50), rafting and tubing on the lesser-known Río Colorado (US$45 to US$60), hanging bridges (US$15 to US$20) and, everyone's favorite cash-burner, canopy tours (US$50). If you're staying in Liberia, it's possible to organize these activities in advance either through your hotel or by contacting the lodges directly.

🛏 Sleeping & Eating

Note that most of these hotels are a long way from any eateries, so you're stuck with paying for (usually pricey) meals at your hotel restaurant.

🛏 Santa María Sector

Rinconcito Lodge LODGE $
(☎ 2200-0074; www.rinconcitolodge.com; standard s/d US$25/39, superior s/d incl breakfast US$46/63; P 🖤) Just 3km from the Santa Maria sector of the park, this recommended budget option has attractive, rustic cabins that are surrounded by some of the prettiest pastoral scenery imaginable. Cheaper rooms are just as clean and fresh as the larger variety, but they're tiny. Inexpensive transportation and tours are also available.

🛏 Las Pailas Sector

Cropping up on the road to the park is an eclectic collection of truly lovely lodges that are worth considering if you've got your own wheels. The following lodges are located on (or just off) the road from the Interamericana to the national park.

El Sol Verde CAMPGROUND $
(☎ 2665-5357; www.elsolverde.com; campsites US$7.50, tent houses US$26, d/q US$49/69; P 🖤) 🏄 The lovely Dutch couple here in Curubandé village offer three Spanish-tiled, wood-walled rooms. Alternatively, bed down in the camping area, where there are a few furnished tent houses, a shared outdoor kitchen, solar-heated showers and plenty of space to pitch your own tent. The mural-painted terrace is a lovely place to relax, and you'll find hiking, swimming and wildlife in the immediate vicinity.

Casa Rural Aroma de Campo HOTEL $$
(☎ 2665-0008, reservations 7010-5776; www.aromadecampo.com; s/d/tr/q incl breakfast

US$53/76/104/123; (P🛜🍽) A secluded, sweet spot, this serene, epiphyte-hung, hammock-strung oasis has six rooms with polished hardwood floors, open bathrooms, colorful wall art, mosquito nets and classy rural sensibility. Delicious meals are served family-style in the courtyard. Warning: the pet parrot is an early riser.

Rancho Curubandé Lodge   LODGE $$
(📋2665-0375; www.ranchocurubande.com; s/d/tr/villas incl breakfast US$50/60/70/90; P❄🛜) Set on a working *finca*, this is a pleasant, family-run place with horses for hire. There are 16 spotless and simple rooms with beamed ceilings and a wide common front porch lit by tasteful wrought-iron chandeliers. The two-bedroom villas are particularly good value.

Hacienda Guachipelín   HOTEL $$
(📋2666-8075; www.guachipelin.com; s/d/tr/q incl breakfast US$81/99/128/148; P❄@🛜🍽) This appealing 19th-century working cattle ranch is set on 12 sq km of primary and secondary forest. The 54 rooms are simple and spacious with traditional wood furniture and wide, welcoming verandas. All rooms enjoy lovely views of the volcano and surrounding grounds. You'll appreciate the welcome drink that awaits you when you check in.

Be warned that the onsite 'adventure center' makes this place feel a little like a vacation factory, catering largely to package-tour clientele who descend for organized horse tours, in-house canopy tours and guided hikes in the national park.

Rincón de la Vieja Lodge   LODGE $$
(📋2200-0238; www.hotelricondelaviejacr.com; s/d incl breakfast from US$60/70; P@🍽) 🏊 Closest to the Las Pailas entrance, this rustic hacienda is on 400 hectares of protected land in breezy horse country. In addition to the 49 rustic rooms, there is a small pond, a family-style restaurant and a canopy tour. The staff are utterly charming.

🛏 Cañas Dulces Area

North of the road to Las Pailas is another, nearly roadless flank of the park, accessible from the charming *pueblo* Cañas Dulces. This is where dramatic shark-fin mountains draped in forest jut from pasturelands, and spectacular waterfalls thunder into valleys and bowls steaming with hot springs and scalding volcanic mud.

Buena Vista Lodge   LODGE $$
(📋2690-1414; www.buenavistalodgecr.com; d incl breakfast US$88-99; P@🍽) Part cattle ranch and part adventure lodge, this expansive place is set on 2000 acres. On the grounds are three waterfalls, thermal pools, a canopy tour, hanging bridges and a thrilling 400m mountain water slide. Choose between rustic stained-wood rooms and more private log cabins with glorious views. This lodge caters to package tourists big time.

Borinquen Mountain Resort & Spa   RESORT $$$
(📋2690-1900; www.borinquenresort.com; d incl breakfast US$218-373; ⊘Anáhuac Spa 9am-6pm; ❄🛜) Splurge. The most luxurious resort in the area features nicely appointed bungalows with private decks and jaw-dropping mountain views. All the expected adventure tours are on offer. The hot springs, mud baths and natural saunas are gorgeous and surrounded by greenery; and a treatment at the elegant Anáhuac Spa – suspended over the steaming jungle – is the icing on this decadent mud pie.

❶ Information

Each of the two main entrances to the park has its own ranger station, where you sign in and get free maps. Most visitors enter through **Las Pailas ranger station** (📋2661-8139; www.acguanacaste.ac.cr; adult/child 6-12yr/child 5yr & under US$10/1/ free; ⊘8am-4pm Tue-Sun, no entry after 3pm) on the western flank. Most of the trails begin here. The **Santa María ranger station** (📋2661-8139; www.acguanacaste. ac.cr; adult/child US$10/1; ⊘8am-4pm Tue-Sat), to the east, is in the Hacienda Santa María, a 19th-century *rancho* (small house) that was reputedly once owned by US President Lyndon Johnson. Closest to the sulfurous hot springs, it has a small public exhibit, an observation tower and a nearby waterfall.

❶ Getting There & Away

The Las Pailas sector is accessible via a good 20km road that begins at a signed turnoff from the Interamericana, 5km north of Liberia. It's paved for the first part of the drive past Curubandé. If you're not staying at the Hacienda Guachipelín, you'll have to pay to drive on its private road, which costs US$1.50 per person and takes you to the park gates. The Santa María ranger station, to the east, is accessible via a rougher gravel road beginning at Barrio La Victoria in Liberia. Both roads are passable to regular cars throughout the dry season, but a 4WD is required during the rainy season and is highly

SANTA ROSA IN HISTORY

This stretch of coast is famous among Ticos (Costa Ricans) as a national stronghold. Costa Rica has been invaded three times, and the enemy has always surrendered in Santa Rosa.

The best known of these incidents is the Battle of Santa Rosa, which took place on March 20, 1856, when the soon-to-be-self-declared president of Nicaragua, an uppity American named William Walker, invaded Costa Rica. Walker was the head of a group of foreign pirates and adventurers known as the 'Filibusters' that had already seized Baja and southwest Nicaragua and were attempting to gain control over all of Central America. In a brilliant display of military prowess, Costa Rican president Juan Rafael Mora Porras guessed Walker's intentions and managed to assemble a ragtag group of fighters who proceeded to surround Walker's army in the main building of the old Hacienda Santa Rosa, known as La Casona. The battle was over in just 14 minutes, and Walker was forever driven from Costa Rican soil.

Santa Rosa was also the site of battles between Costa Rican troops and invading forces from Nicaragua in the 20th century. The first – in 1919 – was a somewhat honorable attempt to overthrow the Costa Rican dictator General Federico Tinoco. Then, in 1955, Nicaraguan dictator Anastasio Somoza led a failed coup d'état. Today you can still see Somoza's abandoned tank, which lies in a ditch beside the road just beyond the entrance to the park.

Santa Rosa's military history didn't end with Somoza. In the 1980s US Marine Lieutenant-Colonel Oliver North illegally sold weapons to Iran and used the profits to fund the Nicaraguan Contras during the Sandinistas-Contra war. The troops' staging area was right here in Santa Rosa (near the famous surf break now known as Ollie's Point).

recommended at all other times (or it will take you twice as long).

There's no public transportation to the park entrances, but a bus travels from Liberia to Curubandé three times daily in each direction (40 minutes). Any of the lodges can arrange transport from Liberia to the park for around US$20 to US$30 per person each way (two or three people minimum). Alternately, you can hire a 4WD taxi from Liberia for about US$35 to Las Pailas, or US$65 to Santa María, each way.

To travel between the two sectors you needn't double back to Liberia. One kilometer from the Las Pailas park entrance is the turn toward Rincón de la Vieja lodge, Río Negro hot springs, the Santa María sector, and eventually San Jorge, Guayabo and Bagaces.

The road to Cañas Dulces and beyond, toward Buena Vista Lodge and Borinquen Mountain Resort & Spa, is well signed about 11.5km north of Liberia, where it intersects with the Interamericana.

Área de Conservación Guanacaste

Among the oldest (established in 1971) and largest protected areas in Costa Rica, this sprawling 386-sq-km national refuge on the Península Santa Elena protects the largest remaining stand of tropical dry forest in Central America, some of the most important nesting sites of several species of sea turtle, and deep historical gravitas. Almost all of the worthy diversions can be found in a vast area known as the Santa Rosa sector (☑2666-5051; www.acguanacaste.ac.cr; adult/child US$10/1, surfing surcharge US$15; ☺8am-4pm).

Although the park was established mainly due to historical and patriotic reasons, Santa Rosa has also become extremely important to biologists. Upon seeing its primordial acacia thorn trees and tall jaragua grass, first impressions of the park are likely to have you believe you've suddenly landed in the African savanna, though closer inspection reveals more American species of plants, including cacti and bromeliads. Santa Rosa is also home to Playa Nancite, which is famous for its *arribadas* (mass nesting) of olive ridley sea turtles – they can number up to 8000 at a time.

However, the majority of travelers are here for one reason: the chance to surf the near-perfect beach break at Playa Naranjo, which is created by the legendary offshore monolith known as Witch's Rock (also known locally as Roca Bruja). The park is home to another break of arguably equal fame, namely Ollie's Point, which was immortalized in the film *Endless Summer II*.

Difficult access means that most of the Santa Rosa sector is fairly empty, though it can get reasonably busy on weekends in the dry season, when Ticos flock to the park in search of their often-hard-to-find history. And, unfortunately, those breaks can get busy in the dry season too. But in the wet months from July through December, particularly in September and October, you'll often have the park virtually to yourself.

The park's **Sector Murciélago** (Bat Sector) encompasses the wild northern coastline of the Península Santa Elena and is not accessible from Santa Rosa. Here you'll find the isolated white-sand beach of **Playa Blanca** and the trailhead for the Poza el General watering hole, which attracts birds and animals year-round. The famous surf break Ollie's Point is in this sector near Playa Portero Grande, but it can only be reached by boat from Playa del Coco or Tamarindo. Or you can do as Patrick and Wingnut did in *Endless Summer II* and crash-land your chartered plane on the beach (ahem, not actually recommended).

◎ Sights & Activities

La Casona
HISTORIC BUILDING

(☏ 2666-5051; www.acguanacaste.ac.cr; ◷ 8-11:30am & 1-4pm) La Casona is the main edifice of the old Hacienda Santa Rosa. The battle of 1856 was fought around this building, and the military action is described with wonderful displays detailing (in English and Spanish) the old gold-rush route, William Walker's evil imperial plans, and the 20-day-battle breakdown. There are also exhibits on the region's natural history. Two hiking trails leave from behind the museum.

La Casona is located near the park headquarters in the Santa Rosa sector.

Wildlife-Watching

The wildlife is both varied and prolific, especially during the dry season, when animals congregate around the remaining water sources and the trees lose their leaves. More than 250 bird species have been recorded, including the raucous white-throated magpie jay, unmistakable with its long crest of manically curled feathers. The forests contain parrot and parakeet, trogon and tanager, and as you head down to the coast you'll be rewarded by sightings of a variety of coastal birds.

Dozens of species of bats have been identified in Santa Rosa. Other mammals you

have a reasonable chance of seeing include deer, coati, peccary, armadillo, coyote, raccoon, three kinds of monkey and a variety of other species – about 115 in all. There are also many thousands of insect species, including about 4000 moths and butterflies (just bring insect repellent).

Reptile species include lizards, iguanas, snakes, crocodiles and four species of sea turtle. The olive ridley sea turtle is the most numerous, and during the July to December nesting season tens of thousands of turtles make their nests on Santa Rosa's beaches. The most popular beach is Playa Nancite, where, during September and October especially, it's possible to see as many as 8000 of these 40kg turtles on the beach at the same time. The turtles are disturbed by light, so flash photography and flashlights are not permitted. Avoid the nights around a full moon – they're too bright and turtles are less likely to show up. Playa Nancite is strictly protected and entry is restricted, but permission may be obtained from park headquarters to observe; call ahead.

The variety of wildlife reflects the variety of habitat within park boundaries. Apart from the largest remaining stand of tropical dry forest in Central America, habitats include savanna woodland, oak forest, deciduous forest, evergreen forest, riparian forest, mangrove swamp and coastal woodland.

Hiking

Near Hacienda Santa Rosa is **El Sendero Indio Desnudo**, an 800m trail with signs interpreting the ecological relationships among the animals, plants and weather patterns of Santa Rosa. The trail is named after the common tree, also called *gumbo limbo,* whose peeling orange-red bark can photosynthesize during the dry season, when the trees' leaves are lost (resembling a sunburned tourist...or 'naked Indian', as the literal translation of the trail name implies). Also seen along the trail is the national tree of Costa Rica, the *guanacaste*. The province is named after this huge tree species, which is found along the Pacific coastal lowlands. You may also see birds, monkeys, snakes and iguanas, as well as petroglyphs (most likely pre-Columbian) etched into rocks along the trail.

Behind La Casona a short 330m trail leads up to the **Monumento a Los Héroes** and a lookout platform. There are also longer trails through the dry forest, including a gentle 4km hike to the **Mirador**, with spectacular views of Playa Naranjo, which is accessible to hikers willing to go another 9km along the deeply rutted road to the sea. The main road is lined with short trails to small waterfalls and other photogenic natural wonders.

On the road to Playa Naranjo, and about 8km from shore, you'll pass a trailhead for the **Mirador Valle Naranjo**. It's a short 600m hump to a viewpoint with magical Naranjo vistas.

From the southern end of Playa Naranjo there are two hiking trails: **Sendero Carbonal** is a 5km trail that swings inland along the mangroves and past Laguna El Limbo, where the crocs hang out; **Sendero Aceituno** parallels Playa Naranjo for 13km and terminates near the estuary across from Witch's Rock.

There's also a 6km hiking trail that starts where the northern branch of the access road terminates – this leads to the biological research station at Nancite; you'll need prior permission to access this beach. You'll also need to park in Naranjo and walk the 3.5km back to the **Sendero Nancite** trailhead, from where it's an additional 7km to the secluded beach, where there's no water source, so plan extensively and carefully.

Surfing

The surfing at Playa Naranjo is truly world-class, especially near **Witch's Rock**, a beach break famous for its fast, hollow 3m rights (although there are also fun lefts when it isn't pumping). Beware of rocks near the river mouth, and be careful near the estuary as it's a rich feeding ground for crocodiles during the tide changes. Oh, and by the way, the beach is stunning, with a sweet, rounded boulder-strewn point to the north and shark-fin headlands to the south. Even further south, Nicoya and Papagayo peninsular silhouettes reach out in a dramatic attempt to outdo each other.

The surfing is equally legendary at **Ollie's Point** off Playa Portero Grande, which has the best right in all of Costa Rica, with a nice long ride, especially with a south swell. The bottom here is a mix of sand and rocks, and the year-round offshore is perfect for tight turns and slow closes. Shortboarding is preferred by surfers at both spots.

PARQUE NACIONAL GUANACASTE

With the addition of this national park in 1989, the Área de Conservación Guanacaste became part of a protected nature corridor that stretches from the Pacific to the Caribbean coast. The 345-sq-km park is one of the least-visited parks in the country because tourist access is highly restricted. For information on visiting the park, contact the **ACG headquarters** (☑ 2666-5051; www.acguanacaste.ac.cr; adult/child US$10/1) in Parque Nacional Santa Rosa.

In its lower western reaches, the park is composed of the dry tropical rainforest characteristic of much of Guanacaste, but the terrain soon begins to climb toward two volcanoes: Volcán Orosí (1487m) and Volcán Cacao (1659m). Here the landscape slowly transitions to the humid cloud forest of the highland Cordillera de Guanacaste. This habitat provides a refuge for altitudinal migrants that move between the coast and the highlands.

PN Guanacaste is more the domain of biologists than tourists (admission is by reservation only), and there are two active research stations within the borders of the park. From **Maritza Biological Station** (☑ 2666-5051; www.acguanacaste.ac.cr; adult/child $10/1, dm US$15-20), there are rough trails to the summits of Volcán Orosí and Volcán Cacao (about five to six hours). A better trail leads to a site of ancient petroglyphs. To get here, turn east off the Interamericana opposite the turnoff for Cuajiniquíl. The station is about 17km east of the highway along a rough dirt road.

The **Pitilla Biological Station** (☑ 2666-5051; adult/child US$10/1, dm US$15) lies on the northeastern side of Volcán Orosí, which is on the eastern side of the continental divide. The surrounding forests here are humid, lush and unlike anything you'll find in the rest of Guanacaste. To get to the station, turn east off the Interamericana about 12km north of the Cuajiniquíl turnoff, or 3km before reaching the small town of La Cruz. Follow the paved eastbound road for about 28km to the community of Santa Cecilia. From here, a dirt road in truly terrible condition heads 11km south to the station – you'll need a 4WD year-round.

🛏 Sleeping & Eating

Campground CAMPGROUND

(per person US$2) There's a shady developed campground close to the park headquarters, with picnic benches, grills, flushing toilets and cold-water showers. Playa Naranjo has pit toilets and showers but no potable water – bring your own, and don't expect complete solitude. Everyone shares one sandy flat basin, only moderately sheltered from gusty wind by thin trees. There's a 25-person, two-night maximum.

There's also a small campsite with pit toilets and showers near the ranger station in the Sector Murciélago, though you'll have to bring your own food and water.

Research Station HOSTEL

(☑ 2666-5051; www.acguanacaste.ac.cr; dm US$10) Make reservations in advance to stay in basic to grim eight-bed dorms with cold showers and electricity. Researchers get priority, but there's usually some room for travelers. Good food (meals US$6 to US$7) is available in the *comedor* (cheap eatery).

❶ Getting There & Around

SANTA ROSA SECTOR

Access to the Santa Rosa sector park entrance is on the west side of the Interamericana, 35km north of Liberia and 45km south of the Nicaragua border. The well-signed main park entrance can be reached by public transportation: take any bus between Liberia and the Nicaraguan border and ask the driver to let you off at the park entrance; rangers can help you catch a return bus. You can also arrange private transportation from the hotels in Liberia for about US$20 to US$30 per person round trip.

From the entrance it's another 7km to park headquarters, where you'll find the administrative offices, scientists' quarters, an information center, three basic campgrounds, a museum and a nature trail. This office administers the Área de Conservación Guanacaste (ACG).

From this complex, a very rough track leads down to Playa Naranjo, 12km away. Even during the dry season this road is only passable by a high-clearance 4WD, and you must sign an eerie waiver at the park entrance stating that you willingly assume all liability for driving this road. The park also requires that you be completely self-sufficient should you choose to undertake the trip, which means bringing all your own water and knowing how to do your own car repair. During the rainy months (May to November) the road is open to hikers and horses but closed to all vehicles; if you want to surf here, it's infinitely easier

to gain access to the beach by hiring a boat from Playa del Coco or Tamarindo, further south.

SECTOR MURCIÉLAGO

The park's Sector Murciélago (Bat Sector) encompasses the wild northern coastline of the Península Santa Elena and is not accessible from the main body of the park.

To get to the northern Sector Murciélago, continue north on the Interamericana past the entrance to the Santa Rosa sector for 10km and then turn left once you pass through the police checkpoint. Continue on this road for a few more kilometers until you reach the village of Cuajiniquíl and then bear left. Continue on this road for another 15km, which will bring you past such historic sights as the former hacienda of the Somoza family (it's currently a training ground for the Costa Rican police) and the airstrip that was used by Oliver North to 'secretly' smuggle goods to the Nicaraguan Contras in the 1980s. Continue straight until you cross a river, then hang a right and keep going straight over two more rivers until you reach the village of Murciélago and the park entrance. You can camp at the Murciélago ranger station or continue another 12km on a dirt road to the remote bays and beaches of Bahía Santa Elena and Bahía Playa Blanca. A 4WD is a must, and even then the road may be impassable in the wet season. Also, signage is nonexistent.

Ollie's Point in Playa Portero Grande is in this sector of the park and can only be reached by boat from Playa del Coco or Tamarindo.

Refugio Nacional de Vida Silvestre Bahía Junquillal

This 505-hectare wildlife refuge is part of the ACG, administered from the park headquarters at Santa Rosa. There's a **ranger station** (☑ 2666-5051; www.acguanacaste.ac.cr; adult/child 6-12yr/child 5yr & under US$13/5/free, camping per person US$2; ⊙ 8am-5pm) in telephone and radio contact with Santa Rosa.

The quiet bay and protected beach provide gentle swimming, boating and snorkeling opportunities, and there are tropical dry forest and mangroves. Two short trails (totaling 1.7km) hug the coast and take the visitor to a lookout for marine bird-watching in one direction and to the mangroves in the other. Pelicans and frigate birds are seen, and turtles nest here seasonally. Volcán Orosí can be seen in the distance. This is a very popular campground among domestic tourists, and it's outfitted with brick grills and picnic tables at every site. Campers should note that, during the dry season especially, water is at a premium and is turned on for only one hour a day. There are pit latrines.

There's no sign pointing the way from Cuajiniquíl. Once you enter town, continue for about 2km on the paved road and turn right onto a dirt road after you pass Super-Compro. Continuing 4km along the dirt road (passable to ordinary cars) brings you to the entrance to Bahía Junquillal. You'll know you're getting close when that glorious cobalt bay appears from out of nowhere on your left. From the entry post there's a sign pointing out the 700m dirt road leading to the beach, ranger station and camping area. If you miss the turn to the refuge you'll land in an estuary fishing village where stilted houses overlook a tidal channel, and several *sodas* serve fresh seafood. The refuge road is passable to all cars.

La Cruz

POP 4800

La Cruz is the closest town to the Peñas Blancas border crossing with Nicaragua, and it's the principal gateway to Bahía Salinas, Costa Rica's premier kitesurfing destination. La Cruz itself is a fairly sleepy provincial town set on a mountaintop plateau, with lots of Tico charm and magical views of an epic windswept bay. At the time of writing, the town was rebuilding a *mirador* (lookout point) and tourist-information center, with an amazing panorama stretching all the way to Nicaragua.

🏃 Activities

Spider Monkey Canopy Tour CANOPY TOUR
(☑2679-8227; spidermonkeytours@hotmail.com) On the road to Bahía Salinas you'll find the requisite canopy tour, with 11 cables and a Tarzan swing. The place also organizes hiking and horseback riding in the surrounding dry forest. It's worth stopping just to eat lunch at **La Casa del Abuelo** (☑2679-8227; mains $3-8; ⊙11am-9pm).

🛏 Sleeping & Eating

Amalia's Inn INN **$**
(☑2679-9618; s/d US$25/35; P🌊) This yellow stucco house on a cliff isn't a bad place to spend the night. For starters, the shared terracotta terraces have stupendous bay views. Inside, homey rooms are furnished rather randomly, but the brick floors and

wooden ceilings are attractive. Walls in the meandering house are hung with modernist paintings by Amalia's late husband, Lester Bounds.

Amalia's niece is now the lady of the house, and short of offering meals she'll make you feel right at home.

Hotel La Mirada HOTEL **$**
(☑2679-9702; www.hotellamirada.com; s/d/tr US$28/44/56; P❄️🐕) Just off the Interamericana you'll find the town's spiffiest spot. Family owned and lovingly cared for, rooms are spacious and clean, with high, beamed ceilings and loft sleeping spaces. The biggest rooms have kitchenettes. Despite the name, there's no view to speak of. The place was up for sale at the time of writing, so everything is subject to change.

Hotel Bella Vista HOTEL **$**
(☑2679-8060; s/d/tr/q US$20/30/40/50; P🐕🌊) With a lovely mosaic-bottomed pool and breezy restaurant at the top of the hill, this Dutch-run hotel is a great place for a beer in the evenings. Fan-cooled rooms are crowded but reasonably clean. Ask for one on the second level for more light and outstanding views. Big discounts for backpackers; just ask.

Cañas Castillas CABIN **$$**
(☑8381-4030; www.canas-castilla.com; s/d/tr/q US$40/56/68/79; P🐕) On the banks of the peaceful Río Sapoa, a half-dozen quaint cabins are surrounded by 68 hectares of tropical forest and farmland. The family *finca* includes cattle and horses, as well as oranges, passion fruit and loads of other tempting fruit trees, making for amazing bird-sighting opportunities. Hearty, home-cooked meals are available.

The *finca* is about 5km north of La Cruz in Sonzpote. It's a perfect place to recover from a border crossing. Or if you're headed north, staff can help with that too.

ℹ️ Information

Changing money at the border post often yields a better exchange rate than in town.

Banco Nacional (☑2679-9296) At the junction of the short road into the town center; has a 24-hour ATM.

Banco Popular (☑2679-9352) In the town center; has an ATM.

Cruz Roja (☑2679-9004, emergency 2679-9146) A small clinic just north of the town center on the road toward the border.

ⓘ HEADING NORTH OF THE BORDER

Peñas Blancas is a busy **border crossing** (◷6am-10pm Mon-Sat, to 8pm Sun), which can be a major hassle at peak times. Avoid trying to cross the border in the days leading up to major holidays.

You won't be charged to exit or enter Costa Rica, but entering and leaving Nicaragua costs US$10. Driving a car across the border is another $27, but most car-rental companies in Costa Rica won't allow you to cross borders; check before you sign your contract. Alternatively, leave your car in the 'no-man's-land' parking area between borders. Banks on either side will change local colones and córdobas for dollars but, inconveniently, not for each other. Independent money changers will happily make the exchange for you – at whatever rates they feel like setting.

The border posts are about 1km apart. Hordes of generally useless touts will offer to 'guide' you through the simple crossing – let them carry your luggage if you like, but agree on a fee beforehand. You'll also be charged US$1 to enter the state of Rivas. Should you have any hard currency left at this point, there's a fairly fabulous duty-free shop waiting for you in Sapoá, the Nicaraguan equivalent of Peñas Blancas.

Relax with your purchases on the 37km bus ride (US$1, 45 minutes), departing every 30 minutes, to Rivas. The city is a quiet transport hub, though its well-preserved 17th-century center is worth exploring (think a more run-down version of Granada without all the crowds).

If you're good at bargaining (and you will have to bargain hard), there are a number of taxis waiting on the Nicaraguan side of the border to whisk you to Rivas (US$30).

ⓘ Getting There & Away

The bus station is located on the western edge of town, just north of the road to Bahía Salinas. A **Transportes Deldú counter** (www.transportesdeldu.com; ◷7:30am-12:30pm & 1:30-6pm) sells tickets and stores bags. To catch a TransNica bus to Peñas Blancas and on to Managua you'll need to flag down a bus on the Interamericana. Buses to the beaches depart from the bus terminal near Hotel Bella Vista; a taxi to the beach costs US$16 to US$20.

Liberia (Transportes Deldú) US$2.50; 1½ hours; departs every 45 minutes from 5:30am to 6:30pm. Alternatively, catch any San José–bound bus.

Peñas Blancas US$1; 45 minutes; 10 departures per day from 5am to 5:30pm.

Playa Jobó US$1.50; 30 minutes; departs four times daily from 8:30am to 5:30pm.

San José via Liberia (Transportes Deldú) US$7; five hours; departs almost every hour from 7:30am to 5:30pm.

Bahía Salinas

Welcome to the kitesurfing capital of Costa Rica, where giddy riders shred beneath magnificent rainbows that arch over a wide bay, extending all the way to Nicaragua. The destination has a deconstructed nature: communities congregate on empty beaches, clumped with tropical forests that are home to howler tribes, and linked by dirt roads. The result is a pleasingly *tranquilo*, rural vibe.

By the way, Bahía Salinas is a stunning, under-the-radar destination even if you don't ride wind. But not for long. The glorious sands of Playa Jabó won't be deserted after the opening of a 400-room, five-star resort. After that the road might be paved and more development will certainly follow. For better and for worse.

◉ Sights & Activities

A road (paved for the first few kilometers, but gravel for the remaining 9km) leads down from the lookout point in La Cruz past the small coastal fishing community of Puerto Soley. It then heads out along the curve of the bay to the consistently windy beaches of **Playa Papaturro** and **Playa Copal**, the kiting vortex. It's an incredibly wide beige beach backed by scrubby *manzanillo* trees with views across the sea all the way to Nicaragua. It does get crazy windy here, so, though picturesque, it's not about beachcombing. Copal is for launching kites and riding, and Papaturro is only a safe launch for advanced riders.

If wind isn't your thing, head around the point to **Playa Jobó**, a perfect, 300m-wide horseshoe of a bay with calm water and headlands sprouting with flowering trees, or **Playa Rajada,** set on the southernmost arm of Salinas. Rajada is ruggedly gorgeous and sheltered enough to be almost placid. In September and October, humpback whales often congregate here.

Boats can be rented, in the village of El Jobó or at one of the local resorts, to visit Isla Bolaños, a seabird refuge home to the endangered brown pelican (visits are restricted to April through November to avoid disturbing nesting seabirds). Ask around about fishing and diving trips to Isla Despense, Isla Caballo and Isla Murcielago, with its resident bull sharks.

Kitesurfing

Bahía Salinas is an internationally known mecca for kitesurfers between November and March, when the wind howls fairly consistently. The shape of the hills surrounding the bay funnels the winds into a predictable pattern (though it can be gusty, ranging between 20 and 40 knots), and the sandy, protected beaches make this a great place for beginners and experienced riders alike. It's important to remember that there are inherent dangers to kiting (namely the risk of losing a limb – yikes!), so seek professional instruction if you're not experienced. The Professional Air Sports Association (PASA) and the International Kiteboarding Organization (IKO) have set standards for beginner instruction. You'll need to take a nine-hour certification course to rent gear and safely go out on your own.

Kitesurf School 2000   KITESURFING
(☑2676-1042, 8826-5221; www.bluedreamhotel; lessons per hr US$30-40, 9hr certification US$319, gear rental per day US$65; ☺8am-8pm) Make reservations in advance to take lessons or rent gear at Kitesurf School 2000, the area's original kite shop (IKO certified). Located at Blue Dream Hotel, it's 250m from Papaturro, or the hotel provides a shuttle to Copal. Lessons are available in Spanish, English and Italian. It also has an excellent and incredibly swift repair service.

Bob's Cometa Copal   KITESURFING
(☑2676-1192; www.kiteincostarica.com; lessons per hr US$30-45, 9hr certification US$360; ☺Nov-Jun) Bob is an American instructor, lifeguard and emergency medical technician who runs this reputable kitesurfing school on Playa Copal. It's certified by the PASA but only open seasonally.

KiteHouse   KITESURFING
(☑2676-1045, 8370-4894; www.kiteboardingcostarica.com; lessons per hr US$45-65) Instruction and rentals on Playa Copal. It also offers the option for lessons on the island in the middle of the bay, which means better wind and fewer obstacles. IKO-certified instructors speak French and English.

🛏 Sleeping & Eating

Most hotels in Bahía Salinas offer transfers from San José or Liberia airports.

Blue Dream Hotel   HOTEL $
(☑8826 5221, 2676 1042; www.bluedreamhotel.com; dm US$17, standard s/d US$35/45, bungalow s/d US$42/52; ☺Sep-Jul; 🅿❄@🛜) Home base of Kitesurf School 2000, this friendly, groovy hotel offers marvelous views over Playa Papaturro from its terraced hillside, 200m away. There are simple, comfortable Spanish-tiled rooms and more spacious chalet-style rooms with private balconies. Along with the hammock-strung garden, there's the Mediterranean restaurant, serving hearty breakfasts and good pizzas.

Bob's Cometa Copal   CABINA $$
(☑2676-1192; www.kiteincostarica.com; cabinas US$40-60; 🅿❄🛏) A seasonal operation with clean, colorful little faux-dobe *cabinas* at the top of a hill with gorgeous views of the bay. *Cabinas* are quite sweet, with Spanish tiles, vaulted beamed ceilings and kitchenettes. Walk to the beach when you're ready to ride. And when you're done, walk back, lounge around the pool or grab a bite at the excellent restaurant.

Bolaños Bay Resort   HOTEL $$
(☑2676-1163; www.hotel-bolanos.com; d incl breakfast US$80; 🅿❄🛜🛏) Walk through the overly dramatic *palapa* (shelter with a thatched, palm-leaf roof and open sides) entryway and through the deserted restaurant, and feast your eyes on the seaside pool and the epic bay views beyond. That's what you came for. The rooms are cheery – with polished-concrete floors and whitewashed wood furnishings – but nothing special. Overall, it's a decent option if you can get past the atmosphere of abandonment.

Ecoplaya Beach Resort   HOTEL $$
(☑2676-1010; www.ecoplaya.com; s/d US$80/90, villas from US$130; 🅿♿@🛏) First things first: there's nothing particularly 'eco' about this place, and the *playa* is thin and gray.

But this chilled-out resort has a few things going for it. The huge rooms have sustainable teak furnishings and cool design elements like soaring slanted ceilings and epic views from the 2nd floor. Most importantly, it's a hop and a skip away from gorgeous Playa Jobó.

★ **Plaza Copal** SODA **$**

(☑8994-5292; meals US$6-10; ⊘8am-10pm) There's a fantastic vibe at this outdoor *soda*, located on the road down to Copal. Hungry kitesurfers congregate here to get their fill before and after riding the waves. They can vouch for the home-cooked meals, which are filling and downright delectable. Service is slow, but it's worth the wait for amazing coconut curry, grass-fed beef steaks and fresh fish.

If you want easy access to the goods from the kitchen, you can stay here in one of the basic wooden rooms with shared bathrooms (doubles US$25). The owner, Ulf, is also good for travel information, including tips and trips for getting to Nicaragua.

Vista Copal RESTAURANT **$$**

(☑2676-1006; mains US$8-15; ⊘5-9pm; [P][☎]) Take a talented New York–trained chef and put him in a kitchen with drop-dead-gorgeous views of the ocean, and you've got yourself a winner of a restaurant. This stunning, thatched wooden dining room is the place to come for giant, juicy steaks and super-fresh seafood, cooked to make your mouth water and your head spin. Whatever they've got is on the chalkboard.

❶ Getting There & Away

Buses (US$1.50) make the 30-minute run between the La Cruz bus terminal and the village of Jobó three times a day in either direction. A taxi to the beaches costs about US$16 to US$20.

To get to Playa Jobó, take the road past Bolaños Bay Resort for about 2km. It dead ends at the beach. For Playa Rajada, double back to the main road, make a right (away from La Cruz) and veer right again at the Mini Super in El Jobó; 3km later the road ends at the beach.

Arenal & Northern Lowlands

Best Places to Eat

➡ Restaurant Don Rufino
(p257)

➡ Rainforest Café (p256)

➡ Gingerbread Hotel &
Restaurant (p265)

➡ Café y Macadamia (p267)

Best Wildlife-Watching

➡ Ecocentro Danaus (p248)

➡ Refugio Nacional de Vida
Silvestre Caño Negro (p271)

➡ Chilamate Rainforest Eco
Retreat (p281)

➡ Estación Biológica La
Selva (p285)

Why Go?

You know about the region's main attraction: the now-dormant Volcán Arenal, surrounded by old lava fields, bubbling hot springs and a stunning lake. Venture further onto the wild rivers and into the tropical jungle of the northern lowlands and you will discover real-life Costa Rica, where agricultural commerce and ecological conservation converge as a work in green progress. Stretching from the borderlands of Nicaragua south to the Cordillera de Tilarán, banana, sugarcane and pineapple *fincas* (farms) roll across humid plains. Community tourism lives and breathes here, creating added revenue for a historically farm-based economy. You can spot a macaw in the wild, paddle into roaring rapids and cruise inky lagoons, all with lifelong resident guides, then nest in lodges that double as private rainforest reserves. When the tourist hordes get you down, make your way here for a refreshing blast of rural realism and an invigorating dose of wild beauty.

When to Go

➡ There's no dry season in the northern lowlands: the lush jungles surrounding the rivers in the region, such as the Río Frío and the Río Sarapiquí, receive rainfall at almost any time of year.

➡ There is a less-wet season, though, from January to April, when rainfall is lower.

➡ Because there's so much rain, you can run the rivers any time of year, but they flow faster from July to December.

Arenal & Northern Lowlands Highlights

❶ Hiking up the Cerro Chato at **Parque Nacional Volcán Arenal** (p259) and gazing across the turquoise-blue crater lake at its summit.

❷ Marvelling at sweeping lake and volcano views from your perch in **El Castillo** (p261).

❸ Exploring the lagoons of the **Refugio Nacional de Vida Silvestre Caño Negro** (p271) to take a gander at spoonbills or a stab at tarpon.

❹ Riding the rapids through the jungle on the **Río Sarapiquí** (p280).

❺ Spotting howlers, sloths, peccaries and all manner of birdlife while exploring the grounds of your ecolodge near **Puerto Viejo de Sarapiquí** (p283).

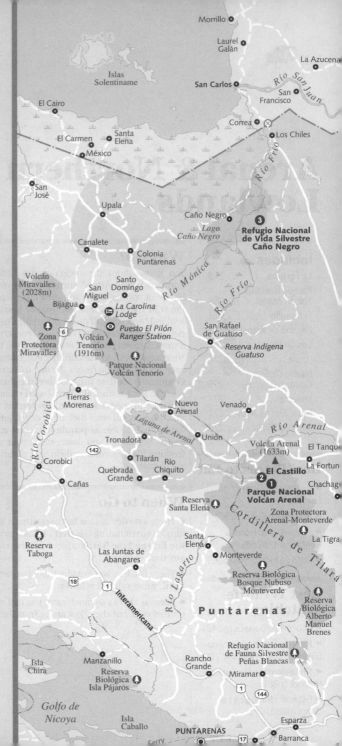

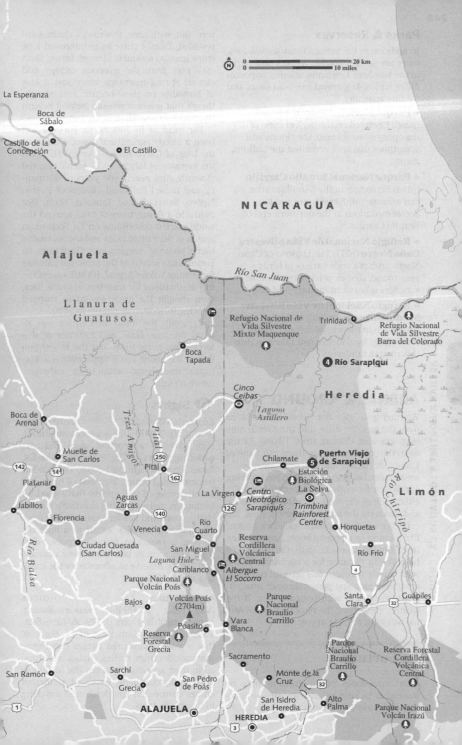

N | 0 _____ 20 km
0 _____ 10 miles

La Esperanza

Boca de
Sábalo

Castillo de la
Concepción

El Castillo

NICARAGUA

Alajuela

Río San Juan

**Llanura de
Guatusos**

Refugio Nacional de
Vida Silvestre
Mixto Maquenque

Trinidad

Refugio Nacional
de Vida Silvestre
Barra del Colorado

Boca
Tapada

4 Río Sarapiquí

Cinco
Ceibas

*Laguna
Astillero*

Heredia

Boca de
Arenal

Tres Amigos

Pital

Muelle de
San Carlos

(142)

(141)

Pital

(250)

(162)

Chilamate

5 **Puerto Viejo
de Sarapiquí**

Estación
Biológica
La Selva

Río Chirripó

Limón

Platanar

Aguas
Zarcas

(140)

La Virgen

(126)

*Centro
Neotrópico
Sarapiquís*

Tirimbina
Rainforest
Centre

Jabillos

Florencia

Venecia

Río
Cuarto

Horquetas

Río Balsa

Ciudad Quesada
(San Carlos)

San Miguel

Reserva
Cordillera
Volcánica
Central

Río Frío

Laguna Hule

Cariblanco

*Albergue
El Socorro*

(4)

Parque Nacional
Volcán Poás

Bajos

Volcán Poás
(2704m)

Parque
Nacional
Braulio
Carrillo

Santa
Clara

Guápiles

Poasito

Vara
Blanca

Reserva Forestal
Grecia

Parque
Nacional
Braulio
Carrillo

(32)

San Ramón

Sarchí

Sacramento

Reserva Forestal
Cordillera
Volcánica
Central

Grecia

San Pedro
de Poás

Monte de la
Cruz

(32)

ALAJUELA

San Isidro
de Heredia

Alto
Palma

Parque Nacional
Volcán Irazú

(1)

HEREDIA

(3)

Parks & Reserves

In addition to the famous must-see volcano, there are several notable refuges and parks in the Northern Lowlands, offering opportunities for low-key, crowd-free boat tours and wildlife-watching.

➡ **Parque Nacional Volcán Arenal** (p259) Centered on the perfect cone of the eponymous volcano, the clouds will sometimes disperse, revealing the hulking giant.

➡ **Parque Nacional Braulio Carrillo** (p144) Ecolodges in the Sarapiquí area can arrange rainforest tours and have accommodations at the northern end of Braulio Carrillo.

➡ **Refugio Nacional de Vida Silvestre Caño Negro** (p271) The lagoons of Caño Negro attract a wide variety of birds year-round, though prime time for birdwatchers is between January and July.

➡ **Refugio Nacional de Vida Silvestre Mixto Maquenque** (p279) Though there isn't much in the way of infrastructure at this refuge, local lodges can take you into this remote rainforest.

ARENAL & AROUND

Whether you approach from the west or from the east, the drive into the Arenal area is spectacular. Coming from Tilarán in the west, the paved road hugs the north bank of Laguna de Arenal. The lake and forest vistas are riveting, but pay attention to your driving and watch for potholes and coati jams. On either side of the road – up the green slope and down on the lakeside – lovely inns, hip coffeehouses and eccentric galleries appear like pictures in a pop-up book. Approaching from Ciudad Quesada (San Carlos), you'll have Volcán Platanar for a backdrop, the road winds through this green, river-rich agrarian region and passes through prosperous towns bright with bougainvillea. If the weather cooperates, the resolute peak of Arenal will loom in front of you.

La Fortuna

POP 10,000

First impressions of La Fortuna may be somewhat lacking, what with all the tourists and uninspired cinder-block architecture. But, with time, this town's charms are revealed. Horses graze in unimproved lots, spiny iguanas scramble through brush, sloth eyes peer from the riverside canopy and eternal spring mornings carry just a kiss of humidity on their breath. And always, there's that massive volcano lurking behind the clouds or sparkling in the sun.

For most of its history La Fortuna has been a sleepy agricultural town, 6km from the base of **Cerro Arenal** (Arenal Hill). On the morning of July 29, 1968, Arenal erupted violently after nearly 400 years of dormancy, and buried the small villages of Pueblo Nuevo, San Luís and Tabacón. Soon, like moths to a flame, tourists from around the world started descending on La Fortuna in search of fiery night skies and the inevitable blurry photo of creeping lava. Since then, La Fortuna has served as the principal gateway for visiting Volcán Arenal. It's still one of the top destinations for travelers in Costa Rica, even though the great mountain stopped spewing its molten discharge in 2010.

Certainly, the influx of tourism has altered the face, fame and fortunes of this former one-horse town. But the longer you linger, the more you'll appreciate La Fortuna's underlying, small-town *sabanero* (cowboy) feel.

◉ Sights

Ecocentro Danaus   BUTTERFLY FARM
(Map p250; ☎2479-7019; www.ecocentrodanaus. com; admission with/without guide US$16/11, guided night tours US$35; ☽8am-4pm Mon-Sat, 9am-3:30pm Sun, night tour 5:30pm) This reader-recommended center, 2km east of town, has a well-developed trail system that's good for birding, as well as spotting mammals such as sloths, coatis and howler monkeys. The price of admission includes a visit to a butterfly garden, a ranarium featuring poison-dart frogs and a small lake containing caimans and turtles. Reserve in advance for the excellent night tour.

Arenal Natura   ECO-PARK
(Map p250; ☎2479-1616; www.arenalnatura. com; day/night/bird tours US$29/35/40; ☽8am-5:30pm) Located 6km west of La Fortuna, this is a well-manicured nature experience that includes frogs, turtles, snakes and crocs, all in their appointed places. The birdlife is also prodigious here. Excellent naturalist guides ensure that you don't miss anything hiding in the trees.

La Fortuna

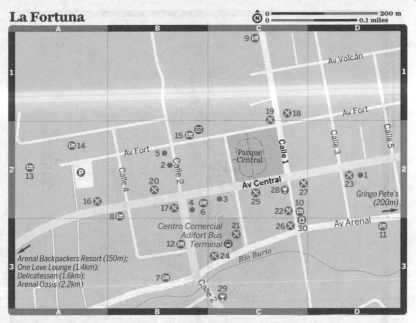

N 0 — 200 m
0 — 0.1 miles

La Fortuna

🏃 Activities

La Catarata de la Fortuna   WATERFALL
(Map p250; admission US$10; ⊙8am-5pm) You can glimpse the sparkling 70m ribbon of clear water that pours through a sheer canyon of dark volcanic rock covered in bromeliads and ferns with minimal sweat equity. But it's worth the climb down and out to see it from the jungle floor. Though it's dangerous to dive beneath the thundering falls, a series of perfect swimming holes with spectacular views tiles the canyon in aquamarine. This is also the trailhead for the hike to Cerro Chato (p261).

From the turnoff on the road to San Ramón, it's about 4km uphill to the falls. If you decide

Around La Fortuna

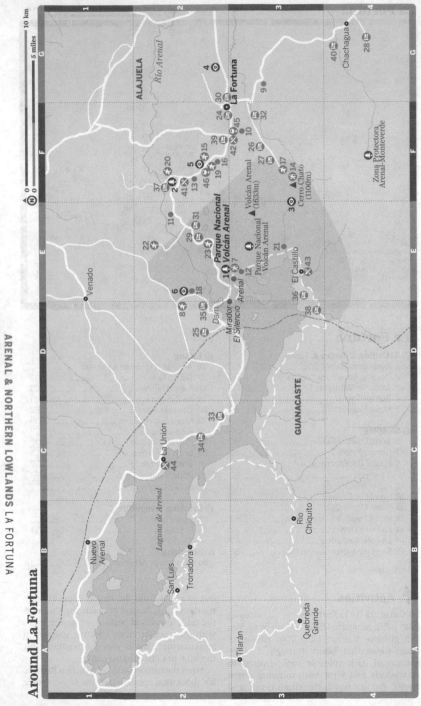

Around La Fortuna

ARENAL & NORTHERN LOWLANDS LA FORTUNA

to walk up, you'll enjoy spectacular views of Cerro Chato as you hike through pastures and past the small hotels lining the road.

Bike Arenal CYCLING
(☎2479-7150; www.bikearenal.com; rental per day/week US$25/150, half-/full-day tour US$67/96; ☺8am-5pm Mon-Fri) This outfit offers a variety of bike tours for all levels of rider, including a popular ride around the lake and a half-day ride to El Castillo. You can also do versions of these rides on your own. Make advance arrangements for rental and an English-speaking bike mechanic will bring the bicycle to you.

Hot Springs
Beneath La Fortuna the lava is still curdling and heating countless bubbling springs. There are free, natural hot springs in the area that any local can point you toward. If you're after a more comfortable experience, consider one of the area's resorts.

Eco Termales Hot Springs HOT SPRING
(Map p250; ☎2479-8787; www.ecotermalesfortunacr.com; adult/child US$34/29; ☺10am-9pm; ♿) ⊘ A large, forbidding gate leads to this recommended, reservation-only complex. Everything from the natural circulation systems in the pools to the soft, mushroom lighting is understated yet luxurious. Just 100 visitors per four-hour slot are welcomed at 10am, 1pm and 5pm. Dinner is served in the evening.

Paradise Hot Springs HOT SPRING
(Map p250; paradisehotspringscr.com; adult/child US$23/15; ☺11am-9pm) A relative newcomer to the spring scene, this low-key place has one lovely, large pool with a waterfall, and several smaller pools, surrounded by lush vegetation and tropical blooms. The pools vary in temperature (up to 40°C), some with hydromassage. Paradise is much simpler than the other larger spring settings, but there are fewer people, and your experience is bound to be more relaxing and more romantic. Lockers, towels and non-alcoholic drinks are included with admission.

There's a nice restaurant if you want to eat or drink something more potent.

Springs Resort & Spa HOT SPRING

(Map p250; ☑2401-3313, in USA 954-727-8333; www.thespringscostarica.com; 2-day admission US$50; ☺8am-10pm; 🖳) If you're looking for a luxurious hot-spring experience, the Springs features 18 free-form pools with various temperatures, volcano views, landscaped gardens, waterfalls and swim-up bars, including a jungle bar with a water slide. The whole scene is human-made, but it's lovely.

Tabacón Hot Springs HOT SPRING

(Map p250; ☑2519-1999; www.tabacon.com; day pass incl lunch or dinner adult/child US$85/30; ☺10am-10pm) 🍴 Some say it's cheesy and some say it's fun. (We say it's both.) Broad-leaf palms, rare orchids and other florid tropical blooms part to reveal a 40°C waterfall pouring over a fake cliff, concealing constructed caves complete with camouflaged cup holders. Lounged across each well-placed stonelike substance are overheated tourists of various shapes and sizes, relaxing.

The spa, 14km west of La Fortuna, is on the site of a 1975 volcanic eruption that killed one local. The former village of Tabacón was destroyed in the 1968 eruption, when 78 people were killed. Don't sweat it: the mountain is once again dormant. For now.

✺ Festivals & Events

Fiestas de la Fortuna CULTURAL FESTIVAL

(☺mid-Feb) The big annual bash features two weeks of Tico-rules bullfights, colorful carnival rides, greasy festival food, craft stands and unusual gambling devices. It's free, except for the beer (which is cheap), and you'll have a blast trying to decide between the reggaetón go-go dancers and the live *ranchero* and salsa.

☞ Tours

Although it's no longer erupting, Volcán Arenal is the big draw here. But you don't need a guide to take a hike into the upper reaches of the national park. It's perfectly feasible to show up at the park and follow the well-marked trail system. Organized Arenal tours are often combined with a dip in the hot springs (US$25 to US$65 per person). Make sure you understand whether or not your tour includes entry fees to the park and hot springs.

It has become common in La Fortuna to sell tourists pricey tours to distant destinations, such as Caño Negro. If you're short

of time, this is a fine option, though you'll save yourself a ton of money (and probably have a much better experience) if you actually go to the place and organize a tour upon arrival.

Commissions in La Fortuna amount to big money. Shop around before you book, and treat all unsolicited advice with a degree of skepticism.

Arenal Wilberth Stables HORSEBACK RIDING

(Map p250; ☑2479-7522; www.arenalwilberth-stable.com; per person US$58; ☺7:30am, 11am & 2:30pm) Three-hour horse-riding tours depart from these stables at the foot of Arenal. The ride takes in forest and farmland, as well as lake and volcano views. The stables are opposite the entrance to the national park, but there's an office in town next to Arenal Resort Hostel.

Alberto's Horse Tours HORSEBACK RIDING

(☑2479-7711, 2479-9043; per person US$65) Alberto and his son lead popular horse-riding trips to the Catarata de la Fortuna. It's a three- or four-hour trip, but you'll spend about an hour off your horse, when you hike down to the falls for a swim or a photo op. Beautiful setting, beautiful horses.

Canoa Aventura CANOEING

(☑2479-8200; www.canoa-aventura.com; canoe trip US$67, full-day trip to Caño Negro US$113; ☺6:30am-9:30pm) 🍴 This long-standing family-run company specializes in canoe and float trips led by bilingual naturalist guides. Most are geared toward wildlife- and bird-watching. One popular paddle is the full-day trip to Caño Negro.

Wave Expeditions RAFTING, KAYAKING

(Map p249; ☑2479-7262; www.waveexpeditions.com; cnr Calle 2 & Av Fort; river trips US$70-100, kayaking US$53; ☺7am-9pm) Wave Expeditions runs the wild Toro and mellower Balsa rivers. You can also run the smooth Río Arenal on an inflatable kayak. Hiking, horse riding, caving, canyoning, and tortilla making are also available.

Aguas Bravas RAFTING, KAYAKING

(☑2479-7645; www.costaricaraftingvacation.com; safari float trip US$80, Class III/Class IV trips US$80/95; ☺7am-7pm) This rafting specialist offers a few options in the area, including a gentle safari float trip on Peñas Blancas, as well as Class III and IV trips. It can also organize hiking, horse riding and kayaking on Lago Arenal.

PureTrek Canyoning
CANYONING

(Map p250; ☎1-866-569-5723, 2479-1313; www.
puretrekcanyoning.com; 4hr incl transportation &
lunch US$98; ☺7am-10pm; ☻) ✎ The reputa-
ble PureTrek leads guided rappels down four
waterfalls, one of which is 50m high. Check
in at PureTrek headquarters, located in a
tree house 6km west of town.

Arenal Paraíso Canopy Tours
CANOPY TOUR

(Map p250; ☎2479-1100; www.arenalparaiso.com;
tours US$45; ☺8am-5pm) A dozen cables zip
across the canyon of the Río Arenal, giving a
unique perspective on two waterfalls, as well
as the rainforest canopy.

Ecoglide
CANOPY TOUR

(Map p250; ☎2479-7120; www.arenalecoglide.
com; adult/student & child US$55/45; ☺7am-4pm;
☻) Opened in 2008, Ecoglide is the biggest
canopy game in town, featuring 13 cables,
15 platforms and a 'Tarzan' swing. The dual-
cable safety system provides extra security
and peace of mind.

Canopy Los Cañones
CANOPY TOUR

(Map p250; ☎2479-1000; www.canopyloscanones.
com; adult/child US$50/35) ✎ Located at the
Hotel Los Lagos, the Canopy Los Cañones
has 12 cables over the rainforest, ranging
from 50m to 500m long. The price includes
admission to a frog farm, butterfly farm, hot
springs and natural pools, which are all on
the hotel grounds.

Arenal Oasis
BIRD-WATCHING, NIGHT WALK

(Map p250; ☎2479-9526; night walks US$55;
☺5:45pm) The Rojas Bonilla family has created this wild frog sanctuary, home to some
28 species of croaking critters. The frogs are
just the beginning of the night walk, which
continues into the rainforest to see what
other nocturnal animals await. If you're
more of a morning person, you can do a
bird-watching tour. Reservations are recommended.

Arenal Mundo Aventura
ADVENTURE TOUR, HIKING

(Map p250; ☎2479-9762; www.arenalmundoaven-
tura.com; adult/child adventure tours US$70/50,
hiking US$48/33; ☻) An all-in-one adventure
park, this place offers various guided hikes,
rappelling and horse riding, as well as a
canopy tour. It also hosts performances of
indigenous Maleku dance and song. It is
2km south of La Fortuna, on the road to
Chachagua.

Desafío Adventure Company
ADVENTURE TOUR

(Map p249; ☎2479-0020; www.desafiocostarica.
com; Calle 2; tours US$65-85; ☺6:30am-9pm) De-
safío has the widest range of river trips in
Fortuna, including paddling trips on the Río
Balsa, horse-riding treks to Volcán Arenal,
adventure tours rappelling down waterfalls,
and mountain-bike expeditions. It can also
arrange your transfer to Monteverde by
horse, boat or bike.

Aventuras Arenal
TOUR

(Map p249; ☎2479-9133; www.aventurasarenal.
com; Av Central; hiking from US$51, horse riding
from US$66; ☺7am-8pm) Operating for over
15 years, this outfit organizes a variety of
local day tours on bike, boat and horseback.
It also does trips further afield, including to
Caño Negro and Río Celeste.

Jacamar Naturalist Tours
HIKING, ADVENTURE TOUR

(Map p249; ☎2479-9767; www.arenaltours.com;
Av Central; ☺7am-9pm) Recommended for its
variety of naturalist hikes, including Arenal
and Cerro Chato. It does adventure tours
too, including canyoning and ATV riding.
It's located on the ground level of Hotel Arenal Carmela.

Sunset Tours
ADVENTURE TOUR

(Map p249; ☎2479-9800; www.sunsettourcr.com;
Calle 2; ☺6:30am-9pm) Recommended for
high-quality tours with bilingual guides.
Offers canyoning, kayaking and trips around
the region, including to the Venado Caves.

🛏 Sleeping

There are loads of places to stay in town. In
the low season room rates plummet by as
much as 40%.

If you have your own transport, consider
staying at the **Arenal Observatory Lodge**
(Map p250; ☎lodge 2479-1070; www.arenalobserv-
atorylodge.com; day pass US$6, museum admission
free; P) or closer to the volcano in the small
town of El Castillo, as you'll be rewarded
with fewer crowds and a more rustic vibe.

🛏 La Fortuna

★Sleeping Indian Guesthouse
GUESTHOUSE $

(Map p249; ☎8446-9149, 2479-8431; sleepingin-
dianguesthouse@gmail.com; Av Fort; d US$45; ☎)
Ethnic insensitivities aside, this is a delightful 2nd-story guesthouse just north of the
church. Six sweet fan-cooled rooms have

lofty ceilings, tile floors, colorful paint jobs and big windows. The spacious common area includes a fully-equipped kitchen, two balconies with volcano views, and a homey living room, well stocked with books, games and funky artwork. The live-in owner is a gracious host.

Arenal Hostel Resort HOSTEL $

(Map p249; ☑ 2479-9222; www.arenalhostelresort. com; Av Central; dm/s/d/tr/q US$16/48/58/75/88; P✳@☎☷) Offering the best of hostel and resort, this welcoming place is arranged around a landscaped garden, complete with hammocks, small pool, party-place bar, and volcano view. All rooms are clean, spacious and air-conditioned, with en suite bathrooms. Service is top notch, if a tad impersonal.

Pay attention: Arenal Hostel Resort and Arenal Backpackers Resort do essentially the same thing, but they are not actually the same place.

Hostel Backpackers La Fortuna HOSTEL $

(Map p249; ☑ 2479-9129; www.hostelbackpack-erslafortuna.com; dm/s/d/tr US$14/44/52/69; P✳@☎☷) This is the most 'grown-up' hostel in town. The rooms are done in whites and beiges, and the courtyard is lush, lovely and strung with hammocks. Guests are invited to go down the street to the sister property, Arenal Hostel Resort (p254), to join the party (swimming pool, bar) and then to return here for quiet, comfort and a good night's sleep.

The hostels in this town are not very creative with their names. This place should not be confused with La Fortuna Backpackers, which is a different beast altogether.

Arenal Backpackers Resort HOSTEL $

(Map p250; ☑ 2479-7000; www.arenalbackpack-ersresort.com; Av Central; dm US$15-16, tents s/d US$25/35, d with/without bathroom US$56/45; P✳@☎☷) The original hostel-resort in La Fortuna, this self-proclaimed 'five-star hostel' with volcano views is pretty cushy. Sleep on orthopedic mattresses and take hot showers in your en suite bathroom (even in the dorms). Somewhere between dormitory and hotel is the covered tent city: raised tents have air mattress and electricity (but no proper walls, so you'll hear your neighbors loud and clear).

The main attraction is the landscaped pool with swim-up bar, where backpackers spend lazy days lounging with a cold beer.

You'll be in a traveler's party bubble here. Not that there's anything wrong with that.

La Choza Inn INN $

(Map p249; ☑ 2479-9361; www.lachozainnhostel. com; Av Fort btwn Calles 2 & 4; incl breakfast dm US$10, s/d US$35/50, air-con US$10; P@☎) With all the budget 'resorts' in town, it's refreshing to find a charming, old-fashioned, family-run inn, where kids and puppies interact with the guests and where facilities are basic but the staff is always accommodating. Take your pick from the dark, palm-wood dorms or the attractive doubles boasting Arenal views from the balconies.

Hotel Pepito's Place HOTEL $

(Map p249; ☑ 2479-9238; pepitoplace.com; Calle 2; d incl breakfast US$50; P✳@☎) Lovely blooming flowers deck the 2nd-floor terrace, inviting you into this cute motel-style lodging. Inside, you'll find good value and personable service. Spotless rooms are painted in pastels, with beds dressed in tasteful quilts and walls hung with tropical paintings. The place is small, however, and once you leave your room you're as good as on the street.

Gringo Pete's HOSTEL $

(Map p250; ☑ 2479-8521; www.gringopetes.com; Calle 7; dm US$7, r US$20-24; P@☎) The purple place is one of the cheapest in town. The rooms are completely bare save the colorful paint job and some rustic tree-trunk bunk beds. But you'll find everything you need, including a communal kitchen, hammocks hanging in the garden and volcano views. If it's full, they'll send you a few blocks away to Gringo Pete's Too (Map p249).

La Fortuna Suites GUESTHOUSE $$

(Map p249; ☑ 8577-1555; www.lafortunasuites.com; d incl breakfast US$96; P✳☎) Here's a chance to luxuriate in some high-end amenities at midrange prices. We're talking high-thread-count sheets and memory-foam mattresses, custom-made furniture and flat-screen TVs, gourmet breakfast on the balcony and killer views. Despite all these perks, guests agree that the thing that makes this place special is the hospitality shown by the hosts.

Hotel Monte Real HOTEL $$

(Map p249; ☑ 2479-9357; www.monterealhotel. com; Av Arenal btwn Calles 3 & 5; incl breakfast standard/premium r US$62/90, ste US$112; P✳☎) A smart modern motel property on the edge of town, next to the Río Burio.

This excellent location combines the convenience of town with the nature and rusticity of the forest – meaning lovely gardens and wildlife at your doorstep. Spacious rooms have Spanish-tile floors, stained-wood ceilings and sliding-glass doors; spring for a superior for a private balcony with volcano views.

Hotel Arenal Rabfer
HOTEL $$

(Map p249; ☑ 2479-9187; www.arenalrabfer.com; Calle 1; s/d/tr/q incl breakfast US$62/75/87/101; P❄@🛜🏊) Arguably the most architecturally appealing of the downtown options, with a striking shingled 2nd floor. Set up around a pebbled pool area and shady palm garden, the rooms are spacious with high slanted ceilings and fresh coats of paint. The whole place is immaculate. Located on a quiet side street, two blocks from the action.

Hotel Las Colinas
HOTEL $$

(Map p249; ☑ 2479-9305; www.lascolinasarenal. com; Calle 1 btwn Avs Central & Arenal; incl breakfast s/d/tr economy US$49/63/79, standard US$72/82/102; P❄@🛜) 🍃 Stay here and you're likely to spend most of your time on the 2nd-story 'terrace garden', with ample sun lounges and spectacular views of the volcano. The rooms are simple but stylish, with tile floors and cherry-stained furnishings. The economy rooms on the 1st floor are dark, so you'll pay more for the sunlit standard units with balconies.

🛏 West of Town

The road to the Arenal turnoff is lined with places to stay, ranging from quaint *cabinas* to luxurious lodges. Most of the area's high-end accommodations are located along this stretch. It's not particularly convenient if you don't have your own transportation.

★ Roca Negra del Arenal
GUESTHOUSE $$

(Map p250; ☑ 2479-9237; www.hotelrocanegradelarenal.com; d/tr/q US$60/70/80, breakfast US$6; P❄🛜🏊) Plenty of feathered and furry friends roam the grounds at this gem of a guesthouse, located 2km west of town. Along with the ever-charming owner, they make for quite a welcome party. There are seven spacious rooms, each with stained-wood accents, huge tile bathrooms and semi-private terraces facing the garden (complete with rockers).

But what makes this place so special? It's the paradisaical setting. The luscious tiled pool and Jacuzzi are surrounded by tropical gardens that are bursting with blooms and buzzing with bees and birds. If you came for R&R in exotic environs, look no further.

Hotel Campo Verde
BUNGALOW $$

(Map p250; ☑ 2479-1080; www.hotelcampoverde. com; s/d/tr/q incl breakfast from $75/90/110/130; P@🛜) An absolutely darling family-owned property, located 9km west of town. Canary-yellow wooden bungalows have vaulted beamed ceilings, two queen beds, lovely drapes and chandeliers, and a sweet tiled patio blessed with two waiting rockers. Book the wooden bungalows furthest from the road at the foot of the mountain, where the views are unbeatable.

Erupciones Inn B&B
B&B $$

(Map p250; ☑ 2479-1400; www.erupcionesinn. com; d incl breakfast US$80-90; P❄🛜) You can admire Arenal from every single colorful *cabina* at this riverside property 11km from La Fortuna. Take a seat on your private patio and take it in. Otherwise, the *cabinas* are a bit tired, but service is sweet and the recent change in ownership means that an overhaul is in the works.

El Silencio del Campo
LODGE $$$

(Map p250; ☑ 2479-7055; www.hotelsilenciodelcampo.com; d/tr/q incl breakfast US$195/220/245; P❄🏊) This lovely lodge has 24 stand-alone cabins that are luxurious without being showy. The property's pièce de résistance, though, is the hot spring. For guests only, it has half a dozen decadent pools in a range of temperatures. Guests can also experience life on a working farm (try your hand at milking a cow) and feast on fresh eggs for breakfast.

El Silencio del Campo is about 4km west of town.

Nayara Hotel, Spa & Gardens
HOTEL $$$

(Map p250; ☑ 2479-1600; www.arenalnayara.com; r/ste incl breakfast US$280/390; P❄@🛜🏊) This intimate and indulgent hotel, 6km west of town, has amassed a slew of awards for its Asian-inspired architecture, minimalist decor and richly romantic setting. The 24 rooms have exquisite furnishings and bedding, rich woods, high-tech gadgetry, an outdoor shower and a private outdoor Jacuzzi where you can soak up views of Volcán Arenal. Exquisite.

ARENAL & NORTHERN LOWLANDS LA FORTUNA

🛏 South of Town

Just a few kilometers south of town, a partially paved road trundles to the base of Cerro Chato, and hotels now dot either side of it. Even further flung is the village of Chachagua, 12km south along the road to San Ramón. Crisscrossed by local rivers, this authentic, agrarian, market *pueblo* (small town or village) is an antidote to the touristy brouhaha of La Fortuna.

Villas Josipek   CABINA $$
(Map p250; ☑2430-5252; www.costaricavillas-josipek.com; per person incl breakfast US$34; P ✳ 🛜 ⊠) Just north of the village of Chachagua, these immaculate, simple, wooden cabins with full kitchens and volcano views are surrounded by private rainforest trails that penetrate the Bosque Eterno de Los Niños. Your hosts, Suhey and Edgar, are delightful, as is the sly sloth that inhabits the guarumo tree near the lobby.

On the grounds, you can take an 1100m stroll through the **Jardín Botánico Josipek** (admission US$10), which includes rose gardens, rainforest and medicinal plants, as well as a contemplative labyrinth.

Hotel Cerro Azul   BUNGALOW $$
(Map p250; ☑2479-9212; www.ranchocerroazul.com; d/tr/q US$72/86/100; P ✳ 🛜) Five cute, shingled cabins face the parking lot but back up to the forest, with private porches overlooking the trees. A 200m trail leads to the rushing river, with the volcano beyond. The cabins have woody interiors and stylish details. Think simple, natural, beautiful, comfortable.

Catarata Eco-Lodge   LODGE $$
(Map p250; ☑2479-9522; www.cataratalodge.com; s/d/tr incl breakfast US$71/77/92; P @ 🛜 ⊠) Set at the base of Cerro Chato and surrounded by forest, this place is ideal if you want to get away from it all (but not too far away, as you're still just 4km from town). The digs are decent little Spanish-tile and wood rooms, with hammocks strung on the terrace. The restaurant is also recommended.

Our only complaint is that we're not sure what makes this an *eco*-lodge. Sure, they care about the environment and they obviously talk the talk, but do they walk the walk?

Chachagua Rainforest Hotel   HOTEL $$$
(Map p250; ☑2468-1010; www.chachaguarainforesthotel.com; d/bungalows incl breakfast US$236/290; P ⊖ ✳ 🛜 ⊠) Situated on a private reserve that abuts the Bosque Eterno de Los Niños, this hotel is a naturalist's dream. Part of the property is a working orchard, cattle ranch and fish farm, while the rest is humid rainforest. Explore it on hiking trails or on horseback. The rooms are nice but arguably overpriced, while the stylish, spacious bungalows are gorgeous as all get-out.

Drive 11km south of La Fortuna. On the south side of Chachagua, fork right off the main road and follow the signs on a 2km dirt track that may require a 4WD in the rainy season.

Casa Luna Hotel & Spa   HOTEL $$$
(Map p250; ☑2479-7368; www.casalunahotel.com; s/d incl breakfast US$135/145; P ✳ @ 🛜 ⊠) The snazziest joint on this rustic road, this walled-off complex initially seems like a gated community. But, once inside, you'll see that the landscaped gardens and adobe-style lodgings are lovely. Wooden doors open into 36 elegant, split-level duplexes with tiny private patios. There's a full menu of spa treatments (facial/massage from US$25/50), and guests rave about the attentive service.

🍴 Eating

Unless you're eating exclusively at *sodas* (cheap lunch counters) you'll find the restaurants in La Fortuna to be more expensive than in other parts of the country. If you're cooking for yourself, stock up at the **Mega Super** (Map p249; Av Arenal; ⊙7am-9pm Mon-Sat, to 8pm Sun) near the bus station or **Super Cristian 2** (Map p249; cnr Av Central & Calle 1; ⊙7am-9pm), west of town.

🍴 In Town

Rainforest Café   CAFE $
(Map p249; ☑2479-7239; Calle 1 btwn Avs Central & Arenal; mains US$4-6; ⊙7am-8:30pm; 🛜) We know it's bad form to start with dessert, but the irresistible sweets at this popular spot are beautiful to behold and delicious to devour. The savory menu features burritos, *casados* (set meals) and other excellent traditional fare. There's also a full menu of hot and cold coffee, including some tempting specialty drinks (Mono Loco = coffee, banana, milk, chocolate and cinnamon).

There's a dash of urban-coffeehouse atmosphere here. Must be the writing in the milk foam.

Soda Viquez
SODA $

(Map p249; ☑ 2479-7133; cnr Calle 1 & Av Arenal; mains US$6-10; ⊙ 7am-10pm) Insanely popular among travelers, this friendly spot takes *tipica* (typical Costa Rican food) and adds something to it. Soda Viquez has a tasty, saucy steam table but also makes chicken, beef and fish six different ways if you choose to order off the menu. Prices are reasonable, portions ample.

Soda la Hormiga
SODA $

(Map p249; Av Arenal; mains US$3-5; ⊙ 6am-8pm) Locally beloved and set conveniently next door to the bus station, this open-air lunch counter is one of the quaintest, cheapest *sodas* in town. It does all the *casados,* as well as big breakfasts and burgers.

Anch'io Ristorante & Pizzeria
ITALIAN $$

(Map p249; ☑ 2479-7024; Av Central; mains US$10-18; ⊙ noon-10pm) If you have a hankering for pizza, you can't do better than Anch'io, where it is cooked in a wood-fired oven, the crust is crispy thin and the toppings are plentiful. Start yourself off with a traditional antipasto. Accompany with cold beer or a bottle of red. Add super service and pleasant patio seating, and you've got yourself a winner.

Kappa Sushi
SUSHI $$

(Map p249; Calle 1 & Ave Fort; sushi & rolls US$7-10; ⊙ noon-10pm) When you're surrounded by mountains and cattle farms, who's thinking of sushi? Well, think of it. The fish is fresh (you're not *that* far from the ocean) and the preparations are innovative. The ponzu roll (tuna with sriracha, avocado, cucumber and chives) is a favorite. Sit at an outside table and enjoy the view of Arenal while you feast on raw fish.

La Cascada
INTERNATIONAL $$

(Map p249; ☑ 2479-9145; cnr Av Fort & Calle 1; mains US$6-26; ⊙ 11am-late) This landmark has been around so long that its *palapa* (thatched palm-leaf roof) is almost as big an institution as the volcano it mimics. It has a small bar and acquires a drinking crowd at night, but tourists consider it a lunch and dinner option too. Look for well-prepared roast- and grilled-meat dishes, pastas, sandwiches and a few veggie options.

Lava Lounge
INTERNATIONAL $$

(Map p249; ☑ 2479-7365; www.lavaloungecostarica.com; Av Central btwn Calles 4 & 2; mains US$8-12; ⊙ 11am-10:30pm; P🖥🍴) This hip, open-air restaurant is a breath of fresh air

when you just can't abide another *casado*. There is pasta, burgers and five kinds of tacos, as well as bigger plates. Both food and service are variable, but the picnic tables and *palapa* roof create a cool, rustic vibe. Add occasional live music and you find you can't help but go back.

If you prefer breakfast or a light lunch, go across the street to Gecko Gourmet (Map p249; ☑ 2479-8905; cnr Calle 2 & Av Central; mains US$4-8; ⊙ 8am-6pm Wed-Mon; 🍴), which is under the same management. It serves sandwiches, salads and icy blended-coffee drinks.

Soda La Parada
SODA $$

(Map p249; ☑ 2479-9547; www.restaurantelaparada.com; Av Central; mains US$5-19; ⊙ 24hr) Facing Parque Central and all the street action, this popular *soda* does a brisk trade in, well, everything, from decent pizzas to satisfying *tipica*. Prices are high for a *soda* – how much are you willing to pay to beat the midnight munchies?

★ Restaurant Don Rufino
INTERNATIONAL $$$

(Map p249; ☑ 2479-9997; www.donrufino.com; cnr Av Central & Calle 3; mains US$16-40; ⊙ 11am-11pm) In almost every way, this indoor-outdoor bar and grill is light years ahead of the competition. The highlight of the menu is the grilled meats, which include rib eye, filet, peppercorn tenderloin medallions, and a porterhouse with gorgonzola sauce. If you're cutting back on red meat, look for crab risotto, ginger-glazed grilled tuna, and chicken in coconut curry.

The vibe is trendy and the place is hopping. Reservations recommended.

✖ Around La Fortuna

Delicatessen
SODA $

(Map p250; ☑ 2479-7038; mains US$6-8; ⊙ 7am-9pm) Take a break from the hustle and bustle of La Fortuna to have lunch at this friendly place, 2km west of town. It's essentially a *soda*, with big breakfasts and excellent *casados,* as well as burritos, burgers and some very tempting desserts. Portions are big, prices are small.

Benedictus Steakhouse
STEAKHOUSE $$$

(Map p250; ☑ 2479-1912; mains US$14-30; ⊙ noon-10pm) 🌿 Turn off the highway and drive about 1km up a steep, rough dirt road to arrive at this spectacularly situated steak house (tricky in the dark, so arrive before the sun goes down). You'll be rewarded with a gorgeous view, followed by an amazing meal. In addition to the meats, there is heavenly homemade bread, fantastic ceviche and tantalizing desserts.

The steaks come from free-range cattle that graze on grass in the pastures below the restaurant. They also raise lambs, chickens and pigs. Veggies come from the organic greenhouse.

🍷 Drinking & Nightlife

One Love Lounge   BAR
(Map p250; ☑ 8872-9703; Av Central; ☺ 6pm-2am) You can't miss this place, west of town, with its magic-bus facade. La Fortuna's favorite bar has a new roots-reggae theme. Sometimes there's live music and sometimes there's DJ Tío Matteo, but there are always good vibes and lots of love. On Friday and Saturday nights you can catch a free lift from the church at 9:45pm, 10:45pm or 11:40pm.

Volcán Look   CLUB
(Map p250; ☑ 2479-9690; men's cover charge US$4; ☺ 8pm-3am Wed-Sat) This club is reportedly Costa Rica's biggest discotheque outside of San José. It's about 5km west of town, though it's virtually abandoned except on weekends: don't bother showing up until after 11pm unless you want to dance to the *cumbia* alone.

El Establo   BAR
(Map p249; Calle 2; ☺ 5pm-2am Wed-Sat) La Fortuna's raucous bar with an attached disco fronts the bull ring and attracts an ever-enthusiastic local following. The age demographic here ranges from 18 to 88. That's almost always a good thing.

Cosechos   JUICE BAR
(Map p249; Calle 1 btwn Avs Central & Arenal; US$2-3.50; ☺ 10am-9pm) A branch of Costa Rica's favorite juice bar is tucked in across the street from Hotel Las Colinas, and it does wonderful alchemy with fruits and veggies, including a mango-strawberry-pineapple smoothie, a watermelon-passionfruit milkshake, and the delicious watermelon-strawberry-lemon combo.

🛈 DANGERS & ANNOYANCES

Beware of pickpockets and bag thieves on buses between Monteverde and La Fortuna. Keep your eyes on your valuables and your valuables at your feet.

🛍 Shopping

Local artisans converge on the Lava Lounge (p257) in the evening to display exquisite beaded, silver and braided bracelets, earrings and necklaces. They'll be lined up and waiting by the front door almost every night.

Neptune's House of Hammocks   HOMEWARES
(☑ 2479-8269; hammocks US$50-170; ☺ 8am-6pm) On the road to La Catarata de la Fortuna (p249), it sells soft drinks and hammocks. Take a breather and try one out.

Handmade Art Shop   HANDICRAFTS
(Map p249; ☑ 8611-0018; Calle 1; ☺ 10am-6pm) There's no shortage of souvenirs for sale in La Fortuna. But this unique shop is something special, carrying an excellent selection of arts and crafts by local and national artists. You'll find representative pieces from Costa Rica's many subcultures, including Boruca masks, Rasta handicrafts, lots of macramé and some lovely handmade jewelry.

🛈 Information

INTERNET ACCESS

Arenal Rocks Internet (☑ 8854-2892; Av Central; per hr US$1.20; ☺ 8am-11pm) Located under the Hotel Arenal Carmella.

Expediciones Internet (☑ 2479-9101; cnr Av Central & Calle 1; per 30/60min US$0.80/1.20; ☺ 7am-9pm Mon-Sat) Most tour operators in town also provide internet access, but if you're not interested in hearing a sales pitch, there are no hassles here.

MEDICAL SERVICES

Centro Médico Arenal Vital (☑ 2479-7027; www.secmesa.com; Calle 1; ☺ 24hr) Located in the Hotel Las Colinas building, this private clinic is open 24/7 and has English-speaking staff.

Clínica Fortuna (☑ 2479-9142, 2479-9501; Calle 3 btwn Avs Volcán & Fort; ☺ 8am-8pm Mon, 8am-10pm Tue-Thu, 24hr Fri-Sun) For minor injuries and illnesses.

MONEY

BAC San José (cnr Av Fort & Calle 3)
Banco de Costa Rica (Av Central)
Banco Nacional (cnr Calle 1 & Av Fort)
Banco Popular (cnr Av Central & Calle 5)

POST

Correos de Costa Rica (Map p249; Av Fort; ☺ 8am-5:30pm Mon-Fri, 7:30am-noon Sat)

ℹ Getting There & Away

BUS

Most domestic buses stop at the **Centro Comercial Adifort** (Map p249; Av Arenal). Keep an eye on your bags, particularly on the weekend San José run.

Ciudad Quesada (Auto-Transportes San José–San Carlos) US$1.60, one hour, 14 departures per day from 4:30am to 7pm.

San José (Auto-Transportes San José–San Carlos) US$4.25, 4½ hours, departs 12:45pm and 2:45pm. Alternatively, take a bus to Ciudad Quesada and change to frequent buses to the capital.

Tilarán, with connection to Monteverde (Auto-Transportes Tilarán, departs from the Parque Central) US$2.60, 3½ hours, departs 8am and 4:30pm. To reach Monteverde (US$3.60, six to eight hours), take the early bus to Tilarán, where you'll have to wait a few hours for the onward bus to Santa Elena.

HORSEBACK

Several tour companies offer horse-riding trips between La Fortuna and Monteverde. The trip (which also involves a boat ride) takes five to seven hours and costs about US$85, including separate transport of your luggage. Desafío Adventure Company (p253) can make these arrangements, as can any of the Monteverde horse-riding companies (see p199).

JEEP-BOAT-JEEP

The fastest route between Monteverde–Santa Elena and La Fortuna is the jeep-boat-jeep combo (US$25 to US$40, three hours). The 'jeep' is actually a minivan with the requisite yellow 'turismo' tattoo. It's still a terrific transportation option and can be arranged through almost any hotel or tour operator in either town. The minivan from La Fortuna takes you to Laguna de Arenal and meets a boat that crosses the lake, where a 4WD taxi on the other side continues to Monteverde. This is increasingly becoming the primary transportation between La Fortuna and Monteverde as it's incredibly scenic and reasonably priced and it'll save you half a day of travel over rocky roads.

ℹ Getting Around

BICYCLE

Biking is a reasonable option to get around town and reach some of the top tourist attractions. The challenging 7km ride from town to La Catarata is a classic. Make advance arrangement to rent a bike from Bike Arenal (p251) and they'll drop it off at your hotel.

CAR

La Fortuna is easy to access by public transportation, but nearby attractions such as the hot springs, Parque Nacional Volcán Arenal and Laguna de Arenal demand lots of waiting, cursing and walking. Luckily, you can rent cars in town.

Adobe Rent a Car (☑2479-7202; www.adobe-car.com; Calle 1; ⊙7am-7pm)

Alamo (☑2479-9090; www.alamocostarica.com; cnr Av Central & Calle 2; ⊙7:30am-5:30pm)

Parque Nacional Volcán Arenal

Arenal was just another dormant volcano surrounded by fertile farmland from about AD 1500 until July 29, 1968, when huge explosions triggered lava flows that destroyed three villages, killing 78 people and 45,000 cattle. The area was evacuated and roads throughout the region were closed. Eventually, the lava subsided to a relatively predictable flow and life got back to normal. Sort of.

Although it occasionally quieted down for a few weeks or even months, Arenal produced menacing ash columns, massive explosions and streams of glowing molten rock almost daily. It all ended quite abruptly in 2010, leaving the alarmed local tourist industry to gasp and spew in its place. Still, any obituary on the Arenal area is premature given the fact that the volcano has retained its picture perfect conical shape and there is still plenty of forest on its lower slopes and in the nearby foothills.

While the molten night views are gone for now (one never knows what lies beneath or beyond), this mighty mountain is still worthy of your time. Clouds may shroud her at any time, but there are excellent trails to explore. And even if it does rain and there is a chill in the air, you are just a short drive away from hot springs.

Arenal was made a national park in 1995, and it is part of the Área de Conservación Arenal, which protects most of the Cordillera de Tilarán. This area is rugged and varied, and the biodiversity is high; roughly half the species of land-dwelling vertebrates (birds, mammals, reptiles and amphibians) known in Costa Rica can be found here. Commonly seen mammals include howler monkeys, white-faced capuchins and even anteaters (northern

ARENAL & NORTHERN LOWLANDS PARQUE NACIONAL VOLCÁN ARENAL

tamandua). Coatis are surprisingly tame: don't feed them. With more than 400 species, birdlife is rich in the park and includes such species as trogons, rufous motmots, fruitcrows and lancebills.

🏃 Activities

From the ranger station (which has trail maps available) you can hike the **Sendero Los Heliconias**, a 1km circular track that passes by the site of the 1968 lava flow. A 1.5km-long path branches off this trail and leads to an overlook. The **Sendero Las Coladas** also branches off the Heliconias trail and wraps around the volcano for 2km past the 1993 lava flow before connecting with the **Sendero Los Tucanes**, which extends for another 3km through the tropical rainforest at the base of the volcano. To return to the car-parking area, you will have to turn back. You'll get good views of the summit on the way to the parking lot.

From the park headquarters (not the ranger station) is the 1.3km **Sendero Los Miradores**, which leads down to the shores of the volcanic lake and provides a good angle for volcano viewing. Also from park headquarters, the **Old Lava Flow Trail** is an interesting and strenuous lower elevation trail following the flow of the massive 1992 eruption. The 4km round trip takes two hours to complete. If you want to keep hiking, combine it with the **El Ceibo trail**, a scenic 1.8km trail through secondary forest.

There are additional trails departing from Arenal Observatory Lodge and on a nearby private reserve.

Waterfall Trail
HIKING

(Map p250; www.arenalobservatorylodge.com; Arenal Observatory Lodge; day pass per person US$6) This scenic hike, which departs from the Arenal Observatory Lodge, is an easy, 2km round-trip hike that takes about an hour to complete. The terrain starts out flat then descends into a grotto where you'll find a thundering gusher of a waterfall that's about 12m high. You'll feel the mist long before you see its majesty.

FEELIN' HOT, HOT, HOT!

Volcanoes are formed over millennia as a result of the normal shifting processes of the earth's crust. For example, when oceanic crust slides against continental crust, the higher-density oceanic crust is pushed into a deep region of the earth known as the asthenosphere. This process, along with friction, melts the rocky crust to form magma, which rises through weak areas in the continental crust due to its comparatively light density. Magma tends to collect in a chamber below the earth's crust until increasing pressure forces it upward through a vent and onto the surface as lava. Over time, lava deposits can form large, conical volcanoes with a circular crater at the apex from which magma can escape in the form of gas, lava and ejecta.

Although our understanding of volcanoes has greatly progressed in the past few decades, scientists are still unable to predict a volcanic eruption with certainty. However, it is possible to monitor three phenomena – seismicity, gas emissions and ground deformation – in order to predict the likelihood of a volcanic eruption. Seismicity refers to the ongoing seismic activity that tends to accompany active volcanoes. For example, most active volcanoes have continually recurring low-level seismic activity. Although patterns of activity are difficult to interpret, generally an increase in seismic activity (which often appears as a harmonic tremor) is a sign that an eruption is likely.

Scientists also routinely monitor the composition of gas emissions as erupting magma undergoes a pressure decrease that can produce a large quantity of volcanic gases. For example, sulfur dioxide is one of the main components of volcanic gases, and an increasing airborne amount of this compound is another sign of an impending eruption. Finally, scientists routinely measure the tilt of slope and changes in the rate of swelling of active volcanoes. These measurements are indicators of ground deformation, which is caused by an increase in subterranean pressure due to large volumes of collecting magma.

Volcán Arenal is still considered by scientists to be active, despite its recent appearance to the contrary, and comprehensive monitoring of the volcano occurs frequently.

Cerro Chato Trail
HIKING

(Map p250; arenalobservatorylodge.com; Arenal Observatory Lodge; day use per person $6) The ultimate hike in the national park, the Cerro Chato Trail starts at the Arenal Observatory Lodge and meanders through pasture before climbing quite steeply through remnant forest and into patches of virgin growth reaching into misty sky. Eventually the trail crests Cerro Chato, Arenal's dormant partner, and ends in a 1100m-high volcanic lake that is simply stunning. The hike is only 8km round trip, but it will take two to three hours each way.

There is an alternative, even more strenuous route that departs from La Catarata de la Fortuna (p249).

Arenal 1968
HIKING

(Map p250; ☑ 2462-1212; www.arenal1968.com; per person US$10; ☉ 7am-10pm) This new trail system, a private network of trails and lookouts along the original 1968 lava flow, is worth checking out. It's located 1.2km from the highway turnoff to the park, just before the ranger station.

🛏 Sleeping & Eating

Arenal Observatory Lodge
LODGE $$$

(Map p250; ☑ 2479-1070, 2290-7011; www.arenalobservatorylodge.com; d/tr/q without bathroom US$97/$112/127, with bathroom from US$133/147/176; [P] ⊕ ❷ ❸ ❄) Set high on the Arenal slopes, this sensational, sprawling lodge is the only accommodation in the national park. Rooms range from La Casona's rustic doubles with shared bathrooms and views from the porch, to junior suites, with king-size beds, local art and huge picture windows framing the volcano. Most of the rooms fall somewhere in the middle of this range.

There's a decent international restaurant on the grounds (as there's obviously nowhere else to eat in the area). There is also a small museum with exhibits on the history, volcanology and hydrology of Arenal. Rates include access to the swimming pool and hiking trails, as well as a free guided walk each morning.

❶ Information

The **ranger station** (☑ 2461-8499; adult/child US$10/1; ☉ 8am-4pm) is on the western side of the volcano, and the complex housing it also includes an information center and parking lot. From here, trails lead 3.4km toward the volcano.

❶ Getting There & Away

To get to the ranger station by car, head west from La Fortuna for 15km, then turn left at the 'Parque Nacional' sign and take the 2km good dirt road to the entrance on the left side of the road. You can also take an 8am bus toward Tilarán (tell the driver to drop you off at the park) and catch the 2pm bus back to La Fortuna.

If you are heading to Arenal Observatory Lodge, continue driving on the dirt road. About 3km past the ranger station you will come to a small one-lane bridge and parking area. After crossing the bridge you'll reach a fork in the road; left goes to Arenal Observatory Lodge and right goes to the village of El Castillo. Turn left and continue 2.6km to reach the lodge. This steep, hard-packed gravel and partially paved road is fine for most vehicles, but a 4WD is recommended.

A taxi from La Fortuna to either the lodge or El Castillo will cost about US$30.

El Castillo

The tiny mountain village of El Castillo is a wonderful alternative to staying in La Fortuna – it's bucolic and reasonably untouristed (although there is a tight expat community), and it has easy access to Parque Nacional Volcán Arenal. It also offers amazing, up-close views of the looming mountain. It's best to have your own wheels out here, as buses don't serve this little enclave.

◉ Sights & Activities

El Castillo-Arenal Butterfly Conservatory
WILDLIFE RESERVE

(☑ 2479-1149; www.butterflyconservatory.org; adult/student US$14/10; ☉ 8:30am-4:30pm) This is more than just a butterfly conservatory (although it houses one of the largest butterfly exhibitions in Costa Rica). Altogether there are six domed habitats, a ranarium, an insect museum, a medicinal herb garden, and an hour's worth of trails through a botanic garden and along the river. The birding is also excellent at this peaceful place.

Arenal EcoZoo
ZOO

(El Serpentario; ☑ 2479-1059; www.arenalecozoo.com; adult/child US$16/10; ☉ 8am-7pm) Meet 36 of the most dangerous snake species in the world, including Eliza, a 5m-long Burmese python, then handle and milk a venomous snake. The EcoZoo is also home to vibrant frogs, amphibious lizards, spiny iguanas, shy turtles, vengeful scorpions, hairy tarantulas and floating butterflies.

Big Forest Hike
HIKING

(☑ 2479-1747; per person US$130) Offered by the adventurous folks at La Gavilana, this is a two-day round-trip 'extreme hike' between El Castillo and San Gerardo (near Santa Elena). Traversing old-growth forests and raging rivers, hikers stay overnight at the rustic Rancho Maximo in San Gerardo. Dinner and breakfast are provided, but hikers should bring food and water to sustain them for the hike.

☞ Tours

Rancho Adventure Tours
BIKING, KAYAKING, HORSE RIDING

(Map p250; ☑ 8302-7318; www.ranchomargot.com; bike rental per day US$15, tours US$45) Rancho Margot has a good selection of guided tours, including horse riding on the south side of Lake Arenal, kayaking on Lake Arenal and hiking to Cerro Chato. If you wish to explore the area on your own, you can rent a mountain bike for a day.

Sky Trek
CANOPY TOUR

(Map p250; ☑ 2479-4100; www.skyadventures. travel; adult/child Sky Tram only US$44/28, Sky Walk US$35/22, Sky Trek & Sky Tram US$77/48; ◷ 7:30am-4pm) El Castillo's entry in the canopy-tour category has zip lines (Sky Trek), a tram (Sky Tram) and a series of hanging bridges (Sky Walk). It's safe and well run, and visitors tend to leave smiling. An all-new adventure (Sky River Drift) combines a zip line with tree-climbing (and jumping) and river tubing.

🛏 Sleeping & Eating

Essence Arenal
HOSTEL $

(☑ 2479-1131; www.essencearenal.com; d/tr/q from US$43/54/65, d without bathroom US$32, tents US$32; ◷ restaurant 7am-8pm; P@🛜🍽) ✦ Perched on a 22-hectare hilltop with incredible volcano and lake views, this 'boutique hostel' is the best cheap sleep in the Arenal region. Bed down in a basic but clean room or a fine hippified tent, done up with plush bedding and wood furnishings. It's an eclectic, positive-energy place, offering group hikes, yoga classes and good vibes.

Guests participate in the loving preparation of vegetarian meals that will delight even the most hardcore carnivore. If you don't have your own wheels, the hostel can arrange transportation from La Fortuna. Otherwise, turn left towards the Butterfly Conservatory and continue 1km uphill to the hostel.

Cabinas Los Tucanes
HOTEL $

(☑ 2479-1076; www.arenalcabinaslostucanes.com; d/tr/q US$55/65/70, breakfast US$5) Here you'll find huge, bright, spotless and spacious rooms, with plain decor but fabulous vistas from the picture windows. The top-floor rooms catch a nice breeze off the terrace. Fanny and Licho take care of this place, and they'll take care of you too.

Nepenthe
B&B $$

(☑ 8892-5501; www.nepenthe-costarica.com; d incl breakfast US$95; P❄🛜🍽) The highlight of this sweet place is the spectacular infinity pool overlooking the lake. Lodge-like rooms are simple, tiled numbers with colorful artisanal accents, set in a gentle arc of a ranch-style building. There are hammocks on the patio and its Blue Lagoon spa comes highly recommended.

Majestic Lodge
GUESTHOUSE $$

(Map p250; ☑ 8703-1561, 2469-1085; www.majesticlodgecostarica.com; r $95; P❄🛜🍽) It looks like a private villa, but it's actually a lovely boutique lodge overlooking Laguna de Arenal. Plush rooms have beautiful handcrafted wooden furniture and exquisite tiled bathrooms. The wooden deck is a perfect place to relax, sip a cold drink and enjoy the gorgeous lake views (or watch the flat-screen TV).

Hummingbird Nest B&B
B&B $$

(Nido del Colibri; ☑ 2479-1174, 8835-8711; www. hummingbirdnestbb.com; d/tr/q incl breakfast US$85/95/100; P) At the entrance to town, a small path leads up the steep hill to this charming B&B, owned by a former flight attendant and all-round world traveler who found a small slice of paradise to call her own. Her quaint complex has two guest rooms and a garden full of hummingbirds. Soak the night away in a huge outdoor Jacuzzi in the garden. Two-night minimum.

★ Rancho Margot
RESORT, LODGE $$$

(Map p250; ☑ 8302-7318; www.ranchomargot. org; incl meals dm per person US$75, bungalow s/d US$165/245; P🛜🍽) ✦ Part resort lodge, part organic farm, Rancho Margot is 152 acres of cinematic loveliness, set along the rushing Río Caño Negro and surrounded by rainforested mountains. There are comfortable dorm-style bunkhouse accommodations. If your budget allows, spring for a beautiful teak-furnished bungalow, its deck strung with a hammock and blessed with views of hulking mountains, weeping jungle and placid lake. Two-night minimum.

Prices include all meals, a two-hour guided tour of the farm and two daily yoga classes. Hiking trails and (free) hot springs are at hand. There's also a handful of tours on offer, as well as a full-service spa. Staff are predominantly students and volunteers, so professionalism can be hit-and-miss.

La Gavilana Herbs & Art   BAKERY, GALLERY **$**
(📞2479-1747; lagavilana.discoverelcastillo.com; items US$2-6; ⊙8am-5pm Mon-Fri, 9am-2pm Sat) Meet Thomas and Hannah. He's Czech and makes the hot sauce and vinegar; she's American and bakes the cookies and breads. Their place is decked with paintings (by Hannah), while the grounds contain a food forest (by Thomas), filled with medicinal herbs and fruit trees. The whole place is filled with love, beauty and creativity. It's 100m uphill from Essence Arenal hostel.

La Mesa de Mama   COSTA RICAN **$**
(Map p250; 📞2479-1954; mains US$6-9; ⊙7am-8pm) Sit down at the picnic tables for Mama's tasty, *tipica* home cooking.

❶ Getting There & Away

El Castillo is located 8km past the entrance to Parque Nacional Volcán Arenal. It's a rough gravel road, and it only gets worse once you pass through the village. A 4WD is required in the rainy season and recommended year round. There is no public transportation, but Essence Arenal runs a shuttle to La Fortuna (6$).

Laguna de Arenal & Around

About 18km west of La Fortuna you'll arrive at a 750m-long causeway across the dam that created Laguna de Arenal, an 88-sq-km lake and the largest in the country. A number of small towns were submerged during its creation, but the lake now supplies valuable water to Guanacaste and produces hydroelectricity for the region. High winds also produce power with the aid of huge steel windmills, though windsurfers and kitesurfers frequently steal a breeze or two.

If you have your own car (or bicycle), this is one of the premier road trips in Costa Rica. The road is lined with odd and elegant businesses, many run by foreigners who have fallen in love with the place. Strong winds and high elevations give the lake a temperate feel. And the views of lakeside forests and Volcán Arenal are about as romantic as they come.

But things are changing – quickly. Gringo baby boomers, lured to the area by the eternal-spring climate, are snapping up nearly every spot of land with a 'For Sale' sign on it. Some Ticos (Costa Ricans) are not all that happy about the impending loss of their lakeside paradise and, in fact, this part of the country doesn't actually feel much like Costa Rica at all. Still, it is nourishing to have Laguna de Arenal in your life – rain or shine, be it a quick and lively affair or one that lasts.

The paved road is in decent condition, but watch for potholes. Buses run about every two hours; hotel owners can tell you when to catch your ride.

WORLD-CLASS WIND

Some of the world's most consistent winds blow across northwestern Costa Rica, attracting wind riders. Laguna de Arenal is rated one of the best windsurfing spots in the world and kitesurfers flock here too, especially from late November to April, when **Tico Wind** (📞8383-2694, 2692-2002; www.ticowind.com; kitesurf/windsurf per day US$80/84, lessons per hr US$50) sets up camp on the lake shore. It has state-of-the-art boards and sails, with equipment to suit varied wind conditions. First-timers should consider the 'Get on Board' package (US$120). Beginner kitesurf instruction ($530) is much more detailed and requires nine hours, but students will graduate International Kiteboarding Oranization (IKO) certified. The launch is located 15km west of Nuevo Arenal. The entrance is by the white chain-link fence with 'ICE' painted on it. Follow the dirt road 1km to the shore.

It gets a little chilly on Laguna de Arenal, and rentals usually include wetsuits, as well as harnesses and helmets. For a warmer experience, head up to Bahía Salinas (p242) on Costa Rica's far-northwestern coast. Resorts at that budding kitesurf mecca and drop-dead-gorgeous bay offer seasonal rentals and instruction. When the wind is right, riders insist that Salinas conditions wildly surpass even world-class Laguna de Arenal. The seasons in Salinas are the same as for the lake.

Around Laguna de Arenal

Forget for a moment that there are always ecological issues associated with dams and revel in the fact that this one created a rather magnificent lake. In the absence of wind the glassy surface reflects the volcano and the surrounding mountains teeming with cloud forest. Crowds congregate to admire the view and snap photos. (Unfortunately, there's no convenient place to stop, so you'll often encounter a minor traffic jam, especially at the dam's western end.)

◉ Sights & Activities

Laguna de Arenal offers scores of secluded bays and coves to explore and a forested island too. You'll find a kayak concession usually set up on the western end of the dam, but take care because when the wind kicks in it can be hard work to make it back home.

Motmot Jungle   BUTTERFLY GARDEN
(Map p250; ☑ 2479-1170, 8859-4992; admission US$10; ⊙ 7am-4pm) High above the dam, this is not only a butterfly breeding center but also a wildlife sanctuary set amidst primary rainforest. After you observe the life cycle of your fluttering friends and admire the 15 species that are breeding at the facility, you can wander the trails and watch for birds and wildlife.

Arenal Hanging Bridges   FOREST
(Puentes Cogantes de Arenal; Map p250; ☑ 2290-0469; www.hangingbridges.com; admission adult/student/child US$24/14/free, tours US$36-47; ⊙ 7:30am-4pm, tours 6am, 9am & 2pm) Unlike the fly-by view you'll get on a zip-line canopy tour, a walk along the hanging bridges allows you to explore the rainforest and canopy from six suspended bridges and 10 traditional bridges at a more natural and peaceful pace. The longest swaying bridge is 97m long and the highest is 25m above the earth. All are accessible from a single 3km trail that winds through a tunnel and skirts a waterfall.

Reservations are required for guided bird-watching tours or informative naturalist tours. The Tilarán bus can drop you off at the entrance, but it's a 3km climb from the bus stop. There are also loads of tours from La Fortuna.

La Roca Canyoneering   CANYONEERING
(Map p250; ☑ 2479-9800; US$79) Rappelling into river canyons, zip lining, cross-ing hanging bridges, swinging on a Tarzan rope, swimming and snacking are packed into this adrenaline-pumping half-day tour. Make sure you bring a change of clothes, as you will get wet. La Roca is 4km from the dam, but it also has an office in La Fortuna at Sunset Tours (p253).

⌒ Sleeping & Eating

NEAR THE LAKE

Arenal Lodge   LODGE $$$
(Map p250; ☑ 2479-1881; www.arenallodge.net; incl breakfast d standard/superior US$102/160, f US$190, junior ste US$198, chalets US$208; P❋☎❄) Arenal Lodge is at the top of a steep 2.5km ascent, though the entire lodge is awash with views of Arenal and the surrounding cloud forest. Standard rooms are just that, but the spacious junior suites are tiled and have wicker furniture and a picture window or balcony with volcano views. A blue macaw hangs out in the lobby.

The ground is crisscrossed by hiking trails, and the lodge also has a Jacuzzi, a billiards room, a restaurant and private stables.

Lost Iguana Resort   RESORT $$$
(Map p250; ☑ 2479-1559, 2479-1557; www.lostiguanaresort.com; r/ste incl breakfast US$245/275; P❋@☎❄) This stylish and splashy tropical resort, just 1.5km from the dam, is set among lush rainforest and rushing streams with glorious volcano views at every turn. Luxurious rooms have private balconies looking out on Arenal, beds made with Egyptian cotton sheets, a terra-cotta wet bar, and an invaluable sense of peace and privacy. Upgrade to a suite for a Jacuzzi or outdoor rain shower.

Also on the grounds are a romantic restaurant, a gorgeous bi-level pool with swim-up bar, and the well-equipped Golden Gecko Spa.

UNIÓN AREA

La Ceiba Tree Lodge   LODGE $$
(☑ 8313-1475, 2692-8050; www.ceibatree-lodge.com; d incl breakfast US$89; P❋☎) About 22km west of the dam, this lovely, laid-back lodge overlooks a magnificent 54m ceiba tree. Seven spacious, Spanish-tiled rooms are hung with original paintings and fronted by Maya-inspired carved doors. Each room has rustic artifacts, polished-wood ceilings and vast views of Laguna de Arenal. The tropical gardens and spacious terrace make this mountaintop spot a tranquil retreat.

The ceiba tree is actually on the grounds of the Tropical Garden (admission US$4) next door. The entrance fee gives you access to a blooming orchid garden and several kilometers of trails.

Hotel Los Héroes   HOTEL $$

(Map p250; ☎2692-8013, 2692-8012; www.pequeniahelvecia.com; incl breakfast d with/without balcony US$65/55, tr/apt US$80/115; P☎🛜🏊) Los Héroes looks like a Swiss village, centered on a charming chapel complete with chimes. The alpine chalet, 13.5km west of the dam, has large, immaculate but rather innocuous rooms. There's a working dairy on the grounds. A narrow-gauge train (per person US$10; ⏰11:30am & 1pm) chugs up the hill, bringing guests to the revolving Rondorama Panoramic Restaurant (unique in Costa Rica!).

Villa Decary   B&B $$$

(☎2694-4330, in US or Canada 1-800-556-0505; www.villadecary.com; r/casitas incl breakfast US$112/160; P✴🛜) This country inn is an all-round winner, offering epic views and unparalleled hospitality. Elegant, spacious rooms are decorated with bright serape bedspreads and original artwork, and boast balconies with excellent views of the woodland below and the lake beyond. There are larger *casitas* (sleeping four) with kitchenettes. The trails behind the house offer excellent opportunities for birding.

Villa Decary also boasts one of the best collections of palm trees in Costa Rica, which explains why it's named for the French botanist who discovered a new species of palm. It's 24.5km west of the dam, and 2km east of Nuevo Arenal.

La Mansion Inn Arenal   INN $$$

(Map p250; ☎2692-8018; www.lamansionarenal.com; incl breakfast US$125-175, ste US$175-195) About 15.5km west of the dam, La Mansion enjoys amazing lake views from the cottages, pool and restaurant. The large split-level rooms feature king-size beds, private terraces and mural-painted walls. The fabulous infinity lap pool is surrounded by a relaxing patio and an ornamental garden featuring Chorotega pottery. Lovely all around.

With a bar shaped like the bow of a ship, onsite restaurant Le Bistro is a romantic spot for lunch or dinner, with panoramic views from the dining room and outdoor patio. It has a substantial menu of well-prepared European fare. There's quite a show at sunset.

Toad Hall   RESTAURANT $$

(Map p250; ☎8534-3605; www.toadhallarenal.com; mains US$7-10, P☎🛜🍴) ✎ No need to write a review of this place, as all the info is proudly displayed on a million signs littering the lake road. Toad Hall does have excellent guacamole, tasty fish tacos and cold beer, true enough. There are beautiful views and lake trails, as you will know. Does it live up to the self-hype? We're not so sure.

There are three lovely on-site villas and a fun gift shop filled with hokey souvenirs. The signs are apparently part of a project with local schoolchildren. (To us this doesn't justify the visual pollution and self-promotion, but at least they're good for a laugh.)

★Gingerbread Hotel & Restaurant   RESTAURANT $$$

(☎8351-7815, 2694-0039; www.gingerbreadarenal.com; mains US$18-32; ⏰5-9pm Tue-Sat, lunch by reservation only) Don't miss the chance to eat at one of the best restaurants in northwestern Costa Rica. Chef Eyal is the larger-than-life, New York trained, Israeli chef who turns out transcendent meals from the freshest local fare. Favorites include mushrooms smothered in gravy, blackened tuna salad, and enormous, juicy, grass-fed beef burgers. It's big food that goes down smooth. Cash only.

If you want to sleep where you eat, book one of the sweet boutique rooms upstairs. Each showcases fabulous murals and other artwork by local creatives.

Nuevo Arenal

Although steeped in aging *extranjero cultura* (expat culture), this two-horse town still feels very Tico. A rest stop for travelers heading to Tilarán and points beyond, it's certainly a pleasant (and cheap) place to spend the night. The tiny downtown also has a gas station, a Banco de Costa Rica and a Banco Nacional (both with ATMs), a SuperCompro and a bus stop near the park. It even has a rickety old *plaza del toros* (bullring).

Nuevo Arenal is 27km west of the dam, or an hour's drive from La Fortuna. In case you were wondering what happened to old Arenal, it's about 27m below the surface of Laguna de Arenal. In order to create a large enough reservoir for the dam, the Costa Rican government had to make certain, er, sacrifices, which ultimately resulted in the forced relocation of 3500 people. Today, the humble residents of Nuevo Arenal don't seem to be fazed by history, especially since they now own premium lakeside property.

Just before you reach Nuevo Arenal (coming from La Fortuna) you'll pass a marina, where you can join **Arenal Kayak** (☑2694-4336; www.arenalkayaks.com; 2hr tour US$30) for a guided paddle on the lake.

🛏 Sleeping & Eating

Aurora Hotel
HOTEL $

(☑2694-4245; r US$24; P@🐾🖥) You'd never know it from the street, but these rooms are rather sweet, spotless, spacious, wood-cabin-like constructions with lovely lake views and vaulted beamed ceilings. Located on the east side of the square, it's one of the only budget options on Laguna de Arenal. The attached restaurant does decent pizza.

★ Tinajas Arenal
CAFE $$

(☑8926-3365; mains US$9-15; ⊙9am-9:30pm; 🐾🖥) 🍴 With glorious sunsets and a dock for boat access, this new lakeside retreat is a hidden gem. The chef – who honed his skills at La Mansion Inn Arenal nearby – has created a menu of traditional favorites and new surprises, using fresh seafood and organic ingredients grown right here. Sample the refreshing cocktail *a la casa,* limon hierba (lemonade with mint).

At the southern end of Nuevo Arenal, turn off the main road and follow the signs about 2km to Tinajas Arenal.

Moya's Place
CAFE, PIZZERIA $$

(☑2694-4001; mains US$6-12; ⊙11am-10pm) Murals, masks and other indigenous-inspired art adorn the walls at this friendly cafe. Take your pick from the delicious sandwiches, well-stuffed wraps and burritos, and tasty thin-crust pizza. This place is a sort of local gathering spot, where Ticos and expats alike gather to eat, drink and laugh. The food is good and the beer is cold.

Los Platillos Voladores
ITALIAN $$

(☑2694-5005; mains US$6-14) This new Italian carry-out joint has opened to rave reviews, serving homemade pastas, roast chickens and fresh salads. It's mostly Italian – the eggplant Parmesan is delectable – but the rotating menu features a variety of fish, chicken and meat dishes. If you have nowhere to go, you can enjoy your food on the patio overlooking the lake.

Las Delicias
SODA $$

(☑8320-7102; mains US$4.50-11; ⊙7am-9pm) A cheap and cheerful *soda* near the top of the hill as you approach town, with ample wooden-table seating. It does Western-style breakfasts, pasta dishes, quesadillas and grilled steaks on the cheap, but it's known for its *casados.*

Tom's Pan
BAKERY $$

(☑2694-4547; www.tomspan.com; mains US$9-16; ⊙7:30am-5pm Mon-Sat; P🖥) Better known as 'the German bakery', thanks to the signs that litter the lake road, this landmark is a famous rest stop for road-trippers heading to Tilarán. Its breads, strudels and cakes are all homemade. It also has German sausages, sandwiches and beer. Surprisingly pricey for the setting.

Sunset Grill
PUB $

(☑2694-4557; mains US$5-10; ⊙7am-11pm, bar til 2:30am; 🖥) American owned and patronized, Sunset Grill is an inviting open-air bar known for its fun, friendly atmosphere and good selection of bourbons. Big breakfasts, burgers and pub fare are on the menu.

Nuevo Arenal to Tilarán

West and around the lake from Nuevo Arenal, the scenery becomes even more spectacular just as the road gets progressively worse.

🛏 Sleeping & Eating

La Rana de Arenal
HOTEL $

(☑2694-4031; www.hotel-larana-arenal.com; r incl breakfast US$45; P🖥) About 5.5km from Nuevo Arenal, watch out for the hairpin turnoff at the driveway to La Rana, a quaint German-run spot with seven simple, comfortable rooms. In an airy upstairs pub-style dining room, the restaurant serves good international food with an emphasis on German cuisine. The property has tennis courts, a lakeside walking trail and a nearby swimming spot.

Living Forest
CABINAS $$

(☑8708-8822; www.lakearenalretreats.com; s/d US$50/55, dm/d/tr/q with shared bathroom US$28/45/75/95) Interior designer, massage therapist, yogi and free spirit: Johanna Harmala has combined these traits to create this inviting, inspiring retreat on the banks of the Río Sabalito about 15km west of Nuevo Arenal. The jewel-toned rooms are furnished with attractive walnut beds, with shared or private access to beautiful open-air stone bathrooms.

There's a delicious swimming hole, as well as yoga and spa services.

Mystica Resort
RESORT **$$**

(📞 2692-1001; www.mysticacostarica.com; s/d/tr/q incl breakfast US$102/135/152/165; ⊙ noon-9pm; 🅿 @ 🛜) About 15km west of Nuevo Arenal, this Mediterranean-style retreat has several comfortable, colorful rooms with Spanish-tile floors, woven bedspreads, wooden accents and a wide, inviting front porch with volcano views. If you're not staying here, the restaurant is still a great place to stop for a wood-fired pizza (US$5 to US$14).

Yoga and meditation classes are held in a gorgeous sheltered hardwood yoga space overlooking a gurgling creek, and there's a tree-house healing center for Reiki and massage. Wait, we feel an 'om' coming on.

Agua Inn Spa
B&B **$$**

(📞 2694-4218; www.aguainnspa.com; d incl breakfast US$80, spa treatments US$60-90; 🅿 🛜 ♨) The sound of the rushing river will lull you to sleep at this intimate B&B on the banks of the rainforest-shaded Río Cote. This gorgeous property is designed for total relaxation and rejuvenation, with a jungle-shaded pool and a private lake trail. Four simple rooms feature bold colors and plush linens. Downstairs, the full-service spa does facials, massages and body scrubs.

Surf & Reit Chalets
CABINA **$$**

(📞 8381-8363; www.costa-rica-reise.net; bungalows US$62-85; 🅿 🛜) Nab your hippie-kitesurf habitat in this breezy, tumbledown, disorganized, alluring collection of wooden *cabinas* on a hill. Don't misunderstand: there is elegance here. The rooms are built of wood and polished concrete, and decorated with colorful linens. What's more, the property has a majestic perch over the lake.

The turnoff is about 12.5km from Nuevo Arenal, near the village of Rio Piedras.

Minoa Hotel & Microbrewery
HOTEL **$$**

(📞 2695-5050; www.hotelminoa.com; s/d incl breakfast from US$68/78; ⊙ 11am-9pm; 🅿 ✳ 🛜 ♨) If you like beer, consider staying at the only hotel (that we're aware of) that has a microbrewery onsite, mixing up the hops and barley to bring you delicious pale ales and nut-brown beers. Drink it while feeling the lake breezes and admiring the views at the top-floor restaurant (the food is also good here).

Formerly Volcano Brewing, the whole place has been overhauled by new owners and it's looking fine. The rooms have been refurbished with attractive textured paint jobs and colorful quilts. You'll pay more for lake views and private patios.

Lake Coter Ecolodge
LODGE **$$**

(📞 2694-4084; www.ecolodgecostarica.com; r/cabins incl breakfast US$65/75; 🅿 🛜) 🐾 This aging lodge was in the midst of an ownership change at the time of research, so its future is fuzzy. Suffice to say, the new ownership is committed to preserving its 250 hectares of primary forest and 50 hectares of secondary-growth forest. The 14km of hiking trails aren't going anywhere, either, and nor are those spectacular lake and volcano views.

Look for the sign 4.5km west of Nuevo Arenal, then turn 3km down a steep, unpaved road.

Lucky Bug B&B
B&B **$$$**

(📞 2694-4515; www.luckybugcr.net; d incl breakfast US$99-129; 🅿 ✳ 🛜 ♨) Set on a rainforest lagoon, the five blissfully isolated bungalows at the Lucky Bug feature works and decorative details by local artisans. Here are blond-wood floors, wrought-iron butterflies, hand-painted geckos, and mosaic washbasins and end tables. Each room is unique and captivating. There's a rainforest trail in the grounds and kayaks for use on the lagoon.

There is also the onsite Caballo Negro Restaurant and the fabulously quirky Lucky Bug Gallery. Should you fall in love with a painting of a bug or something bigger, they can ship it for you. It's 3km west of Nuevo Arenal.

★ Café y Macadamia
CAFE **$$**

(📞 2692-2000; cafeymacadamia@yahoo.com; pastries & coffee US$2-4, mains US$6-13; ⊙ 8am-8pm; 🅿 🛜) Pull over for a cup of coffee and maybe an elegant salad or hearty sandwich, but save room for an irresistible dessert. Savor it all along with the spectacular views of Laguna de Arenal. This is your perfect pitstop or sunset vantage point. It's 20.5km west of Nuevo Arenal.

Equus Bar-Restaurant
RESTAURANT **$$**

(📞 8389-2669; mains US$6-14; ⊙ 11am-midnight) Follow your nose to this authentic stone-built tavern, 14.5km west of Nuevo Arenal, where the meat is cooked in an open fire pit, producing decadent, delicious aromas. Take a seat at a wooden-slab picnic table and dig in! A local favorite, this place has been run by the same family for more than a quarter of a century.

San Luis & Tronadora

On the south side of Laguna de Arenal, the main lake road (Rte 142) takes a sharp turn south to head toward Tilarán. If you take the northbound road instead, it quickly turns to gravel and descends into the lakeside hamlets of San Luis and, 3km further, Tronadora. With dramatic lake and volcano views, these villages are surprisingly and delightfully untouristed.

If you're driving between Arenal and Monteverde, consider taking the scenic route through Tronadora and Río Chiquito instead of driving through Tilarán. The distance is a bit longer and the roads are a bit rougher, but the marvelous vistas are well worth it. Look for the turnoff to Río Chiquito about 1km east of Tronadora. Note: if you go this route, there are no gas stations between Nuevo Arenal and Santa Elena, and the gas gets guzzled on the rough mountain roads. Make sure you fill up when you can.

🛏️ Sleeping & Eating

Monte Terras   B&B
(📞 2693-1349; www.monteterras.com; d incl breakfast US$75; 🅿️ 🛜) Set amidst a blooming, bird-filled garden in the village of Tronadora, you'll find a handful of comfy *cabinas*, each with high ceilings, polished-concrete floors, colorful paint jobs and tropical artwork. Rocking chairs deck the shared terrace, where it's easy to while away the day. Dutch owners Kees and Griselda go out of their way to make sure their guests are content.

Brisas Del Lago   SODA $$
(📞 2695-3363; mains US$6-11; ⊙ 11am-10pm Tue-Sat, 1-10pm Sun; 🅿️ 🛜 ♿) Simple Tico fare is done with panache at this dressed-up *soda*. They marinate chicken breasts in their own BBQ sauce, skewer Thai-style shrimp and sauce teriyaki chicken, and the garlic fish is sensational. To get here head toward Tilarán, then make a left at the T-junction toward the community of San Luis. Continue for 800m.

Little Longhorn   TEX-MEX $$
(📞 2695-2035; mains US$8-12; ⊙ noon-8pm Tue-Sun) Jason from Texas knows how to make a good burger, and he'll make one for you, just the way you like it. Veggie burger, if you prefer. There's country music on the radio and football on the TV. Yeehaw! Little Longhorn is in the village of San Luis, about 1km from the turnoff.

Tilarán

POP 8900

Near the southwestern end of Laguna de Arenal, the small town of Tilarán has a laid-back, middle-class charm – thanks to its long-running status as a regional ranching center. This tradition is honored on the last weekend in April with a rodeo that's popular with Tico visitors, and on June 13 with a *fiesta de toros* (bullfight) that's dedicated to patron San Antonio.

Because it's situated on the slopes of the Cordillera de Tilarán, this little hub is a much cooler alternative (in climate and atmosphere) than, say, Cañas, and makes a pleasant stop between La Fortuna and Monteverde. Life unfurls immediately around the main plaza. Wander more than a block in any direction, and things get rather residential. Street signs are a new and limited resource.

The city has several ATMs, two gas stations and an internet cafe.

🛏️ Sleeping & Eating

Cheap meals can be found in the *mercado* (market) beside the bus terminal, or pop into the **SuperCompro** (⊙ 8am-8pm) for groceries; it's across from the park.

Hotel Guadalupe   HOTEL $$
(📞 2695-5943; www.hotelguadalupe.co.cr; s/d/tr US$36/56/74; 🅿️ ❄️ 🛜 🖥️) This modern hotel attracts traveling business types, who make themselves at home in simple rooms, dressed up with jewel tones and tiled floors. Service is friendly and efficient. There is a decent restaurant onsite, as well as swimming pool, kiddie pool and hot tub.

Hotel Cielo Azul   HOTEL $$
(📞 2695-4000; www.cieloazulresort.com; per person incl breakfast US$50; 🅿️ ❄️ 🛜 🖥️) Found 500m before town coming from Nuevo Arenal, this hillside property has eight recently redone rooms with tiled floors, whitewashed walls and new bathrooms. There are spectacular views from the pool and grounds, and it even has a spinning studio. Especially good value for solo travelers.

La Troja   RESTAURANT $$
(📞 2695-4935; mains US$8-12; ⊙ 10am-9pm) This is a popular stop for Ticos and tourists alike, and rightly so. The attractive wooden building has massive windows, offering a lovely vista over Laguna de Arenal. Reli-

ably good Costa Rican fare includes grilled steaks, rotisserie chicken and delicious whole tilapia.

❶ Getting There & Away

Tilarán is usually reached by a 24km paved road from the Interamericana at Cañas. The route on to Santa Elena and Monteverde is paved for the first stretch, but then it becomes steep, rocky and rough. A 4WD is recommended, though ordinary cars can get through with care in the dry season.

Buses arrive and depart from the terminal, half a block west of Parque Central. Be aware that Sunday-afternoon buses to San José may be sold out by Saturday. The route between Tilarán and San José goes via Cañas and the Interamericana, not the Arenal–La Fortuna–Ciudad Quesada route. Regular services go to the following locations:

Cañas US$1, 30 minutes, departs 10 times daily from 5am to 5pm.

La Fortuna US$5, 3½ hours, departs 7am and 12:30pm.

Nuevo Arenal US$1, 1¼ hours, departs 12 times daily from 4:30am to 3:30pm.

Puntarenas US$4, two hours, departs 6am and 1pm.

San José US$7, four hours, departs 5am, 7am, 9:30am, 2pm and 5pm.

Santa Elena/Monteverde US$3, 2½ hours, departs 4am and 12:30pm.

NORTHERN LOWLANDS

Los Chiles

Seventy kilometers north of Muelle on a smooth, paved road through the sugarcane, and just three rutted kilometers south of the Nicaraguan border, lies the sweltering farming and fishing town of Los Chiles. The humid lowland village, arranged with dilapidated grace around a ragged soccer field and along the unmanicured banks of the leisurely Río Frío, is charming by border-town standards, sex workers and foreboding 'import-export' types notwithstanding. It was originally settled by merchants and fisherfolk who worked on the nearby Río San Juan, much of which forms the Nicaragua–Costa Rica border. In recent history, Los Chiles served as an important supply route for the Contras in Nicaragua, and was home to a strong US military presence throughout the 1980s.

Gringo traffic is on the rise in Los Chiles as it's a great base for enjoying the scenic water route to Caño Negro, and an early-morning excursion by small motorized boat is an adventure in itself. The second big draw is the scenic route to Nicaragua, a one-hour boat ride across the border that is becoming increasingly popular among foreign tourists. Crossing the border via the river is a relaxing, hassle-free way to go. Although the road continues past Los Chiles to Nicaragua, this border post is closed. The police patrolling this line in the sand are heavily armed and extremely bored, so don't waste your time or energy there.

☞ Tours

Los Chiles is a convenient base to organize your tours to Caño Negro. The port is also a good jumping-off point for exploring the islands of Lago de Nicaragua, and if you miss the early boat, private transportation to San Carlos in Nicaragua is available.

Just head to the dock, where you can hire boat captains to take you up the lovely, chocolaty Río Frío during the dry season and all the way into Lago Caño Negro during the rainy season, as well as to San Carlos, Nicaragua, if necessary. Three- to four-hour trips cost about US$50 to US$90 for a small group, depending on the size and type of

---

TOP WATERWAYS FOR WILDLIFE-WATCHERS

Head to some of the following waterways for an up-close glimpse of the local wildlife.

Río Sarapiquí (p283) Whether you're resting between rapids or traveling up to Trinidad, keep your eyes peeled for somnolent sloths or mud-covered caimans.

Caño Negro (p271Wake up early to savor a quiet view of breakfasting birds on the lagoons.

Río Frío (p269) Not only is this the kinder, gentler border crossing into Nicaragua but also you'll see trees filled with howler monkeys, and caimans on the riverbanks along the way.

Río San Carlos (p277) Lodges in the Boca Tapada area can get you on the river, where the slow flow near the Río San Juan affords good opportunities for bird-watching.

boat. If possible, make arrangements a day in advance and get an early start in the morning: the earlier out, the more you'll see.

🛏 Sleeping & Eating

Accommodations in town are surprisingly limited, though most people aren't too keen on sticking around. There's a **Palí** (cnr Av 1 & Calle 1) two blocks north of the bus stop, and the local **Supermercado Carranza** (cnr Av 0 & Calle 2) on the west side of the soccer field to meet all of your grocery and bakery needs.

Hotel y Cabinas Carolina   CABINAS **$**
(☑ 2471-1151; r from US$30; 🕸🖥) Not your typical border-town accommodations. This friendly, family-run option gets rave reviews for attentive English-speaking staff, spotless rooms and excellent local food. It's farther from the boat dock than the other options, but it's worth the walk.

Hotel Wilson Tulipán   HOTEL **$**
(☑ 2471-1414; www.hoteleswilson.com; cnr Av 0 & Calle 4; s/d/tr incl breakfast US$30/48/60; 🅿🕸🖥@🖥) Brand-new rooms are set in a somewhat strange, ghost-town motel that's right down the road from the boat dock. There are older but still comfortable rooms in the main building too, but those get night noise from the lively bar and restaurant, which flaunts tasty seafood *tipica* and bad behavior.

Restaurante El Parque   RESTAURANT **$**
(☑ 2471-1090; cnr Calle 2 & Av 0; mains US$4-7; ⏱ 6am-9:30pm) This popular spot facing the plaza has some of the best eats in town, and it's open early if you're looking to get your coffee fix before setting out on the river.

ℹ Information

Banco Nacional (☑ 2212-2000; Av 1 btwn Calles 0 & 1) Close to the central park and soccer field, changes cash and traveler's checks and has a 24-hour ATM.

Cruz Roja (Red Cross; ☑ 2471-2025, 2471-1037; cnr Calle 2 & Av 1; ⏱ 24hr) On the west side of the plaza if you need basic medical assistance or supplies.

Internet.com (☑ 2471-1515; Av 0 btwn Calles 0 & 1; 8am-7pm; ⏱ per hr US$1)

Post office (⏱ 8am-noon & 1-5:30pm Mon-Fri) One block west of the bus station.

ℹ Orientation

The last stretch of paved road along Hwy 35 is home to a few restaurants, the post office and a gas station. If you continue north past Los Chiles on the rutted dirt road, you'll find yourself in the

ARENAL & NORTHERN LOWLANDS LOS CHILES

ℹ GETTING TO SAN CARLOS, NICARAGUA

Although there's a 14km dirt road between Los Chiles and San Carlos, Nicaragua, using this crossing requires special permission generally reserved for federal employees. Most regular folk go across by boat on the Río Frío, which is easily arranged in Los Chiles. You must first get an exit stamp in your passport at the **migración** (Immigration; Calle 4 & Av 0; ⏱ 8am-noon & 1:30-4pm), about 100m east of the dock and directly across the street from Hotel Tulipán. If you are coming from Nicaragua, you must make the *migración* your first stop.

Los Chiles municipality charges a US$1.10 exit and entry fee; after getting your passport stamped at the *migración*, walk down to the docks and pay the exit fee at the yellow Recaudador Municipal office. Reverse this procedure if you are arriving here from Nicaragua.

Regular boats (US$12, 90 minutes) leave Los Chiles at 12:30pm and 3:30pm daily, with extra boats at 11am and 2:30pm if demand is high. Boats leave San Carlos for Los Chiles at around 10:30am and 4pm, with extra boats scheduled as needed. Of course, the Nicaragua–Costa Rica border is not known for its reliability, so confirm these times before setting out. Your boat will make a stop at the actual border post about halfway through the trip. Nicaragua charges a US$7 entry fee and US$2 exit fee.

When you hit the confluence of the Río San Juan, consider keeping your fingers and toes in the boat as there are river sharks (seriously!). Sharks are one of several euryhaline species that are able to survive in both fresh- and saltwater conditions. Every year, sharks that have been tagged by scientists in the Caribbean Sea are later found swimming in Lago de Nicaragua. Although the rapids of the Río San Juan are a deterrent for most species of marine fish, sharks are apparently able to negotiate the river without problems, and presumably head for fresh water in search of food.

dusty no-man's-land en route to a border crossing you won't be allowed to use.

Drivers: hang a left (west) off the highway when you see the sign for Palí grocery store. The bus terminal is tucked behind Soda Pamela on Av 1. The docks are located about 1km west of the bus terminal. Before hopping on the boat to Nicaragua, you need to stop at *migración*, across the street from Hotel Tulipán.

ⓘ Getting There & Away

Drivers usually get here via Hwy 35 from Muelle. Skid marks and reptilian road kill do break up the beautiful monotony of orange groves, sage-blue pineapple fields and dense sugarcane plantations. More scenic, if a little harder on your chassis, is the decent dirt road running for 50km from Upala, through Caño Negro, passable for normal cars throughout the dry season.

Regular boat transportation is limited to quick shuttles across the Nicaraguan border (US$10 to US$12). Boats across the border leave daily at 12:30pm and 3:30pm, but get here early because space is limited and immigration lines are long. In addition to the boat fees, you'll need to pay a US$1.10 departure tax.

All buses arrive and leave from the terminal behind Soda Pamela, near the intersection of Hwy 35. Timetables are flexible, so play it safe and inquire locally.

Ciudad Quesada US$2.25, two hours, departs 12 times daily from 4:30am to 6pm. For transfer to La Fortuna.

San José US$6, five hours, departs 5am and 3pm.

Upala via Caño Negro US$4, 2½ hours, departs 5am, noon and 4:30pm.

Refugio Nacional de Vida Silvestre Caño Negro

This remote, 102-sq-km refuge (☑2471-1309; www.ligambiente.com; adult/child US$10/1; ⊙8am-4pm) has long lured anglers seeking that elusive 18kg snook, and birders hoping to glimpse rare waterfowl. During the dry season water levels drop, concentrating the birds (and fish) in photogenically close quarters. From January to March, when migratory birds land in large numbers, avian density is most definitely world class.

The Río Frío defines the landscape – south of the main Caño Negro dock it's a table-flat, swampy expanse of marsh and lagoon that is similar in appearance, if not size, to other famous wetlands such as the Florida Everglades or the Mekong Delta. North of town, it's a slender river that carves

looming forest. During the wet season, the river breaks its banks to form one immense 800-hectare lake, then contracts during the dry months from January through April, when water levels drop to the point where the river is barely navigable. By April it has almost completely disappeared – until the May rains begin. This cycle has proceeded without fail for millennia, and the small fishing communities that live around the edges of the reserve have adapted to each seasonal nuance.

Thanks to improved roads, tour operators are now able to offer relatively inexpensive trips to Caño Negro from all over the country. However, you don't need them to explore the river. It's much more intriguing and rewarding to rent some wheels (or hop on a bus), navigate the rutted road into the rural flat lands and hire a local guide through the cooperative right in the center of Caño Negro village. It's also a lot cheaper, and it puts money directly into the hands of locals, thus encouraging communities in the area to protect wildlife.

🏃 Activities

Caño Negro is regarded among bird-watchers as one of the premier destinations in Central America. During the dry season, the sheer density of birds in the park is astounding, but the the variety of species is also impressive. At last count, more than 300 species of bird live here at least part of the year. In the winter months, there are huge congregations of migratory ducks, as well as six species of kingfisher, herons, cormorants, three types of egret, ibises, rails, anhingas, roseate spoonbills, toucans and storks. The refuge is also the only reliable site in Costa Rica for olivaceous cormorants, Nicaraguan grackles and lesser yellow-headed vultures.

Conspicuous reptiles include the spectacled caiman, green iguana and striped basilisk. Howler monkeys, white-faced capuchins and two-toed sloths are common, and despite increasing incursions from poachers, pumas, jaguars and tapirs have been recorded here in surprising numbers.

Caño Negro is also home to an abundance of river turtles, which were historically an important part of the Maleku diet. Prior to a hunt, the Maleku would appease the turtle god, Javara, by fasting and abstaining from sex. If the hunt was successful, the Maleku would later celebrate by feasting on smoked turtle meat and consuming large quantities of *chicha* (a spirit derived from maize). And, well, they probably had some sex too.

Mosquitoes in Caño Negro are damn near prehistoric. Bring bug spray or suffer the consequences.

Tours

Hiring a local guide is quick, easy and full of advantages – you'll pay less, you'll be supporting the local economy, and you'll have more privacy when you're out on the water. The local guide cooperative, Real Tour (2471-1621; real.tour@hotmail.com; US$40-60, plus park admission; 8am-4pm), is well signed and set right in the center of town. For a bit more cash you can add in a one-hour turtle and butterfly tour.

If you're looking to do some sportfishing, it's best to organize your trips through one of the lodges in the park. Seasonal fishing licenses, valid for two months, can be arranged through the lodges or at the ranger station for US$34. You'll need a photocopy of your passport and a small photo.

Sleeping & Eating

Kingfisher Lodge   CABINA $

(2471-1116; www.kingfisherlodgecr.com; r US$50-60; P ⊛ ❄) Located about 400m from the village center, these rustic *cabinas* have heavy wood furniture and hammock-strung porches. Your hosts, the Sequera brothers, are recommended refuge guides and boat captains. You can also arrange horse riding here.

★ Hotel de Campo Caño Negro   LODGE $$

(2471-1012; www.hoteldecampo.com; s/d incl breakfast US$79/95; restaurant 7:30am-9:30pm; P ❄ ❄ ❄) Set in an orchard of mango and citrus trees next to the 'Chapel' lagoon, this Italian-Tico–run hotel is a paradise for fishers and bird-watchers. After angling for tarpons or spying on spoonbills, relax in the ceramic-tiled *casitas,* decked with vaulted beamed ceilings and tasteful bedding. The stylish restaurant – adorned with gushing fountains and twirling fans – serves top-notch Italian and seafood.

You can hire boats, guides (who speak English, Spanish, French and Italian), kayaks (four hours US$20) and fishing equipment here at the well-stocked tackle shop.

Caño Negro Natural Lodge   LODGE $$$

(2471-1426; www.canonegrolodge.com; d incl breakfast US$140; P ❄ ❄ ❄) Perched on land that becomes a virtual island in the Río Frío during the rainy season, this lodge is surprisingly upscale. Well-appointed rooms have glass sliding doors, wooden and wrought-iron furnishings and tiny terraces facing the garden. Relax in the pool or Jacuzzi or stroll the leafy grounds, while the staff makes arrangements for boat tours of the lagoon.

Information

Caño Negro refuge is part of the Área de Conservación Arenal–Huetar Norte and is accessible primarily by boat. Close to the park entrance (that'd be the dock) is the tiny community of Caño Negro, which has no banks or gas stations. All visitors to the park must go to the **Real Tour** (2471-1621; 8am-4pm) office to pay the park entrance fees. You can book a local guide here. It's best to arrange an early-morning boat the day before.

The Minae office and ranger station, located about 150m behind (north of) the green-and-pink *pulpería* (corner grocery store), no longer offers service to tourists. For years rumors have swirled that all park offices, research labs and revamped accommodations were scheduled to move to the new Estación Biológica Caño Negro, located 6km north of the church at the end of the gravel road past the radio tower. It may be worth checking in at the ranger station to see if basic accommodations at the new station are up and running.

Getting There & Away

The village of Caño Negro and the entrance to the park lie on the rough road connecting Upala and Los Chiles, which is passable to all cars during the dry season. However, this road is frequently washed out during the rainy season, when a 4WD is required. Coming from Los Chiles, the turnoff is right before the big cell tower (it may or may not be signed); if you get to Escuela Los Angeles you've passed it.

Buses go to Los Chiles (US$2, one hour) at 7am, 1pm and 6pm. The return bus passes through en route to Upala (US$2.50, one hour) at around 6:30am, 1pm, 3pm and 5pm. Both buses stop at Real Tour and circle the village square; ask around as this schedule changes frequently.

During the rainy season and much of the dry season, you can also catch a boat (US$20 to US$25) to and from Los Chiles. This is becoming increasingly popular, especially as more travelers are crossing into and out of Nicaragua on the Río Frío.

THE WEEPING FOREST

Extensive deforestation of the Caño Negro area began in the 1970s in response to increased population density and the subsequent need for more farmland. Although logging was allowed to proceed in the area for almost 20 years, the government took action in 1991 with the creation of the Refugio Nacional de Vida Silvestre Caño Negro. Since its creation, Caño Negro has served as a safe habitat for the region's aquatic and terrestrial birds, and has acted as a refuge for numerous migratory birds.

However, illegal logging and poaching have continued around the perimeter of the park, and wildlife has suffered. In the last two decades, one-time residents of the park including ocelots, manatees, sharks and macaws have vanished. Tarpon and caiman populations are decreasing, and fewer migratory birds are returning to the park each year. Additionally, anglers are reporting record lows in both the size and number of their catches.

Satellite images show that the lake is shrinking each year, and that water levels in the Río Frío are dropping rapidly. It's difficult to say with certainty what is causing these changes, though the farms surrounding Caño Negro require extensive irrigation, and sugarcane is nearly 10 times as water-intensive as wheat.

Locals are extremely worried about the stability of the park, as entire communities are dependent on fishing and tourism for their survival. In response to the growing need to regulate development in the region, residents have formed a number of organizations aimed at controlling development in the northern lowlands. If you want to support the Caño Negro community, book your tour in town and spend your tourist dollar locally.

Upala

Just 9km south of the Nicaraguan border in the northwestern corner of the northern lowlands, Upala is a small *ranchero* town with a bustling market and plenty of tasty *sodas*. It's a center for the area's ranching and rice industries; most visitors are Costa Rican businesspeople who come to negotiate for a few dozen calves or a truckload of grain. Though it's a somewhat convenient public-transit stopover between the Volcán Tenorio area and Caño Negro, there's no reason to linger.

🛏 Sleeping & Eating

The busy market, just behind the bus terminal, opens early with several nice *sodas* dishing up good *gallos* (tortilla sandwiches), *empanadas* (turnovers stuffed with meat or cheese) and just about everything else. There are also a few Chinese restaurants and produce vendors.

Hotel Marakabú HOTEL $
(✆2470-4008; hotelmarakabu@hotmail.com; d US$28; P❋🐾🛜) Coming into town from the southeast, you'll cross a river and come across this attractive two-story stucco building facing a pleasant courtyard. The rooms

are musty but super clean, and they're well equipped, with flat-screen TVs and refrigerators. Spa services and tours are also on offer.

Cabinas Maleku CABINAS $
(✆2470-0142; d/tr US$34/50; P❋🛜) Wrapping around a gravel parking lot, these cute and comfortable *cabinas* are blessed with mosaic-tile patios decorated with hand-painted Sarchí-style wooden chairs and plenty of potted plants. It's a cheerful cheapie, for sure. There's an attached *soda* too.

La Terazza RESTAURANT $$
(✆8514-1563; mains US$6-13; ⏰7am-11pm) For more sophisticated eats and environs come to this 2nd-story, polished-wood wagon wheel of a bar and grill. In addition to three flat-screen TVs and all the ball games, it offers grilled *chuleta* (pork chop) plates, chicken brochettes, beef fajitas and whole-fried-fish dinners.

❶ Getting There & Away

From Upala, the well-maintained, paved Hwy 6 runs south via Bijagua, intersecting with the Interamericana just north of Cañas. Also paved, Hwy 4 runs in a more southeasterly direction to Muelle de San Carlos (near La Fortuna). A rough, unpaved road, usually passable to all cars, skirts the Refugio Nacional de Vida Silvestre Caño Negro on the way to Los Chiles, the official border crossing with Nicaragua.

The bus terminal is right off the park; a **ticket booth** (◷ 4:30-5:15am, 7:30am-1pm & 6:45-8pm Mon-Sat) has information and can store bags. Taxis congregate just outside the bus terminal. The following buses depart from Upala:

Cañas, via Bijagua US$2, two hours, 5am, 6am, 8:30am, 11am, 1pm and 3:30pm.

Liberia US$2, two hours, 7:30am.

Los Chiles, via Caño Negro US$2, two hours, 4am, noon and 4:30pm.

San José, via Cañas US$4, five hours, 4:30am, 5:15am and 9:30am.

San Rafael de Guatuso Area

The main population center of this agricultural area, the small town of Guatuso (shown on some maps as San Rafael) is 19km northeast of Nuevo Arenal and 30km east of Bijagua. Although the town itself is rather humble, it's a decent base for exploring the fantastic Venado Caves to the south and the blue waters of Río Celeste and the Parque Nacional Volcán Tenorio to the west (p221). The area is also home to the few remaining indigenous Maleku, who reside in *palenques* (indigenous settlements) near here.

A BRIEF HISTORY OF THE MALEKU

The Maleku (colloquially referred to as the Guatuso) are one of the few remaining indigenous groups in Costa Rica. Historically, they were organized into 12 communities scattered around the Tilarán-Guanacaste range and the Llanura de San Carlos. Although their numbers dwindled following the arrival of Spanish colonists, the population survived relatively intact until the early 20th century. With the invention of the automobile, the US rubber industry started searching for new reserves to meet the increasing demand for tires. With the aid of Nicaraguan mercenaries, industry representatives scoured Central America for stable rubber reserves, which were found on land inhabited by the Maleku. The resulting rubber war virtually wiped out the Maleku population, and confined survivors to a handful of communities. Today, the Maleku number around 400, and live in the three *palenques* (settlements) of Sol, Margarita and Tonjibe.

As is the situation with most indigenous groups in Costa Rica, the Maleku are among the poorest communities in the country, and they survive by adhering to a subsistence lifestyle. Their diet revolves around corn and the *tipuisqui* root, a traditional food source that grows wild in the region. Fortunately, since the Maleku have a rich artisan tradition, they are able to earn a small income by selling traditional crafts to tourists. Historically, the Maleku were renowned for their impressive jade work and arrow craftsmanship. Nowadays, their crafts primarily consist of pottery, jewelry, musical instruments and other small trinkets for the tourist market.

The Maleku are also famous for their unique style of clothing made from *tana* (tree bark that has been stripped of its outer layer, soaked in water and then pounded thin on wooden blocks). After it has been dried and bleached in the sun, *tana* can be stitched together like leather, and has a soft texture similar to suede. Although today it's rare to see Maleku wearing anything other than Western-style clothing, *tana* articles are often offered for sale to tourists.

Despite being small in number, the Maleku have held on to their cultural heritage, perhaps more than any other indigenous group in Costa Rica. This is especially evident in their language, which is one of the oldest in the Americas and linguistically distinct from the Amazonian and Maya dialects. Today, the Maleku still speak their language among themselves, and a local radio station, Radio Sistema Cultural Maleku, airs daily programs in the Maleku language. The Maleku have also maintained their ceremonial traditions, such as the seasonal custom of crying out to Mother Nature for forgiveness through ritualistic song and dance.

As with all indigenous reservations in Costa Rica, the Maleku welcome tourists, as craft sales are vital to their survival. You can access the *palenques* via Rte 143, though it's best to inquire locally for directions as the roads are poorly maintained and unsigned.

🛏 Sleeping & Eating

★ Cabinas Los Almendros   CABINA $
(☎ 8887-0495; cabinaslosalmendros@hotmail.com; s US$20, d US$24-30; 🅿 ❄ 🤶) A cute family-run motel with well-maintained rooms, blessed with a fresh coat of paint and lovely bedding and window treatments. Each room is named after a different jungle beast or bird, complete with hand-carved wooden sculpture. Set on the edge of town behind the Banco Nacional, this is easily the best choice in the area.

The folks at Los Almendros offer transportation and tours to the Maleku reservation, the Venado Caves and Río Celeste (Parque Nacional Volcán Tenorio).

Cabinas Cristal   CABINA $
(☎ 2464-0016; s/d US$20/24; 🅿 @ 🤶) There are a handful of clean pastel-brushed and tiled rooms, located in a tin-roofed, atrium-style complex. There's no one working on-site, but the manager will supposedly show up if you call.

Soda La Zuyapa   SODA $
(meals US$4; ⊙ 6am-8pm) Recommended by locals as the best *soda* in this humble town, La Zayupa offers a fresh take on the traditional. *Casados* come with noodles and potato salad unless you request otherwise. Drink options include fresh-pressed carrot juice and fresh-squeezed lemonade. There are also burgers and excellent fried chicken.

ℹ Getting There & Away

Guatuso lies on Hwy 4, midway between Upala and Muelle de San Carlos (about 40km from each). Buses leave frequently for Ciudad Quesada, where you can connect to La Fortuna. There is also one daily bus to Tilarán (three hours, departs 7:30pm) via Nuevo Arenal, and three daily buses to San José (five hours, departs 8am, 11:30am and 3pm).

From Guatuso, a rough gravel and dirt road covers the 21km to the entrance of Parque Nacional Volcán Tenorio, and onward to Bijagua. For this route, a 4WD is required in the rainy season and recommended year-round.

Muelle de San Carlos

This small crossroads village – locally called Muelle – was once an important dock as it's the most inland spot from which the Río San Carlos is navigable. These days it is sugarcane country and it serves as a rest stop for truckers and travelers. It's also only 27km east of La Fortuna. If you have your own wheels, Muelle can be a quaint, quiet base for visiting Arenal and its surrounding environs.

The **Centro Turistico Las Iguanas** (Iguana Bridge; ☎ 2462-1107; mains US$6-12) is a popular spot for tourists en route from La Fortuna to Caño Negro – but not for lunch. Countless iguanas hang out in the bamboo above the river, providing a great photo op.

A 24-hour gas station lies at the intersection of Hwy 4 (which connects Ciudad Quesada and Upala) and Hwy 35 (running from San José to Los Chiles). From Hwy 4 you can easily catch Hwy 32, the main artery serving the Caribbean coast.

🛏 Sleeping & Eating

Hotel La Garza   LODGE $$$
(☎ 2475-5222; www.hotellagarza.com; d/tr incl breakfast US$108/124, 2/4hr tours US$35/55; 🅿 ➰ 🤶 🏊) You know you're somewhere special as soon as you enter the landscaped reception via the graceful suspension footbridge. This upscale lodge sits on a 700-hectare working dairy ranch and citrus plantation, with views of the Río Platanar and far-off Volcán Arenal. There are 12 classy, polished wooden bungalows, as well as tennis, basketball and volleyball courts, and 4km of private trails.

Tours include horse rides through primary and secondary tropical forest, and rapelling inside a strangler fig. La Garza is about 5km south of Muelle in the village of Platanar.

Tilajari Resort Hotel   RESORT $$$
(☎ 2462-1212; www.tilajari.com; d incl breakfast from US$112; 🅿 ➰ ❄ @ 🤶 🏊) This country club turned luxury resort has well-landscaped grounds overlooking the Río San Carlos and comfortable, well-appointed rooms. The extensive list of amenities includes a lovely pool area, racquetball and tennis courts, a restaurant, sauna, spa and butterfly garden, plus access to the neighboring 400-hectare private rainforest reserve with several trails.

The resort is 800m west of the intersection at Muelle, on the road to Ciudad Quesada.

Bar La Subasta   RESTAURANT $$
(☎ 2467-8087; mains US$3-11; ⊙ 11am-11pm) Overlooking a bullpen, this place is bustling with hungry *campesinos* (farmers). It has an expansive menu of local dishes, and it's a great spot for a cold beer. Come for lunch on Tuesday or Thursday to see the cattle auction.

WORTH A TRIP

VENADO CAVES

Four kilometers south of Venado (Spanish for 'deer') along a good dirt road, the **Venado Caves** (Cavernas de Venado; ☎2478-8008; cavernasdelvenado@hotmail.com; adult/child under 12yr US$22/12; ⏲9am-4pm, last admission 2pm) are an adventurous excursion into an eight-chamber limestone labyrinth that extends for almost 3km. A bilingual guide leads small groups on two-hour tours through the darkness, squeezing through narrow passes, pointing out the most interesting rock formations and encountering bats and bugs.

The cavern system, composed of soft, malleable limestone, was carved over the millennia by a series of underground rivers. The caves were discovered by chance in 1945 when a farmer fell through a hole in the ground and found himself in an underground chamber surrounded by stalactites and stalagmites.

You'll be provided with rubber boots, headlamps and helmets, as well as a shower afterwards. You'll definitely want to bring a change of clothes. There's a small onsite *soda*, and a few restaurants in Venado, but no lodging.

This popular rainy-day attraction can be organized as a day trip from La Fortuna for US$50 to US$80 per person (including transportation and lunch). Alternatively, visit with your own car; the caves are well signed from Hwy 4. We don't recommend coming by bus; the 'early' bus from Ciudad Quesada drops you off a steep 4km slog from the cave entrance at about 2pm, too late to make the last admission into the caves. A taxi from San Rafael de Guatuso will cost about US$30 to US$40.

Ciudad Quesada (San Carlos)

POP 29,900

The official name of this small city is Ciudad Quesada (sometimes abbreviated to 'Quesada'), but all the locals know it as San Carlos, and local buses often list San Carlos as the destination. It's long been a bustling ranching and agricultural center, known for its *talabaterías* (saddle shops), where a top-quality saddle can cost US$1000. Get a sense of that at **Feria del Ganado** (a cattle fair and auction), which is held every April and accompanied by carnival rides and a *tope* (horse parade).

Although San Carlos is surrounded by pastoral countryside, the city has developed into the commercial center of the region – it's gritty and quite congested. Fortunately, there's no real reason to enter the city, except to change buses. The hot springs and resorts are located about 8km east of town, heading toward Aguas Zarcas.

As it's the regional market town, you'll find plenty of ATMs, internet cafes, groceries and shops around Parque Central.

Termales del Bosque HOT SPRINGS
(☎2460-4740; www.termalesdelbosque.com; hot springs incl lunch adult/child US$21/19; Ⓟ) Luxury here is low-key, with therapeutic soaking available in seven natural hot- and warm-water springs. The stone pools are surrounded by lush greenery and built into the riverbank, in a forested valley populated by morpho butterflies. It's a welcome antidote to the overdone, overpopulated springs in La Fortuna.

In addition to the springs, several airy cottages are arranged around the junglelike grounds at this recommended resort (doubles including breakfast US$95).

El Tucano Resort HOT SPRINGS
(☎2460-6000; www.hoteltucano.com; spa admission US$75; Ⓟ) This posh but ageing resort is set amid gorgeous primary forest. The thermal springs are tapped into three warm pools of varying temperatures – perfect for soaking away your ills. The most unique feature is the spring-fed river that streams through the property, creating warm rapids and hot holes to delight local swimmers.

The spacious, colonial-style rooms (doubles US$120 to US$136, suites US$145 to US$200) enjoy forest views from the terrace.

ℹ Getting There & Away

The Terminal Quesada is about 2km from the center of town. Taxis (US$1) and a twice-hourly bus (US$0.50) make regular runs between town and the terminal. Walking there is fine if you don't mind hauling your luggage uphill. Popular bus routes from Ciudad Quesada:

La Cruz and Peñas Blancas US$7, six hours, 6am (Transnorte) and 2pm (La Cañera).

La Fortuna US$2, 1½ hours, 12 daily between 5:15am and 9:30pm.

Los Chiles (Chilsaca) US$5, two hours, 12 daily from 5am to 7:15pm.

Puerto Viejo de Sarapiquí (Transportes Linaco) US$4, two hours, eight daily from 4:40am to 6:30pm.

San José (Autotransportes San José-Venecia) US$4.50, 2½ hours, 11 daily from 5am to 6pm.

Upala (Empresario Unidos del Norte) US$5, three hours, 5:30am, 10am, 1:30pm and 4:45pm.

Venecia

East of Muelle de San Carlos and Ciudad Quesada, the highway traces the northern limits of the Cordillera Central as flowering vines scramble down the mountains and threaten to overtake the road. In the distance, the northern lowlands appear as a patchwork quilt of cane fields and rice paddies. The road momentarily straightens out as it enters the affluent rural town of Venecia. There's a lively square and a maze of almost suburban streets stretching into the surrounding hills.

If you're looking to break up the driving, spend the night here in a 'medieval castle', **Torre Fuerte Cabinas** (☑2472-2424; s/d US$24/28; P☀☎). It's a sweet, kitschy hotel, family run, with lots of homey touches like silk flowers and plants. It's a perfect roadside cheapie. And yes, there's a turret.

About 3km from downtown, set 700m down a steep dirt road in a seething rainforest is **Recreo Verde** (☑2472-1020; www.recreoverde.com; pools adult/child US$12/8, cabins adult/child US$30/20), a family-friendly lodge with mineral baths. This is a Tico favorite; and though it's not exactly luxurious, it is affordable and fun. It has three pools set just above the roaring river, as well as hiking trails and a campground. Spacious polished-wood cabins have full kitchens and a pair of rockers on the porch.

Boca Tapada Area

Here's an off-the-beaten-track destination for adventurous souls. The rocky roads and lack of signage (even less than usual!) could mean a few unintended detours, but it's worth the effort for a glimpse into the ecological extravaganza of pristine rainforest. On the roads that pass pineapple fields and packing plants, your fellow travelers will be commuting *caballeros* (cowboys) and *campesinos* going about their day-to-day business. And at the end of the road, you'll be rewarded with a luxuriant bit of rainforest replete with the song of frogs and rare birds, and an inkling of the symbiosis that can happen when humans make the effort. Local lodges offer rainforest tours into the Refugio Nacional de Vida Silvestre Mixto Maquenque.

🛏 Sleeping & Eating

Laguna del Lagarto Lodge LODGE $$
(☑2289-8163; www.lagarto-lodge-costa-rica.com; s/d/tr US$51/75/80, P☎) ✈ Surrounded by rainforest, this German-run lodge is legendary among bird-watchers. Rustic screened rooms share large, hammock-strung verandas. It's not fancy, but it's wild and lovely, with chances to get up close and personal with wildlife. There are 10km of trails, and canoes to explore the surrounding lagoons, where caimans dwell and Jesus Christ lizards make tracks across the water's surface.

WORTH A TRIP

PROYECTO ASIS

It's an animal rescue center. It's a volunteer project. It's Spanish classes...**Proyecto Asis** (☑2475-9121; www.institutoasis.com; adult/child US$29/17, incl volunteering US$51/29; ☉tours 8:30am & 1pm) is doing a lot of good, and you can help. The introductory experience is a 90-minute tour of the wildlife-rescue center, which is pricey, but it affords some up-close interaction with the animals and – more importantly – the money goes to a good cause. Pay a bit more to follow up with a volunteer opportunity to help with the care or feeding of the animals. Asis also does homestays in the local community and runs Spanish classes. It's located about 20km west of Ciudad Quesada (San Carlos), past the village of Florencia. Reserve at least a day in advance.

Mi Pedacito de Cielo　　　LODGE $$
(☎2200-4782, 8308-9595; www.pedacitodecielo.
com; s/d/tr US$65/75/85; P🖥) ✐ Perched
above the Río San Carlos, Mi Pedacito de
Cielo ('my little piece of heaven') is a rustic
retreat, with 14 wooden bungalows offer-
ing river and rainforest views. Guests can
swing in the hammock-chairs to watch the
sunset and listen to the rainforest come
alive. The super-friendly service and excel-
lent home-cooked meals are perks, as is
the attached rainforest reserve with hiking
trails.

★**Maquenque Eco-Lodge**　　LODGE $$$
(☎2479-8200; www.maquenqueecolodge.com; r
incl breakfast from US$106; P🖥🏊) ✐ Set on
60 glorious, bird-filled hectares, 14 unique
and lovely bungalows overlook a lagoon and
tropical garden. The place is a birders' paradise, with countless species flocking to feed-
ers and fruit trees on the grounds. There's
also an onsite restaurant which serves excellent home-cooked food, primarily using
ingredients from the 'green garden' on the
grounds.

Prices include a guided morning rainforest hike, a student-led tour of a local school
and use of canoes on the lagoon. The lodge
also offers guests a chance to support sustainable tourism by planting a tree in the
rainforest.

❶ Getting There & Away

Getting to Boca Tapada is an adventure in
itself. The nearest town of note is Pital, north of
Aguas Zarcas. After passing through Pital, turn
right after the church on the right and soccer
field on the left, and continue through the village of Veracruz. At the Del Huerto pineapple-
packing plant, hang a left and continue along
the paved road. About 10km later, where the
pavement ends, turn right at the intersection.
When you come to the gas station, turn right
again and follow the signs to Boca Tapada. It's a
slow, rough 40km, but worth it.

Buses reach Boca Tapada on a two-hour
trip from Pital, departing Pital at 9:30am and
4:30pm. You can reach Pital on frequent buses
from Ciudad Quesada (US$2, 1½ hours) or four
daily buses from San José (US$4, 2½ hours).
Leaving Boca Tapada, the buses to Pital depart
at 5:30am and 12:30pm.

The lodges can also arrange transfers from La
Fortuna or San José.

SARAPIQUÍ VALLEY

This flat, steaming stretch of *finca*-dotted
lowlands was once part of the United Fruit
Company's vast banana holdings. Harvests
were carried from plantations to Puerto
Viejo de Sarapiquí, where they were shipped
downriver on boats destined for North
America. In 1880 a railway connected rural
Costa Rica with the port of Puerto Limón,
and Puerto Viejo de Sarapiquí became a
backwater. Although it's never managed to
recover its former glory, the river again shot
to prominence as one of the premier destinations in Costa Rica for kayakers and rafters in the 1990s. In addition to tasty raging
rapids, there are a slew of stellar lodges in
the region, featuring rainforest trails, suspension bridges, pre-Columbian ruins and
chocolate tours.

San Miguel

If you're driving up from San José or Alajuela, Hwy 126 curves up the slopes of the
Cordillera Central, leaving behind the urban bustle and passing Volcán Poás before
descending again into pastureland. This is
campesino country, where the plodding
hoofbeat of cattle is about the speed of life,
as the hard-to-spot rural speedbumps will
remind you if you take those curves too
quickly. You're off the beaten track now, and
if you're self-driving, you may as well linger,
because there are few Costa Rican corners
quite this beautiful and unheralded.

Albergue El Soccoro (☎8820-2160;
www.alberguelsocorrosarapiqui.com; per person
incl meals US$75; P🅟) is 9km south of San
Miguel, 1000m above sea level, on a plateau surrounded by a magnificent knife's
edge of green mountains, tucked between
the looming Cerro Congo and Volcán Poás.
The owner was born and raised a rancher
here, but in January 2009 a massive earthquake struck the area, destroying the road
from Vara Blanca to San Miguel along with
the family's home and dairy. This wonderful
family rebuilt the ranch from scratch and
incorporated a tourism component. Guests
stay in one of three cozy A-framed cabins,
from which you can explore 4km of trails
in primary and secondary rainforest. It also
has a working dairy. Kids (and grown-ups)
can milk the cows and ride horses.

A GREEN-GREEN SITUATION

The gorgeous green plumage, electric-blue wing tips and red forehead of the great green macaw *(Ara ambiguus)* have long attracted collectors of exotic birds. The (illegal) sale of just one macaw can fetch several thousand dollars, despite the fact that the species' nervous personality causes them to fare poorly in captivity. International trade has depleted the population, even though the macaw is protected by the Convention on International Trade in Endangered Species (Cites).

Deforestation also threatens the great green macaw. The northern lowlands have suffered from heavy deforestation in recent years due to the demand for increased agricultural and pasture land. Furthermore, the *almendro* tree *(Dipteryx panamensis)*, whose nut provides 90% of the macaw's diet and whose high hollows are far and away the preferred nesting tree for breeding pairs, is highly sought after as a luxury hardwood. Extensive logging of the *almendro* has severely cut back potential nesting sites, and as a result the great green macaw is endangered. It's estimated that Costa Rica's population is as low as 200, with as few as 30 breeding pairs left.

But all is not lost! With the leadership of the **Tropical Science Center** (www.cct.or.cr), a coterie of nonprofit organizations and government agencies established the San Juan–La Selva Biological Corridor to protect existing green macaw populations as well as other species in the area. The corridor bridges the gap between existing protected areas. Eventually, all of these protected areas will form a Mesoamerican biological corridor that will stretch from Mexico through Central America.

In 2005 the **Refugio Nacional de Vida Silvestre Mixto Maquenque** was officially declared by then-president Abel Pacheco. Owing to this victory, Maquenque now protects an estimated 6000 species of vascular plant, 139 mammals, 515 birds, 135 reptiles and 80 amphibians. And as a 'mixed-use' wildlife refuge – the first of its kind in Costa Rica – it allows human residents to continue living and working within its boundaries. However, most of the refuge's approximately 500 sq km, which are privately owned, are now bound to certain regulations, such as the drastic reduction of activities including logging. So where does this leave the residents, who depend on forestry and agriculture for subsistence?

Enter the **Costa Rican Bird Route** (www.costaricanbirdroute.com), a project initiated by the non-profit Raintorest Biodiversity Group in partnership with several other nonprofit organizations. The Costa Rican Bird Route has been working with and educating communities within these protected areas to help create viable and sustainable ecotourism opportunities, as economic alternatives to habitat-destructive agriculture and logging. While promoting locally owned lodges throughout the region, the Costa Rican Bird Route is also helping to establish new, community-based ecolodges from the Río San Juan to Parque Nacional Braulio Carrillo. The hope is that green tourism will be more financially beneficial to these poor communities, and will also be salvation for the great green macaw.

La Virgen

Tucked into the densely jungled shores of the wild and scenic Río Sarapiquí, La Virgen was one of a number of small towns that prospered during the heyday of the banana trade. Although United Fruit has long since shipped out, the town remains dependent on its nearby pineapple fields, and it still leans on that river. For over a decade, La Virgen was the premier kayaking and rafting destination in Costa Rica. Dedicated groups of hard-core paddlers spent happy weeks running the Río Sarapiquí. But a tremendous 2009 earthquake and landslide altered its course and flattened La Virgen's tourist economy. Some businesses folded, others relocated to La Fortuna. But independent kayakers are starting to come back and there are now three river outfitters offering exhilarating trips on Class II–IV waters. There are cheap digs in town, or consider staying in one of the more interesting lodges on the outskirts or on the road to Puerto Viejo.

◉ Sights

Snake Garden
ZOO

(☑2761-1059; snakegarden@hotmail.com; adult/student/child US$15/10/10, night tour US$24/18/18; ◷9am-5pm) This wildlife center is an entertaining rainy-day outing. Get face to face with 50 species of reptiles and amphibians, including poison-dart frogs, rattlesnakes, crocs and turtles. The star attraction is a gigantic 80kg Burmese python.

Nature Pavilion
WILDLIFE RESERVE, BIRD-WATCHING

(☑2761-0801; www.costaricanp.com; without/with guide US$20/30; ◷7am-5pm) Father and son Dave and Dave greet all comers to this 10-acre reserve on the Río Sarapiquí. It's a lovely setting in which to spy on feathered friends. There are several viewing platforms, with feeders attracting toucans, trogans, tanagers and 10 species of hummingbird. From here you can follow (or be guided) along a trail system that winds through secondary forest all the way down to the river.

Santuario de Mariposas Aguas Silvestres
WILDLIFE RESERVE

(☑8720-1074, 2761-1095; www.santuariomariposas.jimdo.com; admission US$8.50, guided hikes US$18) You'll need your own wheels to visit this butterfly sanctuary in the mountains. Guided hikes (in Spanish) take you through the rainforest along a waterfall trail, including a tour of the butterfly garden. You can also stay overnight in the rustic bunkhouse (per person US$24) and swim in the nearby lagoon. However long your stay, be sure to bring bug repellent, as butterflies are not the only insects living up there.

To get here, turn onto the Pozo Azul road and follow the brown wooden signs to the sanctuary, which is about 10km up the mountain, near the village of San Ramón.

🏃 Activities

The Río Sarapiquí isn't as wild as the white water on the Río Pacuare near Turrialba, though it will get your heart racing. Even better, the dense jungle that hugs the riverbank is lush and primitive. You can run the Sarapiquí year-round, but December offers the biggest water. The rest of the year, the river fluctuates with rainfall. The bottom line is: if it's been raining, the river will be at its best. Where once there were nearly a dozen outfitters in La Virgen, now there are three. All offer roughly the same Class II–IV options at similar prices.

Sarapiquí Outdoor Center
RAFTING

(☑8506-6889, 2761-1123; www.costaricaraft.com; 2/4hr rafting trip US$65/90, guided kayak trips US$90-120) Here is your local paddling authority. In addition to offering its own rafting excursions, it offers kayak rental, lessons and clinics. Indie paddlers should check in for up-to-date river information. If you need somewhere to sleep before you hit the water, you can pitch a tent here.

Aventuras del Sarapiquí
RAFTING

(☑2766-6768; www.sarapiqui.com; river trips US$55-80) A highly recommended outfitter, Aventuras del Sarapiquí offers mountain biking, and canopy, hiking and horse-riding tours, as well as a variety of river trips. It's set just out of town on the main highway in Chilamate.

Hacienda Pozo Azul Adventures
ADVENTURE TOUR

(☑2438-2616, in USA & Canada 877-810-6903; www.pozoazul.com; tours US$55-85; 🛉) Hacienda Pozo Azul Adventures specializes in adventure activities, including horse-riding tours, a canopy tour over the lush jungle and river, rappelling, mountain biking, and assorted river trips. It is the most polished and best-funded tour concession in the area, catering largely to groups and day-trippers from San José.

Inflatable Duckies
KAYAKING

(☑2761-0095, 8760-3787; adult/child US$65/50; ◷departs 9am & 1pm) Highly recommended for beginners and families, this outfit does tours and instruction in inflatable kayaks, which allow for a fun paddle even when the river is low. Paddle on flat moving water or Class III rapids (or somewhere in between). Reserve ahead.

🛌 Sleeping & Eating

Bar & Cabinas El Río
BUNGALOW $

(☑2761-0138; r with fan/air-con US$15/20; ℗❄) Located at the southern end of town, these seven A-frame bungalows have tiled floors, clean hot-water bathrooms and TV. About 100m further down the steep hill is the lovely open-air Bar El Río, on rough-hewn stilts high above the river.

Cabinas El Bosque
CABINA $

(☑2761-0204; r US$10) Basic but sparkling-new *cabinas* set off the main highway, 1km south of town. Rooms are in little square houses with cold-water bathrooms, fans, new tiles and sweet window treatments.

Hacienda Pozo Azul Adventures
BUNGALOW $$

(📞2438-2616, 2761-1360; www.haciendapozoazul. com; s/d incl breakfast US$80/92; 🅿@📶) 🏄 Located near the southern end of La Virgen, Pozo Azul features luxurious 'tent suites' scattered on the edge of the tree line, all on raised polished-wood platforms and dressed with luxurious bedding and mosquito nets. At night, the frogs and wildlife sing you to sleep as raindrops patter on the canvas roof.

Pozo Azul also has a restaurant-bar in town with a lovely riverside veranda.

Restaurante y Cabinas Tía Rosita
SODA $

(📞2761-1032; meals US$2-6; 🅿📶) Tía Rosita is the best *soda* in La Virgen, with excellent *casados* and Costa Rican–style *chiles rellenos* (stuffed fried peppers). The family also rents several *cabinas* with private hot-water bathrooms and plenty of breathing space, located about 100m down the road.

Restaurante Mar y Tierra
RESTAURANT $

(📞2761-1603; mains US$4-11; ⏰8am-10pm) La Virgen's favorite fine-dining (but still very relaxed) option is this comfortable seafood and steak restaurant that's popular with both locals and travelers.

ℹ️ Information

Most of La Virgen's businesses are strung along the highway, including a gas station, a Banco Nacional with 24-hour ATM, and a couple of small supermarkets.

ℹ️ Getting There & Away

La Virgen lies on Hwy 126, about 8km north of San Miguel and 17km southwest of Puerto Viejo de Sarapiquí. Buses originating in San José, San Miguel or Puerto Viejo de Sarapiquí make regular stops in La Virgen. If you're driving, the curvy road is paved between San José and Puerto Viejo de Sarapiquí, though irregular maintenance can make for a bumpy ride.

La Virgen to Puerto Viejo de Sarapiquí

This scenic stretch of Hwy 126 is home to a few excellent ecolodges. Good news for budget travelers: you don't have to stay at them to take advantage of their private trails and other interesting attractions. Any bus between La Virgen and Puerto Viejo de Sarapiquí can drop you off at the entrances, while a taxi from La Virgen will cost from US$8 to US$10.

👁️ Sights

Sarapiquí al Natural
FARM

(📞8635-7645; admission US$10; ⏰7am-5pm Mon-Fri & 8am-5pm Sat & Sun) In the tiny village of Las Palmitas, Leo Herra welcomes guests to his family farm to spot frogs in the pond, to marvel at spiders, and – most intriguing – to spy on the amazing cutter ants as they go about their business in their nest. Aside from the critters, the farm is dedicated to the cultivation of vanilla beans and peppercorns, so there's a lot to learn (and taste) here.

Finca Corsicana
FARM

(📞tours 2761-1700; www.fincacorsicana.com; adult/ child US$22/18) The world's largest organic-pineapple plantation, Finca Corsicana was founded by the owners of Collin Street Bakery, a Texas-based confectioner famous for fruit cakes. Take a ride through 3000 acres of pineapple fields, learn about planting and harvesting, see the processing and packaging, and – of course – taste the sweet, juicy product. Take the turnoff to La Quinta and follow the signs for 2km to the facility.

🛏️ Sleeping & Eating

⭐ Chilamate Rainforest Eco Retreat
LODGE $$

(📞2766-6949; www.chilamaterainforest.com; dm US$29-35, s/d incl breakfast US$85/102; 🅿📶) 🏄 Family run and family-friendly, this is an inviting and truly innovative retreat, where owners Davis and Meghan are dedicated to protecting the environment and investing in community. Built on 20 hectares of secondary forest, the solar-powered cabins are basic but full of character, with hand-crafted furniture and natural air-cooling. The restaurant serves incredible, fresh breakfast and dinner buffets, using local, organic ingredients.

Covered, flat walkways allow you to move between buildings in the complex without ever getting wet (after all, this is the rainforest!). Behind the cabins, 6km of paths wind through the jungle, where you're likely to spot sloths, monkeys, toucans, frogs, snakes and more. And when you can't take the heat, head to the nearby river swimming hole, complete with Tarzan swing from the bridge. Trail access is US$12.

Centro Neotrópico SarapiquíS
LODGE $$

(📞2761-1004; www.sarapiquis.org; d incl breakfast US$94; 🅿📶) 🏄 About 2km north

ARENAL & NORTHERN LOWLANDS

WORTH A TRIP

CINCO CEIBAS

On the grounds of the huge, 1100-hectare Finca Pangola there is a swathe of dense, green primary rainforest, home to some of the oldest and largest trees in all of Costa Rica. This is Cinco Ceibas (☑ 4000-0606; www.cincoceibas.com; half-day tour incl lunch US$40-60). And yes, there are five glorious ceiba trees that you can gawk at as you walk 1.2km along the raised wooden boardwalk through the jungle. The stroll is paired with horse riding, kayaking, or an ox-cart ride, plus lunch, for a carefully choreographed adventure.

Cinco Ceibas offers transportation for day-trippers from San José or La Fortuna. If you have your own wheels, it's a one-hour drive on mostly gravel roads from La Virgen. From the highway north of town, take the turn off to Pueblo Nuevo. There is supposed to be a new highway in the works, which will make this journey faster and easier, so ask around before you set out.

of La Virgen, this ecolodge offers a place to stay and eat, as well as an education in environmental conservation and pre-Columbian culture. Modeled after a 15th-century pre-Columbian village, the *palenque*-style thatched-roof buildings each contain a clutch of luxuriously appointed rooms with huge solar-heated bathroom and private terrace. The restaurant incorporates ingredients used in indigenous cuisine, many grown on the premises.

What's really special about the lodge is the other attractions scattered about the grounds. The Alma Ata Archaeological Park is a Maleku archaeological site, estimated to be around 600 years old. Currently about 70 small stone sculptures marking a burial field are being excavated by Costa Rican archaeologists who have revealed a number of petroglyphs and pieces of pottery. Nearby is the Sarapaquís Gardens & Museum (www.sarapiquis.org; self-guided adult/child 4-16yr US$8/4, with guide US$15/8; ☺ 9am-5pm), which chronicles the history of the rainforest and of human interactions with it. It also displays hundreds of indigenous artifacts. The gardens boast one of the largest scientific collections of medicinal plants in Costa Rica.

La Quinta de Sarapiquí Lodge   LODGE $$
(☑ 2761-1052; www.laquintasarapiqui.com; d incl breakfast US$95; P ✹ ☏ ✻) ✦ At this family-run lodge on the banks of the Río Sardinal, covered paths crisscross the landscaped garden, connecting thatched-roof, hammock-strung rooms. You can swim in the pretty saltwater pool or in the nearby river swimming hole; observe the creatures in the frog house, the caimen nursery and the butterfly garden; or hike the trails through secondary forest. Day passes are US$10.

Tirimbina Rainforest Center & Lodge   LODGE $$
(☑ 2761-1579; www.tirimbina.org; d incl breakfast US$85-105; P ✹ @ ☏) Located 2km from La Virgen, this is a working environmental-research and education center. The spacious, comfortable accommodations are located at the lodge or at a more remote field station. Tirimbina reserve has more than 9km of trails (access US$15/9 per adult/child), and tours (US$22 to US$27) include birdwatching, frog and bat tours, night walks and a recommended chocolate tour.

The 345-hectare private reserve is connected to the nearby Centro Neotrópico Sarapiquís by two long suspension bridges. Halfway across, a spiral staircase drops to an island in the river. Explore!

Selva Verde Lodge   LODGE $$$
(☑ 2761-1800, in USA & Canada 800-451-7111; www.selvaverde.com; incl breakfast s/d US$116/134, bungalow s/d US$133/163; P ✻) In Chilamate, about 7km west of Puerto Viejo, this former *finca* is now an elegant lodge protecting 200 hectares of rainforest. Choose to stay at the river lodge, elevated above the forest floor, or in a private bungalow, tucked away in the nearby trees. Rooms have shiny wooden floors, solar-heated showers, and wide verandas with views to the forest.

There are three walking trails through the grounds and into the premontane tropical wet forest, as well as medicinal and butterfly gardens, various boat tours on the Río Sarapiquí, and an onsite Italian kitchen.

★ **Rancho Magallanes**   RESTAURANT $$
(☑ 2766-5606; chicken US$5-12; ☺ 10am-10pm) Rancho Magallanes is a sweet roadside restaurant with a wood-burning brick oven

where they roast whole chickens and serve them quite simply with tortillas and banana salsa. You can dine with the truckers by the roadside or in the more upscale riverside dining area, painted with colorful jungle scenes.

Puerto Viejo de Sarapiquí & Around

At the scenic confluence of Ríos Puerto Viejo and Sarapiquí, this was once the most important port in Costa Rica. Boats laden with fruit, coffee and other commercial exports plied the Sarapiquí as far as the Nicaraguan border, then turned east on the Río San Juan to the sea. Today, it is simply a gritty but pleasant palm-shaded market town. The town is adjusting to the new economy, as the local polytechnic high school offers students advanced tourism, ecology and agriculture degrees. The school even has its own reserve, laced with trails. Visitors, meanwhile, can choose from any number of activities in the surrounding area such as bird-watching, rafting, kayaking, boating and hiking. The *migración* (immigration office) is near the small wooden dock.

🏃 Activities & Tours

Taking the launch from Puerto Viejo to Trinidad, at the confluence of Ríos Sarapiquí and San Juan, provides a rich opportunity to see crocodiles, sloths, birds, monkeys and iguanas sunning themselves on the muddy riverbanks or gathering in the trees. This river system is a historically important gateway from the Caribbean into the heart of Central America, and it's still off the beaten tourist track, revealing rainforest and ranches, wildlife and old war zones, deforested pasture land and protected areas.

Ruta Los Heroes   BOAT TOUR
(☑ 2766-5858; 2hr tour per person US$20; ☉ 7am-3pm) The pink building near the dock is a boat-captain cooperative, offering river tours with ecological and historical emphasis. Make arrangements to leave as early as possible to beat the heat and see more wildlife. If the office is closed (as it sometimes is in the low season), you can negotiate directly with the captains you find at the dock. Or, try calling **Oscar** (☑ 8365-3683) or **Rafael** (☑ 8346-1220) directly.

Green Rivers   RAFTING, KAYAKING
(☑ 8884-0187, 2766-5274; tours US$50-70) Operating out of the Posada Andrea Cristina B&B, this is a new outfit run by the ever-amiable Kevín Martínez and his wife. They offer a wide variety of rafting and kayaking tours, from family-friendly floats to adrenaline-pumping, rapid-surfing rides. They also know their nature, so they do natural-history and bird tours, too.

Aguas Bravas   RAFTING
(☑ 2766-6524; www.costaricaraftingvacation.com; Class III-IV US$85, safari float US$65; ☉ 9am-5:30pm) Aguas Bravas no longer maintains an office in the Sarapiquí area, but it does run the river (book at the Souvenir Río Sarapiquí in town). There are two tours on offer: take a gentle safari float to spot birds, iguanas, caimans and other wildlife, or sign up to splash through 14km of 'extreme rapids' on the San Miguel section of the river.

Lago Jalapa   HIKING, CANOEING
(☑ 8955-8869, 8973-8488; per person US$20-45) 📎 Located about 8km north of town, this is a grassroots ecotourism effort, offering hiking and canoeing on the Lago Jalapa. It's not the most professionally run operation, and guides speak no English, but it offers access to the stunning lake in the Refugio de Vida Silvestre Tapiria, surrounded by forest teeming with wildlife.

🛏 Sleeping

This stretch of jungle boasts quite a range of accommodations, from budget bunks in town designed for local long-term plantation workers to several excellent lodges on the outskirts.

Cabinas Laura   CABINA $
(☑ 2766-6316; s/d US$24/30; ᴘ ❄ 🛜) Quiet and cheap; located on the road to the pier. Rooms are simple but spotless, with new tiles, wooden furnishings and cable TV.

Mi Lindo Sarapiquí   HOTEL $
(☑ 2766-6281; s/d US$26/36; ᴘ ❄ @) On the southern side of the soccer field, rooms here are simple, spacious and clean, with hot water and ceiling fans. The onsite restaurant offers some of the freshest seafood in town.

★ Posada Andrea Cristina B&B   B&B $$
(☑ 2766-6265; www.andreacristina.com; s/d incl breakfast from US$38/55; ᴘ 🛜) On the edge

of town and at the edge of the forest, this charming B&B is a gem. The grounds are swarming with birds, sloths and monkeys, not to mention the frogs that populate the pond. Quaint cabins all have high, beamed ceilings, colorful paint jobs and private terraces. Or opt to stay in a funky tree house, built around a thriving Inga tree.

Your delightful host, Alex Martínez, is also a bird guide. He's active in environmental protection and runs Tierra Hermosa (www.tierrahermosacenter.org), a nearby wildlife reserve and rescue center. You'll see some of the 'clients' around the posada (guesthouse).

Hotel Gavilán
HOTEL $$

(☑2234-9507; www.gavilanlodge.com; d US$65-75; P❄🌐✉) Sitting on a 100-hectare reserve about 4km northeast of Puerto Viejo, this former cattle hacienda (estate) is a bird-watching haven, with 5km of private trails on the grounds. The cozy rooms have pastel paint jobs and wide porches, some with river views. Management is quite charming, offering private boat tours (US$50) and bird walks (US$18) upon request.

Hotel Ara Ambigua
HOTEL $$

(☑2766-7101; www.hotelaraambigua.com; d/tr/q incl breakfast from US$86/106/128; P❄@✉) About 1km west of Puerto Viejo, this countryside retreat offers oddly formal but well-equipped rooms, set on gorgeous grounds. There are birds buzzing in the luscious, blooming gardens, poison-dart frogs in the ranario (frog pond) and caimans in the small lake. Even if you're not staying here, the onsite pizzeria, La Casona, is an excellent place to grab lunch and spy on your feathered friends.

Hotel El Bambú
HOTEL $$

(☑2766-6005; www.elbambu.com; d standard/superior incl breakfast US$88/105; P❄🌐✉) This big hotel is smack dab in the middle of town, with a popular restaurant and an inviting pool. The rooms are spacious and attractive enough, though it's worth springing for the 'superior', which has a jacuzzi tub and a private balcony facing the trees.

✖ Eating

Most of the lodgings in and around Puerto Viejo have onsite restaurants or provide meals. Otherwise, there are several sodas in Puerto Viejo de Sarapiquí and a Palí supermarket (⊙8am-9pm) at the western end of town.

Soda Judith
SODA $

(mains US$2-5; ⊙6am-7pm) The excellent Soda Judith, one block off the main road, is where early risers grab brewed coffee and big breakfasts or an empanada to start their day.

Bar y Restaurante Real Sarapiquí
CHINESE $

(☑2766-5590; mains US$3-8; ⊙7:30am-10pm) A popular local Chinese greasy spoon decorated with Christmas lights and Chinese fans emblazoned with caballos (horses). It's a bit kitsch, but does roast quarter-chicken plates, fried rice, wonton soup, chow mein and all the noodle dishes. Located 150m east of Hotel El Bambú.

Restaurante La Casona
RESTAURANT $$

(☑2766-7101; www.hotelaraambigua.com; meals US$8-16; ⊙8am-10pm; 🔌📶) At the Hotel Ara Ambigua, this place is particularly recommended for its oven-baked pizza and typical, homemade cuisine served in an open-air rancho. The deck offers a sweet view of the gardens, where birds flutter by as you enjoy your meal.

ℹ Information

Banco Popular (☑2766-6815) Has an ATM and changes money.

Banco de Costa Rica At the entrance of town; has an ATM.

Cruz Roja (☑administration 2764-2424, emergency 2766-6212) Provides medical care.

Gecko.Net (☑2766-7007; per hr US$1; ⊙8:30am-7pm Mon-Fri, 9am-6pm Sun; 📶) Across from Cruz Roja; has the newest and fastest internet access in town.

ℹ Getting There & Around

Puerto Viejo de Sarapiquí has been a transportation center longer than Costa Rica has been a country, and it's easily accessed by paved major roads from San José, the Caribbean coast and other population centers. There is a taxi stop across from the bus terminal, and drivers will take you to the nearby lodges for US$5 to US$10.

BOAT

The small port has a regular service to the small ranching outpost of Trinidad just across the Río San Juan from Nicaragua. The five-hour trip to Trinidad departs at 12:30pm and returns the following morning at 5am (US$10 per person). There is one guesthouse in Trinidad where you can stay overnight. You can also arrange transportation anywhere along the river (seasonal conditions permitting) through independent boat captains. To get to the dock, make a right from the main road at Banco Nacional and follow it until it ends.

BUS

Right across from the park, the **bus terminal** (☎ 2233-4242; ⏱ 5am-7pm) sells tickets and stores backpacks for a few hours, but not overnight. Local buses run hourly between La Virgen and Puerto Viejo de Sarapiquí (US$1, 30 minutes) from 6am to 8:15pm.

Ciudad Quesada (Transportes Linaco) US$3, two hours, departs eight times daily from 4:40am to 6:30pm.

Guápiles (Empresarios Guapileños) US$2, one hour, departs 10 times daily from 5:30am to 5pm.

San José (Autotransportes Sarapiquí and Empresarios Guapileños) US$2.50, two hours, departs 5am, 5:30am, 7am, 8am, 11am, 1:30pm, 3pm and 5:30pm.

Estación Biológica La Selva

Not to be confused with Selva Verde Lodge in Chilamate, Estación Biológica La Selva (☎ 2524-0607; www.threepaths.co.cr; r per person incl meals from US$98; Ⓟ) is a working biological research station equipped with laboratories, experimental plots, a herbarium and an extensive library. The station is usually teeming with scientists and students researching the nearby private reserve. La Selva does welcome drop-ins, though it's best to phone ahead and reserve your accommodations. Rooms are simple but comfortable, and rates include guided hikes.

The area protected by La Selva is 16 sq km of premontane wet tropical rainforest, much of which is undisturbed. It's bordered to the south by the 476-sq-km Parque Nacional Braulio Carrillo, creating a protected area large enough to support a great diversity of life. More than 886 bird species have been recorded here, as well as 120 mammal species (including 70 species of bat and five species of big cat), 1850 species of vascular plant (especially from the orchid, philodendron, coffee and legume families) and thousands of insect species – with 500 types of ant alone.

La Selva is operated by the Organization for Tropical Studies (OTS; ☎ 2524-0607; www. ots.ac.cr), a consortium founded in 1963 to provide leadership in the education, research and wise use of tropical natural resources.

🏃 Activities

Reservations are required for three-hour **guided hikes** (US$32, departing 8:30am and 1pm daily) with a bilingual naturalist guide. You'll head across the hanging bridge and into 57km of well-developed jungle trails, some of which are wheelchair accessible. Unguided hiking is forbidden, although you'll be allowed to wander a bit after your guided tour. Make reservations for the popular guided bird-watching hikes, led at 5:45am and 7pm, depending on demand. Profits from these walks help to fund the research station.

No matter when you visit La Selva, it will probably be raining. Bring rain gear and footwear that's suitable for muddy trails. Insect repellent and a water bottle are also essential.

❶ Getting There & Away

Public buses between Puerto Viejo and Río Frío/Horquetas can drop you off 1km from the entrance to La Selva. It's about 4km from Puerto Viejo, where you can catch a taxi for around US$5 to US$7.

Horquetas & Around

South of Puerto Viejo de Sarapiquí, plantations line Hwy 4 and sprawl all the way to the marshes and mangroves of the Caribbean coast. To the west, the rugged hills of the Cordillera Central mark the northeastern boundary of Parque Nacional Braulio Carrillo. Most travelers on this scenic stretch of highway are either heading to the Caribbean coast or to the Central Valley. However, some are pulling off the road to visit one of the area's unique off-the-beaten-track destinations, such as the world-class botanical garden at Heliconia Island or the backyard frog habitats at Frog's Heaven.

About 12 smoothly paved kilometers from Puerto Viejo de Sarapiquí is the village of Horquetas, around which you'll find the turnoffs for Frog's Heaven, Heliconia Island and the other resorts. From Horquetas it's another 15km to Hwy 32, which connects San José to the Caribbean coast and bisects Parque Nacional Braulio Carrillo on the way to San José.

◉ Sights

Frog's Heaven
GARDENS

(Cielo de Ranas; ☑8891-8589, 2764-2724; www.frogsheaven.com; ⊙8am-8pm) The frogs hop free in this lovely tropical garden, which provides a perfect habitat for more than 20 species. On guided tours you're likely to see old favorites including the red-eyed tree frog and poison-dart frogs, as well as some lesser-known exotic amphibians, such as the translucent glass frog and the wrinkly Mexican tree frog. Come for the night tour to see a whole different frog world.

This place is also excellent for birding and – occasionally – spotting other creatures. Reserve at least a day ahead.

Heliconia Island
GARDENS

(☑2764-5220; www.heliconiaisland.com; self-guided/guided tours US$10/18; ⊙8am-5pm; ℗⛟) This self-proclaimed 'oasis of serenity' is a masterpiece of landscape architecture that is home to more than 80 varieties of heliconias, tropical flowers, plants and trees. The 2.3-hectare island overlooking the Río Puerto Viejois is also a refuge for 228 species of bird, including a spectacled owl who returns every year to raise her family. There are resident howler monkeys, river otters, sloths, and a few friendly dogs that will greet you upon arrival.

Dutch owners Henk and Carolien offer guided tours to show off the most memorable plants, including rare hybrids of heliconia found only on the island. They also own swatches of secondary forest on either side of the garden, which offers a wild forest buffer and attracts wildlife. The admission fee is waived for overnight guests, who stay in immaculate raised cabins with stone floors and breezy balconies (without/

with air-con US$78/90). Heliconia Island is about 5km north of Horquetas.

🛏 Sleeping & Eating

Sueño Azul Resort
RESORT $$$

(☑2764-1000; www.suenoazulresort.com; d standard/superior US$150/180) Sueño Azul has a stunning perch at the confluence of the Ríos Sarapiquí and San Rafael. The vast property has hiking trails, a suspension bridge, a canopy tour and a waterfall, as well as an enormous stable of gorgeous horses. Rooms are huge, with terracotta floors, log beds and river views. Adventure groups make up the majority of the clientele here.

Rara Avis
CABINA $$$

(☑2764-1111, 2200-4238; www.rara-avis.com; incl meals casitas per person US$70, s/d US$84/160) When they say remote, they mean remote. This private reserve, 13 sq km of high-altitude tropical rainforest, is accessible only to guests who make the three-hour tractor ride up a steep, muddy hill. Accommodations are rustic: there's no electricity, though the kerosene lamps and starry skies are unforgettable. Prices include all meals, transportation from Horquetas and two guided hikes per day.

The private reserve borders the eastern edge of Parque Nacional Braulio Carrillo and has no real dry season. Bird-watching here is excellent, with more than 350 documented species, while mammals including monkeys, coatis, anteaters and pacas are often seen. Since getting here is time-consuming and difficult, a two-night stay is recommended. You can also arrange to travel on horseback instead of by tractor, but you'll have to hike the last 3km yourself.

Península de Nicoya

Best Places to Eat

➡ Mamasa (p303)

➡ Green Papaya (p309)

➡ Koji's (p347)

➡ Playa de los Artistas (p341)

Most Beautiful Beaches

➡ Playa Conchal (p300)

➡ Playa Junquillal (p313)

➡ Playa Carrillo (p327)

➡ Playa San Miguel (p329)

➡ Playa Cocolito (p339)

Why Go?

Maybe you've come to the Península de Nicoya to sample the sapphire waters that peel left and right, curling into perfect barrels up and down the coast. Or perhaps you just want to hunker down on a pristine patch of sand and soak up some sun. By day, you might ramble down rugged roads, fording rivers and navigating ridges with massive coastal views. By night, you can spy on nesting sea turtles or take a midnight dip in the luxuriant Pacific. In between adventures, you'll find no shortage of boutique bunks, tasty kitchens and indulgent spas to shelter and nourish body and soul. Whether you come for the thrills or just to chill, the Nicoya Peninsula delivers. You'll find that the days (or weeks, or months) drift away on ocean breezes, disappearing all too quickly.

When to Go

➡ Northern Península de Nicoya has one of the driest climates in Costa Rica, although rainfall does peak during the green season of September and October, when swollen rivers make some roads impassable.

➡ September and October is when the peninsula is at its most lush: the air isn't nearly as dusty, the whales are migrating and prices are cheap. Yes, even wet season is glorious here.

Península de Nicoya Highlights

1 Catching the morning swell and relish afternoon *asanas* in **Nosara** (p318).

2 Fording rivers and navigating the coastal 4WD tracks between **Santa Teresa** (p344) and **Sámara** (p323).

3 Hiking to the tip of the peninsula at **Reserva Natural Absoluta Cabo Blanco** (p343).

4 Surfing luscious breaks at **Playas Grande** (p301) and **Negra** (p312).

5 Delighting your sweetheart with a romantic dinner at **Playa de los Artistas** (p341) in Montezuma.

6 Sitting beneath the palms at **Playa Carrillo** (p327) and watching the sun set.

7 Glimpsing the turtles on **Playa Grande** (p301) and at the **Refugio Nacional de Fauna Silvestre Ostional** (p322).

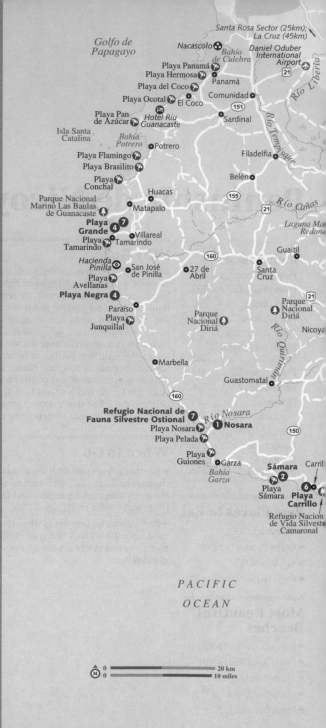

Santa Rosa Sector (25km); La Cruz (45km)

Golfo de Papagayo

Nacascolo
Bahía de Culebra
Daniel Oduber International Airport

Playa Panamá
Playa Hermosa
Panamá
21

Playa del Coco
Comunidad
Playa Ocotal
El Coco
151

Playa Pan de Azúcar
Hotel Riu Guanacaste
Sardinal

Isla Santa Catalina
Bahía Potrero
Potrero
Filadelfia

Playa Flamingo
Playa Brasilito
Belén
Playa Conchal
Huacas
155
Parque Nacional Marino Las Baulas de Guanacaste
Matapalo
21
Río Cañas
Playa Grande **7** **4**
Playa Tamarindo
Tamarindo
Villareal
Laguna Ma Redonda
160
Guaitil
Hacienda Pinilla
San José de Pinilla
27 de Abril
Santa Cruz
Playa Avellanas
Playa Negra **4**
Parque Nacional Diriá
21
Paraíso
Playa Junquillal
Parque Nacional Diriá
Nicoya
Río Quirimán
Marbella
Guastomatal
160
Refugio Nacional de Fauna Silvestre Ostional **7**
Río Nosara
150
Playa Nosara
1 **Nosara**
Playa Pelada
Playa Guiones
Garza
Sámara
Carril
Bahía Garza
Playa Sámara
Playa Carrillo **6**
2
Refugio Nacion de Vida Silvestre Camaronal

PACIFIC OCEAN

N
0 ———— 20 km
0 ———— 10 miles

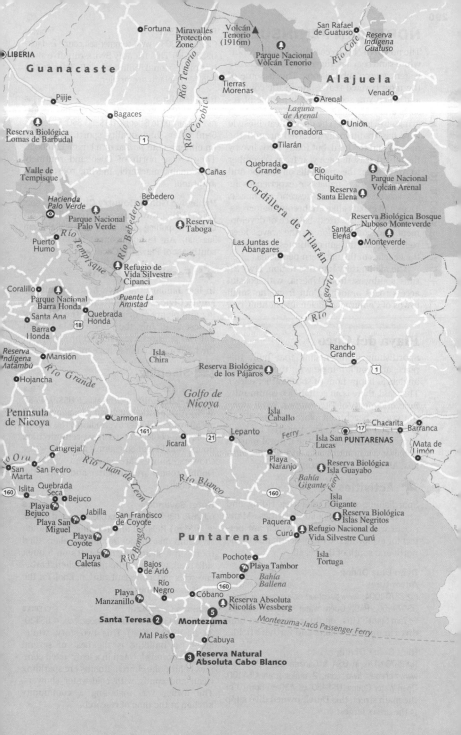

NORTHERN PENINSULA

The northern Nicoya coastline in a snapshot: white-sand beaches, rugged green hills, azure waters, stucco subdivisions. This is some of the most coveted real estate in the country, and when you zoom in, it's a jumble of resorts and retirement properties with a high gringo-to-Tico ratio. The Costa Rican lifestyle here has traditionally revolved around the harvest and the herd, but today Ticos live by the tourist season. Each year from December to April, when the snow falls on Europe and North America, Guanacaste experiences its dry season and tourists descend en masse. Ticos and expats alike are becoming increasingly aware of the tricky balance of development and conservation as the waves keep rolling in, and the sun continues to smile on the beaches of the northern peninsula.

The main artery into this region, Hwy 21, runs southwest from Liberia, with coastal access roads branching out from the small towns of Comunidad, Belén and Santa Cruz.

Playa del Coco

Sportfishing is the engine that built this place, and you'll mingle with the American anglers at happy hour (it starts rather early). That said, there is an actual Tico community here, and plenty of Tico tourists. Stroll along the grassy beachfront plaza at sunset and gaze upon the wide bay, sheltered by long, rugged peninsular arms, the natural marina bobbing with motorboats and fishing *pangas*. All will be right in your world.

🕴 Activities

Sportfishing, sailing, horseback riding and sea kayaking are popular activities. Many places will rent sea kayaks, which are perfect for exploring the rocky headlands to the north and south of the beach.

Deep Blue Diving

Adventures   DIVING, SNORKELING
(☑2670-1004; www.deepblue-diving.com; 2 tanks US$79-150, PADI Open Water Course US$415; ⊙7am-6pm) This outfitter runs two-tank dives in the local waters and further afield.

Rich Coast Diving   DIVING
(☑2670-0176, in USA & Canada 800-434-8464; www.richcoastdiving.com; 2 tanks from US$100, Open Water Course US$450; ⊙7:30am-6pm) On the main street, this Dutch-owned dive shop is the area's largest.

Summer Salt   DIVING
(☑2670-0308; www.summer-salt.com; 2 tanks US$80-110) This friendly Swiss-run dive shop has professional, bilingual staff. Trips to the Isla Murciélago are pricier.

Blue Marlin   SPORTFISHING
(☑2670-0707, 8828-8250; www.sportfishingblue-marlin.com; up to 6 people US$350-860; ⊙departs 6am) Offers high-quality sportfishing trips on either an 8m *panga* or a larger 12m boat. They cruise north of Coco and routinely hook mahi, mackerel, marlin, rooster fish and tuna.

Papagayo Golf & Country Club   GOLF
(☑2697-0169; www.papagayo-golf.com; 9/18 holes US$55/95, putting green US$4-6; ⊙6:30am-5pm Tue-Sun) An 18-hole course located 10km southeast of Playa del Coco.

🎊 Festivals & Events

In late January the town hosts a multiday Fiesta Cívica, with bullfights, rodeos, dancing and plenty of drinking. On the Saturday closest to 16 July, the Fiesta de la Virgen del Mar features a festive boat procession in the harbor and a horse pageant on the land.

🛏 Sleeping

Hotel M&M   HOTEL $
(☑2670-1212; s/d/tr incl breakfast US$27/47/67; 🅿🛜) A romantic beachfront hacienda with an all-wood balcony overlooking the boardwalk. Fan-cooled rooms have ceramic tiled floors, wood-beamed ceilings and cold-water showers. Singles are clean but cramped. Double rooms are far better and worth the extra dosh.

Hotel Savannah   HOTEL $
(☑2670-0367; www.hotelcocopalms.com; d US$50; 🅿❄🛜🐾) Relaxed and relaxing, this motel-style inn has basic but immaculate tiled rooms in a shady longhouse. It's on a quiet side road, with a communal kitchen, barbecue grills and a pleasant garden. Look for the giant monkey mural.

Cabinas Coco Azul   CABINAS $
(☑2670-0431; www.cabinascocoazul.co; d US$30-35, apt US$80; 🅿🛜) This two-story, white-and-brick building is the best of several budget *cabinas* located in a leafy gated complex behind the church. Rooms are sparkling clean and comfy with cold-water showers. The owner was installing a community kitchen at the time of research.

WORTH A TRIP

PARKS & RESERVES

Most of Nicoya's parks and reserves lie along the shoreline, with several stretching out to sea to protect marine turtles and their nesting sites.

Parque Nacional Barra Honda (p316) Best in the dry season; you can go spelunking in underground limestone caves.

Parque Nacional Marino Las Baulas de Guanacaste (p301) Crucial to the survival of the leatherback turtle, this park protects one of the turtle's major Pacific nesting sites.

Refugio Nacional de Fauna Silvestre Ostional (p322) Olive ridleys converge in *arribadas* (mass nestings) at Ostional.

Refugio Nacional de Vida Silvestre Camaronal (p328) This out-of-the-way refuge has good surf and protects the nesting grounds of four marine turtle species.

Refugio Nacional de Vida Silvestre Curú (p335) A privately owned reserve and an unexpected oasis of diverse landscapes.

Reserva Natural Absoluta Cabo Blanco (p343) Costa Rica's first protected wilderness area is at the peninsula's cape.

Pato Loco Inn   GUESTHOUSE **$$**
(☑ 2670-0145; www.patolocoinn.com; d incl breakfast US$58-78; P ❀ @ 🛜 🐾) Richard and Mary Cox offer a warm welcome to Playa del Coco, with a wide range of rooms, a friendly bar and the best American breakfast in town (think biscuits and gravy). Most of the rooms feature stenciling or thematic murals, hand-painted by Mary herself. Stop by for Monday or Friday happy hour to shoot the breeze with the expats.

Hotel Chantel   BOUTIQUE HOTEL **$$**
(☑ 2670-0389; www.hotelchantel.com; r/ste/apt incl breakfast US$99/110/125. P ❀ 🛜 🐾 🐾) Perched on a cliff overlooking the coast, this intimate hotel is a step up from the local lodgings. Eleven rooms have tasteful wood and wicker furniture, contemporary artwork on the walls, and private terraces with stunning vistas of Playa del Coco. The elegant infinity pool and the breezy rooftop restaurant share the same panoramic view.

It's a short drive from town: head west off the main road, just south of Flor de Itabo, and follow the signs.

Toro Blanco   HOTEL **$$**
(☑ 2670-1707; www.toroblancoresort.com; s/d US$50/80; P ❀ 🛜 🐾) This mustard-yellow, three-story colonial-style building surrounds a courtyard with a lovely swimming pool and swim-up bar. Apartments are outfitted with engraved headboards, wooden wardrobes, full kitchens, flat-screen TV and

private balcony or patio. A few steps from the beach, this midrange option offers terrific value.

Villa del Sol   HOTEL **$$**
(☑ 2670-0085, in Canada 866-793-9523, in USA 866-815-8902; www.villadelsol.com; La Chorrera; r incl breakfast US$65-75, apt US$100; P ❀ @ 🛜 🐾) About 1km north of the town center, this leafy, tranquil property attracts monkeys, iguanas and a good variety of birdlife, in addition to the happy travelers lounging on hammocks. The main building has stylish rooms with sunset-view balconies. In the back building, studio apartments (sleeping four) offer excellent value. Walk to the beach in five minutes or less.

Laura's House B&B   B&B **$$**
(☑ 2670-0751; www.laurashousecr.com; La Chorrera; s/d/tr/q incl breakfast US$52/68/79/90; P ❀ 🛜 🐾) Laura was just a kid when she opened this cheerful B&B, 100m north of the main drag and steps from the beach. For more than a decade, she has offered simple, spotless rooms and friendly, familiar service. The swings hanging from the shade tree are the perfect place to while away an afternoon with a book. Discounts for payment in cash.

Hotel La Puerta del Sol   HOTEL **$$$**
(☑ 2670-0195; www.lapuertadelsolcostarica.com; d incl breakfast US$113; P ❀ @ 🛜 🐾) A five-minute walk from town, this unpretentiously luxurious Mediterranean-inspired

hotel has two large suites and eight huge pastel-colored rooms with polished brick and concrete floors, king-sized beds and private terraces. The well-manicured grounds house a glorious pool, a trellis-shaded gym and an Italian restaurant.

Rancho Armadillo HOTEL $$$

(📞 2670-0108, 8336-9645; www.ranchoarmadillo.com; standard/deluxe incl breakfast US$204/244; 🅿️❄️🛜🏊) Near the entrance to town, this private estate is on a hillside about 600m off the main road (all paved), with ocean views to remind you where you are. It's set on 25 acres with plenty of wildlife, and the seven rooms are decorated with individually crafted furniture, hand-woven tapestries and local artwork. Self-catering gourmands will appreciate the fully equipped professional kitchen.

Cafe de Playa BOUTIQUE HOTEL $$$

(📞 2670-1319, 2670-1621; www.cafedeplaya.com; d incl breakfast US$250; 🅿️❄️🛜🏊) Elegant rooms are adorned with gallery-worthy contemporary art, boldly painted walls, beamed ceilings and marble baths. They surround a gorgeous circular tiled pool and tropical gardens. A stained wood boardwalk winds past a gourmet restaurant and down to the beach. It's a hot 15-minute hike north of the town center, but you might not feel the need to leave.

✖️ Eating

Congo CAFE $

(📞 2670-2135; www.costaricacongo.com; mains US$6-10; ⊗8am-8pm Mon-Sat, 8am-6pm Sun; 🅿️🛜🦎) Part cafe, part funky retail boutique, the interior is groovy with arched booths, rattan sofas and a deconstructed wood-and-granite coffee bar. All the espresso drinks are served, as well as an array of healthy sandwiches, salads and breakfasts.

Soda La Teresita SANDWICHES $

(📞 2670-0665; sandwiches US$3-10; ⊗6:30am-8:30pm) Located at the crossroads of the main drag and the beach, this place can't be beaten for people-watching in Coco. It's also your best bet for lunch, whether you're hankering for a *torta* (sandwich) or a traditional *casado* (set meal). Teresita also offers an array of breakfasts, as well as *ceviche* (seafood marinated in lemon or lime juice, garlic and seasonings) and other seafood dishes.

La Vida Loca AMERICAN $$

(📞 2670-0181; www.lavidalocabeachbar.com; mains US$9-12; ⊗11am-11pm) Across a creaky wooden footbridge on the south end of the beach is where you'll find this hangout, popular among gringos and Ticos alike. They specialize in US-style comfort food such as burgers, nachos, meat loaf, chili dogs, clam chowder and more. It's also the best bar in town, with pool tables, live music and good vibes.

Restaurante Donde Claudio y Gloria SEAFOOD $$

(📞 2670-0256; www.dondeclaudioygloria.com; mains US$9-15; ⊗8am-9pm) Founded by Playa del Coco pioneers Claudio and Gloria Rojas, this casual, beachfront seafood restaurant has been a local landmark since 1955. It's a must for seafood-lovers, with such interesting dishes as spicy mahi in an almond, raisin and white-wine sauce. Be warned: service can be painfully slow, but the solid jazz soundtrack will keep you buoyant.

Las Olas SEAFOOD $$

(📞 2670-2003; mains US$9-16; ⊗11am-10pm) Just north of the cramped commercial vortex on the main road, this is a dressed-up seafood *soda* (inexpensive eatery) with tablecloths, bamboo design accents, and recommended fresh seafood in the kitchen. The lounge area is quite cool, featuring molded concrete booths and dripping candles, whirling fans and a bubbling fountain.

La Dolce Vita ITALIAN $$

(📞 2670-1384; www.ladolcevitacostarica.com; La Chorerra; mains US$10-18; ⊗8am-10pm) Set in the Pueblito Sur development about 500m north of the main drag, this is the local expat choice for wood-fired pizza in Playa del Coco. The restaurant is lovingly set in a brick courtyard around a gurgling fountain, sprinkled with candlelit tables. It also does a range of pastas, unique preparations of seafood and traditional grills.

Citron FUSION $$$

(📞 2670-0942; www.citroncoco.com; mains US$15-20; ⊗5:30-10pm Mon-Sat) The contemporary menu features fresh ingredients and innovative preparations, including a few enticing specials from the wok (think sea bass poached with scallions, soy sauce and sesame oil). Save room for a decadent Mediterranean dessert. Despite the shopping-mall setting, you can dine in the sophisticated, minimalist dining room or on an open-air deck, surrounded by pochote trees.

Cafe de Playa
ITALIAN $$$

(☎ 2670-1621; www.cafedeplaya.com; mains US$15-25; ⊙8am-9pm; 🛜) Take a stroll north of town and treat yourself to a delightful, delicious meal at this romantic beachside restaurant. The fare is mostly Mediterranean, with a few more exotic flavors on the menu for good measure. Fresh and tropical seafood are prominently featured. Bonus: the best selection of wine on the peninsula.

🍷 Drinking & Nightlife

Tiki Coco Place
BAR

(☎ 2670-0711; www.tikicocoplace.com; ⊙10am-11pm; 🛜) Get a front-row seat for the ongoing beach volleyball match or, even better, a killer sunset. This new open-air beach bar offers tasty American fare, ice-cold beers and standard fruity cocktails, not to mention service with a smile.

La Vida Loca
BAR

(☎ 2670-0181; ⊙11am-2am) Keep the party moving at La Vida Loca, with live music on some weekends.

Zi Lounge
CLUB

(☎ 2670-1978; ⊙11:30am-2:30am; 🛜) A snazzy night spot, trying oh so hard to be Ibiza sleek while stuck in a beer-drinking fishing port. Still, this bass-thumping outdoor mosh pit draped in bold tapestries is not unattractive. Thursday is ladies' night.

ⓘ Information

The police station and a small post office are southeast of the plaza by the beach. The few people arriving at Playa del Coco by boat will find the Immigration Office across from Deep Blue Diving Adventures.

BAC Bank (Pacífico Plaza) 24hr ATM.

BCR Bank (⊙9am-4pm Mon-Fri) The ATM is operational from 5am to 10pm.

Main Post Office (⊙8am-noon & 1-5:30pm) Located near the entrance to town next to Flor de Itabo hotel.

ⓘ Getting There & Away

BUS

All buses arrive and depart from the main terminal next to Immigration.

Liberia US$1, one hour, departs hourly from 5am to 7pm.

San José (Pulmitan) US$8, five hours, departs 4am, 8am and 2pm.

CAR

Note that there's no gas station in town; the nearest one is in Sardinal, about 7.5km inland from Playa del Coco.

TAXI

A taxi from Liberia to Playa del Coco costs US$50. Taxis between Playa del Coco and Playas Hermosa or Ocotal will cost about US$20.

Playa Hermosa

Playa Hermosa, or 'beautiful beach', is a lovely, wide and languid sheltered bay, framed by headlands and sprinkled with coconut palms and olive trees. Although it's only 5.5km (by road) north of Playa del Coco, and development is springing up rapidly along this entire coastline, Hermosa feels more remote.

🏃 Activities

Diving Safaris
DIVING

(☎ 2672-1259; www.costaricadiving.net; ⊙7am-5pm) Bobbie Jo and her daughters will show you the best of underwater Costa Rica. Boats leave to local dive sites every morning. Trips also go to Catalinas and Bat Islands, with hopes of sighting manta rays (especially during the dry season) and bull sharks.

Papagayo Gulf Sport Fishing & Surf
SPORTFISHING

(☎ 2670-1564; www.papagayofishing.typepad.com) Captain Mauricio and first mate Daniel are local anglers keen to share their passion for fishing. They will take you on their 8m fishing boat, *Don Manuel*, for coastal fishing, snorkeling and/or surfing. Split-charters available.

🛌 Sleeping

Cabinas La Casona
CABINA $

(☎ 2672-0025; gaviotalouise@hotmail.com; d/apt US$45/90; 🅿 ❄ 🛜) One block away from the beach, seven cozy *cabinas* have whitewashed rooms with metal furnishings and hot-water bathrooms. Two newer apartments are snazzier, with tile floors and attractive wood furniture. All rooms include kitchenettes, making this an ideal spot for self-caterers.

Congo's Hostel & Camping
HOSTEL $

(☎ 2672-1168; www.congoshostel.com; dm incl breakfast US$12-15; 🅿 ❄ 🛜) This decent, friendly budget option is on the main drag into town, just one block from the beach.

It's a ramshackle place with hammocks, offering secure parking and an open-air communal kitchen. The four-bed dorm rooms have metal beds with worn mattresses and a bathroom in each. Breakfast is coffee and bread.

Hotel Villa Bel Mar   HOTEL $$
(☑ 2672-0276; www.sevillaresort.es; d incl breakfast US$80-90; P ✳ ☎ ☀) A sweet, Spanish-owned beachfront inn with a pool that leads to a lawn that leads to the sand. Rooms are super clean and bright with colorful paint jobs and whimsical bathroom tile. Pay more for an ocean view, or enjoy the vista from the breezy restaurant.

Hotel El Velero   HOTEL $$
(☑ 2672-0036, 2672-1017; www.costaricahotel. net; d US$78; P ✳ ☎ ☀) Just steps from the beach, this resort hotel has 22 spacious rooms decorated with woodwork, bamboo beds with colorful bedspreads, wicker ceiling fans, and granite washbasins. Ask for a seafront room on the 2nd floor for maximum views. The attached restaurant hosts a biweekly barbecue dinner (Wednesday and Saturday) that is good fun.

La Gaviota Tropical   HOTEL $$$
(☑ 2672-0011; www.lagaviotatropical.com; ste US$158-181; P ✳ ☎ ☀) This brand new facility is essentially a vertical hotel, so that all five huge suites – fully equipped and impeccably decorated – are facing the glorious sea. Climb to the top floor to cool off in the small but spectacular infinity pool. Downstairs, you can enjoy an excellent meal at Roberto's restaurant or walk a few steps to the sand.

Hotel La Finisterra   BOUTIQUE HOTEL $$$
(☑ in USA 877-413-1139; www.lafinisterra.com; d incl breakfast US$170; P ✳ @ ☎ ☀) At the southern end of Playa Hermosa, this stylish boutique hotel has only 10 rooms and suites, all with ocean views. Original artwork and big picture windows enhance the interiors. Outside, the swimming pool, Jacuzzi and landscaped patios all enjoy a fabulous panorama of surf, sand and sky.

Bosque del Mar   HOTEL $$$
(☑ 2672-0046; www.hotelplayahermosa.com; s/d/ tr/q ste US$200/226/260/294; P ✳ @ ☎ ☀) ⦿ Notched into the southern headland, this lovely all-suite hotel offers a stunning location. Guests relish the gorgeous gardens, private terraces and spectacular, modern design elements. Pay more for beachfront suites, which allow you to enjoy the view of the waves while soaking in your own open-air Jacuzzi. Get here via the first beach access road.

✖ Eating & Drinking

Supplies are available at **Mini Super Cenizaro**, on the paved road into town.

Aqua Sport   COSTA RICAN $$
(☑ 2672-0050; mains US$9-23; ⊙ 10am-10pm; ☎) This colorful, fun beach bar is an excellent place to pass an evening feasting on burgers or fish tacos and swilling beers. Or sample the Peruvian specialties, such as *lomo saltado* (salted pork), *diabla* octopus (spicy with tomato sauce) and, of course, *ceviche*. Hammocks hang from the rafters and Adirondack chairs sit right on the sand. *¡Que rico!*

Ginger   MEDITERRANEAN $$
(☑ 2672-0041; www.gingercostarica.com; small plates US$5-12; ⊙ 5-10pm Tue-Sun; ✐) If you're driving north, look toward the hills on the right and you'll see this stunner cantilevered into the trees. The chic ambience complements a gourmet list of Asian- and Mediterranean-inspired tapas, fresh-fruit cocktails and a decent wine list.

Roberto's   COSTA RICAN $$
(☑ 2672-0011; mains US$9-18; ⊙ 8am-9pm; ☎) If you want to sip fruity cocktails while you watch the sun drop into the sea, Roberto's is the place for you. For dinner, there is plenty of local seafood and other Tico specialties. Or snack on burgers and sandwiches when you come in from the beach for lunch. It's not the most complicated food you'll ever eat, but it doesn't need to be.

❶ Getting There & Away

BUS
Buses to Liberia and San José depart from the main road on the northern end of the beach and make a stop in Sardinal.

Liberia (La Pampa) US$1, 1¼ hours, departs eight times from 4:50am to 5:30pm.

San José (Tralapa) US$9, six hours, departs 5am and 3:30pm.

CAR
If you're driving from Liberia, take the signed turnoff to Playa del Coco. The entire road is paved.

North of Hermosa, the main coastal road leads to the beaches along the Gulf of Papagayo. Playa Panama is right in the middle of the gulf, with mangroves on one side and a placid bay that feels almost like a lake. In between are the rustic Playa Bonita and Playa Buena, which you can access with your own wheels and a bit of ingenuity.

TAXI

A taxi from Liberia costs about US$40 and a taxi from Coco about US$15.

Playa Ocotal

There isn't an actual town here – just a few vacation rentals and an attractive resort. That's one reason it feels like a rustic outpost amid the condo-mania of the northern peninsula. The beach is gray and wooded, and the northernmost corner is quite picturesque. The water is warm and placid. It's about 4km southwest of Playa del Coco by paved road, so it's worth a trip simply to eat at Father Rooster's.

🏃 Activities

Rocket Frog Divers   DIVING
(📞 2670-1589; www.scuba-dive-costa-rica.com; 2 tanks US$80-135; ⏰ 7:30am-6:30pm) This awesome upstart dive shop on the Los Almendros property hits 22 local dive sites and motors out to the Catalina Islands to dive with mantas. The 11m, purpose-designed *Pacific Express* promises to make it to distant dive sites in half the time of other vessels.

🛏 Sleeping & Eating

Los Almendros de Ocotal   APARTMENT $$
(📞 2670-1744; www.losalmendrosrentals.com; studio/apt/villa US$82/180/237; 🅿✳@🛜❄) Perched on the hillside just above the beach, these studios and apartments are a great option for divers, beach bums and self-caterers. Studios sleep two, apartments sleep four and villas sleep six. The fancier units have a private pool and terrace.

Father Rooster Bar & Grill   PUB $$
(📞 2670-1246; www.fatherrooster.com; mains US$12-16; ⏰ 11am-10pm; 🛜) This colorful gastropub by the sea serves up a good variety of grilled and Tex-Mex dishes. You cannot beat the location, especially if you sit in the rockers on the shaded wooden terrace or at tables under the palms sunk into the sand.

Beaches South of Playa Ocotal

Although they're lined up in a row, Playas Danta, Pan de Azúcar, Potrero, Flamingo, Brasilito and Conchal have relatively little in common. The beaches range from gray to white sand to crushed seashells, with a wide variety of development along the way.

Coming from the north, it's tempting to take the 'road' from Sardinal to Potrero. Keep in mind there's a reason why locals call this route the 'Monkey Trail.' The first 8km of gravel road leading to the small town of Nuevo Colón is fine, but the second half is pretty brutal, and should only be tackled in

---

DIVERS DO IT DEEPER

The northern peninsula is one of the best and most easily accessible dive destinations in the country. Dives are made either around volcanic rock pinnacles near the coast, or from a boat further off at Isla Santa Catalina (about 20km to the southwest) or Isla Murciélago (40km to the northwest, near the tip of Península Santa Elena). Visibility varies greatly (9m to 15m, and sometimes up to 20m), and the water can be chilly.

There is no colorful hard coral that you would see at a reef, but the sites make up for it with abundant marine life. Plenty of turtles and pelagics meander through, including mantas, sharks and whales. You'll be lost in huge schools of smaller tropical fish. These waters are sometimes home to humpback whales, who can be heard underwater during calving season (January to March) and seen during migration season (June and July).

Isla Santa Catalina and Isla Murciélago both host migrant manta rays from December to late April, and Murciélago is also known for its regular sightings of resident bull sharks. Divers also head to Narizones, which is a good deep dive (about 27m), while Punta Gorda is an easy descent for inexperienced divers.

If you haven't been scuba diving before, consider taking a 'Discovery Course,' which costs about US$145. If you're interested in getting your Open Water Diver certification, which allows you to dive anywhere in the world, a three- to four-day course is about US$420.

dry season with a 4WD. The Monkey Trail begins 5km west of El Coco; turn right at the Castrol Oil sign and follow the signs for **Congo Trail Canopy Tour** (2666-4422; US$65; 8am-5pm). At the 'T' intersection in Nuevo Colón, turn left, bear left at the fork and continue for 5km until you reach Congo Trail Canopy. From there, it's a hair-raising 6km drive to Bahía Potrero.

To avoid the rough roads, return to the main peninsular highway from El Coco, then head south through Filadelfia and on to Belén (a distance of 18km), from where a paved road heads 25km west to Huacas. Take the road leading north until you hit the ocean in Brasilito. If you turn right and head north, you'll pass Playa Flamingo and Bahía Potrero before reaching Playa Pan de Azúcar. If you make a left instead and head south, you will end up at Playa Conchal. If you're into sea kayaking, the proximity of the beaches to one another makes for some great day trips.

Bahía Potrero

Several undeveloped beaches are strung along this low-key bay. The black-sand beach is Playa Prieta, while the gorgeous white-sand beach is Playa Penca, where stand-up paddle (SUP) boarders ply the sheltered turquoise bay toward gleaming offshore islets. Further south is the more developed 'town' beach, Playa Potrero.

There's a small fishing *pueblo* at Potrero, just beyond the northern end of the eponymous beach. The bus line ends here, so you won't see the weekend rush found at Brasilito.

Sleeping

Hotel Isolina   HOTEL $$
(2654-4333; www.isolinabeach.com; d/tr/q incl breakfast from US$80/90/102; P✳@🛜🏊) Surrounded by tropical gardens, these attractive yellow buildings are a comfortable and affordable option, with special amenities to welcome families. Simple rooms have plain wood furniture and whitewashed walls; pay more for an in-room kitchenette. At the north end of Playa Potrero, it's a short walk to Playa Penca, so that's a two-fer.

Cabinas Christina   CABINA $$
(2654-4006; www.cabinascristina.com; d with/without kitchen US$68/57; P✳🛜🏊) The cheapest accommodations in town, these simple *cabinas* are scattered under a lovely palm-grove garden. It's about 200m from the beach in Surfside.

Bahía del Sol   RESORT $$$
(2654-4671; www.bahiadelsolhotel.com; d/ste incl breakfast from US$180/275; P✳@🛜🏊) With a prime beachfront location at Playa Potrero, this luxurious resort gets high marks for four-star laid-back elegance. Large, tropically-themed rooms surround a garden with hammocks, offering easy access to the onsite outdoor spa. Out front, the lawn leads to a beach peppered with *palapas* (thatched shelters).

Eating & Drinking

Shack   AMERICAN $
(2654-6038; mains US$5-17; 8am-11pm; P🛜) Set beneath a stilted tin roof twirling with ceiling fans, this fabulous diner is Potrero's favorite spot to grab a bite. Come for breakfast when homemade bagels and sausages are served. Lunch and dinner feature Tex-Mex flavor, but it does lobster rolls and pizzas too. Bonus: live music.

Las Brisas Bar & Grill   COSTA RICAN $
(2654-4047; mains US$5-12; 11am-10pm) Just off the northwest corner of the soccer field in Potrero, this popular beachfront bar has been a local favorite since 1950. Villagers pack the joint nightly for *bocas* (appetizers), beers and brilliant sunsets. There is a weekly beach party on Wednesday nights.

La Perla   AMERICAN $
(2654-4500; mains US$5-12; 4pm-late; 🛜) You need to know La Perla, as it serves as the landmark by which all directions are given (next to La Perla, 300m south of La Perla etc). You might also want to know about its highly lauded Friday-night rib dinners. Live music, bar games and good-old-fashioned comfort food keep the expat community happy.

Getting There & Away

BUS
Buses begin their route in Potrero on the southeast corner of the soccer field. Many (but not all!) buses to Playa Flamingo continue on to Potrero.

San José (Tralapa) US$11, six hours, departs 9am and 2pm.
Santa Cruz US$2, two hours, departs 11 times per day from 5am to 10pm.

CAR
The drive from here to Playa Pan de Azúcar is one of the most scenic stretches of paved road in all of northern Costa Rica.

WORTH A TRIP

PLAYA PAN DE AZÚCAR

Although buses stop at Potrero, travelers with their own ride can head 3km north on a paved road to 'Sugar-Bread Beach,' which derives its name from the strip of white sand that's protected at both ends by rocky headlands. This is one of the most scenic stretches of road in all of northern Costa Rica, as dry rugged cliffs sheer down into aquamarine coves sheltered by offshore islets. Difficult access and the lack of cheap accommodations create an atmosphere of total seclusion, and the ocean here is calm, clear and perfect for snorkeling.

Luxury at the **Hotel Sugar Beach** (☎2654-4242; www.sugar-beach.com; d incl breakfast from US$155; P❋@⬚⬚) ⬚ is simple and understated. The 22 lovely rooms are entered via elaborately hand-carved wooden doors. Deluxe rooms are slightly larger and have stunning ocean views. But the real reason you're here is to slow down and linger on an isolated beach. Overheard in the lobby: 'Now this is vacation.'

Playa Flamingo

Anytime a once-pristine slice of paradise sprouts McMansions and condos and gets stitched up with a network of roads, there is a tendency to point fingers and raise hell about what was and what now is. And, yes, Flamingo does feel like the developers won. But that does not change the fact that this sugary, postcard-worthy white sand and shell beach is glorious. Kissed by a serene blue sea with the rugged keys of the Catalinas floating off in the distance, it attracts a local Tico scene along with package tourists. Nose the air if you must, but why not enjoy the place?

⊁ Activities

Flamingo Adventures　　　ADVENTURE SPORTS
(☎8704-1685; www.flamingoadventures.com) This one-stop adventure outfitter in La Plaza mall can get you into all sorts of action. Think: horseback, ATV, surf, kayak, fishing and much more.

🛏 Sleeping & Eating

Mariner Inn　　　INN $
(☎2654-4081; www.marinerinn.com; d US$34-39, q US$45, ste US$68; P❋@⬚⬚) Overlooking the harbor, this old-school inn is an incredible deal. Rooms are a bit old, but not too shabby, with lovely ceramic tile floors and a fresh coat of paint, and the dark wood beds are IKEA chic. Formerly a sailor's hang, the bar is fantastic.

Marie's　　　DINER $
(☎2654-4136; www.mariesrestaurantincostarica. com; mains US$6-16; ⊙6:30am-9:30pm) In the La Plaza complex, Marie's is an upscale *soda* set under a thatched *palapa* roof. Daily specials feature the freshest seafood of the day, but you'll also find filling favorites like steak dinners, pork chops and chicken and rice.

Tubla　　　ITALIAN $$
(☎2654 4085; mains US$9-18; ⊙11am-10pm Mon-Sat; ⬚⬚⬚) Flamingo's favorite place for thin-crust wood-fired pizza, tried and true. Oven-baked lasagna and eggplant parmesan also come highly recommended. It's a friendly, family-run place that knows how to satisfy its hungry customers, starting with the free mozzarella appetizer for dine-in guests.

Angelina's　　　SEAFOOD $$
(☎2654-4839; www.angelinasplayaflamingo.com; lunch mains US$9-14, dinner mains US$13-28; ⊙11:30am-10pm) Relatively formal for Costa Rica, Angelina's offers fine dining in a breezy, open-air setting. Innovative seafood preparations feature tropical fruits and local flavors. Frugal travelers can feast on thin-crust pizzas with unique toppings or delectable pasta dishes, which come in half-portions.

❶ Getting There & Away

BUS

Buses depart from the traffic circle near the entrance of town and travel via Brasilito. Schedules change often, so ask locally about departure times as well as the best place on the road to wait for the bus.

Liberia (La Pampa) US$2, two hours, departs 5am, 12:30pm and 4pm.

San José (Tralapa) US$11, six hours, departs 9am and 2pm.

Santa Cruz US$2, one hour, departs 15 times per day from 5am to 10pm.

Undiscovered Nicoya

When it comes to beautiful beaches, Península de Nicoya is blessed richly indeed. Notoriety and development are not shared equally here, which means there are plenty of hidden nooks, secluded coves and pristine paradises that remain unexploited.

Playa Penca

Playa Penca (p296) is the kind of unexpected find that appears out of nowhere. A gleaming jewel of a beach that's immediately captivating.

Playas San Miguel & Coyote

Too often overlooked, this pair of virgin beaches (p329) has a certain rustic elegance, and nesting olive ridley turtles bring eco gravitas.

Playa Carrillo

White sand framed by granite, backed by jungle. What's not to love? Carrillo (p327) can be busy with Ticos on weekends and holidays, but otherwise it's empty and sweet.

Playa Pan de Azúcar

A stretch of jaw-dropping raw coastal beauty, a jigsaw of rugged cliffs and pristine coves (p297).

Playa Junquillal

Beachcombing meets the wilderness at this stunning and mostly deserted beach with a 200-hectare estuary just beyond (p313).

Getting There

All the best places are hard to get to. You can't just take a direct flight to paradise, you have to work for it. In Costa Rica, that usually means switching to 4WD and driving over some brutally bumpy, rough and rugged roads. Hang on tight and embrace the adventure: it's worth the effort to escape the crowds and discover your own secret spot.

1. Horse riding, Playa Carrillo 2. Fording a river, Península de Nicoya 3. Playa Carrillo

Playa Brasilito

Unlike the other touristy towns along this stretch, Brasilito feels like an authentic *pueblo*, complete with town square, beachfront soccer pitch, pink-washed *iglesia* (church) and friendly Tico community. All of which makes up for the beach, which has its (much) betters on either side. Still, it's just a short stroll along the sea to sugary Conchal.

🛏 Sleeping

Tropical Fun Cabinas   CABINA $
(✆ 2654-5519; www.diversiontropical.com; s/d/tr US$37/43/49; P❄✿🏠☕) Here's an outstanding deal. Tiled rooms are clean but cramped, with upstairs rooms giving a glimpse of the ocean (which is 300m away). Guests have free use of snorkel gear, while kayaks and mountain bikes are available for rental. Communal facilities (aka the 'Fun Zone') include an outdoor kitchen and grill, book exchange, board games and darts.

Hotel Brasilito   HOTEL $$
(✆ 2654-4237; www.brasilito.com; d/tr/q from US$50/60/70; P❄✿🏠) On the beach side of the plaza, this recommended hotel offers simple, clean rooms with wood floors and ceiling fans, lined up along a wide balcony. Sea-view rooms are a little more, but worth the splurge. Otherwise, the patio's hammocks are ideal for soaking up the sunset.

Hotel y Restaurante Nany   HOTEL $$
(✆ 2654-4320; www.hotelnany.net; s/d US$50/60; P❄@🏠☕) Set well back from the road and shrouded in mango and palm trees, this impressive Tico-run property offers good value. The spacious rooms, painted in cheerful tropical colors, face an enticing saltwater pool. The restaurant is also recommended.

Conchal Hotel   HOTEL $$
(✆ 2654-9125; www.conchalcr.com; d incl breakfast US$96-120; P❄@🏠☕) This bougainvillea- and palm-dappled lodge is a sweet retreat. Spacious rooms are fitted with unique design touches, such as beamed ceilings and wrought-iron furniture. Enjoy the lovely gardens while lounging poolside or from the privacy of your patio. A simple but scrumptious continental breakfast is served at the Papaya Restaurant (which is also recommended for other meals).

🍴 Eating & Drinking

★**Pollo Tropical**   COSTA RICAN $
(✆ 2654-5676; mains US$5-12; ⊙ 11am-9pm) You can't miss this roadside stand, painted mustard-yellow and often crowded with patrons lined up at the self-serve window. It doesn't look like much, but it is. While namesake chicken is indeed succulent, this place also does delicious seafood and other traditional dishes, all served with homemade dipping sauces. Don't miss the refreshing house 'Arnold Palmer' with homemade lemonade.

Papaya Restaurant   SEAFOOD, VEGETARIAN $
(✆ 2654-9125; www.conchalcr.com; mains US$6-18; ⊙ 7am-10pm Thu-Tue; 🏠🍴) Vegetarians and seafood lovers, rejoice! For the former, there are all-day breakfasts, power salads and tofu curries. For the latter, there are seafood salads, fresh grilled fish and jumbo shrimp. Come during the day for big burritos and flatbread sandwiches or come at night for fancier fare. There's also *típica* (typical Costa Rican food) if that's what you're craving. The restaurant is at the Conchal Hotel.

Don Brasilito's   COSTA RICAN
(✆ 2654-5310; bocas US$3-5; ⊙ 5pm-midnight; 🏠) Set a block north of the square, this massive dive is popular with the gritty old-school tourist set who descend from early afternoon. The wall-less interior offers ample seating.

ℹ Getting There & Away

Buses to and from Playa Flamingo travel through Brasilito. There is a bus ticket office at the north end of Brasilito – look for the blue house with the sign for **Tralapa Agencia** (⊙ 8am-noon & 1-6pm Mon & Wed-Sat, 8am-noon & 1-3pm Sun).

Playa Conchal

Just 1km south of Brasilito is Playa Conchal, a gorgeous stretch of sea and sand backed by palms. Conchal rates among the most beautiful beaches in Costa Rica. The name comes from the billions of *conchas* (shells) that wash up on the beach and are gradually crushed into coarse sand. The shallows drift from an intense turquoise to sea-foam green deeper out, a rarity on the Pacific coast. If you have snorkeling gear, this is the place to use it.

On weekends, the beach is often packed with locals, tourists and countless vendors, but on weekdays during low season, Playa Conchal can be pure paradise. The further south you stroll, the wider, sweeter and more spectacular the beach becomes.

The easiest way to reach Conchal is to simply walk 15 minutes down the beach from Playa Brasilito. You can also drive along the sandy beach road, though you'll be charged US$2 to park.

Playa Grande

Playa Grande is a wide, gorgeous beach, famous among conservationists and surfers alike. By day, the offshore winds create steep and powerful waves, especially at high tide. By night, an ancient cycle continues, as leatherback sea turtles bearing clutches of eggs follow the ocean currents back to their birthplace. The beach stretches for about 5km from the Tamarindo estuary, around a dome rock – with tide pools and superb surf fishing – and onto equally grand Playa Ventanas. The water is exquisite: warm, clear and charged with dynamic energy. Even confident swimmers should obey those riptide signs, as people have drowned here.

Since 1991, Playa Grande has been part of the Parque Nacional Marino Las Baulas de Guanacaste, which protects one of the most important leatherback nesting areas in the world. During the day, the beach is free and open to all, which is a good thing as the breaks off Playa Grande are fast, steep and consistent. At night, however, it is only possible to visit the beach on a guided tour, to ensure that nesting cycles continue unhindered.

◉ Sights

**Parque Nacional Marino
Las Baulas de Guanacaste** PARK
(☑ 2653-0470; admission incl tour US$25; ⊙ 8am-noon & 1-5pm, tours 6pm-2am) Playa Grande is considered one of the world's most important nesting areas for the *baula* (leatherback turtle). The park encompasses the entire beach and adjacent land (700 hectares), along with 220 sq km of ocean. In the evenings from October to March, rangers lead tours for visitors to witness this amazing cycle of life.

The ecosystem is primarily composed of mangrove swamp, ideal for caiman and crocodile, as well as numerous bird species, including the beautiful roseate spoonbill. But the main attraction is the nesting of the world's largest species of turtle, which can weigh in excess of 400kg.

Nesting season is from October to March. It's fairly common to see turtles lay their eggs here on any given night, but it may not be a leatherback. Chances of seeing one of these giants hover around 10%, while you are 95% sure to see a green or black turtle.

The leatherback is critically endangered and, despite increased conservation efforts, fewer leatherbacks are nesting on Playa Grande each year. In an effort to protect the dwindling population, park rangers collect eggs and incubate them to increase their chances of survival. Even so, sea turtles must hatch on the beach and enter the water by themselves, otherwise memory imprinting does not occur, and the hatchlings will never return to their birthplace to nest. It's estimated that only 10% of hatchlings survive to adulthood, though leatherbacks can live more than 50 years, and females lay multiple clutches of eggs during a single nesting season.

The park office is by the northern entrance to Playa Grande. Reservations for turtle-watching can be made up to seven days in advance. Many hotels and tourist agencies in Tamarindo also book tours that include transportation, as well as park admission and a guided tour.

The show kicks off anytime after 9pm. (Be prepared to wait. It could be a very long night – but well worth it.) Tourists are not allowed on the beach until the turtles have made it to dry sand. Guards with two-way radios will alert your guide, who will accompany you to a designated viewing area. Photography, filming or lights of any kind are prohibited to protect the turtles. Over the span of one to two hours, you can watch as the turtle digs its nest, lays about 80 to 90 shiny silver eggs and then buries them in the sand (while grunting and groaning).

🏃 Activities

Surfing is most people's motivation for coming to Playa Grande, and it is indeed spectacular.

Frijoles Locos Surf & Spa   SURFING
(☏8354-2044; www.frijoleslocos.com; boards per hour US$10-20, lessons per hour US$30; ☉9am-5pm) An all-purpose surf shop where you can rent surfboards and sign up for lessons. Afterward, you can recover with a deep tissue massage or other spa treatments. This place also rents just about everything you need to guarantee a great day at the beach, including bikes, snorkel gear, body boards and shade tents. Enjoy!

Playa Grande Surf Camp   SURFING
(☏8870-4164; www.playagrandesurfcamp.com; board rental per day US$15-20) Gerry and his cohorts rent short or long boards, and show you how to ride 'em.

Playa Grande Surf School   SURFING
(☏2653-0952; www.micasahostel.com; board rental per day US$15, lessons per person US$40) Based out of Mi Casa Hostel, this well-run surf school offers board rentals and 90-minute lessons.

🛏 Sleeping & Eating

Hotels are signposted from the main road into Playa Grande. Bring a flashlight for walking around at night.

Playa Grande Surf Camp   CABINA $
(☏8870-4164; www.playagrandesurfcamp.com; s/d/q US$35/45/60, surf package US$100; P❄🤖🔌) This great budget option has three thatched A-frame *cabinas* with private porches and hammocks, just steps from the beach. There's also two breezy elevated *cabinas* that sleep four. Sign up for the surf package, which includes bed, board and lessons.

Playa Grande Inn   INN $
(☏2653-0719; www.playagrandeinn.com; r incl breakfast US$50; P❄🤖🔌) Rickety rooms and super-friendly service are the hallmarks of this old standby. The handsome hardwood hotel has nine clean, cramped rooms and a cool restaurant and bar area with paper lanterns. Everyone raves about RAW, the onsite juice and smoothie bar.

★ La Marejada Hotel   BOUTIQUE HOTEL $$
(☏2653-0594, in USA & Canada 800-559-3415; www.hotelswell.com; r incl breakfast US$79; ❄🔌🤖) Hidden behind a bamboo fence, this stylish nest is a gem. The eight elegantly understated rooms have stone tile floors, rattan and wooden furnishings, and queen beds. Owners Gail and Carli are at-

tentive to every need: if you treat yourself to an in-house massage, perhaps after a day of surfing, Carli will personally wring out all of your kinks. The attached restaurant is also recommended.

El Manglar & Mi Casa Hostel   VILLA, HOSTEL $$
(☏2653-0952; www.micasahostel.com; dm/r/villa US$15/40/70; P@🔌) Near the southern end of the beach this funky, friendly faux-dobe villa property offers a room to suit every budget. All categories of rooms are quite smart, with fresh paint and sturdy wood furnishing. The villas offer particularly good value, complete with king-sized beds, kitchen, living area and private patio. The accommodations surround lush grounds in the Palm Beach Estates neighborhood.

Rip Jack Inn   INN $$$
(☏2653-0480, in USA 800-808-4605; www.ripjackinn.com; d from US$102; P❄@🤖🔌) Named for two canine amigos, this comfy, convivial inn has a handful of rooms that are clean, modern and artfully painted, each featuring a small patio with a hammock. In addition to a place to lay your head, Rip Jack has a yoga *shala* with daily classes, surf gear for rent and an amazing 'treetop' restaurant.

The restaurant's menu features delicacies such as sugar-cane-skewered jumbo shrimp in papaya ginger sauce, mahi slathered in mango lime sauce, and flank steak on the grill. Even the burgers are masterful. It's easily the best kitchen on the *playa*.

Hotel Cantarana   INN $$$
(☏2653-0486; www.hotel-cantarana.com; Palm Beach Estates; s/d US$107/124) This is a lovely, intimate inn nestled into the semi-gated Palm Beach Estates neighbourhood. The five spacious rooms each have a private terrace overlooking the glittering pool and gorgeous gardens. A highlight is the restaurant, set on the 2nd-floor terrace amid the treetops. Open for breakfast and dinner, the kitchen creates some tasty concoctions from local ingredients.

Hotel Las Tortugas   HOTEL $$$
(☏2653-0423; www.lastortugashotel.com; economy/standard/ste US$67/107/147; P❄@🤖🔌) 🏄 The granddad of Playa Grande, Louis Wilson is a local hero as he was instrumental in the designation of the national park. Right next to the beach, his hotel was carefully designed to keep ambient light away from the turtle nesting area. The rooms are modest, but only about 15 steps from the waves.

Hotel Bula Bula · HOTEL $$$

(☎2653-0975; www.hotelbulabula.com; r incl breakfast US$120; P✳@🛜☲) Todd and Wally want you to enjoy your vacation in paradise. They've decked the rooms out with tropical paint jobs and whimsical local art. The grounds are gorgeous and the front porch is well equipped with rattan rockers. Most importantly: cocktails. The Great Waltini's hardwood bar puts out some seriously potent drinks, including rum yummies, margaritas and the mysterious Siberian.

★Mamasa · BRUNCH $

(☎5002-5468; www.mamasarestaurant.com; mains US$4-15; ⊙10am-2pm Tue-Sun, 5:30-9pm Wed & Sat) For brunch, feast on eggs Benedict, breakfast burritos or to-die-for lemon ricotta pancakes. Come back when the sun sets, as that's when Jamie really gets creative. Wednesday is for tapas, while Saturday shows off a unique and ever-changing menu of gastronomic delights. If you're sick of *típica*, Mamasa has the cure.

This all takes place in a funky open-air *palapa*. Pull up a tree stump and devour the goodness.

Taco Star · MEXICAN $

(meals US$4-6; ⊙9am-6pm Tue-Sun) Three words: beachfront taco stand. Hefty beef and veggie tacos and fresh *batidos* (fruit shakes) will sustain you for a full day of sun and surf. Can't beat it.

Cafe Del Pueblo · PIZZERIA $$

(☎2653-2315; mains US$10-18; ⊙5-9pm) Just east of town, and recommended by local foodies, this pizzeria also does homemade pasta and fresh seafood dishes. Dine under the stars on the patio.

ℹ Information

Playa Grande Clinic (☎2653-2767, 24hr emergency 8827-7774) If you get rolled too hard in the surf and need a doctor, find this clinic next to Kike's Place.

ℹ Getting There & Away

There are no buses to Playa Grande, but the road was recently paved so it's an easy drive.

Alternatively, catch a boat across the estuary from Tamarindo to the southern end of Grande (around US$1 per person, from 7am to 4pm). From Playa Grande arrange your boat to Tamarindo at Hotel Bula Bula.

Playa Tamarindo

Well, they don't call it Tamagringo for nothing. Tamarindo's status as Costa Rica's top surf and party destination has made it the first and last stop for legions of tourists. It stands to reason, then, that this is the most developed beach on the peninsula with no shortage of hotels, bars and restaurants. Yet, despite its party-town reputation, Tamarindo is more than just drinking and surfing. It forms a part of the Parque Nacional Marino Las Baulas de Guanacaste, and the beach retains an allure for kids and adults alike. Foodies will find some of the best restaurants in the country. Families and students will appreciate the fierce competition that has kept lodging prices reasonably low. And Tamarindo's central location makes it a great base for exploring the northern peninsula.

Amazingly, there's no gas station here. For that, you'll have to drive 15 paved kilometers to Huacas, hang a right and go up the hill. The gas station is 4km ahead, on the right.

🏃 Activities

Sportfishing

There are more than 30 fishing outfitters offering a variety of tour packages. Prices vary wildly depending on boat size, but expect to pay at least US$250 for a half-day tour.

Surfing

Like a gift from the surf gods, Tamarindo is often at its best when neighboring Playa Grande is flat. The most popular wave is a medium-sized right that breaks directly in front of the Tamarindo Diria hotel. The waters here are full of virgin surfers learning to pop up. There is a good left that's fed by the river mouth, though be advised that crocodiles are occasionally sighted here, particularly when the tide is rising (which is, coincidentally, the best time to surf). There can be head-high waves in front of the rocks near Le Beach Club.

More advanced surfers will appreciate the bigger, faster and less crowded waves at Playa Langosta (on the other side of the point); Playas Avellanas, Negra and Junquillal to the south; and Playa Grande to the north.

A number of surf schools and tour operators line the main road in Tamarindo. Surf lessons hover at around US$45 for 1½ to two hours, and most operators will let you keep the board for a few hours beyond that to practice.

Playa Tamarindo

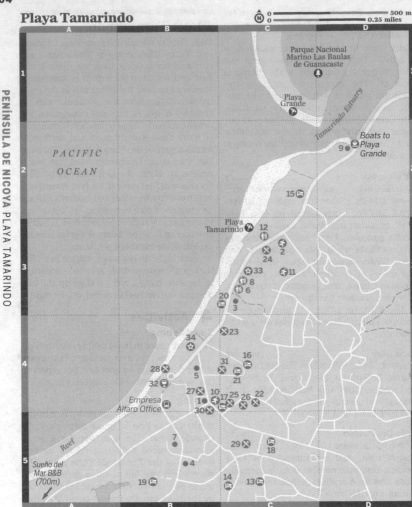

Kelly's Surf Shop SURFING
(📞 2653-1355; www.kellyssurfshop.com; board rental per day/week US$20/120, group/private lesson US$50/90; ⏱ 9am-6pm) One of the very best surf shops in the area, it has a terrific selection of newish boards that it rents by the day or week. Premium boards cost a bit more.

Matos Surf Shop SURFING
(📞 2653-0734, 2653-0845; www.matossurfshop. com; Sunrise Commercial Center; ⏱ 8am-8pm, lessons 9-11am & 2-4pm) The granddaddy of local surf shops is owned by a Uruguyan DJ-photo-entrepreneur. It offer lessons, and rents and sells boards at the cheapest rates in town. There is another outlet in Playa Grande.

Blue Trailz SURFING, CYCLING
(📞 2653-1705; www.bluetrailz.com; board rental per day US$15, group/private surf lesson US$45/80, bike rental per day US$20, bike tours US$55-75; ⏱ 7am-7pm Mon-Sat) Blue Trailz offers surf lessons, board rental and other more comprehensive surf packages. Lodging is at the same-named hostel, just across the street from the beach. This is also the local expert on mountain biking, distance cycling, bike tours and repairs.

Playa Tamarindo

Other Activities

Bike Shop CYCLING
(☎2653-2136; www.bikeshoptamarindo.com; cruisers/mountain bikes per day US$25/35; ☺9am-4:30pm Mon-Sat) Next to Kelly's Surf Shop, this no-nonsense bike garage offers one of the best selections of cruisers and mountain bikes in Tamarindo. New and used bikes are also for sale.

Agua Rica Diving Center DIVING
(☎2653-2023, 2653-0094; www.aguarica.net; 2 tanks US$80-105) Italian-owned Agua Rica Diving Center, the area's scuba-diving expert, offers snorkeling and an assortment of dives in the Catalina Islands, including diving certification classes and trips to the Cocos Islands.

Ser Om Shanti Yoga Studio YOGA
(☎8346-8005; www.seryogastudio.com; classes from US$15) Daily yoga, tai chi and Pilates mat classes are on offer at this airy and bright studio on the top floor of Tamarindo plaza.

Tamarindo Tennis Club TENNIS
(☎2653-0898; court rental per person US$10; ☺7:30am-9pm) Tennis, anyone? There are two well-maintained hard courts at this tiny tennis club on the property of a contemporary B&B.

Hacienda Pinilla GOLF
(☎2681-4318; www.haciendapinilla.com; 9/18 holes US$95/185) Just outside Tamarindo, near the village of San José de Pinilla, Hacienda Pinilla has a 7500yd, par-72 course that was designed by noted architect Mike Young.

Courses

Use your vacation time wisely by learning Spanish. There are several language schools in Tamarindo, all of which charge about US$420 to US$440 for a week-long intensive course (beginner to advanced), including 'homestay' accommodations with a Tico family. Most schools offer multiple-week discounts, and 'Spanish & Surf' packages that include language lessons, surf classes, accommodations and board rentals for about US$600 per week.

Coastal Spanish Institute LANGUAGE COURSE
(☎2653-2673; www.coastalspanish.com; per week from US$310)

Instituto de Wayra LANGUAGE COURSE
(☎2653-0359; www.spanish-wayra.co.cr; per week incl homestay from US$455; ☺7:30am-5:30pm Mon-Fri, 10am-4pm Sun)

Surfing the Península de Nicoya

Ever since surf legend Robert August started riding waves all those decades ago, surfers have descended to this rugged peninsula in search of the perfect wave. The result is a string of epic beach towns – with excellent facilities and good vibrations – blossoming all along the spectacular coastline.

Playa Grande

Playa Grande (p301) is across the river and a world away from Tamarindo. It doubles as a national park that protects leatherback turtle nesting grounds, which means the wide beach, which rambles for miles, is damn near pristine. The wave shapes up beautifully with head-high sets year-round, and the local expat residents have opened up some truly tasty kitchens and comfy inns.

Playa Avellanas

South of Tamarindo, you'll find one of the most celebrated surf spots on the peninsula, though the nearby villages still retain that appealing atmosphere of rusticity and remoteness. Playa Avellanas (p312) is an understated yet elegant place to nest, within reach of white-sand beaches and a break that is kind to beginners.

Playa Negra

Nearby, the surf swells big and gnarly at Playa Negra (p312), breaking on beautiful dark sand. To dodge the crowds at this popular spot, seek out the still-hidden waves tucked between all the big names.

Nosara

Within striking distance of three different beach breaks, Nosara (p318) offers consistent surf and a welcome cloud of hippie-chic comfort. It's a maze of rough dirt roads, backed by lush rainforest, although this town is growing rapidly. Here, yoga studios and spa treatments are the antidote for your surf-sore body.

Mal País & Santa Teresa

At the southern end of the peninsula, Mal País and Santa Teresa (p344) are favored by young, hip and sexy surfers from northern Europe to southern Argentina. The beach is long and the swell is scarily consistent, which means you can generally find some space to yourself – particularly if you drive just a bit north to Playa Hermosa (p293) or Manzanillo (p344).

There's a wonderful farm-to-table movement happening here, so you'll be well fed throughout your stay. Mal País is also a stunning fishing harbor. And when you need a break from the waves, escape to the nearby Reserva Natural Absoluta Cabo Blanco (p343), the country's oldest protected area.

1. Mal País 2. Playa Grande

Tours

Boat tours, snorkeling trips and scooter rentals can be arranged through various tour agencies in town. Many also rent out equipment.

Parque Nacional Marino Las Baulas de Guanacaste Office   ECOTOUR
(☑ 2653-1687; tours to turtle nesting sites US$25) The official Tamarindo branch of the nearby national park, it books turtle-spotting night tours and offers daytime estuary tours. This is also where you'll grab a boat across the river to Playa Grande.

Go Adventures   TOUR
(☑ 2653-1563; www.goadventurescostarica.com; sportfishing US$360) Runs sportfishing trips on its own boats. Other tours include sunset sailing, surfing, canopy tours and wildlife-watching in Palo Verde.

Sleeping

Be mindful, most budget hotels have cold water only, while midrange options generally have hot-water bathrooms. The rates given are high-season rates; low-season rates can be 25% to 40% lower.

Tamarindo Backpackers   HOSTEL $
(☑ 2653-1720; www.tamabackpackers.com; dm US$15, d from US$40; P ❋ @ ❂ ≋) New owners Anne and Chris have spruced up this attractive yellow hacienda with brand new bathrooms and colorful wall murals. Private rooms (mostly with shared bathroom) are excellent value, with Spanish-tiled floors, beamed ceilings and fat flat-screens on the wall. The dorms are quite clean but otherwise unspectacular.

Outside, you'll find lovely tropical gardens, a luxurious veranda, a small pool and hammocks, all surrounded by woods inhabited by howler monkeys.

Blue Trailz Hostel   HOSTEL $
(☑ 2653-1705; dm/r US$14/59; ❋ @ ❂) Across the street from the beach, this immaculate and intimate hostel is popular among the surfer set and other party people. Super-attentive staff go out of their way to make sure everyone is having a good time. Guests get reduced rates on boards, bikes, lessons and tours. Sweet.

Pura Vida Hostel   HOSTEL $
(☑ 8747-8780; www.puravidahostel.com; dm US$12-15, s/d US$35/45; ❂ ❋ @ ❂) Inside this leafy compound are dorms and private rooms

accented by hand-painted flourishes and mirrored mosaics. It's not much of a party place, but the vibe is friendly and super chill, especially in the common *rancho*, furnished with hammocks and rocking chairs. Also: bike rental, yoga classes, Reiki crystals, surf lessons and more.

La Oveja Negra   HOSTEL $
(☑ 2653-0005; www.laovejanegrahostel.com; dm/d US$15/35; P @ ❂) A hip hostel with an international crowd. You'll like the sufficiently clean, tiled rooms; the funky art on the walls; and the groovy furniture and open kitchen in the common areas. It also offers board rentals and surf lessons.

★ **Villa Amarilla**   B&B $$
(☑ 2653-0038; www.hotelvillaamarilla.com; d incl breakfast from US$100; P ❋ ❂) It's hard to resist this fun and funky yellow house backing up to the beach, its facade painted with happy animals and colorful fish. Newly renovated rooms feature flat-screen TVs, tile floors, comfy beds and whimsical paint jobs. An open-air massage area is on the grounds. The whole place is laid-back and lovely.

Casa Bambora   APARTMENT $$
(☑ 2653-0124; www.casabambora.com; studio US$70-110; P ❋ ❋ ≋) These five slick studio apartments include fully equipped kitchens, private balconies and room to sleep three. They are perfectly practical and simply stylish, and enhanced by delicious ocean views. An outdoor kitchen and bar overlook the waterfall-soaked swimming pool. But the best scenery is from the 4th-floor sundeck, which offers 360 degrees of mountains, sea and sky.

Villas Macondo   HOTEL $$
(☑ 2653-0812; www.villasmacondo.com; s/d/tr US$42/52/62, with air-con US$67/77/88, apt US$110-150; P ❋ @ ❂ ≋) Although it's only 200m from the beach, this German-run establishment is an oasis of serenity in an otherwise frenzied town – it's also one of the best deals around. Beautiful modern villas with private hot showers, hammocks and patios surround a solar-heated pool and tropical garden, while larger apartments are equipped with full kitchens, making them ideal for families.

Hotel La Laguna del Cocodrilo   HOTEL $$
(☑ 2653-0255; www.lalagunadelcocodrilo.com; d/tr/q from US$65/76/85, ocean view from US$122; P ❋ ❂) A beachfront location blesses this

charming French-owned hotel, with well-kept rooms overlooking either the shady grounds or the ocean and estuary. Adjacent to a crocodile-filled lagoon (hence the name), the hotel opens onto a rocky garden that rolls to the sand. The spotless rooms are simple rather spartan. Bonus: French bakery onsite. *Mais oui!*

Harry's El Esondite GUESTHOUSE $$
(☑ 8842-3419; www.esconditetamarindo.com; d/tr US$80/100; ☒) Four attractive *cabinas* – with full kitchens and private patios – are arranged around a tropical garden with hammocks and a small swimming pool. Upstairs, guests share an open-air kitchen and sundeck. Free use of surfboards and bikes makes Harry a hero.

15 Love B&B $$$
(☑ 2653-0898; www.15lovebedandbreakfast.com; d/ste incl breakfast US$107/117; ⊞ ✽ 🤶 ☒) A self-proclaimed contemporary B&B, this white-washed, concrete, mod villa with weathered louvered accents overlooks a plunge pool and two tennis hard courts and is within earshot of the sea. Interiors are quite stylish with polished concrete floors, high ceilings, floating beds and designer light fixtures.

Hotel Luamey BOUTIQUE HOTEL $$$
(☑ 2653-1510; www.hotelluamey.com; d from US$135; ⊞ ✽ 🤶 ☒) This brand new boutique hotel is simply exquisite. Spacious *cabaña* suites are decorated in earthy tones, with dark wood furnishings, stone showers and private patios. Service is super accommodating. Free use of surfboards. The onsite restaurant is highly recommended for breakfast or any other meal.

Sueño del Mar B&B B&B $$$
(☑ 2653-0284; www.sueno-del-mar.com; d US$195, casitas US$220-295; ⊞ ✽ @ 🤶 ☒) This exquisite B&B on Playa Langosta is set in a stunning faux-dobe Spanish-style *posada* (inn) The six rooms have four-poster beds, artfully placed crafts and open-air garden showers, while the romantic honeymoon suite has a wraparound window with sea views. There's private beach access beyond the pool and tropical garden, and a priceless, pervasive atmosphere of seclusion and beauty. No children allowed.

✗ Eating

Tamarindo has some of the best restaurants in Costa Rica. But be prepared to pay – a cheap meal in this town is about as common

as a nesting turtle. **Super 2001** (☺ 7am-9:30pm Mon-Sat, 8am-8:30pm Sun) and **Super Compro** (☺ 8am-9pm Mon-Sun) are well stocked with international groceries.

★ Green Papaya TAQUERÍA $
(☑ 2652-0863; mains US$5-10; ☺ 9am-10pm Tue-Sun; ✽ 🞡 🞡) Swing on up to the bar for a breakfast burrito or pull up a tree-stump stool to sample the terrific tacos at this fantastic new addition. The mahi-mahi tacos are perfection in a tortilla, while non-meat-eaters will appreciate the multiple veggie options. You'll go loco for the Coco Loco dessert. Everything is funky, fresh and friendly – don't miss it.

Falafel Bar LEBANESE $
(☑ 2653-1268; mains US$5-8; ☺ 9am-11pm; 🞡) This Middle Eastern cafe serves all the faves: shawarma, falafel, tabbouleh, hummus and kebabs. And like any good shawarma joint it routinely (if not regularly) stays open into the wee hours.

Longboards BBQ AMERICAN $
(☑ 2653-0027; mains US$4-11; ☺ 11am-10pm Thu-Tue) An American-style barbecue joint and expat favorite, with excellent pulled pork, ribs and beef brisket. Belly up to the surfboard-shaped tables and grind some proper barbecue.

El Casado del Carro COSTA RICAN $
(casados US$4-6; ☺ noon-2pm) Doña Rosa has been delivering top-notch *casados* from her late-model Toyota hatchback for more than a decade. Her devoted Tico following lines up daily at noon, and she generally sells out by 2pm. You'll get your meal in a Styrofoam platter (nobody's *perfecto*), usually with yucca or plantains, rice, chicken or beef, and some tasty black beans.

FT's COSTA RICAN $
(☑ 2653-0041; mains US$5-9; ☺ 11am-10pm; 🞡) Eat + Drink + Surf + Sleep. FT's has got you covered for the first two, serving authentic grub like chicken and rice, pork chops and fresh fish. Regulars rave about the gigantic burritos, while ice-cold beers and slushy margaritas go down smooth. Prices are low and service is all smiles.

If you're worried about the last one, FT's also rents a few cheap, clean *cabinas* on the beach. The 'Surf' part is up to you.

Nogui's SEAFOOD $$
(☑ 2653-0029; mains US$9-22; ☺ 11am-11pm) A fish shack with Mediterranean charm, this

fabulously romantic, wooden and stained-glass, tin-roofed gem on the beach flaunts local seafood. Make a dinner reservation, or get sloshed at the bar with the occasionally rowdy (but not too rowdy) regulars.

La Baula
PIZZERIA $$

(✉ 2653-1450; mains US$9-13; ⏲ 5:30-11pm; 🖉 👪) By far the best pizza in Tamarindo – this casual open-air restaurant has real wood-fired pizzas, pastas and other Italian fare. It's also one of the most family-friendly restaurants in town, with a playground to keep the kids entertained.

Dragonfly Bar & Grill
ASIAN $$$

(✉ 2653-1506; www.dragonflybarandgrill.com; mains US$15-22; ⏲ 6-11pm Mon-Sat; P 🛜 🖉) Dragonfly is a local favorite, not just for its refined menu, but also for its lovely tiki-bar atmosphere. The chic open-air dining room has twinkling lights and lanterns, with a subtle dragonfly motif throughout. The menu has an Asian bent, featuring delights such as panko-crusted pork loin and Thai-style crispy fish cakes. The desserts are divine.

Seasons by Shlomy
MEDITERRANEAN $$$

(✉ 8368-6983; www.seasonstamarindo.com; Hotel Arco Iris; mains US$15-19; ⏲ 6-10pm Mon-Sat) Don't leave town without eating here. Israeli chef Shlomy offers a short list of carefully selected and perfectly prepared dishes. Depending on the availability of ingredients, you might start with sashimi, grilled octopus or spicy tuna tartare. Follow up with seared tuna in a honey chili marinade or filet mignon in red wine sauce.

The understated yet elegant open-air restaurant has indoor seating or romantic poolside tables. Reservations are recommended.

🍸 Drinking & Nightlife

On Tamarindo weekends, all you really have to do is follow the scene wherever it happens to go. Cruising the main drag has the festive feel of spring break, and nearly every bar hosts a ladies' night.

Cafe Tico
CAFE

(⏲ 7am-5pm Mon-Fri, 7am-3pm Sat) Walk in. Take a deep breath. Smell the coffee brewing? That's why you are here. Sip it on the shady patio while snacking on a homemade pastry. *Pura vida.*

Eat@Joe's
AMERICAN

(✉ 2653-1262; ⏲ 7am-10pm, bar til 2am) The best snack in town is at this US-run surf camp, where you can order the famous 'nachos as big as your ass' (or sushi rolls), while sucking down cold ones on the outdoor deck until 2am.

Pacífico Bar
BAR

(✉ 2653-4406; ⏲ 6pm-2am) This place thinks it's a dance club, but it's really more of a tropical dive bar, with occasional live bands and DJ. And that's OK. Better in fact. Come on Sunday for reggae and world music.

Sharky's Rock 'n' Roll Sports Bar
SPORTS BAR

(✉ 8729-8274; ⏲ 6pm-2am) If you're looking for a place to watch the big game, look no further than Sharky's. Besides nine screens showing sports, there are burgers and wings and lots of beer. Tuesday is karaoke night and Saturday is ladies' '80s night (girls drink free 9pm to midnight).

Le Beach Club
CLUB

(✉ 2653-0178; ⏲ 11am-close) This place has beds and hammocks on the sand and live DJs on Saturday. It also gets an excellent sundowner crowd who feel the throbbing bass as the orb melts into the sea.

Aqua Disco
CLUB

(✉ 8702-2925; www.aquadiscoteque.com; ⏲ 9pm-2am) Aqua Disco is the only real nightclub in Tamarindo. Monday night is ladies' night. Friday is called 'Open Bar for Everyone', which promises free drinks until they run out. Techno music, overpriced drinks, dressed-up crowd.

El Garito
CLUB

(✉ 2653-2017; Plaza Tamarindo; ⏲ 5pm-2am) With a small bar and dance floor inside and a spacious patio outside, El Garito is a friendly, fun place to get your groove on.

ℹ️ Information

Tourist information is available from any of the tour operators in town, your hotel and the **Tamarindo News** (www.tamarindonews.com).

BAC San José (Plaza Conchal; ⏲ 8:30am-3:30pm) Has an ATM and exchanges US dollars and traveler's checks.

Backwash Laundry (per kg US$2; ⏲ 8am-8pm Mon-Sat) Get your filthy unmentionables washed, dried and folded.

Banco de Costa Rica (Plaza Conchal) 24hr ATM.

Centro Medico Tamarindo (☎ 2653-1974, emergency 8835-8074; ⏰ 24hr)
HSBC 24hr ATM.
Internet Bakanos (per hour US$2.50; ⏰ 8am-10pm) On the 2nd floor above an Italian deli; offers high-speed internet connections and international phone calls.

❶ Getting There & Away

AIR

The airstrip is 3km north of town; a hotel bus is usually on hand to pick up arriving passengers, or you can take a taxi. During high season, **Sansa** (☎ 2653-0012) has two daily flights to and from San José (one way US$114), while NatureAir (one way US$141) has three. Some flights transit through Liberia.

BUS

Buses for San José depart from the Empresa Alfaro office behind the Babylon bar. Other buses depart across the street from Zullymar Hostel. It's possible to get to Montezuma or Mal País and Santa Teresa by bus for about US$11 total, but it will take all day and multiple changes: take the 5:45am bus to Liberia, bus to Puntarenas, ferry to Playa Naranjo, bus to Cóbano and bus to Montezuma or Mal País.
Liberia US$3, 2½ hours, departs 12 times per day from 4:30am to 6pm.
San José US$11, 5½ hours, departs three times from 5:30am to 2:15pm. Alternatively, take a bus to Liberia and change for frequent buses to the capital.
Santa Cruz US$2, 1½ hours, departs 10 times per day from 5:45am to 10pm.

CAR & TAXI

By car from Liberia, take Hwy 21 to Belén, then Hwy 155 via Huacas to Tamarindo. A taxi costs about US$30 to or from Santa Cruz, and US$50 to or from Liberia. Alternatively, consider a mini-bus shuttle service. **Tropical Tours** (☎ 8849-8569, 2640-1900; www.tropicaltourshuttles.com) offers door-to-door service to Montezuma and Mal País (US$50 per person, five hours). **Tamarindo Shuttle** (☎ 2653-4444, 2653-2626; www.tamarindoshuttle.com) services the Aeropuerto Internacional Daniel Oduber Quiros in Liberia (US$20 per person, 1½ hours), and will pick you up or drop you off at your hotel of choice.

❶ Getting Around

BOAT

Boats on the northern end of the beach can be hired to cross the estuary for daytime visits to the beach at Playa Grande at the Parque Nacional Marino Las Baulas De Guanacaste Office (p308). The ride costs US$1 per person (from about 7am to 5pm).

CAR & TAXI

There's no gas station in town, but you can buy expensive gas from drums at the hardware store near the entrance to town. (It's cheaper to fill up in Santa Cruz or at the gas station in Huacas.)
Rental car companies:
Alamo (☎ 2653-0727, www.alamocostarica.com, ⏰ 7:30am-5:30pm)
Hola Rent a Car (☎ 2653-2000, www.hola.net, ⏰ 8am-5pm)
Mapache Rent a Car (☎ 2586-6300, 2586-6363, www.mapache.com, ⏰ 8am-5pm)

PENÍNSULA DE NICOYA PLAYA TAMARINDO

---

❶ WHAT TO DO IF YOU'RE CAUGHT IN A RIPTIDE

Riptides account for the majority of ocean drownings, though a simple understanding of how these currents behave can save your life. Rip currents are composed of three parts: the feeder current, the neck and the head. The feeder current consists of rapidly moving water that parallels the shore. When this water reaches a channel, it switches direction and flows out to sea, forming the neck of the rip. This is the fastest-moving part of the riptide, and can carry swimmers out to sea at a speed of up to 10km/h. The head is formed past the breakers where the current quickly dissipates.

If you find yourself caught in a riptide, it's important to conserve your energy and not to panic and fight the current – this is the principal cause of drownings. It's impossible to swim directly back to shore. Instead, tread water and let yourself be swept out past the breakers. Once you're in the head of the rip, you can swim parallel or diagonally to the shore until you're out of the channel, then swim back to shore with the waves.

Rip currents usually occur on beaches that have strong surf, and there are indicators, such as the brownish color on the surface of the water that is caused by swept-up sand and debris. If you're ever in doubt about the safety of a beach, inquire locally about swimming conditions. Remember, rips are survivable as long as you relax, don't panic and conserve your energy.

Playas Avellanas & Negra

About 15km south of Tamarindo, these popular surfing beaches have some of the best, most consistent waves in the area, made famous in the surf classic *Endless Summer II*. Playa Avellanas is an absolutely stunning pristine sweep of pale golden sand. Backed by mangroves in the center and two gentle hillsides on either end, there's plenty of room for surfers and sunbathers to have an intimate experience even when there are lots of heads in town. The wave here is decent for beginners and intermediate surfers. **Little Hawaii** is the powerful and open-faced right featured in *Endless Summer II*, while **Beach Break** barrels at low tide. Still, advanced surfers get bored here.

Playa Negra is also undeniably romantic. Though the sand is a bit darker and the beach is broken up by rocky outcrops, those gorgeous dusty back roads link tidepools of expat shredders who picked this place to exist (and surf) peacefully. Though there isn't much local soul here, it's still a stunning nook blessed by a world-class right that barrels. Further south is (hush hush) **Playa Tortuga**, an epic break for advanced surfers only. The waves are best between April and November, but start getting good in March.

To get here backtrack from Tamarindo 5km to the village of Villareal, and turn right onto the dirt road. This road gets progressively worse and usually requires a 4WD. If you're not coming from Tamarindo, head west on the paved highway from Santa Cruz, through 27 de Abril to Paraíso, then follow the signs. While you're at the beach, be absolutely certain that nothing is visible in your car as professional thieves operate in this area.

Part of the Hotel Playa Negra complex, **Playa Negra Surf Shop** (☑2652-9134; www.playanegra.com; board rental per day US$20; ☺8am-5pm) rents boards and sells T-shirts, sunglasses and other beachy accessories. **Café Playa Negra** (☑2652-9351; www.cafeplayanegra.com; ☺7am-9pm) has a laundry service and internet access.

🛏 Sleeping & Eating

🛏 Playa Avellanas

If you prefer to sleep out under the stars, you'll find a few places to string a hammock or pitch a tent at the southern end of Playa Avellanas.

Casa Surf GUESTHOUSE $
(☑2652-9075; www.casa-surf.com; per person US$15; 🅿) ✆ Casa Surf is looking tropically terrific after a recent makeover, featuring an all-new bamboo exterior and palm thatch roof. Inside, you'll find simple, clean rooms that share a bathroom and kitchen. The casa offers an excellent-value room, board and board option, which includes two meals daily and surfboard rental. Delicious filling meals (US$5 to US$7) are designed to sate hungry surfers. Also available: bike rental, book exchange, community guitar.

Las Avellanas Villas APARTMENT $$
(☑2652-9212, 8821-3681; www.lasavellanasvillas.com; d/tr/q US$90/100/110; 🅿✳🛜) Thoughtfully designed, these five stunning villas are oases of tranquillity and balance, with private terraces, polished concrete floors, indoor greenery, open-air showers and large windows streaming with natural light. Full kitchens make this option perfect for families or groups. The grounds are about 800m from the beach.

Mauna Loa Surf Resort BUNGALOW $$
(☑2652-9012; www.hotelmaunaloa.com; d/tr/q from US$90/113/136; 🅿✳🛜🏊) This hip Italian-run spot offers a secure location that's a straight shot to the beach. Paths lead from the gorgeous pool area through a lush garden to attractive pod-like bungalows with pastel-brushed walls, and swaying hammocks on terraces.

Cabinas Las Olas BUNGALOW $$
(☑2652-9315; www.cabinaslasolas.co.cr; s/d/tr US$90/100/110, air-con US$20; 🅿✳🛜🏊) ✆ Set on spacious grounds that are bursting with cocobolo, laurel and guanacaste trees, these 10 airy bungalows have shiny woodwork, stone detailing and private decks. There's an open-air restaurant and a surf shop where you can rent boards and kayaks. A purpose-built boardwalk leads 200m through the mangroves (good for wildlife) and down to the beach.

Mediterraneo Surf Camp APARTMENT $$
(☑2653-4169; www.mediterraneo-costarica.com; d US$90-125; 🅿✳🛜🏊) Mediterraneo is all about the surf, offering board rental, lessons and a free shuttle to the beach. The six apartments are simple but practical, with extra living space and equipped kitchens. The place is surrounded by the dry tropical forest, with views to the beach. Ask about custom surf packages.

Lola's on the Beach

CAFE $

(☑2652-9097; meals US$8-13; ⊘10am-5pm Tue-Sun) If the water is looking glassy, this hauntingly stylish beach cafe is the place to hang out. Minimalist slanted wood chairs are planted in the sand beneath thatched umbrellas. A tree-stump bar overlooks an open kitchen, where the beachy cuisine is tops. In case you're wondering, Lola was an enormous and lovable pig, aka the queen of Avellanas. She has since passed, but her legacy lives on in 'little' Lolita!

Playa Negra

Kon Tiki

HOSTEL $

(☑2652-9117; www.kontikiplayanegra.com; r per person US$20; P☎) Along the road from Avellanas, this low-key place run by a splendid young couple has a rambling collection of colorful cabins on stilts that are frequented by both surfers and howlers. In the middle of it all is a rickety pavilion where guests swing in hammocks and devour pizza. Bathroom facilities are shared.

Café Playa Negra

GUESTHOUSE $$

(☑2652-9351; www.cafeplayanegra.com; s/d/tr/q US$45/65/80/90; P☀☎☲) These stylish, minimalist digs upstairs from the cafe have polished concrete floors and elevated beds dressed with colorful bedspreads and other artistic touches. There's a groovy shared deck with plush lounges and an inviting swimming pool. The downstairs cafe (mains US$7 to US$13) serves delectable sandwiches, *ceviche* and super fresh seafood.

★ Villa Deevena

BOUTIQUE HOTEL $$$

(☑2653-2328; www.villadeevena.com; d US$107; P☀☎☲) With a Balinese theme and a minimalist aesthetic, this property tempts guests with simple but sensual luxury. Six swish bungalows – decorated with hard wood and soothing tones – surround a glittering saltwater pool. Onsite is an otherworldly good restaurant (mains US$18 to US$28, open 7am to 9pm), brainchild of *chef de cuisine* Patrick Jamon. Look for perfect French preparations, such as mahi baked with preserved lemon and rosemary, slow-braised shortrib and duck confit.

Hotel Playa Negra

BUNGALOW $$$

(☑2652-9134; www.playanegra.com; s/d/tr/q from US$102/113/124/136; P☀☎☲) This sweet compound of circular *rancho* bungalows is steps from a world-class reef break. The traditional thatch-roof *ranchos* have high ceilings and breezy porches. Higher-priced suites are further from the beach, but they have air-con, private decks with hammocks and outdoor showers. Restaurant and surf shop onsite.

🛈 Getting There & Away

There is no public transportation to/from Playa Tamarindo to Playas Avellanas or Negra, though surf camps often organize trips. The only bus connections are heading inland, via Santa Cruz (US$1.50, 1½ hours, two daily). The schedule seems to change frequently, so inquire locally.

Playa Junquillal

Hard to pronounce and almost as difficult to find, Junquillal (say 'hoon-kee-yal') is a 2km-wide gray-sand wilderness beach that's absolutely stunning and mostly deserted. To the south, a dome boulder crumbles into a jutting rock reef and beyond that is a vast, 200-hectare estuary carved by the Río Nanda Mojo. To the north is a narrow rise of bluffs sprouting clumps of palm trees. Sunsets are downright surreal with blinding golds, molten oranges and shocking pinks. The sea does swirl with fierce rip currents, however, and when it gets big, surfers descend from Negra. But even when the surf isn't high, it's dangerous out there and drownings do happen. Don't let kids or even intermediate swimmers venture out alone.

Olive ridley turtles nest in Junquillal from July to November, with a peak from August to October, though in smaller numbers than at the refuges; Junquillal is also an important nesting site for leatherbacks. Though it is not officially protected, conservation groups have teamed up with local communities to protect the nesting sites and eliminate poaching.

With far more Ticos than tourists, Junquillal has an inviting authenticity unique on the northern peninsula. The nearest town is 4km inland at Paraíso, which has a few local *sodas* and bars. Accommodations are spread out along the beach.

🛏 Sleeping & Eating

Aside from the hotel restaurants, your best option for cheap eats is to head to nearby Paraíso, though there are a few small spots on the beach.

El Castillo Divertido
HOTEL $

(☑2658-8428, 8351-5162; www.castillodivertido. com; d US$30-40; P) On a hilltop you'll find the entrance to this funky, colorful faux-dobe lodge, decked out with crenellated walls and carved masks, with panoramic views from the rooftop bar. Take advantage of the one-of-a-kind kayaking tours through the Río Nanda Moja and surrounding mangroves.

★ Mundo Milo Ecolodge
BUNGALOW $$

(☑2658-7010; www.mundomilo.com; d incl break-fast US$67-77; P⛱≋) ✈ The most cre-ative nest in the area is this Dutch-owned ecolodge, where attention to detail is para-mount. Choose between three fan-cooled, sky-lit bungalows, each with a full kitchen and private patio and styled after a different world region (Africa, Mexico, Persia). The pool is an artful arc overlooking the dry trop-ical woodland, with monkeys howling, birds chatting and waves crashing in the distance.

Hotel Iguanazul
HOTEL $$

(☑2658-8123; www.hoteliguanazul.com; d with/ without air-con US$120/89; P⛱@⛱≋) Gor-geously perched on a 19m bluff, this palm-shaded property overlooks the swirling, thrashing sea. The three-star standalone *casitas* are satisfactory, if not fabulous. Even if you're not staying here, the bar is a popular spot to sip happy-hour specials and watch the sun drop into the ocean.

Hotelito Sí Sí Sí
GUESTHOUSE $$$

(☑8376-2284, 2658-7118; www.hotelitosisisi.com; incl breakfast d/casita US$102/123; P⛱⛱≋) Ensconced in the Tierra Pacifica 'eco' devel-opment, this little guesthouse has access to facilities such as tennis courts, gym and yoga studio, swimming pool and Jacuzzi. The villa itself, shrouded in bougainvillea, has three tiled rooms, each with beamed ceiling, king bed and time-sucking front porch, as well as a cute *casita* with a fully equipped kitchen.

❶ Getting There & Away

Buses depart from Junquillal to Santa Cruz (US$2, 1½ hours) at 6am, 9am, 12:30pm and 4:30pm; you can catch the bus anywhere along the main road. Buses from Santa Cruz' Terminal Diria to Junquillal depart at 5am, 10am, 2:30pm and 5:30pm.

If you're driving, it's about 16km by paved road from Santa Cruz to 27 de Abril, and another smooth 17km into town.

From Junquillal, it's possible to drive 35km south to Nosara via the legendary surf spot of Marbella. However, this is a very rough dirt road

for 4WD only and may be impassable in the rainy season. There are no gas stations on the coastal road and there is little traffic, so ask locally before setting out. It's easier to reach beaches south of Junquillal from Nicoya.

A taxi from Santa Cruz to Junquillal costs about US$50.

Santa Cruz

A stop in Santa Cruz, a *sabanero* (cow-boy) town typical of inland Nicoya, pro-vides some of the local flavor missing from foreign-dominated beach towns. Unfortu-nately, there aren't any attention-worthy sights, so most travelers' experience of Santa Cruz consists of changing buses and buying a mango. However, the town is an important administrative center in the region, which gives it a healthy middle-class appeal, and serves as a good base for visiting Guaitil.

About three city blocks in the center of Santa Cruz burned to the ground in a devas-tating fire in 1993. An important landmark is a vacant-lot-looking field known as Plaza de Los Mangos, which was once a large grassy square with three mango trees. Soon after the fire the attractive and shady Parque Bernabela Ramos opened 400m south of Plaza de Los Mangos.

🛏 Sleeping & Eating

Hotel La Pampa
HOTEL $

(☑2680-0586; s/d with air-con US$40/50, without air-con US$36/40; P⛱⛱) A good budget op-tion, this peach-tinted hotel is 50m west of the Plaza de Los Mangos. It isn't all that in-spiring from the outside, but the rooms are clean and modern, providing a decent place to lay your head.

La Calle de Alcalá
HOTEL $$

(☑2680-0000; www.hotellacalledealcala.com; s/d incl breakfast US$63/84; P⛱⛱≋) With its stucco arches and landscaped garden around a pool, this hotel gets points for design. Carved wooden doors open into small tiled rooms with rattan furnishings. It's one block due east of the bus terminal; a convenient stopover option.

Casa Fonda
COSTA RICAN $

(☑2680-4949; mains US$7-15; ⏲6am-10pm) This spot is rather swish for Santa Cruz and is decked out with local pottery, wrought iron and planter boxes. It does upscale *típica*, American bar food and good coffee and espresso drinks.

DON'T MISS

GUAITIL

An interesting excursion from Santa Cruz is the 12km trip by paved road to the small artisanal potter community of Guaitil. Attractive ceramics are made from local clays, using earthy reds, creams and blacks in pre-Columbian Chorotega style. Ceramics are for sale outside the potters' houses and also in San Vicente, 2km beyond Guaitil by unpaved road. If you ask, you can watch part of the potting process, and local residents will be happy to give you a few lessons for a small price.

Take the main highway toward Nicoya and then follow the signed Guaitil road to the left, about 1.5km out of Santa Cruz. This road is lined by yellow corteza amarilla trees and is very attractive when they bloom in April. Unreliable buses (US$0.60, 45 minutes) make the trip from Santa Cruz, or a taxi will cost about US$20, depending on how long you stay.

ℹ Information

There's a gas station off the main intersection with the highway, and one ATM and at least two internet cafes facing Plaza de Los Mangos. Change money at **Banco de Costa Rica** (☏ 2680-3253), three blocks north of Plaza de Los Mangos.

ℹ Getting There & Away

Santa Cruz is 57km from Liberia and 25km south of Filadelfia on the main peninsular highway. A paved road leads 16km west to 27 de Abril, from where dirt roads continue to Playa Tamarindo, Playa Junquillal and other beaches.

Some buses depart from Terminal Tralapa on the north side of Plaza de Los Mangos. For Empresa Alfaro buses, buy tickets at the Alfaro office, 200m south of the plaza, but catch the bus on the main road north of town.

Liberia (La Pampa) US$2, 1½ hours, departs every 30 minutes from 4.10am to 8:40pm.

Nicoya (La Pampa) US$1, one hour, departs every 30 minutes from 4am to 9pm.

San José US$10, five hours, seven buses from 4am to 4:30pm (Tralapa), six buses from 3am to 4:50pm (Empresa Alfaro).

Local buses leave from the terminal in the Mercado Municipal. The bus schedules fluctuate constantly, so ask around to make sure to of departure times.

Bahía Potrero, via Playa Brasilito & Playa Flamingo US$3, one hour, departs about 15 times per day.

Playa Junquillal US$2, 1½ hours, departs 5am, 10am, 2:30pm and 5:30pm.

Playa Ostional US$2, two hours, departs 12:30pm.

Playa Tamarindo US$2, 1½ hours, departs 11 times daily.

CENTRAL PENINSULA

Long the political and cultural heart of Guanacaste, the inland region of the central peninsula looks and feels palpably more 'Costa Rican' than the beach resorts of the northern coast. Over generations, the dry tropical forest has been cut down to make way for the *sabaneros*' cattle, but stands of forest remain, interspersed between *fincas* (farms) and coastal villages, sometimes backing stretches of wild, empty beaches. Though the areas around Sámara and Nosara are developing slowly, most foreigners who are drawn to the rugged coastline are active in its conservation. So it remains rife with secluded beaches, small villages, and endless possibilities for getting 'off the map.'

Snaking through the higher elevations of the interior is Hwy 21, from the population center of Santa Cruz down through Nicoya, where sinuous Hwy 150 branches through the forest toward Sámara.

Nicoya

A hub between the beaches and ranches, the big cities and *pueblitos,* come here for a blast of Tico time. Truckers, road trippers and locals converge around a grid, packed with commerce and crowned with a gorgeous *iglesia* that makes the leafy Parque Central worth a loiter. Now, that's not necessarily an argument to linger longer than you need to. Nicoya is not fabulous. Just real.

Situated 23km south of Santa Cruz, and a good base for exploring Parque Nacional Barra Honda, Nicoya was named after an indigenous Chorotega chief who welcomed

Spanish conquistador Gil González de Ávila in 1523 (a gesture he regretted). In the following centuries, the Chorotega were wiped out by the colonists, though the distinctive facial features of the local residents are a testament to their heritage.

🛏 Sleeping & Eating

Hotel Jenny HOTEL $
(✍2685-5050; www.hoteljenny.com; cnr Calle 1 & Av 4; s/d/tr US$20/30/36; P ✳ 🕲) It ain't Shangri-la, but rooms are bright enough, clean enough, comfy enough and are damned decent value. There are leafy green plants lining the hallways and smiling faces in reception. Ask for a room away from the road for a quieter night's sleep.

Curime Resort HOTEL $$
(✍2685-5238; d from US$80; P ✳ 🕲 ⛲) Set on 3.5 acres, this unexpected nature resort is a surprise in gritty Nicoya. The lodgings are in tired but pleasant bungalows, scattered about the jungly grounds. The place has an Olympic-sized pool and a full-service restaurant. There's not really any reason to spend the night in Nicoya, but if you're going to do it, you might as well enjoy yourself.

Bobo's Burger House FAST FOOD $
(✍8757-8777; mains US$4-8; ⊙10am-10pm Mon-Sat, 5-10pm Sun; 🕲) Bobo knows his burgers. He makes them from premium beef, chicken or fish, and lets you pick the toppings from the organic veggie bar. Even if you're not a meat-eater you have options here. Thick, crispy steak fries round out the meal. And for dessert? Save room for Bobo's *helado burguesa* – vanilla ice cream sandwiched between two chocolate chip cookies.

Cafe Daniela SODA $
(✍2686-6148; www.cafedaniela.com; Calle 3; mains US$4-7; ⊙7am-9pm; 🖉) A popular *soda* serving appetizing *típica* bites. Think: *gallo pinto* in the morning, and fish, beef, chicken and veggie *casados* later on. All served in bright tiled environs.

La Castallena Panaderia CAFE $
(✍2675-3227; Calle 3; sandwiches US$3; ⊙5am-8pm; 🕲) In addition to its countless fresh baked loaves and goodies, this place does espresso drinks and fresh pressed beef, ham and chicken sandwiches on airy crunchy baguettes. It's the ideal picnic supply depot on your way to Barra Honda.

ℹ Information

Área de Conservación Tempisque (ACT; ✍2686-4967; Av Central; ⊙8am-4pm Mon-Fri) The office of the ACT can help with accommodations and cave exploration at Parque Nacional Barra Honda.

Banco de Costa Rica (Calle Central; ⊙8:30am-3pm Mon-Fri) Exchanges US dollars.

Banco Popular (Calle 3; ⊙9am-4:30pm Mon-Fri, 8:15-11:30am Sat) Exchanges US dollars. It also has a 24hr ATM at Hospital La Anexión.

Hospital La Anexión (✍2685-8400) The main hospital on the peninsula is north of town.

ℹ Getting There & Away

Most buses arrive at and depart from the bus terminal southeast of Parque Central.

Liberia US$2.25, 2½ hours, departs every 30 to 60 minutes from 4am to 9pm.

Playa Naranjo, connects with ferry to Puntarenas US$3, two hours, departs 5am, 9am, 1pm and 5pm.

Playa Nosara US$2, two hours, departs 4am, 10am, 12:30pm, 3pm and 5:30pm Monday to Saturday. On Sundays there is no 4am bus.

Sámara and Playa Carrillo US$2, 1½ hours, 13 buses per day from 5am to 9pm.

San José (Empresa Alfaro) US$7.50, five hours, departs five times daily.

Parque Nacional Barra Honda

Situated about halfway between Nicoya and the mouth of the Río Tempisque, this 23-sq-km national park protects a massive underground system of caverns composed of soft limestone, carved by rainfall and erosion over a period of about 70 million years. Speleologists have discovered more than 40 caverns, some reaching as far as 200m deep, though to date only 19 have been fully explored. There have also been discoveries of pre-Columbian remains dating to 300 BC.

Stalagmites, stalactites and a host of beautiful formations have evocative names such as fried eggs, organ, soda straws, popcorn, curtains, columns, pearls, flowers and shark's teeth. However, unlike caverns found elsewhere, Barra Honda is not developed for wide-scale tourism, which means that it feels less like a carnival attraction and more like a scene from *Indiana Jones*. So, don your yellow miner's hat and sturdy boots, and be prepared to get down and dirty.

⊙ Sights

Parque Nacional Barra Honda
Caverns
CAVE

(☑ 2659-1091, 2659-1551; park admission adult/child US$10/1, guided tour per person US$26; ⊙ trails 8am-4pm, caverns 8am-1pm) Arrange for a guide at the ranger station. The descent involves ladders and ropes, so you should be reasonably fit and must be at least 10 years old. Walk the 2km from the park gate to the cavern's mouth or opt for a ride in a 4WD. Tours to the caverns on foot last about four hours. Only groups of five people or less can enter the caverns and they cannot be entered after 1pm.

The only cave with regular access to the public is the 41m-deep La Terciopelo, which has the most speleothems – calcite figures that rise and fall in the cave's interior. The best known of these is El Órgano, which produces several notes when lightly struck. Scientists and visitors must obtain permits to enter other caves. These include Santa Ana, the deepest at 161m; Trampa (Trap), 110m deep with a vertical 52m drop; Nicoya, where early human remains were found; and Pozo Hediondo, or Fetid Pit. It's a cave, not a cavern, famous for its more than 5000 resident bats, which create mountainous piles of guano.

🏃 Activities

Wildlife-Watching
While wildlife-watching underground, you'll have the chance to see such fun-loving creatures as bats, albino salamander, blind fish and a variety of squiggly invertebrates. On the surface, howler and white-faced monkeys, armadillo, coati, kinkajou and white-tailed deer are regularly spotted, as are striped hog-nosed skunk and anteater.

Hiking
The Barra Honda hills have a few hiking trails through deciduous, dry tropical forest which lead to waterfalls (in the rainy season) adorned with calcium formations. It's also possible to hike 3.5km to the top of Cerro Barra Honda, which has a *mirador* (lookout point) with a view of Río Tempisque and Golfo de Nicoya. You won't need a guide to hike the trails.

🛏 Sleeping & Eating

The vast majority of visitors arrive on day trips from the beach, but there is a camping area (per person US$2) with bathrooms and showers near the park gate. The station's dorm-style accommodations are no longer open to visitors.

Hotel Las Cavernas
HOTEL $

(☑ 2659-1574; per person with air-con/fan US$25/18; P ❄ ❄) Located just outside the park gates. Not many folks stay here, but it's up and running and there is a pool and restaurant. Rooms are relatively clean and fresh, floors are concrete and the mountain location is splendid. You will hear the howlers' roar.

ℹ Information

The dry season is the only time that tourists are allowed to enter the caves, though the hiking is fine at any time of year. As always, carry several liters of water and let the rangers know where you are going. Sneakers or, preferably, boots are necessary if you will be caving.

The ranger station in the southwest corner of the park takes admission fees, provides information and arranges guides. It's best to call and arrange your guide at least the day before. Plan to arrive early to tour the caverns, as tours last three to four hours and you'll need to be out of the caverns by 1pm.

ℹ Getting There & Away

The easiest way to get to the park is from Nicoya. No buses go directly to the park; however, buses go to Santa Ana (US$2, 45 minutes, two daily except Sunday), which will get you within striking distance (about 1km away). The better option is to take a taxi from Nicoya, which will cost about US$20 round-trip. You can arrange for your driver to pick you up at a specified time.

If you have your own vehicle, take the peninsular highway south out of Nicoya toward Mansión and make a left on the access road leading to Puente La Amistad. From here, continue another 1.5km and make a left on the signed road to Barra Honda. The dirt road will take you to the village of Barra Honda then wind to the left for another 6km, passing Santa Ana, before ending at the national park gate. The road is clearly marked, and there are several signs along the way indicating the direction of the park. After the village of Barra Honda, the road is unpaved, but in good condition. However, there is no telling what the next rainy season will do, so ask locally before setting out.

If you are coming to the park from Puente La Amistad, you will see the access road to Barra Honda signed about 16km after leaving the bridge. From this point, follow the above directions.

Nosara Area

Nosara is a cocktail of international surf culture, stunning back-road topography, jungled microclimates, moneyed expat mayhem and yoga bliss. It effortlessly recalls Malibu, O'ahu's North Shore and Byron Bay, Australia, while remaining completely its own – only in Costa Rica – incarnation. Here, three stunning beaches are stitched together by a network of swerving, rutted earth roads that meander over coastal hills and kiss the coast just west of the small Tico village of Nosara. From the south, the first beach you'll come to is **Playa Garza**, still a sleepy Tico fishing village with an arc of pale brown sand and headlands on either side of the rippling bay. Fishing boats bob 100m from shore and there's a point break to the Northside. There are a few *cabinas* and *sodas* here too and lots of sand space with precious few tourists.

But there's a reason the majority of visitors descend on **Playa Guiones**. It's quite simply a slice of raw nectar: a wide, generous, undeveloped arc of marbled sand, with a few pebbles and shells mixed in, excellent beach breaks and plenty of space. It's an easygoing place for surfers, surf dogs and surf babies – you might just see unattended strollers lodged in the wet sand at low tide.

Playa Pelada, just north, is rough and rugged, dry and less endowed with surfers and luxury, which could be viewed as a luxury in itself. Things feel at once a touch spookier and more profound in Pelada. This beach lacks surf, so it's wonderful for children. It also has those sheared-away boulders tumbling into a foaming sea, two alluring beachside restaurants and a fishing village intimacy that Guiones lacks.

Inland are remnant pockets of luxuriant vegetation that attract birds and other wildlife. The area has seen little logging, partly because of the nearby wildlife refuge.

The area is spread out along the coast and a little inland (making wheels a necessity). Nosara village, where you'll find supplies and gas, as well as the airport, is 5km inland from the beach. The main areas with accommodations, restaurants and beaches are Playa Pelada to the north and Playa Guiones to the south. There are many unidentified little roads, which makes it hard to get around if you don't know the place – look for hotel and restaurant signs, and ask for help. For a handy map visit the website of **Nosara Travel** (www.nosaratravel.com/map.html).

🏃 Activities

Miss Sky   CANOPY TOUR
(📞2682-0969; www.missskycanopytour.com; adult/child 5-12 US$65/45; ⊗ office 7am-5pm) Miss Sky has brought a canopy tour to Nosara, with a total length of 11,000m above a pristine, private reserve. The zip lines don't go from platform to platform but from mountainside to mountainside, and have double cables for added safety. Your top speed will be about 45km/h. Tours leave twice daily, at 8am and 2pm. The morning tour is slightly longer.

Reserva Biológica Nosara   HIKING
(📞2682-0035; www.lagarta.com; admission US$6, guided nature walks US$15) The private 35-hectare reserve behind the Lagarta Lodge has trails leading through a mangrove wetland down to the river (five minutes) and beach (10 minutes). This is a great spot for birdwatching, and there's a good chance you'll see some reptiles as well (look up in the trees as there are occasionally boa constrictors here). Non-guests can visit the reserve for self-guided hikes or guided nature walks.

Tica Massage   SPA
(📞2682-0096; www.ticamassage.com; US$35-65; ⊗9am-6pm) After a hard day of surfing, treat yourself to a (totally legit) spa treatment at Tica Massage, in the Heart of Guiones Wellness Center. Services cater especially to surfers; or opt for a foot massage, a face massage or an invigorating 'Sea Glow' massage.

Coconut Harry's   SURFING
(📞2682-0574; www.coconutharrys.com; board rental per day US$15-20, lessons US$45; ⊗7am-5pm) At the main intersection in Guiones, this surf shop offers private lessons, board rental and stand-up paddle-board rental, and even rents snorkels and fins. Conveniently, there's a second location near the main break at Playa Guiones.

Nosara Surf Shop   SURFING
(📞2682-0186; www.nosarasurfshop.com; board rental per day US$15-20, surf lessons per hour US$40; ⊗7am-6pm) It rents surfboards, repairs dings and arranges surf lessons and tours.

Juan Surfo's Surf Shop   SURFING
(📞2682-1081; www.surfocostarica.com; board rental per day US$15-20, lessons per hour US$45; ⊗8am-6pm) Juan Surfo is a highly recommended surf teacher. His shop offers lessons and rents boards, as well as organizing transportation and tours. Located on the

northern loop road, 200m from the beach. Juan also rents rooms at the nearby Surf Lodge.

Nosara Yoga Institute YOGA
(📞 2682-0071; www.nosarayoga.com; classes US$15) This well-known yoga institute hosts a wide variety of drop-in classes (six daily during high season) ranging from Vinyasa to restorative to core strengthening. If you want more, it also holds workshops, retreats and instructor training courses for beginner and advanced students in a beautiful jungle setting. In the hills near Playa Guiones.

Pilates Nosara YOGA
(📞 8663 7354; www.pilatesnosara.com; per person US$10) Set in the Heart of Guiones Wellness Center, this studio offers Pilates mat and reformer classes (six daily during the high season). Teacher training and retreats are also held here.

Nosara Wellness YOGA
(📞 2682-0360; www.nosarawellness.com; per class US$10, private sessions from US$60) In Playa Pelada, this wellness center offers everything from massage and acupuncture to Pilates and yoga. If that's all too mainstream for you, sign up for a session of Aerial Yoga, which promises to 'realign you from the compression of gravity.'

🛏 Sleeping & Eating

🛏 Playa Guiones

★ **4 You Hostal** HOSTEL $
(📞 2682-1316; www.4youhostal.com; dm/s/d/bungalow US$18/25/40/55; P ❋ @ 🛜) A fantastic hostel close to the Guiones action. The high-end minimalist design makes this evolutionary flophouse (read: dorm) feel luxurious. Within the dorm are three pods which have walls that don't quite reach the soaring ceiling, allowing for extra privacy. The place is decked out with Balinese furniture and plenty of hammocks, not to mention a spotless community kitchen.

Nosara Beach Hostel HOSTEL $
(📞 2682-0238; www.nosarahostel.com; dm/d US$20/55; 🛜) Lounge in a hammock on the breezy porch, overlooking iguana-filled gardens. You're steps from the surf. You have a stone shower to wash away the sand and a comfy wooden bunk to crash on. There's a big communal kitchen, a spacious TV room

and – bonus – foosball. The vibe is super chill. All is right in your world.

Ask about giving back by volunteering at the reforestation nursery.

Kaya Sol HOSTEL $$
(📞 2682-1459; www.kayasol.com; dm US$18, d US$50-120; ❋ 🛜 🏊) The heart of this sprawling surfer-and-seeker retreat is the dorm-style accommodations. The shared bathrooms are spotless and the pool, with waterfall shower, is perfect for cooling off. There are also a few rooms and private cabins, some of which have kitchenettes. The onsite restaurant-bar is fun and tasty, though it can be noisy at night.

Gilded Iguana HOTEL $$
(📞 hotel 2682-0450, restaurant 2682-0259; www.thegildediguana.com; r with/without air-con from US$85/57, ste US$85-113; P ❋ 🛜 🏊) Down the second access road to Guiones, this long-standing hotel for anglers and surfers has well-furnished rooms with tile floors, big windows and shared terraces. The cheaper rooms are close to the bar and tend to be noisy. The tasty restaurant (mains US$9 to US$14) serves generous platters of fish tacos, fajitas and seafood specials, and the attached bar is a popular gringo hangout, with live music on Tuesday and Friday nights.

Living Hotel & Spa BOUTIQUE HOTEL $$$
(📞 2682-5201; www.livinghotelnosara.com; r incl breakfast with/without bathroom US$108/86; P ❋ @ 🛜 🏊) Relax amid the simplicity and serenity of this tropical paradise. Pristine white rooms have tile floors, shined wood ceilings and pretty stenciled walls. Tropical gardens surround the sparkling swimming pool, with plenty of communal space in the thatch-roof *rancho*. Located on the north beach access road.

Refresh your palette with a freshly-squeezed juice or some other healthy treat from the Living Cafe; refresh your mind and muscles with something from the full menu of spa treatments.

Nosara Suites HOTEL $$$
(📞 2682-1036; www.nosarasuites.com; d US$150; P ❋ @ 🛜 🏊) Clearly the designer was given free rein in these six swish suites, which feature glass-floored lofts, floating staircases and plenty of original artwork. Also, enjoy the king-sized beds and rain showers. Set upstairs from Cafe de Paris, a local landmark and noteworthy bakery, where you should eat breakfast.

Casa Romántica
B&B $$$

(☎ 2682-0272; www.casa-romantica.net; d incl breakfast with/without air-con US$127/119; P ❄ @ 🛜 ☕) Steps from Playa Guiones. Really, you can't get much closer. The rooms aren't fancy and some have funky layouts with odd corners, but the best of the bunch have high-beamed ceilings, wood furnishings and views of the manicured gardens. Management is warm and welcoming. Small recommended restaurant onsite.

L'Acqua Viva Hotel & Spa
HOTEL $$$

(☎ 2682-1087, in Canada 1877-216-0181, in USA 1888-273-1977; www.lacquaviva.com; r US$218, ste US$290-310; P ❄ 🛜 ☕) One of the most luxurious resorts in the central peninsula. Inside and out, the property is stunning, with water, wood and bamboo features throughout. The 36 contemporary rooms are decorated in minimalist style with all the five-star amenities you'd expect. Yet we do have one complaint: the location. It abuts the main Nosara road, and it's too far from the beach.

Nonetheless, the place is a stunner. The open-air restaurant and lounge, as well as the swimming pools, are open to visitors with a day pass (US$15). Well worth it if you need a break from the beach.

Beach Dog Café
CAFE $

(☎ 2682-1293; mains US$6-10, dinner mains US$12-15; ⊘ 7am-3pm daily, to 10pm Wed & Sat; P 🛜 🍴) Just steps from the beach, this groovy cafe is decadent and delicious. Try banana bread French toast for breakfast, or uber-popular fish tacos for lunch. Dinner is only a couple of nights a week, but they occasionally host live music and show movies on the beach.

Robin's Cafe & Ice Cream
CAFE $

(☎ 2682-0617; www.robinsicecream.com; mains US$5-8; ⊘ 8am-5pm Mon-Sat, 10am-4pm Sun; 🛜 🍴) This cafe is perfectly suited to the health-conscious yogis and surfers who live in and visit Nosara. You'll see Robin working the kitchen, preparing a welcome menu of sweet and savory crepes, tempting wraps and sandwiches on homemade, whole-wheat focaccias. If you must indulge your sweet tooth, the ice cream is homemade and sublime.

Taco! Taco!
TAQUERÍA $

(☎ 2682-0574; tacos US$4-8; ⊘ 11am-4pm; 🍴 ♿) Every beach town needs an open-air taquería where surfers and beach bums can get a quick fix. In Nosara, it's Taco! Taco!, right on the main road into town. It does tacos and only tacos, stuffed with slow-cooked meat, fresh fish or grilled veggies, and topped with savory salsas and delectable guacamole. This place has earned its exclamation points.

Rosi's Soda Tica
SODA $

(☎ 2682-0728; mains US$3-6; ⊘ 8am-3pm Mon-Sat) Next to Marlin Bill's on the main highway, this is the only soda in Guiones and it's a damn good one. Things are kept simple with casados for lunch and gallo pinto in the morning. All are served in airy, cheerful environs.

Marlin Bill's
SEAFOOD, BURGERS $$

(☎ 2682-0458; meals US$11-25; ⊘ 11am-10pm Mon-Sat) Across the main road from the Guiones swirl, this is one of the few restaurants with views of the ocean. The casual, open-air dining room is a perfect place to feast on grilled tuna, ceviche and other fresh seafood. Bill is famous for his burgers, so if you are hankering for the taste of home, he's your man.

🛌 Playa Pelada

Paspartu Beach Hotel
BOUTIQUE HOTEL $

(☎ 8718-3255; paspartuCR@hotmail.com; r US$35-40; 🛜) 'A free spot for free thinkers.' Surrounding a small shady garden, six sweet rooms have pastel painted walls, high wood ceilings and windows to the trees. The whole place is painted with creative, colorful murals. Bike rental available. This one is a gem. (Plus, it's next door to the gelato place.)

★ Refugio del Sol
GUESTHOUSE $$

(☎ 8825-9365, 2682-0287; www.refugiodelsol.net; s/d US$35/55, d with kitchen US$65; P 🛜) A short stroll from the sand, this rustic lodge is decked out with ceramic tiled floors, beamed ceilings, wood furnishings, candles and lanterns, and other soulful touches that make it feel like home. Rooms open onto a wide L-shaped patio with hammocks. The gorgeous young owners make tasty Italian food for guests every night, and are generous of heart.

Lagarta Lodge
LODGE $$

(☎ 2682-0035; www.lagarta.com; r s/d/tr/q US$85/90/96/102, ste s/d/tr/q US$120/125/130/136, air-con US$10; P ❄ @ 🛜 ☕) At the northern end of Pelada, a road dead-ends at this 12-room lodge, a recommended choice set high on a steep hill above a 50-hectare reserve (bird-watching and wildlife-spotting are good here). Large rooms have high ceilings, stucco walls and private patios, while suites take advantage of floor-to-ceiling windows and extra living space. The panoramas are priceless.

The balcony restaurant is worth a visit just for the spectacular views of the river, mountains, sea and sunset, though the rotating menu of international and Tico specialties is also appealing.

Villa Mango B&B
B&B $$

(☑2682-1168; www.villamangocr.com; s/d/tr/q incl breakfast from US$78/89/101/112; P ☎ ☒) You can't help but relax at this B&B in the trees, set high on a hillside with views of both bays. The spacious rooms have a Mediterranean flair, with gorgeous views and rustic stone and wood details. Lounge on the luxurious terrace and enjoy views of the ocean, or take a short stroll down to the isolated stretch of beach.

Rancho Suizo
LODGE $$

(☑2682-0975, 2682-0057; www.nosara.ch; s/d/tr incl breakfast US$45/62/94; P ☎ ☒) Well organized and welcoming, this longtime Swiss outpost offers pretty tiled rooms with stucco walls, wood paneling and small terraces overlooking the garden. Shell-studded flagstones weave through the trees, home to howlers and iguanas. The nearby Piratabar is a laid-back nightspot, 200m from the beach.

Nosara Retreat
B&B $$

(☑2682-0209; www.nosararetreat.com; s/d/villa incl breakfast US$55/70/85; ☎) This sweet retreat is set up for yoga camps, but it's open for individual travelers in search of a clean, quiet getaway. A rocky path winds through the shady garden, connecting the appealing rooms in the main house, the larger villas and the open-air yoga pavilion. It's a rugged, five-minute walk to the beach.

★ Seekretspot
GELATO $

(☑2682-1325; gelato US$3-6; ☎) The secret is out: come to this sweet shack for an authentic gelato or sorbetto, made with love by Stefano and Frederica. For local flavor, go for coffee or coconut. If you need a pick-me-up, there are also fresh-brewed espresso drinks. It also has internet (US$4 per hour). Next to Paspartu Beach Hotel.

La Luna
INTERNATIONAL $$

(☑2682-0122; dishes US$9-24; ☎11am-11pm Mon-Fri, 8am-11pm Sat & Sun) Located on the beach, this trendy restaurant-bar has cushy couches right on the sand, perfect for sunset drinks. The interior is equally appealing, with soaring ceilings, a gorgeous hardwood bar and walls adorned with work by local artists. Asian and Mediterranean flourishes round out the eclectic menu, and the views (and cocktails) are intoxicating. Call ahead for reservations.

Olga's Beach Club
COSTA RICAN $$

(☑8848-0403; mains US$9-16; ☎10am-10pm) The *other* beachfront restaurant on Pelada is an old-fashioned beach bar, offering traditional Tico fare, pizza and *batidos* – and the occasional pig roast. The place does not pretend to be anything other than what it is: an open-air *palapa* with tasty food and reggae music, good vibes and good views.

Drinking & Entertainment

Hear live music and get your groove on at the bar at Kaya Sol (p319) or down the street at the Gilded Iguana (p319). The Beach Dog Café (p320) also has live music when open in the evenings. Head to Olga's Beach Club (p321) after dark for drinking and dancing.

Information

There are two gas stations in Nosara village. That strange concrete lotus flower that peaks above the trees and is visible from both beaches is the tumbledown remains of Hotel Las Playas Nosara, and is a good place for a surreptitious photo shoot if not a beach getaway. It looks almost...haunted.

Banco Popular (☑2682-0011, 2682-0267; ☎9am-3pm Mon-Fri) Changes US dollars and traveler's checks, and gives cash advances on Visa cards only; the ATM also only accepts Visa cards.

Nosara Travel (☑2682-0300; www.nosaratravel.com; ☎9am-3pm Mon-Fri) In Playa Guiones, this office books air tickets, arranges car rentals and books hotels or vacation homes.

NosaraNet & Frog Pad (☑2682-4039; www.thefrogpad.com; per hour US$6; ☎9am-7pm Mon-Sat, 10am-6pm Sun; ☎) In addition to internet, the Frog Pad has used books for sale and rents out DVDs, bikes (per day US$10) and surfboards (per day US$15).

Police (☑2682-0317) Next to the Red Cross and post office on the southeast corner of the soccer field in Nosara village center.

❶ Getting There & Away

AIR

NatureAir has two daily flights to and from San José for about US$103 one way.

BUS

Local buses depart from the *pulpería* (corner grocery store) by the soccer field. Traroc buses depart for Nicoya (US$2, two hours, five daily). Empresa Alfaro buses going to San José (US$9, six hours) depart from the pharmacy by the soccer field at 2:45pm. To get to Sámara, take any bus out of Nosara and ask the driver to drop you off at 'la bomba de Sámara' (Sámara gas station). From there, catch one of the buses traveling from Nicoya to Sámara.

CAR

From Nicoya, a paved road leads toward Playa Sámara. About 5km before Sámara (signed), a windy, bumpy (and, in the dry season, dusty) dirt road leads to Nosara village (4WD recommended). It's also possible to drive north (in the dry season), to Ostional, Junquillal and Paraíso, though you'll have to ford a few rivers. Ask around before trying this in the rainy season, when Río Nosara becomes impassable.

There are a handful of rental car agencies in the Nosara area:

Alamo (☑ 2242-7733; www.alamocostarica. com; Playa Pelada)

Economy Rent a Car (☑ 2299-2000; www. economyrentacar.com; Playa Guiones)

Refugio Nacional de Fauna Silvestre Ostional

This 248-hectare coastal refuge extends from Punta India in the north to Playa Guiones in the south, and includes the beaches of Playa Nosara and Playa Ostional. It was created in 1992 to protect the *arribadas,* or mass nestings of the olive ridley sea turtles, which occur from July to November with a peak from August to October. Along with Playa Nancite in Parque Nacional Santa Rosa, Ostional is one of two main nesting grounds for this turtle in Costa Rica.

The olive ridley is one of the smallest species of sea turtle, typically weighing around 45kg. Although they are endangered, there are a few beaches in the world where ridleys nest in large groups that can number in the thousands. Scientists believe that this behavior is an attempt to overwhelm predators.

Prior to the creation of the park, coastal residents used to harvest eggs indiscriminately (drinking raw turtle eggs is thought to increase sexual vigor). However, an imaginative conservation plan has allowed the inhabitants of Ostional to continue to harvest eggs from the first laying, which are often trampled by subsequent waves of nesting turtles. By allowing locals to harvest the first batches, the economic livelihood of the community is maintained, and the villagers in turn act as park rangers to prevent other poachers from infringing on their enterprise.

Rocky Punta India at the northwestern end of the refuge has tide pools that abound with marine life, such as sea anemone, urchin and starfish. Along the beach, thousands of almost transparent ghost crabs go about their business, as do the bright-red Sally Lightfoot crabs. The sparse vegetation behind the beach consists mainly of deciduous trees and is home to iguanas, crabs, howler monkeys, coatis and many birds. Near the southeastern edge of the refuge is a small mangrove swamp where there is good bird-watching.

🕊 Activities

Mass arrivals of nesting turtles occur during the rainy season every three or four weeks and last about a week (usually on dark nights preceding a new moon), though it's possible to see turtles in lesser numbers almost any night during nesting season. In the dry season, a fitting consolation prize is the small number of leatherback and green turtles that also nest here. Many tour operators in the region offer tours to Ostional during nesting season, though you can arrange with local guides to visit independently. Contact the **Association Guias Locales** (☑ 2682-0428) in the center of Ostional town across from Soda La Plaza.

Surfers catch some good lefts and rights here just after low tide. Otherwise, this stretch of sea is notorious for strong currents and isn't suitable for swimming unless you're green and have flippers. But there is 5km of unbroken beach here, sprinkled with driftwood and swaying with coconut palms.

🛏 Sleeping & Eating

Camping (US$3 per person) is permitted behind the centrally located Soda La Plaza, which has a portable toilet available. The *soda* is open for breakfast, lunch and dinner.

Ostional Turtle Lodge LODGE $

(☑2682-0131; www.surfingostional.com; s/d/tr/q from US$26/40/56/70) A great guesthouse with only five simple rooms, equipped with the basics (pay more for air-con). The pièce de résistance is the exquisite community *rancho* with hammocks, backed by mangroves, overlooking pastureland and within earshot of the sea.

Albergue Ecoturismo Arribadas LODGE $$

(☑2682-0790; www.arribadas.com; cabins US$100) Located in the center of town, this lodge offers spotless rooms with high slanted ceilings, new tiles and private bathrooms. It's normally used for groups of students and volunteers tracking turtles. They help arrange turtle tours, as well as offer a two-night turtle camp for kids.

Brovilla Resort Hotel LODGE $$

(☑8519-6059; www.brovillaresorthotel.com; d with/ without kitchen US$107/85, villas from US$118; P☀️📶❄️) In the hills north of town, this is the area's original ecolodge. Attractive rooms are constructed from wood and stone, with gorgeous stone showers and sliding doors opening to sea views. Concrete villas have flagstone accents, built-in cabinetry and loft bedrooms. Look for colorful murals and kitschy seashell accents, lest you forget you are at the beach.

Onsite, there is a *palapa*-style restaurant serving tropical fare and fresh-baked artisan bread. Reservations recommended; cash required.

❶ Getting There & Away

Ostional village is about 8km northwest of Nosara village. During the dry months there is one daily bus from Santa Cruz (two hours), departing Ostional at 5am and returning from Santa Cruz at 12:30pm. Times change, so be sure to confirm. In any case, at any time of the year the road can get washed out by rain. Hitchhiking from Nosara is reportedly easy.

If you're driving, plan on taking a 4WD as a few rivers need to be crossed on the way to Ostional. Ask locally about conditions before setting out. From the main road joining Nosara beach and village, head north and cross the bridge over the Río Nosara. There's a T-junction 2km after the bridge. Take the left fork (which is signed) and continue on the main road north to Ostional, about 6km away.

Beyond Ostional, the dirt road continues on to Marbella before arriving in Paraíso, northeast of Junquillal. Be careful and ask before attempting this drive, and use a 4WD.

Playa Sámara

Is Sámara the black hole of happiness? That's what more than one expat has said after stopping here on vacation and never leaving. And perhaps it is more than the sum of its parts? Because on the surface it's just an easy-to-navigate beach town with barefoot, three-star appeal and a crescent-shaped strip of pale-gray sand spanning two rocky headlands, where the sea is calm and beautiful. Not spectacular, just safe, mellow, reasonably developed, easily navigable on foot and accessible by public transportation. Not surprisingly, you'll find it's popular with vacationing Tico and foreign families and backpackers, who enjoy Sámara's palpable ease and tranquillity. But be careful, the longer you stay the less you'll want to leave.

If you've got some extra time and a 4WD, explore the hidden beaches north of Sámara, such as Playa Barrigona, equally famous for its pristine beach as for its celebrity resident, Mel Gibson.

TRACKING TURTLES

Since 1997 **Programa Restauración de Tortugas Marinas** (Pretoma Marine Turtle Restoration Program; www.pretoma.org) has collaborated with locals to monitor turtle-nesting activity and operate hatcheries. Members of the community are hired as field assistants, and environmental education activities are held with the children in town. The project also involves tagging, measuring and protecting nesting turtles, which has resulted in a drastic reduction in poaching levels.

At the time of writing, Pretoma was operating projects in Playa Caletas, Playa San Miguel, Playa Corozalito (on the central Pacific coast) and Punta Banco, near the border with Panama. For more information on volunteering, visit the website.

⚡ Activities

Experienced surfers will probably be bored with Sámara's inconsistent waves, though beginners will have a blast.

Pato Surf School SURFING
(☑8761-4738; www.patossurfingsafari.com; board rental per day US$15, lessons US$25-35) Set right on the beach, Pato offers inexpensive and quality board rental, and beginner surf instruction. Pay for a lesson and get free board rental for five days! Also on offer: stand-up paddle-board rental and lessons; kayak rental and tours; and snorkel gear. Plus, massage on the beach and occasional beach yoga. What else do you want?

C&C Surf School SURFING
(☑5006-0369; www.cncsurfsamara.webs.com; board rentals per day US$16, lessons semiprivate/private US$30/40; ☺8am-8pm) A great choice, offering private and semiprivate lessons. The school donates 10% from every surf lesson to a local children's school and a turtle conservation project. C&C also organizes surf tours up and down the peninsula.

Wing Nuts CANOPY TOUR
(☑2656-0153; www.wingnutscanopy.com; adult/child US$60/40; ☺tours 8am, 9am, noon & 1pm) One entrepreneurial family found a way to preserve their beautiful, wild patch of dry tropical forest: by setting up a small-scale canopy tour. Family-owned and professionally run, this 10-platform operation is unique for its personal approach, as groups max out at 10 people. The price includes transportation from your hotel in Sámara.

Flying Crocodile SCENIC FLIGHTS
(☑2656-8048; www.flying-crocodile.com; flights 20/30/60min US$110/150/230, lessons per hour US$230) About 6km north of Sámara in Playa Buenavista, the Flying Crocodile offers ultralight flights and lessons.

⚡ Courses

Centro de Idiomas
Intercultura LANGUAGE COURSE
(☑2656-0127, 2260-8480; www.samaralanguageschool.com; courses per week with/without homestay US$483/315) Centro de Idiomas Intercultura claims to be the only Spanish school directly on the beach, which makes for a pleasant – if not always productive – place to study. Language courses can be arranged with or without a family homestay.

🛏 Sleeping

As a general guideline, budget options have cold-water showers, while midrange and top-end facilities have hot water.

Entre Dos Aguas GUESTHOUSE $
(☑2656-0998; www.hoteldosaguas.com; d US$47-52, tr/q US$60/70, ste US$90-105; ℗@☀) This fantastic little inn offers the charming personality and artistic atmosphere of a boutique hotel at the price of a roadside motel. Seven brightly colored rooms have private stone showers, vibrant woven linens and many homey touches – all with access to an inviting common courtyard and lush gardens. It's just north of the main intersection on the road to Nicoya.

El Cactus Hostel HOSTEL $
(☑2656-3224; wwwsamarabackpacker.com; dm/d US$16/38; ☎☀) Brightly painted in citrus colors, El Cactus is a great new addition for Sámara's backpacker set. All rooms are brand new, with wooden furniture, fresh paint jobs, clean linens and hot-water showers. Hammocks hang around a small pool, while a fully equipped kitchen is also available. Located on a side street in the center of town, 100m from the beach.

Hotel Matilori HOSTEL $
(☑2656-0291; hostelmatilori@gmail.com; dm/s/d/tw US$16/30/36/32; ℗☎) A terrific-value hostel with private rooms (and shared bathrooms) in the main house and wooden dorm rooms that sleep six in the newer annex. All the rooms have fresh coats of jewel-toned paints, and guests have use of an updated kitchen. The ownership is quite endearing.

Hostel Mariposas HOSTEL $
(☑2656-0314, 8703-3625; www.hostelmariposas.com; camp US$8, hammock US$8, dm US$16, d without bathroom US$36; ☎) Down a dirt road (on the way to the language school) is a fun hostel that guarantees a good time, as long as you're in the right frame of mind. It's got wooden rooms and dorms, plenty of swaying hammocks, paper lantern lighting and a communal kitchen. It's just 60m from the sand.

Casa Paraiso GUESTHOUSE $
(☑2656-0741; sabinasalvatore@hotmail.com; d US$45; ☎) There's a lovely little guesthouse tucked in behind Ahora Sí. Eight simple rooms are brushed in deep blues and inviting pastels, with thematic murals, high ceilings and comfy beds. Ceiling fans keep you cool while hot-water showers will warm you up.

La Mansion B&B
B&B $

(☑ 2265-0165; www.samarabeach.com; s/d/ste US$40/60/120; ❄️📶) This whitewashed concrete hacienda is on a quiet street, twirling with fans and bursting with colorful knickknacks. There's loads of charm: rooms are spacious and bright, plus the breakfast is huge. Bathrooms are shared.

Hotel Casa Valeria
HOTEL $

(☑ 2656-0511; casavaleria_af@hotmail.com; r with bathroom US$50-70, s/d without bathroom US$25/30; P❄️) A cheery guesthouse with hammocks in the garden and comfy public spaces, located on a sweet slice of beach. Some rooms are bigger than others, and those with private bathroom that sleep up to four are a steal. It's about 100m east of the main road. It only accepts cash.

Tico Adventure Lodge
LODGE $$

(☑ 2656-0628; www.ticoadventurelodge.com; tw/d/q US$57/68/84; P❄️📶) The US owners are proud of the fact that they built this lodge without cutting down a single tree, and they have every reason to be – it's stunning. Nine double rooms and several larger apartments are surrounded by lush vegetation and old-growth trees. There's an outdoor kitchen and cookout area for communal use, as well as an onsite massage studio.

Sámara Palm Lodge
GUESTHOUSE $$

(☑ 2656-1169; www.samarapalmlodge.com; d US$60-80; P❄️📶) An inviting little lodge on the edge of town. Eight spotless rooms feature a tropical decor, with natural wood furniture, tile floors and colorful artwork. They face a lush garden and enticing swimming pool. Hosts Brigitte and Lothar are delightful.

Hotel Casa del Mar
HOTEL $$

(☑ 2656-0264; www.casadelmarsamara.net; d with/without bathroom incl breakfast US$85/45; P❄️📶) 🏊 Surrounding a big mango tree and a tiny swimming pool are 17 rooms with whitewashed stucco walls and tile floors. The rooms that share a bathroom are a steal (and you can still use the Jacuzzi).

Hotel Giada
HOTEL $$

(☑ 2656-0132; www.hotelgiada.net; s/d/q incl breakfast US$70/90/110; P❄️📶) A pleasant place with sponge painted rooms, located in a hacienda huddled between two pools. It's in the center of town so it ain't quiet, but new double-plated windows cut back the street noise. Colorful African art and a leafy landscape offer plenty of charm.

Rancho de la Playa
HOTEL $$

(☑ 2656-0573; www.ranchodelaplaya.com; dm US$20, r with bathroom US$60-70, r without bathroom US$40-50; P❄️@📶) Now under new management, this sprawling place has a wide variety of rooms and apartments with widely varying standards. In the best of them, look for mango-painted walls, high wood ceilings, tile floors and wood furniture. The onsite bar-restaurant is fun, often hosting live music, although it can be loud if you're trying to sleep.

★ El Pequeño Gecko Verde
BUNGALOW $$$

(☑ 2656-1176; www.gecko-verde.com; r US$95-105, bungalows US$100-175; P❄️📶) A hidden slice of heaven. Contemporary and beautifully decorated bungalows have beds dressed in plush linens, artisanal carvings on the walls, private terraces with hammocks and outdoor dining areas, plus our favorite feature – outdoor stone showers. Onsite amenities include a saltwater swimming pool with waterfall, lush gardens and a fabulous open-air restaurant and bar.

Behind the property, a 400m jungle trail and steep cement staircase lead to a secret beach that doesn't appear on any map – Playa Izquierda, a stunning cove backed by high cliffs with amazing sunset views. Located several kilometers west on the road to Nosara.

Las Ranas
LODGE $$$

(☑ 2656-0609; www.lodgelasranas.com; d/tr US$118/135; P❄️📶) A sharp stucco lodge with a king's location. We're talking nearly 180 degrees of ocean vistas from the restaurant, pool and upper rooms. And those rooms are gorgeous, with canopy beds, granite tile floors, balconies and soaring beamed ceilings. It's a few kilometers west of town, so you'll need wheels.

But it's worth the trip, as the leafy grounds are alive with birdlife and other animals. Spotted here: a stunning pair of western tanagers.

Sámara Tree House Inn
BUNGALOW $$$

(☑ 2656-0733; www.samaratreehouse.com; bungalows incl breakfast US$150; P❄️@📶) These five stilted tree houses for grown-ups are so appealing that you might not want to leave. Fully equipped kitchens have pots and pans hanging from driftwood racks, huge windows welcome light and breezes, and hammocks are hung underneath the raised bungalows. Four of the units face the beach. You can't get much closer than this.

✗ Eating

Self-caterers can stock up on supplies at Super Sámara Market, east of the main road, or the smaller Super La Amistad on the main road by the beach.

★ Ahora Sí   VEGETARIAN $

(☑2656-0741; www. ahorasi.isamara.co; mains US$5-11; ⊙noon-9pm; P 🤖 🍴) A Venetian-owned vegetarian restaurant and all-natural cocktail bar. It does smoothies with coconut milk; gnocchi with nutmeg, sage and smoked cheese; soy burgers and yucca fries; wok stir-fries; and thin-crust pizzas. All served on a lovingly decorated tiled patio. Required eating.

Lo Que Hay   MEXICAN $

(☑2656-0811; tacos US$2, meals from US$6; ⊙7am-late) This rocking beachside *taquería* and pub offers six delectable taco fillings (fish, chorizo, chicken, beef, pork, veggie). The grilled avocados stuffed with *pico de gallo* are worth the money. Even *sin* tacos, it's a good time, as the bar crowd sips into the wee hours.

Luv Burger   VEGETARIAN $

(☑2656-3348; www.luvburger.com; mains US$5-8; ⊙8am-5pm; 🍴) 'Luv' is the operative word here. Feel it, veggies. There are burgers, but they are not made of meat. Neither is the pizza, pasta or sandwiches. It's all veggie, all the time, from vegan pancakes for breakfast to cashew no-goat-cheese pizza for lunch. Wash it down with a glass of organic wine or a microbrew beer.

Cafe Carola   CAFE $

(☑8994-9171; items US$4; ⊙7am-6:30pm daily, 7-10pm Wed & Fri; 🍴) Stop by this shady German bakery for breakfast, for sandwiches or for something to sate your sweet tooth. The book exchange, board games and strong espresso drinks complete the picture. This friendly place is also open for live music on Wednesday nights and Chinese food on Friday nights.

Al Manglar   ITALIAN $$

(☑2656-0096; mains US$9-18; ⊙5-10pm; P🍴) This thatched-roof, open-air restaurant serves excellent gnocchi and ravioli, and the pizzas are perfect. It's tucked along a side street behind El Lagarto.

Casa Esmeralda   SODA $$

(☑2656-0489; mains US$9-17; ⊙noon-9:30pm Mon-Sat) A favorite with locals, it's a dressed-up *soda* with tablecloths, faux-dobe walls and tasty salads, pastas, meat, chicken and fish dishes. The *arroz con camarones* (rice and prawns) comes highly recommended.

Gusto Beach   INTERNATIONAL $$

(☑2656-0252; mains US$9-17; ⊙9am-11pm; P🤖) Good food, great location. Enjoy pastas, salads and seafood, as well as phenomenal smoothies and creative cocktails, all while watching the action on the beach. If you care to linger, there are lounge chairs on the sand, lockers and beach volleyball.

El Lagarto   BARBECUE $$

(☑2656-0750; www.ellagartobbq.com; mains US$11-20; ⊙10am-11pm; 🤖) Grilled meats are the big draw at this beachfront alfresco restaurant, studded with old trees. Watching the chefs work their magic on the giant wood-fired oven is part of the fun. Wash it all down with the biggest margaritas you've ever seen.

🍸 Drinking & Nightlife

Lo Que Hay (p326) lures a gringo crowd and keeps it rocking deep into the night.

Zen Den   COCKTAIL BAR

(☑8725-0611, 2656-2323; www.samarabeach/zenden.com; ⊙6pm-2am) Sámara's most grown-up nightspot is this romantic cocktail lounge, where you can hunker down on comfy couches or sit outside and watch the street action. The atmosphere is casual yet sophisticated, with occasional live music to keep you entertained.

La Vela Latina   BAR

(☑2656-2286; http://samarabeach.com/lavelalatina; ⊙11am-midnight; 🤖) Settle into a comfy chair on the sand and order a bucket of icy beers or a perfectly blended cocktail at this beach bar. There's also a menu of sophisticated *bocas* and American-style pub grub.

Bar Arriba   BAR

(☑2656-1052; ⊙5:30pm-2am) Part sports bar, part dance club, total party place. The lighting is sufficiently dim, the flat screen strobes, the sound system thumps and they pour all your favorite kinds of rum. As the name suggests, it's located on the second level of the Centro Comercial Shana.

Shopping

Cocotales JEWELRY
(☎ 8807-7056; ⊙ 7:30am-7:30pm) Carlos travels around South America to procure gorgeous semiprecious stones, which he crafts into fine jewelry right here in the back of his shop. But his most unique and eye-catching pieces are crafted from coco beans (grown locally, of course).

Marea Surf Shop SPORTS
(☎ 2656-1181; www.mareasurfshop.com; ⊙ 7am-6pm) Part cafe, part downtown surf shop, it doesn't rent gear but does have top-quality tees, hats, board shorts and boards for the buying. Bonus: the shopkeeper steams a fine espresso.

ℹ Information

Surf the excellent www.samarabeach.com to get the skinny on Sámara.

Banco Costa Rica (⊙ 9am-4pm Mon-Fri) Just off the main road and across from the cell tower and soccer field, it changes foreign currency and has a 24-hour ATM.

Banco Nacional (☎ 2656-0086; ⊙ 9am-5pm Mon-Fri) Change money at this bank next to the church; there's also an ATM.

La Vida Verde (Green Life; ☎ 2656-1051; per kg US$3; ⊙ 8am-6pm Mon-Sat) Drop your dirty duds off at this laundromat, 75m west of Banco Nacional. Or call ahead for pick-up and delivery.

Post Office (⊙ 8am-noon & 1:15-5:30pm Mon-Fri) Located in the same building as the police station, on the main road where it meets the beach.

Sky Net Tours (Sámara Adventure Company; ☎ 2656-0920; www.samara-tours.com; internet per hour US$2; ⊙ 9am-9pm) Formerly the Sámara Travel Center, this extremely helpful place has an internet cafe, and can book flights and Interbus tickets and arrange tours. It also rents bicycles (per day US$10) and scooters/motorcycles (per day US$30).

ℹ Getting There & Away

The beach lies about 35km southwest of Nicoya on a paved road. No flights were operating out of the Sámara airport (PLD) at research time.

BUS
Empresa Alfaro has a bus to San José (US$8, five hours) that departs at 4am and 8am. All buses depart from the main intersection just south of Entre Dos Aguas guesthouse. Purchase your San José bus tickets at the Alfaro office, located behind Bazar d'Liss on the main intersection in town.

Traroc buses to Nicoya (US$2.50, one hour) depart hourly from 4am to 6pm from the *pulpería* by the soccer field; there's a more limited schedule on Sunday.

Playa Carrillo

About 4km southeast of Sámara, Carrillo is a wide, arcing beach with clean white sand, cracked granite headlands and a jungle backdrop. On weekends and holidays, the palm-fringed boulevard is lined with cars and the beach crowded with Tico families. At other times, it's practically deserted.

The little town is on a hillside above the beach and attracts a trickle of sunbathers and surfers working their way down the coast, as well as schools of American sportfishers chasing billfish.

◉ Sights & Activities

La Selva WILDLIFE RESERVE
(☎ 2656-2236; adult/child US$15/10; ⊙ 8am-7pm) Up the hill and about 200m east of the beach, La Selva is a small but well-maintained wildlife refuge, with monkeys, iguanas, alligators, coatimundis and other critters. You can use your ticket twice: come in the morning before the heat of the day, then return around sunset when the nocturnal creatures wake up. This is a private venture, so the price of admission pays to protect and rehabilitate these animals. Warning: wear open-toed shoes at your own risk (fire ants).

Blue Barrel Surf School SURFING, KAYAKING
(☎ 2656-0086; www.bluebarrelsurfschool.com; surf lessons per hour US$40-50, kayaking US$35-50) Family-run and family-oriented, Blue Barrel offers special packages catering to kids, teenagers and families. Carrillo's surf is small compared to other Nicoya beaches, making it a great place to learn. Combine your family surf vacation with kayaking, turtle tours or Spanish lessons.

Kingfisher Sportfishing SPORTFISHING
(☎ 2656-0091; www.costaricabillfishing.com; excursions from US$800) A well-known local outfit, offering packages including lodging.

⟳ Tours

Carrillo Tours TOUR
(☎ 2656-0543; www.carrillotours.com; ⊙ 8am-7pm) On the road up the hill, Carrillo Tours organizes turtle tours, snorkeling, kayaking, horseback riding and trips to Palo Verde.

🛏 Sleeping & Eating

At the eastern end of the beach, take the turnoff that leads steeply uphill to reach most of the village's hotels and restuarants. It's a five- to 10-minute walk.

La Posada
B&B $

(☎ 6193-7266, 2656-3131; www.laposada.co.cr; d incl breakfast US$40-50; P❉🐾) High on the hill with sweeping panoramas of the trees and the sea, this new B&B is a sweet addition to Carrillo. Simple rooms have tile or concrete floors, wood and wicker furniture and tropical flourishes. It's worth the extra ten for an ocean-view room, which also include a breezy terrace and rocking chairs from which to take it in.

Otherwise, there's a big communal terrace that's also furnished with rockers. Yoga classes are held here several times a week.

★ La Tropicale
BUNGALOW $$

(☎ 8884-9471, 2656-0159; www.playacarrillocostarica.com; d incl breakfast US$60; P❉🐾) Across from La Selva is a fun, funky, fabulous inn that has ramshackle charm and plenty of hip touches. Two colorful macaws stand guard at the porch, from where a stony path winds around the sparkling swimming pool and through mango, papaya and coconut trees. Stand-alone bungalows are draped with bold linens, lit with funky light fixtures and hung with original art. The romantic restaurant is open only for guests to enjoy continental breakfasts, light lunches and exotic Mediterranean dinners.

Cabinas El Colibrí
CABINA $$

(☎ 2656-0656; www.cabinaselcolibri.com; d incl breakfast US$60, apt US$65; P❉🐾) At this relaxed Argentine-owned property, pleasant, spacious *cabinas* have vaulted beamed ceilings and hammocks on the porch. You'll be well fed at the attached steak house, which serves traditional Argentine *parrilladas* (grilled meats), *empanadas* (turnovers stuffed with meat or cheese) and fresh grilled tuna.

Hotel Esperanza
HOTEL $$$

(☎ 2656-0564; www.hotelesperanza.com; d incl breakfast US$124; P❉@🐾) Cheerful rooms at this recently remodeled hotel are set back from a columned promenade, opening on to the pool area. The rooms are smallish, but nicely decorated, featuring mahogany furniture, excellent mattresses and tile bathrooms. All the expected amenities

are here, and you can also book tours or – even better – a massage in the lovely garden. Located 100m west of the soccer field.

Hideaway Hotel
BOUTIQUE HOTEL $$$

(☎ 2656-1145; www.thehideawayplayasamara.com; d incl breakfast US$145; P❉🐾) Midway between Carrillo and Sámara, this attractive whitewashed place is noteworthy for its super service and intimate atmosphere. A dozen spacious tiled suites all overlook the pleasant pool and blooming gardens. The airy restaurant is excellent. There is a small beach at the end of the road; alternatively Playa Carrillo is a 15-minute walk.

ℹ Getting There & Away

Sansa flights were no longer servicing the airstrip just northwest of the beach at research time. The Traroc buses from Nicoya to Sámara continue on the well-paved road to Playa Carrillo (US$2.50, 90 minutes, 12 daily).

Islita Area

The coast southeast of Playa Carrillo remains one of the peninsula's most isolated and wonderful stretches of coastline, mainly because much of it is inaccessible and lacking in accommodations. But if you're willing to tackle rugged roads or venture down the coastline in a sea kayak (or possibly on foot), you'll be rewarded with abandoned beaches backed by pristine wilderness and rugged hills.

There are a few small breaks in front of the Hotel Punta Islita, where you'll find a gorgeous cove punctuated with that evocative wave-thrashed boulder that is Punta Islita. At high tide the beach narrows, but at low tide it is wide and as romantic as those vistas from above. Another good beach and point break lies north of Punta Islita at **Playa Camaronal**, a charcoal gray stretch of sand strewn with driftwood and sheltered by two headlands. This beach also happens to be a protected nesting site for leatherback, olive ridley, hawksbill and black turtles, and is officially known as **Refugio Nacional de Vida Silvestre Camaronal** (⊙8am-6pm). Nearby hotels and tour operators such as Carrillo Tours can make arrangements for nighttime turtle tours.

Playas Corzalito and **Bejuco** to the south of Punta Islita are both backed by mangrove swamps, and offer good opportunities for bird- and wildlife-watching.

Islita is a pretty little town centered on a church and a soccer field, spruced up by artwork. The place looks unexpectedly prosperous, thanks to the efforts of the Hotel Punta Islita, which channels funding into the local community. Case in point: **Museo Islita** (⊙8am-4pm Mon-Sat), an imaginative contemporary art house crusted with mosaic murals, and featuring carvings and paintings that adorn everything from houses to tree trunks. Worth a peek.

The hotel's most recent sustainability project is a partnership with the **Ara Project** (www.thearaproject.org), a local NGO dedicated to the conservation of Costa Rica's two species of macaw: the great green macaw and the scarlet macaw. Thanks to the hotel's donation, the Ara Project has opened a new breeding center in Islita, as well as an education and viewing center, Lapa Lookout, where guests can learn more.

🛏 Sleeping & Eating

You can camp on the beaches (without facilities) if you have a vehicle and are self-sufficient. Aside from the resort, there is one *soda*, a *pulpería* and not much else.

Hotel Punta Islita   RESORT **$$$**
(☎2231-6122; www.hotelpuntaislita.com; d incl breakfast from US$258; [P][✳][@][🛜][🌊]) 🍃 The hotel located on a hilltop, and has 57 fully equipped rooms with staggering ocean views. (If you spring for a suite, you'll enjoy this view from a private outdoor Jacuzzi.) The infinity pool and surrounding grounds are stunning. The amenities onsite do not stop, including a full-service spa, a beach club with a sunken pool bar and lounges on a rolling lawn.

This luxury resort serves as an example of how to ethically operate a hotel. In addition to implementing sustainability measures and organizing community arts projects, it sponsored the construction of various public buildings, including the village church (which hosts many destination weddings, so that was a win-win).

1492 Restaurant   INTERNATIONAL **$$**
(☎2661-4044; Hotel Punta Islita; mains US$14-28; ⊙7am-10pm; [P][🛜]) The movie *1492* was shot on location in Punta Islita, and some of the props adorn the restaurant. The cuisine here, which is a fusion of Costa Rican and international food, is top quality – and the view is superlative.

❶ Getting There & Away

AIR
NatureAir has one flight daily between San José and Punta Islita (one way US$141).

BUS
The closest you can get to Islita by bus is to take one of the two daily Empresa Arsa buses from San José that go through San Francisco de Coyote and on to Playas San Miguel and Bejuco. Keep in mind that from Bejuco there is still a long uphill hike to Islita – and hitchhiking is almost impossible due to the lack of traffic.

CAR
Although Punta Islita is less than 10km by road southeast of Playa Carrillo, the coastal 'road' is wicked and requires some river crossings that are impossible in the wet season.

During the dry season, there is a bridge over the river that makes it easily passable. Otherwise, the 'easiest' route heads inland on the paved road from Playa Carrillo to the village of Estrada. When you come to the fork in the road, bear left. At the T-intersection in Santa Marta, turn right onto the gravel road to Islita. At the next T-intersection, you can turn right on the rough but decent dirt road to reach Islita (11km), or left to reach Playas San Miguel and Coyote via San Pedro, Cangrejal and Bejuco.

Playas San Miguel & Coyote

Just south of Playa Bejuco are arguably two of the most beautiful and least-visited beaches in Costa Rica. Playa San Miguel is a desolate and beautiful beach buffeted by a hulking granite headland and backed by elegant coconut palms. There's a no-name bar at the end of the road, on the beach. Playa Coyote, to the south, is likewise a wilderness beach, but at high tide much of the fine, silver-gray sand gets swallowed up. San Miguel and Coyote serve as nesting grounds for olive ridley turtles.

There are no coastal villages to speak of, though a number of in-the-know foreigners have settled in the area and have built accommodations near the shoreline. The nearest village is San Francisco de Coyote, which is 4km inland and has a few small *sodas*, *cabinas* and an internet cafe. For a good online map of the area, visit www.nicoyapeninsula.com/coyote/map.php.

KEN WELSH / GETTY IMAGES ©

1. Playa Conchal (p300)
One of Costa Rica's most beautiful beaches, Playa Conchal gets its name from the many *conchas* (shells) that wash up on the sand.

2. Playa Grande (p301)
By day surfers come to ride the powerful breaks and by night leatherback sea turtles return to their birthplace to nest.

3. Playa Tamarindo (p303)
Despite its reputation, Tamarindo is not just a party destination – it's also great for surfing, fishing and relaxing by the sea.

CARVER MOSTARDI / GETTY IMAGES ©

◉ Sights & Activities

You can surf crowd-free beach breaks off San Miguel, particularly when the tide is rising. At Coyote there is an offshore reef that can be surfed at high tide. If swimming, you are advised to take precautions as the surf can pick up, and there are not many people in the area to help you in an emergency. If you have your own sea kayak, these beaches (as well as nearby Islita) are perfect for coastal exploration.

Mike's Jungle Butterfly Farm   GARDENS
(☑ 8719-1703, 2655-8070; www.junglebutterfly farm.com; tours adult/child US$20/10, cottages US$65; ⊗9am-3pm Mon-Sat) Mike's beautiful 47-acre mountainside property includes walking trails and a butterfly *rancho*. In addition to the butterflies, you might spot howler monkeys, agoutis and iguanas. He also has colonies of wild bees, and you can buy their honey in the gift shop. Book ahead for a tour.

If you need a place to lay your weary head, Jungle Mike has two cute cottages on a hill overlooking a sublime stretch of coast. You can also pitch a tent on his farm.

🛏 Sleeping & Eating

You can camp on both beaches if you're self-sufficient, as there are no services.

★ Flying Scorpion   HOTEL $$
(☑ 2655-8080; www.escorpionvolador.com; d/ ste incl breakfast US$55/70, houses US$100-200; 🅿 ❄ 🛜) Once you find this mellow inn, you won't want to leave. A handful of clean, comfortable rooms are decked out with teak beds and eclectic folk art. The place has direct beach access for long days of surfing. Afterward the onsite restaurant will sate you with homemade bread, pastas and ice cream.

Turn right at the Blue Pelican and continue on the dirt road along the beach for 200m.

Laguna Mar   BOUTIQUE HOTEL $$
(☑ 2655-8181, in USA 704-851-8181; www.lagu namarhotel.com; d US$92; 🅿 ❄ 🛜 🏊) A swanky, modern hotel on a deserted beach: what's not to love? The rooms are simple but sophisticated, with high-thread-count linens, flat-screen TVs and contemporary flare. They are set around the sublime three-in-one swimming pool. Extra props for the excellent European restaurant.

Rhodeside B&B   B&B $$
(☑ 2655-8006; www.rhodesidebedandbreak fast.com; d incl breakfast US$65; 🅿 ❄ 🛜) An American-owned coffee shop and B&B on the hillside between San Miguel and Pueblo Nuevo. The iconoclastic owners do exquisite espresso drinks (from locally sourced beans) and delicious breakfasts. They also have quaint, spotless, tiled rooms with lovely patio views.

Casa Caletas   BOUTIQUE HOTEL $$$
(☑ 2655-1271; www.casacaletas.com; s/d/tr/ste US$98/124/146/158; 🅿 ❄ 🛜 🏊) Sitting pretty on a bank of the Río Coyote, this gorgeous property is at once blessedly intimate and blissfully isolated. Gorgeously decorated with heavy wood furniture and folksy art, all the rooms have private terraces, with views to the ocean. Taking advantage of the same panorama, the infinity pool lives up to its name. A walking trail leads to the beach. To get here, take the road from San Francisco de Coyote toward Mal País and follow the signs for the hotel.

Pizza Tree   PIZZERIA $$
(☑ 2655-8063; pizzas US$9-12; ⊗noon-10pm; 🅿 🍴) If there is anything more fun than eating pizza in a tree house, we're not sure what it is. Take a seat at the top of this ramshackle, Seuss-like structure and feast on thin-crust pizzas and focaccia from the wood-fired brick oven. The owner is Italian but the concept is purely Tico.

ℹ Getting There & Away

Empresa Arsa (☑ 2650-0179) has two daily buses from San José that take about four hours (optimistically). Buses depart San José at 6am and 3:30pm. Return buses leave Bejuco at 4:45am and 2:30pm, passing through the beach towns a half-hour or an hour later. This service is sketchy in the rainy season and the trip may take longer if road conditions are bad.

SOUTHERN PENINSULA

Word has spread about the hippie-chic outposts of Montezuma and dusty yet glamorous Mal País. During the dry season, packs of international surfers and wanderers arrive hungry for the wild beauty and soul-stirring waters on either side of the peninsula. In between, and at the very southern tip of the Península de Nicoya, lies the first natural reserve in Costa Rica. It used to require hours of sweaty bus rides and sluggish ferries from the mainland to access this tropical land's end, but these days there are more roads and regular boat shuttles, making the southern peninsula altogether more accessible. But if you have the time and money (and a thirst for adventure), embrace the gritty, arduous drive down the rugged western coast, which requires river crossings and low-tide beach traverses, muddy jungle slogs and steep narrow passes. It's hard work, but your arrival in paradise is all the sweeter.

Playa Naranjo

This tiny village next to the ferry terminal is nothing more than a few *sodas* and small hotels that cater to travelers either waiting for the ferry or arriving from Puntarenas. There isn't any reason to hang around, but if you do get stuck at the port for a night, you can bed down at **Playa Naranjo Inn** (2641-8290; d incl breakfast US$40;), a motel-style accommodation facing a swimming pool. The rooms are comfortable enough, with heavy wood and wicker furniture, though the showers are cold. There is a restaurant here, too.

ⓘ Getting There & Away

All transportation is geared to the arrival and departure of the Puntarenas ferry, so don't worry – if one is running late, the other will wait.

BOAT

The **Coonatramar ferry** (2661-1069; www. coonatramar.com; adult/child/bicycle/motorcycle/car US$2/1/4/6/18) to Puntarenas departs daily at 8am, 12:30pm, 5:30pm and 9pm, and can accommodate both cars and passengers. The trip takes 1½ hours. If traveling by car, get out and buy a ticket at the window, get back in your car and then drive on to the ferry. You cannot buy a ticket on board. Show up at least an hour early on holidays and busy weekends, as you'll be competing with a whole lot of other drivers to make it on.

BUS

Buses meet the ferry and take passengers on to Nicoya (US$3, three hours). You can also catch a bus to Paquera at 10:30am and 5:30pm, though it's not clear why you would want to. If you're headed to Montezuma or Mal País, take the other ferry from Puntarenas to Paquera.

CAR & TAXI

It's possible to get to Paquera (and further to Mal País or Montezuma) via a scenic, rugged and steep but passable road over three inland ridges with magical vistas of Bahía Gigante. A 4WD is recommended, especially in the rainy season when there might be rivers to cross. A 4WD taxi costs around US$40.

Islands near Bahía Gigante

The waters in and around the isolated Bahía Gigante, 9km southeast of Playa Naranjo, are studded with rocky islets and deserted islands. Since there is very little here, and a 4WD is a necessity almost year-round, the area feels very quiet and unhurried. However, travelers are drawn here for its range of activities, namely sportfishing, snorkeling, diving and kayaking, which can all be arranged through hotels and travel agencies from Paquera to Montezuma.

Isla San Lucas

The largest island in Bahía Gigante (just over 600 hectares) is about 5km off the coast from Playa Naranjo, and from a distance seems like a beautiful desert island. However, the 'Island of Unspeakable Horrors' has a 400-year history as one of the most notorious jails in Latin America. The island was first used by Spanish conquistadors as a detention center for local tribes in the 16th century. In 1862 the job of warden was inherited by the Costa Rican government, which used the island to detain political prisoners until 1992.

Visitors can expect to see the 100-year-old remains of the prison. The prison and grounds are open to explore and most trips to the island include tours of the prison.

Isla Gigante

In the middle of Bahía Gigante is the 10-hectare Isla Gigante, which is shown on most maps as Isla Muertos (Island of the Dead) because it is home to a number of Chara burial sites (and is believed by locals to be haunted).

Isla Guayabo, Islas Negritos & Los Pájaros

This cluster of islands was recently established as a biological reserve to protect nesting seabird populations, including the largest breeding colony of brown pelicans in Costa Rica. No land visitors are allowed except researchers with permission from the park service. However, the reserves can be approached by boat, and the bird populations are plainly visible from the ocean.

Isla Tortuga

Isla Tortuga, which consists of two uninhabited islands just offshore from Curú, is widely regarded as the most beautiful island in Costa Rica. The white-sand beaches feel like baby powder, there are gargantuan coconut palms overhead, and the coral reef is perfect for snorkeling. Unfortunately, Tortuga receives heavy boat traffic from tour operators from Montezuma and Jacó, but if you visit during the week in low season it can be magical.

☞ Tours

Most travelers arrange tours either through the hotels listed here or with an operator in Montezuma or Jacó. However, this is one region where independence (and language skills) can make for a good adventure – inquire locally to find out if someone with a boat is willing to take you where you want to go for a fair price. Turismo Curú, in Paquera, offers a variety of low-key itineraries to the islands.

Bay Island Cruises BOAT TOUR
(☑ 2258-3536; www.bayislandcruises.com; tours US$115) Board the catamaran *The Great Bay Princess* for a day trip to pristine Isla Tortuga or historic Isla San Lucas. The trip includes transportation from San José, a bilingual guide, meals and drinks, as well as entertainment on board.

Calypso Tours BOAT TOUR
(☑ 2256-2727; www.calypsocruises.com; tours from US$139) Calypso Tours takes passengers to Isla Tortuga in a luxurious 21m motorized

catamaran. It's all very flash, with a couple of outdoor Jacuzzis, an underwater viewing window and a kayaking option. It's not a bad deal considering that the price includes transportation from San José, Jacó, Manuel Antonio or Monteverde, as well as food and drinks.

❶ Getting There & Away

There is no public transportation in the area. The dirt road from Playa Naranjo to Paquera requires a 4WD for most of the year.

Paquera

The tiny village of Paquera is about 12km by road from Playa Naranjo and 4km from the ferry terminal. Paquera is more of a population center than Playa Naranjo, though there's little reason to stay here longer than you have to.

There are a number of *cabinas* in the village, though **Cabinas & Restaurante Ginana** (☑ 2641-0119; d US$40; ℙ ❄ @ 🛜 ⛵) is the best option, with 28 simple and clean, tiled rooms. The quality restaurant (dishes US$3 to US$6) turns out tasty seafood in tiled *palapa* environs if you need a bite to eat before getting on the ferry.

❶ Information

Banco Popular (⊘ 8:15am-4pm), on the side street, can change US dollars and traveler's checks. On the main road, across from the gas station, you'll find **Turismo Curú** (☑ 2641-0004; www.curutourism.com; ⊘ 8am-9pm), operated by the knowledgeable Luis Schutt of the Curú refuge. Luis offers a tour that combines a visit to Curú and a snorkeling trip to Isla Tortuga for US$30 per person (a great deal!). They also run dive trips (two tanks US$100) to Isla Tortuga, and offer internet access in their Paquera office.

COSTA RICAN WILDCAT CONSERVATIONISTS

Since 1992 Programa para la Conservación de Felinos (Profelis; Feline Conservation Program) has taken care of confiscated felines that were given to the center by the Ministerio del Ambiente y Energía (Minae; Ministry of Environment and Energy). The project concentrates on smaller felines, including the margay, ocelot and jaguarundi, and aims to rehabilitate and, when possible, reintroduce animals into the wild. In addition, a large component of the program involves the environmental education of the public.

Profelis (☑ 2641-0646, 2641-0644; www.grafischer.com/profelis) is headquartered in Hacienda Matambú, a private wildlife reserve in San Rafael de Paquera, about 5km west of Paquera. Volunteers are sought after, especially those who have experience either in veterinary science or in keeping animals.

ℹ Getting There & Away

All transportation is geared to the arrival and departure of the Puntarenas ferry. If either is running late, the other will wait.

BOAT

Ferry Naviera Tambor (📞 2661-2084; www.navieratambor.com; adult/child/bicycle/motorcycle/car US$1.65/1/4.50/7/23) leaves daily at 5:30am, 9am, 11am, 2pm, 5pm and 8pm. The trip to Puntarenas takes about an hour. Buy a ticket at the window, reboard your car and then drive onto the ferry; you can't buy a ticket on board. Show up at least an hour early on holidays and busy weekends. The terminal contains a *soda* where you can grab a bite while waiting for the boat.

BUS

Buses meet passengers at the ferry terminal and take them to Paquera, Tambor and Montezuma. The bus can be crowded, so try to get off the ferry fast to get a seat.

Most travelers take the bus from the terminal directly to Montezuma (US$3, two hours). Many taxi drivers will tell you the bus won't come, but this isn't true. There are no northbound buses.

TAXI

Getting several travelers together to share a taxi is a good option since the ride will take half as long as the bus. The ride to Montezuma is about US$12 per person, and to Mal País it's about US$20 – provided you can get enough people together.

A 4WD taxi to Playa Naranjo costs about US$40 for up to four people.

Refugio Nacional de Vida Silvestre Curú

Situated at the eastern end of the peninsula and only 6km south of Paquera, the tiny, 84-hectare **Refugio Nacional de Vida Silvestre Curú** (📞 2641-0100; www.curuwildliferefuge.com; day fee adult/child 3-11/child 2 & under US$10/5/free; ⏰ 7am-3pm) holds a great variety of landscapes, including dry tropical forest, semi-deciduous forest and five types of mangrove swamp. The rugged coastline is also home to a series of secluded coves and white-sand beaches that are perfect for snorkeling and swimming. The entrance to the refuge is clearly signed on the paved road between Paquera and Tambor (it's on the right-hand side). Day visitors can show up anytime during operating hours and pay the day fee to hike the 17 well-marked,

easy to moderate trails, or join a variety of tours – from horseback riding and kayaking through the estuary to snorkeling and guided hikes. Local fauna includes deer, three types of monkey, agouti and paca, and three species of cat. Iguana, crab, lobster, chiton, shellfish, sea turtle and other marine creatures can be found on the beaches and in the tide pools. Bird-watchers have recorded more than 232 bird species.

Camping is not allowed in the reserve, though there are six rustic **cabinas** (r per person US$30, meals US$10) with private cold showers. Stays must be arranged in advance either through the Turismo Curú office in Paquera, or at the reserve's entrance.

Playas Pochote & Tambor

These two mangrove-backed, gray-sand beaches are protected by Bahía Ballena, the largest bay on the southeastern peninsula, and are surrounded by small fishing communities. In the past 15 years, the area has slowly developed as a resort destination, but for the most part, Pochote and Tambor are mellow, authentic Tico beaches, providing plenty of opportunities for hiking, swimming, kayaking and even whale-watching.

The beaches begin 14km south of Paquera, at the mangrove shrouded, fishing *pueblo* of Pochote, and stretch for about 8km south west to Tambor. They're divided by the narrow estuary of the Río Pánica, where you'll find two seafood *sodas* on the Pochote side, overlooking the river. Tambor is the area's access point. It should also be said that there is one rather conspicuous all-inclusive megaresort in the Tambor area. Hotel Barceló Playa Tambor has a convention center and golf course, but once you're in the *pueblo*, you won't even know it's there.

🏃 Activities

Both beaches are safe for swimming, and there are occasional whale sightings in the bay. The gentle waters also make this a good spot for kayaking, and Curú's hiking trails are just down the road.

🛏 Sleeping & Eating

Mar y Sol CABINA $
(📞 8980-0040, 2683-1065; www.marysolcr.com; d/q US$30/50; 🅿❄🛜) The location is a bit odd – stuck on a side road with no beach in sight – but this Canadian-owned joint has

undergone an impressive renovation, making it an excellent budget option. The eight rooms have been thoughtfully designed and decked out with custom furniture, handcrafted light fixtures and hardwood ceilings. Air-con and hot water are available on request.

Out front, the gorgeous wood bar (also handhewn) is lit by wine-bottle lamps, invented and designed by the owner. It's an excellent place to grab a *cerveza*, or a pizza from the wood-fired oven.

Cabinas Cristina   CABINA $
(☑ 2683-0028; r US$36-56; P 🐾) 🏂 Just 50m from the beach, and across from Tambor's rather romantically ramshackle Victorian church, this old standby has simple and spotless rooms, and a small but tasty home-style restaurant. The owners are warm and welcoming and offer valuable travel tips. Room prices vary depending on size and amenities.

Cabinas El Bosque   CABINA $
(☑ 2683-0039; s/d from US$23/35; ❄️ 🐾 🍽️) Nine *cabinas* are set back from the road, strewn across the forested lawn. Basic but clean, they have TVs and fresh coats of paint. The swimming pool is tiny, but the place is only 200m from the beach.

Tambor Tropical   BOUTIQUE HOTEL $$$
(☑ 2365-2872; www.tambortropical.com; ste incl breakfast US$160-248; P 🐾 🍽️) Romantically set on the beach amid a palm-fringed garden, Tambor Tropical is a lovely boutique hotel with stunning architecture. The 12 roomy, hexagonal suites all have dark wood interiors, full kitchen, wet bar and private veranda. The ocean breeze will keep you cool on all but the hottest days. The higher prices are for rooms on the 2nd floor.

🛈 Getting There & Away

The airport is just north of the entrance to Hotel Barceló Playa Tambor. Hotels will arrange pickup at the airport for an extra fee. Between them, Sansa and NatureAir (one way from US$87) have up to 10 daily flights to and from San José. There's a **Budget** (☑ 2683-0500; www.budget.co.cr; ⊙ 8am-6pm Mon-Sat, 8am-4pm Sun) car-rental place 4km from the Tambor airport. It has a free shuttle to and from the 'terminal'.

Paquera–Montezuma buses pass through here.

Montezuma

Montezuma is an immediately endearing beach town that demands you abandon the car to stroll, swim and, if you are willing to stroll even further, surf. The warm and wild ocean and that remnant, ever-audible jungle has helped this rocky nook cultivate an inviting, boho vibe. Typical tourist offerings such as canopy tours do a brisk trade here, but you'll also bump up against Montezuma's internationally inflected, artsy-rootsy beach culture in yoga classes, volunteer corps, veggie-friendly dining rooms and neo-Rastas hawking uplifting herbs. No wonder locals lovingly call this town 'Montefuma.' It's not perfect. The lodging is particularly poor value, and the eateries can be that way too (though there are some absolute gems). But in this barefoot *pueblo,* which unfurls along several kilometers of rugged coastline, you're never far from the rhythm and sound of the sea, and that is a beautiful thing.

⊙ Sights

Picture-perfect white-sand beaches are strung along the coast, separated by small rocky headlands, offering great beachcombing and ideal tide-pool contemplation. Unfortunately, there are strong riptides, so inquire locally before going for a swim.

The beaches in front of the town are nice enough, but the best beach is just north of Cocolores restaurant, where the sand is powdery and sheltered from big swells. This is your glorious sun-soaked crash pad, and the further northeast you walk the more solitude you'll find. The water's shade of teal is immediately nourishing, the temperature is perfect and fish are abundant.

During low tide, the best snorkeling is at **Playa Las Manchas**, 1km west of downtown.

★**Montezuma Waterfalls**   WATERFALL
(parking US$2) A 40-minute river hike leads to a waterfall with a delicious swimming hole. Further along the trail, a second set of falls offers a good clean 10m leap into deep water. (Reach the 'diving platform' from the trail: do not try to scale the slippery rocks!) Daring souls can test their Tarzan skills on the rope that swings over a third set. A lot of travelers enjoy these thrills but a few of them have died; do it at your own risk.

Montezuma

Montezuma

◎ Sights
1 Montezuma Gardens............................B5

◈ Activities, Courses & Tours
  Cabo Blanco Travelers...............(see 27)
2 Devaya Yoga.....................................A3
3 La Escuela del Sol..............................A2
4 Montezuma EcoTours.........................A3
  Montezuma Yoga.......................(see 13)
5 Proyecto Montezuma..........................B3
6 Sun Trails...A3
7 Young Vision Surf School B1
  Zuma Tours ....(see 6)

⊜ Sleeping
8 Downtown Montezuma Hostel...........A3
9 El Sano Banano..................................A3
10 Hotel Amor de Mar...........................B5
11 Hotel El Jardín...................................A3
12 Hotel La Cascada...............................B5
13 Hotel Los Mangos..............................B4
14 Hotel Lucy..B4
15 Hotel Pargo Feliz...............................B2
16 Luna Llena A2
17 Luz de Mono.....................................B1
18 Luz en el Cielo..................................A2
19 Montezuma Pacífico...........................A2

⊗ Eating
20 Bar Restaurante Moctezuma.............B3
21 Cocolores...B2
22 Kalibó..A3
23 Orgánico..B2
24 Playa de los Artistas..........................B4
25 Puggo's...A3
  Soda Monte Sol....................(see 6)
26 Super Montezuma.............................A3

⊜ Drinking & Nightlife
27 Chico's Bar.......................................B2

As you head south past Hotel La Cascada, there's a parking area, then take the trail to the right just after the bridge.

Montezuma Gardens GARDENS
(☑8888-4200, 2642-1317; www.montezumagardens.com; adult/student/child US$8/6/4; ⊙8am-4pm) About 1km south of town, alongside the waterfall trail, you can take a tour through this lush *mariposario* (butterfly garden) and nursery where the mysterious metamorphoses occur. You'll learn about the life cycles and benefits of a dozen local species, of which you'll see many colorful varieties. There's also a B&B here (rooms US$57 to US$80).

Playa Grande BEACH
About 7km north of town, Playa Grande is the best surf beach in the area. It's a 3km-plus stretch of waves and sand, which doesn't get too crowded as it requires a 30-minute hike to get here. But what a hike it is, wandering along between the turquoise waters of the Pacific and the lush greenery of the Montezuma Biological Reserve.

Because of the town's carefree boho feel, topless and (sometimes) nude sunbathing have become de rigueur on some beaches, especially Playa Grande. Be aware that many residents find this disrespectful so please be discreet.

🏃 Activities

Young Vision Surf School   SURFING
(☎ 8669-6835; www.youngvisiontest.net76.net; lessons from US$40) Manny and Alvaro get rave reviews for their knowledge, enthusiasm and patience with new surfers of all ages. Daily lessons include two hours of instruction, the use of a surfboard and rash guard, and fresh fruits.

Montezuma Yoga   YOGA
(☎ 8704-1632; www.montezumayoga.com; per person US$14; ⊗ classes 8:30am Mon-Fri, 6pm Fri-Sun) Anusara-inspired instruction, which pairs Iyengar alignment principles with a Vinyasa flow, is available in a gorgeous studio kissed by ocean breezes, lit by paper lanterns and sheltered by a peaked tin roof. On the grounds of Hotel Los Mangos.

Devaya Yoga   YOGA
(☎ 8833-5086; www.devayayoga.com; per class US$12; ⊗ classes 8:30am & 4pm Mon-Sat) A studio smack in the middle of town, upstairs from Pizzeria L'Angolo Allegro, it offers morning and afternoon classes, as well as massage therapy and astrology readings.

Proyecto Montezuma   VOLUNTEERING
(☎ 8314-0690;   www.proyectomontezuma.com) Proyecto Montezuma is an innovative volunteer program that not only gives to the community but also fosters cultural exchange, pays fair wages to its employees and gives back for donating your time and energy. You choose the project in which you'd like to participate, such as teaching or trash removal (privileges that you will pay for). Or you can sign up for a sustainable adventure tour or surf lessons in and around Montezuma.

Sun Trails   CANOPY TOURS
(☎ 2642-0808; www.montezumatraveladventures. com; tours US$40; ⊗ 9am-3pm) After you've flown down nine zip lines, this 2½-hour canopy tour winds up with a hike down – rather than up – to the waterfalls; bring your swimsuit. Book at the office in town.

🎓 Courses

La Escuela del Sol   DANCE, LANGUAGE COURSE
(☎ 8884-8444; www.laescueladelsol.com) Based at the Hotel El Tajalin, this electic educational vortex offers Spanish, surf, yoga, fire dance and scuba instruction. In other words, there is no excuse to leave Montezuma without a bilingual, underwater, surf warrior, dreadlocked hippie soul.

☞ Tours

Tour operators around town rent everything from snorkeling gear to body boards and bikes. They can also arrange speed-boat transfers to Jacó as well as private shuttle transfers.

The most popular tour is a boat trip to Isla Tortuga, which costs around US$50 and should include lunch, fruit, drinks and snorkeling gear. Although the island is certainly beautiful, travelers complain that the whole outing feels like a tourist circus, especially during high season when the entire island is full of boat tours.

Also popular are guided hikes in Cabo Blanco and horseback riding to Playa Cocolito.

Cabo Blanco Travelers   TOUR
(☎ 2642-1439, 8835-0270; www.caboblancotravelers.com) Local guide Gerardo Canti leads nature hikes in Cabo Blanco, sharing the knowledge of local flora and fauna garnered from his Chorotega ancestors. He also does horseback-riding tours and rents a few bungalows.

Montezuma EcoTours   TOUR
(☎ 2642-0467, 2642-1000; www.montezumaecotours.com; ⊗ 8am-9pm) Specializing in snorkel trips to Isla Tortuga, as well as horseback riding, sportfishing and canopy tours.

Zuma Tours   TOUR
(☎ 2642-0024; www.zumatours.net) Snorkeling trips to Isla Tortuga, horseback riding in Cabo Blanco and more. This office also has the only public internet access in town.

🎉 Festivals & Events

Costa Rica Film Festival   FILM
(www.costaricafilmfestival.com) Now held in June, this fabulous festival attracts filmmakers from all over the region and the world. Screenings take place at El Sano Banano and Amor de Mar.

🛏 Sleeping

The high season gets crowded, though with so many hotels dotting such a small town you're bound to find something even if you have to search for it. More importantly, Montezuma is a town distinguished by poor-value lodging, so it does make sense to book a good room ahead of time. Note that some hotels have a three-night minimum during Christmas and Easter weeks.

WORTH A TRIP

PLAYA COCOLITO

Here's your chance to see a waterfall crashing down a cliff, straight onto the rocks and into the ocean. And yes, it is as spectacular as it sounds. **El Chorro Waterfall** is the pièce de résistance of **Playa Cocolito**, which is itself pretty irresistible. The waters here are a dreamy, iridescent azure, with pink rocky cliffs creating two inviting swimming areas. It's far enough away from the action that you are likely to have the place to yourself.

It's a hot, two-hour, 12km hike from Montezuma: leave at sunrise to spot plenty of wildlife along the way. Alternatively, this is a popular destination for horseback riding. In any case, be sure to bring water and snacks as there are no facilities here.

Camping is technically illegal on the beaches, but there is a small, shaded campground with bathrooms (200m away) and cold-water showers only a 10-minute walk north of town on the beach. It's got a communal ethos, and there's no charge for space. Kick in for meals and all will be groovy.

There are a sprinkling of long-term rentals and boutique three-star hotels above Montezuma off the road to Cóbano, all of which are only suitable if you have wheels.

★**Luna Llena** HOSTEL $
(✆2642-0390; www.lunallenahotel.com; dm/s US$15/28, d with/without bathroom from US$55/38; P⊙) On the northern edge of town on a hilltop overlooking the bay is this delightful budget option. There's an inviting dorm and 12 varied, private rooms, all of them spotless, most with balconies and shared bathroom facilities. There are two fully equipped kitchens, a barbecue grill and a breezy communal lounge with rattan chair-swings and stunning ocean views. Wildlife abounds in this area (keep your food in the communal kitchen).

Luz en el Cielo HOSTEL, B&B $
(✆8811-3700, 2642-0030; www.luzenelcielo.com; dm US$15-27, s/d/tr/q US$54/78/98/112; P⊙) In the heart of the jungle but two minutes from town, this homey hostel and B&B is an inviting retreat. Crowded dorm rooms are super clean with sturdy wood furniture and lockers, while the new 'luxury' dorms are more spacious, with TVs, private balconies and en suite bathrooms. The treetop *cabinas* are also wonderful. Amazing breakfasts (included in rates), enticing hammocks and super-friendly staff.

Hotel Pargo Feliz CABINA $
(✆2642-0064; d US$30-45; ⊙) You can't beat the location of these beachfront *cabinas* in the heart of Montezuma. Rooms are simple,

clean and fan-cooled. The communal balcony and garden terrace have relaxing hammocks with sea views, and at night the surf will lull you to sleep.

Hotel Los Mangos HOTEL $
(✆2642-0076; www.hotellosmangos.com; d/q US$35/75, tr bungalows US$90; P✲⊙⊛) Scattered across mango-dotted gardens, this whimsical hotel has simple, bright, jewel-toned rooms in the main building and attractive (though dark) octagonal bungalows that offer more privacy. Monkeys populate the mango trees and yoga classes are held in the gorgeous, ocean-view yoga pavilion.

Downtown Montezuma Hostel HOSTEL $
(✆2642-0284; dm US$10, d with/without bathroom US$30/24; ⊙) The new kid on the block is this funky little two-story hostel, run by the ever-accommodating and amiable Elena. She's got four-person dorm rooms and some private doubles, all with cold-water bathrooms. Rates all include breakfast. There's a communal kitchen and plenty of hammocks. The facilities are nothing special, but the place has a fun, friendly vibe that guarantees a good time.

Hotel Lucy GUESTHOUSE $
(✆2642-0273; dm/d US$15/35; P⊙) This beachside *pensión* is popular with shoestring travelers, thanks to the hammocks on shared terraces overlooking a rocky beach. Rooms are small and drab and service is lackluster, but the views from the upstairs veranda are terrific.

Luz de Mono LODGE $$
(✆2642-0090; www.luzdemono.com; standard/ ste incl breakfast US$75/90; P⊙⊛) A sweet stone lodge built into a lush inlet of remnant jungle, just a few steps from the beach. The upstairs 'suites' have high palm-beamed ceilings, wood furnishings and new tile

throughout. The cheaper downstairs rooms are not all that, but they all have access to a lovely pool area (with kiddie pool), an open-air *rancho* and shady grounds with abundant wildlife.

Hotel La Cascada
HOTEL $$
(☏ 2642-0057; www.lacascadamontezuma.com; d incl breakfast US$60, air-con US$10; P ✳ ☎ ☞) At the mouth of the river, en route to the waterfalls, this classic Montezuma hotel has 15 simple, sharp wooden rooms with flowy curtains and crisp white sheets. A huge 2nd-floor terrace faces the ocean and has hammocks perfect for swinging, snoozing or spying on the local troop of howlers.

Hotel El Jardín
CABINA $$
(☏ 2642-0548; www.hoteleljardin.com; d US$60-80, casas US$95-115; P ✳ ☎ ☎) This hillside hotel has 15 stained-wood *cabinas,* some with stone bathrooms, wide balconies and ocean views. The grounds are landscaped with tropical flowers and lush palms. There's even a humble spa, making it quite a nice little three-star resort.

El Sano Banano
BOUTIQUE HOTEL $$
(☏ 2642-0638; d US$86; P ✳ @ ☎ ☎) A well-run boutique hotel in the center of town. Although its many businesses take up an entire city block, it has just 12 prim and comfortable rooms. The attached restaurant has appetizing baked goods and an inviting terrace on the main drag. It's also worth showing up in the evening when the restaurant shows nightly films in the garden out back.

Montezuma Pacifico
GUESTHOUSE $$
(☏ 2642-0204; www.montezumapacifio.com; r US$45-65; P ✳ ☎) This small property is tucked away from the action (and the noise) but close to the beach. Rooms in this older atrium-style guesthouse won't wow you, but the mosaic mix-match tile is cool. Plus, the owner is a charming gentleman.

Casacolores
BUNGALOW $$
(☏ 2642-0283; www.casacolores.com; 1/2-bedroom casa US$68/113; P ☎ ☎) Seven bright houses (each painted and named for a color of the rainbow) are fully equipped with kitchens, and big porches with hammocks. They're set amid blooming tropical gardens, with a stone-rimmed swimming pool on-site. The location is sort of a no-man's land (a 20-minute uphill hike from town) but the price is right.

Nature Lodge
LODGE $$
(☏ 2642-0124; www.naturelodge.net; d incl breakfast U$97-165; P ✳ ☎ ☎) About 3km north of Montezuma on the road to Cóbano, this 16-hectare ranch is adjacent to the Reserva Absoluta Nicolás Wessberg. The lodge has 12 simple but elegant rooms in a lovely hacienda, beautifully landscaped, with a pool deck blessed with ocean and woodland views. There's also a spa offering a variety of wellness treatments.

★ Hotel Amor de Mar
B&B $$$
(☏ 2642-0262; www.amordemar.com; d with/without ocean view US$135/102, villas from US$278; P ☎) A lovable, German-owned B&B with 11 unique rooms, replete with exquisite touches like timber-framed mirrors, organic lanterns, and rocking chairs on a terrace laced with fishing netting and dotted with hundreds of potted plants. Then there's the palm-dappled lawn that rolls out to the tide pools and the Pacific beyond. Hotel Amor de Mar also has two exquisite private beach villas.

Ylang-Ylang Beach Resort
RESORT $$$
(☏ 2642-0636, in USA 888-795-8494; www.ylangylangresort.com; standard/ste/bungalow incl breakfast & dinner US$237/288/322; ✳ ☎ ☎) Walk 15 minutes north along the beach to this lush four-star property, complete with beautifully appointed rooms and bungalows, a palm-fringed swimming pool, yoga center, gourmet organic restaurant and spa. The decor is lovely and tropical, with tile floors, stenciled walls and colorful tapestries. All accommodations have outdoor terraces facing the glorious sea. You can't actually drive here, though staff will pick you up in their custom beach cruisers from El Sano Banano.

✗ Eating

Self-caterers should head to the **Super Montezuma** for fresh food.

Kalibó
CAFE $
(☏ 2642-4545; mains US$3-8; ◷ 6am-9pm) A tiny place with an open kitchen and half a dozen tables, across from the bus stop. This perfect breakfast stop does homemade pastries, fresh fruit smoothies and strong local coffee. It also serves salads and sandwiches and proper meals. Everything is fresh and delicious and made with love.

Orgánico

ORGANIC **$**

(mains US$7-11; ⊙8am-9pm; ⊘) When they say 'pure food made with love,' they mean it – this healthy cafe turns out vegetarian and vegan dishes such as spicy Thai burgers, a *sopa azteca* (tortilla soup) with tofu, burritos, falafel, smoothies and other meat-free treats you can feel good about. But it does meat dishes, like spaghetti Bolognese, too. Whaddaya want? They're Italian. There's live music almost nightly, including an open mike on Monday nights.

Soda Monte Sol

COSTA RICAN **$**

(⊘8849-4962; mains US$5-14; ⊙7am-9pm) A cute hole-in-the-wall *soda* that does all the *típica* dishes, tasty and affordable *casados,* pastas, burgers and a variety of juices and smoothies. All is served on pressed tablecloths in a humble dining room touched with grace. Great people-watching spot.

★ Playa de los Artistas

INTERNATIONAL **$$**

(⊘2642-0920; www.playamontezuma.net/playa-delosartistas.htm; mains US$9-13; ⊙5-9pm Mon-Fri, noon-9pm Sat) Most romantic dinner ever. If you're lucky, you'll snag one of the tree-trunk tables under the palms. The interior tables – covered by a bamboo roof but open to sea breezes – are also inviting. The international menu with heavy Mediterranean influences changes daily depending on locally available ingredients, though you can always count on fresh seafood roasted in the wood oven. The service is flawless, the cooking is innovative and delicious, and the setting is downright dreamy. Cash only (back to reality).

Puggo's

MIDDLE EASTERN **$$**

(⊘2642-0308; mains US$9-20; ⊙noon-11pm) A locally beloved restaurant decorated like a bedouin tent that specializes in Middle Eastern cuisine, including falafel, hummus, kebabs and aromatic fish dressed in imported spices and herbs and roasted whole. Cap it off with a strong cup of Turkish coffee.

Bar Restaurante Moctezuma

MEDITERRANEAN **$$**

(⊘2642-0058; mains US$9-23; ⊙7:30am-11pm; ☎⊛) The long menu has just about everything, especially when it comes to seafood. Look for steamed mussels, broiled octopus, fish carpaccio and grilled shrimp, not to mention basics like burgers and *casados*. You're bound to find something you like, and you can't beat the prime beachfront location.

Cocolores

INTERNATIONAL **$$**

(⊘2642-0348; mains US$9-22; ⊙5-10pm Tue-Sun) Set on a beachside terrace lit with lanterns, Cocolores is one of Montezuma's top spots for an upscale dinner. The wide-ranging menu includes curries, pasta, fajitas and steaks, all prepared and served with careful attention to delicious details. Prices aren't cheap but portions are ample.

🍸 Drinking & Entertainment

If you're not down for drinks, you can stop by the restaurant at El Sano Banano to check out which movie is screening that night.

Chico's Bar

BAR

(⊙11am-2am) A sprawling complex of bars, tables, beach chairs and a wide dance floor. It can get loud, especially on Thursday, which is reggae night. If you can score a table outside, it can be sort of romantic. Bar-keeps are well stocked with all manner of spirits, and the old weathered bones are built to withstand a hurricane.

ℹ Information

Internet access is at Zuma Tours (p338). The only ATM in town is a BCR *cajero* located across from Chico's Bar. The nearest full-service bank is in Cóbano. For money exchange, tour operators in town will take US dollars, euros or traveler's checks.

El Parque (⊘2642-0164; laundry per kg US$2, bikes/scooters/ATVs per day US$10/40/75; ⊙7am-8pm) The best place in town to get your laundry done. It also rents bikes, scooters and ATVs.

Librería Topsy (⊘2642-0576; ⊙8am-4pm Mon-Fri, 8am-noon Sat) Has US newspapers and magazines, and a large lending library with mostly used books in several languages. Accepts trade-ins but doesn't offer straight swaps.

ℹ Getting There & Away

BOAT

A fast passenger ferry connects Montezuma to Jacó in an hour. At US$40 or so, it's not cheap, but it'll save you a day's worth of travel. Boats depart at 9:30am daily and the price includes van transfer from the beach to the Jacó bus terminal. Book in advance from any tour operator. Dress appropriately; you will get wet.

BUS

Buses depart Montezuma from the sandy lot on the beach, across from the soccer field. Buy tickets directly from the driver. To get to Mal País and Santa Teresa, go to Cóbano and change buses.

Cabo Blanco via Cabuya US$1.50, 45 minutes, departs 8:15am, 10:15am, 12:15pm and 4:15pm.

Paquera, via Cóbano US$3, two hours, departs 5:30am, 8am, 10am, noon, 2pm and 4pm.

San José US$14, five hours, departs 6:20am and 2:20pm.

CAR & TAXI

During the rainy season the stretch of road between Cóbano and Montezuma is likely to require a 4WD. In the village itself, parking can be a problem, though it's easy enough to walk everywhere.

A 4WD taxi can take you to Mal País (US$70) or Cóbano (US$12).

Montezuma Expeditions (www.montezumaexpeditions.com) operates private shuttles to San José (US$50), La Fortuna (US$55), Monteverde (US$55), Jacó, (US$55), Manuel Antonio (US$60), Dominical (US$70), Tamarindo (US$45), Sámara (US$45) and Liberia (US$55).

Cabuya

This tiny, bucolic village is populated by a community of Ticos and expats, and unfurls along a rugged dirt road about 7km south of Montezuma. It is a hidden gem, ideal for those looking to chill, with easy access to the Cabo Blanco reserve. Don't miss the amazing Cabuya ficus tree, which claims to be the largest strangler fig in Costa Rica, measuring 40m high and 22m in diameter!

The beach here is rocky and not great for swimming or surfing. But you're a short walk from Playa los Cedros, a great surf spot that is halfway between Montezuma and Cabuya. Alternatively, at low tide you can walk across the natural bridge to Isla Cabuya, which has a small sandy beach and good snorkeling spots. It's also worth visiting the cemetery, where you'll find a few modest graves marked by crosses. Make sure you keep an eye on the tides or you'll have to swim back!

🍴 Sleeping & Eating

El Ancla De Oro   CABINA $

(☎ 2642-0369; www.hotelelancladeoro.com; s/d US$15/25, cabinas US$35-45; P 🞲) The rustic, Dutch outpost is a great option for budget travelers who want to experience life in the treetops. Simple but super-clean accommodations include regular rooms in the main building as well as more secluded standalone 'jungalows'. If you stay in the latter, you're likely to spot howlers and white-faced monkeys from bed. Located on the road to Montezuma.

★ Hotel Celaje   CABINA $$

(☎ 2642-0374; www.celaje.com; s/d/tr/q incl breakfast US$78/90/106/121; P 🞲 @ 🞲 🞲) This sweet spot is a collection of spacious, stained-wood A-frame bungalows set on a sublime palm-dappled slice of shore. The place is decorated with beachy artistic touches, like coconut lamps and seashell mobiles. Your hosts – a Dutch couple and their dogs – are delightful. This is the first property you'll reach coming from Montezuma.

Howler Monkey Hotel   HOTEL $$

(☎ 2642-0303; www.howlermonkeyhotel.com; s/d US$50/70; P 🞲 🞲) Follow the signs down the side road to find these large rustic A-frame bungalows with kitchenettes (useful, as eating options are limited in Cabuya). They are clean and comfortable, and the place is right on a slice of very quiet, rocky beach, while the friendly Irish owner also rents bikes, ATVs and kayaks. And yes, it's called Howler Monkey Hotel for a reason: expect a wake-up call.

Panadería Cabuya   BAKERY, CAFE $

(☎ 2642-1184; cabuyabakerycafe.crcena.com; mains US$3-17; ⊘ 6:30am-8pm Mon-Sat, 6:30am-6pm Sun; 🞲) A local landmark. Set on a tropical patio, this inviting cafe serves up a stellar menu including fresh bread, pastries and strong coffee for breakfast, as well as soups, sandwiches and sushi for later in the day. If you have a thing for tall, dark and handsome, you should meet the chocolate cake.

Café El Coyote   PIZZERIA $

(☎ 2642-0354; www.cabuyabeach.com; mains US$5-11; ⊘ 8am-10pm) Jenny can help you with just about anything you need, from calling a taxi, organizing an adventure outing, pouring you a cold *cerveza* or making you a tasty pizza (her specialty). She also offers delicious breakfast options and other meals to sate your appetite at any time of day.

Soda Marvin   SODA $

(mains US$4-10; ⊘ 7am-9pm; 🖉) Here's your local family-run *soda*, offering all your Tico favorites. Non-meat-eaters will be surprised and delighted by the excellent vegetarian *casado*, but there's also seafood pasta, fish fajitas, filling breakfasts and ever-important, strong, dark coffee. You'll find this delightful place set under a thatch roof across from Super David.

Reserva Natural Absoluta Cabo Blanco

Just 11km south of Montezuma is Costa Rica's oldest protected wilderness area. Cabo Blanco comprises 12 sq km of land and 17 sq km of surrounding ocean, and includes the entire southern tip of the Península de Nicoya. The moist microclimate on the tip of the peninsula fosters the growth of evergreen forests, which are unique when compared with the dry tropical forests typical of Nicoya. The park also encompasses a number of pristine white-sand beaches and offshore islands that are favored nesting areas for various bird species.

The park was originally established by a Danish-Swedish couple, the late Karen Mogensen and Olof Nicolas Wessberg, who settled in Montezuma in the 1950s and were among the first conservationists in Costa Rica. In 1960 the couple was distraught when they discovered that sections of Cabo Blanco had been clear-cut. At the time, the Costa Rican government was primarily focused on the agricultural development of the country, and had not yet formulated its modern-day conservation policy. Karen and Nicolas, as he was known, were instrumental in convincing the government to establish a national park system, which eventually led to the creation of the Cabo Blanco reserve in 1963. The couple continued to fight for increased conservation of ecologically rich areas, but, tragically, Nicolas was murdered in 1975 during a campaign in the Península de Osa. Karen continued their work until her death in 1994, and today they are buried in the Reserva Absoluta Nicolás Wessberg, the site of their original homestead.

Cabo Blanco is called an 'absolute' nature reserve because prior to the late 1980s visitors were not permitted. Even though the name hasn't changed, a limited number of trails have been opened to visitors, but the reserve remains closed on Monday and Tuesday to minimize environmental impact.

🏃 Activities

Wildlife-Watching

Monkey, squirrel, sloth, deer, agouti and raccoon are usually present, and armadillo, coati, peccary and anteater are occasionally sighted.

The coastal area is known as an important nesting site for the brown booby, mostly found 1.6km south of the mainland on Isla Cabo Blanco (White Cape Island). The name 'Cabo Blanco' was coined by Spanish conquistadors when they noticed that the entire island consisted of guano-encrusted rocks. Seabirds in the area include the brown pelican and the magnificent frigatebird.

Hiking

From the ranger station, the Sendero Sueco (Swedish Trail) leads 4.5km down to a wilderness beach at the tip of the peninsula, while the Sendero Danes (Danish Trail) is a spur that branches from Sendero Sueco and reconnects 1km later. So, you can make this small 2km loop and stay in the woods, or take on the considerably more difficult but much more rewarding hike to the cape, heading down one way and taking the other path back up. Be advised that the trails can get very muddy (especially in the rainy season) and are fairly steep in certain parts – plan for about two hours in each direction.

The wide, sandy pebble beach at the end of the trail is magnificent. It's backed by jungle, sheltered by two rugged headlands including one that stretches out into a rock reef with island views just offshore. The water is striped turquoise at low tide, but the cool currents still make for a refreshing dip. Visibility isn't always great for snorkeling but you may want to bring a mask anyway. Driftwood is smooth, weathered and piled haphazardly here and there. There are even picnic tables and a grill, if you care to get ambitious. Simply put, it is a postcard, and frankly a must do. Leave the beach by 2pm to get out before the park closes.

ℹ Information

The **ranger station** (📞2642-0093; www.caboblancopark.com; adult/child under 12 yr US$10/1; ⊘8am-4pm Wed-Sun) is 2km south of Cabuya at the entrance to the park, and trail maps are available. It is not possible to overnight in the park, though there are plenty of options in nearby Cabuya or Montezuma. Bring drinks and snacks as there is no food or water available.

The average annual temperature is about 27°C (80°F) and annual rainfall is some 2300mm at the tip of the park. Not surprisingly, the trails can get muddy, so it's best to visit in the dry season, from December to April, and start your hike early before it gets too steamy.

❶ Getting There & Away

Buses (US$1.50, 45 minutes) depart from the park entrance for Montezuma at 7am, 9am, 11am and 3pm. A taxi from Montezuma to the park costs about US$16.

During dry season, you can drive (4WD required) for 7km from Cabuya to Mal País via the stunningly scenic Star Mountain Rd. It's a rough road and there is one river crossing but it's all good.

Mal País & Santa Teresa

Get ready for tasty waves, creative kitchens and babes in board shorts and bikinis, because the southwestern corner of Península de Nicoya has all that and more. Which is why it's become one of Costa Rica's most life-affirming destinations. Here, the sea is alive with wildlife and is almost perfect when it comes to shape, color and temperature. The hills are dotted with stylish boutique sleeps and sneaky good kitchens run by the occasional runaway, top-shelf chef. Sure, there is a growing ribbon of mostly expat development on the coastline, but the hills are lush and that road is still rutted earth (even if it is intermittently sealed with aromatic vats of molasses). The entire area unfurls along one coastal road that rambles from Santa Teresa in the north through Playa el Carmen, the area's commercial heartbeat, then terminating in the fishing hamlet of Mal País. The whole region is collectively known as Mal País.

The road from Cóbano meets the beach road next to Frank's Place, on the western side of the peninsula. To the left (south) lies Mal País and to the right (north) is Santa Teresa. Dead ahead is the beach at Playa el Carmen. In the dry season you might also arrive on the 4WD road from Montezuma via Cabuya, which terminates at the southern end of Mal País village.

🏃 Activities

Surfing is the be-all and end-all for most visitors to Mal País, but the beautiful beach stretches north and south for kilometers on end, and many accommodations can arrange horseback-riding tours and fishing trips. Or you could find the fishing harbor in Mal País and arrange your own fishing tour. It does help to speak some Spanish, however.

Surfing

The following beaches are listed from north to south.

About 8km north of the Playa el Carmen intersection, **Playa Manzanillo** is a combination of sand and rock that's best surfed when the tide is rising and there's an offshore wind.

The most famous break in the area is at **Playa Santa Teresa**, and it's fast and powerful. This beach can be surfed at virtually any time of day, though be cautious as there are scattered rocks. To get here take the lane just north of La Lora Amarilla from the main road. The beach down the alley from Casa Zen is our favorite. White and powdery, it's great for swimming and surfing as the small cove is protected by rock reefs on both sides.

Playa el Carmen, downhill from the main intersection, is a good beach break that can also be surfed anytime. The beach is wide and sandy and curls into successive coves, so it makes good beachcombing and swimming terrain too.

The entire area is saturated with surf shops, and competition has kept prices low. This is a good place to pick up an inexpensive board, and you can probably get most of your money back if you sell it elsewhere. Most of the local shops also do rentals and repairs, and may clue you into secret surf spots.

Al Chile Surf Shop
SURFING

(📞 2640-0959; www.alchilesurfshop.com; board rental per day US$10, lessons per person US$40-45) 'Al Chile' is a slang phrase that means something like 'For real!' As in 'In one lesson you'll be riding the white water – *al chile!*' The charming husband-wife team here guarantees it. If you don't want a lesson, they will still rent you a top-notch board. And if you're bringing your own board, check out the custom surfboard art by local surfer-artist William Borges.

Nalu Surf School
SURFING

(📞 2649-9391, 2640-0714; board rental per day US$10-20, lessons per person US$40) Located 300m north of the intersection at Playa el Carmen, this surf school has a good reputation. It rents boards by the half- and full day, offers daily lessons for all skill levels and has a good range of new and used boards for sale in the surf shop.

Kina Surf Shop SURFING

(☑2640-0627; www.kinasurfcostarica.com; lessons per person US$50, board rentals per day US$12-20; ⏰9am-5pm) A terrific, efficient surf shop near the break in Santa Teresa. The 90-minute lessons for beginner, intermediate and advanced surfers come highly recommended, plus it has an excellent selection of boards to buy or rent.

Freedom Ride SUP SURFING

(☑2640-0521; www.sup-costarica.com; rental half-/full day US$25/35, lessons per person US$50; ⏰9am-6pm) A stand-up paddle (SUP) place with sharp, English-speaking management, set in Mal País proper. It offers half- and full-day rentals, as well as SUP lessons and tours. Lessons should be arranged in advance.

Yoga

Yoga naturally complements surfing, and if you haven't been in the water for a while, the stretching can be the perfect antidote to sore flippers.

Casa Zen YOGA

(☑2640-0523; www.zencostarica.com; per person US$9) Offers two or three classes daily, in a lovely 2nd-story, open-air studio, surrounded by trees. Most of the classes are a Hatha-inspired Vinyasa flow, but there's also a more relaxing flow class, cardio fit and other styles. Multi-class packs available.

Horizon Yoga Hotel YOGA

(☑2640-0524; www.horizon-yogahotel.com; per person US$12) Offers two classes daily, in a serene environment overlooking the ocean. Classes include Sivananda, Vinyasa and Pilates. A massage from the Horizon Spa is a nice follow-up.

Yoga Studio at Nautilus YOGA

(☑2640-0991; www.hotelnautiluscostarica.com; yoga US$10) Twice-daily yoga classes are held on the deck at the Nautilus Boutique Hotel, offering lovely views over the village. Private lessons are also available.

🛏 Sleeping & Eating

Frank's Place occupies the corner of the main intersection in Playa el Carmen; this is also where shuttles will drop you off and pick you up. Entries are listed in order from the main Playa el Carmen intersection.

🛏 Santa Teresa

Horizon Yoga Hotel HOTEL $$$

(☑2640-0524; www.horizon-yogahotel.com; d US$120-140, q US$210; ⓟ❄🅰🏊) Replete with fountains and profound beauty, this stunning terraced property on the Santa Teresa hillside offers barefoot elegance at its best. There is a range of rooms, including family-friendly villas with private pools. A better choice is the stilted bamboo bungalows, which have decks with hammocks and massive 180-degree ocean views.

The same views are available at the nearby teahouse that plays jazz, blends smoothies and brews a delicious house-made herbal tea.

Brisas del Mar SEAFOOD $$

(☑2640-0941; www.buenosairesmalpais.com; mains US$14-18; ⏰8-11am & 4-10pm Tue-Sun; ⓟ🅰) It's worth the steep climb for sensational views and delectable seafood at the poolside patio restaurant at the Hotel Buenos Aires. Begin with a specialty cocktail as you peruse the day's menu written on the blackboard. Look for fresh *fruits de mer* prepared with international influences, such as chipotle lime-marinated tuna with roasted-tomato salsa and jalapeño cilantro cream. Brisas del Mar is open for breakfast too.

Hostel 7 HOSTEL $

(Casa de Gingi; ☑2640-0268; http://hostelseven.wix.com/hostelseven7; dm US$12, r US$30-35; ⓟ❄🅰) Gingi's place is beloved by surfers and backpackers for its welcoming, laid-back vibe, clean accommodations and awesome extras. The whitewashed rooms are excellent for the price. On grounds filled with fruit trees, there's also a communal kitchen, pool table, basketball court and TV lounge. Gingi is a gem: he goes above and beyond to ensure you have a great time.

Atrapasueños Lodge BOUTIQUE HOTEL $$$

(Dream Catcher Lodge; ☑2640-0080; www.atrapasuenos.net; d/apt incl breakfast US$130/200; ⓟ❄🅰🏊) One of the few properties right on the beach, this family-owned place offers the intimacy of a B&B and the luxury of a boutique hotel. With a balcony or terrace overlooking lush gardens, the rooms have hardwood floors, exotic art and tapestries, and big glass sliding doors. A lovely mosaic pool is surrounded by a sun terrace with an outdoor shower.

Wavetrotter
HOSTEL $

(☑2640-0805; www.wavetrotterhostel.com; dm US$15, r without bathroom US$35; P⊛) An excellent option for hostel hoppers, not just surfers. Italian-owned Wavetrotter is a simple but classy place, with all-wood six-bed dorms overlooking a vast common area. There are private rooms in the garden, which is also home to howler monkeys and iguanas. There is a huge communal kitchen and – major bonus – the whole place is spotless. This place is one block east of the main road: turn off right before Pizza El Pulpo.

Casa Zen
GUESTHOUSE $

(☑2640-0523; www.zencostarica.com; dm/d/tr/q US$15/34/42/50; P@⊛) This recommended Asian-inspired guesthouse is decked out in Zen art, celestial murals and enough happy Buddha sculptures to satisfy all your belly-rubbing needs. The goal is to help guests 'chill and recreate on their own time.' There is also an eclectic restaurant that has everything from veggie sandwiches and burgers to fresh sushi and Thai curries. Rates all include breakfast.

Funky Monkey Lodge
BUNGALOW $$

(☑2640-0272; www.funky-monkey-lodge.com; dm US$15-20, d US$92-97, apt US$135-170; P⊛@⊠) Up the hill from Tuanis, this funky lodge has sweet, rustic bungalows built out of bamboo. Each has an open-air shower, balcony with hammock and access to a communal kitchen. One huge bungalow is sometimes used as a dorm, as are smaller, less interesting quads in the main building. Also: ping-pong, pool and board games...good times! Located on the main drag, just past the soccer field.

Don Jon's
BUNGALOW $

(☑2640-0700; www.donjonsonline.com; dm/d US$12-18, bungalow US$45-75, apt US$75-110; P⊛⊛) Just past the soccer field, Don Jon's place is the perfect base for surfers and anybody looking to 'relax to the max'. Rustic teak bungalows are creatively decorated and quite appealing, while attractive Spanish-tiled dorms have high-beamed ceilings and plenty of hammocks.

The restaurant knows its audience, serving filling breakfasts, giant burritos, delicious fish tacos and strong drinks. Located 100m from the surf.

Zwart Cafe
CAFE $

(☑2640-0011; mains US$4-8; ⊙7am-5pm; ⊛) Zwart means 'black' in Dutch, but this shabby-chic, artist-owned gallery and cafe is all white (or mostly, damn dust!). You'll love the surf-inspired technicolor canvases, the lively outdoor patio and popular breakfasts including three flavors of crepes and two varieties of French toast. At lunch it's all about the burritos. There's a dynamite used-book store here too.

Canaima Chill House
APARTMENT $$$

(☑2640-0410; www.hotel-canaima-chill-house. com; d US$100-130; P⊛⊠) A 'chill house' is an apt desciptor for this eight-room boutique eco-chic hotel. Super-stylish suites have breezy indoor-outdoor living areas, awesome hanging bamboo beds and loads of natural materials (such as stone grotto showers). Guests share the Jacuzzi and plunge pool off the sunken pillow lounge. It's set in the hills, 500m from the main road, so you'll want wheels.

Nautilus Boutique Hotel
BOUTIQUE HOTEL $$$

(☑2640-0991; www.hotelnautiluscostarica.com; villa d/q US$150/250; P⊛⊛⊠) ✿ If you're looking for a healthy, relaxing retreat with a bit of luxury, Nautilus is for you. Each villa has a living area, fully equipped kitchen and private deck. Even better, the design incorporates plenty of wood and natural elements, local artwork and fine linens.

Besides being a boutique hotel, Nautilus is also a 'wellness center', offering twice-daily yoga classes (US$10) and amazing, healthy food at the onsite restaurant Olam.

Rumbo Surf Lodge
HOTEL $$

(☑2640-1122; www.rumbosurf.com; apt US$70, surf camp from US$900; P⊛⊛) Simple and sweet, Rumbo has four clean, tile apartments with kitchenettes and balconies with hammocks. They're not fancy, but they have everything you need – if not, Nico will find it for you. He can also teach you to surf, with weekly packages that include lessons and board rental. Rumbo is 100m from the waves.

Cuesta Arriba
HOSTEL $$

(☑2640-0607; www.cuestaarriba.com; dm US$15, d US$50-60; P⊛⊛⊠) This is a thinking person's hostel attracting an older, more polished crowd. Colorful, loft-style dorms have en suite bathrooms, polished concrete floors and creative mosaic tile embellishments. The lovely private rooms are similar, but there are fewer beds. Communal areas include a big well-stocked kitchen area, a breezy terrace upstairs and a garden with hammocks. Rates all include breakfast.

★ Koji's   JAPANESE $$$
(2640-0815; www.santa-teresa.com/kojis; sushi US$5-10; ⊙5:30-9:30pm Wed-Sun) Koji Hyodo's sushi shack in nearby Playa Hermosa is a twinkling beacon of fresh raw excellence. The atmosphere and service are superior, of course, but his food is a higher truth. The grilled octopus is barely fried and sprinkled with sea salt; and there's a sweet crunch to his lobster sashimi, sliced trace-paper thin and sprinkled with fresh ginger.

There are generally bar seats available, but if you want a table, book ahead. Koji's is located 2km north of Florblanca. If you cross the bridge, you've gone too far.

🛏 Playa el Carmen

Frank's Place   HOTEL $$
(2640-0096; www.franksplacecr.com; s/d standard US$55/75, superior US$95/115; P❅@🛎🏊) Coming into town from Cóbano the first place you'll see is this historic surfer outpost. But Frank has grown up, and this is no longer the backpackers' paradise it once was. The rooms are plain but clean and comfortable (all include breakfast). The location has its advantages: not the least, the road is paved here so it's not nearly as dusty as elsewhere in town.

Pizzeria Playa Carmen   PIZZERIA $
(2640-0110; mains US$8-23; ⊙11am-9pm) Playa el Carmen's most conspicuous pizza joint is this splashy restaurant right on the *playa*, which makes it ideal for sundowners. The tasty pizza is cooked in the wood-fired oven and beer is cheap.

Casa Azul   GUESTHOUSE $$
(2640-0379; www.hotelcasaazul.com; r with/without ocean view US$125/60, casita US$150, ste US$400; P🛎🏊) You can't get much closer to the waves than this fabulous electric-blue house, looming over the garden, pool and beach. Sharing a communal kitchenette and an outdoor barbecue, the three downstairs rooms are attractive with ceramic-tile floors, wrought-iron beds and plenty of light. The secluded garden *casita* has a private patio with sea views.

🛏 Mal País

The Place   BOUTIQUE HOTEL $$
(2640-0001; www.theplacemalpais.com; d/bungalow incl breakfast US$69/135; P❅🛎🏊) A waterfall-fed pool is surrounded by cushy blood-red lounge chairs and day beds at this Euro-chic boutique hotel. Attractive tile rooms are draped in linens, but it's absolutely worth it to splurge on the more expensive bungalows. Set amid tropical gardens, each one is creatively and uniquely decorated according to a different theme.

Malpaís Surf Camp & Resort   LODGE $$
(2640-0357; www.malpaissurfcamp.com; camp US$11, dm US$17, d with/without bathroom US$73/40; P❅@🛎🏊) There are comfortable, private *cabañas* and more luxurious digs, but the best deal at this surfers' lodge is the open-air *rancho*, with a tin roof and pebble floors, which you can share with three other surfers. Wander the landscaped tropical grounds, swim in the luscious pool, grab a cold beer in the open-air lounge and soak up the good vibes.

Blue Jay Lodge   BUNGALOW $$
(2640-0089; www.bluejaylodgecostarica.com; d/tr/q incl breakfast US$83/100/115; P🛎🏊) These charming stilted bungalows are built along a forest-covered hillside, each with a huge, screened-in veranda with hammocks. Though they're a bit on the rustic side, the luxury is in their spaciousness and openness to the dramatic surroundings. The lodge is 200m from the beach.

Caracolas   SODA $
(2291-1470; mains US$4-13; ⊙7am-9pm; P🛎📶) The lone *soda* on this end of the coast. It serves *típica* on timber tables in a garden that rolls onto the rocky beach, and does all the usual chicken, beef and seafood dishes, as well as sandwiches and salads. But the reason to come here is to feel the ocean breeze and stare at the setting sun. There are also rooms available from US$45 to US$100.

Pachamama   HOTEL $$
(2640-0195; www.pacha-malpais.com; bungalows US$65-75, house US$160; P🛎) This sweet earth-loving property offers tremendous value, especially in its quaint fauxdobe bungalows, each with a kitchenette and lovely shady front porch. There's also a wicked two-story two-bedroom house with a romantic wooden loft. All choices

are romantic and recommended. Wildlife abounds in the tropical garden, and it's about 50m from the beach.

Camping Elimar CAMPGROUND $
(☑ 8892-2005; per person US$6) Set on a stunning slice of rocky coastline is this humble family-run campsite where a pebble beach rolls onto a rock reef that becomes tide pools. There's ample shade and flat ground where you can pitch your tent, and a shared grill, showers, bathrooms and electricity.

★**Moana Lodge** BOUTIQUE HOTEL $$$
(☑ 2640-0230, in USA 888-865-8032; www.moanalodge.com; r standard/deluxe US$99/135, ste US$235-260) A simply stunning boutique property etched into the wooded hillside above Mal País. Standard rooms are all-wood garden cottages, decked out with African art, and close to the pool and reception. Make the climb to the junior suites for 180-degree views of the coast, as well as wood floors throughout, rain showers inside and outside, a wet bar and sliding glass door entry. The top-shelf **Papaya Lounge** (☑ 2640-0230; tapas US$6-9; ☺ 7:30-10am & 5-10pm) shares that stunning perch.

★**Mary's Restaurant** INTERNATIONAL, ORGANIC $
(☑ 8348-1285; www.maryscostarica.com; mains US$7-17; ☺ 5:30-10pm Thu-Tue) At the far end of Mal País village, this unassuming, open-air restaurant has polished concrete floor, wood oven, pool table and chalkboard menu. It offers delicious wood-fired pizzas, homemade bacon and sausage, grilled seafood, sashimi tasting plates and fresh produce straight from the farm. It's all fabulous. Its secret? Using only fresh, organic ingredients from local farms and fishermen.

🍸 Drinking & Entertainment

Rocamar BAR
(☑ 2640-0250; ☺ noon-9pm; 🛜) Tucked away on the sand deep in Santa Teresa is this beach lounge that has become a popular local expat hang at sunset. There's a thatched dining area (meals US$8 to US$16), timber tables and beanbags stuck in the sand, and hammocks slung in the trees – all perfectly positioned for sunset.

Kika LIVE MUSIC
(☑ 2640-0408; ☺ 5pm-2am) This Argentine-owned restaurant is a popular spot for dinner and drinks by candlelight (Grandma's pork gets rave reviews). But things really pick up after dark on Thursday, when the local punk-rock-ska cover band takes the stage, attracting a lively crowd for drinking and dancing. Good band, bad band? Don't think too hard, rockers, there's music in the air!

La Lora Amarilla CLUB
(☑ 2640-0132; ☺ 7pm-2am) The town's enormous concrete hangar of a dive bar and disco. It is a stone's throw from Kika, making for an easy flow between both on Thursday (reggae-dub) nights.

ℹ️ Information

Next door to Frank's Place, **Banco de Costa Rica** (☺ 9am-4pm Mon-Fri) has a 24hr ATM. Directly across the street at the Centro Comercial Playa El Carmen you'll find a branch of **Banco Nacional** (☑ 2640-0598; ☺ 1-7pm) that can change US dollars and has an ATM.

You can find internet access all over Mal País, but for a start, try Frank's Place (p347) on the main intersection.

There are several grocery stores along the coast. The largest is **Super La Hacienda** (☺ 7am-8pm), located 100m north of Cuesta Arriba hostel. The closest gas station is 2km up the Cóbano road from Playa el Carmen.

A useful website for local information is www.malpais.net.

ℹ️ Getting There & Around

All buses begin and end at Ginger Café, 100m south of Cuesta Arriba hostel; you can flag the bus down anywhere along the road up to Frank's Place, at which point buses turn left and head inland toward Cóbano.

A direct bus from Mal País to San José via the Paquera ferry departs at 6am and 2pm (US$13, six hours). Local buses to Cóbano (US$2, 45 minutes) depart at 7am and noon.

A taxi to or from Cóbano costs approximately US$32. Taxis between Mal País, Playa el Carmen and Santa Teresa range from US$4 to US$8. A taxi to the ferry in Paquera is US$55.

Montezuma Expeditions (☑ 2642-0919; www.montezumaexpeditions.com; Centro Comercial Playa el Carmen) organizes shuttle-van transfers to San José, Tamarindo and Sámara (US$50); Jacó, La Fortuna, Liberia and Monteverde (US$50); Manuel Antonio (US$60); and Dominical (US$70).

For car rental:

Alamo (☑ 2242-7733; www.alamocostarica.com; ☺ 7:30am-5:30pm) Located at Frank's Place.

Budget (☑ 2640-0500; www.budget.co.cr; ☺ 8am-6pm Mon-Sat, 8am-4pm Sun) Next to Banco Nacional.

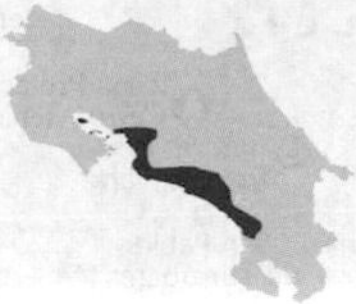

Central Pacific Coast

Best Places to Eat

➡ Citrus (p406)

➡ Exotica (p406)

➡ Graffiti (p367)

➡ Sabor Español (p403)

➡ Tropical Sushi (p376)

Out-of-the-Way Beaches

➡ Matapalo (p395)

➡ Playa Colonia (p401)

➡ Playa Esterillos (p371)

➡ Playa Hermosa (p370)

➡ Playa Palo Seco (p376)

Why Go?

Stretching from the rough-and-ready port of Puntarenas to the tiny town of Uvita, the central Pacific coast is home to both wet and dry tropical rainforests, sun-drenched sandy beaches and a healthy dose of wildlife. On shore, national parks protect endangered squirrel monkeys and scarlet macaws, while offshore waters are home to migrating whales and pods of dolphins.

With so much biodiversity packed into a small geographic area, it's no wonder the coastal region is often thought of as Costa Rica in miniature. Given its close proximity to San José and the Central Valley and highlands, and its well-developed system of paved roads, this part of the country is a favorite weekend getaway for domestic and international travelers.

While threats of unregulated growth and environmental damage are real, it's also important to see the bigger picture, namely the stunning nature that first put the central Pacific coast on the map.

When to Go

➡ West of the Cordillera Central, rains fall heavily between April and November. The hillsides are particularly lush and green during this time

➡ In summer (December to March) little rain falls, leaving the countryside dry and barren looking.

➡ Festival fans will want to visit from around mid-January to late February, when music and art gatherings light up Jacó and Uvita.

Puntarenas

6 17

Isla San Lucas

Playa Doña Ana

Reserva Biológica Isla Guayabo

Mata de Limón

Puerto Caldera

Playa Tivives & Valor

Chacarita

Esparza

Alajuela

Barranca
Boca Barranca

Zona Protectora Río Grande

Atenas

Zona Protectora Cerro Atenas

San Mateo

3

Orotina

Turu Ba Ri Tropical Park

San Pablo de Turrubares

Santiago de Puriscal

Zona Protectora Cerros de Turrubares

San José

Lepanto

Playa Naranjo

Península de Nicoya

Paquera

Curú

Reserva Biológica Islas Negritos

Refugio Nacional de Vida Silvestre Curú

Isla Tortuga

Pochote

Playa Tambor

Tambor

Golfo de Nicoya

Punta Leona

Reserva Absoluta Nicolás Wessburg

Montezuma

Cabuya

Reserva Natural Absoluta Cabo Blanco

Tárcoles

4 Parque Nacional Carara

Bijagual

34

Reserva Indígena Zapatón

Playa Herradura

Jacó 2

Playa Hermosa 2

Refugio Nacional de Playa Hermosa

Playa Esterillos

Valle de Parrita

Playa Pa Se

Parrita

PACIFIC

OCEAN

N 0   30km
0   20 miles

Central Pacific Coast Highlights

❶ Watching troops of monkeys, lazy sloths and gliding brown pelicans at **Parque Nacional Manuel Antonio** (p389).

❷ Surfing the beach breaks of **Jacó** (p362), **Playa Hermosa** (p370) and **Dominical** (p397) – or learning how.

❸ Sampling some of the coast's most sophisticated cuisine in **Ojochal** (p405).

❹ Listening for squawking pairs of scarlet macaws flying

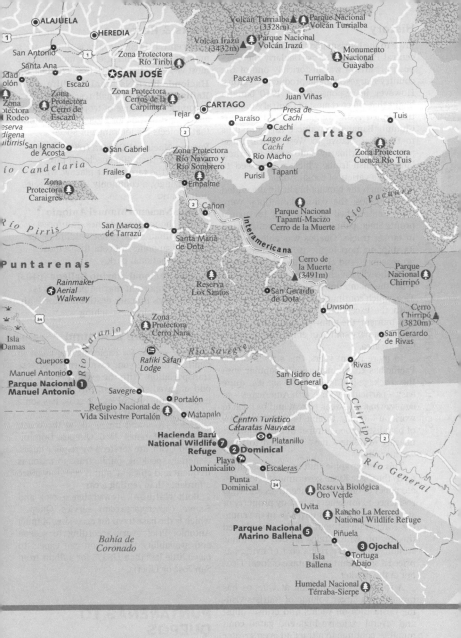

overhead at **Parque Nacional Carara** (p356).

5 Scanning the horizon for pods of breaching humpback whales from the deserted

beaches of **Parque Nacional Marino Ballena** (p403).

6 Unearthing the ramshackle historic charms of **Puntarenas** (p353).

7 Getting a guided animal-spotting tour at the **Hacienda Barú National Wildlife Refuge** (p395).

History

Prior to the tourism boom in Costa Rica, the central Pacific coast – particularly the Quepos port area – was historically one of the country's largest banana-producing regions. However, in response to the 1940 banana blight that affected most of Central America, the United Fruit Company (also known as Chiquita Banana) introduced African palms to the area. Native to West Africa, these palms are primarily cultivated for their large, reddish fruits, which are pressed to produce a variety of cooking oils.

Although the banana blight finally ended in the 1960s, the palm plantations were firmly entrenched and starting to turn a profit. Since palm oil is easily transported in tanker trucks, Quepos was able to close its shipping port in the 1970s, which freed up resources and allowed the city to invest more heavily in the palm-oil industry. In 1995 the plantations were sold to Palma Tica, which continues to operate them today. With the exception of commercial fishing and tourism, the palm-oil plantations serve as the primary source of employment in the Quepos area.

In more recent years, this stretch of the Pacific has grown increasingly popular with the package-holiday crowd, as it's quite easy – particularly for North Americans – to squeeze in a one-week retreat and be back to work on Monday. Unable to resist the draw of paradise, a good number of baby boomers nearing retirement have relocated to these warmer climes.

This demographic shift has been facilitated by the Costa Rican government's decades-old policy of offering tax incentives and legal residence to foreigners who buy property or start businesses and enterprises in the country. Foreign investment has thus far blessed this region with vitally needed economic stimuli, though the rising cost of living has priced a significant percentage of local Ticos out of the market.

A sparkling new marina at Quepos has brought in a larger volume of tourists visiting Costa Rica on yachts and cruise ships, and several exclusive high-end gated communities continue to attract an even greater number of wealthy immigrants. Things are indeed changing quickly along this stretch of coastline, though it's difficult to imagine that the authenticity of the coastal fishing villages, agricultural plantations and protected areas could ever be lost.

Parks & Reserves

The central Pacific coast is home to a number of parks and reserves, including the most visited national park in Costa Rica.

Hacienda Barú National Wildlife Refuge (p395) This small reserve encompasses a range of tropical habitats and is part of a major biological corridor that protects a wide range of species.

Parque Nacional Carara (p356) Home to no fewer than 400 species of bird, including the rare scarlet macaw, which is, amazingly, a commonly sighted species in the park.

Parque Nacional Manuel Antonio (p389) The pristine beaches, rainforest-clad mountains and dense wildlife never fail to disappoint in Costa Rica's most touristed national park.

Parque Nacional Marino Ballena (p403) A vitally important marine park, this is the country's premier destination for both whale- and dolphin-watching.

Getting There & Around

The best option for exploring the coast in depth is to have your own form of private transportation. With the exception of a few odd unpaved stretches of dirt off the main highways, the central Pacific coast has some of the country's best roads.

Major cities and towns along the coast, such as Puntarenas, Jacó, Quepos, Dominical and Uvita, are serviced by regular buses. Generally speaking, public transportation is frequent and efficient, and is certainly more affordable than renting a car.

Both NatureAir (www.natureair.com) and Sansa (www.flysansa.com) service Quepos, which is the base town for accessing Manuel Antonio. Prices vary according to season and availability, though you can expect to pay a little less than US$75 for a flight from San José or Liberia.

PUNTARENAS TO QUEPOS

The northern reaches of the central Pacific coast extend from the maritime port of Puntarenas, a historic shipping hub that has fallen on harder times, to the booming town of Quepos, which is the main access point for Parque Nacional Manuel Antonio. In between are vast swaths of forested hillsides and wilderness beaches, which together protect large concentrations of remarkable wildlife. However, the local spotlight is fixed firmly on the surf city of Jacó, which plays host to a colorful cast of characters.

Puntarenas

Port cities the world over have a reputation for polluted waters, seedy streets and slow decay, which might be a traveler's first impression of little Puntarenas, Costa Rica's gateway to the Pacific. But just under the surface are some down-to-earth charms – ones largely absent in the country's most heavily traveled regions. As the closest coastal town to San José, Puntarenas has long been a popular escape for landlocked Ticos (Costa Ricans) on the weekend, but during the week activity along the oceanfront promenade slows to an amenably languid pace, all the better to enjoy the beachfront *sodas* (informal lunch counters), tiny museums and busy market.

The city's ferry terminal is a convenient way to connect to pristine beaches on the central Pacific coast or to southern Nicoya. While most travelers are only stopping by en route to the greener pastures and bluer seas elsewhere, those who get stuck here overnight could do a lot worse.

History

Prior to the mid-20th century, Puntarenas was the largest and most significant open-water port in Costa Rica. Some of the finest coffees to fill European cups were carried to the continent on Puntarenas-registered freighters, and the steady flow of capital transformed Puntarenas into the 'Pearl of the Pacific.' However, after the construction of the railway leading from the Central Valley to Puerto Limón in 1890, a more direct shipping route to Europe initiated the city's decline in importance, though Puntarenas did manage to remain a major port on the Pacific coast. Visitors get a whiff of the city's glory in the lovely stone church at its center, but modern history has left many unattractive sights: polluted waters, eroding structures and tacky souvenir stands that close up when the hulking cruise ships leave port.

⊙ Sights & Activities

Museo Histórico Marino MUSEUM
(☑2661-5036, 2256-4139; Av Central btwn Calles 3 & 5; ⊙8am-1pm & 2-5pm Tue-Sun) FREE This museum describes the history of Puntarenas through audiovisual presentations, old photos and artifacts.

Casa de la Cultura GALLERY
(☑2661-1394; Av Central btwn Calles 3 & 5; ⊙10am-4pm Mon-Fri) Casa de la Cultura has an art gallery with occasional exhibits as well as a performance space offering seasonal cultural events.

Parque Marino del Pacífico AQUARIUM
(☑2661-5272; www.parquemarino.org; adult/child under 12yr US$10/5; ⊙9am-5pm Tue-Sun) This marine park has an aquarium that showcases manta rays and other creatures from the Pacific. The park sits on the site of the old train station and has a tiny splash pool, snack bar, gift shop and information center.

Paseo de los Turistas PROMENADE
(Tourists' Promenade) Stroll beside the beach on the Paseo de los Turistas, a pedestrian boulevard stretching along the southern edge of town. Cruise ships make day visits to the eastern end of this road, and a variety of souvenir stalls and *sodas* are there to greet passengers. On weekend nights, this is the place to knock back beers and find the party.

☞ Tours

Tour operators will greet passengers disembarking from cruise ships. Quality and price are greatly variable, but a few come highly recommended.

Calypso Cruises BOAT TOUR
(☑2256-2727, 2661-0585; www.calypsocruises.com; Av 3, near Calle 9; day trips adult/student/child under 7yr US$139/129/75) This long-established, top-class, gringo-owned catamaran makes day trips to Tortuga's brilliant white beaches. Trips come with a picnic lunch, fresh fruit, snacks and booze. The same company also operates Puntarenas' only fine-dining establishment, El Shrimp Shack.

Odyssey Tours ADVENTURE TOUR
(☑8994-6245, 2635-2221, 8319-1315; www.odysseytourscr.com; ⊕) Diego and Alvaro, a pair of friendly bilingual brothers, host a variety of customizable day tours and come with a

slew of excellent recommendations. Costa Rica's full suite of adventures are on offer: white-water rafting, trips to local canopy walks and nearby national parks.

⚜️ Festivals & Events

Puntarenas is one of the seaside towns that celebrates the **Fiesta de La Virgen del Mar** (Festival of the Virgin of the Sea) on the Saturday closest to July 16. Fishing boats and elegant yachts are bedecked with lights, flags and decorations and sail around the harbor, seeking protection from the Virgin as they begin another year at sea. There are also boat races, a carnival, and plenty of food, drinking and dancing.

🛏️ Sleeping

There's no shortage of accommodations in Puntarenas, though plenty of the very cheapest ones cater to the clientele that want to pay by the hour. Also, high humidity and lots of rain makes even the most upscale options muggy, so make sure there's a fan.

Hotel Cabezas HOTEL $
(☑2661-1045; Av 1 btwn Calles 2 & 4; s/d without bathroom US$14/24, with bathroom US$20/30; P🛜) This no-nonsense budget option is an excellent choice. Pastel-painted rooms have functional overhead fans and screened windows, which means you'll sleep deeply without needing air-con. Although you certainly shouldn't leave your valuables strewn about, this hotel is safe, secure and surprisingly quiet.

Cabinas Joyce CABINA $
(☑8706-9101, 2661-4290; cnr Calle 4 & Av 2; s from US$24, d US$30-60; P🌀❄️🛜) This is the best option near the bus station; a spotless little joint of tiled rooms overseen with a hawkish eye by the cantankerous, if lovable, Joyce.

Hotel La Punta HOTEL $$
(☑2661-0696; www.hotellapunta.net; cnr Av 1 & Calle 35; s/d US$70/80; P❄️🛜🏊) For early-morning ferry departures, Hotel La Punta is an appealing choice. Conveniently located one block from the dock, its 10 rooms are arranged around a landscaped courtyard and small pool. Comfortable accommodations feature terra-cotta floors, cable TV and fridge.

Hotel Tioga HOTEL $$
(☑2661-0271; www.hoteltioga.com; Paseo de los Turistas btwn Calles 17 & 19; d deluxe/balcony incl breakfast from US$85/96; P❄️🛜🏊) Opened

in 1959, this is the most established hotel in Puntarenas. It's worth paying a bit more for the balcony rooms, which have sweeping views of the beachfront.

Double Tree Resort by Hilton Central Pacific RESORT $$$
(☑2663-0808, 800-555-5555; www.doubletree-centralpacific.com; all-inclusive packages per person from US$290, child under 12yr US$51; P❄️@🛜🏊) This all-inclusive, family-friendly resort gets top billing for its enormously curvaceous swimming pool, immense offering of water sports and around-the-clock entertainment. While there are certainly nicer beaches down the coastline, there is excellent value to be had here, especially if you book in advance online.

🍴 Eating

The freshest, cheapest food is available in the small stands and *sodas* near the Central Market. This is also the stomping ground of a motley mix of sailors, drunks and prostitutes, but the scene is raffish rather than dangerous – during the day, at least. There are more *sodas* along the Paseo de los Turistas between Calles Central and 3, but most of the sit-down options around there are touristy and overpriced.

Self-caterers can head to the **MegaSuper** (☑2661-5301; Calle 3 btwn Avs 1 & 3) supermarket or the Central Market, where you can find cut-to-order tuna steaks for a pittance.

La Casona COSTA RICAN $
(☑2661-1626; cnr Av 1 & Calle 9; casados US$5-12; ⏰8am-8pm) This bright-yellow house is marked with a small, modest sign, but it's an incredibly popular lunch spot, attracting countless locals who jam onto the shaded, greenery-laden deck across from Parque Mora y Cañas. Portions are heaped, and soups are served in bathtub-sized bowls – bring your appetite.

Marisquería Kaite Negro SEAFOOD $
(☑2661-5566; cnr Av 1 & Calle 19; dishes US$6-12; ⏰10am-late) On the north side of town, this rambling restaurant is popular with locals, and serves good seafood and a variety of tasty *bocas* (appetizers). If you really want to see the place swinging, the open-air courtyard comes to life on weekends with live music and all-night dancing.

El Shrimp Shack SEAFOOD $$
(☑2661-0585; Av 3 btwn Calles 7 & 3; meals US$7-18; ⏰11:30am-3:30pm Tue-Sun; ❄️) Offering

the most upscale dining in Puntarenas, El Shrimp Shack's silly name belies a gracious interior – wood-paneled walls, marble-topped tables, antique light sconces and a stunning stained-glass ceiling, all within a century-old house with harbor views. Shrimp dishes feature prominently, though other options include burgers and excellent *ceviche* (seafood marinated in lemon or lime juice, garlic and seasonings).

La Yunta Steakhouse   STEAKHOUSE $$

(☑2661-3216; Paseo de los Turistas btwn Calles 19 & 21; meals US$6-20; ☺8am-midnight) A favorite with the cruise-ship crowd, this long-running steakhouse has professional service (bow ties!), a tiered veranda overlooking the boardwalk and ocean, and impressive portions of well-prepared, tender meat. The menu is rounded out by seafood.

Drinking & Nightlife

Entertainment in the port tends to revolve around boozing and flirting, though occasionally there's a more highbrow offering at the Casa de la Cultura (p353). On the weekends, follow crowds of Ticos to the countless bars lining the Paseo de los Turistas.

El Oasis del Pacífico   BAR

(☑2661-6368; cnr Paseo de los Turistas & Calle 5; ☺9am-10pm Sun-Thu, to 1am Fri & Sat) A popular spot with a lengthy bar and a warehouse-sized dance floor; during the day, pay a small fee to use the shower facilities.

Capitán Moreno's   CLUB

(☑2661-6888; cnr Paseo de los Turistas & Calle 13; ☺11am-6pm Mon-Fri, 10am-8pm Sat & Sun) A time-honored spot for shaking some booty, with a huge dance floor right on the beach.

Orientation

Situated at the end of a sandy peninsula (8km long but only 100m to 600m wide), Puntarenas is just 110km west of San José by paved highway. The city has 60 *calles* (streets) running north to south, but only five *avenidas* (avenues) running west to east at its widest point. As in all of Costa Rica, street names are largely irrelevant, and landmarks are used for orientation.

Information

The major banks along Av 3, to the west of the market, exchange money and are equipped with 24-hour ATMs. There's also a Banco de Costa Rica (BCR) ATM opposite the pier on the Paseo de los Turistas.

Puntarenas Tourism Office (Catup, Cámara de Turismo de Puntarenas; ☑2661-2980, 24hr 2284-6600; ☺11am-6pm Tue-Fri, 9am-4pm Sat; ☎) Opposite the pier on the 2nd floor of Plaza del Pacífico. It closes for lunch.

Getting There & Away

BOAT

Car and passenger ferries bound for Paquera and Playa Naranjo depart several times a day from the **northwestern dock** (Av 3 btwn Calles 31 & 33); other docks are used for private boats. If you are driving and will be taking the car ferry, arrive at the dock early to get in line. The vehicle section tends to fill up quickly and you may not make it on. In addition, make sure that you have purchased your ticket from the walk-up ticket window before driving onto the ferry. You will not be admitted onto the boat if you don't already have a ticket.

Schedules change seasonally and can be affected by inclement weather. Check with the ferry office by the dock for any changes. Many of the hotels in town also have up-to-date schedules posted.

To Playa Naranjo (for transfer to Nicoya and points west), **Coonatramar** (☑2661 1069; www.coonatramar.com; adult/child US$2/1, bike/car US$4/18) has daily departures at 6:30am, 10am, 2:30pm and 7:30pm.

To Paquera (for transfer to Montezuma and Mal País), **Naviera Tambor** (☑2661-2084; www.navieratambor.com; adult/child US$1.60/1, bike/car US$4.50/23) also has several daily departures between 5am and 8:30pm.

BUS

Buses for San José depart from the large navy-blue building on the north corner of Calle 2 and the Paseo de los Turistas. Book your ticket ahead of time on holidays and weekends. Buses for other destinations leave from across the street, on the beach side of the Paseo.

Jacó US$2.30, 1½ hours, departs 10 times daily between 5am and 5:30pm.

Quepos US$4, 3½ hours, departs 10 times daily between 5am and 5:30pm.

San José US$5, 2½ hours, departs every hour from 4am to 9pm, stopping en route at the Alajuela airport.

Santa Elena, Monteverde US$3, 3½ hours, departs 8:30am and 1pm.

Getting Around

Buses marked 'Ferry' run up Av Central and go to the ferry terminal, 1.5km from downtown. The taxi fare from the San José bus terminal in Puntarenas to the northwestern ferry terminal is about US$2.

Buses for the port of Caldera (also going past Playa Doña Ana and Mata de Limón) leave from the market about every hour and head out of town along Av Central.

Around Puntarenas

The road heading south from Puntarenas skirts the coastline, and a few kilometers out of town you'll start to see the forested peaks of the Cordillera de Tilarán in the distance. Just as the port city fades away, the water gets cleaner, the air crisper and the vegetation more lush. At this point, you should take a deep breath and heave a sigh of relief – the Pacific coastline gets a whole lot more beautiful as you head further south.

About 8km south of Puntarenas is **Playa San Isidro**, the first 'real' beach on the central Pacific coast. Although it is popular with beachcombers from Puntarenas, surfers prefer to push on 4km south to **Boca Barranca**, which some say is the third-longest left-hand surf break in the world. Conditions are best at low tide, and it is possible to surf here year-round. However, be advised that there isn't much in the way of services out here, so be sure that you're confident in the water and seek local advice before hitting the break.

Just beyond the river mouth is a pair of beaches known as **Playa Doña Ana** and **El Segundo**, which are relatively undeveloped and have an isolated and unhurried feel to them. Surfers can find some decent breaks here, too, though, like Playa San Isidro, they are more popular for Tico beachcombers on day trips from Puntarenas, especially during weekends in high season. There are snack bars, picnic shelters and changing areas, and supervised swimming areas.

The next stop along the coast is **Mata de Limón**, a picturesque little hamlet that is situated on a mangrove lagoon and locally famous for its bird-watching. If you arrive during low tide, flocks of feathered creatures descend on the lagoon to scrounge for tasty morsels. Mata de Limón is divided by a river, with the lagoon and most facilities on the south side.

A major port on the Pacific coast is **Puerto Caldera**, which you pass soon after leaving Mata de Limón. There aren't any sights here, and the beach is unremarkable unless you're a surfer, in which case there are a few good breaks to be had (though be careful, as the beach is rocky in places).

Buses heading for the Caldera port depart hourly from the market in Puntarenas, and can easily drop you off at any of the spots described here. If you're driving, the break at Boca Barranca is located near the bridge on the Costanera Sur (South Coastal Hwy), while the entrance to Playa Doña Ana and El Segundo is a little further south (look for a sign that says 'Paradero Turístico Doña Ana'). The turnoff for Mata de Limón is about 5.5km south of Playa Doña Ana.

Parque Nacional Carara

Situated at the mouth of the Río Tárcoles, this 52-sq-km park is only 50km southeast of Puntarenas by road or about 90km west of San José via the Orotina highway. During our last visit, the visitor center visible from the road was a half-remodeled mess, though there were murmurs of a renovation. A short paved trail begins at the **Carara ranger station** (3km south of Río Tárcoles; admission US$10; ◷ 7am-4pm Dec-Apr, 8am-4pm May-Nov), where there are bathrooms, picnic tables and a short, wheelchair-accessible nature trail. Guides can be hired here for US$25 per person (two-person minimum) for a two-hour hike.

The dry season from December to April is the easiest time to go, though the animals are still there in the wet months. March and April are the driest months. Rainfall is almost 3000mm annually, which is less than in the rainforests further south. It's fairly hot, with average temperatures of 25°C (77°F) to 28°C (82°F), but it's cooler within the rainforest. An umbrella is important in the wet season and occasionally needed in the dry months. Make sure you have insect repellent.

◉ Sights

With the help of a hired guide, it's possible to visit the archaeological remains of various indigenous **burial sites** located within the park, though they're tiny and unexciting compared to anything you might see in Mexico or Guatemala. At the time of the Europeans' arrival in Costa Rica, these sites were located in an area inhabited by an indigenous group known as the Huetar (Carara means 'crocodile' in the Huetar language). Unfortunately, not much is known about this group, as little cultural evidence was left behind. Today the few remaining

Huetar are confined to several small villages in the Central Valley.

If you're driving from Puntarenas or San José, pull over to the left immediately after crossing the Río Tárcoles bridge, also known as **Crocodile Bridge**. If you scan the sandbanks below the bridge, you'll have a fairly good chance of seeing as many as 30 basking crocodiles. Although they're visible year-round, the best time for viewing is low tide during the dry season. Binoculars will help a great deal.

Crocodiles this large are generally rare in Costa Rica as they've been hunted vigorously for their leather. However, the crocs are tolerated here as they feature prominently in a number of wildlife tours that depart from Tárcoles. And, of course, the crocs don't mind, as they're hand-fed virtually every day.

🏃 Activities

Wildlife-Watching

The most exciting bird for many visitors to see, especially in June or July, is the brilliantly patterned scarlet macaw, a rare bird that is commonly seen in the Parque Nacional Carara. Its distinctive call echoes loudly through the canopy, usually moments before a pair appears against the blue sky. If you're having problems spotting them, it may help to inquire at the ranger station, which keeps tabs on where nesting pairs are located.

Dominated by open secondary forest punctuated by patches of dense, mature forest and wetlands, Carara offers some superb bird-watching. More than 400 species of bird inhabit the reserve, though your chances of spotting rarer species will be greatly enhanced with the help of an experienced guide. Some commonly sighted species include orange-billed sparrows, five kinds of trogon, crimson-fronted parakeets, blue-headed parrots, golden-naped woodpeckers, rose-throated becards, gray-headed tanagers, long-tailed manikins and rufous-tailed jacamars (just to name a few!).

Birds aside, the trails at Carara are home to several mammal species, including red brockets, white-tailed deer, collared peccaries, monkeys, sloths and agoutis. The national park is also home to one of Costa Rica's largest populations of tayras, weasel-like animals that scurry along the forest floor. And, although most travelers aren't too keen on stumbling upon an American crocodile, some truly monstrous specimens can be viewed from a safe distance at the nearby Crocodile Bridge.

According to the park rangers, the best chance of spotting wildlife is at 7am, when the park opens.

Hiking

Some 600m south of the Crocodile Bridge on the left-hand side is a locked gate leading to the **Sendero Laguna Meándrica**. This trail penetrates deep into the reserve and passes through open secondary forest and patches of dense mature forest and wetlands. About 4km from the entrance is Laguna Meándrica, which has large populations of heron, smoothbill and kingfisher. If you continue past the lagoon, you'll have a good chance of spotting mammals and the occasional crocodile, though you will have to turn back to exit.

Another 2km south of the trailhead is the Carara ranger station.

SCARLET MACAWS

With a shocking bright-red body, blue-and-yellow wings, a long, red tail and a white face, the scarlet macaw (*Ara macao*) is one of the most visually arresting birds in the neotropical rainforest. It also mates for life and can live up to 75 years, flying across the forest canopy in pairs, squawking like pterodactyls – there are few birds in Costa Rica with such character, presence and beauty.

Prior to the 1960s the scarlet macaw was distributed across much of Costa Rica, though trapping, poaching, habitat destruction and increased use of pesticides devastated the population. By the 1990s the distribution was reduced to two isolated pockets: the Península de Osa and Parque Nacional Carara.

Fortunately, these charismatic creatures are thriving in large colonies at both locales, and sightings are virtually guaranteed if you have the time and patience to spare. Furthermore, despite this fragmentation, the International Union for the Conservation of Nature continues to evaluate the species as 'Least Concern,' which bodes well for the future of this truly emblematic rainforest denizen.

About 1km further south are two loop trails. The first, **Sendero Las Araceas**, is 1.2km long and can be combined with the second, **Sendero Quebrada Bonita** (another 1.5km). Both trails pass through primary forest, which is characteristic of most of the park.

🛏 Sleeping & Eating

Camping is not allowed, and there's nowhere to stay in the park. As a result, most people come on day trips from neighboring towns and cities such as Jacó.

Restaurante Los Cocodrilos   COSTA RICAN **$**
(📞 2428-2308; mains US$5-12; ☺ 6am-8pm; 🅿) Located on the north side of the Río Tárcoles bridge, this is the nearest place to get a decent meal. It has inexpensive, filling meals and is extremely popular with travelers stopping to check out the crocodiles.

❶ Information

DANGERS & ANNOYANCES

Increased tourist traffic along the Pacific coast has resulted in an unfortunate increase in petty theft. Vehicles parked at the Laguna Meándrica trailhead are routinely broken into, and although there may be guards on duty, it is advised that drivers leave their cars in the lot at the Carara ranger station and walk along the Costanera Sur for 2km north or 1km south. Alternatively, park beside Restaurante Los

Cocodrilos (be sure to tip the parking attendants on your return).

❶ Getting There & Away

Any bus traveling between Puntarenas and Jacó can leave you at the park entrance. You can also catch buses headed north or south in front of Restaurante Los Cocodrilos. This may be a bit problematic on weekends, when buses are full, so go midweek if you are relying on a bus ride. If you're driving, the entrance to Carara is right on the Costanera and is clearly marked.

Tárcoles & Around

The small, unassuming town of Tárcoles is little more than a few rows of houses strung along a series of dirt roads that parallel the ocean. As you'd imagine, this tiny Tico town isn't much of a tourist draw, though the surrounding area is perfect for fans of the superlative, especially if you're interested in seeing the country's tallest waterfall and some of its biggest crocodiles.

About 2km south of the Carara ranger station (p356) is the Tárcoles turnoff to the right (west) and the Hotel Villa Lapas turnoff to the left. To get to Tárcoles, turn right and drive for 1km, then go right at the T-junction to the village. Local buses between Orotina and Bijagual can drop you off at the entrance to the Parque Nacional Carara.

GARABITO

The area encompassed by Parque Nacional Carara was once home to a legendary indigenous hero, a local *cacique* (chief) named Garabito. Commanding a vast area from the Golfo de Nicoya to the Central Valley, he led a fierce struggle against the Spanish in the mid-16th century.

At the time, a favorite tactic of the Spanish conquistadors throughout Latin America to weaken native resistance was to turn tribes against each other and decapitate the tribal leadership – literally. Although each story has grisly variations, the fate of captured *caciques* often involved public humiliation at a show trial, brutal torture and decapitation. Sometimes, the heads of *caciques* would be mounted and displayed.

Garabito was a different story. The popular chieftain constantly disrupted the Spanish establishment in the Pacific region and, in 1560, Guatemalan high command dispatched a military force to arrest him. Garabito, who claimed to have never spent two nights in the same bed, eluded capture, but the Spanish managed to seize his wife, Biriteka, as a hostage. Garabito countered by having one of his followers dress up as the chieftain and allow himself to be captured. While the camp celebrated catching who they thought was Garabito, the real Garabito escaped with his wife. The ruse is a celebrated victory of Costa Rica's indigenous underdogs, but eventually Garabito too had to accept defeat at the hands of the Spanish. Senior in years and lacking the support that had fueled his earlier series of rebellions, Garabito surrendered in the 1570s, and was even baptized as a Christian.

⊙ Sights & Activities

**Catarata Manantial de
Agua Viva** WATERFALL
(☑8831-2980; admission US$20; ⊙8am-3pm)
This 200m-high waterfall is claimed to
be the highest in the country. From the
waterfall, it's a steep 3km hike down into
the valley; at the bottom, the river continues through a series of natural swimming
holes. The falls are most dramatic at their
fullest, during the rainy season, though the
serene rainforest setting is beautiful any
time of year.

Keep an eye out for brightly colored
poison-dart frogs as well as the occasional
pair of scarlet macaws. A 5km dirt road past
Hotel Villa Lapas leads to the primary entrance to the falls.

Jardín Pura Vida GARDENS
(☑2637-0346; admission US$20; ⊙8am-5pm)
In the town of Bijagual, this private botanical garden offers great vistas of Manantial
de Agua Viva cascading down the side of a
cliff, and there are some easy but altogether
pleasant hiking trails. There is a small restaurant on the grounds, and you can also
arrange horseback riding and tours through
the area.

At the time of writing the Jardín was up
for sale, so its future is uncertain.

☞ Tours

This area is known for crocodile-watching
tours, and travelers anywhere near this part
of the coast will be bombarded with advertisements and flyers for them. Although it
will be hard for adrenaline junkies to resist,
these tours have a dubious impact on the
natural habitat of the magnificent animals
who lurk in the mudflats of the Río Tárcoles.
Although they are definitely a spectacle to
behold, it's frustrating to watch the crocodiles being hand-fed by the tour guides. If
you do visit the crocodiles on a tour, ask a lot
of questions and do your part to encourage
responsible interaction with the animals.
Tours usually cost US$25 per person for two
hours.

Both **Crocodile Man** (☑2637-0771; www.
crocodilemantour.com) and **Jungle Crocodile
Safari** (☑2637-0656; www.junglecrocodilesafari.
com) have offices in Tárcoles. The tours leave
from town or you can arrange to be picked
up at your hotel.

⊨ Sleeping & Eating

Hotel Villa Lapas RESORT $$$
(☑2439 1816, 2637-0232; www.villalapas.com; all-
inclusive r from US$130; ⓟ❄️📶🍽️) ✈ Located
on a private reserve comprising both sec-
ondary rainforest and tropical gardens, this
resort offers rooms housed in an attractive
Spanish colonial–style lodge. Guests can un-
wind in relative comfort in between guided
hikes, bird-watching trips, canopy tours and
soaks in the pool. Geared towards a birding
crowd, the pace here is slow and low-key.

Alongside the Río Tarcolito, the hotel
grounds include the kitschy 'Santa Lucia
Town,' which has a couple of souvenir shops
and a wedding chapel.

❶ Getting There & Away

There are no buses to Tárcoles, but any bus be-
tween Puntarenas and Jacó can leave you at the
entrance. If you're driving, the entrance to the
town is right on the Costanera Sur and is clearly
marked. If you're staying at Hotel Villa Lapas,
it's possible to arrange a pick-up from either San
José or Jacó with an advance reservation.

Playa Herradura Area

Until the mid-1990s, Playa Herradura was a
rural, palm-sheltered beach of grayish-black
sand that was popular mainly with campers
and local fishers. In the late 1990s, however,
Herradura was thrown into the spotlight
when it was used as the stage for the movie
1492. Rapid development ensued, result-
ing in the construction of one of the most
high-profile marinas in the country, the Los
Sueños marina.

While parts of the beach today look like
one giant gravel pit, Playa Herradura repre-
sents one possible future for the central Pa-
cific coast. Sprawling complexes of condos
and high-rise apartments are slowly encir-
cling the bay and snaking up the mountain-
side, while the marina boasts rows of luxury
yachts and sportfishing vessels. Although
opinionated detractors of Playa Herradura
are quick to lob insults, there are some truly
world-class hotels on the beach and high
up in the surrounding mountains that are
worth seeking out.

⊨ Sleeping & Eating

You have to pay to play in Playa Herradura,
so consider moving further down the coast
to Jacó if you're not prepared to bunk down
in the top-end price bracket.

★**Hotel Villa Caletas**　　BOUTIQUE HOTEL **$$$**
(☑2630-3000;　www.hotelvillacaletas.com;　r
US$224-641; P❋🌐≋) ✒ Although the views
of the Pacific are amazing, what makes this
blufftop hotel truly unique is its fusion of ar-
chitectural styles, incorporating elements as
varied as tropical Victorian, Hellenistic and
French colonial. The ultraexclusive accom-
modations are located on the tiny headland
of Punta Leona, perched high on a dramatic
hillside at the end of a serpentine driveway.

Each room is arranged amid the tropical
foliage of the terraced property, affording a
singular sense of privacy and isolation. The
interiors of the rooms are tastefully deco-
rated with art and antiques, with windows
looking onto spectacular views. There is also
a French-influenced restaurant, several semi-
private infinity pools, and a private 1km trail
leading down the hillside to the beach.

Los Sueños Marriott Ocean &
Golf Resort　　　　　　　RESORT **$$$**
(☑2630-9000; www.marriott.com/sjols; r US$383-
666; P🌐❋@🌐≋) With golf course behind
and marina in front, this sprawling 200-
room resort at Playa Herradura embodies
the upscale comfort envisioned for the development, all wrapped up in a hacienda-style
aesthetic. Interconnected pools meander
through the landscaped property, while luxurious rooms include such comforts as hair
dryers, iPod docks, and windows that actually open to catch the ocean breezes.

Zephyr Palace　　　　BOUTIQUE HOTEL **$$$**
(☑2637-3000; www.zephyrpalace.com; r US$399-
1824; P❋@🌐≋) On the same property as
the elegant Villa Caletas, its over-the-top
sibling takes the decadence to another level
of luxury. At this veritable marble palace,
seven individually decorated theme rooms
that wouldn't look out of place in Las Ve-
gas evoke the splendor of ancient Rome,
pharaonic Egypt and the Orient.

Jimmy T's Provisions　　SELF-CATERING
(☑2637-8636; www.jimmytsprovisions.com; Los
Sueños Marina; ☉6:30am-7pm Mon-Sat, 7:30am-
5pm Sun) For gourmets looking to self-cater
in style, Jimmy T's is a dream come true. His
small store on the docks of the Los Sueños
marina might cater mostly to the yachting
set, but it's stacked floor to ceiling with or-
ganic, imported and rare-in-Costa-Rica deli-
cacies. Italian cheeses, grass-fed meat, Asian
foods – it's a delight for travelers who love
to cook.

❶ Getting There & Away

The Herradura turnoff is on the Costanera Sur,
about 6km after the Costanera Sur leaves the
edge of the ocean and heads inland. From here,
a paved road leads 3km west to Playa Herradura.
There are frequent local buses (US$2.25, 20
minutes) connecting Playa Herradura to Jacó.

Jacó

Few places in Costa Rica generate such di-
vergent opinions and paradoxical realities
as Jacó. Partying surfers, North American
retirees and international developers laud it
for its devil-may-care atmosphere, bustling
streets and booming real-estate opportuni-
ties. Observant ecotourists, marginalized
Ticos and loyalists of the 'old Costa Rica' ab-
solutely despise the place for the *exact* same
reasons.

Jacó was the first town on the central
Pacific coast to explode with tourist devel-
opment and, despite ups and downs over
the years, it remains a major draw for back-
packers, surfers, snowbirds and city-weary
josefinos (inhabitants of San José). Al-
though working-class Tico neighborhoods
are nearby, open-air trinket shops and tour
operators line the tacky main drag which, at
night, is given over to a safe but somewhat
seedy mix of binge-drinking students, weed-
slinging surfers and scantily clad working
girls.

While Jacó's lackadaisical charm is not
for everyone, the surfing is excellent, the
restaurants and bars are generally great
and the nightlife can be a blast. Tourist in-
frastructure here is among the best in the
country, and all around the greater Jacó area
you can expect some high-quality service for
your money. Despite its more off-putting
features, it's impossible to deny Jaco's good
side, which put it on the map in the first
place: the sweeping beauty of the beach, the
consistently fine surf and the lush tropical
backdrop.

History

Jacó has a special place in the hearts of Ti-
cos, as it is the quickest oceanside escape
for landlocked denizens of the Central
Valley. Many Ticos recall fondly the days
when weekend shuttle buses would pick up
beach-seekers in the city center and whisk
them away to the then-undeveloped Pacific
paradise.

Jacó Center

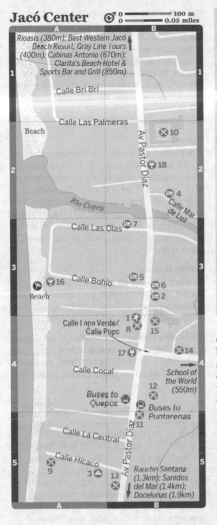

Jacó Center

🌀 Activities, Courses & Tours
1 Serenity Spa	B4

🛏 Sleeping
2 Buddha House	B3
3 Camping El Hicaco	A5
4 Hotel Mar de Luz	B2
5 Hotel Poseidon	B3
6 Jacó Inn	B3
7 Posada Jacó	B3

🍴 Eating
8 Caliche's Wishbone	B4
9 El Hicaco	A5
10 Graffiti	B2
11 Lemon Zest	B5
12 Más x Menos	B4
13 Soda a Cachete	B5
14 Taco Bar	B4
15 Tsunami Sushi	B4

🍷 Drinking & Nightlife
16 Bohio Beach Bar & Bubba's Fish Tacos	A3
17 Le Loft	B4
18 Monkey Bar	B2

The secret got out in the early 1990s, when Canadians on package tours started flooding in, though for the most part tourism remained pretty low-key. Things picked up a bit in the late 1990s, when surfers and anglers the world over started visiting Costa Rica en masse, though Jacó remained the dominion of Central Valley Ticos looking for a little fun and sun. However, things changed dramatically as soon as retiring baby boomers in search of cheap property began to relocate here.

In only a few years' time, Jacó became the most rapidly developing town in all of Costa Rica. Plots of land were subdivided, beachfronts cleared and hillsides leveled, and almost overnight Jacó became the exclusive enclave of moneyed expats. Ticos were happy that development brought coveted Western institutions such as paved roads and fast-food restaurants, but as the initial flash of cash and glitz started to fade, some began to wonder if they had inadvertently sold out the ground beneath them. The global economic crisis of 2008 was in some ways a blessing in disguise for little Jacó, halting construction of high-rise condo developments, whose empty shells now languish amid razed open space.

Jacó's future is anything but certain. Optimists point out that the town is simply experiencing growing pains, and argue that drugs and prostitution have subsided with the increasingly stable infrastructure. Pessimists are quick to retort that wealth attracts opportunism, especially of the illicit kind, and that the problems in Jacó are just getting started.

Regardless of which camp you fall into, what is certain is that the country is casting a watchful eye on Jacó, and will ultimately point to the city as either an example of development gone awry or a success story of wealth creation.

🏃 Activities

Swimming

Jacó is generally safe for swimming, though you should avoid the areas near the estuaries, which are polluted. Be advised that the waves can get crowded with beginner surfers who don't always know how to control their boards, so keep your wits about you and stay out of their way. Riptides occasionally occur, especially when the surf gets big, so inquire about local conditions and keep an eye out for red flags marking the paths of rips.

Surfing

Although the rainy season is considered best for Pacific coast surfing, Jacó is blessed with consistent year-round breaks. Even though more advanced surfers head further south to Playa Hermosa, the waves at Jacó are strong, steady and a lot of fun. Jacó is also a great place to start a surf trip as it's easy to buy and sell boards here.

If you're looking to rent a board for the day, shop around as the better places will rent you a board for US$15 to US$20 for 24 hours. There are too many surf shops for us to list them all. Our favorite place to rent is **Carton Surf Shop** (☑ 2643-3762; www. cartonsurfboards.com; Calle Madrigal; ⊘ 8am-5pm Mon-Sat, 10am-3pm Sun), run by the friendly Villalobos brothers, near the beach at the southern end of the main drag on Calle Madrigal.

Six-time national surf champion Álvaro Solano runs the highly respected **Vista Guapa Surf Camp** (☑ 2643-2830, in USA 409-599-1828; www.vistaguapa.com), which is recommended by readers. Weekly rates including full board start at around US$1000. Check the website for directions.

Hiking

A popular local pastime is following the trail up Mt Miros, which winds through primary and secondary rainforest and offers spectacular views of Jacó and Playa Hermosa. The trail actually leads as far as the Central Valley, though you only need to hike for a few kilometers to reach the viewpoint. Note that the trailhead is unmarked, so ask a local to point it out to you.

Horse Riding

Be wary of winging it here; readers have reported incidents of horse abuse in Jacó and visitors will see malnourished and mistreated animals on offer near the beach.

Discovery Horseback Tours HORSE RIDING (☑ 8838-7550; www.horseridecostarica.com; rides from US$75) Nearby beach and rainforest rides are available through this highly rec-

---

JACÓ FOR CHILDREN

Jacó has long been on the radar of Tico families looking to swap the congestion of San José for the ocean breezes of the central Pacific coast. Therefore, you'll find that your children are very well cared for in Jacó, and there is enough going on to keep even those with the shortest attention spans amused for days on end.

Families flock to the beach, and, compared with more famed surfing destinations up and down the coast, the waves here are modest. As with any water-based activities, the usual amount of parental watch is required, though young children can safely splash about on most days. However, strong surges often accompany ill weather, so it's always best to survey the scene and inquire locally about conditions.

Beyond the beach you'll find a laundry list of activities on offer, and a good number of operators offer discounts for young children.

There is a tremendous diversity of accommodations in the Jacó area, and aside from the more backpacker-oriented youth hostels and the upmarket boutique hotels, the vast majority welcome children. Smaller, more intimate B&B types are good for maintaining a comfortable, familial atmosphere, while larger resorts have a range of child-friendly amenities. If possible, book in advance if you need to reserve child beds or have other special requests. Hotels with pools can save the day, especially when the mercury starts to rise.

Eating out with children is a breeze, since nearly all of the places in town offer English menus and/or have English-speaking staff, and there are plenty of familiar takeout options. Fruit smoothies are an excellent way to keep your kids properly hydrated and happy.

ommended outfit, run by an English couple who offer an extremely high level of service and professionalism.

Kayaking

Kayak Jacó
KAYAKING

(☎2643-1233, 8869-7074; www.kayakjaco.com; tours from US$70) This reliable company facilitates kayaking and sea-canoeing trips that include snorkeling excursions to tropical islands, in a wide variety of customized day and multiday trips. Though it does have a presence at Playa Agujas, 250m east of the beach, it's best to phone or email in advance.

Spas

Serenity Spa
SPA

(☎2643-1624; www.serenityspacr.com; Av Pastor Díaz; ⏱9:30am-7pm Mon-Sat, to 5pm Sun) Serenity Spa, east of Calle Bohío, offers the full range of spa services.

🎓 Courses

School of the World
LANGUAGE COURSE

(☎2643-2463, www.schooloftheworld.org; 1-4 week packages US$540-2225) This popular school and cultural-studies center offers classes in Spanish, surfing, yoga, art and photography. The impressive building and activities center also houses a cafe and art gallery. Rates include kayaking and hiking field trips and onsite lodging. Spanish and surfing are the most popular programs. See the website for directions.

👉 Tours

Tours around the area include visits to Parque Nacional Carara (from about US$50) as well as longer-distance trips around the country. Another popular destination is Isla Damas – you can organize tours here or in Quepos, further south. Isla Damas is not technically an island but the tip of a pointed mangrove forest that juts out into a small bay just south of Parrita. During high tide, as the surrounding areas fill with water, this point becomes an island, offering an incredible opportunity for bird- and other wildlife-watchers. Boating tours can be arranged from Jacó for around US$70 per person, but more avid adventurers can opt for a sea-kayaking expedition with several operators that work with local hotels.

Virtually every shop, hotel and restaurant in town books tours, as Jacó operates on a lucrative commission-based system. As you'd imagine, it's hard to know who is greasing whose palms and who is running tours, though usually it works out. Still, you shouldn't book anything from touts on the streets, and if an offer from a vendor seems too good to be true, then most likely it is.

In Jacó there is also a handful of competing companies offering similar package canopy tours.

Gray Line Tours
TOUR

(☎2220-2126; www.graylinecostarica.com; Best Western Jacó Beach Resort, Av Pastor Díaz) Gray Line Tours is one longstanding agent that receives good reviews. It books tours throughout the country as well as private intercity transportation.

Vista Los Sueños
Canopy Tour
ADVENTURE TOUR

(☎2637-6020, in USA 321-220-9631; www.canopyvistalossuenos.com; tours from US$80; ⏱hourly tours 8am-3pm) The longest zip lines in the area belong to Vista Los Sueños, which offers 14 cables accessed by tractor cart though the lush hillside.

✨ Festivals & Events

Mid-January in Jacó brings with it the **Jungle Jam** music festival. Featuring international acts (heavy on the reggae) as well as local up-and-comers, the four-day event is based at Docelunas (p366) but hosts shows throughout Jacó's venues.

🛏 Sleeping

Jacó has hosted a variety of tourists for years, and there's a wide spread of places to lay your head. From spare concrete-block dives with little more than a bed and a fan to upscale resorts with full amenities, there's a lot to choose from in just a few blocks.

The center of town, with its many bars and discos, can mean that noise will be a factor in where you choose to stay. The far northern and southern ends of town have more relaxed and quieter accommodations.

Reservations are highly recommended on weekends in the dry season and become critical during Easter, the week between Christmas and New Year's Eve, and in mid-January during the Jungle Jam music festival.

The rates given are high-season rates, but low-season rates could be as much as 30% to 40% lower. If you plan on a lengthy stay (more than five days), ask about long-term rates.

MINT IMAGES - FRANS LANTING / GETTY IMAGES ©

1. Parque Nacional Corcovado (p458)
One of the most biologically diverse places in the world, this national park is home to countless endangered species.

2. Yellow tree frog, Parque Nacional Manuel Antonio (p387)
Costa Rica's smallest national park is full of wildlife, swaying palms and coconuts.

3. Fungi, Parque Nacional Manuel Antonio (p387)
The forest is full of living organisms – from animals, birds and reptiles, to epiphytes and fungi.

DENIS-HUOT DENIS-HUOT / GETTY IMAGES ©

★**Buddha House** GUESTHOUSE $
(☎2643-3615; www.hostelbuddhahouse.com; Av Pastor Díaz; dm US$15, d with/without bathroom US$65/35; P❄@☎☀) An oasis of calm in the midst of hustling Jacó. Bold colors and modern art create an artistic atmosphere at this 'boutique hostel'. Communal areas include a breezy patio and a spotless kitchen. This place is perfect for budget travelers who don't want the party in their living room.

Jacó Inn HOSTEL $
(☎2643-1935; www.jacoinn.com; Av Pastor Díaz near Calle Bohío; dm US$12, r US$25-45; P☎) Situated down a shaded alley in the middle of town, Jacó Inn is a fantastic deal for the price. Cozy dorms in the main house share a chilled-out living area and homey kitchen, while private rooms in the hangar-like addition are spare and spotless. Surfboards can be rented and surf lessons arranged with the friendly staff, who foster a welcoming vibe.

Cabinas Antonio CABINAS $
(☎2643-3043; cnr Av Pastor Díaz & Bulevar; s/d US$30/40; P☎☀) Something of an institution among shoestringers and local Tico families, this clutch of *cabinas* at the northern end of Jacó is one of the best deals in town. Basic rooms are uninteresting at best, but they are clean and cozy, and come with private cold shower and cable TV. Most importantly, they're just steps from the surf.

Camping El Hicaco CAMPGROUND $
(☎2643-3004; Calle Hicaco; campsites per person US$7; P) The only proper campground in town: there are picnic tables, bathrooms and a lockup for gear, though its proximity to the bars and clubs means you might not get much shut-eye. Don't leave valuables in your tent as theft is a big problem here.

AparHotel Vista Pacífico HOTEL $$
(☎2643-3261; www.vistapacifico.com; d incl breakfast US$68-121; P⊝@☎☀) Located on the crest of a hill just north of Jacó (off Bulevar), this gem of a hotel is run by a warm young Canadian couple. Homey, comfortable rooms and suites with kitchen facilities come in a variety of configurations. Its favorable elevation offers not only panoramic views of the coastline and valley but also blessedly cool breezes.

Posada Jacó HOTEL $$
(☎2643-1951; www.posadajaco.com; Calle Las Olas; r US$100; P❄☎☀) Surprisingly quiet for being steps from Jacó's main drag, this

tiny creekside hotel has a well-kept garden and pool area with a communal barbecue. Suites are the best deal here, complete with kitchenettes and terraces in low-key, friendly environs.

★**Sonidos del Mar** GUESTHOUSE $$$
(☎2643-3912, 2643-3924; www.sonidosdelmar. com; Calle Hidalgo; houses US$250; P❄@☎☀) Set within a mature tropical garden, these guesthouses may be two of the most beautiful in Costa Rica. The design is impeccable, from the vaulted Nicaraguan hardwood ceilings to the hand-laid volcanic-rock and pebble showers. Owner Lauri is a skilled artist and a collector who has lovingly filled each room with original paintings, sculptures and indigenous crafts.

Each house comes with a fully equipped gourmet kitchen and secure parking, and the beach is only 50m away. The houses can accommodate up to six people each, though they can more comfortably put up eight between them. Cheaper weekly and monthly rates are available.

Docelunas HOTEL $$$
(☎2643-2211; www.docelunas.com; Costanera Sur; d/junior ste incl breakfast US$169/197; P⊝❄@☎☀) Situated in the foothills across the highway, 'Twelve Moons' is a heavenly mountain retreat consisting of only 20 rooms sheltered in a pristine landscape of tropical rainforest. Each teak-accented room is uniquely decorated with original artwork, and the luxurious bathrooms feature double sinks and bathtubs. Yoga classes, offered regularly, are free with room rates.

A full spa uses the hotel's own line of beauty products, and you can swim in a free-form, waterfall-fed pool. The open-air restaurant serves everything from marlin *ceviche* to vegan delicacies. To reach the hotel, make a left off the Costanera just after the third signed entrance for Playa Jacó.

Hotel Poseidon HOTEL $$$
(☎2643-1642; www.hotel-poseidon.com; Calle Bohío; d incl breakfast from US$107; P❄@☎☀) It's hard to miss the huge Grecian wooden carvings that adorn the exterior of this small American-run hotel. On the inside, sparkling rooms are perfectly accented with stylish furniture and mosaic tiles, and include amenities like fridges and hair dryers. There's a pool with swim-up bar, a small Jacuzzi and an open-air restaurant serving some of the best food in Jacó.

Hotel Mar de Luz
HOTEL **$$$**

(☎ 2643-3259; www.mardeluz.com; Calle Mar de Luz; d incl breakfast US$109; **P ✳ @ ☎ ⛱**) This adorable little hotel with Dutch-inspired murals of windmills and tulips has tidy and attractive air-conditioned rooms (outfitted with fridges, microwaves and coffeemakers) that are perfect for a little family fun in the sun. The friendly Dutch owners (who also speak Spanish, English, German and Italian) offer two swimming pools, several BBQ grills and plenty of useful information.

The owners are also extremely committed to fighting drugs and prostitution in Jacó, and are at the forefront of an admirable campaign to clean up the city.

Best Western Jacó Beach Resort
HOTEL **$$$**

(☎ 2643-1000; www.bestwesternjacobeach.com; Av Pastor Díaz btwn Bulevar & Calle Ancha; s/d from US$160/240; **P ✳ @ ☎ ⛱**) Though there are excellent smaller lodges for families in Jacó, the Best Western remains a solid choice for its all-inclusive resort packages. Rooms are predictably bland but comfortable and well maintained. The pools, beach access, myriad resort activities and bounteous meals more than make up for the slightly dated accommodations. It pays to check for internet specials.

🍴 Eating

The quality of fare in Jacó is high, and aside from the Quepos and Manuel Antonio area, the city proudly boasts the most diverse offering of international cuisine on the central Pacific coast. While the vast majority of eateries cater primarily to Western palates, there are still a few local spots that have weathered the storm of change.

It's worth pointing out that hours can fluctuate wildly, especially in the rainy season, when many shops close sporadically, so it's best to eat early.

⭐ Taco Bar
MEXICAN **$**

(☎ 2643-0222; Calle Pops; meals US$6-12, breakfast from US$3; ⏱ 7am-10pm Tue-Sun, noon-10pm Mon; 🐾 🚸) A one-stop shop for Mexican, seafood, salads and smoothies. Get your drink in the gargantuan 1L size or your greens at the salad bar featuring more than 20 kinds of exotic and leafy components. And, of course, there's the obligatory fish taco, which may be one of the planet's greatest food combinations.

Soda a Cachete
COSTA RICAN **$**

(☎ 8633-1831; Av Pastor Díaz; meals US$4-8; ⏱ 7am-7pm Thu-Tue) Although many of the local *sodas* have been pushed out by gringo palates, this little place survives through its loyal following, who drop by for huge, excellent breakfasts and set lunches. A few bucks will get you rice, beans, a fish or meat dish of the day and some juice. It's across from the Red Cross.

Más x Menos
SELF-CATERING **$**

(Av Pastor Díaz; ⏱ 8am-9pm Mon-Fri, to 10pm Sat, 7am-9pm Sun) This Western-style supermarket has an impressive selection of fresh produce, and local and international culinary items.

⭐ Graffiti
INTERNATIONAL **$$**

(☎ 2643-1708; www.graffiticr.com; mains US$8-22; ⏱ 5-10pm Mon-Sat; 🚸) The decor is what you might expect from the name, and live music on weekends ups its game, but the spotlight here is fixed on the plate. Those in the know come for the famous cacao-and-coffee-encrusted filet mignon, macadamia-and-passionfruit catch of the day, decadent cheesecake and creative cocktails. Reservations are highly recommended.

Caliche's Wishbone
INTERNATIONAL **$$**

(☎ 2643-3406; Av Pastor Díaz; meals US$9-18; ⏱ noon-10pm Thu-Tue) Overseen by the charming Caliche, this has been a Jacó favorite for years and years. The eclectic menu includes pizzas, pitas, stuffed potatoes, pan-seared sea bass and tuna-sashimi salads, though its justifiable fame comes from the fact that everything is quite simply fresh, delicious and good value. It's south of Calle Bohío.

Rancho Santana
COSTA RICAN **$$**

(☎ 2643-4234; Calle Hidalgo; mains US$5-9; ⏱ 11am-midnight) Though slightly out of the way, this Tico-run spot is worth a leisurely dinner under the breezy *rancho* (house-like building), with its tree-trunk beams, thatched roof and rustling palms. Traditional fare – the *casados* and *ceviche* rule – is served by friendly staff in a completely unpretentious setting.

Tsunami Sushi
JAPANESE **$$**

(☎ 2643-3678; www.tsunamisushicr.com; Av Pastor Díaz; meals US$10-30; ⏱ 5-10pm Sun-Thu, to 1am Fri) Reservations are recommended at this popular sushi spot, one of the best on the central Pacific coast. Play your cards right and the half-off specials throughout the week can save you some serious colones. Find it in the mall Il Galeone.

Rioasis
PIZZERIA $$

(☑2643-3354; Plaza Jacó, Av Pastor Díaz; pizzas US$9-13; ⊙11:30am-10pm; 🛜) Admit it – sometimes pizza seems like *the best thing ever* in the moment. When it comes to Rioasis' wood-fired pie, topped with all kinds of gourmet goodness, it usually is. The place is next to BCR.

El Hicaco
SEAFOOD $$$

(☑2643-3226; www.elhicaco.net; Calle Hicaco; mains US$15-30; ⊙11am-midnight) This oceanside spot brims with casual elegance and is regarded as one of the finer dining experiences in Jacó. Although the menu is entirely dependent on seasonal offerings, both from the land and the sea, the specialty of the house is seafood, prepared with a variety of sauces highlighted by Costa Rica's tropical produce.

Lemon Zest
FUSION $$$

(☑2643-2591; www.lemonzestjaco.com; Av Pastor Díaz; mains US$10-30; ⊙5-10pm; ▣🛜🚗) Chef Richard Lemon (a former instructor at Le Cordon Bleu Miami) wins many accolades for Jacó's most swish menu. The roster of upscale standards – including Caribbean-style jerk pork chop and seared duck in blackberry sauce – might lack a creative concept, but the dishes are carried out with due sophistication, accompanied by a well-matched wine list.

🍸 Drinking & Nightlife

Jacó isn't the cultural capital of Costa Rica: it's where people go to get hammered and party the night away. There are numerous raging bars and dance clubs that cater to good-times-seeking expats and travelers, but choose your venues carefully, as prostitution figures prominently.

Le Loft
CLUB

(☑2643-5846; Av Pastor Díaz; cover US$10; ⊙9pm-2am) The Loft is Jacó's sleekest nightlife venue, offering some much-needed urban sophistication. Live DJs spin essential mixes while the pretty people preen and be seen. There's a calendar of special events and a balcony perch for checking out the street life.

Monkey Bar
CLUB

(☑2643-2357; Av Pastor Díaz; ⊙9pm-2:30am Tue-Sun) Attracting a younger crowd of locals and visitors, Monkey Bar pumps with good times, reggaetón and pheromones.

Bohio Beach Bar & Bubba's Fish Tacos
BAR

(☑2643-3112; Calle Bohío) Fortification for a surf session (or a long day of lounging on the beach) is sometimes an immediate need. In such scenarios, Bohio Bubba's meets the basic requirements: huge fish tacos, ice-cold Imperials and a beachfront locale. Decidedly better during daylight hours.

Clarita's Beach Hotel and Sports Bar and Grill
SPORTS BAR

(☑2643-3327; www.claritashotel.com) Catch the game on the big screen, day-drink with a fun crowd, enjoy live Tico-style music played by local oldsters and stay the night if you don't want to leave – the hotel is quite comfortable and offers rooms (set back from the raucous beachfront bar) from US$60. It's at the western end of Bulevar.

ℹ Orientation

Playa Jacó is about 2km off the Costanera, 3.5km past the turnoff for Herradura. The beach itself is about 3km long, and hotels and restaurants line the road running just inland. The areas on the northern and southern fringes are the most tranquil and attractive, and are the cleanest.

Note that, in an effort to make foreign visitors feel more at home, the town has placed street-name signs on most streets. These names are shown on the map, but the locals continue to use the traditional landmark system.

ℹ Information

There's no independent tourist-information office, though several tour offices will give information. Look for the free monthly *Jaco's Guide* or the quarterly *Info Jaco*. For cash, there are ATMs everywhere, though the best rates will be found at the big branches like Banco Popular.

DANGERS & ANNOYANCES
Aside from occasional petty crime such as pickpocketing and breaking into locked cars, Jacó is not a dangerous place by any stretch. However, the high concentration of wealthy foreigners and comparatively poor Ticos has resulted in a thriving sex and drugs industry. To be fair, the local council has done an admirable job cleaning things up in recent years, and these vices are not as public as they once were. But this is not to say that Jacó is now squeaky clean.

ℹ BATTLING THE BLOOD SUCKERS

Whether you call them skeeters, mozzies or midges, everyone can agree that fending off mosquitoes is one of the most annoying parts of traveling in the tropics. Although the scientific evidence surrounding effective mosquito-bite prevention is circumstantial at best, the following is a list of road-tested combat strategies for battling the blood-suckers.

➡ Wear socks, long trousers and a long-sleeved shirt, especially at dusk, when mosquitoes feed.

➡ Eat lots of garlic (not recommended if you're traveling with your significant other).

➡ Fill your room with the smoke of the ever-present burnable Costa Rican mosquito coils.

➡ Invest in a good-quality mosquito net, preferably one that has been chemically treated.

➡ Never underestimate the power of spraying yourself with DEET.

Jacó is the epicenter of Costa Rica's prostitution scene. Assuming that the working girl or guy is over 18 (not always a given), prostitution is legal in Costa Rica, but travelers who wish to explore this dark corner of Costa Rican nightlife should carefully consider the health and safety risks and negative social impacts.

ℹ Getting There & Away

AIR

NatureAir (www.natureair.com) and **Alfa Romeo Aero Taxi** (www.alfaromeoair.com) offer charter flights. Prices are dependent on the number of passengers, so it's best to try to organize a larger group If you're considering this option.

BOAT

The Jet-boat transfer service that connects Jacó to Montezuma is, far and away, the most efficient way to travel between the central Pacific coast and the Península de Nicoya. The journey across the Golfo de Nicoya only takes about an hour (compared to about seven hours overland), though at US$40 it's definitely not cheap. (For a small extra fee you can bring a bicycle or surfboard.) The bonus? Sometimes travelers see dolphins along the ride. Several boats leave daily from Playa Herradura, 2km north of town. Reservations are required and can be made at most tour operators in town (the most consistent daily departure is at 10:45am). It's a beach landing, so wear the right shoes.

BUS

Buses for San José stop at the Plaza Jacó mall, north of the center. The bus stop for other destinations is opposite the Más x Menos supermarket on Av Pastor Díaz. (Stand in front of the supermarket if you're headed north; stand across the street if you're headed south.) The departure times listed here are approximate since buses originate in Puntarenas or Quepos. Get to the stop early!

Puntarenas US$2, 1½ hours, departs 6am, 9am, noon and 4:30pm.

Quepos US$2, 1½ hours, departs hourly from 6:30am to 2:30pm, 6pm and 7pm.

San José US$5, three hours, departs 5am, 7am, 9am, 11am, 1pm, 3pm and 5pm.

ℹ Getting Around

Getting around in Jacó is easy on foot; strolling the length of town in flip-flops takes about 20 minutes.

BICYCLE & SCOOTER

Several places around town rent out bicycles, mopeds and scooters. Bikes can usually be rented for about US$3 to US$5 an hour or US$8 to US$15 a day, though prices change depending on the season. Mopeds and small scooters cost from US$25 to US$50 a day (many places ask for a cash or credit-card deposit of about US$200).

CAR

There are several rental agencies in town, so shop around for the best rates.

Budget (☑ 2643-2665; Av Pastor Díaz, near Calle Bohío; ☻8am-5pm Mon-Sat, to 4pm Sun)

Economy (☑ 2643-1719; Av Pastor Díaz; ☻8am-6pm) South of Calle Ancha.

TAXI

Taxis to Playa Hermosa from Jacó cost between US$10 and US$15. To arrange for a pick-up, call **Taxi 30-30** (☑ 2643-3030), or negotiate with any of the taxis along Av Pastor Díaz.

Playa Hermosa

Regarded as one of the most consistent and powerful breaks in the whole country, Hermosa serves up serious surf that commands the utmost respect. You really need to know what you're doing in these parts – huge waves and strong riptides are unforgiving, and countless surfboards here have wound up broken and strewn about on the shoreline. Still, even if you're not a pro, the vibe is excellent, the surfers are chilled out and the beach lives up to its name.

Several places on the Pacific coast have names that translate to 'beautiful beach' in Spanish, but none is more deserving than this lovely 10km-long strip of gray sand. It has seen significant investment in recent years: billed as an upscale alternative to Jacó, the shore sports a couple of brand-new top-end hotels and notably more tony visitors, but in comparison with that in neighboring Jacó and Playa Herradura, development is modest. For the time being, Hermosa is very much a slow-paced beach town edged by the Costanera Sur and the surf-washed shores of the Pacific.

🏃 Activities

Surfing

Most of the wave action takes place at the northern reaches, where there are no fewer than half a dozen clearly defined beach breaks. These have tons of power and break very near the shore, particularly in the rainy season between May and August. Conditions are highly variable, but you can expect the maximum height to top out around high tide. Swell size is largely dependent on unseen factors such as current and offshore weather patterns, but when it gets big, you'll know. At times like these, you really shouldn't be paddling out unless you have some serious experience under your belt. Playa Hermosa is not for beginners, and even intermediate surfers can get chewed up and spat out here. To watch and appreciate, park at the small road by the Backyard Hotel and wander out to the beach.

Yoga

Vida Asana Retreat Center   YOGA
(☎ 2643-7108; www.vidaasana.com) High in the hills above Playa Hermosa lies this retreat, which offers fully customizable packages combining yoga, surfing and healthy organic meals. Reservations are highly recom-

mended, and prices are dependent on the size of your party, the season and the extent of requested instruction. The accommodations are breezy, rustic and set amid lush jungle.

✨ Festivals & Events

If you don't think you can hack it with the aspiring pros, you might want to give the surf on this beach a miss. However, consider stopping by in late July or early August, when local pro surfers descend for the annual **national surf competition**. Dates vary, though the event is heavily advertised around the country, especially in neighboring Jacó.

🛌 Sleeping

Most accommodations in Playa Hermosa are clustered along a few hundred meters of highway and the beach road paralleling it, which basically comprise the village. Rates vary wildly depending on season, demand and the whims of proprietors, and they're often negotiable.

Cabinas Las Arenas   CABINA $
(☎ 8729-4532, 2643-7013; www.cabinaslasarenas. com; s/d/tr/q US$44/55/64/72, ste US$64-76, villas US$141; 🅿 ❄ @ 🛜) Las Arenas caters to the backpacking surfer crowd by sticking to the basics in an effort to keep prices on the low side. The property comprises 10 cabins that can each sleep up to four, providing tremendous bang for your buck if you're traveling in a group. There's also a good restaurant on the premises.

Cabinas Brisa del Mar   CABINA $
(☎ 8816-2294, 2643-7076; cabinasbrisadelmar@ hotmail.com; s/d/tr US$25/40/45; 🅿 ❄ 🛜) A classic no-frills surfers' crash pad, this Floridian-run spot has basic rooms with air-con, private hot shower and cable TV, as well as a communal kitchen where you can self-cater. If the surf is looking too small (or too big!), you can pass the time on the basketball court or with a few games of table tennis.

★ Tortuga del Mar   LODGE $$
(☎ 2643-7132; www.tortugadelmar.net; r US$89, studios from US$99; 🅿 ❄ @ 🛜 🛁) Top-end accommodations with a recession-proof midrange price tag, this newish lodge is sheltered amid shady grounds, and has just a handful of rooms housed in a two-story building. Tropical modern is the style, mak-

ing excellent use of local hardwoods to construct lofty ceilings that catch every gust of the Pacific breezes.

The larger studios are spacious and even feature mini kitchenettes that make self-catering a real possibility within this price bracket.

Cabinas Las Olas Hotel CABINA $$
(2643-7021; www.lasolashotel.com; r US$45-75, skyboxes US$100; P❉🛜🏊) This distinctive three-story A-frame building is home to an awesome 'skybox room', a teak-accented, ocean-facing penthouse where you can fall asleep to the sounds of the surf and wake to a surf check. If that's booked, you can also rent one of several beachside rooms, from spartan budget digs to bigger rooms that include kitchenettes and sleep up to three.

Costanera B&B $$
(2643-7044; www.costaneraplayahermosa.com; d incl breakfast without/with air-con US$50/55; P🛜🏊) Blink and you may miss Costanera, a tidy Italian-run B&B – so look carefully for the yellow buildings, as it's a great deal in this neighborhood. Five rooms of various sizes and shapes have vaulted wooden ceilings and beachfront terraces, each offering a fair degree of privacy and intimacy.

Hermosa Beach Bungalows BUNGALOW $$$
(2643-7190, 2643-1513; www.hermosabeach-bungalows.com; bungalows US$200-250) These attractive, two-bedroom bungalows on stilts are individually owned, but a third are managed by onsite concierge Twinka. Most are pet-friendly, and all have modern bathrooms, washers, dryers and balconies. Trimmed in bright, tropical colors, the bungalows surround a pool and community *rancho,* and the property faces a long stretch of beach 1km south of town.

Backyard Hotel HOTEL $$$
(2643-7011; www.backyardhotel.com; r/ste incl breakfast from US$150/260; P❉@🛜🏊) Right next door to Playa Hermosa's perenially popular Backyard Bar – upside or downside? Your call! – Backyard Hotel offers cool, tiled rooms that are enticingly cushy for little Hermosa. Outfitted with quality linens and mattresses, mini-bars, hair dryers and alarm clocks, they also come with private terraces, most of which have beach or jungle views.

🍴 Eating & Drinking

Backyard Bar BREAKFAST $
(2643-7011; meals US$5-10; ☺noon-late; 🛜) Backyard Bar's expansive menu reaches beyond the usual surfer fare, though the burritos are a good bet if you're in the mood for the usual. As the town's de facto nightspot, the Backyard Bar occasionally hosts live music, heavy pours at its nightly happy hour and a local surf contest every Saturday from 4pm until sunset.

Bluegrass Cafe & Bakery BAKERY $
(8945-9885; Costanera Sur; mains US$2-6; ☺7am-3pm Wed-Mon; P) Hot cinnamon rolls, whole-grain and jalapeño-cheddar bread, banana-cream pies and cinnamon-fig loaves are all lovingly made by a super-friendly Texan – who also serves up pulled-pork and chicken curry with rice or in sandwich form. Well worth a stop for quality baked goods and Shannon's impromptu bluegrass stylings. (There's also a bluegrass jam every Sunday afternoon.)

Jungle Surf Café CAFE $
(meals US$4-9; ☺8am-9pm Thu-Tue high season only) If you're looking for a quick bite between sets, this terminally laid-back cafe is a local institution that offers everything from kebabs and fish tacos to cold beer and fruit smoothies.

ℹ Getting There & Away

Located 5km south of Jacó, Playa Hermosa can be accessed by any bus heading south from Jacó, see p369 for detailed information. Frequent buses running up and down the Costanera Sur can easily pick you up, though determined surfers can always hail a taxi (with surf racks) or hitchhike.

Playa Esterillos

Fifteen minutes south of Jacó but a veritable world away, Playa Esterillos lures those who simply want to catch some surf, sun and scenery (sans scene), as there isn't much else to do along this miles-long expanse of beach. Playa Esterillos is signed off the highway in several sections: Esterillos Oeste (West), Centro (Central) and Este (East). Esterillos Oeste has a mini-supermarket a couple of *sodas,* a tiny tour office and a Tico-village vibe absent in Jacó; Esterillos Este has more of a resort feel, with upscale accommodations and a string of holiday homes along the beachfront.

WORTH A TRIP

RAINMAKER AERIAL WALKWAY

Rainmaker is a privately owned rainforest that offered the first aerial walkway (www.rainmakercostarica.org; guided tour only) through the forest canopy in Central America. Although its star has faded a bit, the place is still regarded as one of the region's best. From its tree-to-tree platforms there are spectacular panoramic views of the surrounding primary and secondary rainforest, as well as occasional vistas out to the Pacific Ocean. The reserve is also home to the full complement of tropical wildlife, which means that there are myriad opportunities here for great bird-watching as well as the occasional monkey sighting. The trips are often completed by a swim in a natural pool at the base of a waterfall.

Tours with naturalist guides leave hotels in Manuel Antonio and Quepos daily except Sunday; reservations can be made at most hotels or by calling the Rainmaker office (☑ in Quepos 2777-3565, in USA 540-349-9848). A self-guided trip through the aerial walkway costs only US$15 per person (kids are free!) and for US$35 a guide is included. Bird-watching and amphibian and reptile tours (US$90) are also on offer. Binoculars are invaluable for watching wildlife, as are water and sun protection for staying hydrated and sunburn-free.

There are short interpretive trails that enable the visitor to identify some of the local plants, and some long and strenuous trails into the heart of the 20-sq-km preserve. Keep your eye out for poison-dart frogs, which are very common along the trails.

Rainmaker also offers opportunities for volunteers to participate for two weeks to one month in one of the four departments needed to run and preserve the project. There are also opportunities to work with local schools and various community-outreach programs. Contact it for more information regarding fees and placements.

A large colorful sign marks the turnoff for Rainmaker on the Costanera Sur at the northern end of Pocares (10km east of Parrita or 15km west of Quepos). From the turnoff it's 7km to the parking area.

The most luxe of the resorts is the modern Alma del Pacífico (☑ 2778-7070; www.almadelpacifico.com; bungalows US$236-293, villas US$349-519; P ❋ @ 🖥 🌊), located in Esterillos Este. Each individually designed villa encompasses a range of intriguing elements, including wooden-lattice ceilings, sheer walls of glass framing private gardens, concrete-poured furniture done up with custom leatherwork and impossibly intricate mosaic tiling. The onsite restaurant specializes in gourmet and organic cuisine.

If such a splurge will sink your budget, check out the laid-back Hotel Pelicano (☑ 2778-8105; www.pelicanbeachcostarica.com; r US$96-153; P ⊜ ❋ 🖥 🌊 ✻) a bit further south: it's affordable, safe and homey, and on the same dreamy stretch of the Pacific. Fairly basic rooms with wooden or tile floors surround a small pool, and the open-air restaurant is the perfect refuge from the sun after a day at the beach – the *ceviche* paired with a cold Imperial is the bomb.

In Esterillos Oeste, seek out the intimate Hotel La Dolce Vita (☑ 2778-7015; www.resortladolcevita.com; s/d from US$58/85; P ❋ 🖥 🌊), where tidy rooms are steps from the beach.

Parrita & Around

A bustling town on a river of the same name, Parrita is home to a tremendous palm-oil processing plant. If the wind is blowing right, the fried-food odor of the plant can be smelled from several kilometers away. Although palm oil doesn't perhaps have the immediate recognition of olive oil, the product finds its way into just about everything, from chocolate bars to french fries. If the smell whets your appetite, stop by Café Café (☑ 2779-9851; mains US$3-5; ⊙ 6am-7pm; 🖥) in Parrita, in a yellow corner building about 100m north of the river, for a surprisingly good selection of pastries, wraps, pizzas, sandwiches and coffee drinks.

While you're rolling through the area, a glimpse of the day-to-day maintenance of the palms is fascinating. To keep them free of insects, workers clear growth on the forest floor and apply poison to the trunks. To encourage fruit growth and provide easy access to the pod the fronds are regularly clipped. Pods are then transported to processing plants, where the fruits are separated and pressed. Huge big-rigs full of fruit come flying down this relatively poor stretch of the Costanera Sur – be careful on the road out there!

Parrita is about 40km south of Jacó, and can be reached on any bus heading south from there. Just south of the Río Parrita is the signed turnoff for Playa Palo Seco (p376). After Parrita, the coastal road dips inland through more palm-oil plantations on the way to Quepos.

PARQUE NACIONAL MANUEL ANTONIO & AROUND

As visitors find themselves along this small outcrop of land that juts into the Pacific, the air becomes heavy with humidity, scented with thick vegetation and alive with the call of birds and monkeys, making it suddenly apparent that *this* is the tropics. The reason to come here is the stunning Parque Nacional Manuel Antonio, one of the most picturesque bits of tropical coast in Costa Rica.

If you get bored of cooing at the baby monkeys that scurry in the canopy and scanning for birds and sloths, the turquoise waves and perfect sand provide endless entertainment. However, there's no pretending that Manuel Antonio is anyone's secret (despite being the smallest of Costa Rica's national parks, it's also one of the most popular.) See Tours, p375 for more information.

Little Quepos, the once sleepy fishing and banana village on the park's perimeter, has ballooned with this tourism-based economy (although it is, admirably, clinging to its roots despite ongoing socioeconomic transformation), and the road leading from Quepos to the park is overdeveloped. However, the rainforested hills sweeping down to the sea and the blissful beaches make the park a stunning destination worthy of the tourist hype.

Note that, for purposes of clarity, we've divided our coverage into four sections: Quepos proper (the area's only proper small city), the road from Quepos to Manuel Antonio, the tiny Manuel Antonio Village and the national park itself.

Quepos

Located just 7km from the entrance to Manuel Antonio, the small, busy town of Quepos serves as the gateway to the national park, as well as a convenient port of call for travelers in need of goods and services. Although the Manuel Antonio area was rapidly and irreversibly transformed following the ecotourism boom, Quepos has largely retained an authentic Tico feel, particularly when you get out of the middle of town. Exuding an ineffable charm absent from so much of the central Pacific, Quepos still has glimmers of traditional Latin America, even while being a heavily traveled stop on the tourist-packed gringo trail.

While most visitors to the Manuel Antonio area prefer to stay outside Quepos, accommodations are generally cheaper and better in town, though you will need to organize transportation to both the national park and the beaches. Quepos can be an appealing place to stay, especially since it's home to a burgeoning restaurant scene that belies its small size, as well as one of the country's best hostels. Quepos is also gridded with easy-to-walk streets, which provide the opportunity to interact with the friendly locals, who have thus far weathered the storm of change with cheerfulness and optimism.

History

The town's name was derived from the indigenous Quepoa, a subgroup of the Brunka (Boruca), who inhabited the area at the time of the Spanish conquest. As with many indigenous populations across the region, the Quepoa were quickly decimated by newly introduced European diseases. By the end of the 19th century no pure-blooded Quepoa were left, and the area proceeded to be colonized by farmers from the highlands.

Quepos first came to prominence as a banana-exporting port in the early 20th century, though a huge bout of banana blight in the mid-20th century obliterated the industry. African oil palms, which currently stretch toward the horizon in dizzying rows around Quepos, soon replaced bananas as the major local crop, though unfortunately they generated a lot less employment for the locals.

The future, on the other hand, is looking bright for locals, as foreign visitors are

Quepos

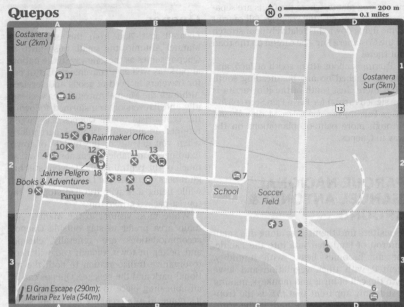

N 0 — 200 m
0 — 0.1 miles

Quepos

coming to the Manuel Antonio area by the boatload, and more people means more jobs in the area's rapidly expanding tourism industry. The opening of the Marina Pez Vela may also have profound effects on this humble town, though questions of sustainability and the need for balanced growth continue to be fiercely debated in the local media.

Activities

Titi Canopy Tours   CANOPY TOUR
(2777-3130; www.titicanopytour.com; Costanera Sur; daytime/nighttime tours US$65/80; ⊙ tours 7:30am, 11am & 2:30pm) Offering zip-lining adventures during the day and night, this outfit has friendly, professional guides and a convenient location just outside of central Quepos (150m south of the hospital). Tour rates include drinks, snacks and local transportation; group discounts are available.

H2O Adventures   RAFTING
(Ríos Tropicales; 2777-4092; www.h2ocr.com) The venerable Costa Rican rafting company Ríos Tropicales has a franchise in Quepos called H2O Adventures. Rates for Class II to IV rapids start at US$67 in low season. In summer they are US$82.

Diving

The dive sites are still being developed in the Quepos and Manuel Antonio area, though the following operator has been recommended by readers. The dive sites are away from the contaminated beaches, so water pollution is not a problem when diving.

Oceans Unlimited DIVING
(☑ 2777-3171; www.scubadivingcostarica.com; 2-tank dive US$98) 🤿 This shop takes its diving very seriously, and runs most of its excursions out to Isla Larga and Isla del Caño, which is south in Bahía Drake (connected via a two-hour bus trip). It also has a range of specialized PADI certifications, and regular environmental-awareness projects that make it stand out from the pack. It's located 400m up the road to Parque Nacional Manuel Antonio.

Sportfishing

Sportfishing is big here, and offshore ventures are said to be best from December to April, when sailfish are being hooked. By and large this is a high-dollar activity and you can expect to pay upwards of US$1000 to hire a boat for the day. If you want to shop around a bit, visit the office of **Marina Pez Vela** (☑ 2774-9000; www.marinapezvela.com), 500m south of the town center, which can connect you with captains of boats best suited to your needs.

Quepos Sailfishing Charters FISHING
(☑ 2777-2025, toll free in USA 800-603-0015; www.quposfishing.com) This Quepos-based outfitter gets good reviews from travelers and offers charters on a fleet of variously sized boats. Rates vary significantly depending on season, number of people and size of boat. It also offers packages that include accommodations and transfers.

☞ Tours

There are numerous reputable tour operators in the Quepos area, but the scene can be a bit tricky because of the abundance of third-party booking agents who work on commission. The best way to arrange a tour is through your hotel or hostel. Travelers also give glowing reviews of tours booked out of foreign-language bookstore Jaime Peligro (p378).

Iguana Tours ADVENTURE TOUR
(☑ 2777-2052; www.iguanatours.com; ⊙ 6:30am-9pm) 🤿 With tours that leave for destinations all over the central Pacific coast, this adventure-travel shop offers reputable river rafting, sea kayaking, horseback riding, mangrove tours and dolphin-watching excursions. It's no fly-by-night operation – it's been around since 1989 – and has a proven commitment to ecotourism principles.

Planet Dolphin DOLPHIN- & WHALE-WATCHING TOUR, CRUISE
(☑ 2777-1647, toll free 800-943-9161; www.planet-dolphin.com) Steve Wofford at Planet Dolphin offers dolphin- and whale-watching tours; starlight sailing cruises are also available. The cruises include lunch and transfers to your hotel, and depart from Marina Pez Vela in Quepos. Prices vary depending on the size of your group and the itinerary.

🛏 Sleeping

Staying in Quepos offers a cheaper alternative to the sky-high prices at many lodges on the road to Manuel Antonio. It can also be more convenient, as all the banks, supermarkets and bus stops are in Quepos. Still, those who save a bit here on a room may have to spend it on taxi rides to the park. Reservations are recommended during high-season weekends and are necessary during Easter and the week between Christmas and New Year's Eve.

★ **Wide Mouth Frog Backpackers** HOSTEL $
(☑ 2777-2798; www.widemouthfrog.org; dm US$12, r with/without bathroom US$50/40; 🅿 ❄ @ 🛜 ⛱) Friendly, secure and ideally outfitted for travelers of all stripes – this backpacker outpost is one of the best hostels in the country. Brightly tiled rooms and dorms with clean shared bathrooms are situated around the pool, which is fenced for children's safety but also attractively landscaped. The communal kitchen is fully equipped and has a spacious, open-air dining area.

Breakfast is available for only US$3, and there's a TV lounge with a free DVD rental library and wi-fi, a couple of lazy dogs padding around and a security guard watching the place and cars (street parking only) after hours. WMF is a perfect staging area for Manuel Antonio.

Hotel Sirena HOTEL $$
(☑ 2777-0572; www.lasirenahotel.com; s/d/tr incl breakfast from US$82/94/105; 🅿 ❄ @ 🛜 ⛱) This intimate boutique hotel is a welcome and warm addition to the Quepos scene, and is easily the best midrange option in town. The Sirena's whitewashed walls, blue trim

PLAYA PALO SECO

Playa Palo Seco (aka Isla Palo Seco) is a quiet, unhurried black-sand beach that's off the beaten track, located near mangrove swamps with good opportunities for bird-watching. A 6km dirt road connects the eastern edge of town to the beach. Another popular excursion is to visit **Isla Damas**, which is actually the tip of a mangrove peninsula that becomes an island at high tide. Most people arrive here on package tours from Jacó or Quepos, though you can hire a boat to take you to and from the island.

It's worth making a detour to stay at **Beso del Viento** (📞2779-9674; www.besodelviento.com; r without/with air-con & incl breakfast from US$99/107; P❄️🎫🛜🏊) if you relish privacy – this lovely French-run B&B lives up to its name ('Kiss of the Breeze'), located in a garden setting across the road from the isolated beach. Charming wooden-floored rooms are comfortably outfitted and decorated with an elegant eye for detail, with tiled bathrooms and immaculate linens. Your lovely hosts serve superb French meals, rent kayaks and bikes, and can arrange tours for guests, who must be aged 15 or older.

and aromatherapy offer a slice of breezy Mediterranean serenity. In their rooms, guests enjoy crisp white linens, air-conditioning, cable TV and a minifridge. Rooms upstairs get much better light.

Best Western Hotel Kamuk HOTEL $$$
(📞2777-0379; www.kamuk.co.cr; r incl breakfast from US$80-147; P🐶❄️@🛜🏊) While the Best Western standard ensures professional service, the Hotel Kamuk is all Costa Rican, from the bones of its historic building to the colonial decorative elements. Rooms are on the small side but have all of the modern conveniences, as well as a pool and open-air restaurant overlooking the waterfront. Check the internet for discounts.

Hotel Villa Romántica HOTEL $$$
(📞2777-0037; www.villaromantica.com; s/d incl breakfast from US$77/111; P❄️@🛜🏊) A short walk southeast from the town center brings you to this peaceful garden oasis, which is overflowing with verdant greens and tropical flowers; rooms are bright and open. If you're looking for a compromise between the convenience of staying in Quepos and the intimate proximity to nature found in Manuel Antonio, this is an excellent choice.

🍴 Eating

One benefit of staying in Quepos proper is the accessibility of a wide range of dining opportunities – from cheap local *sodas* to the best sushi on the central Pacific coast – all within a short stroll. The **mercado central** (Central Market; ⏰hours vary) is packed with produce vendors and good *sodas* too numerous to list, so follow your nose and

the locals. Self-caterers should also check out the **farmers market** (⏰4pm Fri-noon Sat) near the waterfront, where you can buy directly from farmers, fisherfolk, bakers and other food producers.

Soda Come Bien SODA $
(📞2777-2550; mains US$3-6; ⏰6am-5pm Mon-Sat, to 11am Sun) The daily rotation of delicious cafeteria options might include fish in tomato sauce, *olla de carne* (beef soup with rice) or chicken soup, but everything is fresh, the ladies behind the counter are friendly and the burly portions are a dream come true for hungry shoestringers. Or, pick up a fresh *empanada* (savory turnover) before or after a long bus ride.

Super Mas SUPERMARKET $
(📞2777-1162; ⏰8am-8pm Mon-Sat, to 1pm Sun; 🛜) Don't mistake this market for your average supermarket: the wondrous aisles of Super Mas have an astonishing array of imported goods, fresh bread and liquor.

Tropical Sushi JAPANESE $$
(📞2777-1710; meals US$10-27, all-you-can-eat sushi US$26; ⏰4-10:30pm) This is without doubt the best sushi on the central Pacific coast. Chef Fuji (originally from Japan, and a resident of Costa Rica for 15 years) serves up delicious sushi and other authentic Japanese cuisine in this cozy little spot. As he's the only one manning the kitchen, expect to have a leisurely dining experience.

Although the sushi is a sure bet, the other menu offerings are also worth a try, such as the *donburi* (pork or chicken and egg over rice), steamed dumplings and tempura.

Gran Inca
PERUVIAN $$

(☑2777-4347; mains US$7-15; ⊘5-10pm Tue-Sun) The no-frills look of this Peruvian-run spot belies the excellent food you'll find here. The menu encompasses a variety of traditional dishes, ranging from Peruvian-style *ceviche* to steak sautéed with peppers and onions. While the dishes might sound similar to Tico fare found everywhere, the flavors are lively and distinctive, and a welcome change of pace.

Escalofrío
ITALIAN $$

(☑2777-1902; gelato $2, mains US$9-20; ⊘2:30-10:30pm Tue-Sun; 🛜) Gelato lovers should make a point of stopping here, to choose from more than 20 flavors of the heavenly stuff. This spacious alfresco restaurant may also be the only game in town on Sunday night during slow season, a godsend especially if you enjoy wood-fired pizza, pasta and gnocchi.

Across the street, its deli makes excellent sandwiches with imported Italian meats and cheeses, perfect for toting on excursions to Manuel Antonio.

Monchados
CARIBBEAN $$

(☑2777-1972; dishes US$8-15; ⊘5pm-midnight) Although the food is inconsistent, this counts as a Quepos institution among gringos. The long-standing Mex-Carib spot offers traditional Limón-style dishes and Mexican standards. Food here is eclectic, innovative and never bland, a theme that's also reflected in the vibrant decorations and fairly regular live music.

🍸 Drinking & Nightlife

Nightlife in Quepos has a good blend of locals and travelers, and it's cheaper than anything you'll find in the Manuel Antonio area. If you are looking for something a bit more sophisticated, however, it's easy enough to jump in a taxi. Keep in mind that the action won't start warming up until around 10pm.

Café Milagro
CAFE

(☑2777-1707; www.cafemilagro.com; drinks US$3-6; ⊘7am-5pm Mon-Sat) Café Milagro sources its coffee beans from all over Costa Rica and produces a variety of estate, single-origin and blended roasts to suit any coffee fiend's palate. Aside from the glorious caffeine buzz, you can feel good about purchasing its bagged beans, as it donates 1% of its profits to environmental causes via international nonprofit 1% for the Planet.

Dos Locos
BAR

(☑2777-1526; ⊘7am-11pm Mon-Sat, 11am-10pm Sun) This popular Mexican restaurant is the regular watering hole for the local expat community, and serves as a venue for the occasional live band. Opening onto the central cross streets of town, it's fun for people-watching (and cheap Imperials). There's an English-language trivia night every Thursday. Added bonus: breakfast is served here all day.

El Gran Escape
BAR

(☑2777-0395; ⊘6am-11pm) This longstanding pub, formerly located in central Quepos, had moved to a swish new location at Marina Pez Vela at the time of writing. Sportsfishers can disembark to find cold beers and pub grub awaiting them right at the marina (a short taxi ride from town).

Cuban Republik Disco Lounge
CLUB

(☑8345-9922; cover US$4; ⊘9pm-3am Thu-Sun) Cuban Republik hosts the most reliable party in central Quepos, and it has some kind of drink special nearly every night if

---

QUEPOS FOR CHILDREN

The entire Quepos and Manuel Antonio area is one of Costa Rica's leading family-friendly destinations. With beaches and rainforest in close proximity – not to mention a healthy dose of charismatic wildlife – the region can enchant young minds regardless of their attention spans.

You'll find that most families with children congregate in the hotels and resorts lining the Quepos–Manuel Antonio road, but this is more due to accommodations density than other factors. In fact, the appeal of Quepos for children is that there is plenty to explore beyond the hotel walls, which can give parents a bit of fresh air and breathing room.

All in all, the town's excellent restaurant scene is kid-friendly, and the local Ticos are very welcoming to little ones. And finally, while you're not exactly on the beach or up in the forest, it's just a short and uneventful ride out to Manuel Antonio if the kids need an idyllic day on the beach.

you arrive early (before 10:30pm or 11pm). Later, the volume gets loud, the drinks get more pricey and things tend to career out of control. Women get in for free before 11pm on Friday night.

Musik CLUB
(☑ 2777-7060; ⊙ 4pm-2am Mon-Sat) The decor of this futuristically themed place (white plastic furniture and lasers) is a bit heavy-handed, but the centrally located club has theme nights, requisite (dangerously cheap) ladies' specials and a molar-rattling sound system.

Casino CASINO
(⊙ slot machines 11am-6pm, all games 6pm-4am) If you feel like putting your cash on the line, there's a small but suitable casino at the Best Western Hotel Kamuk, but the scene gets a bit seedy.

ⓘ Orientation

Downtown Quepos is a small checkerboard of dusty streets that are lined with a mix of local- and tourist-oriented shops, businesses, markets, restaurants and cafes. The town loses its well-ordered shape as it expands outward, but the sprawl is kept relatively in check by the mountains to the east and the water to the west.

Southeast of the town center is the Marina Pez Vela, whose marine slips opened to much fanfare in 2010. Though the global economic crisis slowed development somewhat, the next phase of shops and restaurants debuted in late 2013, with longtime Quepos bar El Gran Escape relocating to a shiny new spot in the marina's commercial hub.

ⓘ Information

Look out for *Quepolandia,* a free English-language monthly magazine that can be found at many of the town's businesses. Both Banco de San José and Coopealianza have 24-hour ATMs on the Cirrus and Plus systems. Other banks will all change US dollars and traveler's checks.

The best source of books for travelers within miles is **Jaime Peligro** (☑ 2777-7106; www.queposbooks.com; ⊙ 9:30am-5:30pm Mon-Sat), which has a complete selection of local guides, literature in a number of languages and tons of local information.

DANGERS & ANNOYANCES

As in other well-traveled parts of Costa Rica, theft is a problem, and the usual common-sense precautions apply: lock valuables in a hotel safe and never leave anything in a car.

When leaving bars late at night, walk in a group or take a taxi. Women should keep in mind that the town's bars attract rowdy crowds of plantation workers on weekends.

Note that the beaches in Quepos are polluted and not recommended for swimming. Go over the hill to Manuel Antonio instead, where some of the dreamiest waters in Costa Rica await.

ⓘ Getting There & Away

AIR

Both **NatureAir** (www.natureair.com) and **Sansa** (www.sansa.com) service Quepos. Prices vary according to season and availability, though you can expect around US$75 for a flight from San José or Liberia. Flights are packed in the high season, so book (and pay) for your ticket well ahead of time and reconfirm often. The airport is 5km out of town, and taxis make the trip for a few thousand colones (do not pay more than US$8), depending on traffic.

BUS

All buses arrive at and depart from the busy, chaotic main terminal in the center of town. If you're coming and going in the high season, buy tickets for San José in advance at the **Transportes Morales ticket office** (☑ 2777-0263; ⊙ 7-11am & 1-5pm Mon-Sat, 7am-1pm Sun) at the bus terminal; *colectivo* fares (not listed) to San José are slightly cheaper and take two hours longer.

Jacó US$2.80, 1½ hours, 10 departures daily from 4:30am to 5:30pm.

Puntarenas US$3.90, three hours, 10 departures daily from 4:30am to 5:30pm.

San Isidro de El General, via Dominical US$4, three hours, departs 5:30am, 11:30am and 3:30pm.

San José (Tracopa) US$9, three hours, departs 4am, 6am, 7:30am, 9:30am, noon, 1pm, 2:30pm and 5pm.

Uvita, via Dominical US$8, two hours, departs 6:30am, 9:30am and 5:30pm.

ⓘ Getting Around

BUS

Buses between Quepos and Manuel Antonio (US$0.60) depart roughly every 30 minutes from the main terminal between 7am and 7pm, and less frequently after 7:30pm. The last bus departs Manuel Antonio at 10pm. There are more frequent buses in the dry season.

CAR

A number of American car-rental companies operate in Quepos; reserve ahead and reconfirm to guarantee availability.

Budget (☑ 2774-0140; www.budget.co.cr; Quepos airport; ⊙ 8am-5pm Mon-Sat, to 4pm Sun)

X MARKS THE SPOT

Locals have long believed that a treasure worth billions and billions of dollars lies somewhere in the Quepos and Manuel Antonio area, waiting to be discovered. The legend was popularized by English pirate John Clipperton, who befriended the coastal Quepoa during his years of sailing to and from the South Pacific. Clipperton's belief stemmed from a rumor that in 1670 a number of Spanish ships laden with treasure escaped from Panama City moments before it was burned to the ground by Captain Henry Morgan. Since the ships were probably off-loaded quickly to avoid being raided at sea, a likely destination was the San Bernadino de Quepo Mission, which had strong loyalty to the Spanish crown.

John Clipperton died in 1722 without ever discovering the legendary treasure, and the mission closed permanently in 1746, as most of the Quepoa had succumbed to European diseases. Although the ruins of the mission were discovered in 1974, they were virtually destroyed and had long since been looted. However, if the treasure was indeed as large as it's described in lore, it is possible that a few gold doubloons could still be lying somewhere, waiting to be unearthed.

TAXI

Colectivo taxis between Quepos and Manuel Antonio will usually pick up extra passengers for a few dollars. A private taxi will cost a few thousand colones. Call **Quepos Taxi** (☑2777-0425) or catch one at the taxi stand south of the market. The trip between Quepos and the park should cost about US$15. At night, there is an abundance of private taxis; have the front desk of your hotel call one.

Quepos to Manuel Antonio

From the Quepos waterfront, the road swings inland for 7km before reaching the beaches of Manuel Antonio Village and the entrance to the national park. This route passes over a number of hills awash with picturesque views of forested slopes leading down to the palm-fringed coastline.

This area is home to some of Costa Rica's finest hotels and restaurants, though navigating the area without a car is challenging. While shoestringers and budget travelers are catered for, this is one part of the country where those with deep pockets can bed down and dine out in the lap of luxury.

Note that the road to Manuel Antonio is steep, winding and very narrow. Worse, local bus drivers love to careen through at high velocities, and there are almost no places to pull over in the event of an emergency. At all times, you should exercise caution and drive and walk with care, especially at night. Be particularly aware of pedestrians.

◉ Sights & Activities

Manuel Antonio Nature Park & Wildlife Refuge
WILDLIFE RESERVE
(☑2777-0850; www.wildliferefugecr.com; adult/child US$15/8; ⊙8am-4pm; 🖈) Formerly known as Fincas Naturales, this private rainforest preserve and butterfly garden breeds about three dozen species of butterfly – a delicate population compared to the menagerie of lizards, reptiles and frogs that inspire gleefully grossed-out squeals from the little ones. A jungle night tour (US$39 for adults, US$29 for children) showcases the colorful local frogs and their songs.

Amigos del Río
ADVENTURE TOUR
(☑2777-0082; www.adradventurepark.com; tours US$130; ⊙tours depart 6:45am, 8:30am & 10:30am) Pack all of your canopy-tour jungle fantasies into one day on Amigos del Ríos' '10-in-One Adventure', featuring zip lining, a Tarzan swing, rappelling down a waterfall and more. The seven-hour adventure tour includes a free transfer from the Quepos and Manuel Antonio area as well as breakfast and lunch. Amigos del Río is also a reliable outfit for white-water rafting trips.

Cala Spa
SPA
(☑2777-0777, ext 220; www.sicomono.com; Hotel Sí Como No; treatments US$65-140; ⊙10am-7pm) If you're sunburned and sore from exploring Manuel Antonio – even better if you're not – the Cala Spa offers aloe body wraps, citrus salt scrubs and various types of massage to restore body and spirit. Open daily by appointment only.

Manuel Antonio Area

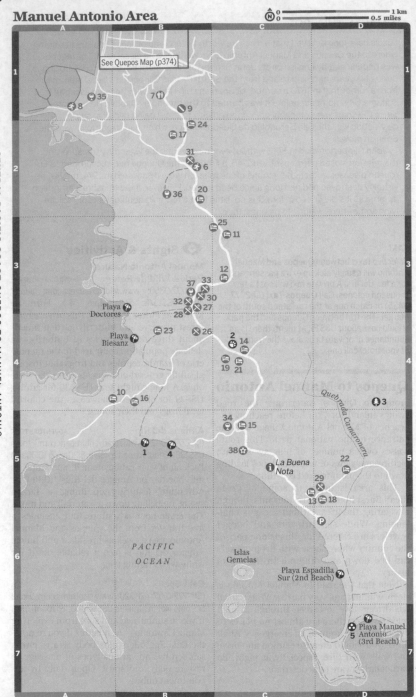

See Quepos Map (p374)

Playa Doctores

Playa Biesanz

PACIFIC OCEAN

Islas Gemelas

La Buena Nota

Quebrada Camaronera

Playa Espadilla Sur (2nd Beach)

Playa Manuel Antonio (3rd Beach)

Manuel Antonio Area

Manuel Antonio Surf School   SURFING
(MASS; ☑ 2777-1955, 2777-4842; www.manuelantonlosurfschool.com; group lessons US$65) MASS offers friendly, safe and fun small-group lessons daily, lasting for three hours and with a three-to-one student-instructor ratio. Find its stand about 500m up the Manuel Antonio road south of Quepos.

🛏 Sleeping

The Quepos–Manuel Antonio road is heavily skewed towards ultra-top-end hotels, but plenty of noteworthy midrange accommodations and excellent budget hostels are hidden along the way. High-season rates are provided throughout this section, though – as elsewhere in the region – low-season rates can be as much as 40% lower. Reservations are an absolute must for busy weekends and holiday seasons.

Although the sleeping options along the Quepos–Manuel Antonio road are closer to the park than those in Quepos, many of them will still require a taxi or a long walk along the busy road to reach the park.

★**Vista Serena Hostel**   HOSTEL $
(☑ 2777-5162; www.vistaserena.com; incl breakfast dm US$10-16, bungalows without bathroom US$45-60; ℗ @ 🛜) In an area that is hopelessly overpriced, it's a relief to find such a great budget hostel. Perched scenically on a quiet hillside, this memorable spot allows guests to enjoy spectacular ocean sunsets from a hammock-filled terrace and strum the communal guitar. The spick-and-span white-tiled dorms have shared bathrooms, a communal kitchen and a TV lounge.

For those who want a bit more privacy, there are also bungalows and a house that sleeps up to eight. Super-friendly owners Sonia, Conrad and Alex speak fluent English, and are commendable for their efforts in assisting countless travelers. To top it off, a short trail hike through local farmland leads to a remote wilderness beach.

Backpackers Manuel Antonio   HOSTEL $
(☑ 2777-2507; www.backpackersmanuelantonio. com; dm/d incl breakfast US$12/35; ℗ @ 🛜 🗮) This locally owned hostel has a very sociable vibe and a good location – relatively near the entrance of the park and walking

distance from a good grocery store and bakery. The dorms are clean and secure and there's a grill and pool out back. Larger rooms, with a bunk and double bed, are good for families.

★ Hotel Mono Azul   HOTEL $$

(☑ 2777-2572; www.monoazul.com; r US$55-85, ste from US$115, child under 12yr free; P❋@ 🛜🏊) The Mono Azul represents terrific value as well as being a great family option – nestled in a tropical garden and decorated throughout in a rainforest theme, rooms are arranged around three pools and a game room. Ten percent of hotel receipts are donated to Kids Saving the Rainforest (KSTR), founded here by two local schoolchildren in 1999.

The girls were concerned about the endangered *mono tití* (Central American squirrel monkey). Many of these adorable critters were run over on the narrow road to the national park or electrocuted on overhanging electrical cables, so KSTR purchased and erected monkey 'bridges' across the road (you can see them, often in use, as you head to the park). All proceeds from the hotel's onsite souvenir shop also go directly to KSTR.

Mimo's Hotel   HOTEL $$

(☑ 2777-0054; www.mimoshotel.com; d/ste from US$73/119; P❋@ 🛜🏊) Run by a delightful Italian couple, this whitewashed and wood-trimmed hotel has spacious, clean, terra-cotta-tiled rooms. The property is connected by lovely stone paths, bringing guests to two palm-fringed swimming pools, a glowing Jacuzzi and a restaurant serving Italian-influenced dishes. The owners speak half a dozen languages, and have a wealth of knowledge about Costa Rica.

Hotel Tres Banderas   HOTEL $$

(☑ 2777-1871; www.hoteltresbanderas.com; d/ ste incl breakfast US$90/113; P❋@ 🛜🏊) This welcoming roadside inn is owned by a Polish-born US citizen who lives in Costa Rica – hence the very appropriate moniker, *tres banderas* (three flags). Fourteen doubles and three suites are spacious affairs with imported tiles and local woods and, while some could use a bit of air, all come with jungle-facing terraces furnished with leather rocking chairs.

Dinner is often prepared on an outdoor grill and guests congregate to dine together around the deep central pool, which lends a communal flourish to the property.

Babaloo Inn   HOTEL $$

(☑ 2777-3461; www.babalooinn.com; d standard/ king US$90/202; P❋🛜🏊) Standard rooms at the Babaloo Inn come with private balcony overlooking a lush tropical garden. However, we're partial to the larger king rooms featuring dramatic ocean views, comfortable sitting area, oversized beds and shower, small kitchenette and enough space for a family of four. All rooms come with fully stocked minibar and DVD player, perfect for a rainy day.

Makanda by the Sea   VILLA $$$

(☑ 2777-0442; www.makanda.com; studios/villas incl breakfast US$299/452; P❋@ 🛜🏊) Comprising just six villas and five studios, Makanda has an unmatched air of intimacy and complete privacy. Villa 1 (the largest) will take your breath away – one entire wall is open to the rainforest and the ocean. The other villas and studios are air-conditioned and enclosed, though they draw upon the same minimalistic, Eastern-infused design schemes.

QUEPOS TO MANUEL ANTONIO FOR CHILDREN

The Quepos to Manuel Antonio stretch of road is home to the lion's share of accommodations and restaurants in these parts, and you will see plenty of vacationing families wherever you go. But it's worth pointing out that many of the high-end boutique hotels and upscale eateries are not always very welcoming to babies and young children. Assuming, however, that you avoid anything with obvious over-the-top glitz and glamour, your children will be well catered for at many of the establishments covered in this section.

A word of caution: driver visibility is limited along parts of the narrow, steep and winding road, particularly during low-light and foul-weather conditions. If you find yourself walking along the road (there is no shoulder), keep a close eye on your children at all times, and warn them to be careful of passing cars. Likewise, always drive carefully, and return the favor by keeping an eye out for pedestrians.

The grounds are also home to a beautiful infinity pool and Jacuzzi, both offering superb views out to sea, as well as a series of flawless Japanese gardens in which you can stroll and reflect on the beauty of your surroundings. And, if you're still not impressed, you can access a private beach by taking the 552 steps down the side of the mountain – bliss! Note that guests must be 16 or older.

Hotel Costa Verde
HOTEL $$$

(☎2777-0584; www.costaverde.com; efficiency units/studios from US$130/168, Boeing 727 fuselage home US$565; P❄@🐶❄) The collection of comfortable rooms and studios at Costa Verde occupy a verdant setting frequented by troops of monkeys. Efficiency units incorporating teak trim and furnishings are attractively tiled and face the encroaching forest, while more expensive studios have full ocean views. But the most coveted accommodation is the airplane-tree-house hybrid made out of a decommissioned Boeing 727 fuselage.

The 727, which juts out of the jungle in the most surreal way, has two bedrooms with three queen-sized beds, two bathrooms, kitchenette and private terrace. The owners of Costa Verde are also the masterminds behind several eateries along the road to Manuel Antonio, including El Avión (p385), which was also fashioned from a retired fuselage.

Arenas del Mar
BOUTIQUE HOTEL $$$

(☎2777-2777; www.arenasdelmar.com; r incl breakfast US$350-825; P❄@🐶❄) 🍴 This visually arresting hotel and resort complex is consistently shortlisted among Costa Rica's finest upscale hotels. Despite the extent and breadth of the grounds, there are only 40 rooms, which ensures an unmatched degree of personal service and privacy. It has won numerous ecotourism awards since its establishment and was designed to incorporate the beauty of the natural landscape.

In short, the overall effect is breathtaking, especially when you're staring down the coastline from the lofty heights of your private open-air Jacuzzi.

Hotel Sí Como No
HOTEL $$$

(☎2777-0777; www.sicomono.com; r US$260-328, ste US$401-424, child under 6yr free; P❄@🐶❄) 🍴 The flawless design of this hotel is an example of how to build a resort while maintaining environmental sensibility. Ecofriendliness aside, the hotel is also gorgeous and packed full of family-friendly amenities. The rooms themselves are accented by rich woods and bold splashes of tropical colors, and they feature enormous picture windows and sweeping balconies.

The hotel has two pools (one with a slide for kids, one for adults only, both with swim-up bars), two solar-heated Jacuzzis, a health spa, a THX movie theater and two excellent restaurants. Sustainable construction and practices include energy-efficient air-con units, recycling its water for landscaping use and solar-powered water heaters. No surprise, then, that Sí Como No is one of the 30-odd hotels in the country to have been awarded five out of five leaves by the government-run Certified Sustainable Tourism (CST) campaign.

Hotel La Mariposa
BOUTIQUE HOTEL $$$

(☎2777-0355; www.lamariposa.com; r US$243-475, ste US$531; P❄@🐶❄) This internationally acclaimed hotel was the area's first luxury accommodations option, so unsurprisingly it snatched up the best view of the coastline. Fifty-plus pristine rooms of various sizes are elegantly decorated with hand-carved furniture. This hotel was listed in the book *1000 Places to See Before You Die*, principally for the immaculate gardens and world-class views from every corner.

Hotel Casitas Eclipse
HOTEL $$$

(☎2777-0408; www.hotelcasitaseclipse.com; r/ste/casitas from US$158/215/373; P❄@🐶❄) Casitas Eclipse consists of nine attractive, bright-white houses spread around three swimming pools. The bottom floor of each house is an enormous junior suite, while the upper floor is a standard room with private terrace. These have a separate entrance, but a staircase (with lockable door) combines the two and, *voilà*, you have a sumptuous *casita* sleeping five.

🍴 Eating & Drinking

Many hotels listed previously have good restaurants open to the public. As with sleeping venues, eating and drinking establishments along this stretch are skewed upmarket. Reservations are recommended on weekends and holidays and during the busy dry season.

There are more eating options in the surrounding area in Quepos and Manuel Antonio Village.

Falafel Bar
MEDITERRANEAN $

(☎2777-4135; mains US$5-9; ⊙11am-7pm; 🖉🖢) Adding to the diversity of cuisine to be found along the road, this new falafel spot dishes up authentic Isaeli favorites. You'll also find plenty of vegetarian options, including couscous, fresh salads, stuffed grape leaves and even french fries for the picky little ones.

Super Joseth SELF-CATERING $
(☑2777-1095; ☺7am-10pm; 🅿) Although it's a godsend for self-caterers, Super Joseth is a grocery stop that's reflective of its location – a bit pricey, stocked for foreign travelers and very busy. It has a full selection of booze (Campari?), sunblock and upscale picnic goods.

★Café Milagro CAFE $$
(☑2777-0794; www.cafemilagro.com; mains US$6-19; ☺7am-9:30pm; 🅿🛜🍽) With a menu full of vibrant, refreshing delectables – like gazpacho, or salads tossed with mango and chayote squash in passionfruit dressing, or fish tacos with chunky guacamole, or banana-macadamia pancakes – this appealing cafe is worth a stop morning, noon or night. Like its sister cafe in Quepos, it also serves a mean cuppa joe.

Agua Azul INTERNATIONAL $$
(☑2777-5280; www.cafeaguaazul.com; meals US$7-18; ☺11am-10pm Thu-Tue) Perched on the 2nd floor with uninterrupted ocean views, Agua Azul is a killer lunch spot on this stretch of road – perfect for early-morning park visitors who are heading back to their hotel. The breezy, unpretentious open-air restaurant, renowned for its 'big-ass burger', also serves up excellent fajitas, panko-crusted tuna and smoked-trout salad.

Claro Que Sí SEAFOOD $$
(☑2777-0777; Hotel Sí Como No; meals US$8-20) 🍃 A casual, family-friendly restaurant that passes on pretension without sacrificing quality, Claro Que Sí proudly serves organic and locally sourced food items that are in line with the philosophy of its parent hotel, Sí Como No. Guilt-free meats and fish are expertly complemented with fresh produce, resulting in flavorful dishes typical of both the Pacific and Caribbean coasts.

Restaurante Barba Roja SEAFOOD $$
(☑2777-0331; www.barbarojarestaurant.com; meals US$7-20; ☺10am-10pm Tue-Sun) A Manuel Antonio area institution, the Barba Roja has morphed into a seafood-and-steak spot with an unexpected but respectable sushi menu. The terrace affords fantastic ocean views, best enjoyed with a local Libertas y La Segua craft brew (pints are US$5) and some *edamame* (steamed soybeans) as you contemplate your dining options.

Kapi Kapi Restaurant FUSION $$$
(☑2777-5049; www.restaurantekapikapi.com; meals US$15-40; ☺4-10pm) While there is some stiff competition for the title of best restaurant in the area, this Californian creation certainly raises the bar on both quality and class. The menu at Kapi Kapi (*kapi kapi* is a traditional greeting of the indigenous Maleku people) spans the globe from America to Asia. Pan-Asian-style seafood features prominently, brought to life with rich continental-inspired sauces.

South American wines and Costa Rican coffees complete this globetrotting culinary extravaganza. True to its name, Kapi Kapi welcomes diners with soft lights, earthy tones and soothing natural decor, which perfectly frame the dense forest lying just beyond the perimeter.

La Luna INTERNATIONAL $$$
(☑2777-9797; mains US$8-55; ☺7am-11pm; 🍽) Unpretentious, friendly and first rate, La Luna makes a lovely spot for a special-occasion dinner, with a spectacular backdrop of jungle and ocean. An international menu offers everything from pizza to lobster tails, with a Tico-style twist – such as grouper baked *en papillote,* with plantain purée and coconut milk. Or enjoy the inexpensive tapas menu from 4pm to 6pm.

Salsipuedes BAR
(☑2777-5019; tapas US$6-8; ☺7am-10pm Wed-Mon) With fantastic views at sunset, Salsipuedes ('leave if you can') is a great place for tapas and beer – or for the more adventurous, cocktails made with *guaro* (a local firewater made with sugarcane). Quesadillas, *ceviche,* and white bean and chicken stew are some of the tasty tapas on offer.

Ronny's Place BAR
(☑2777-5120; www.ronnysplace.com; mains US$6-14; ☺noon-10pm) The insane views at Ronny's Place, of two pristine bays and jungle on all sides, make it worth a detour (just for a drink; don't bother eating here). While plenty of places along this stretch of road boast similar views, the off-the-beaten-path location makes it feel like a secret find. Look for the well-marked dirt road off the main drag.

El Avión   BAR

(☎ 2777-3378; mains US$6-14; 🛜🏍) This unforgettable bar-restaurant was constructed from a 1954 Fairchild C-123. Allegedly, the plane was purchased by the US government in the '80s for the Nicaraguan Contras, but it never made it out of its hangar in San José because of the Iran-Contra scandal that embroiled Oliver North and his cohorts. (The plane is lovingly referred to as 'Ollie's Folly'.)

In 2000 the enterprising owners of El Avión purchased it for the surprisingly reasonable sum of US$3000 and proceeded to cart it piece by piece to Manuel Antonio. It now sits on the side of the main road, where it looks as if it had crash-landed into the side of the hill. It's a great spot for a beer, guacamole and a Pacific sunset, and in the evenings during the dry season there are regular live-music performances.

☆ Entertainment

Sí Como No Cinema   CINEMA

(☎ 2777-0777; www.sicomono.com; Hotel Sí Como No; ⊙ 8:30pm) This 45-seat theater shows a fun rotation of popular American movies. If you spend US$10 at the hotel's restaurant or bar, admission is free.

❶ Getting There & Away

A good number of visitors who stay in this area arrive by private or rented car. The public bus from Quepos will let you off anywhere along the road.

GAY GUIDE TO MANUEL ANTONIO

For jet-setting gay and lesbian travelers the world over, Manuel Antonio has long been regarded as a dream destination. Homosexuality has been decriminalized in Costa Rica since the 1970s – a rarity in all-too-often machismo-fueled, conservative Central America – and a well-established gay scene blossomed in Manuel Antonio soon after. Gay and lesbian travelers will find that it's unlike any other destination in the country.

It's not hard to understand why Manuel Antonio first started attracting gay travelers. Not only is the area stunningly beautiful but also it's long attracted liberal-minded individuals. There is a burgeoning artist community and a sophisticated restaurant scene.

Sights & Activities

During daylight hours, the epicenter of gay Manuel Antonio is the famous La Playita, a beach with a long history of nude sunbathing for gay men. Alas, the days when you could sun in the buff are gone, but La Playita is still widely regarded as a playful pick-up scene for gay men.

Sleeping

A significant number of hotels in the Manuel Antonio area advertise themselves as being gay-friendly and even the ones that don't are unlikely to discriminate. If you want to enjoy the freedom and peace of mind that comes with staying at exclusively gay accommodations, book a room at the gay-owned and -operated **Hotel Villa Roca** (☎ 2777-1349; www.villaroca.com; d/apt incl breakfast from US$113/192; 🅿 @ 🛜 🌊), a collection of brightly whitewashed rooms and apartments situated around a central pool and sundeck. The expansive view from the pool takes in an uninterrupted view of the water and rocky offshore islands. This is also the place to catch incredible sunsets.

Eating & Drinking

The Manuel Antonio area has always been proud to host one of the most sophisticated and cosmopolitan restaurant scenes on the central Pacific coast. A few venues have particularly good gay-oriented events. **Bar Mogambo** (☎ 2777-6310; ⊙ 4pm-midnight Tue-Sun) is a friendly spot with an excellent happy hour, and **Liquid** (☎ 2777-5158; ⊙ 9pm-3am Tue-Sun), a club near the bottom of the hill, is a good place for young gay guys to party. After enough deceptively strong, colorful cocktails the dance floor is a blast. It has theme parties every night of the week and a raucous annual 'Mr Liquid' competition.

386

1. Crested caracara 2. Parque Nacional Marino Ballena
3. Scarlet macaw 4. Punta Uvita ('Whale Tail'), Parque Nacional
Marino Ballena

Reserves of the Central Pacific Coast

Costa Rica's best road trip follows the Costanera Sur, along a string of fantastic natural parks. With wet and dry tropical forests and long beaches, these parks are alive with brightly colored birds, curious monkeys and a veritable army of iguanas – all of which show off the country's stunning biodiversity.

Rancho La Merced National Wildlife Refuge

Surrounding Parque Nacional Marino Ballena on the southern part of the central Pacific coast, this former cattle ranch (p402) has excellent horse trails, primary and secondary forest and miles of mangrove channels.

Parque Nacional Marino Ballena

It's appropriate that this lovely, relatively quiet national park (p403) is shaped like a whale's tail; from the beaches it's possible to spot the migrating giants as they swim near shore.

Hacienda Barú National Wildlife Refuge

Excellent trails and naturalist-led hikes make this the best bird-watching spot on the central Pacific coast (p395). And just in case spotting rare tropical birds doesn't thrill you, there's also a zip line.

Catarata Manantial de Agua Viva

With macaws overhead, this picture-perfect jungle waterfall (p359) drops 183m from one swimmable pool to the next. It's best during the rainy season, when the flows are full.

Manuel Antonio Village

As you travel the road between Quepos and Parque Nacional Manuel Antonio, the din from roaring buses, packs of tourists and locals hunting foreign dollars becomes increasingly loud, reaching its somewhat chaotic climax at Manuel Antonio Village, whose beer advertisements and barkers have inched right up to the gates of the park. Hordes descend on this tiny oceanside village at the entrance to one of the country's most celebrated tourist destinations. Don't show up all bright-eyed and bushy-tailed, expecting deserted beaches and untouched tropical paradise. Higher primates tend to be the most frequently sighted species, especially during the congested dry season, when tour groups arrive en masse.

While it can be difficult at times to have a quiet moment to collect your thoughts, the environs here really do look as glossy and polished as the travel brochures suggest. And, when troops of monkeys climb down from the forest canopy to the tropical sands, you can get up close and personal with some marvelous wildlife. The moral is to arrive in Manuel Antonio with some realistic expectations, though you're likely going to have a memorable visit.

◉ Sights & Activities

Body boards and kayaks can be rented all along the beach at Playa Espadilla. Whitewater rafting and sea kayaking are also popular in this area. Don't worry about finding a place to rent equiptment; they'll find you. The possibility of good snorkeling in the area is nearly nonexistent due to crowded waters and low visibility.

Also, don't be fooled – you do not need to pay to use the beaches, as they're outside the park.

Playa Espadilla   BEACH
There's a good beach, Playa Espadilla, near the entrance to the Parque Nacional Manuel Antonio, though you need to be wary of rip currents. There are some lifeguards working at this beach, though not at the other beaches in the area. For years Playa Espadilla was one of Costa Rica's only nude beaches, but the nearby construction of a big hotel seems to have ended that tradition, and those who bathe in the buff have been known to suffer police harassment.

La Playita   BEACH
At the far western end of Playa Espadilla, beyond a rocky headland (wear sandals), is one of Costa Rica's most famous gay beaches and a particular draw for young men. The beach is inaccessible one hour before and after the high tide, so time your walk well.

🛏 Sleeping & Eating

The village of Manuel Antonio is the closest base for exploring the national park, though the selection of eating and sleeping options is not as varied as in Quepos proper or the Quepos to Manuel Antonio stretch of road. It's also completely overrun with foreigners.

**Backpackers Paradise
Costa Linda**   HOSTEL $
(📞 2777-0304; www.costalindabackpackers.com; r per person from US$12; P🅿❄@🛜) Calling this backpacker pad a paradise is most definitely a stretch, but you can't really beat the price when you can amble out to the beach or the national park in just a few minutes. While the staff is a bit harried, and the shared bathrooms could be cleaner, the food is good and the place eminently budget-friendly.

**Hotel Playa &
Cabinas Espadilla**   HOTEL $$$
(📞 2777-0903, 2777-2113; www.espadilla.com; cabinas/r from US$120/189; P❄🛜🏊) Two favorably located properties in one: the hotel is centered on a large swimming pool and tennis courts, and the more affordable *cabinas* across the road are slightly closer to the beach. While the accommodations are fairly bland for the price, compared to swisher properties up the road, you do have extremely convenient access to park and *playa* from here.

La Posada   BUNGALOW $$$
(📞 2777-1446; www.laposadajungle.com; bungalows incl breakfast US$141-266; P❄@🛜🏊) These private jungle bungalows each sleep four to six guests, and all come equipped with kitchenette, TV with DVD player, safe and terrace. But the real beauty of staying here is the location right next to the park – from your bungalow you'll see squirrel monkeys and other wildlife crisscrossing the trees and rooftops.

MONKEY BUSINESS

There are a number of stands on the beach that cater to hungry tourists, though everything is exuberantly overpriced and of dubious quality. Plus, all the food scraps have negatively impacted the monkey population. Before you offer a monkey your scraps, consider the following risks to their health:

➡ Monkeys are susceptible to bacteria transmitted from human hands.

➡ Irregular feeding will lead to aggressive behavior as well as create a dangerous dependency (picnickers in Manuel Antonio suffer downright intimidating mobs of them sometimes).

➡ Bananas are not their preferred food, and can cause serious digestive problems.

➡ Increased exposure to humans facilitates illegal poaching as well as attacks from dogs.

It should go without saying: don't feed the monkeys. And, if you do happen to come across someone doing so, take the initiative and ask them politely to stop.

Hotel Vela Bar & Restaurant   SEAFOOD $
(☑ 2777-0413; www.velabar.com; meals US$6-13, s/d US$49/64; P ❄ 🛜) Hotel Vela is primarily known for its justifiably famous thatched-roof bar and restaurant, which serves up some of the freshest seafood in the area. However, the attractive little hotel is also surprisingly affordable – rooms here are fairly basic, but it's hard to beat the price, considering that you can stroll over to the park entrance in two minutes.

ℹ Information

La Buena Nota (☑ 2777-1002), at the northern end of Manuel Antonio Village, serves as an informal tourist information center. It sells maps, guidebooks, books in various languages, English-language newspapers, beach supplies and souvenirs; it also rents out body boards. You can inquire here about guesthouses available for long-term stays. Look for a free copy of the English-language *Quepolandia*, which details everything to see and do in the area. If you're looking for a quick online overview, visit www.manuelantonio.net.

ℹ Getting There & Away

Buses depart Manuel Antonio for San José (US$9, three hours) at 4am, 6am, 7:30am, 9:30am, noon, 1pm, 2:30pm and 5pm. These will pick you up at the beach, or from the Quepos bus terminal, after which there are no stops. Buy tickets well in advance at the Quepos bus terminal. This bus is frequently packed and you will not be able to buy tickets from the driver. Buses for destinations other than San José also leave from the main terminal in Quepos.

Parque Nacional Manuel Antonio

A place of swaying palms and playful monkeys, spakling blue water and riotous tropical birds, **Parque Nacional Manuel Antonio** (☑ 2777-0644; park entrance US$10, parking US$3; ⏰ 7am-4pm Tue-Sun) embodies Costa Rica's postcard charms. It was declared a national park in 1972, preserving it (with just minutes to spare) from being bulldozed and razed to make room for a coastal development project.

Although Manuel Antonio was enlarged to its present-day size of 19.83 sq km in 2000, it is still the country's smallest national park. Space remains at a premium, and as this is one of Central America's top tourist destinations, you're going to have to break free from the camera-clicking tour groups and actively seek out your own idyllic spot of sand.

That said, Manuel Antonio is absolutely stunning, and on a good day, at the right time, it's easy to convince yourself that you've died and gone to a coconut-filled paradise. The park's clearly marked trail system winds through rainforest-backed tropical beaches and rocky headlands, and the views across the bay to the pristine outer islands are unforgettable. As if this wasn't enough, add a ubiquitous population of iguanas, howlers, capuchins, sloths and squirrel monkeys.

Parque Nacional Manuel Antonio

There's good reason that Manuel Antonio is Costa Rica's most popular national park: this stunning green gem has excellent beaches, accessible trails and lots of wildlife. It can be crowded, but at times it seems like the monkeys outnumber the people.

Although not as untamed as some of Costa Rica's other parks, Manuel Antonio's light hiking makes a good primer on the tropical rainforest environment. Here, you spend a leisurely morning navigating trails and scanning the canopy for wildlife before spending dreamy afternoons picnicking under swaying beach palms and swimming in the turquoise Pacific. The day ends as sundown sets the horizon ablaze and dinner is served at a cliffside restaurant. This is the Costa Rica you've been dreaming about.

1. Suspension bridge 2. Coastline of Parque Nacional Manuel Antonio 3. Three-toed sloth

WILDLIFE CHECKLIST

White-faced capuchin monkeys Often seen near the beach; keep your eyes peeled for cute babies.

Mantled howler monkeys You'll likely hear these beasts before you spot them; their call makes an iconic soundtrack to Costa Rica's rainforest.

Squirrel monkeys These tiny monkeys, which often live in groups of between 20 and 75, are absolutely adorable.

Sloths Two-toed and three-toed varieties can be seen lazing about in Manuel Antonio's canopy.

Toucans These memorable birds of paradise are among the park's 180 winged species.

Black spiny-tailed iguanas (ctenosaurs) They might lazily pose for your camera, but they're the fastest-running lizards on earth.

⊙ Sights & Activities

Hiking & Swimming

After the park entrance, it's about a 30-minute hike to **Playa Espadilla Sur** and **Playa Manuel Antonio**, the park's idyllic beaches, which is where most people spend a good part of their time in the park. There will be numerous guides leading clusters of groups along the flat hike, so a bit of eavesdropping will provide solo shoestring travelers an informal lesson on the many birds, sloths and monkeys along the way. Eventually, the obvious, well-trodden trail veers right and through forest to an isthmus separating Playas Espadilla Sur and Manuel Antonio. This is also where there's a park ranger station and information center (its hours are random, but we've yet to see it open, so be pleasantly surprised if it is staffed).

Geography fun fact: this isthmus is called a *tombolo* and was formed by the accumulation of sand between the mainland and the peninsula beyond, which was once an island. Along this bridge are the park's two amazing beaches, Playa Manuel Antonio, on the ocean side, and the slightly less visited (and occasionally rough) Playa Espadilla Sur, which faces Manuel Antonio Village. With their turquoise waters, shaded hideouts and continual aerial show of brown pelicans, these beaches are dreamy.

At its end, the isthmus widens into a rocky peninsula, with thick forest in the middle. Several informal trails lead down the peninsula to near the center of it, the **Punta Catedral**. If you bushwhack your way through, there are good views of the Pacific Ocean and various rocky islets that are bird reserves and form part of the national park. Brown boobies and pelicans nest on these islands.

At the western end of Playa Manuel Antonio you can see a semicircle of rocks at low tide. Archaeologists believe that these were arranged by pre-Columbian indigenous people to function as a **turtle trap**. (Turtles would swim in during high tide, but when they tried to swim out after the tide started receding, they'd be trapped by the wall.) The beach itself is an attractive one of white sand and is popular for swimming. It's protected and safer than the Espadilla beaches.

Beyond Playa Manuel Antonio, if visitors return towards the trail from the entrance of the park, the trail divides and leads deeper into the park. The lower trail is steep and slippery during the wet months and leads to the quiet **Playa Puerto Escondido**. This beach can be more or less completely covered by high tides, so be careful not to get cut off. The upper trail climbs to a **lookout** on a bluff overlooking Puerto Escondido and Punta Serrucho beyond – a stunning vista. Rangers reportedly limit the number of hikers on this trail to 45.

The trails in Manuel Antonio are well marked and heavily traversed, though there are some quiet corners near the ends of the trails. Off-trail hiking is not permitted without prior consent from the park service.

Watch out for the *manzanillo* tree *(Hippomane mancinella)* – it has poisonous fruits that look like little crab apples, and the sap exuded by the bark and leaves is toxic, causing the skin to itch and burn. Warning

SAVING THE SQUIRREL MONKEY

With its expressive eyes and luxuriant coat, the *mono tití* (Central American squirrel monkey) is a favorite among Costa Rica's four monkey species. It is also in danger of extinction, as there are only roughly 1500 of these animals left in Manuel Antonio, one of its last remaining native habitats.

Overdevelopment is one of the animal's greatest threats. To remedy this problem, a conservation project known as the **Tití Conservation Alliance** (☑ 2777-2306; www.monotiti.org) is taking bold measures to prevent further decline. This coalition of organizations is helping to create a sustainable wildlife corridor between Parque Nacional Manuel Antonio and the Zona Protectora Cerro Nara in the northeast.

To achieve this aim, it is reforesting the Río Naranjo, a key waterway linking the two locations. More than 10,000 trees have already been planted along 8km of the Naranjo. This not only has the effect of extending the monkeys' habitat but also provides a protected area for other wildlife to enjoy. Scientists at the Universidad Nacional de Costa Rica have mapped and selected sites for reforestation, and business owners in the area as well as private donations support the project financially.

signs are prominently displayed beside examples of this tree near the park entrance.

Wildlife-Watching

Increased tourist traffic has taken its toll on the park's wildlife, as animals are frequently driven away or – worse still – taught to scavenge for tourist handouts. To its credit, the park service has reacted by closing the park on Monday and limiting the number of visitors to 600 per day during the week and 800 per day on weekends and holidays.

Even though visitors are funneled along the main access road, you should have no problem seeing animals here, even as you line up at the gate. White-faced **capuchins** are very used to people, and normally troops feed and interact within a short distance of visitors; they can be encountered anywhere along the main access road and around Playa Manuel Antonio.

You'll probably also hear **mantled howler monkeys** soon after sunrise. Like capuchins, they can be seen virtually anywhere inside the park and even along the road to Quepos – watch for them crossing the monkey bridges that were erected by several local conservation groups.

Coatis can be seen darting across various paths and can get aggressive on the beach if you're eating. Three-toed and two-toed **sloths** are also common in the park. Guides are extremely helpful in spotting sloths, as they tend not to move around all that much.

However, the movements of the park's star animal and Central America's rarest primate, namely the **Central American squirrel monkey**, are far less predictable. These adorable monkeys are more retiring than capuchins, and though they are occasionally seen near the park entrance in the early morning, they usually melt into the forest well before opening time. With luck, however, a troop could be encountered during a morning's walk, and they often reappear in beachside trees and on the fringes of Manuel Antonio Village in the early evening.

Offshore, keep your eyes peeled for pantropical spotted and bottle-nosed **dolphins**, as well as humpback **whales** passing by on their regular migration routes. Other possibilities include orcas (killer whales), false killers and rough-toothed dolphins.

Big **lizards** are also a featured sighting at Manuel Antonio – it's hard to miss the large ctenosaurs and green iguanas that bask along the beach at Playa Manuel Antonio and in the vegetation behind Playa Espadilla

Sur. To spot the well-camouflaged basilisk, listen for the rustle of leaves along the edges of the trails, especially near the lagoon.

Manuel Antonio is not usually on the serious bird-watchers' trail of Costa Rica, though the **bird** list is respectable. The usual suspects include the blue-gray and palm tanagers, great-tailed grackles, bananaquits, blue dacnises and at least 15 species of hummingbird. Among the regional endemics you should look out for are the fiery-billed aracaris, black-hooded antshrikes, Baird's trogons, black-bellied whistling ducks, yellow-crowned night herons, brown pelicans, magnificent frigate birds, brown boobies, spotted sandpipers, green herons and ringed kingfishers.

White-Water Rafting & Kayaking

While not as popular as Turrialba, Manuel Antonio is emerging as a white water rafting and sea-kayaking center. Although you shouldn't expect the same level of world-class runs here as in other parts of the country, there are certainly some adrenaline kicks to be had.

☞ Tours

Hiring a guide costs US$25 per person for a two-hour tour. The only guides allowed in the park are members of Aguila (a local association governed by the park service), who have official ID badges, and recognized guides from tour agencies or hotels. This is to prevent visitors from getting ripped off and to ensure a good-quality guide. Aguila guides are well trained and multilingual (French-, German- or English-speaking guides can be requested). Visitors report that hiring a guide virtually guarantees wildlife sightings.

TOP PICKS: KIDDY FUN IN MANUEL ANTONIO

➡ Buy a wildlife picture book and make a game out of spotting animals.

➡ Teach your kids how to read a map and use a compass to navigate.

➡ If your older children have an adventurous streak, take them rafting.

➡ Cool off by splashing in the gentle surf at Playa Manuel Antonio.

➡ When in doubt, even the fussiest of tykes love playing in the sand.

ℹ Information

Visitors who drive themselves will be accosted with parking touts as they approach Manuel Antonio Village; the charge is usually US$3. There have been reader reports of break-ins and thefts, so, as anywhere in the country, never leave anything in your car. Note that the road here is also very narrow and congested, so it's suggested that you leave your car at your hotel and take an early-morning bus to the park entrance instead, then simply walk in.

The park entrance is at the end of the road that forks northeast before you arrive at the beach roundabout. The ticket window is on the left side of the road; count your change carefully to ensure you've been given the right amount back. Here you can hire naturalist guides to take you into the park.

The ranger station and **national park information center** (☑ 2777-0644) is just before Playa Manuel Antonio. Drinking water is available, and there are toilets, beach showers, picnic tables and a refreshment stand. There is no camping and guards will come around in the evening to make sure that no one has remained behind. The information center keeps woefully unpredictable hours.

The beaches are often numbered – most people call Playa Espadilla (outside the park) '1st beach', Playa Espadilla Sur '2nd beach', Playa Manuel Antonio '3rd beach', Playa Puerto Escondido '4th beach' and Playa Playitas '5th beach'. Some people begin counting at Espadilla Sur, which is the first beach in the park, so it can be a bit confusing trying to figure out which beach people may be talking about. Regardless, they're all equally pristine, and provide ample opportunities for swimming or restful sunbathing.

The average daily temperature is 27°C (80°F) and average annual rainfall is 3875mm. The dry season is not entirely dry, merely less wet, so you should be prepared for rain (although it can also be dry for days on end). Make sure you carry plenty of drinking water, sun protection and insect repellent. Pack a picnic lunch if you're spending the day.

To exit the park, you can either backtrack to the entrance or follow the trail along Playa Espadilla Sur to the Camaronera estuary, which can be anywhere from ankle to thigh deep, depending on the tides and the season. A small trail leads to the shallowest spot to cross. However, in an impressive display of opportunism, there are boaters here to transport you 100m for the small fee of about US$1.

ℹ Getting There & Away

The entrance and exit to Parque Nacional Manuel Antonio lies in Manuel Antonio Village.

QUEPOS TO UVITA

South of Quepos, the well-trodden central Pacific tourist trail begins to taper off, evoking the feel of the Costa Rica of yesteryear – surf shacks and empty beaches, roadside *ceviche* vendors and a little more space. Intrepid travelers can have their pick of any number of deserted beaches and great surf spots. The region is also home to the bulk of Costa Rica's African-palm-oil industry, which should be immediately obvious after the few dozen kilometers of endless plantations lining the sides of the Costanera.

Known as the Costa Ballena, the beauteous length of coastline between Dominical and Ojochal is more accessible than ever since the completion of the Costanera Sur. For the time being, the area retains an easygoing, unjaded allure despite the growing numbers discovering its appeal.

Rafiki Safari Lodge

Nestled into the rainforest, with a prime spot right next to the Río Savegre, the **Rafiki Safari Lodge** (☑ 2777-5327, 2777-2250; www.rafikisafari.com; s/d/ste incl all meals US$189/327/420, child under 5yr free; ℗ @ 🛜 ➿) 🏊 combines all the comforts of a hotel with the splendor of a jungle safari – and getting here is half the fun. The owners, South African expats who have lived in the area for years, have constructed 10 luxury tents on stilts equipped with modern bathroom, private porch and hydroelectric power. All units are screened in, allowing you to see and hear the rainforest without actually having creepy-crawlies in your bed. There's a spring-fed pool with a serious waterslide and ample opportunity for horseback riding, bird-watching (more than 350 species have been identified), hiking, white-water rafting and unplugging. And of course, South Africans are masters on the *braai* (barbecue), so you know that you'll eat well alongside other guests in the *rancho*-style restaurant. This place makes for a great three-day stay; it's too remote to warrant the transport for only one night, but guests exhaust all the activities on offer after three days.

The entrance to the lodge is located about 15km south of Quepos in the small town of Savegre. From here, a 4WD dirt road parallels the Río Savegre and leads 7km inland, past the towns of Silencio and Santo Domingo, to the lodge. However, if you don't have private transportation, the lodge can ar-

OFF THE BEATEN TRACK

MATAPALO

For years, Matapalo has been off most travelers' radars, though without good reason, as this palm-fringed, gray-sand beach has some truly awesome surf. With two river-mouth breaks generating some wicked waves, Matapalo is recommended for intermediate to advanced surfers who are comfortable dealing with rapidly changing conditions. As you might imagine, Matapalo is not the best beach for swimming as the transient rips here are about as notorious as they come.

The first hotel you'll see after turning off the Costanera is **El Coquito del Pacífico** (☎ 2787-5031; www.elcoquito.com; bungalows from US$65, houses US$125; P ✽ ✖ ✸), which consists of a small batch of bungalows highlighted by their beaming whitewashed walls and rustic furnishings. The entire complex is attractively landscaped with shady gardens of almond and mango trees, and centered on an open-air bar and restaurant.

Dreamy Contentment (☎ 2787-5223; www.dreamycontentment.com; r/bungalows/ houses US$28/102/226; P ✽) has something for everyone – it's a Spanish-colonial property with impressive woodworking and towering trees throughout. The bungalows are equipped with functional kitchenettes, though the real star attraction is the main house, which has the kitchen of your dreams, a beachfront veranda and a princely bathroom complete with hot tub. Budget travelers will find basic but reasonably comfortable backpacker rooms that put you in front of the surf without having to dig too deep.

Near the end of the road you'll find the friendly and laid-back **Rafiki Beach Camp** (☎ 2787-5014; www.rafikibeach.com; d/tents incl breakfast US$60/125; ✖), with luxury safari-style beachfront tents and *cabinas*. All of the tents are fully furnished and have electricity, tiled bathroom with hot shower, hand-painted sink and ocean views. The *cabinas* across the road are also beautifully decorated and come ornamented with fresh flowers. There's a pool overlooking the ocean, adjacent to a *rancho* with communal kitchen.

Buses between Quepos and Dominical can drop you off at the turnoff to the village; from there it's a couple of kilometers to this off-the-beaten-track beach.

range all of your transfers with advance reservations. Word to the wise: bring your own flashlight to supplement the standard-issue loaner that comes with your room keys.

Hacienda Barú National Wildlife Refuge

Located on the Pacific coast 3km northeast of Dominical on the road to Quepos, this **wildlife refuge** (☎ 2787-0003; www.haciendabaru.com; admission US$7, each extra day US$2, guided tours US$20-60) forms a key link in a major biological corridor called the 'Path of the Tapir'. It comprises more than 330 hectares of private and state-owned land that has been protected from hunting since 1976. The range of tropical habitats that may be observed here include pristine beaches, riverbanks, mangrove estuaries, wetlands, selectively logged forests, secondary forests, primary forests, tree plantations and pastures.

This diversity of habitat plus its key position in the Path of the Tapir account for the multitude of species that have been identified in Hacienda Barú. These include 351 birds, 69 mammals, 94 reptiles and amphibians, 87 butterflies and 158 species of tree, some of which are more than 8.5m in circumference. Ecological tourism provides this wildlife refuge with its only source of funds with which to maintain its protected status, so guests are assured that money spent here will be used to further the conservation of tropical rainforest.

There is an impressive number of guided tours on offer. You can experience the rainforest canopy in three ways – a platform 36m above the forest floor, tree climbing and a zip line called 'Flight of the Toucan'. In addition to the canopy activities, Hacienda Barú offers bird-watching tours, hiking tours, and two overnight camping tours in both tropical rainforest and lowland beach habitats. Hacienda Barú's naturalist guides come from local communities and have lived near the rainforest all of their lives. Even if you don't stop here for the sights, the onsite store carries an excellent selection of specialist titles for bird-watchers.

For people who prefer to explore the refuge by themselves, there are 7km of well-kept and marked, self-guided trails, a bird-watching tower, 3km of pristine beach, an orchid garden and a butterfly garden.

The **Hacienda Barú Lodge** (d incl breakfast US$96) consists of six clean, two-bedroom cabins located 350m from Barú beach. Guests staying here receive free admission to the refuge. The red-tile-roofed, open-air restaurant serves a variety of tasty Costa Rican dishes (US$6 to US$10).

The Quepos–Dominical–San Isidro de El General bus stops outside the hacienda entrance. The San Isidro de El General–Dominical–Uvita bus will drop you off at the Río Barú bridge, 2km from the hacienda office. A taxi from Dominical costs about US$5.

If you're driving, the El Ceibo gas station, 50m north of the Hacienda Barú Lodge, is the only one for a good distance in any direction. Groceries, fishing gear, tide tables and other useful sundries are available, and there are clean toilets.

Dominical

Dominical hits a real sweet spot with the travelers who wander up and down its rough dirt road with a surfboard under an arm, balancing the day's activities between surfing and hammock hang time. And although some may decry the large population of expats and gringos who have hunkered down here, proud residents are quick to point out that Dominical recalls the mythical 'old Costa Rica' – the days before the roads were all paved, and when the coast was dotted with lazy little towns that drew a motley crew of surfers, backpackers and affable do-nothings alike. Dominical has no significant cultural sights, no paved roads and no chain restaurants, and if you're not here to learn to surf or to swing in a hammock it might not be the place for you.

But the overall picture is a bit more complex, especially since Dominical is starting to stretch its legs, seeking to attract more than the college-aged and shoestringer sets. The completion of the Costanera Sur, which runs right by town, is facilitating the spread of development further south along the coast, which has brought along with it an intense wave of foreign investment. Although reliable wi-fi is now available throughout town, the dirt roads are still unpaved and Dominical remains the sort of place where

it's best to just slow down, unwind and take things as they come.

◉ Sights & Activities

Dominical owes its fame to its seriously sick point and beach breaks, though surf conditions here are variable. There is a great opportunity to learn surfing in the white water beach breaks, but beware of getting in too deep, as you can really get trashed out here if you don't know what you're doing. If you're just getting started, stay in the white water or make for the nearby Playa Dominicalito, which is a bit tamer.

Centro Turístico Cataratas Nauyaca   WATERFALL
(☑ 2787-0542, 2787-0541; www.cataratasnauyaca.com; horseback tour US$60, hike admission US$5; ◉ tours depart 8am Mon-Sat; ♿) This Costa Rican family-owned and -operated center is home to a series of wonderful waterfalls that cascade through a protected reserve of both primary and secondary forest. The family runs horseback-riding tours to the falls, where visitors can swim in the inviting natural pools. Led by experienced guides, the six-hour tours include breakfast, lunch and transfers from Dominical – reservations required. Alternatively, you can pay US$5 and hike to the falls independently if you're in decent shape.

The center is located 10km up the road to San Isidro de El General; you'll find the junction just north of the turnoff for Dominical. Accommodations in Dominical can also arrange tours.

Parque Reptilandia   ZOO
(☑ 8308-8855, 2787-0343; www.crreptiles.com; adult/child US$12/6; ◉ 9am-4:30pm) Though Parque Reptilandia is a reptile lover's dream come true on any day, keep in mind that Friday is feeding day. If you're traveling with kids who love slick and slimy reptiles and amphibians, or you yourself just can't get enough of these prehistoric creatures, don't miss the chance to get face to face with Costa Rica's most famous reptiles. The animal park is home to everything from alligators and crocodiles to turtles and poison-dart frogs.

Our favorite is the viper section, home to such infamous critters as the deadly fer-de-lance. The park is located in the town of Platanillo, which is 7km up the road to San

Isidro de El General. Find the junction just north of the turnoff to Dominical.

Bamboo Yoga Play   YOGA
(☎2787-0229, in USA 323-522-5454; www.bambooyogaplay.com; classes US$14) Complementary as yoga is to surfing, it's no wonder the practice is sweeping across Costa Rica. This lovely Dominical studio offers a variety of classes for all levels, including unique dance-yoga-flow hybrid styles and even burlesque dance. The studio also serves as a center for yoga and arts retreats and offers several tidy accommodations for people interested in yoga-intensive stays.

Dominical Surf Adventures   RAFTING, SURFING
(☎8897-9540, 2787-0431; www.dominicalsurfadventures.com; ⊗8am-5pm Mon-Sat, 9am-3pm Sun) A bit of an adventurer's one-stop shop; visitors can book white-water trips, kayaking, snorkel and dive trips and surf lessons from this humble little desk on the main drag. Rafting trips start at US$80 (for runs on the Class II and III Guabo) and include a more challenging run on the Rio Coto Brus' Class IV rapids. Thankfully, there's no hustling sales pitch.

Pineapple Kayak Tours   KAYAKING
(☎8362-7655, 8873-3283; www.pineapplekayaktours.com; tours US$) Run by a friendly young Tico-American couple, Pineapple Kayak Tours runs kayaking and stand-up paddle trips to local caves, rivers and mangrove forests. Find the office next to the police station in Dominical.

🍃 Courses

Adventure Education Center   LANGUAGE COURSE
(☎2787-0023, in USA & Canada 800-237-2730; www.adventurespanishschool.com) This school runs one-week Spanish-language programs, starting at US$260 without accommodations. Private lessons are available, as are discounts for longer periods of study. Various lodging options are available, from homestays to hotels.

☞ Tours

Dominical has emerged as a jumping-off point for trips to Parque Nacional Marino Ballena and, further south, Parque Nacional Corcovado. Get details at **Dominical Information Center** (☎8651-9090, 2787-0454; www.dominicalinformation.com), which can hook you up with local tour operators who can customize tours to your interests. Dominical Surf Adventures also has a suite of tours. Excellent kayak and stand-up paddleboard (SUP) day trips are on offer from Pineapple Kayak Tours, in local rivers, mangrove forests and Ventanas Caves.

🛏 Sleeping

Dominical proper is home to the majority of the area's budget accommodations, while midrange and top-end places are popping up on the outskirts of town. The rates given here are for high season, but low-season rates could be 30% to 40% lower. Note that there are additional accommodations options in the nearby mountaintop village of

---

LEARNING TO SURF IN DOMINICAL

Although Dominical attracts some serious surfers and the waves can be gnarly, the quality of surf instruction here is among the best and most affordable in the country. For beginners who need lots of time and attention, the two most important questions to ask are about the ratio of students to instructors and if rates include board rental. There are scores of shops and instructors who offer services with a wide range of quality; the following come highly recommended.

Costa Rica Surf Camp (☎2787-0393, 8812-3625; www.crsurfschool.com; Hotel DiuWak; all-inclusive packages per week from US$1105) This fantastic, locally owned surf school prides itself on a two-to-one student-teacher ratio, with teachers who have CPR and water-safety training and years of experience. The amiable owner, Cesar Valverde, runs a friendly, warm-hearted program.

Sunset Surf (☎8827-3610, 8917-3143; www.sunsetsurfdominical.com; Domilocos; all-inclusive packages per week from US$1315; ⊗8am-4:30pm) Operated by Dylan Park, who grew up surfing the waves of Hawaii and Costa Rica, Sunset offers a variety of packages (including one for women only). It has a three-to-one student-instructor ratio and Park is an excellent teacher.

Escaleras. Although most of the year Dominical has an unflappably laid-back vibe, the place goes bananas over the holidays, when Ticos from around the country flock to the coast. Travelers on the thinnest of shoestrings can probably get away with camping on the beach, but the local police are likely to move you along after a few days.

🛏 In Town

In addition to the spots listed below, there are several budget places right along the beach road. Because they're in the middle of party central, be aware that late-night noise is an issue.

★ Posada del Sol   HOTEL $
(☑ 2787-0085, 2787-0082; d from US$30; P 🛜) There are only five rooms at this charming, secure, tidy little place, but if you score one, consider yourself lucky (no advance reservations are taken). Posada del Sol hits the perfect price point and has basic comforts – hammocks outside each room, a sink to rinse out your salty suit and a clothesline to dry it. It's no place to party (it's a short stroll to the beach or to the bars in town), but the warm-hearted, watchful proprietor, Leticia, makes the place so inviting. Single travelers should check out the tiny single in the back – a great deal. Located 30m south of the school.

Cool Vibes Hostel   HOSTEL $
(Piramys; ☑ 8353-6538, 8353-6428; www.hosteldominical.com; dm US$10; P @ 🛜) Run by a sweet young French couple, this lovely hostel is a quiet beachfront haven at the southern end of town. Taking full advantage of ocean views, the hostel has two open-air dormitories with single and double beds draped in mosquito nets. A huge, airy lounge has hammocks, wi-fi and TV, and there's a communal kitchen and surfboards for rent.

Accommodations are quite limited, so it's first come, first served.

Que Nivel   CABINA $
(☑ 2787-0127; r US$35-45) Que Nivel may not be the best choice for restless sleepers or lovers of light, but it's affordable and near the beach. Concrete rooms downstairs are quite dark, although they come with air-con and are decorated in cheery colors with a surprisingly modern look. Upstairs, fan-only rooms get better light. There's a shared kitchen, as well as a lively restaurant-bar.

Domilocos   HOTEL $$
(☑ 2787-0244; www.domilocos.com; r incl breakfast US$75; P 🛜 @ 🛜 ⛱) On the road in the southern end of town, Domilocos is a solid midrange option, with Mediterranean-inspired grounds, an attractive plunge pool lined with potted plants and one of the town's best restaurants, ConFusione. Tile-floored rooms with solid beds and bamboo furniture are basic but spacious and clean.

Hotel Villas Río Mar   HOTEL $$
(☑ 2787-0052; www.villasriomar.com; bungalows US$89, ste US$140; P 🛜 @ 🛜 ⛱) ✈ From the turnoff into town, a right turn will bring you to this property about 800m from the village. Here you'll find a few dozen polished-wood bungalows, each with a private hammock-strung terrace, as well as a handful of luxury suites that accommodate small groups. Río Mar also offers a pool, Jacuzzi, tennis court, playground, equipment rental, restaurant and bar.

Hotel DiuWak   HOTEL $$$
(☑ 2787-0087; www.diuwak.com; r US$105-145, ste US$200; P 🛜 @ 🛜 ⛱) While the location in the center of town is super-convenient, this hotel could use a bit of an upgrade for these prices. Rooms range greatly in size and are quite comfortable, with hot water and all the modern conveniences you would expect, amid a lovely tropical garden. Onsite amenities include a bar, restaurant, convenience store, fitness center and spa.

🛏 Around Dominical

Albergue Alma de Hatillo   B&B $$
(☑ 8850-9034; www.cabinasalma.com; r US$70-140; P 🛜 @ 🛜) One of the most loved B&Bs on the entire Pacific coast, this hidden gem is run by Sabina, a charming Polish woman who has legions of dedicated fans the world over. If you're looking for a quiet base from which to explore the Dominical area, this tranquil spot is home to immaculate cabins spread among several hectares of fruit trees.

Guests rave about the organic produce on offer at Sabina's restaurant, as well as the daily yoga classes in her open-air studio. The B&B often hosts yoga retreats, so it's best to book ahead as early as possible. You'll find it in the village of Hatillo, about 6km north of town along the Costanera Sur.

Hotel y Restaurante Roca Verde   HOTEL $$
(☑ 2787-0036; www.rocaverde.net; r US$85; P 🛜 @ 🛜 ⛱) Overlooking the beach about

ANDRES POVEDA ON COSTA RICAN PRIDE

The founder of the Costa Rican Hostel Network has spent the last several years raising the bar for Costa Rica backpackers.

What does it mean to be Costa Rican? To understand this, all you need to do is spend some time hanging out with us Costa Ricans, or, as we prefer to call ourselves, Ticos. I think one of the most infectious qualities of Ticos is that we don't think too much about the future, and instead prefer to have a great time and simply enjoy the moment. You know, almost immediately upon arriving in this country, travelers are greeted with the words *pura vida*, which really is a catch-all phrase for Ticos. Although it directly translates as 'pure life', *pura vida* really is a philosophy of living that all of us strive to uphold.

What is the best way for travelers to experience Costa Rica? The great thing about this country is that it has a youthful spirit, so you don't have to be 18 or 21 to have a good time here. In Costa Rica the great social equalizer is beer, so all you have to do is grab a bottle and just interact with the people around you.

1km south of town, this US-owned hotel has common spaces with tile mosaics, festive murals and rock inlays. Ten tropical-themed rooms are comfortable and have terra-cotta tile floors and pretty handpainted flora and fauna decorating the walls. Still, the real action takes place in the festive communal areas, which include an open-air bar and pool.

There's also a restaurant, open 8am to 9pm Tuesday to Saturday, 8am to 5pm Sun.

Costa Paraíso BOUTIQUE HOTEL **$$$**
(☑ 2787-0025; www.costa-paraiso.com; d US$140-150; P✹🖥❄) In a prime spot overlooking a rocky cove in Playa Dominicalito, this snug hideaway lives up to its name. Each of the five rooms is beautifully appointed in a modern tropical style, with cool tile floors, wood beams and furniture and windows oriented to catch ocean breezes and views. Bonus: the in-house restaurant (p400) is a destination in itself.

All but one room (which does come with fridge and coffeemaker) has a kitchenette. Keep an eye out for the tiny sign on the ocean side, 2km south of Dominical – it's a sharp turn that goes steeply downhill.

Cascadas Farallas LODGE **$$$**
(☑ 2787-8378; www.waterfallvillas.com; ste/villas from US$125/190; P✹❄) Although it's a bit outside Dominical proper, this spiritual retreat is located beside a series of cascading waterfalls. Balinese-style suites and villas are decked out from floor to ceiling with Asian art, and all have balconies facing the waterfalls. Regular yoga and meditation sessions are balanced with exclusively vegan cuisine. This eco-retreat has no TV and no wi-fi.

To reach the property, take the San Isidro de El General fork (just north of the Dominical turnoff) for 6km, and look out for the sign marking the entrance.

🍴 Eating & Drinking

The restaurant scene in Dominical is of a high standard, catering mostly to foreign guests. The town also loves to party, though the scene changes from night to night. Maracutú hosts lots of live music and DJs; the late-night scene unfolds at San Clemente on Friday and Hotel y Restaurante Roca Verde on Saturday.

🛏 In Town

★ Soda Nanyoa COSTA RICAN **$**
(☑ 2787-0195; mains US$3-7; ⊘ 6am-10pm) In a town that caters to gringo appetites with inflated price tags, Nanyoa is a gratifying find: an authentic, moderately priced, better-than-most Costa Rican *soda*. The big pinto breakfasts and fresh-squeezed juice are ideal after a morning session on the waves, and at night it lets patrons bring their own beer from the grocery across the street.

Chapy's Healthy Subs & Wraps DELI **$**
(☑ 2787-0283; meals US$5-10; ⊘ 11am-6:30pm; 🖉🖐) With crunchy wraps and thick, grilled-veg sandwiches stacked high on homemade focaccia, Chapy's is a vegetarian's delight. As healthy as they are delicious, the sandwiches can be dressed in spicy hummus and homemade sauces. If you need a lunch to grab and go, this place has the best stuff in town.

Moca Café
CAFE $

(☑8783-2806; mains US$3-9; ☺6am-6pm; 🅿🛜 📶) Best espresso in town, hands down. The airy riverside cafe also dishes up tasty, simple breakfasts and lunches, using organic local produce. Find it at the junction of the road into town and the main drag.

Café de Ensueños
CAFE $

(meals US$4-8; ☺6am-8pm) Run by a lovely Tico family, this cafe is tucked away at the end of the southern spur road. Organic coffee drinks, fresh juices and hearty breakfasts are served alfresco under a covered terrace – an excellent spot for a quiet, unhurried morning.

Maracutú
VEGETARIAN, ASIAN $$

(☑2787-0091; www.maracatucostarica.com; meals US$6-12; ☺11am-1am; 📶) This 'natural restaurant and world music' spot hits a lovely high note in Dominical, serving mostly vegetarian and vegan dishes of international provenance, but skewing towards Asian. From vegan pad thai to shiitake soba salad, the food is made from organic and locally sourced produce as much as possible. For your aural pleasure, the musical rotation changes genres nightly.

San Clemente Bar & Grill
BAR

(☺9am-midnight) Near the center of the village away from the beach, this classic Dominical watering hole is decorated with broken surfboards on the walls and serves up big breakfasts and Tex-Mex dishes (meals US$5 to US$12). It's also one of the more popular places to drink with like-minded travelers from around the world.

Tortilla Flats
BAR

(☑2787-0033) The beachfront Tortilla Flats is the de facto place for surfers to enjoy session beers and tacos after a morning in the water. Its open-air atmosphere is pleasant, the surf videos on continuous loop and the good times abundant, but the staff is unfortunately surly.

✖ Around Dominical

★ ¿Por Qué No?
FUSION $$

(☑2787-0025; www.cpporqueno.com; mains US$5-14; ☺7am-2pm & 5:30-9:30pm, closed Mon night) Blackberry-and-cream-cheese-stuffed French toast, anyone? (Served with *real* maple syrup – this Canadian-run establishment doesn't mess around.) If breakfast doesn't turn you on, it's worth making a reservation for any other time of day, as the creative, well-executed Tico fusion cuisine at this restaurant at the Costa Paraíso hotel represents some of the best eats around here.

Organic, locally sourced ingredients are used whenever possible. Dishes like mango jerk chicken, vegetarian cassoulet and wood-fired pizza are quite reasonably priced, especially considering the quality and freshness, and the gorgeous oceanfront location can't be beat.

🛍 Shopping

Bookstore by the Seashore
BOOKS

(bookstorebytheseashore@gmail.com; ☺11am-4pm Mon-Sat) The central Pacific coast is a virtual desert when it comes to good English-language bookshops, so readers who love actual paper books will want to stock up at this oasis. A shop on the road into town, Bookstore by the Seashore is packed with well-curated used fiction, nonfiction and genre titles – in excellent condition, and most for five bucks a pop.

ℹ Orientation

The Costanera Sur bypasses the town entirely; the entrance to the village is immediately past the Río Barú bridge. There's a bone-rattling main road through the village, where many of the services are found, and a beach road parallel to the ocean. About 100m south of this intersection is a southern spur road with a couple of accommodations, a laundry and a cafe.

ℹ Information

There's a **Banco de Costa Rica** (BCR; ☑2787-0381; ☺9am-4pm Mon-Fri) on the highway just outside of town, and a postal service upstairs in the same small shopping center.

DANGERS & ANNOYANCES

Waves, currents and riptides in Dominical are very strong, and there have been drownings in the past. Watch for red flags (which mark riptides), follow the instructions of posted signs and swim at beaches that are patrolled by lifeguards. If you're smart, this is no problem, but people die here every year.

Also, Dominical attracts a heavy-duty party crowd, which in turn has led to a burgeoning drug problem.

ℹ Getting There & Away

BUS

Buses pick up and drop off passengers along the main road in Dominical.

Palmar US$2, 1½ hours, departs 4:45am, 10:30am and 3pm.

Quepos US$8, two hours, departs 5:30am, 8:30am, 1pm, 1:20pm and 3pm.

Uvita US$1.20, 20 minutes, departs 4:45am, 8:30am, 10:30am, 12:40pm, 1pm, 3pm, 5pm and 9:40pm.

TAXI

Taxis to Uvita cost US$10 to US$20, while the ride to San Isidro de El General costs US$25 to US$35, US$55 to US$65 for Quepos. Cars accommodate up to five people, and can be hailed easily in town from the main road.

Escaleras

Escaleras, a small community scattered around a steep and narrow dirt loop road that branches off the Costanera, is famed for its sweeping views of the coastline. If you want to make it up here, you're going to need a 4WD to navigate one of the country's most notoriously difficult roads. Needless to say, the locals weren't kidding when they named the place *escaleras* (staircase). Aside from the scenic views, travelers primarily brave the road to relax in a mountain retreat.

The first entrance to Escaleras is 4km south of the San Isidro de El General turnoff before Dominical, and the second is 4.5km past the first one. Both are on the left-hand side of the road and poorly signed.

One of the first places you'll come to along the main road is **Bella Vista Lodge** (☑ in USA 305-975 0003; www.bellavistalodge. com; cabins $65-75; ℗), a remote *finca* (farm) with several shiny-wood cabins on the property.

About 2km up the road, **Villa Escaleras** (☑ 8823-0509, in USA & Canada 866-658-7796; www.villa-escaleras.com; villas for 4/6/8 people US$240/280/320, casas US$70; ℗❄@🛜🏊) is a spacious four-bedroom villa accented by cathedral ceilings, tiled floors, colonial furnishings and a palatial swimming pool. Twice-weekly maid service and a wraparound balcony awash with panoramic views make the setting complete. The smaller *casa* has a three-night minimum stay when it's not housing a longer-term tenant. Inquire about discounted weekly and monthly rates.

Located on a different access road that's 1.2km south of the first entrance is **Pacific Edge** (☑ 8935-7905, 2200-5428; www.pacificedge.info; cabins/bungalows from US$70/100; ℗❄🛜🏊). The owners are a worldly North American–British couple who delight in

MOVIES IN THE JUNGLE

The decade-long (give or take) tradition of Friday and Saturday night movies, high on the hillside in Escaleras, had taken an indefinite hiatus on our last visit. The creators of this magical event may revive **Cinema Escaleras** (☑ 2787-8065; www.moviesinthejungle. com) at some point in the future; check the website for signs of life.

showing guests their slice of paradise. Four cabins are perched on a knife-edge ridge about 200m above sea level, while larger family-friendly bungalows accommodate up to six and come with fully stocked kitchen.

If you have a hankering for chicken wings, **Bar Jolly Roger** (☑ 8706-8438; 10 wings US$9; ⊘4-10pm) offers 19 varieties, in addition to cold beers and good margaritas. This friendly expat outpost is up the southern entrance to Escaleras. Look for the smiley-face Jolly Roger sign.

Uvita

Just 17km south of Dominical, this sweet little hamlet is really nothing more than a loose straggle of farms, houses and tiny shops, though it should give you a good idea of what the central Pacific coast looked like before the tourist boom. Uvita serves as the base for visits to Parque Nacional Marino Ballena, a pristine marine reserve famous for its migrating pods of humpback whales and its virtually abandoned wilderness beaches.

Sights & Activities

Uvita is a perfect base for exploring Costanera Sur, which is home to some truly spectacular beaches that don't see anywhere near the number of tourists that they should attract. All the better for you, if crowds aren't your thing.

Surfers passing through the area tend to push on to more extreme destinations further south, though there are occasionally some swells at **Playa Hermosa** (not to be confused with the one south of Jacó) to the north and **Playa Colonia** to the south. However, if you've just come from Dominical, or you're planning on heading to Pavones, you might be a bit disappointed with the mild conditions here. If you're a beginner, this can be a good place to practice.

Reserva Biológica Oro Verde OUTDOORS
(☑ 8843-8833, 2743-8072) A few kilometers before Uvita you'll see a signed turnoff to the left on a rough dirt road (4WD only) that leads 3.5km up the hill (look over your shoulder for great views of Parque Nacional Marino Ballena) to this private reserve. Two-thirds of the 150-hectare property is rainforest, and there are guided hikes, horseback-riding tours and bird-watching walks. Tour prices vary.

The reserve is on the farm of the Duarte family, who have lived in the area for more than three decades.

Rancho La Merced National Wildlife Refuge OUTDOORS
(☑ 8861-5147, 2743-8032; www.rancholamerced. com) A few kilometers before Uvita, opposite the turnoff to Oro Verde, is this 506-hectare national wildlife refuge (and former cattle ranch) with primary and secondary forests and mangroves lining the Río Morete. Here you can take guided nature hikes, horse-back-riding tours to Punta Uvita and bird-watching walks. Tour prices vary.

You can also stay at La Merced in a 1940s farmhouse, which can accommodate up to 10 people in double rooms of various sizes (doubles US$85).

👉 Tours

Bahía Aventuras ADVENTURE TOUR
(☑ 8846-6576, 2743-8362; www.bahiaaventuras. com) A well-regarded tour operator in Uvita, Bahía Aventuras has tours running the gamut, from surfing to diving to hiking, and spanning the Costa Ballena to Corcovado. Tour rates are variable.

✨🎪 Festivals & Events

Best Fest MUSIC
(www.thebestfestival.com) Adding to the festival season that's developing along the central Pacific coast, this new music festival kicks off at the beginning of February and features a great mix of danceable, up-and-coming Tico and American bands.

Envision Art, Music & Sacred Movement Festival ART, MUSIC
(www.envisionfestival.com) Four days of spoken word, music, yoga, performance art, permaculture, dreadlocks and DJs descend on Uvita in late February. Attendees set up camp in a jungle setting near the beach in Uvita.

🛏 Sleeping & Eating
The main entrance to Uvita leads inland, east of the highway, where you'll find a number of eating and sleeping options. More guesthouses, *sodas* and local businesses are along the bumpy dirt roads that surround the edges of the park.

★ Flutterby House HOSTEL $
(☑ 2743-8221, 8341-1730; www.flutterbyhouse.com; campsites US$6, dm US$12, d US$30-80; P @ 🛜) 🌿 Is it possible to fall in love at first sight with a hostel? If so, the ramshackle collection of colorful *Swiss Family Robinson*-style tree houses and dorms at Flutterby has us head over heels. Run by a pair of beaming Californian sisters, the hostel is friendly, fun and well situated within a short stroll of Marino Ballena's beaches.

It rents out boards and bikes, sells beer for a pittance, has a tidy, open-air communal kitchen as well as a new restaurant, and it employs downright visionary sustainability practices. Follow the signs from the main highway; it's near the south entrance gate of the park.

Cabinas Los Laureles CABINA $
(☑ 2743-8008, 2743-8235; www.cabinasloslaureles.com; campsites US$10, s/d from US$30/35; P @ 🛜) Set up on a forested property with a short trail running through it, this 14-room spot in Uvita offers authentic Costa Rican hospitality. Of the friendly Tico family that runs the place, son Victor is bilingual and conscientious about referring guests to other locally-run businesses. He also runs good kayaking and mountain-biking tours via **Uvita Adventure Tour** (☑ 8918-5681, 2743-8008; www.uvitadventuretours.com; mountain-biking/kayaking tours from US$35/65).

Cascada Verde HOSTEL $
(☑ 8593-9420, 2743-8191; www.cascadaverde-costarica.com; dm US$11, r US$14-54; P @ 🛜) 🌿 If you're looking for a quiet retreat in the jungle, this hostel is for you. About 2km inland and uphill from Uvita, it's run by a young German couple who keeps the atmosphere peaceful and the facilities spotless. There's a large communal kitchen, plenty of indoor and outdoor spaces for relaxing, and a waterfall and pools a short walk away.

Because of the open architecture style, be aware that there's very little noise privacy – but you'll also hear the jungle symphony surrounding you.

Tucan Hotel   HOSTEL $

(☏ 2743-8140; www.tucanhotel.com; campsites/hammocks/dm US$6/6/10, d from US$25; P ❄ @ 🛜) Located 100m inland from the main highway, this is a most popular hostel for international travelers. There is a variety of accommodations to suit all budgets, from simple tents and hammocks to dorms, private rooms and the lofty tree house. With a shared kitchen, daily movies at 4pm and a convivial atmosphere, Tucan Hotel is a reliable budget choice.

Bungalows Ballena   BUNGALOW $$$

(☏ 8309-9631, 2743-8543; www.bungalowsballena.com; apt/bungalows US$125/250; P 🛜 ❄) These fully outfitted apartments and stand-alone bungalows are an excellent mid-market option for families and large groups. All have kitchens, wi-fi and satellite television. The place is outfitted for kids – there's a playground and a big, welcoming pool in the shape of a whale's tail. Find it 300m north of the park's main entrance.

Sabor Español   SPANISH

(☏ 8768-9160, 2743-8312; Playa Colonia; mains US$7-22; ⊙ noon-3pm & 6-9:30pm Tue-Sun) Having had a successful run in Monteverde, charming Spanish couple Heri and Montse realized that they wanted to live by the ocean – to Uvita's good fortune. Thus, their sublime *gazpacho, paella, tortilla española* and other Spanish specialties can now be savored with sangria at the end of a dirt road in Playa Uvita, in a lovely *rancho* setting.

❶ Orientation

The area off the main highway is referred to locally as Uvita, while the area next to the beach is called Playa Uvita and Playa Bahía Uvita (the southern end of the beach). The beach area is reached through two parallel roads that are roughly 500m apart – they make a C-shape connecting back to the road. The first entrance is just south of the bridge over the Río Uvita and the second entrance is in the center of town. At low tide you can walk out along Punta Uvita, but ask locally before heading out so that the rising water doesn't cut you off.

❶ Information

You can find bus schedules, an area map and other useful information at www.uvita.info. Also keep an eye out for the free print magazine *Ballena Tales*, a wonderful resource for visitors, with bilingual articles, tide charts and listings of local businesses from Dominical to the Península de Osa.

DANGERS & ANNOYANCES

When enjoying the local beaches, be aware that personal possessions that are left unattended have been known to melt away into the jungles that fringe the shorelines.

In fact, it's best not to bring anything valuable to the beach with you. Until recently, petty theft was the worst problem around the national park and area beaches, but unfortunately, a few in-person (non-violent) robberies had been reported at the time of research. Get the latest word from the staff at your accommodations.

❶ Getting There & Away

Most buses depart from the two sheltered bus stops on the Costanera in the main village.

San Isidro de El General US$1.25, two hours, departs 6am and 2pm.

San José US$5, 3½ hours, departs 5:15am and 1:15pm.

Parque Nacional Marino Ballena

This stunner of a marine park (☏ 2743-8236; admission US$7) protects coral and rock reefs surrounding several offshore islands. Its name comes not only from the humpback whales that breed here but also because of the Punta Uvita 'Whale Tail', a distinctive sandbar extending into a rocky reef that, at low tide, forms the shape of a whale's tail when viewed from above. Despite its small size, the importance of this area cannot be overstated, especially since it protects migrating humpback whales, pods of dolphins and nesting sea turtles, not to mention colonies of seabirds and several terrestrial reptiles.

Although Ballena is relatively off the radar of many coastal travelers, this can be an extremely rewarding destination for beach lovers and wildlife-watchers. The lack of tourist crowds means that you can enjoy a quiet day at the beach in near solitude – a rarity in Costa Rica. And, with a little luck and a bit of patience, you just might catch a glimpse of a humpback breaching or a few dolphins gliding through the surf.

⊙ Sights & Activities

The beaches at Parque Nacional Marino Ballena are a stunning combination of golden sand and polished rock. All of them are virtually deserted and perfect for peaceful swimming and sunbathing. And the lack of visitors means you'll have a number of quiet opportunities for good bird-watching.

From the ranger station you can walk out onto Punta Uvita and snorkel (best at low tide). Boats from Playa Bahía Uvita to Isla Ballena can be hired for up to US$45 per person for a two-hour snorkeling trip, though you are not allowed to stay overnight on the island.

To delve into the underwater beauty of the park, take a dive with the Argentine-run **Mad About Diving** (☏ 2743-8019; www.madaboutdivingcr.com).

There is also some decent surfing near the river mouth at the southern end of Playa Colonia.

Wildlife-Watching

Although the park gets few human visitors, the beaches are frequently visited by a number of animal species, including nesting seabirds, bottle-nose dolphins and a variety of lizards. And from May to November, with a peak in September and October, olive ridley and hawksbill turtles bury their eggs in the sand nightly. However, the star attraction are the pods of humpback whales that pass through the national park from August to October and December to April.

Scientists are unsure as to why humpback whales migrate here, though it's possible that Costa Rican waters may be one of only a few places in the world where the whales mate. There are actually two different groups of humpbacks that pass through the park – whales seen in the fall migrate from Californian waters, while those seen in the spring originate from Antarctica.

❶ Information

Heading southeast from Punta Uvita, the park includes 13km of sandy and rocky beaches, mangrove swamps, estuaries and rocky headlands. All six kinds of Costa Rican mangrove occur within the park. There are coral reefs near the shore, though they were heavily damaged by sediment run-off from the construction of the coastal highway. Entrance is at the **ranger station** (☏ 2743-8236; admission US$6; ☉ dawn–dusk) in Playa Bahía Uvita, the seaside extension of Uvita.

❶ Getting There & Away

Parque Nacional Marino Ballena is best accessed from Uvita or Ojochal, by either private vehicle or a quick taxi ride; inquire at your accommodations for the latter.

Ojochal Area

Beyond Uvita, the Costanera Sur follows the coast as far as Palmar, approximately 40km away. This route provides a coastal alternative to the Interamericana, as well as convenient access to points in the Península de Osa. En route, about 15km south of Uvita, you'll pass the tiny town of Ojochal, on the inland side of the highway.

Ojochal also serves as a convenient base for exploring nearby Parque Nacional Marino Ballena, and there are plenty of accommodations here to choose from, despite its small size. Though Ojochal has attracted quite a multicultural expat population, its friendly, well-integrated vibe has a distinctly different cultural feel from that of surfer-dominated Dominical.

Just north of Ojochal, about 14km south of Uvita, is the wilderness beach of Playa Tortuga, which is largely undiscovered and virtually undeveloped, but home to some occasional bouts of decent surf.

⏾ Sleeping

There's not much of a nucleus to Ojochal – most of the sleeping and eating options are spread out along the Costanera Sur.

Lookout at Playa Tortuga BOUTIQUE HOTEL $$
(☏ 2786-5074; www.hotelcostarica.com; d US$79-110; P ✳ @ 🕱 ☀) This beautiful hilltop sanctuary is home to a dozen brightly painted bungalows awash in calming pastels. The grounds are traversed by a series of paths overlooking the beaches below, but the highlight is the large deck in a tower above the pool. Here you can pursue some early-morning bird-watching, or perhaps better yet, some late-afternoon slothful lounging.

It also has a wood-fired BBQ, excellent for grilling a fresh catch. Look for the signed turnoff on the eastern side of the road just after Km 175.

Hotel Villas Gaia CABINA $$
(☏ 8382-8240; www.villasgaia.com; r incl breakfast from US$85, casa US$153; P @ 🕱 ☀) ⚑ Along the beach side of the road is this beautifully kept collection of shiny wooden cabins

with shaded porches, set in tranquil forested grounds. An excellent restaurant serves a variety of international standards, and the hilltop pool boasts a panoramic view of Playa Tortuga. The beach is a pleasant 20-minute hike along a dirt path that winds down the hillside.

Diquis del Sur
B&B $$

(☑2786-5012; www.diquiscostarica.com; r per day/week from US$55/330; 🅿✴@🛜🐾) In Ojochal proper, this bed and breakfast is run by a delightful French-Canadian couple who make it feel like a home away from home. Accommodations are in a variety of fairly modest rooms, though all have kitchenettes conducive to self-catering. There's also a good restaurant onsite, and the well-maintained property is landscaped with flowers and fruit trees.

There are also villas for long-term rental. An interesting side fact: the property is named after the 'Diquis Spheres', which are pre-Columbian stone balls, many of which were found in this area (for more, see p449).

Finca Bavaria
BOUTIQUE HOTEL $$

(☑8355-4465; www.finca-bavaria.de; s/d from US$64/74; 🅿🛜🐾) This quaint German-run inn comprises a handful of pleasing rooms with wooden accents, bamboo furniture, romantic mosquito-net-draped beds and... high-tech German toilets. The lush grounds are lined with walkways and hemmed by forest, though you can take in sweeping views of the ocean from the hilltop pool. Look for the signed dirt road at Km 167.

An amazing German breakfast buffet is available for an additional US$8.

★ La Cusinga
ECOLODGE $$$

(☑2770-2549; www.lacusingalodge.com; Finca Tres Hermanas; s/d US$136/172; 🅿) 🍃 Awarded five out of five leaves by government-run Certified Sustainable Tourism (CST) program, this lovely ecolodge is a model of sustainable practices. It's also a relaxing place to unplug – in place of televisions there are yoga classes. Located on a private reserve that borders on Parque Nacional Marino Ballena, it has access to hiking, bird-watching, snorkeling and swimming in the national park.

Accommodations are in natural-style wooden and stone rooms with terra cotta tiled floors and crisp white linens. The restaurant offers a savory, sustainable menu of upcale Costa Rican rural dishes that includes locally raised chicken, fresh seafood and organic produce. Its location, about 5km south of Uvita, is well signed on the highway.

✗ Eating

Ojochal is an enclave of excellent cuisine, from Mediterranean to Indonesian, and it's home to a patisserie, pizzeria, butcher and farmers market. There are too many eateries to list here, but you can find them at www.elsabordeojochal.com.

Ballena Bistro
CAFE $$

(☑2786-5407; Costanera Sur, Km 169; ⏱11am-4pm Tue-Sun, to 8pm Thu; 🅿🐾✏) The main attraction of multiuse Goathouse 169, this bistro offers substantial and fresh dishes,

---

REVIVING ROOTS
· ·

Ojochal's namesake, once on the verge of extinction in the area, is making a slow comeback. Though the tall, leafy *ojoche* tree (*Brosimum alicastrum*) takes about 30 years to mature, making this a long-term project, the local community has begun putting the *ojoche* back into Ojochal.

As Ojochal's population grew through the 1950s, most stands of *ojoche* were felled for cattle grazing and lumber. But in the same decade the tree's starchy fruit provided nourishment to many local families during severe drought. The pulp of the fruit can be eaten raw, boiled, or made into flour. The fruit (also known as the 'Maya nut', though not a true nut) has a low glycemic index and high protein content, and it's rich in fiber, fat, folate, iron and antioxidants.

Around 2009, the grass-roots community group Comité de Ojoche began to replant *ojoche* trees in the area in an effort to reestablish Ojochal's connection with its roots (so to speak), and to save the tree from local extinction while reforesting the area with a nutritious and culturally valuable food source.

Hotel Villas Gaia offers walking tours of the 'Ojoche Route', and you can buy *ojoche* flour from the local women's entrepreneurial association, which helps to fund the *ojoche*-revival project.

such as lentil, beet and feta salad, Brazilian coconut fish soup and Belgian beef stew. Salads, burgers, wraps, fresh juices and cold beers round out the menu. This is a smashing spot to break up a long drive or pick up some damn good picnic fixings.

★ **Citrus** INTERNATIONAL **$$$**
(☑ 2786-5175; meals US$10-30; ☺ 11am-9pm Mon-Sat; ☑) With its fresh, bright, Moroccan-inspired flavors Citrus is a standout, even among the excellent choices within strolling distance. Offering New World dishes that are heavily influenced by Southeast Asian and north African culinary traditions, and benefiting from its candlelit riverside location, Citrus welcomes patrons with flair and bravado.

★ **Exotica** INTERNATIONAL **$$$**
(☑ 2786-5050; dishes US$10-30; ☺ 11am-9pm Mon-Sat) This phenomenal gourmet restaurant certainly sets a high benchmark for Ojochal. The nouveau French dishes each emphasize a breadth of ingredients brought together in masterful combinations. Some of the highlights include oil-drizzled fish carpaccio, wild-duck breast topped with tropical-fruit tapenades and homemade desserts.

With more than a decade in the business, yet only nine tables for diners to choose from, this is an intimate culinary experience that is certainly worth seeking out.

❶ Getting There & Away

Daily buses between Dominical and Palmar can drop you off near any of the places described here. However, given the infrequency of transportation links along this stretch of highway, it's recommended that you explore the area by private car.

Southern Costa Rica & Península de Osa

Best Ecolodges

➡ Danta Corcovado Lodge (p441)

➡ El Remanso Lodge (p448)

➡ Esquinas Rainforest Lodge (p434)

➡ Luna Lodge (p448)

Best Off-the-Beaten Track

➡ Isla del Coco (p439)

➡ Parque Internacional La Amistad (p430)

➡ Santa María & Valle de Dota (p411)

➡ Playas San Josecito, Nicuesa & Cativo (p435)

Why Go?

From the chilly heights of Cerro Chirripó (3820m) to the steamy coastal jungles of the Península de Osa, this sector of Costa Rica encompasses some of the country's least-explored and least-developed land. Vast tracts of wilderness remain untouched in Parque Internacional La Amistad, and the country's most visible indigenous groups – the Bribrí, Cabécar, Brunka and Ngöbe – maintain traditional ways of living in their remote territories.

Quetzal sightings around San Gerardo de Dota are not unusual, and scarlet macaw appearances throughout the coastal region are the norm. Besides the easily spotted birds, and monkeys, sloths and coatis roaming the region's abundant parks and reserves, in Parque Nacional Corcovado there's also the rare chance to spy on slumbering tapir. Meanwhile, the rugged coasts of the Golfo Dulce and Península de Osa captivate travelers with abandoned wilderness beaches, world-class surf and opportunities for rugged exploration. This is the land for intrepid travelers yearning for something truly wild.

When to Go

➡ While the rainforests are always wet, it absolutely pours between October and December. Wet weather in the Osa can make roads impassable and logistics challenging, so if you're planning a Corcovado trek, aim for the 'dry' season (late December through March). For surfers, the upside to rainy season is that it's the best time of year for swells.

➡ Southern Costa Rica gets as much rain as much of the coast, and at higher elevations it can get very chilly at night. The best time for serious bird-watching (particularly for quetzal sightings) is between November and May. The week leading up to Easter and the Christmas period are both super-high season, when many Ticos flee to the beaches or cooler mountain climes.

Southern Costa Rica & Península de Osa Highlights

1 Hiking the remote coast and rich rainforest of **Parque Nacional Corcovado** (p458), the country's premier wilderness experience.

2 Shivering atop Costa Rica's tallest peak to watch the sunrise from **Cerro Chirripó** (p419).

3 Communing with hammerhead sharks and colorful reef fish in the waters of **Reserva Biológica Isla del Caño** (p457).

4 Catching a ride on one of the world's longest left breaks at the slow-paced surfing paradise of **Pavones** (p437).

5 Looking for resplendently feathered quetzal in the cool highlands of **San Gerardo de Dota** (p440).

6 Celebrating the vibrant **Fiesta de los Diablitos** (p423) at the Reserva Indígena Boruca.

7 Watching the sun rise over the Golfo Dulce and set over the Pacific from the deserted beaches on **Cabo Matapalo** (p446).

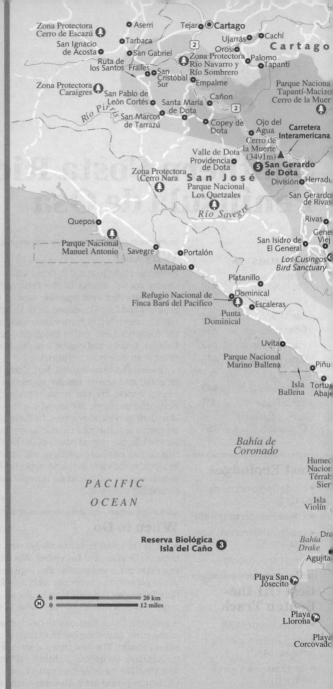

Zona Protectora Cerro de Escazú · Aserri · Tejar ○ ●Cartago
Tarbaca · Ujarrás ○ ·Cachí
San Ignacio de Acosta ○ ·San Gabriel · Orosí · Cartago
Ruta de los Santos Frailes · Zona Protectora Río Navarro y Río Sombrero · Palomo ○ ·Tapantí
San Cristóbal Sur
Zona Protectora Caraigres · San Pablo de León Cortés · Empalme · Parque Nacional Tapantí-Macizo Cerro de la Muer
Cañón
Santa María de Dota · ②
San Marcos de Tarrazú · Copey de Dota · Ojo del Agua · Carretera Interamericana
Valle de Dota · Cerro de la Muerte (3491m) ▲
Providencia de Dota · **5** San Gerardo de Dota
Zona Protectora Cerro Nara · San José · División○ ·Herradu
Parque Nacional Los Quetzales · San Gerardo de Rivas
Río Savegre
Quepos ○ · Rivas ○
San Isidro de El General · Gene Viej
Parque Nacional Manuel Antonio · Savegre ○ · Portalón · Los Cusingos Bird Sanctuary
Matapalo ○
Platanillo
Refugio Nacional de Finca Barú del Pacífico · Dominical
Escaleras
Punta Dominical
Uvita ○
Parque Nacional Marino Ballena · Piñu
Isla Ballena · Tortu Abaje

Bahía de Coronado

PACIFIC OCEAN

Humec Nacior Térrab Sier

Isla Violín

Reserva Biológica Isla del Caño 3

Bahía Drake
Agujita

Playa San Josecito

Playa Llorona

Playa Corcovado

0 — 20 km
0 — 12 miles

History

Costa Rica's indigenous population was almost entirely wiped out through both the direct and indirect effects of colonization. Spanish conquistadors eventually gave way to Catholic missionaries, though the end result was the same, namely the complete disruption of pre-Columbian life in the New World.

Even as late as the 20th century, indigenous groups were actively disenfranchised from the Spanish-dominated society. In fact, citizenship was not granted to the indigenous population until 1949, and reservations were not organized until 1977. In the intervening decades, indigenous groups have been allowed to engage in their traditional languages and customs.

On the Osa, the vast majority of the peninsula was never populated or developed by Ticos (Costa Ricans). In fact, because of the remoteness of the region, commercial logging was never a threat until the early 1960s. Although this tumultuous decade saw the destruction of much of Costa Rica's remaining primary forests, Osa was largely spared. By 1975, however, international companies were greedily eyeing the peninsula's timber and gold. Fortunately, these ambitions were halted when researchers petitioned President Daniel Oduber to establish a national park.

In recent years the peninsula has attracted the attention of wealthy foreigners, who have snatched up some prime real estate, but there's hope that development will be more sustainable in this part of the country, particularly since there is a vested interest in keeping the peninsula green.

Climate

Given the southern zone's geographic diversity, the climate varies considerably. In the lowlands, it remains hot and humid year-round, with marked rainfall from mid-April through mid-December. In the Osa, most rainy-season months boast more than 500mm of precipitation. In the highlands, you can expect much cooler temperatures year-round (getting as low as 4°C/40°F at times).

Parks & Reserves

As the country's premier ecotourism destination, the Península de Osa has a plethora of parks, reserves and wildlife refuges. Beyond the Osa, the southern zone has its own wealth of less-visited protected lands. The following is only a list of absolute highlights.

➡ **Parque Internacional La Amistad** (p430) This enormous bi-national park is shared with Panama and protects a biological corridor of incredible ecological significance.

➡ **Parque Nacional Chirripó** (p419) Home to Costa Rica's highest and most famous peak, Cerro Chirripó, which on a clear day offers views of both the Pacific and the Caribbean.

➡ **Parque Nacional Corcovado** (p458) Osa's shining crown jewel, and one of Costa Rica's last true wilderness areas.

➡ **Parque Nacional Isla del Coco** (p439) Visually stunning, utterly pristine and by far the country's most remote and difficult spot to access.

➡ **Reserva Biológica Isla del Caño** (p457) A tiny but spectacular marine and terrestrial park, popular with snorkelers, divers and biologists.

ℹ Getting There & Around

Because of complicated, frequently changing bus schedules, it's best to have your own 4WD ride if you want to explore southern Costa Rica in depth. That said, it's fairly easy to connect via bus to departure points for Amistad and Chirripó. Note that addresses in this part of the country are virtually nonexistent, and the numbered posts (counting the kilometers from San José) along the Carretera Interamericana are used to locate things.

Getting to Osa demands one of two things: lots of patience or a chartered flight. Given the reasonable cost of flights, the best option for exploring the peninsula is to fly in if your time is limited. If you choose to drive, you'll need a 4WD, a spare tire, a whole day to get here from San José and steely nerves: roads in Osa are extremely poor, as most of the peninsula is still off the grid. Getting in and out via public transportation is possible, but slow going.

Major towns in the southern zone are serviced by regular buses, though public transportation can get sporadic once you leave these major hubs.

NatureAir (www.natureair.com) and **Sansa** (www.sansa.com) service Palmar, which is a jumping-off point for the southern zone. Prices vary according to season and availability, but usually you can expect to pay a little less than US$75 for a flight from San José or Liberia.

THE ROAD TO CHIRRIPÓ

Traveling south from San José, the road to Parque Nacional Chirripó passes through gorgeous countryside of redolent coffee plantations and cool, misty cloud forests. The first major area of interest is the Zona de los Santos (Zone of the Saints), a collection of highland villages that famously bear sainted names: San Pablo de León Cortés, Santa María de Dota, San Marcos de Tarrazú, San Cristóbal Sur and San Gerardo de Dota. Further south in the Valle de El General, family-run *fincas* (farms) dot the fertile valley, though the action tends to center on San Isidro de El General, southern Costa Rica's largest town and major transportation hub.

Santa María & Valle de Dota

Centered on a green, grassy soccer field and surrounded by lavish plantations, Santa María de Dota is a picturesque Costa Rican town that merits at least a quick stop if you're driving (on bus, the detour would likely cost you a whole day). It's a quiet, sleepy place where mist rolls across the mountains and coffee production is the economic lifeblood. It seems as if the Coopedota processing facility employs half the town.

Coopedota (2541-2828; www.coopedota.com; 7am-5pm Mon-Fri, 7am-4pm Sat & Sun) can give you the complete picture of where your caffeine fix comes from: the Coffee Experience is a half-day tour (US$32) that takes guests to a coffee farm, visits the production facility and offers tastings. Harvest season (November to March) is the best time to visit. Coopedota is the first coffee co-op in the world to be certified carbon-neutral by the British Standards Institution. It's on the south side of the Coopedota building, across from the soccer field.

Those who linger in the area should spend the night at El Toucanet Lodge (2541-3131; www.eltoucanet.com; Copey de Dota; s/d incl breakfast & bird-watching walk from US$76/124; P), a lovely country lodge perched at 1850m and offering seven rustic hardwood cabins with wonderful views of Valle de Dota. It's accessible from the Interamericana at Km 58 or via the beautiful country road from Santa María de Dota; find detailed directions on its website.

One of our favorite *sodas* (lunch counters) in the region is Soda G&A (2541-1289; meals US$5-10; 7am-7pm Mon-Sat), a cute little family-run joint serving up *casados* (set meals), *olla de carne* (beef stew) and other local specialties made with more inspiration and verve than the norm. In Santa María de Dota (300m west of the park), it's on the road to San Marcos de Tarrazú.

Most drivers from San José take the Interamericana south to Empalme, almost 30km from Cartago. Just south of the gas station a signed turnoff leads west on a paved road and turns to Santa María de Dota (10km away), San Marcos de Tarrazú (7km beyond) and San Pablo (4km further). Six daily buses (US$4, 2½ hours) connect these towns to San José.

San Gerardo de Dota

San Gerardo de Dota is unlike any other place in Costa Rica – a bucolic mountain town run through by a clear, rushing river and surrounded by forested hills that more resemble the alps than the tropics. It's set deep within a mountain valley; the air is crisp and fresh, and chilly at night, and orchard-lined Savegre basin hosts high-altitude species that draw bird-watchers from around the world. The elusive quetzal is such a celebrity in these parts that in 2005 the national government demarcated a national park in its honor.

Visiting the national park is largely a self-organized, DIY affair since it has no permanent infrastructure, but the town of San Gerardo provides easy access to the trailheads and offers a wide assortment of tourist lodges. In stunning contrast to Costa Rica's famous tropical regions, San Gerardo de Dota is a charmer, well worth seeking out for a quiet couple of days of fresh mountain air.

History

The banks of the Río Savegre were long protected by the steep flanks of the Talamanca mountains, prohibiting settlement in this area. It wasn't until 1952 that Efraín Chacón and his brothers – driven by drought – came south from Copey de Dota and established a farm on the western slopes of Cerro de la Muerte.

In the early days, they planted typical subsistence crops but soon brought in dairy cattle, stocked the streams with trout and planted orchards. Trout attracted anglers from San José, while the fruit trees (along with the abundant wild avocado trees) attracted the quetzal.

Quetzals are spotted frequently every April and May (during breeding season) and are fairly common throughout the rest of the year.

Activities

Sportfishing

The trout-fishing in the Río Savegre is excellent: May and June is the time for fly-fishing and December to March for lure-fishing. A number of trout farms surround the village as well.

Bird-Watching & Hiking

The best place to go bird-watching and hiking in the area is Parque Nacional Los Quetzales. Unfortunately there are no information facilities for tourists in the park, so inquire at the lodges in San Gerardo before you set out. You can hire local guides through the hotels. Travelers who wish to do extensive hiking in the area are advised to collect maps before they arrive.

Sleeping & Eating

Note that many of the lodges offer dinner with their accommodation and have access to Parque Nacional Los Quetzales.

Ranchos la Isla & Restaurante Los Lagos CAMPGROUND $
(2740-1009, 2740-1038; campsites per person US$5; P) If you're heading to Chirripó and are geared up for a little bit of camping, this attractive property offers a handful of campsites on metal-roofed platforms alongside a small river. The accommodating Chinchilla families go all out to make sure their guests are entertained by guiding hikes to nearby waterfalls in the hope of spotting the elusive quetzal.

If you're looking for a hot meal, the on-site restaurant is a modest affair serving up wholesome, country-style *casados* (US$6 to US$10).

Cabinas El Quetzal CABINA $$
(2740-1036; www.cabinaselquetzal.com; per person incl 3 meals US$69; P) This simple cluster of four family-run *cabinas* (cabins) has an elegantly homespun feel. The included meals are lovingly prepared – naturally, fresh trout is on offer. The rooms are simple and without frills (tile floors, small sitting areas, no TVs), but they're clean, comfortable and

---

TALAMANCA TROUT FISHING

While most sportfishers flock to the coast for a big catch, the crystal-clear waters and the cool air of the Talamanca cloud forest make for a hypnotic, tranquil setting, and the fish – here, rainbow trout – are no less tasty.

The trout here are not native. Supposedly, they were first introduced to Central American rivers by the US military in Panama and the healthy fish made their way north into Costa Rican waters.

In order to maintain healthy populations, fishers are strongly encouraged to limit stream fishing to catch-and-release. If you want to take home your trout for dinner, fish in one of the local spring-fed ponds, which are well stocked with 30cm to 50cm trout. Success is guaranteed and you just pay for what you take home (about US$4 per kilogram). This is a great option for kids and folk with poor fishing karma.

Truchas Selva Madre (2571-1817, 2571-1364; www.truchasselvamadre.com; 2km north of Km 64, Interamericana Sur; 8am-5pm) A popular local fishing spot that is home to a well-stocked trout pond and hiking trails – good for a full day of fun.

Ranchos La Isla (2740-1038; San Gerardo de Dota; hours vary) Borrow equipment to fish in the river and ponds, then bring your catch back and have the staff fry it up for dinner.

Savegre Hotel de Montaña (2740-1028; San Gerardo de Dota; 8am-4pm) This lodge provides equipment and guides for fly-fishing in the Río Savegre, or you can fish in the picturesque pond and pay for what you catch.

stocked with a pile of blankets in the likely event of a chilly night.

Some *cabinas* come with a wood-burning stove. There's a small playground and tons of space for little ones to run around, and the riverside setting is a tranquil perch from which to take in the fresh air.

★ **Dantica Cloud Forest Lodge** LODGE **$$$**
(📞 2740-1067; www.dantica.com; r/ste incl breakfast from US$189/217; 🅿 ❄ @ 🛜) Definitely the most elegant place in San Gerardo, if not the whole southern zone, this upscale lodge consists of lovely stucco bungalows with colorful Colombian architectural accents. The modern comforts – leather sofas, plasma TVs, Jacuzzis and track lighting – are nice, but the stunning vistas over the cloud forest steal the scene.

Ethanol-burning stoves keep rooms toasty (and redolent of rum). A nature reserve complete with private trails is just steps away, as well as a spa for post-hike pampering. If the price tag is too steep, stop by to browse the gallery's collection of art from all over Latin America or book a romantic dinner at the Tico-continental Restaurant Le Tapir (mains US$10 to US$19).

Savegre Hotel de Montaña LODGE **$$$**
(📞 2740-1028, in USA & Canada 866-549-1178; www.savegre.com; s/d/ste incl 3 meals US$136/190/254; 🅿 @ 🛜) Owned and operated by the Chacón family since 1957, this lodge is a local institution, especially among bird-watchers keen to catch a glimpse of the quetzal. The rooms and suites are gorgeous: wrought-iron chandeliers hang from the high wooden ceilings, while rich wooden furniture surrounds a stone fireplace.

Set on a 160-hectare orchard and reserve, this riverside lodge is hemmed in by avocado trees, the favorite perch of the bird of paradise. It also has a roster of professional guides and an onsite spa.

La Comida Típica Miriam COSTA RICAN **$**
(📞 2740-1049; meals US$5-10; ⏰ 7am-7pm; 🅿) One of the first places you will pass in San Gerardo, about 6km from the Interamericana, is the cozy house advertising *comida típica* (literally, 'typical meals') – regional specialties. Eating is almost like receiving a personal invitation to dine in a Tico home: the food is delicious and abundant and the hospitality even more so.

Miriam also rents a few cabins (US$35) in the woods behind the restaurant: a modest but comfortable place to spend a night or two.

Café Kahawa CAFE **$**
(📞 2740-1081; mains US$5-10; ⏰ 7am-8pm; 🅿) With alfresco tables sitting above the river, funky skull art and sparkling fish tanks filled with fingerling trout, this atmospheric spot prepares trout in eleventeen excellent ways. There isn't much on the menu that doesn't feature this local fish, but variations on the theme – such as trout in coconut sauce and trout *ceviche* (marinated in lemon or lime juice, garlic and seasonings) – can't be found just anywhere.

🛈 Getting There & Away

The turnoff to San Gerardo de Dota is near Km 80 on the Interamericana. From here, the steep road alternates between paved and dirt. Take it slowly, as two-way traffic necessitates a bit of negotiation. Buses between San José and San Isidro de El General can drop you at the turnoff.

Parque Nacional Los Quetzales

Formerly known as Reserva Los Santos, **Parque Nacional Los Quetzales** (📞 2206-5020; admission US$5; ⏰ 7:30am-3:30pm) officially became a national park in 2005. Spread along both banks of the Río Savegre, at an altitude of 2000m to 3000m, Los Quetzales covers 50 sq km of rainforest and cloud forest lying along the slopes of the Cordillera de Talamanca.

The lifeblood of the park is the Río Savegre, which starts high up on the Cerro de la Muerte and feeds several mountain streams and glacial lakes before pouring into the Pacific near the town of Savegre. Although relatively small, this region is remarkably diverse – the Savegre watershed contains approximately 20% of the registered bird species in Costa Rica.

True to the park's new name, the beautiful quetzal is here, along with the trogon, hummingbird and sooty robin. Avians aside, the park is home to endangered species including jaguars, Baird's tapirs and squirrel monkeys. The park is also home to premontane forests, the second-most endangered life zone in Costa Rica.

The park has no facilities for tourists aside from the small ranger station, which collects fees. From here, a modest network of bird-watching trails radiates into the forest. All the lodges around San Gerardo de Dota organize hiking and bird-watching tours; to arrange multiday hiking trips into this unique ecosystem and its nearby villages, contact the ranger station, which has a list of reputable local guides.

The park is bordered by the Interamericana; the entrance is just past Km 76. Any bus along this route can drop you off at the ranger station, though most people arrive in a private vehicle.

Cerro de la Muerte

Between Empalme and San Isidro de El General, the Interamericana reaches its highest point along the famed Cerro de la Muerte (3491m). The 'Hill of Death' received its grisly moniker before it was paved, but it's still a white-knuckle drive, snaking the fog-shrouded spine along a path riddled with blind corners, masochistic bus drivers and hair-raising cliffs. The upside? Travelers who catch a small break in the fog will enjoy exquisite panoramic views of the Cordillera de Talamanca.

Cerro de la Muerte marks the northernmost extent of the *páramo,* a highland shrub and tussock grass habitat typical of the southern zone. This Andean-style landscape is rich in wildlife and home to many of the same species found in nearby Parque Nacional Chirripó. The area is also part of Parque Nacional Tapantí-Macizo Cerro de la Muerte, which offers even more opportunities for hiking and bird-watching.

DON'T MISS

MEETING YOUR MAKER

Although the treacherous drive across the Cerro de la Muerte might offer ample opportunities to meet your maker, look to the heavens about 6km north of San Isidro. There you'll see a towering statue of Christ, perched precariously on the edge of a cliff above.

Sleeping & Eating

Note that addresses in this part of Costa Rica are nonexistent. The following are listed by their Km distance marker.

Mirador de Quetzales   HOTEL $
(☑ 8381-8456, 2200-4185; www.elmiradordequetzales.com; Interamericana Km 70; cabins per person incl 2 meals US$60; P) About 1km west of the Interamericana, this excellent budget option has painted wood walls and colorful curtains and, importantly, electric heaters. Prices also include an early-morning 'quetzal walk' – the bright beauties reside in these forested hills year-round, but sightings are virtually guaranteed between November and April. You can wander its system of trails for a small fee (US$6).

Mirador Vista del Valle   LODGE $
(☑ 8384-4685, 2200-5465; www.valledelgeneral.com; Interamericana Km 119; s/d incl breakfast US$40/55; P) Aptly named, the 'View of the Valley Lookout' boasts a windowed restaurant offering panoramic views that perfectly complement local specialties such as fried trout, and fresh-brewed coffee. Below the restaurant, spotless cabins built entirely from cultivated wood are brightened by colorful indigenous tapestries and the spectacular valley views.

Bosque del Tolomuco   B&B $$
(☑ 8847-7207; www.bosquedeltolomuco.com; Interamericana Km 118; d from US$65; P 🖥 ❄) Named for the sly tayra (tree otter) which can be spotted on the grounds, this cutesy B&B is run by a lovely, chatty Canadian couple. There are four spacious, light-filled cabins, the most charming of which is the secluded 'Hummingbird Cabin.' The grounds offer 5km of hiking trails, ample opportunities to indulge in bird-watching and some magnificent views of Los Cruces and Chirripó.

A made-to-order gourmet dinner is available with advance notice. Day hikers who want to stretch their legs and get off the road can hike the network of trails for $2.

❶ Getting There & Away

Frequent buses running between San José and San Isidro de El General can drop you off at any of the lodges listed here.

San Isidro de El General

With a population of only 45,000, San Isidro de El General is little more than a sprawling, utilitarian town at the crossroads between some of Costa Rica's prime destinations. Still, the strolling lovers and teenage trouble-makers give the town square some charm, as does its unexpectedly lively bar scene.

'El General' (often referred to as Pérez Zeledón, the name of the municipality) is the region's largest population center and major transportation hub. If you're traveling to the southern Pacific beaches or Chirripó, a brief stop is inevitable. Some accommodations options just outside the town environs are worthy destinations in their own right.

And – a curious footnote – the women of San Isidro de El General are widely regarded as Costa Rica's finest. Perhaps it's the fresh mountain air and strong coffee?

The heart of San Isidro is the network of narrow streets clustered around the Parque Central. An uncharacteristic but neverthe-less impressive neo-Gothic cathedral lords over the eastern end.

👉 Tours

Aratinga Tours   BIRD-WATCHING
(📞 2574-2319; www.aratinga-tours.com) 🖋 Pieter Westra runs this highly recommended com-pany, and the Belgian expat is fluent in Eng-lish, Spanish and many dialects of bird. His website provides an excellent introduction to bird-watching in Costa Rica. All-inclusive two-week tours start at around US$1800, but custom trips can be arranged.

🎎 Festivals & Events

Agricultural Festival   AGRICULTURE
(🕐 1st week of Feb; 🎪) This fair is a chance for local farmers to strut their stuff – and that they do, by taking over the central square with fresh flowers, fruits of the region and culinary delights. There are also bullfights and livestock competitions.

🛏 Sleeping

Options in San Isidro proper serve as one-night crash pads of varying levels of style and sophistication, while options outside the town generally have more character and warrant a longer stay.

San Isidro de El General

🛏 Sleeping
1 Hotel Chirripó	B2
2 Hotel Los Crestones	A3
3 Thunderbird Hotel & Casino	A1

🍴 Eating
4 Farmers Market	B3
5 Kafe de la Casa	A1
6 La Casa del Marisco	A3
7 Supermercados Coopeagri	A2

🍸 Drinking & Nightlife
8 Bar El Balcón	A2

🛏 In Town

Hotel Chirripó   HOTEL $
(📞 2771-0529; www.hotelchirripo.com; Av 2 btwn Calles Central & 1; d with/without bathroom US$49/34; 🅿❄🛜) Let's put it bluntly: if you're traveling through town, weary and cash-poor, this is *the* choice. Popular with discerning budget travelers, this centrally located hotel is a two-minute stroll from the bus station and filled with bare, white-washed rooms that are barren but utterly dirt- and grime-free.

A few flowering plants and a festive mural in the lobby brighten otherwise monastic surroundings. The larger rooms have air-con and cable TV for a few extra dollars.

Hotel Los Crestones　　　　HOTEL **$$**
(☑2770-1500, 2770-1200; www.hotelloscrestones.com; cnr Calle Central & Av 14; s/d from US$50/65; P⚹🛜🐕) This sharp motor court is decked with blooming flowerboxes and climbing vines outside – indeed a welcome sight to the road-weary traveler. Inside, functional rooms feature modern furnishings and fixtures, which are made all the better by the attentive staff who keep this place running efficiently. There's even a cozy onsite restaurant.

Thunderbird Hotel & Casino　　HOTEL **$$**
(☑2770-6230; www.tbrcr.com/hotelcostarica; cnr Av 3 & Calle 4; r standard/luxury from US$49/62; P⚹@🛜) 'Executive Elegance' is the boast of this upscale business hotel. After a series of upgrades it's surprisingly swish. The quarters are brightly painted and fitted with shiny black-lacquer furniture. There's a small casino downstairs where you can drink for free while feeding the slots.

🛏 Around San Isidro

Finca Ipe　　　　　HOMESTAY **$**
(www.fincaipe.com; 2-bedroom house rental per week/month from US$300/900; P) 🐕 Located approximately 20km west of San Isidro, this self-sufficient, sustainable organic farm draws a group of devoted staff and volunteers who experiment with holistic medicine and permaculture. If you want to roll up your sleeves and volunteer time and energy you'll get a dorm bed, clean sheets and all the seasonal produce you can stomach, for about US$400 a month.

Talari Mountain Lodge　　　LODGE **$$**
(☑2771-0341; www.talari.co.cr; Rivas; s/d incl breakfast US$62/90; P🛜🐕) This secluded mountain lodge is a bird-watcher's haven, with over 200 species of bird spotted on the riverside property. Accommodations are in simple wooden cabins hemmed in by the forest. To get here from San Isidro, follow the road to San Gerardo de Rivas for 7km; the driveway will be on the right (find directions on the website).

🍴 Eating & Drinking

Central San Isidro is loaded with inexpensive local eateries – travelers really counting their colones should head for inexpensive *casados* in the Mercado Central, or the **Supermercados Coopeagri** (☑2785-0227; Av 6 btwn Calles Central & 2; ⊘7am-9pm Mon-Sat, 8am-4pm Sun), one block south. The largest *feria* in the region, the **farmers market** starts early Thursday morning and usually winds down by early afternoon on Friday; organic produce, prepared foods and goods are bountiful.

⭐**La Casa del Marisco**　　SEAFOOD **$**
(☑8366-1880, 2772-2862; mains US$4-10; ⊘10am-10pm Mon-Sat) Since this unpretentious seafood spot is usually slammed at lunchtime, it's best to come during off hours for its several daily varieties of *ceviche*, fresh fish or shrimp prepared as you like it, and pastas, burgers, salads and soups. The crowd of local clientele not-so-subtly hints at the choice sustenance served here.

Kafe de la Casa　　　　CAFE **$**
(☑2770-4816; Av 3 btwn Calles 2 & 4; meals US$6-13; ⊘6am-8pm Mon-Fri, 7am-3pm Sun; 🛜) Set in an old Tico house, this bohemian cafe features eclectic artwork, an open kitchen and breezy garden seating. The menu has excellent breakfasts, light lunches, gourmet dinners and plenty of coffee drinks.

Bar El Balcón　　　　　　BAR
(☑2771-1112; cnr Calle 2 & Av 2; dishes US$5-10; ⊘11pm-midnight) On an open 2nd-floor corner spot in the heart of town, this spacious bar brings in local businesspeople all day and a mix of locals, visitors and expats for boozy cultural exchange at night.

ⓘ Getting There & Away

BUS

In San Isidro the local bus terminal (known as Mercado) is on Av 6 and serves nearby villages. Long-distance buses leave from points near the Interamericana and are frequently packed, so buy tickets early. Note that buses heading south to Golfito or Ciudad Neily will go through Palmar Norte.

From Terminal Tracopa

You will find Terminal Tracopa on the Interamericana, just southwest of Av Central.

Neily US$8.50, four hours, departs 4:45am, 7am, 12:30pm and 3pm.

Palmar Norte US$4.25, two hours, departs 8am, 10am, 11:30am, 1pm, 4pm, 4:30pm, 5:30pm, 6:30pm, 7:30pm and 9:30pm.

Paso Canoas US$9.25, 4½ hours, departs 8am, 10:30am, 4pm, 6:30pm and 9:30pm.

San José US$7, three hours, departs 7:30am, 8:30am, 9am, 10:30am, 1pm, 4pm, 5:30pm and 8:30pm.

San Vito US$8, 3½ hours, departs 5:30am, 9am, 11am, 2pm and 7pm.

From Terminal Quepos

Terminal Quepos is on the side-street west of the Interamericana.

Dominical US$3, 1½ hours, departs 7am, 9am, 11:30am, 3:30pm and 4pm.

Puerto Jiménez (via Palmar Norte) US$9.50, five hours, departs 6:30am, 11am and 3pm.

Quepos US$5, three hours, departs 7am, 11:30am and 3:30pm.

Uvita US$3.50, 2 hours, departs 9am and 4pm.

From Other Bus Stops

The following buses originate in San Isidro.

Buenos Aires US$2.25, 1½ hours, departs hourly from Terminal Gafeso from around 5am to 7:30pm.

San Gerardo de Rivas (for Parque Nacional Chirripó) US$3, 1½ hours, departs from the local terminal on Av 6 at 5:30am and 2pm.

TAXI

A 4WD taxi to San Gerardo de Rivas will cost between US$25 and US$30. To arrange one, it's best to inquire through your accommodations.

San Gerardo de Rivas

If you have plans to climb Chirripó, you're in the right place – the tiny, tranquil town of San Gerardo de Rivas is at the doorstep of the national park. This is a place to get supplies, a good night's rest and a hot shower before embarking on the trek.

Although hikers are keen to press on to the park as quickly as possible, the logistics of getting up the mountain and the infrequent bus schedule will almost certainly require a night in San Gerardo before the hike, the night after or both. Luckily, the boulder-strewn Río Chirripó and bird-filled alpine scenery make it a beautiful place to linger. Those who don't have the time or energy to summit Chirripó have lovely, less-difficult hikes in the Cloudbridge Nature Reserve.

The road to San Gerardo de Rivas winds its way 22km up the valley of the Río Chirripó. The road is paved for the first 10km or so until the town of Rivas (note that this town is different from San Gerardo de Rivas). After Rivas, it gets bumpy, narrow and steep. The 'center' of San Gerardo de Rivas consists of the soccer field and the *pulpería* (corner grocery store) opposite. Otherwise, there's not much here – just the family farms and *cabinas* strung along the road and the river.

Sights & Activities

★ Cloudbridge Nature Reserve
NATURE RESERVE

(⊘ in USA 917-494-5408; www.cloudbridge.org; admission by donation; ☉ sunrise-sunset) About 2km past the trailhead to Cerro Chirripó you will find the entrance to the mystical, magical Cloudbridge Nature Reserve. Covering 182 hectares on the side of Cerro Chirripó, this private reserve is an ongoing reforestation and preservation project spearheaded by New Yorkers Ian and Genevieve Giddy. A network of trails traverses the property, which is easy to explore independently. Even if you don't get far past the entrance, you'll find two waterfalls, including the magnificent Catarata Pacifica. Volunteer reforestation and conservation opportunities are listed on the reserve's website.

Cocolisos Truchero
FISHING

(⊘ 2742-5023; ☉ 8am-6pm Sat & Sun, & by appointment; ♿) Down the hill 500m from the middle of town is this lovely little trout farm, operated by the Marin family. If you're hanging out the day before or after a trip into the park, a perfect afternoon can be made out of sitting by the trout pools and taking in the celebrated orchid collection. Naturally, the fish is the best part; matronly Garita puts together a homemade feast of trout and home-cooked sides for US$7.

Thermal Hot Springs
HOT SPRINGS

(Aguas Termales; ⊘ 2742-5210; Herradura; admission US$6; ☉ 7am-5:30pm) About 2km north of San Gerardo above the ranger station the road forks; take the left fork and walk for about 1km on a paved road for these hot springs. Turn right and take the rickety suspension bridge over the river. A switchback trail will lead you another 1km to a house with a *soda,* which is the entrance to the springs.

🛏 Sleeping & Eating

Most options are situated along the narrow road parallel to the river. The majority rent out equipment (sleeping bags, air mattresses, cooking stoves etc), though supplies are limited and quality varies. The services on hand reflect the fact that many Chirripó-bound travelers are young, ready to rough it and on a shoestring budget. Many hotels and *cabinas* allow camping for a small fee. Note that many accommodations close when Chirripó closes, during the last half of May and all of October.

★ **Casa Mariposa** HOSTEL $
(📞 2742-5037; www.hotelcasamariposa.net; dm US$15, d US$36-60; P @) 🏃 Just a short walk from the entrance of the park, this adorable lodge is built into the side of the mountain and has a warm, glowing atmosphere. Traveler-oriented details – warm clothes to borrow for the hike, laundry service, assistance with booking the Chirripó lodge – make it ideal.

In the evening, guests gather around the wood stove in the communal living room to read, plan hikes, and welcome weary hikers returning from the summit. There's a tidy kitchen, a lookout with hammocks on the roof and a stone soaking tub. There's only space for 15 guests, so advance booking is recommended.

Restaurante & Hotel de Montaña El Descanso CABINA, HOTEL $
(📞 2742-5061; www.hoteleldescansocr.com; campsites per person US$5, d per person with/ without bathroom US$48/24; P @) This quaint and quiet homestead, run by the accommodating Elizondo family, is an excellent budget choice. The spare, cell-like single rooms on the ground floor are a fine option, although brighter, more spacious ones on the 2nd floor come with bathroom and balcony for a few dollars more. All rates include transportation to the park entrance for trekkers.

The onsite restaurant dishes out simple, good meals, and the family organizes tours and a guiding service.

El Urán Hotel y Restaurante HOSTEL $
(📞 2742-5003; www.hoteluran.com; r per person without bathroom US$21, d/tr with bathroom US$53/80, all incl breakfast; P 🛜) Located just 50m below the trailhead, this no-nonsense youth hostel is a longtime mecca for hikers heading to and from Chirripó. Budget-friendly rooms are fine for a restful snooze, while the onsite restaurant, grocery store and laundry facility all cater to those on a shoestring budget. Note that it's possible to buy beer here (the *pulpería* doesn't sell alcohol).

★ **Talamanca Reserve** HOTEL $$
(📞 2742-5080; www.talamancareserve.com; r/ste US$70/80; P @🛜) 🏃 With over 16-sq-km of primary and secondary cloud forest, this private reserve has trails leading to its 10 waterfalls and cabins nestled into a garden and forest setting. The lovely garden and river cabins on the property have hot water, terraces and beautifully embellished wood and tile interiors. There's also a good onsite restaurant and a cozy lounge area.

The accommodations and hiking tours are managed by the friendly, bilingual Kenneth, who was born and raised on the reserve, and whose family still maintains the gardens, fruit trees, trails and a reforestation project here. Find the reserve entrance about 1km south of the trailhead for Chirripó.

Hotel de Montaña El Pelícano HOTEL $$
(📞 2742-5050; www.hotelpelicano.net; r with/ without bathroom US$66/30, cabins from US$72; P @🛜🏊) 🏃 About 300m below the ranger station, this simple, functional lodge has a collection of spartan but spotless rooms that overlook the river valley. The highlight of the property is the gallery of the owner, a late-blooming artist who sculpts whimsical wood pieces.

Monte Azul BOUTIQUE HOTEL $$$
(📞 2742-5222, in USA 415-967-4300; www. monteazulcr.com; Rivas; s/d incl 2 meals from US$359/416; P 🛜) 🏃 The luxurious, elegant and carbon-neutral Monte Azul single-handedly boosts the quality of accommodations within a stone's throw of Chirripó. Set on a private 125-hectare reserve, the excellent riverfront suites have tasteful contemporary art, small kitchens, luxury mattresses and linens, and custom-

designed furniture. The gourmet restaurant offers international fusions using organic produce from its garden. Note that this place is in the village of Rivas, which is down the mountain from San Gerardo de Rivas.

Río Chirripó Retreat HOTEL $$$

(☑ 2742-5109; www.riochirripo.com; Canaán; d/cabin/casita incl breakfast US$95/137/147; P@❦≋) This upscale lodge is centered on both a beautiful yoga studio overlooking the river, and a vast open-air, Santa Fe–style communal area. You can hear the rush of the river from eight secluded cabins, where woven blankets and stenciled walls evoke the southwest USA. Grounds include hiking trails, a heated swimming pool and a hot tub with sweeping mountain views. The lodge lies about 1.5km below the ranger station, in Canaán.

ⓘ Information

The Chirripó **ranger station** (Sinac; ☑ reservations 2742-5083; ☉ 6:30am-noon & 1-4:30pm) is about 1km below the soccer field on the road from San Isidro. Stop by early to check for availability at Crestones Base Lodge (p421), and to confirm and pay fees before setting out. The Base Lodge holds 10 first-come-first-served beds, which can only be reserved the day prior to arrival.

ⓘ Getting There & Away

Arriving via public transportation requires a connection through San Isidro. Buses to San Isidro depart from the soccer field at 5:15am, 11:30am and 4pm (US$1.80, 1½ to 2 hours). Any of the hotels can call a taxi for you (about US$30).

Driving from San Isidro, head south on the Interamericana and cross Río San Isidro south of town. About 500m further on, cross the unsigned Río Jilguero and take the first, steep turn up to the left, about 300m beyond the Jilguero. Note that this turnoff is not marked (if you miss the turn, it *is* signed from the northbound side).

The ranger station is about 18km up this road from the Interamericana. The road is paved as far as Rivas but beyond that it is steep and graveled. It is passable for ordinary cars in the dry season, but a 4WD is recommended. If you are driving past the village of San Gerardo de Rivas, to Albergue Urán or to Cloudbridge Nature Reserve, you will need a 4WD.

PARQUE NACIONAL CHIRRIPÓ

Costa Rica's mountainous spine runs the length of the country in four distinct cordilleras (mountain ranges), of which the Cordillera de Talamanca is the highest, longest and most remote. While most of the Talamanca highlands are difficult to access, Costa Rica's highest peak, **Cerro Chirripó**, at 3820m above sea level, is the focus of popular **Parque Nacional Chirripó** (☑ 2742-5083; park fee for two days $15, plus $15 for each additional day; ☉ closed 2nd half of May & all of Oct). Of course, while Chirripó is the highest and most famous summit in Costa Rica, it is not unique: two other peaks inside the park top 3800m, and most of the park's 502 sq km lies above 2000m.

Like a tiny chunk of the South American Andes, Parque Nacional Chirripó's rocky high-altitude features are an entirely unexpected respite from the heat and humidity of the rainforest (it's downright cold at night). Above 3400m, the landscape is *páramo*, which is mostly scrubby trees and grasslands, and supports a unique spectrum of highland wildlife. Rocky outposts punctuate the otherwise barren hills, and feed a series of glacial lakes that earned the park its iconic name: Chirripó means 'eternal waters.'

The bare *páramo* contrasts vividly with the lushness of the cloud forest, which dominates the hillsides between 2500m and 3400m. Oak trees (some more than 50m high) tower over the canopy, which also consists of evergreens, laurels and lots of undergrowth. Epiphytes – the scraggly plants that grow up the trunks of larger trees – thrive in this climate. However, the low-altitude cloud forest is being encroached upon by agricultural fields and coffee plantations in the areas near San Gerardo de Rivas.

The only way up to Chirripó is by foot. Although the trekking routes are long and challenging, watching the sunrise from such lofty heights, literally above the clouds, is an undeniable highlight of Costa Rica. You will have to be prepared for the cold – and at times wet – slog to the top, though your efforts will be rewarded with some of the most sweeping vistas that Costa Rica can offer. The vast majority of travelers visit Chirripó over three days: one to get to San Gerardo de Rivas to secure permits, one to hike to Crestones Base Lodge and one to summit the peak and return to San Gerardo. An extra day of day hiking at the top is advisable for those who really wish to soak up the amazing sights.

The dry season (from late December to April) is the most popular time to visit Chirripó. February and March are the driest months, though it may still rain. On weekends, and especially during holidays, the trails can get a bit crowded with Tico hiking groups. The park is closed in May and October, but the early months of the rainy season are still good for climbing as it usually doesn't rain in the morning. In any season, temperatures can drop below freezing at night, so warm clothes (including hat and gloves), rainwear and a three-season sleeping bag are necessary. In exposed areas, high winds seem even colder. The ranger station in San Gerardo de Rivas is a good place to check on the weather conditions.

The maps available at the ranger station are serviceable for the major trails. Getting highly detailed topographical maps of the region is difficult, though some bookstores in San José stock them occasionally. If you know your trip will include a lot of time in Chirripó's less-traveled regions, order maps in advance through www.cartographic.com.

🏃 Activities

Wildlife-Watching

The varying altitude means an amazing diversity of fauna in Parque Nacional Chirripó. Particularly famous for its extensive birdlife, the national park is home to several endangered species, including the harpy eagle (the largest, most powerful raptor in the Americas) and the resplendent quetzal (especially visible between March and May). Even besides these highlights, you might see

> ### ℹ️ DAY HIKING CHIRRIPÓ
>
> Although it might be possible to leave San Gerardo de Rivas, summit Chirripó and return to town in a single day, don't do it. It would be an utterly exhausting slog for even the most fit hikers, and nearly guarantee returning in the dark over the muddiest parts of the trail.
>
> If you don't have the time, consider a long day hike in the Cloudbridge Nature Reserve (p417).

highland birds including the three-wattled bellbird, black guan and tinamou. The Andean-like *páramo* guarantees volcano junco, sooty robin, slaty finch, large-footed finch and the endemic volcano hummingbird, which is found only in Costa Rica's highlands.

In addition to the prolific birdlife, the park is home to some unusual high-altitude reptiles, such as the green spiny lizard and the highland alligator lizard. Mammals include puma, Baird's tapir, spider monkey, capuchin and – at higher elevations – Dice's rabbit and the coyotes that feed on them.

Although spotting rarer animals is never a guaranteed proposition, here are a few tips to maximize your chances: pumas stick to the savanna areas and use the trails at dawn and dusk to move about; Baird's tapirs gravitate to various highland lagoons, mainly in the rainy season, so stake out the muddy edges at dawn or dusk if you see recent tracks; and at nighttime, coyotes can be seen feeding at the rubbish bins near Crestones Base Lodge.

Climbing Chirripó

The park entrance is at San Gerardo de Rivas, which lies 1350m above sea level; from here the summit is 2.5km straight up! A well-marked 16km trail leads all the way to the top and no technical climbing is required. It would be nearly impossible to get lost.

The amount of time it takes to get up varies greatly – it can take as little as five and as many as 14 hours to cover the 10km from the trailhead to the hostel, depending on how fit you are: the recommended departure time is 5am or 6am. The trailhead lies 50m beyond Albergue Urán in San Gerardo de Rivas (about 4km from the ranger station). The main gate is open from 4am to 10am to allow climbers to enter; no one is allowed to begin the ascent after 10am (although it is unlikely that a fast-moving latecomer would be turned away). Inside the park the trail is clearly signed at every kilometer.

The open-sided hut at **Llano Bonito**, halfway up, is a good place for a lunch break. There is shelter and water, but it is intended for emergency use, not overnight stays.

About 6km from the trailhead, the Monte Sin Fe (which translates as 'Mountain Without Faith'; this climb is not for the faint of heart) is a preliminary crest that reaches 3200m. You then enjoy 2km with gravity in your favor, before making the 2km ascent to Crestones Base Lodge at 3400m.

Reaching the hostel is the hardest part. From there the hike to the summit is about 5km on relatively flatter terrain (although the last 100m is very steep): allow at least two hours if you are fit, but carry a warm jacket, rain gear, water, snacks and a flashlight just in case. From the summit on a clear day, the vista stretches to both the Caribbean Sea and the Pacific Ocean. The deep-blue lakes and the plush-green hills carpet the Valle de las Morenas in the foreground. It's recommended to leave the base camp at 3am to arrive in time to watch the sunrise from the summit – a spectacular experience.

A minimum of two days is needed to climb from the ranger station in San Gerardo to the summit and back, leaving no time for recuperation or exploration. It is definitely worthwhile to spend at least one extra day exploring the trails around the summit and/or the Base Lodge.

Hiking Other Trails

Most trekkers follow the main trail to Chirripó and return the same way, but there are several other attractive destinations that are accessible by trails from the base camp. This will require at least another day and real topographical maps. An alternative, longer route between the base lodge and the summit goes via Cerro Terbi (3760m), as well as Los Crestones, the moonlike rock formations that adorn many postcards. If you are hanging around for a few days, the glorious, grassy Sabana de los Leones is a popular destination that offers a stark contrast to the otherwise alpine scenery. Peak-baggers will want to visit Cerro Ventisqueros (3812m), which is also within a day's walk of Crestones. These trails are fairly well maintained, but it's worth inquiring about conditions before setting out.

For hard-core adventurers, an alternative route is to take a guided three- or four-day loop trek that begins in the nearby village of Herradura and spends a day or two traversing cloud forest and *páramo* on the slopes of Fila Urán. Hikers ascend Cerro Urán (3600m) before the final ascent of Chirripó and then descend through San Gerardo. This trip requires bush camping and carrying a tent. Costa Rica Trekking Adventures (☑2771-4582; www.chirripo.com) can make arrangements for this tour.

🛏 Sleeping & Eating

The only accommodations in Parque Nacional Chirripó are at Crestones Base Lodge (Centro Ambientalista el Parámo; dm US$10), which houses up to 60 people in dorm-style bunks that have serviceable vinyl-coated mattresses. The basic stone building has a solar panel that provides electric light for limited hours and sporadic heat for showers. Amazingly, it also has wi-fi. All crude comforts – sleeping bags, cooking stoves, blankets and the like – should be rented in San Gerardo de Rivas, where they're ubiquitous.

Reservations are absolutely necessary at Crestones Base Lodge. Independent travelers will find it's virtually impossible to make reservations before arriving in Costa Rica. In-country, it's fairly easy to get a reservation at the ranger station directly. Payment is required to confirm the reservation. If you reserve in advance you must present your reservation and payment confirmation at the ranger station in San Gerardo de Rivas on the day before you set out.

Fortunately, the lodge reserves 10 spaces per night for travelers who show up in San Gerardo and are ready to hike on the following day. This is far and away the more practical option for most travelers. Even though there is no certainty that there will be space available on the days you wish to hike, showing up immediately when the ranger station opens at 6:30am is usually guaranteed to work. Space is at a premium during holiday periods and on weekends during the dry season. Your chances are best when you have a day or two to spare, in case multiday visitors max out the accommodations.

Crestones Base Lodge provides drinking water, but no food. Hikers must bring all of their own provisions.

Camping is allowed only at a special designated area near Cerro Urán – not at Crestones or anywhere else in the park.

ℹ Information

It is essential that you stop at the Chirripó ranger station (p419) at least one day before you intend to climb Chirripó so that you can get a space at the mountaintop hostel and pay your park entry fee (US$15 for two days, plus US$15 for each additional day). Even if you have a reservation, you must stop here the day before to confirm (bring your reservation and payment confirmation). You can also make arrangements here to hire a porter (a fixed fee of US$60 for up to 15kg of luggage) or to store your luggage while you hike. The hike is popular with Tico hikers and busiest the dry weeks before Easter. Although the trails are well marked, they can be a muddy mess.

❶ Getting There & Around

Travelers connect to the trails via the mountain village of San Gerardo de Rivas, which is also home to the ranger station. See details under San Gerardo de Rivas for directions on how to get there. From opposite the ranger station, in front of Cabinas El Bosque, there is free transportation to the trailhead at 5am. Also, several hotels offer early-morning trailhead transportation for their guests.

THE ROAD TO LA AMISTAD

From San Isidro de El General, the Interamericana winds its way southeast through glorious rolling hills and coffee and pineapple plantations backed by striking mountain facades, towering as much as 3350m above. Along this stretch, a series of narrow, steep, dirt roads leads to some of the country's most remote areas – some nearly inaccessible due to the prohibitive presence of the Cordillera de Talamanca. But it's worth enduring the thrilling road for the chance to visit Parque Internacional La Amistad, a true wilderness of epic scale.

Reserva Biológica Dúrika

A perfect example of sustainable tourism in action, the 85-sq-km Reserva Biológica Dúrika is home to a small but thriving community of about 40 Ticos and resident foreigners who are committed to local conservation, natural medicine and the preservation of indigenous culture. Since the late 1980s Dúrika has welcomed travelers interested in their inspiring social experiment, and its beautiful location and community spirit make it an excellent way to connect to this corner of the country, which lies adjacent to Parque Internacional La Amistad.

Originally a 350-hectare piece of cattle-grazed land, the reserve has benefited from 20 years of reforestation and is a naturalist's paradise. Tours of the farm demonstrate the principles and processes of organic agriculture that Dúrika employs, such as producing organic fertilizer and making cheese from the milk of farm-raised goats. Guests can also arrange short hikes into the reserve, day-long forays to the Cabécar indigenous village of Ujarrás and multiday treks.

Those who stay in Dúrika can take a variety of excellent day hikes to check out local waterfalls (which fuel the community's hydroelectric power) and banana groves. Comfortable, rustic cabins (per person from US$65) are available to guests; cabin rates include guided hikes on the reserve and organic vegetarian meals made from locally grown foods. Reservations (recommended) and information are available from the **Fundación Dúrika office** (☎2730-0657; www.durika.org) in Buenos Aires. Volunteer opportunities are also available; these require prior arrangement and a commitment of at least five days.

Driving the 18km to Dúrika in a 4WD takes about one hour. Alternatively, the office in Buenos Aires can arrange transportation to the reserve (one-way US$50) and watch over your car while you're staying at the reserve.

Reserva Indígena Boruca

The picturesque valley of the Río Grande de Térraba cradles several mostly indigenous villages that make up the reserve of Brunka (Boruca) peoples. At first glance it is difficult to differentiate these towns from typical Tico villages, aside from a few artisans selling their handiwork. In fact, these towns hardly cater to the tourist trade, which is one of the main reasons why traditional Brunka life has been able to continue without much distraction.

Be sensitive when visiting these communities – dress modestly, avoid taking photographs of people without asking permission, and respect the fact that these living communities are struggling to maintain traditional culture amid a changing world.

History

Historians believe that the present-day Brunka have evolved out of several different indigenous groups, including the Coto, Quepos, Turrucaca, Burucac and Abubaes, whose territories stretched all the way to the Península de Osa in pre-Columbian times. Today, however, the entire Brunka population is largely confined to the small villages of Rey Curré, which is bisected by the Carretera Interamericana, and Boruca, 8km north.

Festivals & Events

Fiesta de los Diablitos   CULTURAL

A three-day Brunka event that symbolizes the struggle between the Spanish and the indigenous population. Sometimes called the Danza de los Diablitos (Dance of the Little Devils), the festival culminates in a choreographed battle between the opposing sides. Villagers wearing wooden devil masks and burlap costumes play the role of the natives in their fight against the Spanish conquerors. The Spaniards, represented by a man in a bull costume, get whipped by branches and lose the battle. There's a lot of homemade corn-based alcohol involved. This festival is held in Boruca from December 30 to January 2 and in Curré from February 5 to 8.

Fiesta de los Negritos   RELIGIOUS

Lesser-known than the Fiesta de los Diablitos, this festival is held during the second week of December to celebrate the Virgin of the Immaculate Conception. Traditional indigenous music (mainly drumming and bamboo flutes) accompanies dancing and costumes.

Sleeping & Eating

Although the little dirt streets of Boruca village have almost no structured tourism other than basic craft stalls, simple meals are available and travelers can find rooms to rent by inquiring locally. Mileni Gonzalez (2730-5178; laflordeboruca@gmail.com). a local community organizer, can help arrange cabina accommodations or homestays, which are an excellent way to connect with the community and contribute to the local economy.

Galería Namu (2256-3412; www.galerianamu.com; Av 7 btwn Calles 5 & 7, San José) in San José can arrange local tours of the Boruca area, which include homestays, hiking to waterfalls, handicraft demonstrations and storytelling. These cost US$65 per person per day, and include meals, but not transportation to the village itself, which is relatively simple to work out by bus via Buenos Aires. Visit the website for more details.

Shopping

The Brunka are celebrated craftspeople and their traditional art plays a leading role in the survival of their culture. While most make their living from agriculture, some indigenous people have begun producing fine handicrafts for tourists. The tribe is most famous for its ornate masks, carved from balsa or cedar, and sometimes colored with natural dyes and acrylics. Brunka women also use pre-Columbian backstrap looms to weave colorful, natural cotton bags, placemats and other textiles. These crafts are not widely available elsewhere in the country.

Information

Rey Curré (usually just 'Curré' on maps) is about 30km south of Buenos Aires, right on the Interamericana. Drivers can stop to visit a small cooperative (9am-5pm Mon-Fri, 2-5pm Sat) that sells handicrafts. In Boruca, local artisans post signs outside their homes advertising their handmade balsa masks and woven bags. Exhibits are sometimes on display in the tiny museum (2730-0045, 2730-2514; 100m west of the pulpería; 9am-4pm). The community operates an excellent website with historical information and more at www.boruca.org. or tune in locally to 88.1 FM, a community radio station.

Getting There & Away

Buses (US$1.75, one hour) leave the central market in Buenos Aires at 11:30am and 1:30pm daily, traveling to Boruca via a poor dirt road. The bus returns the following morning, which makes Boruca difficult for a day trip relying on public transportation. A taxi from Buenos Aires to Boruca is about US$30.

Drivers will find a better road that leaves the Interamericana about 3km south of Rey Curré – look for the sign. This route follows a ridgeline and affords spectacular views of the valleys below. In total, it's about 8km to Boruca from Rey Curré, though the going is slow, and a 4WD is recommended.

Palmar

At the intersection of the country's two major highways, this crossroads town serves as a gateway to the Península de Osa and Golfo Dulce. Although Palmar serves as an important banana-growing center, there isn't much of interest to most travelers, who simply transit through here.

Palmar is actually split in two – to get from Palmar Norte to Palmar Sur, take the Interamericana southbound over the Río Grande de Térraba bridge, then take the first right beyond the bridge. Most facilities are in Palmar Norte, clustered around the intersection of the Carretera Interamericana and the Costanera Sur – if you're heading to Bahía Drake via Sierpe, this is your last chance to hit an ATM. Palmar Sur is home to the airstrip and an appealing little park with plenty of shade for a pleasant picnic stop.

🛏 Sleeping & Eating

Self-caterers will want to hit the **Supermercado BM** (🕿 2786-6556; ⊗ 8am-9pm Mon-Sat, 8am-8pm Sun), 200m north of the Interamericana–Costanera intersection, before heading to the Osa, as shopping opportunities are limited in Bahía Drake.

Brunka Lodge   HOTEL **$$**
(🕿 2786-7489; s/d from US$40/50; ✳@🛜🛁)
The Brunka Lodge is undoubtedly the most inviting option in Palmar Norte. Sun-filled, clean-swept bungalows are clustered around a swimming pool and a popular, pleasant open-air restaurant, and all rooms have hot-water bathrooms, cable TV and high-speed internet connections. The suite is particularly nice as it has a private entrance to the pool.

❶ Getting There & Away

AIR
Departing from San José, **Sansa** (www.flysansa.com) has daily flights to the Palmar airstrip. Prices vary according to season and availability, though you can expect to pay around US$75 to/from San José.

Taxis meet incoming flights and charge up to US$8 to Palmar Norte and US$15 to US$30 to Sierpe. Otherwise, the infrequent Palmar Norte–Sierpe bus goes through Palmar Sur – you can board it if there's space available.

BUS
Buses to San José and San Isidro stop on the east side of the Interamericana. Other buses leave from in front of the Pirola's Pizza and Seafood restaurant or the Tracopa window across the street. Buses to Sierpe depart from in front of the Gollo store.

Neily (Transportes Térraba) US$3.20, 1½ hours, departs 5:30am, 6:15am, 9:25am, 11:40am, noon, 2:10pm and 4:30pm.

San Isidro (Tracopa) US$6.20, 2½ hours, 11 departures daily between 4:40am and 6:30pm.

San José (Tracopa) US$11.50, 5½ hours, 11 departures daily between 4:40am and 6:30pm.

Sierpe (Transportes Térraba) US$0.75, 40 minutes, departs 4:30am, 7am, 9:30am, 11am, 1:30pm, 2:30pm and 5:30pm.

Neily

Although it is southern Costa Rica's second-largest 'city,' Ciudad Neily has retained the friendly atmosphere of a rural town, much like neighboring Palmar. At just 50m above sea level, steamy Neily serves as a regional transportation hub and agricultural center, but is decidedly lacking in tourist appeal.

If you wind up stranded here, the one good option is **Hotel Andrea** (🕿 2783-3715, 2783-3784; www.hotelandreacr.com; d with/without air-con US$46/37; 🅿⊜✳@🛜). Paths of terracotta tiles lead guests to cool, whitewashed rooms. The heavy-handed Romanesque columns might look a bit like Caesar's Palace (the Las Vegas one), but the rooms are good value and very secure. Conveniently, the hotel's onsite restaurant is one of the best in town.

❶ Information

There is a **Banco Coopealianza** (⊗ 8am-3pm Mon-Fri), just southwest of the *mercado* (market), with a 24-hour ATM.

❶ Getting There & Away

BUS
The following buses leave from the main terminal on the east side of town, which is attached to a *mercado* with a clutch of busy *sodas*:

Dominical US$5.10, three hours
Golfito US$1.65, 1½ hours
Palmar US$1.40, 1½ hours
Paso Canoas US$0.75, 30 minutes
Puerto Jiménez US$4.30, three hours
San Isidro US$8.50, four hours

San José US$14.75, six to seven hours
San Vito US$1.50, 1½ hours
Zancudo US$4, two hours

TAXI

Taxis with 4WD wait at the taxi stand southeast of the park. The fare from Neily to Paso Canoas is about US$8, but note that negotiation for prices is par for the course along the busy borderland.

Paso Canoas

The main port of entry between Costa Rica and Panama is like most border outposts the world over – hectic, slightly seedy and completely devoid of charm. As you might imagine, most travelers leave Paso Canoas with little more than a passing glance at their passport stamp.

Both BCR (Banco de Costa Rica; ☎ 2732-2613; ⊙9am-4pm Mon-Sat, 9am-1pm Sun) and Banco Nacional (⊙ATM 5am-10pm) have ATMs near the Costa Rican Migración and Customs (☎2732-2150, 2299-8007; ⊙6am-10pm). Rates for converting excess colones into dollars are not good, but they will do in a pinch. Colones are accepted at the border, but are difficult to get rid of further into Panama.

The Instituto Panameño de Turismo (☎2727-6524; ⊙6:30am-9:30pm), in the Panamanian immigration post, has basic information on travel to Panama.

The hotels in Paso Canoas aren't particularly inviting, but Cabinas Romy (☎2732 1930; s/d from US$28/48; [P][※][🖘]) will do if necessary. Set around a pleasant courtyard, shiny rooms are decked with pastel-colored walls, wooden doors and floral bedspreads, which add a surprising bit of warmth to an otherwise drab town.

Tracopa buses leave for San José (US$15.40, 7½ hours) at 3:30am, 8am, 11am and 4:30pm. The Tracopa bus terminal (☎2732-2119; ⊙7am-4pm), or window really, is north of the border post, on the east side of the main road. Sunday-afternoon buses are full of weekend shoppers, so buy tickets as early as possible. Buses for Neily (US$0.75, 30 minutes) leave from in front of the post office at least once an hour from 6am to 6pm. Taxis to Neily cost about US$7.

Wilson Botanical Garden

Covering 12 hectares and surrounded by 254 hectares of natural forest, Wilson Botanical Garden (☎2773-4004; www.ots.ac.cr/lascruces; Las Cruces Biological Station; admission US$8, half-/full-day guided tours US$28/54; ⊙7am-5pm Mon-Fri, 8am-5pm Sat & Sun) lies about 6km south of San Vito. This world-class garden was established by Robert and Catherine Wilson in 1963 and thereafter became internationally known for its collection.

In 1973 the area came under the auspices of the Organization for Tropical Studies (OTS) and today the well-maintained garden – part of Las Cruces Biological Station – holds more than 1000 genera of plants from about 200 families. Species threatened with extinction are preserved here for possible reforestation in the future.

The gardens are well laid out, many of the plants are labeled and a trail map is available for self-guided walks featuring exotic species such as orchids, bromeliads and medicinal plants. The gardens are very popular among bird-watchers, who look for a number of rare species.

PARADISE TROPICAL GARDEN

Indigenous groups use tropical flowers, herbs and plants to treat all kinds of illnesses, from diabetes to a slipped disk. If you'd like to learn a bit more about rainforest medicine, pay a visit to the Paradise Tropical Garden (☎2789-8746; http://paradise-garden.tripod.com; Río Claro; admission by donation; ⊙8am-3pm with one day's advance notice), where Robert and Ella Beatham have created a wonderfully sensual introduction to tropical fruits and rainforest remedies that they call the 'Tropical Fruit See, Smell, Taste & Touch Experience.' Besides this interactive display, visitors learn about the production of African palm oil and how it came to be the dominant crop of this region following the collapse of the banana industry. Robert and Ella are wonderful hosts, but you should call a day in advance if you want their full attention. The gardens are located just west of the town of Río Claro – follow the Interamericana for 1km, cross the Río Lagarto and turn right at the end of the bridge. From here, the garden is just 200m beyond.

If you want to stay overnight at the botanical gardens, make reservations well in advance: facilities often fill with researchers. Accommodations are in comfortable cabins (singles/doubles including meals US$98/186) in the midst of the gorgeous grounds. The rooms are simple but they each have a balcony with an amazing view.

Buses between San Vito and Neily pass the entrance to the gardens. Take the bus that goes through Agua Buena, as buses that go through Cañas Gordas do not stop here.

San Vito

Although the Italian immigrants who founded little San Vito in the 1850s are long gone, this hillside village proudly bears traces of their legacy in linguistic, cultural and culinary echoes. As such, the town serves as a base for travelers in need of a steaming plate of pasta and a good night's sleep before descending into the deep wilderness.

The proximity of the town to the Reserva Indígena Guaymí de Coto Brus means that indigenous peoples pass through this region (groups of Ngöbe – also known as Guaymí – move back and forth across the border with Panama). You might spot women in traditional clothing – long, solid-colored *nagua* dresses trimmed in contrasting hues – riding the bus or strolling the streets.

Tucked in between the Cordillera de Talamanca and the Fila Costeña, the Valle de Coto Brus offers some glorious geography, featuring the green, rolling hills of coffee plantations backed by striking mountain facades. The principal road leaves the Interamericana at Paso Real (near Rey Curré) and follows the Río Jaba to San Vito, then continues south to rejoin the Interamericana at Neily. This winding mountain road offers spectacular scenery and a thrilling ride.

KNOWING THE NGÖBE

The earliest inhabitants of Costa Rica's far southern corner were the Ngöbe, historically referred to as the Guaymí. The name Guaymí was a Spanish transliteration of what another indigenous group had dubbed the Ngöbe – and while 'Guaymí' is not considered offensive, necessarily, the Ngöbe rightly prefer the name that they call themselves.

Having migrated over generations from neighboring Panama, the Ngöbe now inhabit indigenous reserves in the Valle de Coto Brus, the Península de Osa and southern Golfo Dulce; however, they retain some seminomadic ways and are legally allowed to pass freely over the border into Panama. This occurs frequently during the coffee-harvesting season, when many travel to work on plantations.

The Ngöbe have been able to preserve – to some degree – their customs and culture, and it is not unusual to see women wearing the traditional brightly colored, ankle-length *nagua* dress. Unlike other indigenous groups, the Ngöbe still speak Ngöbere, their native language, and teach it in local schools.

One reason the culture has been able to preserve its traditional ways is that the Ngöbe reserves are largely inaccessible. But as tourism filters into the furthest reaches of the country, the growing interest in indigenous traditions and handicrafts may actually encourage their preservation, so long as it is managed with community participation and visitor respect.

The easiest way to visit a Ngöbe reserve is to head to the visitor center at La Casona or the community museum (open 8am to 5pm) at Villa Palacios in the Coto Brus reserve, about 8km north of San Vito and another 8km off the Interamericana (the turnoff is marked by a hard-to-miss statue of a woman in Ngöbe dress).

To get the total immersion experience (and fully off the beaten track), stay for a few nights at **Tamandu Lodge** (☎ 8821-4525; www.tamandu-lodge.com; r per person US$55) on the northern Península de Osa. The lodge is run by the Carreras, a Ngöbe family. This unique lodge provides a rare chance to experience the Ngöbe lifestyle firsthand, with the family. This is hands-on stuff: gather crabs and fish with palm rods; harvest palmito and yucca; and learn how to prepare these specialties over an open fire. Accommodations are in rustic, wooden houses, built on stilts with thatch roofs. Make reservations and find out details about the journey on the website.

Sights

Finca Cántaros
PARK

(☎2773-3760, www.fincacantaros.com; admission US$5; ⏰7am-5pm; 🚸) About 3km south of town, Finca Cántaros is a recreation center and reforestation project. Over 7 hectares of grounds – formerly coffee plantations and pastureland – are now a lovely nature reserve with trails, picnic areas and a dramatic lookout over the city. Especially interesting are the pre-Columbian cemetery and a large petroglyph that was discovered on the property in 2009. Though its meaning and age are unclear, the petroglyph is estimated to be about 1600 years old.

Another point of interest, reachable by self-guided hike, is the 3000-year-old Laguna Zoncho – picnic at one of the small shelters and watch for rare birds as you contemplate the history of this place. The reserve's reception is housed in a pretty, well-maintained cabin that contains a small but carefully chosen selection of local and South American crafts.

Sleeping & Eating

★ Casa Botania
B&B $$

(☎2773-4217; www.casabotania.com; s/d incl breakfast US$62/73; 🌐🐾) 🍽 This, the freshest B&B in the region, is exquisitely run by a sweet young Belgian-Tico couple. It hits every note with pitch-perfect elegance, from the modern, beautifully adorned rooms, to the library of bird-watching guides, to the gourmet meals, which are served on a polished deck overlooking the steaming foliage of the valley below. If you don't stay, book a dinner reservation; the three-course, locally sourced, ever-changing menu of smart European-touched Costa Rican fare wins raves. It's located 5km south of town on the road between the Wilson Botanical Garden and San Vito.

Cascata del Bosco
BUNGALOW $$

(☎2773-3208; www.cascatadelbosco.com; camping US$20, d US$75; 🅿🐾) The four round cabins at Cascata del Bosco overlook the forested valley below and enclose guests in tree-house-like comfort. Each cabin has a large terrace, kitchenette and lovely interior of bamboo and tile. A short trail winds through the property (there are also plans for a canopy walkway) to the roadside restaurant, a convivial gathering spot for locals and expats. Located 200m north of Wilson Botanical Garden.

Hotel El Ceibo
HOTEL $$

(☎2773-3025; s/d from US$37/53; 🅿🌐🐾) The best option in town – though fairly subdued by any account – is El Ceibo, conveniently located downtown in a private, secure cul-de-sac (100m east of the park). Simple but functional rooms all come with fans and nice touches like reading lamps, and some have balconies with forest views. In the sky-lit dining room, tuck into some Italian pasta and wine.

Pizzería Liliana
PIZZERIA $

(☎2773-3080; www.ilprosciuttolerici.com; pizzas US$4-9; ⏰10:30am-10pm) This great spot for Italian fare offers more than a dozen different kinds of pizza, all of which are made from scratch. The lovely mountain views and old-world environs make this a pleasant place to spend an afternoon. It's 50m west of the park.

🛈 Information

If you're planning on heading to Parque Internacional La Amistad, San Vito is home to the **Minae parks office** (Ministry of Environment & Energy; ☎2773-3955; Calle 2 btwn Avs 4 & 6; ⏰9am-4pm), which can help you get your bearings before heading to the national park.

🛈 Getting There & Away

BUS

The main **Tracopa bus terminal** (☎2773-3410) is about 150m down the road to Sabalito from downtown.

San Isidro US$7.85, three hours, departs 6:45am and 1:30pm.

San José US$13.45, seven hours, departs 5am, 7:30am, 10am and 3pm.

A local bus terminal at the northwest end of town runs buses to Neily and other destinations.

Neily US$1.50, 1½ hours, departs 4:45am, 5:30am, 7:30am, 9am, 11am, 2pm, 3pm and 5:30pm.

Río Sereno US$1.60, 30 minutes, departs 7am, 10am, 1pm and 4pm.

CAR

The drive north from Neily is a scenic one, with superb views of the lowlands dropping away as the road winds up the hillside. The paved road is steep, narrow and full of hairpin turns. You can also get to San Vito from San Isidro via the Valle de Coto Brus – an incredibly scenic and less-used route with fantastic views of the Cordillera de Talamanca to the north and the lower Fila Costeña to the south.

CHRISTIAN KOBER / GETTY IMAGES ©

JUDY BELLAH / GETTY IMAGES ©

1. Cerro Chirripó (p419)
Costa Rica's highest peak rises 3820m above sea level.

2. Flowers blooming in Cartago (p125)
Although its main attraction is the basilica, Cartago is surrounded by beautiful mountains.

3. Parque Nacional Corcovado (p458)
Corcovado's coastal trails offer endless wildlife-watching opportunities – scarlet macaws, toucans and aracaris are spotted regularly.

PARQUE INTERNACIONAL LA AMISTAD

The 4070-sq-km Parque Internacional La Amistad is an enormous patch of green sprawling across the borders of Panama and Costa Rica (hence its Spanish name La Amistad – 'Friendship'). This is by far the largest protected area in Costa Rica. Standing as a testament to the possibilities of international cooperation and environmental conservation, the park was established in 1982 and declared a Unesco World Heritage Site just eight years later. It then became part of the greater Mesoamerican Biological Corridor, which protects a great variety of endangered habitats. Its cultural importance is also significant as it includes several scattered indigenous reserves.

Sound like an exciting place to visit? Well, not so fast. The vast majority of the park is high up in the Cordillera de Talamanca, and remains virtually inaccessible. Although there's no shortage of hiking and camping available for intrepid, independent travelers at lower altitudes, tourist infrastructure within the park is virtually nonexistent. For their own safety, trekkers are limited to specific areas, and strongly encouraged (in some places required) to go accompanied by local guides.

While tourists flock to Costa Rica's better-known parks in the hopes of having an eco-adventure, La Amistad is truly as rugged as it comes. Tackling this pristine, potentially treacherous environment is no easy task, but La Amistad is brimming with possibilities for hard-core wilderness exploration – if your fear of growing old in an urban jungle drives you to explore verdant ones, you'll find none wilder on the planet.

The primary jumping-off point by which visitors launch into the deepest parts of the park is the tiny mountain town of Altamira, 25km northwest of San Vito. There are four other official entrances to the park: one near Buenos Aires, one near Helechales, and two near San Vito. But Estación Altamira is the only year-round, staffed facility.

Getting here is rough and confusing due to the terrible roads and lack of good maps. A bone-jarring 21km dirt road departs Hwy 237 at the small rest-stop town of Guácimo (marked on some maps as Las Tablas). You'll pass through El Carmen before making a sharp turn uphill for Estación Altamira (the ranger station).

🏃 Activities

Hiking

Of the few visitors who come here to hike, most leave from Estación Altamira. The first trail, **Los Gigantes del Bosque**, is a short 3km circuit named for the 40m trees along the way. Signposts in Spanish provide simple explanations of some of the flora, and the trail is an easy means of seeing some ancient rainforest. It passes two lookout points, one on the edge of the primary forest, and the other overlooking the rural landscape outside the park. The trail is

---

OFF THE BEATEN TRACK

BIOLLEY

Below the wilderness of Parque Internacional La Amistad, a network of rural villages is signposted by Gaudíesque mosaic navigation markers made by a local artist. The community organization Asoprola (p431) acts as the area's information center, but aside from its funky mosaic cafe and the quiet international park above, these farming villages go about their business mostly unperturbed by tourists. While there isn't a lot of action up here, much of what does happen revolves around the coffee bean.

Asoprola organizes coffee tours to **Asomobi** (Asociación de Mujeres Organizadas de Biolley; ☎2200-4250; www.cafecerrobiolley.com; ⊙ shop 8am-4pm Mon-Fri), a women's cooperative founded in 1997 that processes delicious locally grown coffee. In the village of Biolley (pronounced bee-oh-lay; named for a Swiss biologist who settled here) the colorful beneficio (processing plant) uses ecofriendly methods that conserve water and compost organic waste for use as fertilizer. If you arrive independently, you can buy beans at the beneficio. Asoprola can arrange inexpensive accommodations in the Cerro Biolley lodge, or even better, in a Biolley homestay with a friendly local family.

Biolley is 6km west of the crossroads in Altamira village, but the way zigzags and is poorly signed; get detailed directions at Asoprola if traveling independently.

marked, but it is not well maintained. Normally the loop takes two hours.

The longest trail (14km one way) – known as the Valle del Silencio – departs from Estación Altamira and winds its way through pristine and hilly primary forest before ending up at a camping area and refuge at the base of Cerro Kamuk (3549m). The walk takes anywhere from eight to 12 hours, provided you are in very good physical condition. It is spectacular, and traverses one of the most isolated areas in all of Costa Rica, but a local guide is required to make the journey.

Contact the association of guides, Asoprola (☎ 2743-1184, in Canada 877-206-4642, in USA 866-393-5889; www.actuarcostarica.com; Altamira; ☺ 7am-8pm) to inquire about these arrangements. Rates vary depending on the size of your party and your intended course. Visit the organization's excellent website, which has detailed information about all the hikes.

Visiting Indigenous Groups

Besides the massive environmental preservation efforts of the park, La Amistad is also unique for its cultural preservation; the park is home to five different indigenous reservations for the Cabécar and Bribrí groups. These tribes originally inhabited lands on the Caribbean coast (and many still do), but over the past century they have migrated west into the mountains and as far as the Pacific coast. It is possible to visit the Cabécar via the Reserva Biológica Dúrika (p422) and the Bribrí though organizations in Puerto Viejo (p183).

The reserves see relatively few independent foreign visitors (especially those who aren't there doing missionary or volunteer work) and as a result the Cabécar and Bribrí tend to view tourists with deep curiosity. Although the unforgiving habitat in which they live has shaped societies that are tough and resilient, the Cabécar and Bribrí are known for their hospitality.

Of course, you should make an effort to respect the sensibilities of your hosts. Although these villages have connection with the outside world, they are still conservative societies, and it's recommended that you cover up as a sign of respect.

Additionally, most villagers will be happy to pose for a photo, but always ask before snapping away, to respect the dignity of the subject. Generally, people are not asked to pay for a photo, though it's best to ask your guide what is expected from you.

Tourism has a long way to develop in the region, which is one reason why a visit to a Cabécar or Bribrí village is so refreshing.

Wildlife-Watching

Although most of Parque Internacional La Amistad is inaccessible terrain high up in the Talamanca, the park is home to a recorded 90 mammal species and more than 400 bird species. The park has the nation's largest population of Baird's tapirs, as well as giant anteaters, all six species of neotropical cats – jaguar, puma (mountain lion), margay, ocelot, oncilla (tiger cat) and jaguarundi – and many more common mammals.

Bird species (49 unique) that have been sighted – more than half of the total in Costa Rica – include the majestic but extremely rare harpy eagle. In addition, the park protects 115 species of fish and 215 different reptiles and amphibians, as well as innumerable insect species.

🛏 Sleeping & Eating

Only the ranger stations at Santa María de Pittier and Altamira have camping facilities (per person US$6). There's also a basic hostel at the base of Cerro Kamuk (per person US$6). All of these accommodations offer drinking water and toilets, and – in the case of Altamira – electricity. All food and supplies must be packed in and out.

Asoprola (p431) also runs a simple lodge and restaurant in the village of Altamira and can make arrangements for lodging in local homes in Altamira and Santa Elena de Pittier for a reasonable fee (usually US$10 to US$15 per person). For an intimate look at the lives of people living on the fringes of the rainforest, there is no better way than to arrange a homestay.

ℹ Information

To make reservations to camp, call the park headquarters at Estación Altamira (☎ 2200-5355; park fee per person per day US$10) directly. This is the best-developed area of the park, with a camping area, showers, drinking water, electricity and a lookout tower.

The thickly forested northern Caribbean slopes and southern Pacific slopes of the Talamanca are protected in the park, but it is only on the Pacific side that ranger stations are found.

ⓘ Getting There & Away

If you have a tight schedule, a 4WD drive is required to get around this area – the buses are unreliable, the roads are bumpy and things run on a very loose schedule. To reach Altamira, you can take any bus that runs between San Isidro de El General and San Vito and get off in the town of Guácimo (often called Las Tablas). From Guácimo buses depart at noon and 5pm for El Carmen; if the road conditions permit, they continue 4km to the village of Altamira. From the village of Altamira, follow the Minae sign (near the church) leading to the steep 2km hike to the ranger station.

GOLFO DULCE

While the Golfo Dulce is certainly less celebrated than the Península de Osa, an increasing number of travelers are making the arduous journey in search of one of the world's longest left-hand breaks, at Pavones. The region is also home to Parque Nacional Piedras Blancas, a stunning tract of rainforest that used to be part of Corcovado, and still protects the same amazing biodiversity. This far corner of Costa Rica is also home to significantly large indigenous populations, which live in the Reserva Indígena Guaymí de Conte Burica near Pavones.

Golfito

With a long and sordid history, Golfito is a rough-around-the-edges port that stretches out along the Golfo Dulce. The town was built on bananas – the United Fruit Company moved its regional headquarters here in the 1930s. In the '80s, declining markets, rising taxes, worker unrest and banana diseases forced the company's departure.

In an attempt to boost the region's economy, the federal government built a duty-free facility, the so-called Zona Americana, in Golfito. This surreal shopping center attracts Ticos from around the country, who descend on the otherwise dying town for 24-hour shopping sprees. Unless you count this shopping center, Golfito has no attractions whatsoever. And as charmless as it is by day, by night the place is home to surly ex-military men, boozy yachters, prostitutes and shady characters.

Still, as the largest town in Golfo Dulce, Golfito is a transportation hub for hikers heading to Corcovado, surfers heading to

Pavones and sportfishers. Although it's unlikely that you'll want to stick around for any longer than you have to, there is a certain visual appeal to the crooked buildings and long-faded facades of Golfito. Plus, the verdant slopes of the Refugio Nacional de Vida Silvestre Golfito surround the town, providing a picturesque backdrop to the crumbling buildings.

◉ Sights

Refugio Nacional de Vida
Silvestre Golfito   NATURE RESERVE

(☑ SINAC Office in Golfito 2775 2620; park fee US$10; ⊙ 8am-4pm) This small, 28-sq-km reserve encompasses most of the steep hills surrounding Golfito, though it's poorly publicized and easy to miss. It was originally created to protect the town's watershed, though it also protects a number of rare and interesting plant species. It is home to several cycads, which are 'living fossils,' and are regarded as the most primitive of plants. The reserve also attracts a variety of tropical birds, four species of monkeys and several small mammals.

There are no facilities for visitors, save a gravel access road and a few poorly maintained trails, but for those who don't have the time or ability to hike in Corcovado, it provides a quick alternative. About 2km south of the center of Golfito, a gravel road heads inland, past a soccer field, and winds 7km up to some radio towers (Las Torres) 486m above sea level. This access road is an excellent option for hiking, as it has very little traffic.

A very steep hiking trail leaves from Golfito, almost opposite the Samoa del Sur hotel. A somewhat strenuous hike (allow about two hours) will bring you out on the road to the radio towers. The trail is easier to find in Golfito than at the top.

Finally, there are several trails off the road to Playa Cacao. Hikers on these routes will be rewarded by waterfalls and views of the gulf. However, the trails are often obscured, so it's worth asking locally about maps and trail conditions before setting off.

Fundación Santuario
Silvestre de Osa   WILDLIFE RESERVE

(Osa Wildlife Sanctuary; ☑ 8888-3803, 8861-1309; www.osawildlife.org; Caña Blanca; minimum donation US$25; ⊙ 8am-noon) Run by Earl and Carol Crews, who began with a lodge that became a bird santuary, which then turned into a sanctuary for injured and orphaned animals of all kinds, this nonprofit reserve now rehabilitates and releases all manner of local wildlife. Those that can't be reintroduced into the wild – like the resident spider and howler monkeys – remain at the sanctuary, where visitors can meet them up close and personal.

In a remote spot about 25km from Golfito, the sanctuary can arrange boat transport for up to six visitors. Lodges in both Golfito and Puerto Jiménez can also arrange tours.

Playa Cacao   BEACH
Just a quick trip across the bay, this small beach offers a prime view of Golfito, with the rainforest as a backdrop. If you get stuck in Golfito, Playa Cacao is probably the most pleasant spot to spend the day. To reach the beach, catch a water taxi from Golfito for around US$6 per person. You can also get to Playa Cacao by taking the 6km dirt road west and then south from the airport – a 4WD is recommended.

🏃 Activities
Golfito is home to several full-service marinas that attract coastal-cruising yachters. If you didn't bring your own boat, you can hire local sailors for tours of the gulf at any of the docks. You can fish year-round, but the best season for the sought-after Pacific sailfish is from November to May.

Banana Bay Marina   FISHING
(☎ 2775-0255; www.bananabaymarinagolfito.com) Charters can be arranged, and a full day of all-inclusive fishing starts at around US$750.

🛏 Sleeping
Note that the area around the soccer field in town (not far east of the Muellecito) is Golfito's red-light district, so you'd be wise to spend a few more dollars and stay elsewhere. Domestic tax-free shoppers are required to spend the night in Golfito, so hotel rooms can be in short supply on weekends and during holiday periods.

Cabinas y Marisquería
Princesa de Golfito   CABINA $
(☎ 2775-0442; s/d US$15/25; P ❋ 🛜) If you're watching your budget, this cozy little red-roofed house is the best option. The rooms aren't too fancy – they have fans and tile floors, firm beds and mismatched linens –

but it is safe, homey and secure. The *cabinas* are located in the southern part of town, on Rte 14. Look for them on the bay side.

Samoa del Sur   HOTEL $$
(☎ 2775-0233; www.samoadelsur.com; s/d incl breakfast US$79/96; P ❋ 🛜 ⛵) This French-run facility offers comfortable rooms outfitted with tiled floors, wood furniture and thick towels. The bar, with its huge dome ceiling, is a popular spot in the evenings, and the restaurant serves typical Tico fare as well as beautiful French specialties like mussels Provençal. *Colectivo* (shared) boats to Zancudo leave from the Samoa dock, but it's also near the Muellecito.

Casa Roland Marina Resort   RESORT $$$
(☎ 2775-0180; www.casarolandgolfito.com; d from US$170; P ❋ @ 🛜 ⛵) Casa Roland is Golfito's most swish hotel, and primarily caters to duty-free shoppers looking for an amenity-laden base. You can expect to find all the usual top-end standards including a swimming pool, restaurants and bars, tennis courts and a health spa, as well as a few extras such as a movie theater and casino.

🍴 Eating
The small, walkable district of the Pueblo Civil has about a dozen *sodas* of reputable quality. Banana Bay Marina serves the sportfishing set (with gringo prices to match), but is a great spot to have a beer on the bay and shoot some pool. The restaurant at Samoa del Sur hotel is also a good standby.

Restaurante Buenos Días   BREAKFAST $
(☎ 2775-1124; meals US$5-10; ⏱ 6am-10pm; P) Rare is the visitor who passes through Golfito without stopping at this cheerful spot opposite the Muellecito. Brightly colored booths, bilingual menus and a super-convenient location ensure a constant stream of guests – whether for an early breakfast, a typical Tico *casado* or a good old-fashioned burger.

Rancho Grande   COSTA RICAN $
(☎ 2775-1951; meals US$7-12; ⏱ noon-8pm; hours vary) About 3km south of Golfito, this rustic, thatched-roof place serves country-style Tico food cooked over a wood stove. Margarita, the Tica owner, is famous for her *patacones* (fried plantain chips). Her hours are erratic, so stop in during the day to let her know you're coming for dinner.

ℹ Orientation

The southern part of town is where you'll find most of the bars and businesses, including a seedy red-light district. Nearby is the so-called Muellecito (Small Dock), from where the daily ferry to Puerto Jiménez departs. The northern part of town was the old United Fruit Company headquarters, and it retains a languid, tropical air with its large, veranda-decked homes. Now, the Zona Americana is home to the airport and the duty-free zone.

ℹ Information

Immigration Office (☎2775-0423; ⊗8am-4pm Mon-Fri) Situated away from the dock, in a 2nd-floor office above Soda Pavas.

ℹ Getting There & Away

AIR

The airport is 4km north of the town center near the duty-free zone. **NatureAir** (www.natureair. com) and **Sansa** (www.flysansa.com) have daily flights to/from San José. One-way tickets are approximately US$100.

BOAT

There are two main boat docks for passenger service: the Muellecito is the main dock in the southern part of town. There is a smaller dock north of the Muelle Bananero (opposite the ICE building) where you'll find the **Asociación de Boteros** (Abocap; ☎2775-0357), an association of water taxis that can provide services anywhere in the Golfo Dulce area.

Fast ferries travel to Puerto Jiménez from the Muellecito (US$6, 30 minutes), departing at 6am, 11:30am and 2pm daily. Because this schedule changes frequently, it's best to check for current times at the dock; in any event, show up early to ensure a spot.

If it's within your means, you can also take a private water taxi to Puerto Jiménez. You'll have to negotiate, but prices are usually between US$20 and US$30 a person (sometimes with a US$60 minimum).

The boat taxi for Zancudo (US$6, 30 minutes) departs from the dock at Samoa del Sur hotel at noon, Monday through Saturday. The return trip is at 7am the next day (except Sunday). If you're staying at a coastal lodge north of Golfito and you've made prior arrangements for transportation, the lodge will pick you up at the docks.

BUS

Most buses stop at the depot opposite the small park in the southern part of town.

Neily US$1.65, 1½ hours, departs hourly from 6am to 7pm.

Pavones US$4, two hours, departs 10am and 3pm. This service may be affected by road and weather conditions, especially in the rainy season.

San José, via San Isidro de El General (Tracopa) US$14.70, seven hours, departs from the terminal near Muelle Bananero at 5am and 1:30pm.

Zancudo US$4, three hours, departs 1:30pm.

ℹ Getting Around

City buses and *colectivo* taxis travel up and down the main road of Golfito. Although the payment system seems incomprehensible to anyone else but the locals, it shouldn't cost you more than a few coins.

Parque Nacional Piedras Blancas

Formerly known as Parque Nacional Esquinas, this national park was established in 1992 as an extension of Corcovado. Piedras Blancas has 120 sq km of undisturbed tropical primary rainforest, as well as 20 sq km of secondary forests, pastureland and coastal cliffs and beaches.

As one of the last remaining stretches of lowland rainforest on the Pacific, Piedras Blancas is also home to a vast array of flora and fauna. According to a study conducted at the biological station at Gamba, the biodiversity of trees in Piedras Blancas is the densest in all of Costa Rica, even surpassing Corcovado.

🏃 Activities

Because Piedras Blancas is so remote and so little visited, it is the site for several ongoing animal projects, including the reintroduction of scarlet macaws with the hopes of establishing a self-sustaining population, as well as the reintegration of wild cats like ocelot and margay, which were confiscated from private homes. Look for all of the wildlife that you might see in Corcovado: big cats and all four species of monkey, herds of collared and white-lipped peccary, crocodiles, various species of poison-dart frogs (including the endemic Golfo Dulce poison-dart frog) and more than 330 species of bird.

🛏 Sleeping

⭐**Esquinas Rainforest Lodge**   LODGE **$$$** (☎2741-8001; www.esquinaslodge.com; s/d incl meals US$161/256; P🐕📶❄) ⦸ Accommodations at Esquinas Lodge are in spacious, high-ceilinged cabins with ceiling fans and private porches. The lodge's extensive grounds contain a network of well-marked trails and a welcoming stream-fed pool. This lodge was founded by the nonprofit Rainforest of the Austrians, which was also vital in the establishment of Piedras Blancas as a national park.

Now, surrounded by the primary and secondary rainforest of the park, Esquinas is integrally connected with the community of Gamba, employing local workers and reinvesting profits in community projects. By offsetting development with tree planting, it has become 100% carbon neutral. Gamba is 8km north of Golfito and 6km south of the Interamericana.

ⓘ Information

Parque Nacional Piedras Blancas does not have facilities for visitors. However, it is possible to access the park from the Esquinas Rainforest Lodge in Gamba, as well as any of the coastal lodges lining the beaches north of Golfito.

ⓘ Getting There & Away

Piedras Blancas is best accessed from the Esquinas Rainforest Lodge, which has an extensive trail network onsite and can easily arrange guided hikes deeper into the park. If you don't have your own transportation, any bus heading north from Golfito can drop you off at the lodge

If you're staying at any of the coastal lodges north of Golfito, you can inquire about transportation to/from the park as well as guided hikes into the interior.

Playas San Josecito, Nicuesa & Cativo

Idyllic deserted beaches, backed by the pristine rainforest of Parque Nacional Piedras Blancas, define the northeastern shore of the Golfo Dulce. The appeal of this area is only enhanced by its inaccessibility: part of the charm is that very few people make it to this untouched corner of Costa Rica. If you're looking for a romantic retreat or a secluded getaway, all of the lodges along this stretch of coastline are completely isolated and serve as perfect spots for quiet reflection.

🏃 Activities

The beaches along this stretch are excellent for swimming, snorkeling and sunning. Lodges also provide kayaks for maritime exploration. Hiking and wildlife-watching opportunities are virtually unlimited, as the lodges provide direct access to the wilds of Piedras Blancas. Miles of trails lead to secluded beaches, cascading waterfalls and other undiscovered attractions.

🛏 Sleeping

If you're planning on staying at the lodges listed here, advance reservations via the internet are strongly recommended, especially since it can be difficult to contact them by phone. All of these lodges are extremely isolated and accessible only by boat – you can expect a beach landing, so make sure you're wearing appropriate shoes. Prices include three meals per day and boat transportation to/from either Golfito or Puerto Jiménez.

Dolphin Quest LODGE $$
(☎2775-8630, 8811-2099; www.dolphinquest-costarica.com; Playa San Josecito; s/d campsites US$30/55, cabins US$60/100, houses US$70/120) This jungle lodge offers a mile of beach and 750 secluded acres of mountainous rainforest, with accommodations in round, thatched-roof cabins and a large house. Meals – featuring organic ingredients from the garden – are served in an open-air pavilion near the shore. To get here, arrange transportation through the lodge; the hotel is only reachable by private boat.

Playa Nicuesa Rainforest Lodge LODGE $$$
(☎2258-8250, in USA 866-504-8116; www.nicuesalodge.com; Playa Nicuesa; s/d from US$265/430) 🍃 Nestled into a 65-hectare private reserve, this lodge is barely visible from the bay. The rustic, natural accommodations are beautifully decorated with canopied beds and indigenous textile spreads; private hot-water bathrooms have garden showers. Meals are served in a thatched *rancho* featuring a sparkling, polished-wood bar. There's a two-night minimum stay, and the lodge is closed during October and the first half of November.

ⓘ Getting There & Away

All of the lodges offer boat transportation from Puerto Jiménez and/or Golfito by prior arrangement, though you can always hire a water taxi if need be.

Zancudo

Occupying a slender finger of land that juts into the Golfo Dulce, the tiny village of Zancudo is about as laid-back a beach destination as you'll find in Costa Rica. On the west side of town, gentle, warm Pacific waters lap onto black sands, and seeing more than a handful of people on the beach means it's crowded. On the east side, a tangle of mangrove swamps attracts birds, crocodiles and plenty of fish, which in turn attract fishers hoping to reel them in. Unlike nearby Pavones, an emerging surf destination, Zancudo is content to remain a far-flung village in a far-flung corner of Costa Rica.

⚡ Activities

The main activities at Zancudo are undoubtedly swinging on hammocks, strolling on the beach and swimming in the aqua-blue waters of the Golfo Dulce. Here, the surf is gentle, and at night the water sometimes sparkles with bioluminescence – tiny phosphorescent marine plants and plankton that light up if you sweep a hand through the water. The effect is like underwater fireflies.

The mangrove swamps offer plenty of opportunities for exploration: birdlife is prolific, while other animals such as crocodile, caiman, monkey and sloth are also frequently spotted. The boat ride from Golfito gives a glimpse of these waters, but you can also paddle them yourself: rent kayaks from any of the accommodations listings following.

Zancudo is a base for inshore and offshore fishing, river fishing (mangrove snapper, snook and corvina) and fly-fishing. The best sportfishing is from December to May for sailfish and May to September for snook, though many species bite year-round. Trips can be arranged through any of the accommodations listed here.

🛏 Sleeping & Eating

Sol y Mar CABINA $
(☑ 2776-0014; www.zancudo.com; cabins from US$45; 🅿 @ 🛜) This popular hangout offers various lodging options, from smallish dwellings further from the water to private deluxe units with fancy tile showers and unobstructed ocean views. Even if you're not staying here, the open-air restaurant and thatched bar is a Zancudo favorite – and it's the only game in town during low season.

Au Coeur du Soleil CABINA $$
(☑ 2776-0112; www.aucoeurdusoleil.com; d US$50-60; 🅿 🛜) These brightly painted, lovingly maintained cabins have fans, fridges, big windows and a central BBQ – some have kitchenettes and all have a homey charm. The French hosts are warm and gregarious and offer guests the use of bikes for cruising around Zancudo.

Coloso Del Mar CABINA $$
(☑ 2776-0050; www.colosodelmar.com; s/d US$45/50; 🅿 🛜) It's the little things that make Coloso stand out – matching sheets, shiny hardwood floors and coffeemakers. Bigger-picture attractions include its ideal location steps from the surf, a cute cafe and sweet staff.

Cabinas Los Cocos CABINA $$
(☑ 2776-0012; www.loscocos.com; cabins US$79; 🅿) Los Cocos is home to two historic cabins that used to be banana-company homes in Palmar but were transported to Zancudo and completely refurbished. The other two more spacious cabins are also charming, with loft sleeping areas under palm-frond roofs.

El Coquito COSTA RICAN $
(☑ 2776-0000; meals US$7-8; ⊙ 7am-8pm Sun-Wed, later Thu-Sat) Bright, cheerful and right in the middle of Zancudo's main drag, this *soda* is a charmer. It offers a filling *casado* for US$7 of fresh fish, rice and fruit, and the *licuado* (smoothies) are magically refreshing after the long, dusty ride into town. On weekends the adjoining space transforms into a nightclub, with booming music and dancing.

ℹ Information

Zancudo consists of one dirt road, which leads from the boat dock in the north, past the lodges that are strung along the shore, and out of town south toward Pavones. There is no bank in town and very few places accept credit cards, so bring cash from Golfito.

ℹ Getting There & Away

BOAT

The boat dock is near the north end of the beach on the inland, estuary side. A water taxi to Golfito (US$6, 30 minutes) departs from this dock at 7am, returning at noon, Monday through Saturday. Inquire locally, however, as times are subject to change – though you can always find a local boat captain willing to take you for a negotiable price.

BUS

A bus to Neily leaves from the *pulpería* near the dock at 5am and noon (US$4, two hours). The bus for Golfito (US$4) leaves at 5am for the three-hour trip, with a ferry transfer at the Río Coto Colorado. Service is erratic in the wet season, so inquire before setting out.

CAR

It's possible to drive to Zancudo by taking the road south of Río Claro for about 10km. Turn left at the Rodeo Bar and follow the signs across the bridge. From there, 30km of poorly maintained dirt road gets you to Zancudo.

Pavones

Home to what may be the longest left-hand surf break on the planet, Pavones is a legendary destination for surfers the world over. As this is Costa Rica's southernmost point, you'll need to work hard to get down here. However, the journey is an adventure in its own right, especially since the best months for surfing coincide with the rainy season.

Although the village remains relatively off the beaten path, both foreigners and Ticos are transforming Pavones from its days as a relative backwater. Still, development is progressing slowly and sustainably, which means that the palm-lined streets are still not paved, the pace of life is slow and the overall atmosphere remains tranquil.

The name Pavones is used to refer to both Playa Río Claro de Pavones and Punta Banco, which is 6km south.

The road into Pavones comes south and dead-ends at the Río Claro, which is where you'll find a small soccer field. About 200m to the east, a parallel road crosses the Río Claro and continues the 6km to Punta Banco.

◉ Sights

Tiskita Jungle Lodge NATURE RESERVE
(☑ 2776-2194, 2776-2193; www.tiskita.com; guided hike US$25) Set on a verdant hillside between Pavones and Punta Banco, Tiskita Jungle Lodge consists of 100 hectares of virgin forest and a huge orchard, which produces more than 125 varieties of tropical fruit. Trails wind through surrounding rainforest, which contains waterfalls and freshwater pools suitable for swimming. The combination of rainforest, fruit farm and coastline attracts a long list of birds (about 300 species have been recorded here). Hikes led by knowledgeable local guides are available with advance reservations.

🏃 Activities

Surfing

Pavones is one of Costa Rica's most famous surf breaks – when the surf's up, this tiny beach town attracts hordes of international elite. Conditions are best with a southern swell, usually between April and October. However, because Pavones is inside Golfo Dulce, it is protected from many swells so surfers can go for weeks without seeing any waves.

Pavones has become legendary among surfers for its long left. Some claim it is the world's longest, offering a two- or three-minute ride on a good day.

When Pavones has nothing (or when it's too crowded), head south to Punta Banco, a reef break with decent rights and lefts. The best conditions are at mid- or high tide, especially with swells from the south or west.

Yoga

Pavones Yoga Center YOGA
(☑ 8870-2896, 2776-2120; www.pavonesyogacenter.com; Calle Altamira; drop-in class US$5) Priced so that locals can participate, classes at this teacher-training facility are the most affordable ones around; find the class schedule and directions on its website.

Shooting Star Studio YOGA
(☑ 8829-2409, 2776-2107; www.shootingstarstudio.org; drop-in classes US$15) Only 30m from the beach, this yoga studio is open-air and offers several classes per week, including a specialized 'Yoga for Surfers.'

🛏 Sleeping

🛏 Playa Río Claro de Pavones

Cabinas Mira Olas CABINA $
(☑ 8393-7742, 2776-2006; www.miraolas.com; d/tr from US$35/45; P 🔊) This 4.5-hectare farm is full of wildlife and fruit trees, with a lookout at the top of a hill to check the surf. A sweet duplex with comfortable tiled cabins has a terrace in front, while the 'Jungle Deluxe' is a beautiful, open-air lodging with a huge balcony, kitchen and elegant cathedral ceiling. Find detailed directions on the website.

Riviera Riverside Villas VILLA $$
(☑ 8823-5874, 2776-2396; www.pavonesriviera.com; d US$95-160; P ❄ 🔊) This clutch of exclusive villas in Pavones proper offers fully

equipped kitchens, cool tile floors and attractive hardwood ceilings. Big shady porches overlook the landscaped gardens, which offer a degree of intimacy and privacy found at few other places in town.

🛏 Punta Banco

Rancho Burica
LODGE $

(📞2776-2223; www.ranchoburica.com; r per person US$15-40; P🖥) This friendly Dutch-run outpost is literally the end of the road in Punta Banco. All rooms have bathrooms and fans, while the pricier ones have mosquito-netted beds and attractive wood furniture. Hammocks are interspersed around the property, which has convivial common areas, a restaurant and a trail to a romantic jungle lookout. Reservations are recommended in high season.

Yoga Farm
LODGE $$

(www.yogafarmcostarica.org; dm/s/d incl meals & yoga US$43/50/100) 🌿 A unique and welcome addition to Pavones, this retreat has simple, clean rooms with wood bunk beds, three vegetarian meals prepared primarily with ingredients from the organic garden, and daily yoga classes that take place in an open-air studio overlooking the ocean. It's a sweaty 15-minute walk from road's end in Punta Banco: take the road going up the hill to the left, go through the first gate on the left and keep walking up the hill.

Rancho Cannatella
GUESTHOUSE $$

(📞2776-2251; www.pavonesranchocannatella.com; r per person US$25-45; P🖥) About 2km south of Pavones, this perennial surfer's haven is operated by the perenially shirtless Joseph Robertston, an expat who lives to surf and paddleboard the turquoise waves right across the road. There's a small pool, heated by the sun, and four tidy rooms for rent. Surf and paddleboard lessons can also be arranged.

Cabinas La Ponderosa
CABINA $$

(📞2776-2076; www.cabinaslaponderosa.com; r US$60-140, houses US$235-275; P❄🖥) Housed on six lovely landscaped hectares, these cozy cabins are tenderly cared for by Marshall and Angela McCarthy, who have spent years living in their adopted home of Pavones. The common lounge offers all kinds of entertainment, including a table-tennis table and a massive video library, but the real appeal of staying here is the warm hospitality of the McCarthys.

Tiskita Jungle Lodge
LODGE $$$

(📞in San José 2296-8125; www.tiskita-lodge.co.cr; r from US$570 for 3 nights; P@🖥) Set amid extensive gardens and orchards, this lodge is arguably the most beautiful and intimate in all of Golfo Dulce. Accommodations are in various stunning wooden cabins accented by stone garden showers that allow you to freshen up while bird-watching. Rates include all meals and guided walks (there's a three-night minimum). Reservations must be made in advance.

🍴 Eating & Drinking

As many of the places to stay in Pavones come with a refrigerator and burner, it's worth stocking up a bit at the two centrally located markets in Río Claro or the *pulpería* in Punta Banco.

Café de la Suerte
CAFE $

(📞2776-2388; meals US$4-9; ⏰8am-5pm Mon-Sat; 🖥) Simple breakfasts, omelets and veggie dishes dominate the menu here, all light fare to be washed down with a tropical-fruit smoothie. It also has a handful of simple, colorful rooms for rent (from US$35 to US$70).

Soda Doña Dora
COSTA RICAN $

(📞2776-2021; meals US$3.50-8; ⏰6:30am-9:30pm; 🖥) This long-standing family-run spot serves up huge breakfasts of *gallo pinto* (a stir-fry of rice and beans), eggs and toast; banana pancakes; *casados* with fresh seafood; burgers and fries; and cheap beer. Look for the Bar La Plaza sign just inland from the soccer field; the *soda* and bar share this space.

ℹ Information

Pavones has no bank or gas station, so make sure you have plenty of money and gas prior to arrival. Check out more restaurant options and other local info at www.pavonescr.com.

ℹ Getting There & Away

NatureAir (www.natureair.com) and **Alfa Romeo Aero Taxi** (www.alfaromeoair.com) offer charter flights. Prices are dependent on the number of passengers, so it's best to try to organize a larger group if you're considering this option.

Two daily buses go to Golfito (US$4, two hours). The first leaves at 5:15am, departing from the end of the road in Punta Banco and stopping opposite the Riviera. The second leaves 12:30pm from the school. You can also pick up the early bus in Pavones; check locally for the current bus stops. Buses from Golfito depart at 10am (to Pavones) and 3pm (to Punta Banco via Pavones) from the stop at the Muellecito.

A 4WD taxi will charge about US$80 from Golfito, and US$60 from Paso Canoas. If you're driving, follow the directions to Zancudo and look for the signs to Pavones.

PARQUE NACIONAL ISLA DEL COCO

Even though it's a tiny speck of green amid the endless Pacific, Isla del Coco looms large in the imagination of the adventurer: jagged mountains and tales of treasure, a pristine and isolated ecosystem filled with wildlife and some of the world's best diving. Remember the opening shot of *Jurassic Park,* where the helicopter sweeps over a tropical island? That was here.

Isla del Coco (aka Cocos Island) is around 500km southwest of the mainland in the middle of the eastern Pacific. As it's the most far-flung part of Costa Rica, you'll have to pay through the nose to get here, though few other destinations in the country are as wildly exotic and visually arresting.

As beautiful as the island may be, its terrestrial environs pale in comparison to what lies beneath. Named by PADI as one of the world's top 10 dive spots, the surrounding waters of Isla del Coco harbor abundant pelagics including one of the largest known schools of hammerhead sharks in the world.

Since the island remains largely uninhabited and is closed to overnight visitors, visits require either a private yacht or a liveaboard dive vessel. While nondivers are certainly welcome to make the trip, it pays to have some significant underwater experience in your logbook – sites around Isla del Coco are as challenging as they are breathtaking.

History

In 1526 Spanish explorer Joan Cabezas stumbled onto Isla del Coco, though it wasn't noted on maps until its second discovery by French cartographer Nicolás Desliens in 1541. In the centuries that followed, heavy rainfall attracted the attention of sailors, pirates and whalers, who frequently stopped by for fresh water, coconuts and fresh seafood.

Between the late 17th and early 19th centuries, Isla del Coco became a way station for pirates, who are rumored to have hidden countless treasures here. The most famous was the storied Treasure of Lima, a trove of gold and silver ingots, gold laminae scavenged from church domes and a solid-gold, life-sized sculpture of the Virgin Mary. 'X marks the spot,' right? Not really. More than 500 treasure-hunting expeditions have found only failure. In fact, in 1869 the government of Costa Rica organized an official treasure hunt. They didn't find anything, but the expedition resulted in Costa Rica taking possession of the island, a treasure in itself.

Settlers arrived on the island in the late 19th and early 20th centuries, though their stay on Isla del Coco was short-lived. However, they did leave behind domestic animals that have since converted into feral populations of pigs, goats, cats and rats – all of which threaten the natural wildlife.

◉ Sights

Even though this is the turf of hard-core divers, making landfall and exploring is worth the time and effort. Need a second opinion? The famous oceanographer and diving guru Jacques Cousteau famously dubbed Cocos 'the most beautiful island in the world.'

Rugged, heavily forested and punctuated by cascading waterfalls, Cocos is ringed and transected by an elaborate network of trails. The highest point is at **Cerro Iglesias** (634m), where you can soak up spectacular views of the lush, verdant island and the deep blue Pacific.

Note that visitors to the island must first register with the park rangers, though your tour company will most likely make all the necessary arrangements well in advance.

🏃 Activities

Diving

The diving is excellent, and is regarded by most as the main attraction of the island. But strong oceanic currents can lead to treacherous underwater conditions, and Isla del Coco can only be recommended to intermediate and advanced divers with sufficient experience.

The island has two large bays with safe anchorages and sandy beaches: Chatham Bay is located on the northeast side and Wafer

Bay is on the northwest. Just off Cocos are a series of smaller basaltic rocks and islets, which constitute some of the best dive sites.

Isla Manuelita is a prime spot, home to a wide array of fish, ray and eel. Shark also inhabit these waters, including huge schools of scalloped hammerhead as well as whitetips, which are best spotted at night. Dirty Rock is another main attraction – a spectacular rock formation that harbors all kinds of sea creatures.

Wildlife-Watching

Because of its remote location, Isla del Coco is the most pristine national park in the country and one of Costa Rica's great wildlife destinations. Since the island was never linked to the Americas during its comparatively short geological history, Cocos is home to a very large number of rare endemic species.

Heading inland from the coastal forests up to the high-altitude cloud forests, it is possible to find around 235 unique species of flowering plants, 30% of which are found only on the island. This incredible diversity of flora supports more than 400 known species of insects – 65 endemics, as well as a striking range of butterflies and moths, are included in this count. Scientists believe that more remain to be discovered.

Of the 87 recorded species on the island and neighboring rocks, the most pronounced are the aquatic birds: brown and red-footed booby, great frigatebird, white tern and brown noddy. There are also three terrestrial endemics, namely the Cocos cuckoo, Cocos flycatcher and Cocos finch.

The island's marine life is equally varied, with 18 species of coral, 57 types of crustacean and abundant fish, sea turtles, rays, dolphins and sharks. The scalloped hammerhead shark receives top billing, especially since it often schools in the hundreds.

Tours

Even the most fiercely independent travelers will likely have to join a tour to visit Cocos. Liveaboard dive operators, most of them based in Puntarenas, offer guided excursions to the island. Diving and food are included in the tour prices listed, but daily park fees are not.

Undersea Hunter DIVING
(2228-6613, in USA 800-203-2120; www.underseahunter.com) Offers 10- or 12-day land and sea expeditions with room for 14 to 18 people from US$5295 per person.

Okeanos Aggressor DIVING
(in USA & Canada 800-348-2628; www.aggressor.com) Offers 10-day land and sea expeditions with room for 22 from US$5135 per person.

Sleeping

While visitors are permitted to make landfall on Cocos during the day, they must return to their boat at night to sleep.

ℹ Information

In order to protect the conservation status of the island, all visitors must apply for a permit at the **Área de Conservación Marina Isla del Coco** (Acmic; in San José 2291-1215; Sabana Sur; 8am-3pm Mon-Fri) in San José. However, unless you're sailing to the island on a private boat, tour operators will make all the necessary arrangements for you.

ℹ Getting There & Away

With advance reservations, both of the tour companies listed earlier will arrange transfers from either San José or Liberia to Puntarenas, which is the embarkation/disembarkation point for tours.

TO CORCOVADO VIA PUERTO JIMÉNEZ

The first of two principal overland routes to Parque Nacional Corcovado, the Puerto Jiménez route on the eastern side of the peninsula is much more 'developed.' Of course, as this is Osa, development doesn't amount to much more than a single, devastatingly potholed road and a sprinkling of villages along the coast of Golfo Dulce. The landscape is cattle pastures and rice fields, while the Reserva Forestal Golfo Dulce protects much of the inland area. The largest settlement in the area is the town of Puerto Jiménez, which has transitioned from a boomtown for gold miners to an emerging ecotourism hot spot.

Reserva Forestal Golfo Dulce

The northern shore of the Golfo Dulce is home to this vast forest reserve, which links Parque Nacional Corcovado to the Parque Nacional Piedras Blancas. This connecting corridor plays an important role in preserving the biodiversity of the peninsula, and allowing the wildlife to migrate to the mainland. Although much of the reserve is not easily accessible, there are several lodges in the area doing their part to preserve this natural resource by protecting their own little pieces of this wildlife wonderland.

⊙ Sights & Activities

Most travelers skip the northern part of the peninsula and beeline for Puerto Jiménez to make arrangements to get into Parque Nacional Corcovado. If you have time to dawdle, there's lots of DIY wildlife-watching to be had. About 9km southeast of Rincón, the town of La Palma is the origin of the rough road that turns into the trail to Corcovado's Los Patos ranger station. If you're through-hiking Corcovado, this will likely be the starting or ending point of your trek. Before heading out, however, don't miss the chance to get some sun at the beautiful sand-and-coral beach, known as Playa Blanca, at the east end of town. The Reserva Indígena Guaymí de Osa is southwest of La Palma, on the border of Parque Nacional Corcovado. It's possible to arrange a homestay with a Ngöbe family (p426), who will meet you in La Palma for the journey into the reserve.

Just before entering Puerto Jiménez, a turnoff on the road leads 16km to the hamlet of Río Nuevo, also in the forest reserve. A good trail network leads to spectacular mountain viewpoints, some with views of the gulf. Bird-watching is excellent in this area: you can expect to see the many species that you would find in Corcovado. Most of the following lodges offer day-long excursions in this area.

Finca Köbö   OUTDOORS
(📞8398-7604; www.fincakobo.com; 3hr tours US$32; 🖐) ⬤ About 8km south of La Palma, Finca Köbö is a chocolate lover's dream come true (in fact, köbö means 'dream' in Ngöbere). The 20-hectare finca (farm) is dedicated to organic cultivation of fruits and vegetables and – the product of choice – cacao. Tours in English give a comprehensive overview of the life cycle of cacao plants and the production of chocolate (with degustation!). More than half of the territory is dedicated to protecting and reforesting natural ecosystems.

To really experience the beauty and vision of this finca, you can stay in simple, comfortable teak cabins (singles/doubles US$35/66,

meals US$8 to US$13), with lovely open-air bathrooms and quality linens. Those who stay longer can hike the surrounding forest trails and speak with local farmers.

🛏 Sleeping

Many of the accommodations along the northern part of the peninsula are lovely but isolated – great for honeymooners who want to get away, not too exciting for others. Backpackers tend to move past all the following and head to Puerto Jiménez.

★ Danta Corcovado Lodge   LODGE $$
(📞2735-1111; www.dantalodge.com; r/bungalow incl breakfast US$108/137; 🅿🛜) ⬤ Conveniently located midway between the Los Patos ranger station and La Palma, this low-key lodge is an ideal stopover for those starting or ending a Corcovado through-hike at Los Patos. Each of its delightful room and bungalow designs are dreamed up by the staff, ranging from comfortable wood cabins to a funky concrete dome – with open-air bathrooms and hot water. Winding through this family-run property are 4km of trails, and the lodge offers tours and activities, including day trips to Corcovado. Reserve as far in advance as possible, as this lovely spot fills up fast.

Suital Lodge   LODGE $$
(📞8826-0342; www.suital.com; s/d US$55/71) Lots of love has gone into the construction of this tiny clutch of cabinas on the northern shores of Golfo Dulce. It's situated 15km northeast of Rincón on 30 hectares of hilly, forested property (not a single tree has been felled), and guests can take advantage of a network of trails that winds through the property and down to the beach.

Bosque del Río Tigre   ECOLODGE $$$
(📞8705-3729; www.osaadventures.com; Dos Brazos; s/d US$190/324, 4-day package per per-

SOUTHERN COSTA RICA & PENÍNSULA DE OSA RESERVA FORESTAL GOLFO DULCE

son from US$538; P) ✎ On the edge of the Reserva Forestal Golfo Dulce, in the midst of a 13-hectare private reserve, this off-the-beaten-track ecolodge is a bird-watcher's paradise, and a place that's fancy without being pretentious. Four well-appointed guest rooms and one private, open-air cabin have huge windows for viewing birds. Find directions and intermittent closed periods on its website; email reservations preferred.

ⓘ Getting There & Away

The easiest way to travel on the eastern coast of the peninsula is by car. Otherwise, frequent buses ply the sole road between La Palma and Puerto Jiménez (US$0.50, 30 minutes).

Puerto Jiménez

Sliced in half by the swampy, overgrown Quebrada Cacao, and flanked on one side by the emerald waters of the Golfo Dulce, the vaguely Wild West outpost of Puerto Jiménez is shared equally by local residents and wildlife. While walking through the dusty streets of Port Jim (as the gringos are wont to call it), it's not unusual to spot scarlet macaws roosting on the soccer field, or white-faced capuchins traversing the treetops adjacent to the main street.

Then again, it's not too hard to understand why Puerto Jiménez is brimming with wildlife, mainly because the town lies on the edge of Parque Nacional Corcovado. As the preferred jumping-off point for travelers heading to the famed Sirena ranger station, the town is a great place to organize an expedition, stock up on supplies, eat a hot meal and get a good night's rest before hitting the trails.

Indeed, Puerto Jiménez is the 'big city' around these parts, and here you'll find the region's largest and most diverse offering of hotels, restaurants and other tourist services. But Puerto Jiménez is very much a close-knit community at its core, and its small-town charm and languid pace are surprisingly infectious. While it is understandably difficult to resist the pull of the deep jungle just beyond, consider putting the brakes on and lingering here for a few days.

History

Although it appears on maps dating to 1914, Puerto Jiménez used to be little more than a cluster of houses built on a mangrove swamp. With the advent of logging in the 1960s and the subsequent discovery of gold in the local streams, Jiménez became a small boomtown. The logging industry still operates in parts of the peninsula, but the gold rush has quietened down in favor of the tourist rush.

Even so, the town has a bit of a frontier feel, particularly in the low season, when locals huddle in bars to wait out the downpour. Now, instead of gold miners descending on the bars on weekends, it's outdoors types who come to have a shot of *guaro* (local firewater) and brag about the snakes, sharks and alligators they've tussled with.

◉ Sights & Activities

Even though Corcovado is the central attraction, there are plenty of other diversions. Boat tours around the Golfo Dulce are also increasingly popular. The all-day outings often include a mangrove tour, snorkeling excursion and dolphin-watching. Remember that it is illegal to swim with the dolphins, despite your guide's best intentions. These tours are typically booked through your accommodations; rates vary.

**Herrera Gardens & Conservation
Project**   GARDENS
(☏ 2735-5267; admission US$5, 2hr guided tour US$35; ⊙ 6am-5pm) The Herrera Gardens & Conservation Project is a 100-hectare reserve with beautiful botanical gardens. This innovative, long-term reforestation project offers an ecologically and economically sustainable alternative to cattle-grazing. Visitors can explore the 5km of garden trails or 15km of well-marked forest trails. It's located 400m east of the airstrip. Guided tours focus on birding, botany or even tree climbing. Stop by Jagua Arts & Crafts (p446) to buy a map or arrange your tour.

Playa Platanares   BEACH
About 5km east of town, the secluded – and often deserted – Playa Platanares is excellent for swimming, sunning and recovering from too much adventure. The nearby mangroves of Río Platanares are a paradise for kayaking and bird-watching.

☞ Tours

Puerto Jiménez has a host of tour operators, taxi drivers and touts hungry for the tourist dollar. Ask lots of questions, consult with fellow travelers and choose carefully.

Puerto Jiménez

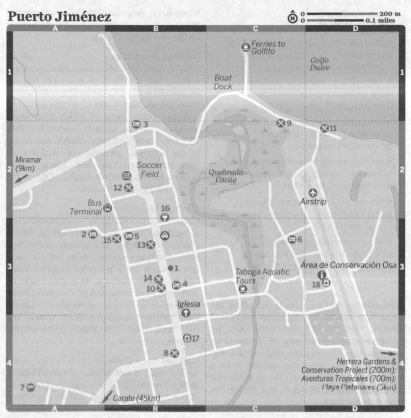

N 0 —————— 200 m
0 —————— 0.1 miles

Puerto Jiménez

Activities, Courses & Tours
Costa Rica Sportsman .... (see 6)
1 Osa Wild B3

Sleeping
2 Cabinas Back Packers A3
3 Cabinas Jiménez B2
4 Cabinas Marcelina B3
5 Cabinas the Corner B3
6 Cabinas Tropicales C3
7 Cacao Monkeys A4

Eating
8 BM Corcovado B4

9 Il Giardino C2
10 Jade Luna B3
11 Los Delfines D2
12 Pizzamail.it B2
13 Restaurant Carolina B3
14 Soda Valeria B3
15 Super 96 .... B3

Drinking & Nightlife
16 Juanita's B2

Shopping
17 Artes de Osa B4
18 Jagua Arts & Crafts D3

★ **Osa Wild**   TOUR
(☎ 8765-3330, 8376-1152, 2735-5848; www.osaw-
ildtravel.com; Rte 245, downtown Puerto Jiménez;
tours from US$25, one-day Corcovado tours US$75;
⊗ 8:30am-noon & 2:30-7pm) ✐ Osa Wild is
the way to connect with Corcovado park

and Osa. Although it's a relatively young
outfit, it's just what the area so desperately
needed: a resource for travelers to connect
with community-oriented initiatives that go
to the heart of the real Osa through homestays, farm tours and sustainable local cul-

DAY TRIPPER

You've got a free day in Puerto Jiménez and you don't want to hang around town? Here's what you can do:

➡ Take a trip to meet a local farmer or learn about rainforest medicine with Osa Wild (p443).

➡ Cross the bay and snuggle a spider monkey at Fundacíon Santuario Silvestre de Osa (p432).

➡ Kayak through the mangrove estuary to look for caimans, birds and monkeys with Aventuras Tropicales.

➡ Indulge your sweet tooth. See (and taste) where chocolate comes from at Finca Köbö (p441).

➡ Slow down and get some sun. Have a picnic on the deserted wilderness beach of Playa Blanca (p441).

tural exchanges. Of course it also offers the more typical stuff like kayaking tours and guided trips through Corcovado. Run by university-trained biologist Ifi, its focus on sustainability, environmental protection and community development put it in a league of its own. It also sets up volunteer programs and rents tents and stoves for trips into the park.

Aventuras Tropicales　　　ADVENTURE TOUR
(☑ 2735-5195; www.aventurastropicales.com) Aventuras Tropicales is a professional, Tico-run operation that offers all sorts of active adventures. Some of its most popular excursions include kayaking tours of the mangroves, which start at US$45 per person. Located 2km east on the road to Platanares.

Costa Rica Sportsman　　　FISHING
(☑ 8997-1445, 2735-5298; www.costaricasportsman.com; charters per day from US$800) This transplanted Florida fisherman has been organizing sportfishing charters in the area for over 20 years, and offers trips on vessels ranging from 7m to 15m. Located 50m west of the airstrip.

🛏 Sleeping

Puerto Jiménez is fairly quiet most times of the year, though reservations are always a good idea on weekends and during busy holidays. You'll find the greatest diversity of accommodations at the budget and midrange levels here, more so than in other parts of the Osa. Top-end options tend to be located on the outskirts of town.

Cabinas Tropicales　　　CABINA $
(☑ 2735-5298, 8997-1445; www.cabinas-tropicales.com; s/d from US$40/45; P ✳ @) The tidy accommodations at Cabinas Tropicales range from simple standards to roomy lofts and a deluxe suite, some of which have lovely outdoor showers. Each is unique, but they all have sturdy furniture, air-con and access to the gorgeous gardens and well-stocked open-air kitchen. Your host, Mark, is both personable and knowledgeable. One of the best-value options in town.

Cabinas Marcelina　　　HOTEL $
(☑ 2735-5007, 2735-5286; www.jimenezhotels.com/cabinasmarcelina; d with/without air-con US$50/45; P ✳ 🛜) Marcelina's place is a long-standing favorite among budget travelers looking for a peaceful night of sleep. The concrete building is painted salmon pink and is surrounded by blooming trees, lending it a homey atmosphere. Rooms have modern furniture, fluffy towels and tile bathrooms. It's 100m north of the church.

Cabinas Back Packers　　　HOTEL $
(☑ 2735-5181; d with/without air-con US$48/38; ✳ 🛜) Puerto Jiménez has a burden of riches with budget digs, but this is among the best of the bunch – it's squeaky clean, relatively quiet and situated directly next to the *colectivo* station leading to the park and just a bit out of the town, so you'll get a good night's sleep. There's a range of room options with differing amenities. It also rents tents and camping gear and there's even a brightly tiled kitchen, available for a US$5 fee.

Cabinas the Corner　　　HOSTEL $
(☑ 2735-5328; www.jimenezhotels.com/cabinasthecorner; dm US$10, d with/without bathroom US$14/12; P @ 🛜) While this family-run backpackers provides little more than a bed in a fan-cooled room for the night, the Corner is kept admirably clean and secure, and resultantly has a growing legion of fans. If all you need is a bit of shut-eye before heading to Corcovado, this is as good a place as any to link up with other trekkers.

★ Cabinas Jiménez　　　CABINA $$
(☑ 2735-5090; www.cabinasjimenez.com; s/d from US$35/50; P ✳ @ 🛜 ⊠) Cabinas Jiménez is

hands-down the nicest place to stay in town. All of the rooms have jungle scenes painted on the walls, with underwater murals in the hot-water bathrooms. Refrigerators and safes are practical, while details such as carved wooden furniture, woven textiles and batik curtains add an elegant flair. Pricier rooms have kitchenettes and fantastic views of the lagoon. Bikes and kayaks are free for guests' use, and the bilingual staff is friendly and helpful.

Cacao Monkeys
CABINA **$$**

(☑ 2735-5248; www.cacaomonkeys.com; s/d incl breakfast from US$40/60; **P** 🛜) On the fringes of downtown on a cacao farm, this jungle joint has a set of five brightly painted wooden *cabinas,* and an excellent riverside cafe (meals US$8). One *cabina* has a small kitchen, two are set up with a double and two single beds for families, and all have shiny hardwood floors and porches. It's a good option for families as it's a bit removed from the noise of town and there is loads of wildlife right out the door.

Iguana Lodge
HOTEL **$$$**

(☑ 8848-0752, in USA & Canada 800-259-9123; www.iguanalodge.com; d incl breakfast US$150, casitas per person incl 2 meals from US$186, villa US$599; **P** ✳) This luxurious lodge fronting Playa Platanares has the most architecturally alluring cabins in the area: four two-story bungalows have huge breezy decks, bamboo furniture, orthopedic beds draped in mosquito netting and lovely stone bathrooms with garden showers. The onsite restaurant serves three delectable meals a day: the creative cuisine is a highlight.

🍴 Eating & Drinking

The restaurant scene in Puerto Jiménez is surprisingly subdued considering all the tourist traffic passing through. Stock up on groceries at the locally run **Super 96** (Super Noventa y Seis; ☑ 2735-5168; ⊙ 6am-8pm Mon-Sat, 7am-7pm Sun) or the **BM Corcovado** (☑ 2735-5009; ⊙ 7am-9pm Mon-Sat, 8am-8pm Sun) across from the gas station.

Soda Valeria
SODA **$**

(Rte 245; mains US$3-8) Clean, cute and smack-dab in the middle of town, this *soda* is a dream – the kind of place you know is good because the local government workers all pile in at lunch. The heaping, fresh *casados* change daily and are delivered with fresh, homemade tortillas and sided with fresh fruit. Add considerate, quick service and Valeria is short-listed among our favorite *sodas* in all of Costa Rica.

Jade Luna
ICE CREAM **$**

(containers US$4; ⊙ 8am-5:30pm Mon-Sat) From a glance at the tastes of the day – boutiquey, inventive flavors like vegan dark-chocolate espresso and sweet-potato cheesecake – Jade Luna might seem a bit out of place in Puerto Jiménez. But the locally sourced, organic flavors are heaven after a sweaty hike in the park. Look for the stand along the main street.

Los Delfines
COSTA RICAN **$**

(☑ 2735-5083; meals US$4-10; ⊙ 10am-10pm) At the end of the beach road that passes the crumbling waterfront walk, Los Delfines is the perfect toes-in-the-sand spot for a late *gallo pinto* breakfast or a beer and delish *ceviche* after sunning on the crescent of beach just beyond.

Restaurant Carolina
COSTA RICAN **$**

(☑ 2735-5185; dishes US$3-8; ⊙ 6am-10pm) This is the hub in Puerto Jiménez. Expats, nature guides, tourists and locals all gather here for food, drinks and plenty of carousing. The food is famous locally and the fresh-fruit drinks and cold beers go down pretty easily on a hot day.

Il Giardino
ITALIAN **$$**

(☑ 2735-5129; www.ilgiardinoitalianrestaurant.com; meals US$9-14; ⊙ noon-10pm) While the possibly overextended menu touts sushi as an offering, Il Giardino shines when it sticks to Italian specialties – homemade pasta, gnocchi and pizza. Both service and cuisine can be inconsistent, but it has a reliably romantic waterfront ambience.

Pizzamail.it
PIZZERIA **$$**

(pizzas US$9-18; ⊙ 4-10:30pm; 🛜) A pizzeria may not instill lots of confidence when its name sounds more like a website. Still, all doubts will be cast aside when a server at Pizzamail.it brings out the pie: a thin-crust, wood-fired piece of Italy in the middle of the jungle. From its small patio, diners can watch squawking macaws in the trees over the soccer pitch. *Bellissimo!*

Juanita's
BAR

(☑ 2735-5056; www.juanitasmexican.com; ⊙ 5pm-2am) Bypass the so-so Mexican food at Juanita's in favor of the *sí-sí* margaritas.

🛍 Shopping

Jagua Arts & Crafts ARTS & CRAFTS
(☑2735-5267; ⊗6:30am-3:30pm) A superb collection of art and jewelry by local and expat craftspeople, including some amazing Boruca masks.

Artes de Osa ARTS & CRAFTS
(☑2735-5317; ⊗7am-7pm) This locally run souvenir shop has interesting handmade carvings, furniture and other handicrafts, all made by Costa Rican artisans.

ℹ Orientation

The compact, gridded and easily walkable town is located to the west of the Río Platanares, which feeds a modest estuary and mangrove forest before reaching the Golfo Dulce and ferry pier. On the east side are the Área de Conservación Osa headquarters and the airstrip. There is also a tiny access road leading to Playa Platanares, which is lined with a few upmarket properties.

ℹ Information

Área de Conservación Osa (ACOSA, Osa Conservation Area Headquarters; ☑2735-5036; Corcovado park fee per person per day US$10; ⊗8am-noon & 1-4pm Mon-Fri) Information about Parque Nacional Corcovado, Isla del Caño, Parque Nacional Marino Ballena and Golfito parks and reserves.

Banco Nacional (☑2735-5020; ⊗8:30am-3:45pm Mon-Fri) Due to completely inscrutable bureaucracy, money orders for the park must be purchased here; it also has an ATM.

BCR (Banco de Costa Rica; ☑2735-5260; ⊗9am-4pm Mon-Fri) Across from the church; it has an ATM.

ℹ Getting There & Around

AIR

NatureAir (☑2735-5428; www.natureair.com; ⊗6am-2pm) and **Sansa** (☑2735-5890; www.flysansa.com) have daily flights to/from San José; one-way flights are approximately US$130.

Alfa Romeo Aero Taxi (☑8632-8150; www.alfaromeoair.com) has light aircraft (for three and five passengers) for charter flights to Golfito, Carate, Drake, Sirena, Palmar Sur, Quepos and Limón. Prices are dependent on the number of passengers, so it's best to try to organize a larger group if you're considering this option. Sometimes, if there's already a trip planned into the park, the cost can be as low as US$60 per person.

BOAT

Several fast ferries travel to Golfito (US$6, 30 minutes), departing at 6am, noon and 2pm daily. Double-check current schedules, as they change often and without notice.

Alternatively, you could opt to hire a private water taxi to shuttle you across the bay. You will have to negotiate, but prices are generally reasonable, especially considering that you set the schedule. Fortunately, waters in the Golfo Dulce are sheltered and generally calm, though it's still good to have a reasonable degree of faith in the seaworthiness of both your captain and his ship before you set out.

Taboga Aquatic Tours (☑8379-0705, 2735-5265; www.tabogatours.com) runs water taxis to Zancudo for about US$50.

BUS

Most buses arrive at the peach-colored terminal on the west side of town. All of these pass La Palma (23km away) for the eastern entry into Corcovado.

Neily US$4.30, three hours, departs 5:30am and 2pm.

San Isidro de El General US$9.50, 5½ hours, departs 5am, 9am and 1pm.

San José US$15, eight hours, departs 5am and 9am.

CAR & TAXI

The *colectivo* (shared truck taxi) runs daily to Cabo Matapalo (1½ hours, US$6) and Carate (2½ hours, US$10) on the southern tip of the national park. Departures are from Soda Deya at 6am and 1:30pm, returning at 8:30am and 4pm.

Otherwise, you can call and hire a 4WD taxi from the **Central Taxi Center** (☑2735-5481). Taxis usually charge up to US$90 for the ride to Carate, about US$55 for the ride to Matapalo, and more than US$100 for the overland trek to Drake.

You can also rent a vehicle from **Solid Car Rental** (☑2735-5777; www.solidcarrental.com; ⊗7am-5pm).

Cabo Matapalo

If you didn't know that it was here, you would hardly suspect that the jungle-obscured community of Matapalo existed. There isn't much to the southern tip of the Osa peninsula save some lodges and homes here at the entrance to the Golfo Dulce. Matapalo lies just 17km south of Puerto Jiménez, but this heavily forested and beach-fringed cape is a vastly different world, and can be very hard to reach. A network of trails traverses the foothills, which are uninhabited except for migrating wildlife from the Reserva Forestal

Golfo Dulce. Along the coastline, miles upon miles of beaches in pristine wilderness are virtually empty, except for handfuls of surfers in the know.

Although facilities in this remote corner are extremely limited, Cabo Matapalo is home to a number of luxurious lodges that cater to travelers searching for peace and seclusion. Of course, it's hard to feel lonely out here given the breadth of animals about: scarlet macaw, brown pelican and all breeds of heron are frequently sighted on the beaches, while all four species of Costa Rican monkey, several wild cat species, sloth, coati, agouti and anteater roam the woods.

From the Puerto Jiménez–Carate road, the poorly marked turnoff for Cabo Matapalo is on the left-hand side, then through a crumbling cement gate (called 'El Portón Blanco').

Those who intended to surf their way down the country will find expert waves at Playa Pan Dulce. The best swell is from the south and it can be surfed at all tides, sometimes reaching double-overhead height.

☞ Tours

Psycho Tours   ADVENTURE TOUR
(Everyday Adventures; ☎ 8353-8619; www.psycho-tours.com; tours US$45-120) Naturalist Andy Pruter runs Psycho Tours, which offers high-adrenaline adventures in Cabo Matapalo. His signature tour is tree climbing (US$55 per person): scaling a 60m ficus tree, aptly named 'Cathedral.' Also popular – and definitely adrenaline inducing – is waterfall rappelling (US$120) down cascades ranging from 15m to 30m.

For the tamer of heart, excellent three- to four-hour guided nature walks (US$45) tap into the extensive knowledge base of Andy and his staff members.

🛏 Sleeping

This area is off the grid, so many places do not have electricity around the clock or hot water. Reservations are recommended in the dry season (mid-December to mid-April). Prices given are high-season rates and include three meals unless otherwise stated.

★ Encanta La Vida   LODGE $$$
(☎ 8376-3209, 2735-5678; www.encantalavida.com; Cabo Matapalo; s/d from US$209/294; P 🛜 ≋) The enchanted life, indeed. Gorgeous breeze-cooled, wood-beamed structures – from round tree houses to romantic, free-standing *casitas* – are scattered at the foot of a jungle-

clad backdrop. Howlers and spider monkeys regularly travel the treetops, while pairs of great curassows stroll shyly below. The food is brilliant, the atmosphere chilled and the location a perfect base for exploring the cape. An ocean-view yoga terrace is available for practice anytime and for classes; surfboards are available to rent; and tours can be arranged by the accommodating staff.

Lapa Ríos   LODGE $$$
(☎ 2735-5130; www.laparios.com; road to Carate, Km 17; s/d US$576/904; P ≋) 🍃 This top-notch all-inclusive wilderness resort combines the right amount of luxury with a rustic, tropical ambience. On the site are 16 spacious, thatched bungalows, all decked out with queen-sized beds, bamboo furniture, garden showers and private decks with panoramic views. An extensive trail system allows exploration of the 400-hectare reserve, while swimming, snorkeling and surfing are within easy reach. Rates include all meals, plus a round-trip transfer from Puerto Jiménez and various tours, classes and workshops. Reservations should be made as far in advance as possible.

Ojo del Mar   BUNGALOW $$$
(☎ 2735-5531; www.ojodelmar.com; road to Carate, Km 16; s/d incl breakfast from US$100/120, tents s/d incl breakfast US$50/70; P 🛜) 🍃 Tucked in amid the windswept beach and lush jungle, this is a little plot of paradise. The six beautifully handcrafted bamboo bungalows are entirely open-air, allowing for all the natural sounds and scents to seep in (though protected by thatch roofs and mosquito nets). Hammocks swing from the palms, while howler monkeys swing above. Rates include breakfast, but Nico – co-owner and cook – also serves an excellent, all-organic dinner. Yoga classes (US$12) are offered every morning.

Ranchos Almendros   CABINA $$$
(Kapu's Place; ☎ 2735-5531; http://home.earthlink.net/~kapu; Cabo Matapalo; r per person with/without meals from US$80/50; P) This is the end of the line on Cabo Matapalo, where the road stops pretending and turns into a sandy beach path. The property includes three cozy *cabañas* that are equipped with solar power, large screened windows, full kitchens and garden showers. Well-suited to surfers and self-sufficient types, these *cabañas* are practically steps from the beach and allow for self-catering. Advance booking recommended.

El Remanso Lodge
LODGE $$$

(☎2735-5569; www.elremanso.com; road to Carate, Km 18; s/d from US$245/320; [P][🛜][❄]) 🅿 Set on 56 hectares of rainforest, El Remanso is a tropical paradise founded by a couple of Greenpeace activists and now run by their daughter. Constructed entirely from fallen tropical hardwoods, the secluded, spacious and sumptuous cabins have shiny wood floors and beautifully finished fixtures. Miles of private trails lead through gardens to the beach, a waterfall and tidepools.

✖ Eating & Drinking

Most lodges in the area offer all-inclusive accommodations as there aren't many places to grab a bite (besides the lodges themselves). If you're planning on hiking, be sure to stock up on lots of fresh water and snacks – once you're out in the woods or on the beach, options are scarce.

Buena Esperanza Bar
BAR

(Casa Martina's; ☎2735-5531; road to Carate, Km 15; meals US$5-15; ⊙9am-10pm) About 1km before the Matapalo turnoff, you'll find this festive, open-air, tropical bar. The menu includes sandwiches, smoothies and vegetarian items, plus a full bar, and it hosts pizza nights on Wednesdays and an artisan market on Fridays starting at 4:20pm. It's Matapalo's only place to eat or drink, and so often attracts a mix of local residents and tourists.

❶ Getting There & Away

If you are driving, a 4WD is highly recommended even in the dry season, as roads frequently get washed out. There are several shallow rivers to cross on the way here. Otherwise, the *colectivo* (US$6) will drop you here; it passes by at about 7:30am and 3pm heading to Carate, and 9:30am and 4:30pm heading back to Jiménez. A taxi will come here from Puerto Jiménez for about US$55.

Carate

If you make it all the way here, congratulations. A bone-rattling 45km south of Puerto Jiménez, this is where the dirt road rounds the peninsula and comes to an abrupt dead end. There's literally nothing more than an airstrip and a *pulpería*. Carate is not a destination in itself, but it is the southwestern gateway for anyone hiking into Sirena ranger station in Parque Nacional Corcovado.

A handful of recommended wilderness lodges in the area make a good night's rest for travelers heading to/from Corcovado. The ride from Puerto Jiménez to Carate is also its own adventure as the narrow, bumpy dirt road winds its way around dense rainforest, through gushing rivers and across windswept beaches. Birdlife and other wildlife are prolific along this stretch: keep your eyes peeled and hang on tight.

🛏 Sleeping & Eating

Many places in Carate don't have 24-hour electricity or hot water. Reservations are recommended in the dry season – communication is often through Puerto Jiménez, so messages may not be retrieved every day. High-season rates are quoted; prices are per person, including three meals, unless otherwise stated. For shoestringers, the best option is to camp in the yard in front of the *pulpería*. The owner is an old Canadian guy who will charge you about US$5 a day to camp in his yard.

West of Carate is the national park, so if you're planning on hiking into Corcovado, you must be self-sufficient from here on. The *pulpería* is the last chance you have to stock up on food and water.

★ Luna Lodge
LODGE $$$

(☎2206-5859, in USA & Canada 888-760-0760; www.lunalodge.com; s/d from US$140/250; [P][🛜][❄]) 🅿 A steep road crisscrosses the Río Carate and up the valley to this enchanting mountain retreat on the border of Parque Nacional Corcovado. Accommodations in this dreamy wilderness retreat range from tent cabins to thatched bungalows with open-air garden showers and private terraces, but all have stunning views of the gardens and the pristine jungle rolling down to the ocean.

The open-air restaurant is a marvelous place to indulge in the expansive views, while an open-air yoga studio provides an even higher vantage point. Lana, the founder and owner of the lodge, is *passionate* about conservation and sustainability and has made the lodge a working practice in both.

Lookout Inn
HUT $$$

(☎2735-5431; www.lookout-inn.com; r per person from US$115; [P][@][❄]) Somehow perched up the side of a steep hillside overlooking the ocean, Lookout Inn has comfortable, open-air quarters with mural-painted walls, hard-

SIERPE SPHERES

Wander Costa Rica long enough and you may notice the odd decorative stone sphere in a garden, or their enormous counterparts gracing local museums. These pre-Columbian artifacts remain something of a mystery, from the methods of their manufacture to their very meaning. Few of these *esferas* (spheres) survive intact in situ, but you'll find two such specimens just outside of Sierpe in a newly established archaeological site maintained by the Museo Nacional de Costa Rica. **Sitio Arqueológico Finca 6** (☏2100-6000; finca6@museocostarica.go.cr; 4km north of Sierpe; admission US$6; ⊗8am-4pm Tue-Sun) offers the rare opportunity to view these spheres in their originally discovered locale, near culturally significant mounds 20m and 30m in diameter. You'll also see several spheres that have been moved, or exploded with dynamite to find the treasure inside (myth: busted). The onsite museum displays other fascinating artifacts discovered here, such as sculptures and *metates* (grain-grinding stones) – mysterious vestiges of Costa Rica's ancient people.

wood floors, beautifully carved doors and unbeatable views. Accommodations are accessible only by a wooden walkway winding through the trees. Interesting gimmick: if you don't spot a scarlet macaw during your stay, your lodging is free!

More traditional rooms are available in the main building. Behind the inn, 360 steps – known as the 'Stairway to Heaven' – lead straight up the side of the mountain to four observation platforms and a waterfall trail.

La Leona Eco-Lodge ECOLODGE **$$$**
(☏2735-5704; www.laleonaecolodge.com; s/d from US$160/280; ☷) ◢ On the edge of Parque Nacional Corcovado, this friendly lodge offers all the thrills of camping, without the hassles. Sixteen comfy forest-green tents are nestled between the palm trees, with decks facing the beach. All are fully screened and comfortably furnished; solar power provides electricity in the restaurant. All guests must hike the 2.5km in from the Carate airstrip.

❶ Getting There & Away

NatureAir (www.natureair.com) and **Alfa Romeo Aero Taxi** (www.alfaromeoair.com) offer charter flights. Prices are dependent on the number of passengers, so it's best to try to organize a larger group if you're considering this option. If you're with others, the rate can be as low as US$60.

The *colectivo* (US$10) departs Puerto Jiménez for Carate at 6am and 1:30pm, returning at 8:30am and 4pm. Note that the *colectivo* often fills up on its return trip to Puerto Jiménez, especially during the dry season. Arrive at least 30 minutes ahead of time or you might find yourself stranded.

Alternatively, catch a taxi from Puerto Jiménez (US$90). If you're driving you'll need a 4WD, even in the dry season, as there are a couple of river crossings. Assuming you don't have valuables in sight, you can leave your car at the *pulpería* (per night US$5) or at any of the tented camps along the road (with prior arrangements) and hike to La Leona station (1½ hours).

TO CORCOVADO VIA BAHÍA DRAKE

The Bahía Drake route is one of the principal overland routes to Parque Nacional Corcovado. This route starts in the town of Sierpe in the Valle de Diquis, at the northern base of the Península de Osa. From here, the valley stretches west to the basin of the Río Grande de Térraba and south to Sierpe, from where the Río Sierpe flows out to Bahía Drake. Although most travelers make a direct route between Sierpe, Drake and Corcovado, those who opt to take it slower may also meander through the Humedal Nacional Térraba-Sierpe, a vast reserve that protects an amazing array of jungle swampland and overgrown mangroves. The Drake route has more options for folks who want to explore the jungle with a few more comforts.

Sierpe

This sleepy village on the Río Sierpe is the gateway to Bahía Drake, and if you've made a reservation with any of the jungle lodges further down the coast, you will be picked up here by boat. Beyond its function as a transit point, there is little reason to spend any more time here than necessary, though you won't have to if you time the connection right.

La Perla del Sur (☎2788-1071, 2788-1082; info@perladelsur.net), the open-air restaurant and info center next to the boat dock, is the hub of Sierpe – arrange your long-term parking (US$6 per night), grab a bite at the lovely riverside restaurant (do not miss the coconut flan), book a tour and take advantage of the free wi-fi before catching your boat to Drake.

If you get stuck here, the dockside **Hotel Oleaje Sereno** (☎2788-1111; www.hoteloleaje-sereno.com; s/d incl breakfast from US$30/50; P❄) is a surprisingly nice little motel overlooking the Río Sierpe. It has pleasant rooms with wood floors and sturdy furniture, and is the most convenient digs in town.

Scheduled flights and charters fly into Palmar Sur, 14km north of Sierpe. If you are heading to Bahía Drake, most upmarket lodges will arrange the boat transfer. Should things go awry or if you're traveling independently, there's no shortage of water taxis milling about – be prepared to negotiate a fair price. Regularly scheduled *colectivo* boats depart Sierpe for Drake at 11:30am (US$15) and 4:30pm (US$20).

Buses to Palmar Norte (US$0.75, 40 minutes) depart from in front of Pulpería Fenix at 5:30am, 8:30am, 10:30am, 12:30pm, 3:30pm and 6pm. A taxi to Palmar costs about US$30.

Humedal Nacional Térraba-Sierpe

The Ríos Térraba and Sierpe begin on the southern slopes of the Talamanca mountains and, nearing the Pacific Ocean, they form a network of channels and waterways that weave around the country's largest mangrove swamp. This river delta comprises the Humedal Nacional Térraba-Sierpe, which protects approximately 330 sq km of wetland and is home to red, black and tea mangrove species. The reserve also protects a plethora of birdlife, especially waterbirds such as herons, egrets and cormorants.

🛏 Sleeping

Veragua River House   B&B $$
(☎2788-1460; www.hotelveragua.com/en; s/d incl breakfast US$50/60; P) Run by an accommodating Italian-Tico couple, this memorable B&B is set on a pair of riverside gardens lovingly planted with fruit trees and tropical flowers. Guests stay in the four garden bungalows, built in a uniquely Costa Rican Victorian architectural style. The B&B is easily reached by car; if you don't have private transportation, arrange a pick-up with the lodge. It's located 3km north of Sierpe. Lunch and dinner (US$15 to US$20) are also available with prior notice.

FLOATING FOREST

As many as seven different species of *manglar* (mangrove) thrive in Costa Rica. Comprising the vast majority of tropical coastline, mangroves play a crucial role in protecting it from erosion. Mangroves also serve as a refuge for countless species of animals, especially fish, crab, shrimp and mollusks, and as a sanctuary for roosting birds seeking protection from terrestrial predators.

Mangroves are unique among plants in that they have distinct methods for aeration (getting oxygen into the system) and desalination (getting rid of the salt that is absorbed with the water). Red mangroves, which are the most common species in Costa Rica, use their web of aboveground prop roots for aerating the plant's sap system. Other species, such as the black mangrove, have vertical roots that stick out above the mud, while buttonwood mangroves have elaborate buttresses.

The most amazing feature of the mangrove is its tolerance for salt, which enables the plant to thrive in brackish and saltwater habitats. Some species, such as the Pacific coast black mangrove, absorb the salinated water, then excrete the salt through their leaves and roots, leaving behind visible crystals. Other species filter the water as it is absorbed – the mangrove root system is so effective as a filter that the water from a cut root is drinkable!

Despite their ecological importance, mangrove habitats the world over are being increasingly threatened by expanding human habitats. Furthermore, mangrove wood is an easily exploitable source of fuel and tannin (used in processing leather), which has also hastened their destruction. Fortunately in the Humedal Nacional Térraba-Sierpe, this fragile yet vitally important ecosystem is receiving the respect and protection that it deserves.

❶ Information

The Térraba-Sierpe reserve has no facilities for visitors, though lodges can organize tours to help you explore the wetlands.

Bahía Drake

As one of Costa Rica's most isolated destinations, Bahía Drake *('drah-kay')* is a veritable Lost World filled with tropical landscapes and abundant wildlife. In the rainforest canopy, howlers greet the rising sun with their haunting bellows, while pairs of macaws soar between the treetops, filling the air with their cacophonous squawking. Offshore in the bay itself, pods of migrating dolphins flit through turquoise waters.

Of course, one of the reasons why Bahía Drake is brimming with wildlife is that it remains largely cut off from the rest of the country. With little infrastructure beyond dirt roads and the occasionally used airstrip, most of the area remains off the grid. However, Bahía Drake is home to a number of stunning wilderness lodges, which all serve as ideal bases for exploring this ecological gem.

History

The bay is named for Sir Francis Drake himself, who visited this area in March 1579, during his circumnavigation in the *Golden Hind*. History has it that he stopped on the nearby Isla del Caño, but locals speculate that he probably landed on the continent as well. A monument at Punta Agujitas, located on the grounds of the Drake Bay Wilderness Resort, states as much.

🏃 Activities

Hiking

All of the lodges offer tours to Parque Nacional Corcovado, usually a full-day trip to San Pedrillo or Sirena ranger stations (from US$85 to US$150 per person), including boat transportation, lunch and guided hikes. Indeed, if you came all the way to the Península de Osa, it's hard to pass up a visit to the national park that made it famous.

Some travelers, however, come away from these tours disappointed. The trails around San Pedrillo station attract many groups of people, which inhibit animal sightings. Furthermore, most tours arrive at the park well after sunrise, when activity in the rainforest has already quietened down.

If you're here to see wildlife, taking the time to spend a night in the park is the way to go, as many animals are at their most active around dawn and dusk. All park visitors are now required to be accompanied by a guide certified by the ICT (Costa Rica Tourism Board), so exploring the beaches and jungles with an eagle-eyed guide will reveal much more than you would likely discover on your own.

If you'd prefer to hike independently, the easiest and most obvious route is the long coastal trail that heads south out of Agujitas and continues about 10km to the border of the national park. A determined, reasonably fit hiker could make it all the way to San Pedrillo ranger station in three to four hours (though visitors intending to enter or spend the night in the park must have secured reservations in advance and must be accompanied by a guide). Hikers along this narrow, muddy trail should remember that sunset descends swiftly at around 5:30pm.

Other popular day hikes along this trail include **Playa Cocalito**, **Playa Caletas** and **Playa San Josecito**, a stunningly remote beach. Other nearby options include **Punta Río Claro Wildlife Refuge** (also called the Marenco Rainforest Reserve), which can be accessed from the Río Claro trail or from Playa San Josecito.

Swimming & Snorkeling

About 20km west of Agujitas, Isla del Caño is considered the best place for snorkeling in this area. Lodges offer day trips to the island (from US$80 per person), usually including the park fee, snorkeling equipment and lunch on Playa San Josecito. The clarity of the ocean and the variety of the fish fluctuate according to water and weather conditions: it's worth inquiring before booking.

There are other opportunities for snorkeling on the coast between Agujitas and Corcovado. Playa San Josecito attracts scores of colorful species, which hide out among the coral reef and rocks. Another recommended spot is Playa Caletas, just in front of the Corcovado Adventures Tent Camp, and Playa Cocalito, a small, pretty beach near Agujitas that is pleasant for swimming and sunbathing.

Scuba Diving

Isla del Caño (p457) is one of Costa Rica's top spots for diving, with attractions including intricate rock and coral formations and an amazing array of underwater life. Divers

Bahía Drake & Around

Bahía Drake & Around

report that the schools of fish swimming overhead are often so dense that they block the sunlight from filtering down.

While the bay is rich with dive sites, a local highlight is undoubtedly the **Bajo del Diablo** (Devil's Rock), an astonishing formation of submerged mountains that attracts an incredible variety of fish species, including jack, snapper, barracuda, puffer, parrotfish, moray eel and shark.

A two-tank dive runs from US$100 to US$150 depending on the site. Several upscale lodges have onsite dive centers, but most lodges in the area can arrange trips through a nearby dive center.

Kayaking & Canoeing

A fantastic way to explore the region's biodiversity is to paddle through it. The idyllic Río Agujitas attracts a huge variety of birdlife and lots of scaly reptiles. The river conveniently empties out into the bay, which is surrounded by hidden coves and sandy beaches ideal for exploring in a sea kayak. Paddling at high tide is recommended because it allows you to explore more territory. Most accommodations in the area have kayaks and canoes for rent for a small fee.

Sportfishing

Bahía Drake claims more than 40 fishing records, including sailfish, marlin, yellowfin tuna, wahoo, cubera snapper, mackerel and roosterfish. Fishing is excellent year-round, although the catch may vary according to the season. The peak season for tuna and marlin is from August to December. Sailfish are caught year-round, but experience a slowdown in May and June. Dorado and wahoo peak between May and August. Other species of fish are abundant year-round, so you are virtually assured to reel in something. Many lodges are able to arrange fishing excursions, but you need to be prepared to pay for the experience – half-/full-day excursions cost around US$600/1000.

Dolphin- & Whale-Watching

Bahía Drake is rife with marine life, including more than 25 species of dolphin and whale that pass through on their migrations throughout the year. This area is uniquely suited for whale-watching: humpback whales come from both the northern and the southern hemispheres to calve, resulting in the longest humpback whale season in the world. Humpbacks can be spotted in Bahía Drake year-round (except May), but the best months to see whales are late July through early November.

Several of the lodges are involved with programs that protect and preserve marine life in Bahía Drake, as well as programs that offer tourists a chance for a close encounter. Tours generally cost about US$100 per person. Note that since 2006 it has been illegal to swim with dolphins.

☞ Tours

Corcovado Info Center   TOUR
(☎8846-4734, 2775-0916; www.corcovadoinfo-center.com) Leading tours into Corcovado and Isla del Caño, all guides with this outfit are local, bilingual and ICT-certified. They're at the beach end of the main road in Agujitas.

Night Tour   TOUR
(☎8701-7462, 8701-7356; www.thenighttour.com; tours US$35; ☉7:30-10pm) Tracie the 'Bug Lady' has created quite a name for herself with this fascinating nighttime walk in the jungle. Tracie is a walking encyclopedia on bug facts, and not just the boring scientific detail – one of her fields of research is the military use of insects! Her Tico naturalist-photographer husband Gian also leads the night tours; reserve in advance.

Original Canopy Tour   CANOPY TOUR
(☎2291-4465, 8371-1598; www.jinetesdeosa.com/canopy_tour.htm; admission US$35; ☉8am-4pm) At Hotel Jinetes de Osa, the Original Canopy Tour has nine platforms, six cables and one 20m-observation deck from where you can get a new perspective on the rainforest. Tours take two to three hours.

🛏 Sleeping & Eating

This area is off the grid, so many places do not have 24/7 electricity. Reservations are recommended in the dry season (mid-December to mid-April).

While budget and midrange options are available in Agujitas, accommodations in Bahía Drake are heavily skewed toward the top end. This is largely because these all-inclusive lodges must incorporate the significant costs of transporting food into this remote area. The upside to upscale: you can expect tremendous quality and service for the money.

High-season rates are quoted; prices include three meals, unless otherwise stated. There are a handful of local restaurants, a bakery and *pulperías* in Agujitas.

All of the midrange and top-end accommodations listed in this section provide transportation (sometimes free, sometimes not) from either Agujitas or the airstrip in Drake with prior arrangements.

For other accommodations, check out the stretch of coastline from Bahía Drake to Corcovado.

Martina's Place   CABINA $
(☎8720-0801; www.puravidadrakebay.com; from US$15-20 per person without meals; ☎) With several crammed-together sheltered tents outside and a few fan-cooled rooms inside, all guests at this budget spot have access to a clean, thoroughly equipped communal kitchen. This friendly, economical place in the middle of Agujitas is an excellent spot to meet other budget travelers, tap into Martina's wealth of Corcovado intel and arrange a variety of local tours.

Cabinas Jade Mar   CABINA $
(☎8845-0394, 2384-6681; www.jademarcr.com; r per person without bathroom US$15, s/d with bathroom from US$25/40, all without meals; ℗❄☎) This quiet, family-run compound 150m up the main road from the beach in Agujitas offers rooms in wood-slat cottages amid a garden frequented by birds. The least

expensive rooms share bathrooms and a kitchen in one house, while the more spacious rooms and bungalows have terraces (some with ocean views). It's a sweet deal for these prices. The family can also arrange tours.

★ **Finca Maresia** BUNGALOW $$
(☑ 8888-1625, 2775-0279; www.fincamaresia. com; Camino a Los Planes; s/d budget US$30/40, standard US$50/60, superior US$75/90, all incl breakfast) After traveling the world for more than 20 years, the owners of this absolute gem of a hotel decided to settle down in their own veritable slice of paradise. Here amid a large *finca* that stretches across a series of hills, Finca Maresia beckons to budget travelers by offering a combination of low prices, high value and good design sense. All seven rooms overlook lush environs, and play a near-continuous audio track of jungle sounds.

Beyond the show-stopping natural setting, the good taste of the owners is evident as you walk from room to room and view the transition from modernist glass walls to Japanese-style sliding rice-paper doors.

Cabinas El Mirador CABINA $$
(☑ 2775-2727; www.miradordrakebay.com; per person incl meals from US$46; P ⑤) High on a hill at the northern end of Agujitas, El Mirador (Lookout Point) lives up to its name, offering spectacular views of the bay from its eight cozy cabins – catch the sunset from the balcony or climb to the lookout that perches above. The hospitable Vargas family ensures all guests receive a warm welcome. Rates include three square meals a day of hearty, home-cooked Costa Rican fare.

Hotel Jinetes de Osa HOTEL $$$
(☑ 2231-5806, in USA 866-553-7073; www.jinetesdeosa.com; s/d standard US$102/108, superior US$147/158, all incl breakfast; ⑤) Ideal for divers, the reasonably priced Jinetes de Osa boasts a choice bayside location that is literally steps from the ocean. Jinetes also runs a canopy tour, as well as one of the peninsula's top PADI dive facilities. Located just outside Agujitas, this sweet collection of rooms strikes the perfect balance between town and country.

Aguila de Osa Inn LODGE $$$
(☑ 2296-2190, toll-free in USA 866-924-8452; www. aguiladeosa.com; s/d 2-night package US$673/1130) On the east side of the Río Agujitas, this swanky lodge consists of roomy quarters with shining wood floors, cathedral ceilings and private decks with expansive ocean views. Diving and sportfishing charters are available to guests, as are significant discounts if you stay beyond two nights. Rates include all meals, plus an Isla del Caño tour and a Corcovado tour.

La Paloma Lodge LODGE $$$
(☑ 2293-7502, 2775-1684; www.lapalomalodge. com; 3-/4-/5-day package per person from US$1119/1379/1667; ✳ ⑤ ✉) Perched on a lush hillside, this exquisite lodge provides guests with an incredible panorama of ocean and forest, all from the comfort of the sumptuous, stylish quarters. Rooms have shiny hardwood floors and queen-sized orthopedic beds, draped in mosquito netting, while shoulder-high walls in all the bathrooms offer rainforest views while you bathe. Each room has a large balcony (with hammock, of course) that catches the cool breeze off the ocean. Rates for stays of three days or more include a tour to both Isla del Caño and Corcovado.

Drake Bay Wilderness Resort CABIN $$$
(☑ 2775-1715; www.drakebay.com; 4-day package s/d from US$1310/1660; ✳ ✉) Sitting pretty on Punta Agujitas, this relaxed resort occupies the optimal piece of real estate in all of Bahía Drake. Naturalists will be won over by the lovely landscaping, from flowering trees to the rocky oceanfront outcroppings, while history buffs will appreciate the memorial to Drake's landing. Accommodations are in comfortable cabins, which have mural-painted walls and ocean-view terraces. Book early, as research and university groups often use the lodge as their home base.

Restaurante Mar y Bosque COSTA RICAN $
(☑ 8313-1366; dishes US$4-16; ⊙ 5:30am-9pm; ⑤) This restaurant up the hill in Agujitas has a spacious terrace from where it's possible to catch a cool breeze and spot pairs of scarlet macaws passing overhead. Serving typical Tico cuisine and an array of desserts, it even has free wi-fi.

ⓘ Orientation

The shores of Bahía Drake are home to two settlements: Agujitas, a tiny town of 300 residents spread out along the southern shore of the bay, and Drake, a few kilometers to the north, which is little more than a few houses alongside the airstrip.

If you're visiting the area on a budget, the best bet is to stay in Agujitas, a one-road town. That road comes south from Rincón and past the airstrip in Drake. At the T, the right branch dead-ends at the water, where the *pulpería*, clinic and school constitute the heart of Agujitas; the left branch heads out of town southeast to Los Planes. From the eastern end of Agujitas, a path follows the shoreline out of town. A swinging, swaying pedestrian bridge crosses the Río Agujitas to Punta Agujitas. From here, the trail picks up and continues south along the coast, all the way to Parque Nacional Corcovado.

The only way to get around the area is by boat or by foot. Fortunately, both forms of transportation are also recreation, as sightings of macaws, monkeys and other wildlife are practically guaranteed.

ⓘ Getting There & Away

AIR

Departing from San José, **NatureAir** (www. natureair.com) and **Sansa** (www.flysansa.com) have daily flights to the Drake airstrip, which is 2km north of Agujitas. Prices vary according to season and availability, though you can expect to pay around US$140 to/from San José.

Alfa Romeo Aero Taxi (☑ 8632-8150; www. alfaromeoair.com) offers charter flights connecting Drake to Puerto Jiménez, Golfito, Carate and Sirena. Flights are best booked at the airport in person; one way fares are typically less than US$100.

Most lodges provide transportation to/from the airport or Sierpe, which involves a jeep or a boat or both, but advance reservation is necessary.

BOAT

Unless you charter a flight, you'll arrive here by an exhilarating boat ride through mangrove channels and the ocean. It's one of the true thrills of visiting the area. Boats travel along the river through the rainforest and the mangrove estuary. Captains then pilot boats through tidal currents and surf the river mouth into the ocean. All of the hotels offer boat transfers between Sierpe and Bahía Drake with prior arrangements. Most hotels in Drake have beach landings, so wear appropriate footwear.

If you have not made advance arrangements with your lodge for a pick-up, two *colectivo*

boats depart daily from Sierpe at 11:30am and 4:30pm, and from Bahía Drake back to Sierpe at 7:15am (US$15) and 2:30pm (US$20).

CAR

A rough dirt road links Agujitas to Rincón, from where you can head south to Puerto Jiménez or north to the Interamericana. A 4WD is absolutely necessary for this route, especially from June to December, as there are several river crossings. The most hazardous crossing is the Río Drake – locals fish many a water-logged tourist vehicle out of the river. Even high-clearance 4WD vehicles have difficulty.

Once in Agujitas, you will likely have to abandon your car as most places are accessible only by boat or by foot. As theft or vandalism is always a very real possibility in Costa Rica, you should park your car in a secure place, and pay someone to watch it for a few days. There are several small *pulperías* where the management would be happy to watch over your 4WD for a nice tip.

HIKING

From Agujitas, it's a three- to four-hour hike along the beachside trail to San Pedrillo ranger station at the north end of Corcovado. For a more relaxed day trip with some downtime on a secluded beach, a round-trip hike from Agujitas to Playa Cocalito or Playa Caletas makes for a beautiful day; you could even stop for a drink or lunch at one of the lodges along the way.

Bahía Drake to Corcovado

This craggy stretch of coastline is home to sandy inlets that disappear at high tide, leaving only the rocky outcroppings and luxuriant rainforest. Virtually uninhabited and undeveloped beyond a few tourist lodges, the setting here is magnificent and wild. If you're looking to spend a bit more time along the shores of Bahía Drake before penetrating the depths of Parque Nacional Corcovado, consider a night or two in some of the country's most remote accommodations.

The only way to get around the area is by boat or by foot, which means that travelers are more or less dependent on their lodges.

⊙ Sights & Activities

A public trail follows the coastline for the entire spectacular stretch, and it's excellent for wildlife-spotting. Among the multitude of bird species, you're likely to see squawking scarlet macaws and the chestnut-mandibled toucan. White-faced capuchin and howler monkeys inhabit the treetops, while eagle-eyed hikers might also spot a sloth or a kinkajou.

Scenic little inlets punctuate this entire route, each with a wild, windswept beach. Just west of Punta Agujitas, a short detour off the main trail leads to the picturesque Playa Cocalito, a secluded cove perfect for sunning, swimming and body surfing. With no lodges in the immediate vicinity, it's often deserted. Playa Caletas, in front of the Corcovado Adventures Tent Camp, is excellent for snorkeling.

Further south, the Río Claro empties out into the ocean. Water can be waist-deep or higher, and the current swift, so take care when wading across. This is also the start of the Río Claro trail, which leads inland into the 400-hectare Punta Río Claro Wildlife Refuge (formerly known as the Marenco Rainforest Reserve) and passes a picturesque waterfall along the way. Be aware that there are two rivers known as the Río Claro: one is located near Bahía Drake, while the other is inside Corcovado near Sirena station.

South of Río Claro, the Playa San Josecito is the longest stretch of white-sand beach on this side of the Península de Osa. It is popular with swimmers, snorkelers and sunbathers, though you'll rarely find it crowded.

The border of Parque Nacional Corcovado is about 5km south of Playa San Josecito (it's about 16km in total from Agujitas to Corcovado). The trail is more overgrown as it gets closer to the park, and in the months after the rainy season it can close completely. Ask around in Agujitas or your lodge before embarking on this route.

🛏 Sleeping & Eating

Reservations are recommended in the dry season (mid-December to mid-April). High-season rates are quoted; prices include three meals, unless otherwise stated. Many places in this area don't have 24-hour electricity (pack a flashlight) or hot water. Stand-alone eating options are virtually nonexistent in this part of the peninsula.

With prior arrangements, all of the accommodations listed in this section provide transportation (free or for a charge) from Agujitas, Sierpe or the airstrip in Drake.

★ **Las Caletas Lodge** LODGE $$
(☑ 8863-9631, 8826-1460, 2560-6602; www.caletas.cr; Playa Caletas; tents/r per person from US$70/80; @ 🛜) 🍽 This adorable lodge consists of cozy wooden cabins and safari tents perched above the picturesque beach of the same name. The Swiss and Tico owners are warm hosts who established this convivial spot before there was phone access or electricity (now mostly solar- and hydro-powered). The food is delicious and bountiful, the staff friendly and the environment beautifully chill.

Proyecto Campanario CAMPGROUND $$$
(☑ 2289-8694, in USA 888-722-6769; www.campanario.org; 4-day package per person US$489) 🍽 Run by a former Peace Corps volunteer, this biological reserve is more of an education center than a tourist facility, as evidenced by the dormitory, library and field station. Ecology courses and conservation camps are scheduled throughout the year, but individuals are also invited to take advantage of the facilities.

Copa de Arbol LODGE $$$
(☑ 8935-1212, in USA 831-246-4265; www.copadearbol.com; Playa Caletas; s/d from US$382/610; 🛜 🌊) Though they look a bit rustic from the outside with their thatch roofs and stilts, these *cabinas* are gorgeously outfitted inside – built with sustainably grown wood and recycled materials, each has a private terrace and air-con. The lodge, located just steps from the beach, is all laid-back luxury, run smoothly by super-friendly staff.

Paddleboards and kayaks are available to rent.

Guaria de Osa LODGE $$$
(☑ 2235-4313, in USA 510-235-4313; www.guariadeosa.com; per person US$150; 🛜) Cultivating a new-age ambience, this Asian-style retreat center offers yoga, tai chi and 'Sentient Experiential' events, along with the more typical rainforest activities. The lovely grounds include an ethnobotanical garden, which features exotic local species. The architecture of this place is unique: the centerpiece is the Lapa Lapa Lounge, a spacious multi-story pagoda built entirely from reclaimed hardwood.

POISON DARTS & HARMLESS ROCKETS

Traversed by many streams and rivers, Corcovado is a hot spot for exquisitely beautiful poison-dart frogs. Two species here, the granular poison-dart frog and the Golfo Dulce poison-dart frog, are Costa Rican endemics – the latter only occurs in and around Corcovado. A search of the leaf litter near Sirena ranger station readily turns up both species, as well as the more widespread green and black poison-dart frog.

You might also find some other members of the family that have one important difference: they're not poisonous! Called rocket frogs because of their habit of launching themselves into streams when disturbed, they are essentially poison-dart frogs without the poisonous punch.

The difference is likely in their diets. Poison-dart frogs have a diet dominated by ants, which are rich in alkaloids, and are thought to give rise to their formidable defenses. Rocket frogs also eat ants but in lower quantities, and rely instead on their astounding leaps to escape predation. They also lack the dazzling warning colors of their toxic cousins.

Costa Rica's poison-dart frogs are not dangerous to humans unless their toxins come into contact with a person's bloodstream or mucous membranes. It's probably best to admire their cautionary colors without touching.

Corcovado Adventures
Tent Camp CAMPGROUND $$$
(☑ 8386-2296, in USA 866-498-0824; www.corcovado.com; 2-day package per person from US$299; ☎) Less than an hour's walk from Agujitas brings you to this rugged family-run spot. It's like camping but comfy: spacious safari tents are set up on covered platforms and fully equipped with sturdy wood furniture. Twenty hectares of rainforest offer plenty of opportunity for exploration, and the beachfront setting is excellent for kayaking, snorkeling and boogie-boarding (equipment rental is free).

Casa Corcovado Jungle Lodge LODGE $$$
(☑ 2256-3181, in USA 888-896-6097; www.casacorcovado.com; s/d 4-day package from US$1025/1830; ☎✱) ◢ A spine-tingling boat ride takes you to this luxurious lodge on 175 hectares of rainforest bordering the national park. Each bungalow is tucked away in its own private tropical garden, and artistic details, including antique Mexican tiles and handmade stained-glass windows, make the Casa Corcovado one of this area's classiest accommodation options.

Guests can also stretch their legs at any time on the lodge's extensive network of trails, which pass a number of watering holes. On site, the Margarita Sunset Bar lives up to its name, serving up margaritas and great sunset views over the Pacific. Discounts are available for longer stays.

❶ Getting There & Away

BOAT
All of the hotels offer boat transfers between Sierpe and Bahía Drake with prior arrangements. If you have not made advance arrangements with your lodge for a pick-up, two *colectivo* boats depart daily from Sierpe at 11:30am and 4:30pm, and from Bahía Drake back to Sierpe at 7:15am (US$15) and 2:30pm (US$20).

HIKING
From Bahía Drake, it's a three- to four-hour hike along the beachside trail to San Pedrillo ranger station at the north end of Corcovado. Note that this trail can be impassable and overgrown depending on the season. Advance reservations are required if you're planning to camp overnight at the ranger station.

Reserva Biológica Isla del Caño

The centerpiece of this biological reserve is a 326-hectare island that is the tip of numerous underwater rock formations. Along the rocky coastline, towering peaks soar as high as 70m, which provides a dramatic setting for anyone who loves secluded nature.

The submarine rock formations are among the island's main attractions, drawing divers to explore the underwater architecture. Snorkelers can investigate the coral and rock formations along the landing beach. Fifteen different species of coral have been recorded,

SOUTHERN COSTA RICA & PENÍNSULA DE OSA RESERVA BIOLÓGICA ISLA DEL CAÑO as well as threatened species that include the Panulirus lobster and the giant conch. The sheer numbers of fish attract dolphins and whales, which – along with hammerhead sharks, manta rays and sea turtles – are frequently seen swimming in these waters.

On the island, at about 110m above sea level, the evergreen trees consist primarily of milk trees (also called 'cow trees' after the drinkable white latex they exude), believed to be the remains of an orchard planted by pre-Columbian indigenous inhabitants. Near the top of the ridge, there are several pre-Columbian granite spheres. Archaeologists speculate that the island may have been a ceremonial or burial site for the same indigenous tribes.

To preserve the ecology of the island, recreational visitors were prohibited from venturing beyond the boat-landing beach at the end of 2013.

Most snorkeling and diving tours are arranged by the nearby lodges. Admission is US$10 per person, plus a US$4 additional charge for divers; the fee is usually included in tour prices.

PARQUE NACIONAL CORCOVADO

Famously labeled by *National Geographic* as 'the most biologically intense place on earth,' this national park is the last great original tract of tropical rainforest in Pacific Central America. The bastion of biological diversity is home to Costa Rica's largest population of scarlet macaws, as well as countless other endangered species, including Baird's tapir, the giant anteater and the world's largest bird of prey, the harpy eagle. Corcovado's amazing biodiversity has long attracted a devoted stream of visitors who descend from Bahía Drake and Puerto Jiménez to explore the remote location and spot a wide array of wildlife.

History

Because of its remoteness, Corcovado remained undisturbed until loggers invaded in the 1960s. The destruction was halted in 1975 when the area was established as government-administered parklands. In the early days park authorities had limited personnel and resources to deal with illegal clear-cutting, poaching and gold mining, the last of which was causing severe erosion in the park's rivers and streams. By 1986 the number of gold miners had exceeded 1000, which promptly caused the government to evict them (and their families) from the park.

Illegal logging has all but subsided, primarily since tourism has led to an increased human presence in the park. Furthermore, a coalition of organizations – including Conservation International, the Nature Conservancy and the World Wildlife Fund – has banded together to help organize and fund the park's antipoaching units.

Since 2003 Corcovado has – much to the chagrin of Minae (the Ministry of Environment and Energy) – remained stagnant on the 'tentative list' of Unesco World Heritage Sites. While no official disclosure has been released as to the reason behind the park's perennial failure to achieve recognition, local media speculate that mismanagement, poor funding and the inability to control illegal poaching may be contributing factors.

🏃 Activities

Wildlife-Watching

The best wildlife-watching in Corcovado is at Sirena, but the coastal trails have two advantages: they are more open, and the constant crashing of waves covers the sound of noisy walkers. White-faced capuchin, red-tailed squirrel, collared peccary, white-nosed coati and northern tamandua are regularly seen on both of the following trails.

The coastal trail from Carate to Sirena produces an endless pageant of birds. Sightings of scarlet macaws are guaranteed, as the tropical almond trees lining the coast are a favorite food. The sections along the beach shelter mangrove black hawk by the dozens and numerous waterbird species.

The Los Patos–Sirena trail attracts lowland rainforest birds such as great curassow, chestnut-mandibled toucan, fiery-billed aracari and rufous piha. Encounters with mixed flocks are common. Mammals are similar to those near coastal trails, but Los Patos is better for primates and white-lipped peccary.

For wildlife-watchers frustrated at the difficulty of seeing rainforest mammals, a stay at Sirena ranger station is a must. Baird's tapirs are practically assured – a statement that can be made at few other places in the world. This endangered and distant relative of the rhinoceros is frequently spotted grazing along the airstrip

Hiking in Parque Nacional Corcovado

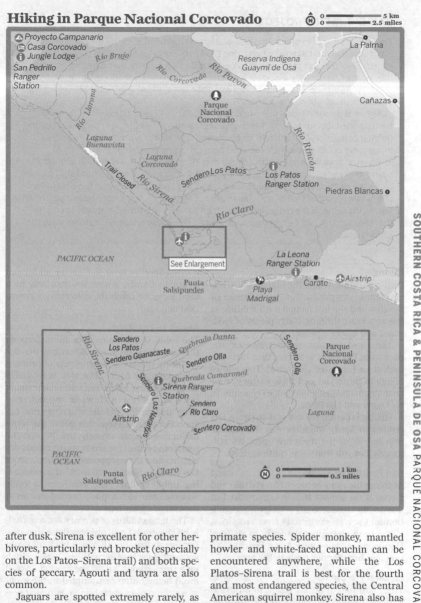

after dusk. Sirena is excellent for other herbivores, particularly red brocket (especially on the Los Patos–Sirena trail) and both species of peccary. Agouti and tayra are also common.

Jaguars are spotted extremely rarely, as their population in the Osa is suspected to be in the single digits. At night look for kinkajou and crab-eating skunk (especially at the mouth of the Río Sirena). Ocelot represents your best chance for observing a cat, but again, don't get your hopes up.

Corcovado is the only national park in Costa Rica with all four of the country's primate species. Spider monkey, mantled howler and white-faced capuchin can be encountered anywhere, while the Los Platos–Sirena trail is best for the fourth and most endangered species, the Central American squirrel monkey. Sirena also has fair chances for the extremely hard-to-find silky anteater, a nocturnal animal that frequents the beachside forests between the Río Claro and the station.

The Río Sirena is a popular spot for American crocodile, three-toed sloth and bull shark.

BAIRD'S TAPIR PROJECT

The Baird's Tapir Project (http://savetapirs.org) has been studying the populations of Baird's tapir around Sirena station since 1994 in the hope of enhancing conservation efforts. Scientists use radio collars to collect data about where the tapirs live, how far they wander, whom they associate with and how often they reproduce. So far, several dozen tapirs around Sirena have been wearing collars, allowing scientists to collect the data without disrupting the animals.

Sirena station is an ideal place to do such research, because there is no pressure from deforestation or hunting, which gives researchers the chance to observe a healthy, thriving population. The animals' longevity and slow rate of reproduction mean that many years of observation are required before drawing conclusions.

So, what have we learned about these river rhinos so far? The nocturnal animals spend their nights foraging – oddly, they prefer to forage in 'disturbed habitats' (such as along the airstrip), not in the dense rainforest. They spend their days in the cool waters of the swamp, out of the hot sun. Tapirs are not very social, but a male-female pair often shares the same 'home range,' living together for years at a time. Scientists speculate that tapirs may in fact be monogamous – who knew these ungainly creatures would be so romantic!

Hiking

Paths are primitive and the hiking is hot, humid and insect-ridden, but the challenge of the trek and the interaction with wildlife at Corcovado are thrilling. Carry plenty of food, water and insect repellent.

The most popular route traverses the park from Los Patos to Sirena, then exits the park at La Leona (or vice versa). This allows hikers to begin and end their journey in or near Puerto Jiménez, offering easy access to La Leona and Los Patos.

Hiking is best in the dry season (from December to April), when there is still regular rain but all of the trails are open. It's still muddy, but you won't sink quite as deep.

San Pedrillo to Sirena   HIKING

At 23km, the route between San Pedrillo and Sirena is the longest trail in Corcovado, but due to its treacherously overgrown condition and several dangerous river crossings, it has been closed permanently to visitors. However, you can camp at San Pedrillo station and hike various trails in the area.

La Leona to Sirena   HIKING

The 16km hike from La Leona to Sirena is a sizzler, following the shoreline through coastal forest and along deserted beaches. It involves one major river crossing at Río Claro, just south of Sirena station.

The journey between La Leona and Sirena takes six or seven hours. You can camp at either ranger station, and Sirena also has dorm accommodations and hot meals (both must be reserved in advance). From Sirena,

it takes another hour to hike the additional 3.5km to Carate, where you can stay in a local lodge or catch the *colectivo* to Puerto Jiménez.

Sirena to Los Patos   HIKING

The route to Los Patos goes 18km through the heart of Corcovado, affording the opportunity to pass through plenty of primary and secondary forest. The trail is relatively flat for the first 12km. You will hike through secondary forest and wade through two river tributaries before reaching the Laguna Corcovado. From this point, the route undulates steeply (mostly uphill!) for the remaining 6km. One guide recommends doing this hike in the opposite direction – from Los Patos to Sirena – to avoid this exhausting, uphill ending. Near Los Patos, a lovely waterfall provides a much-needed shower at the end of a long trek.

The largest herds of peccary are reportedly on this trail. Local guides advise that peccary sense fear, but they will back off if you act aggressively. Alternatively, if you climb up a tree – about 2m off the ground – you'll avoid being bitten or trampled in the event of running into a surly bunch. Fun fact: peccary herds emit a strong smell of onions, so you usually have a bit of a heads-up before they come crashing through the bush.

You can camp at Los Patos, or continue an additional 14km to the village of La Palma. This four-hour journey is a shady and muddy descent of the valley of the Río Rincón. If you are traveling from La Palma to Los Patos, be prepared for a steep climb. The Danta Corcovado Lodge (p441) also makes a heavenly overnight near the Los Patos station.

👉 Tours

Changes to park regulations in early 2014 mean that all visitors to Corcovado must be accompanied by an ICT-certified guide. Besides their intimate knowledge of the trails, local guides are amazingly informed about flora and fauna, including the best places to spot various species. Most guides also carry telescopes, allowing for up-close views of wildlife.

Guides are most often hired through the Área de Conservación Osa park office (p446) in Puerto Jiménez, or through hotels and tour operators. Two recommended local offices are the super-reliable, locally run Osa Wild (p443) in Puerto Jiménez and Corcovado Info Center (p453) in Bahía Drake. Prices vary considerably depending on the season, availability, size of your party and type of expedition you want to arrange. In any case, you will need to negotiate a price that includes park fees, meals and transportation.

🛏 Sleeping & Eating

Camping costs US$4 per person per day at any of the ranger stations; facilities include potable water and latrines. Sirena station has a covered platform, but other stations have no such luxuries. Remember to bring a flashlight or a headlamp, as the campsites are pitch black at night. Camping is not permitted in areas other than the ranger stations.

Simple dormitory lodging (US$8 per person) is available at Sirena station only. Here, you'll find vinyl mattresses and simple bunk beds. The station serves decent meals (breakfast is US$20, lunch or dinner is US$25) by advance reservation only; if packing in your own food, no cooking is allowed, so be sure it's edible as is or with cold preparation.

All visitors are required to pack out all of their trash.

ℹ Information

Information and maps are available at the office of Área de Conservación Osa (p446) in Puerto Jiménez. If you hire a guide through a tour agency, the agency will make all the arrangements for you and include the required fees in the package price. If you hire a guide independently, you may have to make the reservations for lodging and meals yourself. Be sure to make these arrangements a few days in advance, especially in dry season, as there's a daily limit to the number of visitors allowed in the park and facilities sometimes hit their maximum capacity.

Park headquarters are at Sirena ranger station on the coast in the middle of the park. Other ranger stations are located on the park boundaries: San Pedrillo station in the northwest corner on the coast; La Leona station in the southeast corner on the coast (near the village of Carate); and Los Patos ranger station in the northeast corner (near the village of La Palma).

ℹ Getting There & Away

AIR

Alfa Romeo Aero Taxi (☎ 2735-5353; www.alfaromeoair.com) offers charter flights connecting Puerto Jiménez, Drake and Golfito to Carate and Sirena. Flights are best booked at the airport in person, and one-way fares are typically less than US$100. Note that long-term parking is not available at any of these locations, so it's best to make prior arrangements if you need to leave your car somewhere.

FROM BAHÍA DRAKE

From Bahía Drake, you can walk the coastal trail that leads to San Pedrillo station (about

ℹ CORCOVADO LOGISTICS

As of February 2014, Minae (Ministry of Environment & Energy) made the Osa-shaking announcement that *all* visitors to Parque Nacional Corcovado – including day-trippers – must be accompanied by a guide certified by the ICT (Costa Rica Tourism Board). While this change puts the kibosh on DIY expeditions and represents a significant addition to travelers' expenses, it does mean that all visitors will receive a more in-depth Corcovado experience, enhanced by the rich expertise of a local guide. It will also allow a greater number of qualified guides to make a living, while lessening the environmental impact on this increasingly popular wilderness area.

Though hiring a guide may require a bit more advance planning, guides or agencies will typically organize all of the reservations and logistical arrangements for your party. Guides' fees are usually on a per-day basis, so if you can round up another fellow traveler or three, the cost is more than reasonable.

four hours from Agujitas). Many lodges run day tours here, with a boat ride to San Pedrillo (30 minutes to an hour, depending on the departure point) or Sirena (one to 1½ hours). You can make camping reservations at San Pedrillo or Sirena stations.

FROM CARATE

In the southeast, the closest point of access is Carate, from where La Leona station is a one-hour, 3.5km hike west along the beach.

Carate is accessible from Puerto Jiménez via a poorly maintained, 45km dirt road. This journey is an adventure in itself, and often allows for some good wildlife-spotting along the way. A 4WD *colectivo* travels this route twice daily for US$10. Otherwise you can hire a 4WD taxi; prices depend on the size of your party, the season (prices increase in the rainy months) and your bargaining skills.

If you have your own car, the *pulpería* in Carate is a safe place to park for a few days, though you'll have some extra peace of mind if you tip the manager before setting out.

FROM LA PALMA

From the north, the closest point of access is the town of La Palma, from where you can catch a bus or taxi south to Puerto Jiménez or north to San José.

Heading to Los Patos station, you might be able to find a taxi to take you partway; however, the road is only passable to 4WD vehicles (and not always), so be prepared to hike the 14km to the ranger station. The road crosses the river about 20 times in the last 6km. It's easy to miss the right turn shortly before the ranger station, so keep your eyes peeled.

If you have a car, it's best to leave it with a hotel or lodge in La Palma instead of traversing the route to Los Patos, though it certainly is an adventure. Furthermore, once at Los Patos there is no reliable place to park your car while trekking in the park.

Understand Costa Rica

Costa Rica Today

Still slowly bouncing back from the global economic crisis of 2008, Costa Rica remains its peacefully stable, if ever-so-mildly stirred-up self. The 2014 presidential election will provide plenty of conversational fodder when the results shake out, and new disputes over the Nicaraguan border have whipped up old resentments. But the economy is regaining strength as tourists return in increasing numbers.

Best in Print

Tropical Nature: Life and Death in the Rain Forests of Central and South America (Adrian Forsyth and Ken Miyata; 1987) Easy-to-digest natural-history essays explain rainforest phenomena.

Costa Rica: The Last Country the Gods Made (Adrian Colesberry and Brass MacLean; 1993) Beautiful photographs by Kimberly Parsons are accompanied by quirky vignettes.

Costa Rica: A Traveler's Literary Companion (Barbara Ras, foreword by Óscar Arias; 1994) Collection of stories reflecting distinct regions of Costa Rica.

Best on Film

El Regreso (The Return; 2011) Featuring a realistic, contemporary plot, this is the first Tico (Costa Rican) film to earn international acclaim; Hernán Jiménez wrote, directed, starred in and crowdfunded it.

Agua Fría de Mar (Cold Ocean Water; 2010) Directed by Paz Fábrega, this social commentary unfolds at a paradisiacal Pacific beach; the film won several international awards.

Caribe (Caribbean; 2004) The first Costa Rican film ever to be submitted for Oscar consideration; drama set in Limón.

Changing of the Guard

Costa Rica acquired a new president after a runoff election (the second in history) in April 2014. Following the departure of the country's first female president, Laura Chinchilla, who termed out, the runoff between Johnny Araya and Luis Guillermo Solís was a formality, as Araya stopped campaigning in March 2014 after it became clear that Solís was overwhelmingly likely to prevail.

Though Costa Rica's political landscape is unlikely to change dramatically, Solís' win may signal a sea change for the National Liberation Party (PLN), which has dominated Costa Rican politics for more than half a century. Araya, a member of the PLN, had attempted to distance himself during his campaign from Chinchilla's PLN administration, which was dogged by corruption scandals.

Solís, affiliated with the center-left Citizens' Action Party (PAC), ran on promises to fight corruption and to address the country's social and economic inequality. As a scholar of Latin American studies, Solís was formerly a professor at the University of Costa Rica and a published writer specializing in Latin American politics and social issues. As such, he is still considered somewhat of a political outsider, despite serving as an advisor to Óscar Arias as a foreign-ministry official. From the results of the election, it seems that many Costa Ricans view Solís as an agent of much-needed but not-too-radical change. Of course, only time will tell.

Carbon Neutrality

Costa Rica has long had a reputation for being green, but, to paraphrase Kermit: it ain't easy. Back in 2009, then-president Óscar Arias set an ambitious goal – that Costa Rica achieve carbon neutrality by the year 2021.

Meeting this goal would make Costa Rica the first carbon-neutral country in the world and would co-incide auspiciously with the country's bicentennial.

Although some measures have not yet been implemented as scheduled, the numbers suggest that it's still possible to hit the 2021 target. The first phase – as yet incomplete – addresses energy and agriculture, both major contributors to carbon-dioxide emissions. Proposed changes for the energy sector, for example, include transitioning buses and taxis to natural-gas, electric and hybrid vehicles, and imposing stricter emissions regulations on these companies. Agricultural changes include government-sponsored training programs for smaller farms, teaching them to implement organic methods such as composting, using biochar and creating biodigester systems to trap methane gases and use them as onsite fuel. For larger-scale agriculture, like the country's sprawling banana plantations, government incentives encourage reforestation and conservation of existing rainforest in order to offset carbon-dioxide emissions (most of which are generated from overseas shipping).

The progress made in the next few years will reveal whether Costa Rica's vision of carbon neutrality can coalesce into reality by 2021. In the meantime, one of the proposals announced by new president Luis Guillermo Solís during his electoral campaign is an extension of the carbon-neutrality goal to 2025.

Río San Juan Saga

Forming the eastern stretch of the border between Nicaragua and Costa Rica is the Río San Juan, a silty river studded with small marshy islands and floating rafts of water lettuce. This quiet waterway has been the source of much discord between the two countries, to the extent that the International Court of Justice in The Hague has had to preside over several legal disputes in the last 20 years as both countries attempt to lay claim to territory.

The border area is complicated, not only because the river flows from Lago de Nicaragua to the Caribbean Sea and as such, is an evolving geographical entity. The 1858 Cañas-Jerez Treaty asserts that Nicaragua owns the Río San Juan but that Costa Rica retains navigation rights on its side of the river. Though spats have arisen over the years, mostly over the territory on the eastern half, both countries have kept these tensions in relative check. But they've been bubbling over recently.

The latest flap started with Nicaragua dredging Isla Calero's river delta in late 2010. This involved trees being felled and earth being dumped into the river. With Nicaraguan soldiers present during the process, the Costa Rican government decided that

POPULATION: **4.7 MILLION**

ADULT LITERACY: **96.3%**

POPULATION LIVING BELOW THE POVERTY LINE: **20%**

AREA: **51,100 SQ KM**

CARBON DIOXIDE EMISSIONS: **1.85 METRIC TONS PER PERSON PER YEAR**

if Costa Rica were 100 people

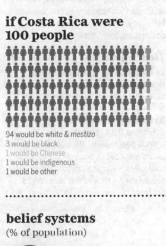

94 would be white & *mestizo*
3 would be black
1 would be Chinese
1 would be indigenous
1 would be other

belief systems
(% of population)

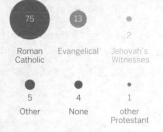

75 Roman Catholic
13 Evangelical
2 Jehovah's Witnesses
5 Other
4 None
1 other Protestant

population per sq km

COSTA RICA   MEXICO   USA

♦ ≈ 6 people

Gringo Media

Tico Times Costa Rica's biggest English-language newspaper is high quality, though news and views are often geared toward the expat community (www.ticotimes.net).

Radio Dos Broadcasting across the country on 99.5FM, Radio 2 spins an amazing selection of US Top 40 music spanning several decades; probably most appealing to Gen X and older.

Costa Rican Times This online, English-language newcomer focuses on Costa Rica happenings but also features international news (www.costaricantimes.com).

Tico Travel Tips

La hora Tica Don't be put off if your local host views an appointment as more of a ballpark suggestion of when to meet.

Directo, directo When asking directions, it's a good idea to ask several people along the way, as some locals will – out of an abundance of politeness – want to say something helpful even if they're not sure how to get there.

this was reason enough to claim invasion, and the situation deteriorated from there. In March 2011, when the International Court of Justice considered the case and reiterated the validity of the Cañas-Jerez Treaty, both sides interpreted the language as a win.

Subsequently, then-president of Costa Rica Laura Chinchilla called for emergency funds to begin construction of a road along the Costa Rican bank of the river, without proper environmental or engineering reviews. This caused consternation not only in Nicaragua but also on Costa Rican soil about the road's environmental and political impact. Nicaraguan president Daniel Ortega, for his part, has proposed the construction of a transoceanic canal in the Río San Juan.

The latest development comes from Ortega, who has hinted that he wishes to extend an olive branch across the river to the incoming president. Stay tuned.

History

Like that of many Central American countries, Costa Rica's history remains a loose sketch during the reign of its pre-Columbian tribes, and it has traced a similar path to that of its neighbors since the European 'discovery' of the New World. But it's in the mid-20th century that Costa Rica radically departed from the standard Central American playbook by abolishing its army, diversifying its economy and brokering peace in the region, thus paving the way for the stable and environmentally friendly nation we know today.

Lost Worlds of Ancient Costa Rica

The coastlines and rainforests of Central America have been inhabited by humans for at least 10,000 years, but ancient civilizations in Costa Rica are largely the subject of speculation. It is thought that the area was something of a backwater straddling the two great ancient civilizations of the Andes and Mesoamerica. On the eve of European discovery some 500 years ago, an estimated 400,000 people were living in today's Costa Rica, though sadly our knowledge about these pre-Columbian cultures is scant. What wasn't destroyed by Spanish colonization was overgrown by jungle, and most traces of indigenous Costa Ricans simply disappeared.

Unlike the massive pyramid complexes found throughout other parts of Latin America, the ancient towns and cities of Costa Rica (with the exception of Guayabo) were loosely organized and had no centralized government or ceremonial centers. However, tales of lost cities still survive in the oral histories of Costa Rica's indigenous communities and there is hope among archaeologists that a great discovery lies in waiting. Considering that so much of the country consists of inaccessible mountains and rainforests, perhaps these dreams aren't so fanciful.

The indigenous people of Costa Rica make up only about 1% of the population, and represent several ethnic groups (the Boruca, Dribrí, Cabécar, Chorotega, Huetar, Kèköldi, Maleku, Ngöbe and Térraba) and six surviving languages.

Heirs of Columbus

On his fourth and final voyage to the New World in 1502, Christopher Columbus was forced to drop anchor near present-day Puerto Limón after a hurricane damaged his ship. While waiting for repairs,

TIMELINE

11,000 BC
The first humans occupy Costa Rica and populations quickly flourish due to the rich land and marine resources found along both coastlines.

1000 BC
The Huetar power base in the Central Valley is solidified following the construction and habitation of the ancient city of Guayabo, continuously inhabited until its mysterious abandonment in AD 1400.

100 BC
Costa Rica becomes part of an extensive trade network that moves gold and other goods and extends from present-day Mexico down though to the Andean empires.

Columbus ventured into the verdant terrain and exchanged gifts with hospitable and welcoming chieftains. He returned from this encounter claiming to have seen 'more gold in two days than in four years in Española'. Columbus dubbed the stretch of shoreline from Honduras to Panama 'Veraguas', but it was his excited descriptions of *costa rica* (the 'rich coast') that gave the region its lasting name. At least, that's how the popular story goes.

Anxious to claim its bounty, Columbus petitioned the Spanish Crown to have himself appointed governor. But by the time he returned to Seville, his royal patron Queen Isabella was on her deathbed, which prompted King Ferdinand to award the prize to Columbus' rival, Diego de Nicuesa. Although Columbus became a very wealthy man, he never returned to the New World. He died in 1506 after being worn down by ill health and court politics.

PRE-COLUMBIAN COSTA RICA

The early inhabitants of Costa Rica were part of an extensive trading zone that extended as far south as Peru and as far north as Mexico. The region hosted roughly 20 small tribes, organized into chiefdoms with a *cacique* (permanent leader), who sat atop a hierarchical society that included shamans, warriors, toilers and slaves.

Adept at seafaring, the Carib dominated the Atlantic coastal lowlands and served as a conduit of trade with the South American mainland. In the northwest, several tribes were connected to the great Mesoamerican cultures. Aztec religious practices and Maya jade and craftsmanship are in evidence in the Península de Nicoya, while Costa Rican quetzal feathers and golden trinkets have turned up in Mexico. In the southwest, three chiefdoms showed the influence of Andean indigenous cultures via the presence of coca leaves, yucca and sweet potatoes.

There is also evidence that the language of the Central Valley, Huetar, was known by all of Costa Rica's indigenous groups, which may be an indication of their power and influence. The Central Valley is home to Guayabo, the only major archaeological site uncovered in Costa Rica thus far.

Thought to be an ancient ceremonial center, Guayabo once featured paved streets, an aqueduct and decorative gold. Here archaeologists uncovered exquisite gold ornaments and unusual life-size stone statues of human figures, as well as distinctive types of pottery and *metates* (stone platforms that were used for grinding corn). Today the site consists of little more than ancient hewed rock and stone, though Guayabo continues to stand as testament to a once-great civilization of the New World.

Still a puzzle, however, are the hundreds of hand-sculpted, monolithic stone spheres that dot the landscape of the Diquis Valley in Palmar and the Isla del Caño. Weighing up to 16 tons and ranging in size from a baseball to a Volkswagen, the spheres have inspired many theories: an ancient calendar, extraterrestrial meddling or pieces of a giant game.

1522	1540	1562	1563
Spanish settlement develops in Costa Rica, though it will be several decades before the colonists can get a sturdy foothold on the land.	The Kingdom of Guatemala is established by the Spanish and includes much of Central America – Costa Rica, Nicaragua, Honduras, El Salvador, Guatemala and the Mexican state of Chiapas.	Spanish *conquistador* Juan Vásquez de Coronado arrives in Costa Rica under the title of governor, determined to move the fringe communities of Spanish settlers to the more hospitable Central Valley.	The first permanent Spanish colonial settlement in Costa Rica is established in Cartago by Juan Vásquez de Coronado, who chooses the site based on its rich and fertile volcanic soils.

To the disappointment of his *conquistador* (conqueror) heirs, Columbus' tales of gold were mostly lies and the locals were considerably less than affable. Nicuesa's first colony in present-day Panama was abruptly abandoned when tropical disease and warring tribes decimated its ranks. Successive expeditions launched from the Caribbean coast also failed as pestilent swamps, oppressive jungles and volcanoes made Columbus' paradise seem more like a tropical hell.

A bright moment in Spanish exploration came in 1513 when Vasco Núñez de Balboa heard rumors about a large sea and a wealthy, gold-producing civilization across the mountains of the isthmus – these almost certainly referred to the Inca empire of present-day Peru. Driven by equal parts ambition and greed, Balboa scaled the continental divide, and on September 26, 1513, he became the first European to set eyes upon the Pacific Ocean. Keeping up with the European fashion of the day, Balboa immediately proceeded to claim the ocean and all the lands it touched for the king of Spain.

The thrill of discovery aside, the *conquistadors* now controlled a strategic western beachhead from which to launch their conquest of Costa Rica. In the name of God and king, aristocratic adventurers plundered indigenous villages, executed resisters and enslaved survivors throughout the Nicoya peninsula. However, none of these bloodstained campaigns led to a permanent presence as intercontinental germ warfare caused outbreaks of feverish death on both sides. Since the area had scarce mineral wealth and indigenous laborers, the Spanish eventually came to regard it as the 'poorest and most miserable in all the Americas'.

New World Order

It was not until the 1560s that a Spanish colony was firmly established in Costa Rica. Hoping to cultivate the rich volcanic soil of the Central Valley, the Spanish founded the village of Cartago on the banks of the Río Reventazón. Although the fledgling colony was extremely isolated, it miraculously survived under the leadership of its first governor, Juan Vásquez de Coronado. Some of Costa Rica's demilitarized present was presaged in its early colonial government: preferring diplomacy over firearms to counter the indigenous threat, Coronado used Cartago as a base to survey the lands south to Panama and west to the Pacific, and secured deed and title over the colony.

Though Coronado was later lost in a shipwreck, his legacy endured: Costa Rica was an officially recognized province of the Viceroyalty of New Spain (Virreinato de Nueva España), which was the name given to the viceroy-ruled territories of the Spanish empire in North America, Central America, the Caribbean and Asia.

For an investigation of Costa Rica's mysterious stone spheres, visit World Mysteries at www.world-mysteries.com/sar_12.htm

HISTORY NEW WORLD ORDER

Pre-Columbian Sites

Monumento Nacional Arqueológico Guayabo (Turrialba)

Hacienda Barú (Dominical)

Sitio Arqueológico Finca 6 (Sierpe)

Finca Cántaros (San Vito)

1737	1821	Apr 1823	Dec 1823
The future capital of San José is established, sparking a rivalry with neighboring Cartago that will culminate in a civil war between the two dominant cities.	Following a unanimous declaration by Mexico on behalf of all of Central America, Costa Rica finally gains its independence from Spain after centuries of colonial occupation.	The Costa Rican capital officially moves to San José after intense skirmishes with the conservative residents of Cartago, who take issue with the more liberal longings of the power-hungry *josefinos*.	The Monroe Doctrine formerly declares the intentions of the USA to be the dominant imperial power in the western hemisphere, despite protests from European powers.

For roughly three centuries, the Captaincy General of Guatemala (also known as the Kingdom of Guatemala), which included Costa Rica, Nicaragua, Honduras, El Salvador, Guatemala and the Mexican state of Chiapas, was a loosely administered colony in the vast Spanish empire. Since the political and military headquarters of the kingdom were in Guatemala, Costa Rica became a minor provincial outpost that had little if any strategic significance or exploitable riches.

As a result of its status as a swampy, largely useless backwater, Costa Rica's colonial path diverged from the typical pattern in that a powerful landholding elite and slave-based economy never gained prominence. Instead of large estates, mining operations and coastal cities, modest-sized villages of smallholders developed in the interior Central Valley. According to national lore, the stoic, self-sufficient farmer provided the backbone for 'rural democracy' as Costa Rica emerged as one of the only egalitarian corners of the Spanish empire.

Equal rights and opportunities were not extended to the indigenous groups and, as Spanish settlement expanded, the local population decreased dramatically. From 400,000 at the time Columbus first sailed, the population was reduced to 20,000 a century later, and to 8000 a century after that. While disease was the main source of death, the Spanish were relentless in their effort to exploit the natives as an economic resource. Central Valley groups were the first to fall, though outside the valley several tribes managed to survive a bit longer under forest cover, staging occasional raids. However, as in the rest of Latin America, repeated military campaigns eventually forced them into submission and slavery.

British explorer, government-sponsored pirate and slaver Sir Francis Drake is believed to have anchored in Bahía Drake in 1579. Rumor has it that he buried some of his plundered treasure here, but the only solid memorial to the man is a monument that looks out to his namesake bay.

Fall of an Empire

Spain's costly Peninsular War with France from 1808 to 1814 – and the political turmoil, unrest and power vacuums that it caused – led Spain to lose all its colonial possessions in the first third of the 19th century.

In 1821 the Americas wriggled free of Spain's imperial grip following Mexico's declaration of independence for itself as well as the whole of Central America. Of course, the Central American provinces weren't too keen on having another foreign power reign over them and subsequently declared independence from Mexico. However, all of these events hardly disturbed Costa Rica, which learned of its liberation a month after the fact.

The newly liberated colonies pondered their fate: stay together in a United States of Central America or go their separate national ways. At first they came up with something in between, namely the Central American Federation (CAF), though it could neither field an army nor collect taxes. Accustomed to being at the center of things, Guatemala also

1824	1856	1889	1890
The Nicoya-Guanacaste region votes to secede from Nicaragua and become a part of Costa Rica, though the region's longing for independence from both countries continues to this day.	Costa Rica quashes the expansionist aims of the war hawks in the USA by defeating William Walker and his invading army at the epic Battle of Santa Rosa.	Costa Rica's first democratic elections are held, a monumental event given the long history of colonial occupation, though blacks and women were prohibited by law to vote.	The construction of the railroad between San José and Puerto Limón is finally completed despite years of hardships and countless deaths due to accidents, malaria and yellow fever.

THE LITTLE DRUMMER BOY

You may notice, during your travels through the countryside, statues of a drummer boy from Alajuela named Juan Santamaría. He is one of Costa Rica's most beloved national heroes.

In April 1856 the North American mercenary William Walker and his ragtag army attempted to invade Costa Rica during an ultimately unsuccessful campaign to conquer all of Central America. Walker had already managed to sieze control of Nicaragua, taking advantage of the civil war that was raging there. It didn't take him long after that to decide to march on Costa Rica, though Costa Rican president Juan Rafael Mora Porras guessed Walker's intentions and managed to recruit a volunteer army of 9000 civilians. They surrounded Walker's army as they lay waiting in an old hacienda (estate) in present-day Parque Nacional Santa Rosa. The Costa Ricans won the battle and Walker was forever expelled from Costa Rican soil. During the fighting, Santamaría was killed while daringly setting fire to Walker's defenses – and a national legend was born.

attempted to dominate the CAF, alienating smaller colonies and hastening its demise. Future attempts to unite the region would likewise fail.

Meanwhile, an independent Costa Rica was taking shape under Juan Mora Fernández, first head of state (1824–33). He tended toward nation building, and organized new towns, built roads, published a newspaper and coined a currency. His wife even partook in the effort by designing the country's flag.

Life returned to normal, unlike in the rest of the region, where post-independence civil wars raged on. In 1824 the Nicoya-Guanacaste region seceded from Nicaragua and joined its more easygoing southern neighbor, defining the territorial borders. In 1852 Costa Rica received its first diplomatic emissaries from the USA and Great Britain.

Coffee Rica

In the 19th century the riches that Costa Rica had long promised were uncovered when it was realized that the soil and climate of the Central Valley highlands were ideal for coffee cultivation. Costa Rica led Central America in introducing the caffeinated bean, which transformed the impoverished country into the wealthiest in the region.

When an export market was discovered, the government actively promoted coffee to farmers by providing free saplings. At first Costa Rican producers exported their crop to nearby South Americans, who processed the beans and re-exported the product to Europe. By the 1840s, however, local merchants had already built up domestic capacity and

1900	1914	1919	1940
The population of Costa Rica reaches 50,000 as the country begins to develop and prosper due to the increasingly lucrative international coffee and banana trades.	Costa Rica is given an economic boost following the opening of the Panama Canal. The canal was forged by 75,000 laborers, many thousands of whom died during construction.	Federico Tinoco Granados is ousted as the dictator of Costa Rica in one of the few episodes of brief violence in an otherwise peaceful political history.	Rafael Ángel Calderón Guardia is elected president and proceeds to improve working conditions in Costa Rica by enacting minimum-wage laws as well as an eight-hour day.

learned to scope out their own overseas markets. Their big break came when they persuaded the captain of HMS *Monarch* to transport several hundred sacks of Costa Rican coffee to London, percolating the beginning of a beautiful friendship.

The Costa Rican coffee boom was on. The drink's quick fix made it popular among working-class consumers in the industrializing north. The aroma of riches lured a wave of enterprising German immigrants, enhancing technical and financial skills in the business sector. By century's end, more than one-third of the Central Valley was dedicated to coffee cultivation, and coffee accounted for more than 90% of all exports and 80% of foreign-currency earnings.

The coffee industry in Costa Rica developed differently from those in the rest of Central America. As elsewhere, there arose a group of coffee barons, elites that reaped the rewards for the export bonanza. But Costa Rican coffee barons lacked the land and labor to cultivate the crop. Coffee production is labor intensive, with a long and painstaking harvest season. The small farmers became the principal planters. The coffee barons, instead, monopolized processing, marketing and financing. The coffee economy in Costa Rica created a wide network of high-end traders and small-scale growers, whereas in the rest of Central America a narrow elite controlled large estates worked by tenant laborers.

Coffee wealth became a power resource in politics. Costa Rica's traditional aristocratic families were at the forefront of the enterprise. At midcentury, three-quarters of the coffee barons were descended from just two colonial families. The country's leading coffee exporter at this time was President Juan Rafael Mora Porras (1849–59), whose lineage went back to the colony's founder, Juan Vásquez de Coronado. Mora was overthrown by his brother-in-law after the president proposed to form a national bank independent from the coffee barons. The economic interests of the coffee elite would thereafter become a priority in Costa Rican politics.

Banana Empire

The coffee trade unintentionally gave rise to Costa Rica's next export boom – bananas. Getting coffee out to world markets necessitated a rail link from the central highlands to the coast, and Limón's deep harbor made an ideal port. Inland was dense jungle and insect-infested swamps, which prompted the government to contract the task to Minor Keith, nephew of an American railroad tycoon.

The project was a disaster. Malaria and accidents churned through workers as Tico (Costa Rican) recruits gave way to US convicts and Chinese indentured servants, who were in turn replaced by freed Jamaican slaves. To entice Keith to continue, the government turned over 3200

GREEN COFFEE

The coffee-processing cooperative Coopedota, located in Costa Rica's Valley of the Saints (famous for growing delicious highland coffee) launched the country's first carbon-neutral coffee in 2011, certified to the British Standards Institution's PAS2060 specifications for carbon neutrality.

1940s	1948	1949	1963
José Figueres Ferrer becomes involved in national politics and opposes the ruling conservatives. Figueres' social-democratic policies and criticism of the government angers the Costa Rican elite and President Calderón.	Conservative and liberal forces clash, resulting in a six-week civil war that leaves 2000 Costa Ricans dead and many more wounded and destroys much of the country's fledgling infrastructure.	Hoping to heal old wounds and look forward, the temporary government enacts a new constitution abolishing the army, desegregating the country, and granting women and blacks the right to vote.	Reserva Natura Absoluta Cabo Blanco at the tip of the Nicoya peninsula becomes Costa Rica's first federally protected conservation area through the efforts of Swedish and Danish conservationists.

sq km of land along the route and provided a 99-year lease to run the railroad. In 1890 the line was finally completed and running at a loss.

Keith had begun to grow banana plants along the tracks as a cheap food source for the workers. Desperate to recoup his investment, he shipped some bananas to New Orleans in the hope of starting a side venture. He struck gold, or rather yellow. Consumers went crazy for the elongated finger fruit. By the early 20th century, bananas surpassed coffee as Costa Rica's most lucrative export and the country became the world's leading banana exporter. Unlike in the coffee industry, the profits were exported along with the bananas.

Costa Rica was transformed by the rise of Keith's banana empire. He joined another American importer to found the infamous United Fruit Company, soon the largest employer in Central America. To the locals, it was known as *el pulpo* (the octopus) – its tentacles stretched across the region, becoming entangled with the local economy and politics. United Fruit owned huge swaths of lush lowlands, much of the transportation and communication infrastructure and bunches of bureaucrats. The company drew a wave of migrant laborers from Jamaica, changing the country's ethnic complexion and provoking racial tensions. Amazingly, you can still see the marks that *el pulpo* left on Costa Rica – look for the rusting train tracks and a locomotive engine in Palmares.

Birth of a Nation

The inequality of the early 20th century led to the rise of José Figueres Ferrer, a self-described farmer-philosopher and the father of Costa Rica's unarmed democracy. The son of Catalan immigrant coffee planters, Figueres excelled in school and went to Boston's MIT to study engineering. Upon returning to Costa Rica to set up his own coffee plantation, he organized the hundreds of laborers on his farm into a utopian socialist community and appropriately named the property La Luz Sin Fin (The Struggle Without End).

In the 1940s Figueres became involved in national politics as an outspoken critic of President Calderón. In the midst of a radio interview in which he badmouthed the president, police broke into the studio and arrested Figueres. He was accused of having fascist sympathies and was banished to Mexico. While in exile he formed the Caribbean League, a collection of students and democratic agitators from all over Central America who pledged to bring down the region's military dictators. When he returned to Costa Rica, the Caribbean League, now 700 men strong, went with him and helped protest against the powers that be.

When government troops descended on the farm with the intention of arresting Figueres and disarming the Caribbean League, it touched off

BITTER FRUIT

For details on the role of Minor Keith and the United Fruit Company in lobbying for a CIA-led coup in Guatemala, pick up a copy of the highly readable *Bitter Fruit* by Stephen Schlesinger and Stephen Kinzer.

1977	1987	1994	2000
The Indigenous Law of 1977 is passed, protecting indigenous communities' ownership of their territories.	President Óscar Arias Sánchez wins the Nobel Peace Prize for his work on the Central American peace accords, which brought about greater political freedom throughout the region.	The indigenous people of Costa Rica are finally granted the right to vote.	The population of Costa Rica tops four million, though many believe the number is far greater due to burgeoning illegal settlements on the fringes of the capital.

a civil war. The moment had arrived: the diminutive farmer-philosopher now played the man on horseback. Figueres emerged victorious from the brief conflict and seized the opportunity to put into place his vision of Costa Rican social democracy. After dissolving the country's military, Figueres quoted HG Wells: 'The future of mankind cannot include the armed forces'.

As head of a temporary junta government, Figueres enacted nearly a thousand decrees. He taxed the wealthy, nationalized the banks and built a modern welfare state. His 1949 constitution granted full citizenship and voting rights to women, African Americans, indigenous groups and Chinese minorities. Today Figueres' revolutionary regime is regarded as the foundation of Costa Rica's unarmed democracy.

Thirty-three out of 44 Costa Rican presidents prior to 1970 were descended from just three original colonizing families.

The American Empire

Throughout the 1970s and '80s, the sovereignty of the small nations of Central America was limited by their northern neighbor, the USA. Big sticks, gunboats and dollar diplomacy were instruments of a Yankee policy to curtail socialist politics, especially the military oligarchies of Guatemala, El Salvador and Nicaragua.

In 1979 the rebellious Sandinistas toppled the American-backed Somoza dictatorship in Nicaragua. Alarmed by the Sandinistas' Soviet and Cuban ties, fervently anticommunist president Ronald Reagan decided it was time to intervene. Just like that, the Cold War arrived in the hot tropics.

The organizational details of the counterrevolution were delegated to Oliver North, an eager-to-please junior officer working out of the White House basement. North's can-do creativity helped to prop up the famed Contra rebels to incite civil war in Nicaragua. While both sides invoked the rhetoric of freedom and democracy, the war was really a turf battle between left-wing and right-wing forces.

Under intense US pressure, Costa Rica was reluctantly dragged in. The Contras set up camp in northern Costa Rica, from where they staged guerrilla raids. Not-so-clandestine CIA operatives and US military advisers were dispatched to assist the effort. A secret jungle airstrip was built near the border to fly in weapons and supplies. To raise cash for the rebels, North allegedly used his covert supply network to traffic illegal narcotics through the region.

The war polarized Costa Rica. From conservative quarters came a loud call to re-establish the military and join the anticommunist crusade, which was largely underwritten by the US Pentagon. In May 1984 more than 20,000 demonstrators marched through San José to give peace a chance, though the debate didn't climax until the 1986 presidential election. The victor was 44-year-old Óscar Arias Sánchez, who, despite be-

2006	2007	2010	2010
Óscar Arias Sánchez is elected president for the second time in his political career on a pro-Cafta (Central American Free Trade Agreement) platform, though he wins by an extremely narrow margin.	A national referendum narrowly passes Cafta. Opinion remains divided as to whether opening up trade with the USA will be beneficial for Costa Rica in the long run.	Costa Rica elects its first female president, National Liberation Party candidate Laura Chinchilla.	Volcán Arenal, the country's most active volcano for over four decades, stops spitting lava and enters a resting phase.

ing born into coffee wealth, was an intellectual reformer in the mold of Figueres, his political patron.

Once in office, Arias affirmed his commitment to a negotiated resolution and reasserted Costa Rican national independence. He vowed to uphold his country's pledge of neutrality and to vanquish the Contras from the territory. The sudden resignation of the US ambassador around this time was suspected to be a result of Arias' strong stance. In a public ceremony, Costa Rican schoolchildren planted trees on top of the CIA's secret airfield. Most notably, Arias became the driving force in uniting Central America around a peace plan, which ended the Nicaraguan war and earned him the Nobel Peace Prize in 1987.

In 2006 Arias once again returned to the presidential office, winning the popular election by a 1.2% margin and subsequently ratifying the controversial Central American Free Trade Agreement (Cafta).

Prior to his re-election, Óscar Arias Sánchez founded the Arias Foundation for Peace and Human Progress; on the web at www.arias. or.cr.

HISTORY THE AMERICAN EMPIRE

2011	2013	2014	2014
Central American drug wars encroach on Costa Rica's borders, and the country is listed among the USA's major drug-trafficking centers.	The murder of 26-year-old environmentalist Jairo Mora Sandoval in Limón province brings international attention to the dangers and lack of police protection that conservationists face on the Caribbean coast.	Costa Rica advances to the 2014 FIFA (Fédération Internationale de Football Association) World Cup in Brazil.	Luis Guillermo Solís is elected president by default when his opponent withdraws from the race.

The Tico Way of Life

Blessed with natural beauty and a peaceful, armyless society, it's no wonder that Costa Rica has long been known as the Switzerland of Central America. While nowadays the country is certainly challenged by its lofty ecoconscious goals, modern intercontinental maladies such as drug trafficking and a disparity in wealth between the haves and have-nots, the Tico attitude remains sunny and family-centered.

Pura Vida

The most comprehensive and complete book on Costa Rican history and culture is *The Ticos: Culture and Social Change in Costa Rica* by Mavis, Richard and Karen Biesanz.

Pura vida – pure life – is more than just a slogan that rolls off the tongues of Ticos (Costa Ricans) and emblazons souvenirs; in the laid-back tone in which it is constantly uttered, the phrase is a bona fide mantra for the Costa Rican way of life. Perhaps the essence of the pure life is something better lived than explained, but hearing '*pura vida*' again and again while traveling across this beautiful country – as a greeting, a stand-in for goodbye, 'cool', and an acknowledgement of thanks – makes it evident that the concept lives deep within the DNA of this country.

The living seems particularly pure when Costa Rica is compared with its Central American neighbors such as Nicaragua and Honduras: there's little poverty, illiteracy or political tumult, the country is crowded with ecological jewels and the standard of living is high. What's more, Costa Rica has flourished without an army for the past 60 years. The sum of the parts is a country that's an oasis of calm in a corner of the world that has been continuously degraded by warfare. And though the Costa Rican people are justifiably proud hosts, a compliment to the country is likely to be met simply with a warm smile and an enigmatic two-word reply: *pura vida*.

Daily Life in Costa Rica

With its lack of war, long life expectancy and relatively sturdy economy, Costa Rica enjoys the highest standard of living in Central America. For the most part, Costa Ricans live fairly rich and comfortable lives, even by North American standards.

As in many places in Latin America, the family unit in Costa Rica remains the nucleus of life. Families socialize together and extended families often live near each other. When it's time to party it's also largely a family affair; celebrations, vacations and weddings are a social outlet for rich and poor alike, and those with relatives in positions of power – nominal or otherwise – don't hesitate to turn to them for support.

Given this mutually cooperative environment, it's no surprise that life expectancy in Costa Rica is almost the same as in the USA. In fact, most Costa Ricans are more likely to die of heart disease or cancer as opposed to the childhood diseases that plague many developing nations. A comprehensive socialized health-care system and excellent sanitation systems account for these positive statistics, as do a generally stress-free lifestyle, tropical weather and a healthy and varied diet – the *pura vida*.

Still, the divide between rich and poor is broad. The middle and upper classes largely reside in San José, as well as in the major cities of the Central Valley highlands (Heredia, Alajuela and Cartago), and enjoy a level of comfort similar to their economic brethren in Europe and the USA. City dwellers are likely to have a maid and a car or two, and the lucky few have a second home on the beach or in the mountains.

The home of an average Tico is a one-story construction built from concrete blocks, wood or a combination of both. In the poorer lowland areas, people often live in windowless houses made of *caña brava,* a local cane. For the vast majority of *campesinos* (farmers) and *indígenas* (people of indigenous origin), life is harder than in the cities, poverty levels are higher and standards of living are lower than in the rest of the country. This is especially true along the Caribbean coast, where the descendants of Jamaican immigrants have long suffered from lack of attention by the federal government. However, although poor families have few possessions and little financial security, every member assists with working the land or contributing to the household, which creates a strong safety net.

As in the rest of the world, globalization is having a dramatic effect on Costa Ricans, who are increasingly mobile, international and intertwined in the global economy – for better or for worse. These days, society is increasingly geographically mobile – the Tico who was born in Puntarenas

NICA VERSUS TICO

Ticos (Costa Ricans) have a well-deserved reputation for friendliness, and it's rare for travelers of any sex, race or creed to experience prejudice in Costa Rica. However, it's unfortunate and at times upsetting that the mere mention of anything related to Nicaragua is enough to turn an average Tico into a stereotype-spewing anti-Nica (note that though the term 'Nica' is used colloquially by Nicaraguans, it is used by some Ticos in a somewhat derogatory manner – when in doubt, err on the side of '*nicaragüense*' to refer to a Nicaraguan person). Despite commonalities in language, culture, history and tradition, Nica-versus-Tico relations are at an all-time low, and rhetoric (on both sides) of *la frontera* (the border) isn't likely to improve any time soon.

Why is there so much hostility between Nicaraguans and Ticos? The answer is as much a product of history as it is of misunderstanding, though economic disparities between the countries are largely to blame.

Though Nicaragua was wealthier than Costa Rica as recently as 25 years ago, decades of civil war and a US embargo quickly bankrupted it, and today Nicaragua is the second-poorest country in the western hemisphere (after Haiti). For example, the 2013 CIA World Factbook lists the GDP-per-capita purchasing-power parity of Costa Rica as US$12,900, while Nicaragua's is listed at only US$4500. The main problem facing Nicaragua is its heavy external debt, though debt-relief programs implemented by the International Monetary Fund (IMF) and the free-trade zone created by the Central American Free Trade Agreement (Cafta) are both promising signs.

In the meantime, however, Nicaraguan families are crossing the border in record numbers, drawn to Costa Rica by its growing economy and impressive education and health systems. However, immigration laws in Costa Rica make it difficult for Nicaraguans to find work, and the majority end up living in shantytowns. Also, crime is on the rise throughout Costa Rica, and though it's difficult to say what percentage is actually attributable to Nicaraguan immigrants, some Ticos are quick to point the finger in their direction.

It's difficult to predict whether relations between the countries will improve, although current signs are fairly negative. Costa Rica, whose civil guard is better funded than many countries' militaries, has a bad habit of being caught on the Río San Juan (the border with Nicaragua) with a patrol boat of combat troops. Nicaragua, on the other hand, has passed a law requiring all visiting Ticos to be in possession of a valid visa. As with all instances of deep-rooted prejudice, the solution is anything but clear.

might end up managing a lodge on the Península de Osa. And, with the advent of better-paved roads, cell coverage, and the increasing presence of North American and European expats (and the accompanying malls and big box stores), the Tico family unit is subject to the changing tides of a global society.

Women in Costa Rica

In conjunction with two indigenous women, Paula Palmer wrote *Taking Care of Sibö's Gifts*, an inspiring account of the intersection between the spiritual and environmental values of the Bribrí.

By the letter of the law, Costa Rica's progressive stance on women's issues makes the country stand out among its Central American neighbors. A 1974 family code stipulated equal duties and rights for men and women. Additionally, women can draw up contracts, assume loans and inherit property. Sexual harassment and sex discrimination are also against the law, and in 1996 Costa Rica passed a landmark law against domestic violence that was one of the most progressive in Latin America. With women holding more and more roles in political, legal, scientific and medical fields, Costa Rica has been home to some historic firsts: in 1998 both vice presidents (Costa Rica has two) were women, and in February 2010 Arias Sánchez's former vice president, Laura Chinchilla, became the first female president.

Still, the picture of sexual equality is much more complicated than the country's bragging rights might suggest. A thriving legal prostitution trade has fueled illicit underground activities such as child prostitution and the trafficking of women. Despite the cultural reverence for the matriarch (Mother's Day is a national holiday), traditional Latin American machismo is hardly a thing of the past and antidiscrimination laws are rarely enforced. Particularly in the countryside, many women maintain traditional societal roles: raising children, cooking and running the home.

Sports

From the scrappy little matches that take over the village pitch to the breathless exclamations of 'goal!' that erupt from San José bars on the day of a big game, no Costa Rican sporting venture can compare with *fútbol* (soccer). Every town has a soccer field (which usually serves as the most conspicuous landmark) where neighborhood aficionados play in heated matches.

The *selección nacional* (national selection) team is known affectionately as La Sele. Legions of rabid Tico fans still recall La Sele's most memorable moments, including an unlikely showing in the quarterfinals at the 1990 World Cup in Italy and a solid (if not long-lasting) performance in the 2002 World Cup. More recently, La Sele's failure to qualify for the 2010 World Cup led to a top-down change in leadership and the reinstatement of one-time coach Jorge Luis Pinto, a Colombian coach who has had mixed results on the international stage. In general, Pinto seems to be a good fit for the team's ferocious young leaders such as record-setting scorer Álvaro Saborío, goalkeeper Keylor Navas and forward Bryan Ruiz. And in fact, Pinto led the team to qualify for the 2014 World Cup in Brazil, which is, needless to say, heady news for Costa Rica.

Get player statistics and game schedules and find out everything you ever needed to know about La Sele, the Costa Rican national soccer team, at www.fedefutbol.com.

With such perfect waves, surfing has steadily grown in popularity among Ticos, especially those who grow up shredding in surf towns. Costa Rica annually hosts numerous national and international competitions that are widely covered by local media, as well as holding regular local competitions such as the weekly contest at Playa Hermosa (south of Jacó).

Bullfighting is also popular, particularly in the Guanacaste region, though the bull isn't killed in the Costa Rican version of the sport. More aptly described, bullfighting is really a ceremonial opportunity to watch an often tipsy cowboy run around with a bull.

Arts

Literature

Costa Rica has a relatively young literary history and few works of Costa Rican writers or novelists are available in translation. Carlos Luis Fallas (1909–66) is widely known for *Mamita Yunai* (1940), an influential novel that took the banana companies to task for their labor practices, and he remains very popular among the Latin American left.

Carmen Naranjo (1928–2012) is one of the few contemporary Costa Rican writers who have risen to international acclaim. She was a novelist, poet and short-story writer who also served as ambassador to India in the 1970s, and a few years later as minister of culture. In 1996 she was awarded the prestigious Gabriela Mistral medal by the Chilean government. Her collection of short stories, *There Never Was a Once Upon a Time,* is widely available in English. Two of her stories can also be found in *Costa Rica: A Traveler's Literary Companion.*

José León Sánchez (1930–) is an internationally renowned memoirist of Huetar descent from the border of Costa Rica and Nicaragua. After being convicted for stealing from the famous Basílica de Nuestra Señora de los Angeles in Cartago, he was sentenced to serve his term at Isla San Lucas, one of Latin America's most notorious jails. Illiterate when he was incarcerated, Sánchez taught himself how to read and write, and clandestinely authored one of the continent's most poignant books: *La isla de los hombres solos* (called *God Was Looking the Other Way* in the translated version).

Music & Dance

Although there are other Latin American musical hotbeds of more renown, Costa Rica's central geographical location and colonial history have resulted in a varied musical culture that incorporates elements from North and South America and the Caribbean islands.

San José features a regular lineup of domestic and international rock, folk and hip-hop artists, but you'll find that the regional sounds also survive, each with their own special rhythms, instruments and styles. For instance, the Península de Nicoya has a rich musical history, most of it made with guitars, maracas and marimbas. The traditional sound on the Caribbean coast is calypso, which has roots in Afro-Caribbean slave culture.

Popular dance music includes Latin dances, such as salsa, merengue, bolero and *cumbia*. Guanacaste is also the birthplace of many traditional dances, most of which depict courtship rituals between country folk. The most famous dance – sometimes considered the national dance – is the *punto guanacasteco*. What keeps it lively is the *bomba,* a funny (and usually racy) rhymed verse shouted by the male dancers during the musical interlude.

Painting & Sculpture

The visual arts in Costa Rica first took on a national character in the 1920s, when Teodórico Quirós, Fausto Pacheco and their contemporaries began painting landscapes that differed from traditional European styles, depicting the rolling hills and lush forest of the Costa Rican countryside, often sprinkled with characteristic adobe houses.

The contemporary scene is more varied and it is difficult to define a unique Tico style. Several individual artists have garnered acclaim for their work, including the magical realism of Isidro Con Wong, the surreal paintings and primitive engravings of Francisco Amighetti and the mystical female figures painted by Rafa Fernández. The Museo de Arte

THE TICO WAY OF LIFE ARTS

ALFONSO CHASE

Although he is yet untranslated, poet Alfonso Chase is a Fulbright scholar and a contemporary literary hero. In 2000 he won the nation's highest literary award, the Premio Magón.

KILLING THE SNAKE

The expression *matando la culebra* (meaning 'to be idle', literally 'killing the snake') originates with *peones* (expendable laborers) from banana plantations. When foremen would ask what they were doing, the response would be *'¡Matando la culebra!'*

y Diseño Contemporáneo in San José is the top place to see this type of work, and its permanent collection is a great primer.

Many art galleries are geared toward tourists and specialize in 'tropical art' (for lack of an official description): brightly colored, whimsical folk paintings depicting flora and fauna that evoke the work of French artist Henri Rousseau.

Folk art and handicrafts are not as widely produced or readily available here as in other Central American countries. However, the dedicated souvenir hunter will have no problem finding the colorful Sarchí oxcarts that have become a symbol of Costa Rica. Indigenous crafts, which include intricately carved and painted masks made by the Boruca, as well as handwoven bags and linens, can also be found in San José and more readily in southern Costa Rica.

Film

Artistically, while film is not a new medium in Costa Rica, young filmmakers have been upping the country's ante in this arena. Over the last decade or so, a handful of Costa Rican filmmakers have submitted their work for Oscar consideration, and many others have received critical acclaim for their pictures nationally and internationally. These films range from adaptations of Gabriel García Márquez's magical-realism novel *Del amor y otro demonios* (Of Love and Other Demons, 2009), directed by Hilda Hidalgo, to a comedic coming-of-age story of young Ticos on the cusp of adulthood in contemporary Costa Rica in *El cielo rojo* (The Red Sky, 2008), written and directed by Miguel Alejandro Gomez.

A film-festival calendar has also been blossoming in Costa Rica, though dates vary year on year. Sponsored by the Ministerio de Cultura y Juventud, the Costa Rica Festival Internacional de Cine (www.costaricacinefest.com) takes place in San José (check the website for current dates) and features international films fitting the year's theme. The longer-running Costa Rica International Film Festival (CRIFF; www.costaricafilmfestival.org) hits Montezuma in early June, with an associated documentary film festival the week following.

Landscapes & Ecology

Despite its diminutive size – at 51,000 sq km it is slightly smaller than the USA's West Virginia – Costa Rica's land is an explosion of Technicolor contrasts and violent contradictions. On one coast are the breezy skies and big waves of the Pacific. Only 119km away lie the muggy and languid shores of the Caribbean. In between there are several active volcanoes, alpine peaks and crisp high-elevation forest. Few places on earth can compare with this little country's spectacular interaction of natural, geological and climatic forces.

The Land
The Pacific Coast

Two major peninsulas hook out into the ocean along the 1016km-long Pacific coast: Nicoya in the north and Osa in the south. Although they look relatively similar from space, on the ground they could hardly be

Above Volcán Arenal (p259)

more different. Nicoya is one of the driest places in the country and holds some of Costa Rica's most developed tourist infrastructure; Osa is wet and rugged, run through by wild, seasonal rivers and rough dirt roads that are always under threat from the creeping jungle.

Just inland from the coast, the Pacific lowlands are a narrow strip of land backed by mountains. This area is equally dynamic, ranging from dry deciduous forests and open cattle country in the north to misty, mysterious tropical rainforests in the south.

The world-famous Organization for Tropical Studies runs three field stations and offers numerous classes for students seriously interested in tropical ecology. See www.ots.ac.cr.

Central Costa Rica

Move a bit inland from the Pacific coast and you immediately ascend the jagged spine of the country: the majestic Cordillera Central in the north and the rugged, largely unexplored Cordillera de Talamanca in the south. Continually being revised by tectonic activity, these mountains are part of the majestic Sierra Madre chain that runs north through Mexico.

A land of active volcanoes, clear trout-filled streams and ethereal cloud forest, these mountain ranges generally follow a northwest to southeast line, with the highest and most dramatic peaks in the south near the Panamanian border. The highest in the country is the windswept 3820m peak of Cerro Chirripó.

In the midst of this powerful landscape, surrounded on all sides by mountains, are the highlands of the Meseta Central – the Central Valley. This fertile central plain, some 1000m above sea level, is the agricultural heart of the nation and enjoys abundant rainfall and mild temperatures. It includes San José and cradles three more of Costa Rica's five largest cities, accounting for more than half of the country's population.

The Caribbean Coast

Cross the mountains and drop down the eastern slope and you'll reach the elegant line of the Caribbean coastline – a long, straight 212km along low plains, brackish lagoons and waterlogged forests. A lack of strong tides allows plants to grow right over the water's edge along coastal sloughs. Eventually, these create the walls of vegetation along the narrow, murky waters that characterize much of the region. As if taking cues from the slow-paced Caribbean-influenced culture, the rivers that rush out of the central mountains take on a languid pace here, curving through broad plains toward the sea.

Compared with the smoothly paved roads and popular beaches of the Pacific coast, much of the land here is still largely inaccessible except by boat or plane.

The Geology

If all this wildly diverse beauty makes Costa Rica feel like the crossroads between vastly different worlds, that's because it is. Part of the thin strip of land that separates two continents with hugely divergent wildlife and topographical character and right in the middle of the world's two largest oceans, it's little wonder that Costa Rica boasts such a colorful collision of climates, landscapes and wildlife.

The country's geological history began when the Cocos Plate, a tectonic plate that lies below the Pacific, crashed headlong into the Caribbean Plate, which is off the isthmus' east coast. Since the plates travel about 10cm every year, the collision might seem slow by human measure, but it was a violent wreck by geological standards, creating the area's subduction zone. The plates continue to collide, with the Cocos Plate pushing the Caribbean Plate toward the heavens and making the area prone to earthquakes and ongoing volcanic activity.

Despite all the violence underfoot, these forces have blessed the country with some of the world's most beautiful and varied tropical landscapes.

Refugio Nacional de Vida Silvestre Gandoca-Manzanillo (p190)

Out on a Reef

Compared with the rest of the Caribbean, the coral reefs of Costa Rica are not a banner attraction. Heavy surf and shifting sands along most of the Caribbean coast produce conditions that are unbearable to corals. The exceptions are two beautiful patches of reef in the south that are protected on the rocky headlands of Parque Nacional Cahuita and Refugio Nacional de Vida Silvestre Gandoca-Manzanillo. These diminutive but vibrant reefs are home to more than 100 species of fish and many types of coral and make for decent snorkeling and diving.

Unfortunately, the reefs themselves are in danger due to sediment washing downriver from logging operations and toxic chemicals that wash out of nearby agricultural fields. Though curbed by the government, these factors persist. Also, a major earthquake in 1991 lifted the reefs as much as 1.5m, stranding and killing large portions of this fragile ecosystem. More recently, climate change has led to warmer water in the Caribbean, which puts the reefs at the greatest peril – scientists released a report in 2008 that found that over half of Caribbean reefs were dead due to increased temperatures.

Wildlife

Nowhere else are so many types of habitats squeezed into such a tiny area, and species from different continents have been commingling here for millennia. Costa Rica has the world's largest number of species per 10,000 sq km: 615, compared with wildlife-rich Rwanda's 596 and the comparatively impoverished USA's 104. This simple fact alone makes Costa Rica the premier destination for nature lovers.

Excellent, contemplative books on birds by the esteemed Dr Alexander Skutch include *A Naturalist in Costa Rica* and *The Minds of Birds*.

Río Corobicí, Guanacaste province

The tallest tree in the rainforest is usually the ceiba (silk-cotton tree). The most famous example is a 70m elder in Corcovado.

The large number of species here is also due to the country's relatively recent appearance. Roughly three million years ago Costa Rica rose from the ocean, and formed a land bridge between North and South America. As species from these two vast biological provinces started to mingle, the number of species essentially doubled in the area where Costa Rica now sits.

For more information see the Wildlife Guide on p489.

Flora

Simply put, Costa Rica's floral biodiversity is mind-blowing – close to 12,000 species of vascular plants have been described, and the list gets more and more crowded each year. Orchids alone account for about 1400 species. The diversity of habitats created when this many species mix is a wonder to behold.

Rainforest

The humid, vibrant mystery of the tropical rainforest connects acutely with a traveler's sense of adventure. These forests, far more dense with plant life than any other environment on the planet, are leftover scraps of the prehistoric jungles that once covered the continents. Standing in the midst of it and trying to take it all in can be overwhelming: tropical rainforests contain over half of the earth's known living organisms. Naturally, this riotous pile-on of life requires lots of water – it typically gets between 5m and 6m of rainfall annually (yes, that's *meters*!).

Classic rainforest habitats are well represented in the parks of southwestern Costa Rica or in the mid-elevation portions of the central mountains. Here you will find towering trees that block out the sky, long, looping vines and many overlapping layers of vegetation. Large trees often show buttresses – winglike ribs that extend from their trunks for added structural support. And plants climb atop other plants, fighting for a bit of sunlight. The most impressive areas of primary forest (a term designating completely untouched land that has never been disturbed by humans) exist on the Península de Osa.

Cloud Forest

Visiting the unearthly terrain of a cloud forest is a highlight for many visitors; there are amazing swaths of it in Monteverde, along the Cerro de la Muerte and below the peaks of Chirripó. In these regions, fog-drenched trees are so thickly coated in mosses, ferns, bromeliads and orchids that you can hardly discern their true shapes. These forests are created when humid trade winds off the Caribbean blow up into the highlands, cool and condense to form thick, low-hanging clouds. With constant exposure to wind, rain and sun, the trees here are crooked and stunted.

Cloud forests are widespread at high elevations throughout Costa Rica and any of them warrant a visit. Be forewarned, however, that in these habitats the term 'rainy season' has little meaning because it's always dripping wet from the fog – a cloud forest often hovers around 100% humidity.

Tropical Dry Forest

Along Costa Rica's northwest coast lies the country's largest concentration of tropical dry forest – a stunningly different scene than the country's wet rainforests and cloud forests. During the dry season many trees drop their foliage, creating carpets of crackling, sun-drenched leaves and a sense of openness that is largely absent in other Costa Rican habitats. The large trees here, such as Costa Rica's national tree, the guanacaste, have broad, umbrella-like canopies, while spiny shrubs and vines or cacti dominate the understory. At times, large numbers of trees erupt into spectacular displays of flowers, and at the beginning of the rainy season everything is transformed with a wonderful flush of new, green foliage.

This type of forest was native to Guanacaste and the Península de Nicoya, though it suffered generations of destruction for its commercially valuable lumber. Most was clear-cut or burned to make space for ranching. Parque Nacional Guanacaste and Parque Nacional Santa Rosa are good examples of the dry forest and host some of the country's most accessible nature hiking.

Mangroves

Along brackish stretches of both coasts, mangrove swamps are a world unto themselves. Growing on stilts out of muddy tidal flats, five species of trees crowd together so densely that no boats and few animals can penetrate. Striking in their adaptations for dealing with salt, mangrove trees thrive where no other land plant dares tread and are among the world's most relentless colonizers. The mangrove seeds are heavy and fleshy, blooming into flowers in the spring before falling off to give way to fruit. By the time the fruit falls, it is covered with spiky seedlings that anchor in the soft mud of low tides. In only 10 years, a seedling has the potential to mature into an entire new colony.

Mangrove swamps play extremely important roles in the ecosystem. Not only do they buffer coastlines from the erosive power of waves, they also have high levels of productivity because they trap nutrient-rich sediment and serve as spawning and nursery areas for innumerable species of fish and invertebrates. The brown waters of mangrove channels – rich with nutrients and filled with algae, shrimp, crustaceans and caimans – form tight links in the marine food chain and are best explored in a kayak, early in the morning.

There are miles of mangrove channels along the Caribbean coast, and several patches of mangrove on the Pacific, near Bahía Drake.

Costa Rica's national tree is the guanacaste, commonly found on the lowlands of the Pacific slope.

Mangroves can survive in highly saline environments by secreting salt via the surface of their leaves, filtering it at the root level and accumulating it in bark and leaves that eventually fall off.

LANDSCAPES & ECOLOGY WILDLIFE

Above Three-toed sloth
Left Scarlet macaw

Poison-dart frog

SLOTHS

Fauna

Though tropical in nature – with a substantial number of tropical animals such as poison-dart frogs and spider monkeys – Costa Rica is also the winter home for more than 200 species of migrating bird that arrive from as far away as Alaska and Australia. Don't be surprised to see one of your familiar backyard birds feeding alongside trogons and toucans. Birds are one of the primary attractions for naturalists, who scan endlessly for birds of every color, from strawberry red scarlet macaws to the iridescent jewels called violet sabrewings (a type of hummingbird). Because many birds in Costa Rica have restricted ranges, you are guaranteed to find different species everywhere you travel.

Visitors will almost certainly see one of Costa Rica's four types of monkey or two types of sloth, but there are an additional 230 types of mammal awaiting the patient observer. More exotic sightings might include the amazing four-eyed opossum or silky anteater, while a lucky few might spot the elusive tapir, or have a jaguarundi cross their path. The extensive network of national parks, wildlife refuges and other protected areas are prime places to spot wildlife.

If you are serious about observing birds and animals, the value of a knowledgeable guide cannot be underestimated. Their keen eyes are trained to notice the slightest movement in the forest, and they recognize the many exotic sounds. Most professional bird guides are proficient in the dialects of local birds, greatly improving your chances of hearing or seeing these species.

No season is a bad one for exploring Costa Rica's natural environment, though most visitors arrive during the peak dry season, when trails are less muddy and more accessible. An added bonus of visiting between December and February is that many of the wintering migrant birds are

Two-toed sloths descend from the trees once every two weeks to defecate.

Olive ridley sea turtle

still hanging around. A trip after the peak season means fewer birds, but this is a stupendous time to see dried forests transform into vibrant greens and it's also when resident birds begin nesting.

Endangered Species

As expected in a country with unique habitats and widespread logging, the populations of numerous species are declining or in danger of extinction. Currently, the number-one threat to most of Costa Rica's endangered species is habitat destruction, followed closely by hunting and trapping.

Costa Rica's four species of sea turtle – olive ridley, leatherback, green and hawksbill – deservedly get a lot of attention. All four species are classified as endangered or critically endangered, meaning they face an imminent threat of extinction. While populations of some species are increasing, thanks to various protection programs along both coasts, the risk for these *tortugas* (turtles) is still very real.

The seven species of poison-dart frog in Costa Rica are beautiful to look at but have exceedingly toxic skin secretions that cause paralysis and death.

Destruction of habitat is a huge problem. With the exception of the leatherbacks, all of these species return to their natal beach to nest, which means that the ecological state of the beach directly affects that turtle's ability to reproduce. All of the species prefer dark, undisturbed beaches, and any sort of development or artificial lighting (including flashlights) will inhibit nesting.

Hunting and harvesting eggs are two major causes of declining populations. Green turtles are hunted for their meat. Leatherbacks and olive ridleys are not killed for meat, but their eggs are considered a delicacy – an aphrodisiac, no less. Hawksbill turtles are hunted for their unusual shells, which are sometimes used to make jewelry and hair

(continued p499)

JONATHAN GREGSON / LONELY PLANET ©

Wildlife Guide

Costa Rica's reputation as a veritable Eden precedes it – with its iconic blue morpho butterflies, four species each of monkey and sea turtle, scarlet and great green macaws, two- and three-toed sloths, a rainbow of poison-dart frogs, mysterious tapirs and cute coatis. What follows is merely an introduction to the country's wildlife.

Contents
➡ **Birds**
➡ **Reptiles & Frogs**
➡ **Marine Animals**
➡ **Land Mammals**
➡ **Insects & Arachnids**

Above Squirrel monkey

1. Fiery throated hummingbird 2. Scarlet macaw
3. Keel-billed toucan 4. Resplendent quetzal

MARCO SIMONI / GETTY IMAGES ©

Birds

Toucan

Six species of this classic rainforest bird are found in Costa Rica. Huge bills and vibrant plumage make the commonly sighted chestnut-mandibled toucan and keel-billed toucan hard to miss. Listen for the keel-billed's song: a repetitious 'carrrick!'

Scarlet Macaw

Of the 16 parrot species in Costa Rica, none is as spectacular as the scarlet macaw. Unmistakable for its large size, bright-red body and ear-splitting squawk, it's common in Parque Nacional Carara and the Península de Osa. Macaws have long, monogamous relationships and can live 50 years.

Resplendent Quetzal

The most dazzling bird in Central America, the quetzal once held great ceremonial significance for the Aztecs and the Maya. Look for its iridescent-green body, red breast and long green tail at high elevations and near Parque Nacional Los Quetzales.

Roseate Spoonbill

This wading bird has a white head and a distinctive spoon-shaped bill, and feeds by touch. Common around the Península de Nicoya, Pacific lowlands and on the Caribbean side at the Refugio Nacional de Vida Silvestre Caño Negro.

Tanager

There are 42 species of tanager in the country – many are brightly colored and all have bodies about the size of an adult fist. Look for them everywhere except at high elevation. Their common name in Costa Rica is *viuda,* meaning widow.

Hummingbird

More than 50 species of hummingbird have been recorded – and most live at high elevations. The largest is the violet sabrewing, with a striking violet head and body and dark-green wings.

Reptiles & Frogs

Green Iguana

The stocky green iguana is regularly seen draping its 2m-long body along a branch. Despite their enormous bulk, iguanas are incessant vegetarians, and prefer to eat young shoots and leaves. You'll see them just about everywhere in Costa Rica – in fact, if you're driving, beware of iguanas sunning on or skittering across the roads.

Red-Eyed Tree Frog

The unofficial symbol of Costa Rica, the red-eyed tree frog has red eyes, a green body, yellow and blue side stripes, and orange feet. Despite this vibrant coloration, they're well camouflaged in the rainforest and rather difficult to spot. They are widespread apart from the Península de Nicoya, which is too dry for them. You'll have a particularly good chance of seeing them at Estación Biológica La Selva (p285).

Poison-Dart Frog

Among the several species found in Costa Rica, the blue-jeans or strawberry poison-dart frog is the most commonly spotted, from Arenal to the Caribbean coast. These colorful, wildly patterned frogs' toxic excretions were once used to poison indigenous arrowheads.

Crocodile

Impressive specimens can be seen from Crocodile Bridge (p357) on the central Pacific coast or in a more natural setting on boat trips along the Tortuguero canals.

Viper

Two serpents you'll want to avoid (and are unlikely to encounter outside of vivariums) are the fer-de-lance pit viper, which lives in agricultural areas of the Pacific and Caribbean slopes, and the eyelash pit viper, which lives in low-elevation rainforest. To avoid serious or fatal bites, remember to watch your step, and look before you grab onto any vines when hiking.

1. Green and black poison-dart frog 2. Gaudy leaf frog
3. Green iguana 4. Eyelash pit viper

Marine Animals

Olive Ridley Turtle

The smallest of Costa Rica's sea turtles, the olive ridley is easy to love – it has a heart-shaped shell. Between September and October they arrive in massive numbers to nest at Playa Ostional in the Refugio Nacional de Fauna Silvestre Ostional (p322), Guanacaste province.

Leatherback Turtle

The gigantic 360kg leatherback sea turtle is much, much bigger than the olive ridley, and is distinguished by its soft, leathery carapace, which has seven ridges. It nests on the Pacific beaches of the Osa and Nicoya peninsulas.

Whale

Migrating whales, which arrive from both the northern and southern hemispheres, include orca, blue and sperm whales and several species of relatively unknown beaked whale. Humpback whales are commonly spotted along the Pacific coast.

1. Manta ray **2.** Humpback whale **3.** Bottlenose dolphins

Bottle-Nose Dolphin

These charismatic, intelligent cetaceans are commonly sighted, year-round residents of Costa Rica. Keep a lookout for them on the boat ride to Bahía Drake.

Whale Shark

Divers may encounter this gentle giant in the waters off Reserva Biológica Isla del Caño, the Golfo Dulce or Isla del Coco. The world's biggest fish, whale sharks can reach 6m long and can weigh over 2000kg.

Manta Ray

With wings that can reach 7m, the elegant manta ray is common in warm Pacific waters, especially off the coast of Guanacaste and around the Bat and Catalina islands.

Hammerhead Shark

The intimidating hammerhead has a unique cephalofoil that enables it to maneuver with incredible speed and precision. Divers can see enormous schools of hammerheads around the remote Isla del Coco.

PAUL SOUDERS / GETTY IMAGES ©

1. White-faced capuchin 2. Three-toed sloth 3. White-nosed coati
4. Jaguar

ISTVAN KADAR / GETTY IMAGES ©

Land Mammals

Sloth

Costa Rica is home to the brown-throated three-toed sloth and Hoffman's two-toed sloth. Both species tend to hang seemingly motionless from branches, their coats growing moss. Look for them in Parque Nacional Manuel Antonio.

Howler Monkey

The loud vocalizations of a male mantled howler monkey can carry for more than 1km even in dense rainforest, and echoes through many of the nation's national parks.

White-Faced Capuchin

The small and inquisitive white-faced capuchin has a prehensile tail that is typically carried with the tip coiled – one is likely to steal your lunch near Volcán Arenal or Parque Nacional Manuel Antonio.

Squirrel Monkey

The adorable, diminutive squirrel monkey travels in small- to medium-sized groups during the day, in search of insects and fruit. They live only along the Pacific and are common in Parque Nacional Manuel Antonio and the Península de Nicoya.

Jaguar

The king of Costa Rica's big cats, the jaguar is extremely rare, shy and well camouflaged, so the chance of seeing one is virtually nonexistent (the best chance is in Parque Nacional Corcovado, p458).

White-Nosed Coati

A frequently seen member of the raccoon family, with a longer, slimmer and lighter body than your average raccoon. Has a distinctive pointy, whitish snout and a perky striped tail.

Baird's Tapir

A large browsing mammal related to the rhinoceros, the tapir has a characteristic prehensile snout and lives deep in forests ranging from the Península de Osa to Parque Nacional Santa Rosa.

Blue morpho butterfly

Insects & Arachnids

Blue Morpho Butterfly

The blue morpho butterfly flutters along tropical rivers and through openings in the forests. When it lands, the electric-blue upper wings close, and only the mottled brown underwings become visible, an instantaneous change from outrageous display to modest camouflage.

Leaf-Cutter Ant

Long processions of busy leaf-cutter ants traverse the forest floors and trails of Costa Rica, appearing like slow-moving rivulets of green leaf fragments. Leaf-cutter ants are actually fungus farmers – in their underground colonies, the ants chew the harvested leaves into a pulp to precipitate the growth of fungus, which feeds the colonies.

Tarantula

Easily identified by its enormous size and hairy appendages, the Costa Rican red tarantula is an intimidating arachnid that can take down a mouse, but it is completely harmless to humans. They are most active at night while foraging and seeking mates.

Hercules Beetle

Turn on your flashlight while visiting one of Costa Rica's old-growth forests and you might draw out the Hercules beetle, one of the largest bugs in the world, a terrifying-looking but utterly harmless scarab beetle that can be as big as a cake plate. Fun fact: it can carry more than 100 times its own body weight.

(continued from p488)

ornaments. Of course, any trade in tortoiseshell products and turtle eggs and meat is illegal, but a significant black market exists.

The legendary quetzal – the bird at the top of every naturalist's must-see list – teeters precariously as its home forests are felled at an alarming rate. Seeing a noisy scarlet macaw could be a bird-watching highlight in Costa Rica, but trapping for the pet trade has extirpated these magnificent birds from much of their former range. Although populations are thriving in the Península de Osa, the scarlet macaw is now extinct over most of Central America, including the entire Caribbean coast.

National Parks & Protected Areas

The national-park system began in the 1960s, and has since been expanded into a Sistema Nacional de Áreas de Conservación (Sinac; National Conservation Areas System) with an astounding 186 protected areas, including 32 national parks, eight biological reserves, 13 forest reserves and 51 wildlife refuges. At least 10% of the land is strictly protected and another 17% is included in various multiple-use preserves. Costa Rican authorities enjoy their claim that more than 27% of the country has been set aside for conservation, but multiple-use zones still allow farming, logging and other exploitation, so the environment within them is not totally protected. The smallest number might be the most amazing of all: Costa Rica's parks are safe haven to approximately 5% of the world's wildlife species.

In addition to the system of national preserves, there are hundreds of small, privately owned lodges, reserves and *haciendas* (estates) that have been set up to protect the land. Many belong to longtime Costa Rican expats who decided that this country was the last stop in their journey along the 'gringo trail' in the 1970s and '80s. The abundance of foreign-owned protected areas is a bit of a contentious issue with Ticos (Costa Ricans). Although these are largely nonprofit organizations with keen interests in conservation, they are private and often cost money to enter.

Although the national-park system appears glamorous on paper, national conservation body Sinac still sees much work to be done. A report from several years ago amplified the fact that much of the protected area is, in fact, at risk. The government doesn't own all of this land – almost half of the areas are in private hands – and there isn't the budget to buy it. Technically, the private lands are protected from development, but there have been reports that many landowners are finding loopholes in the restrictions and selling or developing their properties, or taking bribes from poachers and illegal loggers in exchange for access.

On the plus side is a project by Sinac that links national parks and reserves, private reserves and national forests into 13 conservation areas. This strategy has two major effects. First, these 'megaparks' allow greater numbers of individual plants and animals to exist. Second, the administration of the national parks is delegated to regional offices, allowing a more individualized management approach. Each conservation area

Sidebar (right margin):

LANDSCAPES & ECOLOGY NATIONAL PARKS & PROTECTED AREAS

GREEN TURTLES

Tales of the green turtle's resurgence in Tortuguero are told by Archie Carr in *The Windward Road: Adventures of a Naturalist on Remote Caribbean Shores.*

DON'T DISTURB THE DOLPHINS

Swimming with dolphins has been illegal since 2006, although shady tour operators out for a quick buck may encourage it. Research indicates that in some heavily touristed areas, dolphins are leaving their natural habitat in search of calmer seas. When your boat comes across these amazing creatures of the sea, avoid the temptation to jump in with them – you can still have an awe-inspiring experience peacefully observing them without disturbing them.

Pineapple plantation, Sarapiquí Valley

For maps and descriptions of the national parks, go to www.costarica-nationalparks.com.

has regional and subregional offices charged with providing effective education, enforcement, research and management, although some regional offices play what appear to be only obscure bureaucratic roles.

In general, support for land preservation remains high in Costa Rica because it provides income and jobs to so many people, plus important opportunities for scientific investigation.

Environmental Issues

No other tropical country has made such a concerted effort to protect its environment and in 2012 a study published by Yale and Columbia Universities ranked Costa Rica in the top five nations for its overall environmental performance. At the same time, as the global leader in the burgeoning ecotourism economy, Costa Rica is proving to be a case study in the pitfalls and benefits of this kind of tourism. The pressures of overpopulation, global climate change and dwindling natural resources have also made it a key illustration of the urgency of environmental protection.

Deforestation

The National Biodiversity Institute is a clearinghouse of information on both biodiversity and efforts to conserve it; see www.inbio.ac.cr.

Sometimes, when the traffic jams up around the endless San José sprawl, it is hard to keep in mind that this place was once covered in a lush, unending tropical forest. Tragically, after more than a century of clearing for plantations, agriculture and logging, Costa Rica lost about 80% of its forest cover before the government stepped in with a plan to protect what was left. Through its many programs of forest protection and reforestation, 52% of the country is forested once again – a stunning accomplishment.

Despite protection for two-thirds of the remaining forests, cutting trees is still a major problem for Costa Rica, especially on private lands

Costa Rican coffee beans

that are being cleared by wealthy landowners and multinational corporations. Even within national parks, some of the more remote areas are being logged illegally because there is not enough money for law enforcement.

Apart from the direct loss of tropical forests and the plants and animals that depend on them, deforestation leads directly or indirectly to a number of other severe environmental problems. Forests protect the soil beneath them from the ravages of tropical rainstorms. After deforestation, much of the topsoil is washed away, lowering the productivity of the land and silting up watersheds and downstream coral reefs.

Cleared lands are frequently planted with a variety of crops, including acres of bananas, the production of which entails the use of pesticides as well as blue plastic bags to protect the fruit. Both the pesticides and the plastic end up polluting the environment. Cattle ranching has been another historical motivator for clear-cutting. It intensified during the 1970s, when Costa Rican coffee exports were waning in the global market.

Because deforestation plays a role in global warming, there is much interest in rewarding countries such as Costa Rica for taking the lead in protecting their forests. The USA has forgiven millions of dollars of Costa Rica's debt in exchange for increased efforts to preserve rainforests. The Costa Rican government itself sponsors a program that pays landowners for each hectare of forest they set aside, and has petitioned the UN for a global program that would pay tropical countries for their conservation efforts. Travelers interested in taking part in projects that can help protect Costa Rica's trees should look to volunteer opportunities in conservation and forestry (see p516 for more information).

Green Phoenix, by science journalist William Allen, is an absorbing account of his efforts, alongside scientists and activists, to conserve and restore the rainforest in Guanacaste.

Tourism

The other great environmental issue facing Costa Rica comes from the country being loved to death, directly through the passage of more than two million foreign tourists a year, and less directly through the development of extensive infrastructure to support this influx. For years resort hotels and lodges continued to pop up, most notably on formerly pristine beaches or in the middle of intact rainforest. Too many of these projects were poorly planned, and they necessitate additional support systems, including roads and countless vehicle trips, with much of this activity unregulated and largely unmonitored.

As tourism continues to become a larger piece of the Costa Rican economy, the bonanza invites more and more development. Taking advantage of Costa Rica's reputation as a green destination, developers promote mass tourism by building large hotels and package tours that, in turn, drive away wildlife, hasten erosion and strain local sewer and water systems. The irony is painful: they threaten to ruin the very environment that they're selling.

It's worth noting that many private lodges and reserves are also doing some of the best conservation work in the country, and it's heartening to run across the ever-increasing homespun efforts to protect Costa Rica's environment, spearheaded by hardworking families or small organizations tucked away in some quiet corner of the country. These include projects to boost rural economies by raising native medicinal plants, efforts by villagers to document their local biodiversity, and resourceful fundraising campaigns to purchase endangered lands.

The number-one reason for forest clearing in Central America is to graze cattle, mostly for export.

Sustainable Travel

Presently, Costa Rica's visitors account for the largest sector of the national economy and thus have unprecedented power to protect this country. How? By spending wisely, asking probing questions about sustainability claims and simply avoiding businesses that threaten Costa Rica's future.

In its purest form, sustainable tourism simply means striking the ideal balance between the traveler and their surrounding environment. This often includes being conscientious about energy and water consumption, and treading lightly on local environments and communities. Sustainable tourism initiatives support their communities by hiring local people for decent wages, furthering women's and civil rights and supporting local schools, artists and food producers.

On the road, engage with the local economy as much as possible: for example, if a local artisan's handiwork catches your eye, make the purchase – every dollar infuses the micro-economy in the most direct (and rewarding) way.

Due to deforestation it is best to avoid products made from tropical hardwoods if you're uncertain of the origin.

How to Know if a Business Is Really Ecofriendly

Interpreting the jargon – 'green,' 'sustainable,' 'low carbon footprint', 'ecofriendly' – can be confusing when every souvenir stall and ATV tour operator claims to be ecofriendly. Since sustainable travel has no universal guidelines, here are some things to look for:

➡ For hotels and restaurants: obvious recycling programs, effective management of waste water and pollutants, and alternative energy systems and natural illumination, at a bare minimum.

➡ A high rating from a legitimate sustainability index. In Costa Rica, the government-sanctioned Certificado para la Sostenibilidad Turística

Above Hanging bridge, Bosque Nuboso Monteverde (p212)
Right Ecolodge, Puerto Viejo de Sarapiquí (p283)

BRIAN BAILEY / GETTY IMAGES ©

Wind turbines, Guanacaste province

Few organizations are as involved in building sustainable rainforest-based economies as the Rainforest Alliance. See the website for special initiatives in Costa Rica: www.rainforest-alliance.org.

(CST; www.turismo-sostenible.co.cr) offers a 'five-leaf' rating system. Factors considered by the CST include physical-biological parameters, infrastructure and services, and socioeconomic environment, including interaction with local communities. Its website has a complete directory.

➡ Partnership with environmental conservation programs, education initiatives or regional or local organizations that work on solving environmental problems.

➡ Grassroots connections: sourcing a majority of employees from the local population, associating with locally owned businesses, providing places where local handicrafts can be displayed for sale, serving foods that support local markets, and using local materials and products in order to maintain the health of the local economy.

Survival Guide

Directory A–Z

Accommodations

Accommodations come at every price and comfort level: from luxurious ecolodges and sparkling all-inclusive resorts to backpacker palaces and spartan rooms with little more than a bed and four cinderblock walls. The variety and number of rooms on offer means that advance booking is not usually mandatory.

Rates provided are for the high (dry) season, generally between December and April. Many lodges lower their prices during the low (rainy) season, from May to November. Prices change quickly, so view prices as approximations. Expect to pay a premium during Christmas, New Year and Easter week (Semana Santa). Prices are inclusive of tax and given in US dollars, which is the preferred currency for listing rates in Costa Rica. However, colones are accepted everywhere and are usually exchanged at current rates without an additional fee.

Paying with a credit card sometimes incurs additional fees. Note that many hotels charge per person rather than per room – read rates carefully.

The term *cabina* (cabin) is a catch-all that can define a wide range of prices and amenities – from very rustic to very expensive.

Apartments & Villas

The network of long-term rentals has grown dramatically in recent years. These can be an excellent option for families, as they typically include a kitchen and several bedrooms. The following networks of rental apartments are peer reviewed and cover a spectrum of prices, sophistication and amenities.

Airbnb Costa Rica (www.airbnb.com)

Escape Villas (www.villas-costarica.com) Has high-end villas across Costa Rica, most near Manuel Antonio. Suitable for families and honeymooners looking for luxury.

Vacation Rentals by Owner (VRBO; www.vrbo.com) Worldwide network of vacation rentals by owner; has hundreds of properties listed in Costa Rica.

B&Bs

Generally speaking, B&Bs in Costa Rica tend to be midrange to top-end affairs, often run by resident European and North American expats. You can find B&Bs listed in the *Tico Times* and on the following websites:

BedandBreakfast.com (www.bedandbreakfast.com/costa-rica.html)

Costa Rica Innkeepers Association (www.costaricainnkeepers.com)

Camping

➡ Camping on Costa Rica's coasts is not legal but is widely tolerated. Many local families camp at the beach during the holidays.

➡ Most major tourist destinations have at least one campsite and most budget hotels outside San José accommodate campers on their grounds. Although these usually include toilets, cold showers and basic self-catering facilities (a sink and a BBQ pit), they can be crowded and noisy.

➡ In most national parks campsites are usually of excellent quality and are rigorously cleaned and maintained by staff. As a general rule, you will need to carry in all of your food and supplies and carry out all of your trash.

➡ Theft is a major concern. Camp in a group if possible.

BOOK YOUR STAY ONLINE

For more accommodations reviews by Lonely Planet authors, check out http://lonelyplanet.com/hotels. You'll find independent reviews, as well as recommendations on the best places to stay. Best of all, you can book online.

If not, don't leave anything in the tent unattended.

➡ Don't camp near riverbanks, which are prone to flooding and home to snakes.

➡ Mosquito netting and repellent with DEET are often essential.

Hostels

Although there is still a handful of Hostelling International (HI) hostels left in Costa Rica, the backpacker scene has gone increasingly upmarket. Compared to other destinations in Central America, hostels in Costa Rica tend to be fairly expensive, though the quality of service and accommodations is unequaled. Expect to pay between US$10 and US$15 for a dorm bed.

Hotels

It is always advisable to ask to see a room – and a bathroom – before committing to a stay, especially in budget lodgings. Rooms within a single hotel can vary greatly.

Accommodations Prices
BUDGET

➡ Budget accommodations in the most popular regions of the country are competitive and need to be booked well in advance during the high season.

➡ The cheapest places generally have shared bathrooms, but it's still possible to get a double with a bathroom for US$25 in towns off the tourist trail.

➡ At the top end of the budget scale, rooms will frequently include a fan and a bathroom with hot water.

➡ Hot water in showers is often supplied by electric showerheads, which will dispense hot water if the pressure is kept low.

➡ Most budget hotels also have a few midrange options with more amenities,
including air-con and television.

➡ Wireless internet is increasingly available at budget accommodations, particularly in popular tourist destinations.

MIDRANGE

➡ Midrange rooms will be more comfortable than budget options, and will generally include a bathroom with gas-heated hot water, a choice between fans and air-con, and cable or satellite TV.

➡ Most midrange hotels have wireless internet, though often it is limited to the area near reception or the office.

➡ Many midrange places offer tour services, and will have an onsite restaurant or bar and a swimming pool or Jacuzzi

➡ Many hotels in this price range offer kitchenettes or even full kitchens.

TOP END

➡ This price bracket includes many ecolodges, all-inclusive resorts, and business and chain hotels, in addition to a strong network of intimate boutique hotels, remote jungle camps and upmarket B&Bs.

➡ Top-end places in Costa Rica adhere to the same standards of quality and

service as similarly priced accommodations in North American and Europe.

➡ The staff at hotels of this category will likely speak English.

➡ Many lodgings in this category include amenities such as hot-water bathtubs, private decks, satellite TV and air-con as well as concierge, tour and spa services.

➡ A typical breakfast is usually *gallo pinto* (literally 'spotted rooster'), a stir-fry of rice and beans. This national breakfast dish is usually served with eggs, cheese or *natilla* (sour cream). Tropical-style continental breakfasts are also offered.

RESERVING BY CREDIT CARD

➡ Some pricier hotels will require confirmation of a reservation with a credit card. Before doing so, note that some top-end hotels require a 50% to 100% deposit upfront when you reserve. This rule is not always clearly communicated.

➡ In most cases advance reservations can be canceled and refunded with enough notice. Ask the hotel about its cancellation policy before booking. It is often easier to make the reservation than to unmake it.

➡ Many hotels charge a hefty fee for credit-card use.

➡ Have the hotel fax or email you a confirmation. Hotels often get overbooked, and if you don't have a confirmation, you could be out of a room.

Climate

San José

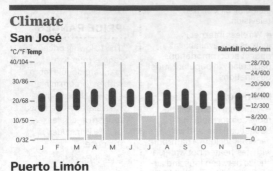

Puerto Limón

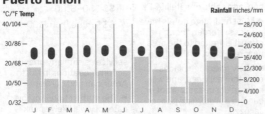

Puntarenas

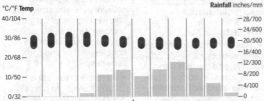

Electricity

120V/60Hz

120V/60Hz

Customs Regulations

➔ All travelers over the age of 18 are allowed to enter the country with 5L of wine or spirits and 500g of processed tobacco (400 cigarettes or 50 cigars).

➔ Camera gear, binoculars, and camping, snorkeling and other sporting equipment are readily allowed into the country.

➔ Dogs and cats are permitted entry to the country provided they have obtained both general health and rabies vaccination certificates.

➔ Pornography and illicit drugs are prohibited.

Discount Cards

Note that discount cards are not universally accepted at museums and parks.

Costa Rica Card (www.costaricacard.org; individual/couple/family US$30/40/60) Hotel and restaurant discounts through affiliated network; must be picked up in-country and used with photo ID.

International Student Identity Card (ISIC; www.isic.org; US$4 to US$25 depending on country of origin) Discounts on museum and tour fees for any full-time students.

International Student Exchange (ISE; www.isecard.com; full-time students between 12 and 26 years old US$25) Offers discounts on museums and tour fees.

Embassies & Consulates

Mornings are the best time to go to embassies and consulates. Australia and New Zealand do not have consular representation in Costa Rica;

their closest embassies are in Mexico City. Most countries are represented in San José.

Canadian Embassy (☎2242-4400; www.costarica.gc.ca; 3rd fl Oficentro Ejecutivo La Sabana, Edificio 5, Sabana Sur; ☺8am-noon & 12:30-4pm Mon-Thu, 7:30am-1pm Fri) Behind La Contraloría.

Dutch Embassy (☎2296-1490; http://costarica.nlambassade.org; 3rd fl, Oficentro La Sabana, Edificio 3, Sabana Sur; ☺by appointment only 8am-noon Mon & Tue, 8am-noon & 1-4pm Wed) Behind La Contraloría.

French Embassy (☎2234-4167; www.ambafrance-cr.org; Curridabat; ☺7:30am-12:30pm Mon-Fri) On the road to Curridabat, 200m south and 50m west of the Mitsubishi agency.

German Embassy (☎2290 9091; www.san-jose.diplo.de; 8th fl, Edificio Torre Sabana, Sabana Norte; ☺7:30am-4:30pm Mon-Thu, to 1:30pm Fri) Two blocks west of the ICE building.

Guatemalan Embassy (☎2220-1297, 2291-6172; www.minex.gob.gt; Sabana Sur; ☺8am-noon Mon-Fri) Situated 100m south and 50m west of Gimnasio Fitsimons.

Honduran Embassy (☎2291 5145, 2232-9506; www.embajadahonduras.co.cr; Blvd Rohrmoser; ☺9am-4pm Mon-Fri)

Israeli Embassy (☎2221-6444; http://embassies.gov.il; 11th fl, Oficentro Colón, Paseo Colón btwn Calles 38 & 40; ☺8am-4pm Mon-Fri)

Italian Embassy (☎2224-6574, 2234-2326; www.ambsanjose.esteri.it; ☺9am-noon Mon-Fri) In Los Yoses.

Mexican Embassy (☎2257-0633; http://embamex.sre.gob.mx/costarica; Av 7 btwn Calles 13 & 15; ☺9am-6pm Mon-Fri) About 250m south of the Subaru dealership, Los Yoses.

Nicaraguan Embassy (☎2221-2884, 2221-2957; www.cancilleria.gob.ni/embajadas; Av Central 2540 btwn Calles 25 & 27; ☺9am-5pm Mon-Fri) In Barrio La California.

Panamanian Embassy (☎2281-2442; www.embajadadepanamaencostarica.org; ☺9am-2pm Mon-Fri) In San Pedro.

Spanish Embassy (☎2222-5745, 2222-1933; www.exteriores.gob.es; Calle 32 btwn Paseo Colón & Av 2; ☺8am-noon Mon-Fri)

Swiss Embassy (☎2221-4829; www.eda.admin.ch/sanjose; 10th fl, Edificio Centro Colón, Paseo Colón btwn Calles 38 & 40; ☺9am-noon Mon-Fri)

UK Embassy (☎2258-2025; www.gov.uk/government/world/costa-rica; 11th fl, Edificio Centro Colón, Paseo Colón btwn Calles 38 & 40; ☺8:30am-4pm Mon-Thu, to 1pm Fri)

US Embassy (☎2519-2000; http://costarica.usembassy.gov; cnr Avenida Central & Calle 120; ☺8am-4:30pm Mon-Fri) Opposite Centro Commercial del Oeste in Pavas.

Food

For information about food in Costa Rica, see p55.

Gay & Lesbian Travelers

In Costa Rica the situation facing gay and lesbian travelers is better than in most Central American countries, and some areas of the country – particularly Quepos and Parque Nacional Manuel Antonio – have been gay vacation destinations for two decades. Homosexual acts are legal. Still, most Costa Ricans are tolerant of homosexuality only at a 'don't ask, don't tell' level. Same-sex couples are unlikely to be the subject of harassment, though public displays of affection might attract unwanted attention.

> **EATING PRICE RANGES**
>
> Throughout this guidebook, the following price ranges refer to a standard meal. Unless otherwise stated, tax is included in the price.
>
> **$** less than $10
> **$$** $10–15
> **$$$** more than $15

Since 1998 there have been laws on the books to protect 'sexual option', and discrimination is generally prohibited in most facets of society, including employment. And though the country is becoming increasingly more gay friendly along with the rest of the world, this traditional culture has not always been quick to adopt equal protection.

Legal recognition of same-sex partnerships has been a hot topic since 2006 and was a major point of contention in the 2010 presidential race. In January 2012 Costa Rica's primary newspaper *La Nación* conducted a poll in which 55% of the respondents believed that same-sex couples should have the same rights as heterosexual couples. Then in July 2013 the Costa Rican legislature 'accidentally' passed a law legalizing gay marriage, due to a small change in the bill's wording. At the time of writing, it had not been vetoed; however, the country's courts have not granted marriage rights to couples who have applied thus far.

The undisputed gay and lesbian capital of Costa Rica is Manuel Antonio; while there, keep an eye out for the gay magazine *Playita*. The monthly newspaper *Gayness* and the magazine *Gente 10* (in Spanish) are both available at gay bars in San José.

Agua Buena Human Rights Association
(☎2280-3548; www.agu-abuena.org) This noteworthy nonprofit organization has campaigned steadily for fairness in medical treatment for people living with HIV/AIDS in Costa Rica.

Center of Investigation & Promotion of Human Rights in Central America
(CIPAC; ☎2280-7821; www.cipacdh.org) The leading gay activist organization in Costa Rica.

International Gay & Lesbian Travel Association (IGLTA; ☎in USA 954-630-1637; www.iglta.org) This association maintains a list of hundreds of travel agents and tour operators all over the world.

Toto Tours (☎800-565-1241, in USA 773-274-8686; www.tototours.com) Gay-travel specialists who organize regular trips to Costa Rica, among other destinations.

Health

Before You Go

➡ Get necessary vaccinations four to eight weeks before departure.

➡ Ask your doctor for an International Certificate of Vaccination (otherwise known as the 'yellow booklet'), which will list all the vaccinations you've received. This is mandatory for countries that require proof of yellow-fever vaccination upon entry. (Costa Rica only requires such proof if you are entering from a country that carries a risk of yellow fever.)

➡ A list of medical evacuation and travel insurance companies can be found on the website of the **US State Department** (www.travel.state.gov) under the 'Before You Go' tab.

➡ Worldwide travel insurance is available at www.lonelyplanet.com/travel_services. You can buy, extend and claim online any time – even if you're already on the road.

In Costa Rica
AVAILABILITY & COST OF HEALTH CARE

➡ Good medical care is available in most major cities but may be limited in rural areas.

➡ For an extensive list of physicians, dentists and hospitals visit http://costarica.usembassy.gov/medical.html.

➡ Most pharmacies are well supplied and a handful are open 24 hours. Pharmacists are licensed to prescribe medication. If you're taking any medication on a regular basis, make sure you know its generic (scientific) name, since many pharmaceuticals go under different names in Costa Rica.

INFECTIOUS DISEASES

➡ **Dengue fever (breakbone fever)** Dengue is transmitted by *Aedes aegypti* mosquitoes, which often bite during the daytime and are usually found close to human habitations, often indoors. Dengue is especially common in densely populated urban environments. It usually causes flulike symptoms including fever, muscle aches, joint pains, headaches, nausea and vomiting, often followed by a rash. Most cases resolve uneventfully in a few days. There is no treatment for dengue fever except taking analgesics such as acetaminophen/paracetamol (Tylenol) and drinking plenty of fluids. Severe cases may require hospitalization for intravenous fluids and supportive care. There is no vaccine. The key to prevention is taking insect-protection measures.

➡ **Hepatitis A** The second-most common travel-related infection (after traveler's diarrhea). It's a viral infection of the liver that is usually acquired by ingestion of contaminated water, food or ice, though it may also be acquired by direct contact with infected persons. Symptoms may include fever, malaise, jaundice, nausea, vomiting and abdominal pain. Most cases resolve without complications, though hepatitis A occasionally causes severe liver damage. There is no treatment. The vaccine for hepatitis A is extremely safe and highly effective.

➡ **Leishmaniasis** This is transmitted by sand flies. Most cases occur in newly cleared forest or areas of secondary growth; the highest incidence is in Talamanca. It causes slow-growing ulcers over exposed parts of the body. There is no vaccine. To protect yourself from sand flies, follow the same precautions as for mosquitoes.

➡ **Malaria** Malaria is very rare in Costa Rica, occurring only occasionally in rural parts of the Limón province. It's transmitted by mosquito bites, usually between dusk and dawn. Taking malaria pills is not necessary unless you are making a long stay in the province of Limón (not Puerto Limón). Protection against mosquito bites is most effective.

➡ **Traveler's diarrhea** Tap water is safe and of high quality in Costa Rica, but when you're far off the beaten path it's best to avoid tap water unless it has been boiled, filtered or chemically disinfected (with iodine tablets). To prevent diarrhea, be wary of dairy products that might contain unpasteurized milk and be highly selective when eating food from street vendors. If you develop diarrhea, be sure to drink plenty of fluids, preferably with an oral rehydration solution containing lots of salt and sugar. If diarrhea is bloody or persists for more than 72 hours, or is accompanied by fever, shaking chills or severe abdominal pain, seek medical attention.

➜ **Typhoid** Caused by ingestion of food or water contaminated by a species of salmonella known as *Salmonella typhi*. Fever occurs in virtually all cases. Other symptoms may include headache, malaise, muscle aches, dizziness, loss of appetite, nausea and abdominal pain. Possible complications include intestinal perforation, intestinal bleeding, confusion, delirium or (rarely) coma. A pretrip vaccination is recommended.

ENVIRONMENTAL HAZARDS

➜ **Animal bites** Do not attempt to pet, handle or feed any animal. Any bite or scratch by a mammal, including bats, should be promptly and thoroughly cleansed with large amounts of soap and water, and an antiseptic such as iodine or alcohol should be applied. Contact a local health authority in the event of such an injury.

➜ **Insect bites** No matter how much you safeguard yourself, getting bitten by mosquitoes is part of every traveler's experience here. The best prevention is to stay covered up – wear long pants, long sleeves, a hat, and shoes, not sandals. Invest in a good insect repellent, preferably one containing DEET. Apply to exposed skin and clothing (but not to eyes, mouth, cuts, wounds or irritated skin). Compounds containing DEET should not be used on children under age the age of two and should be used sparingly on children

under 12. Invest in a bug net to hang over beds (along with a few thumbtacks or nails with which to hang it). Many hotels in Costa Rica don't have windows (or screens), and a cheap little net will save you plenty of nighttime aggravation. The mesh size should be less than 1.5mm. Dusk is the worst time for mosquitoes, so take extra precautions.

➜ **Sun** Stay out of the midday sun, wear sunglasses and a wide-brimmed hat, and apply sunblock with SPF 15 or higher, with both UVA and UVB protection. Drink plenty of fluids and avoid strenuous exercise when the temperature is high.

Internet Access

➜ Costa Rica has plenty of internet cafes and many businesses have wi-fi.

➜ Expect to pay US$1 to US$2 per hour in San José and tourist towns.

➜ Wi-fi is common in all midrange and top-end hotels; most hotels of all budget ranges have a computer for guest use and/or wi-fi.

Language Courses

➜ Spanish-language schools operate all over Costa Rica and charge by the hour for instruction.

➜ Many courses can be found in central San José and the suburb of San Pedro, and the Central Valley.

➜ It is best to arrange classes in advance. A good clearinghouse is the **Institute for Spanish Language Studies** (ISLS; ☎2258-5111, in USA 866-391-0394; www.isls.com), which has eight schools in Costa Rica.

Legal Matters

➜ If you are arrested your embassy can offer limited assistance. Embassy officials will not bail you out and you are subject to Costa Rican laws, not the laws of your own country.

➜ In Costa Rica the legal age for driving and voting is 18 years.

➜ Keep in mind that travelers may be subject to the laws of their own country in regard to sexual relations.

Drivers & Driving Accidents

➡ Drivers should carry their passport and driver's license at all times.

➡ If you have an accident, call the police immediately to make a report (which is required for insurance purposes).

➡ Leave the vehicles in place until the report has been made and do not make any statements except to members of a law-enforcement agency.

Maps

Detailed maps are, unfortunately, hard to come by in Costa Rica; best to purchase one online before your trip.

➡ The excellent, water-resistant 1:350,000 *Costa Rica Adventure Map* published by National Geographic also has an inset map of San José. You can find it in San José, various book and gift shops and online.

➡ Another quality option is the 1:330,000 *Costa Rica* sheet produced by International Travel Map, which is waterproof and includes a San José inset.

➡ The **Fundación Neotrópica** (☎2253-2130; www.neotropica.org) publishes a 1:500,000 map showing national parks and other protected areas; available in San José bookstores and online.

➡ The Instituto Costarricense de Turismo (ICT) publishes a 1:700,000 *Costa Rica* map with a 1:12,500 *Central San José* map on the reverse. Pick it up free at ICT offices in San José.

➡ Online, **Maptak** (www.maptak.com) has maps of Costa Rica's seven provinces and their capitals.

➡ Few national-park offices or ranger stations have maps for hikers. Topographical maps are available for purchase from **Instituto Geográfico Nacional** (IGN; ☎2257-7798; Calle 9 btwn Avs 20 & 22; ☺7:30am-noon & 1-3pm Mon-Fri).

EXPLOITATION & COSTA RICA'S SEX TRADE

Exit the baggage claim at the international airport in San José and you'll be welcomed by a sign that reads 'In Costa Rica sex with children under 18 is a serious crime. Should you engage in it we will drive you to jail'. For decades, travelers have arrived in Costa Rica in search of sandy beaches and lush mountainscapes. Unfortunately, an unknown percentage of them also come in search of sex – not all of it legal.

Prostitution by men and women over the age of 18 is perfectly legal. But the tourist juggernaut of the last few decades has fueled illicit activities at its fringes – namely child prostitution and, to a lesser degree, human trafficking. Sex with a minor in Costa Rica is illegal, carrying a penalty of up to 10 years in jail, but child prostitution has nonetheless flourished. In fact, a number of aid groups, along with the country's national child-welfare agency (Patronato Nacional de la Infancia; PANI), estimate that there may be as many as 3000 child prostitutes in San José alone. In turn, this has led to women and children being trafficked for the purpose of sexual exploitation, as documented in a 2008 report issued by the US Department of State.

Alarm over the problem has increased steadily since 1999, when the UN Committee on Human Rights issued a statement saying that it was 'deeply concerned' about child-sex tourism in Costa Rica. Since then, the government has established national task forces to combat the problem, trained the police force in how to deal with issues of child exploitation and formed a coalition against human trafficking. But enforcement remains weak – largely due to lack of personnel and lack of funding. Meanwhile the USA – the principal source of sex tourists to Costa Rica – has made it a prosecutable crime for Americans to have sex with minors anywhere in the world.

Along with Thailand and Cambodia, Costa Rica is one of the most popular sex-tourism destinations in the world, according to Ecpat International, a nonprofit dedicated to ending child prostitution. The phenomenon has been magnified by the internet: there are entire sex-tourism websites, in which Costa Rica figures prominently.

Various organizations fight the sexual exploitation of children in Costa Rica. See the websites of Ecpat International (www.ecpat.org) and Cybertipline (www.cybertipline.com) to learn more about the problem or to report any incidents you encounter.

→ The *Mapa-Guía de la Naturaleza Costa Rica* is an atlas no longer published by Incafo. The atlas included 1:200,000 topographical sheets, as well as English and Spanish descriptions of Costa Rica's natural areas. Out-of-print secondhand copies can be purchased online.

Money

ATMs

→ *Cajeros automáticos* (ATMS) are ubiquitous in all but Costa Rica's smallest towns.

→ Most ATMs dispense US dollars or Costa Rican colones.

Cash & Currency

→ The Costa Rican currency is the colón (plural colones), named after Cristóbal Colón (Christopher Columbus).

→ Bills come in 1000, 2000, 5000, 10,000, 20,000 and 50,000 notes, while coins come in denominations of five, 10, 20, 25, 50, 100 and 500.

→ Paying for things in US dollars is common, and at times is encouraged, since the currency is viewed as being more stable than colones.

→ Newer US dollars (ie big heads) are preferred throughout Costa Rica.

→ When paying in US dollars at a local restaurant, bar or shop the exchange rate can be unfavorable.

Credit Cards

→ Expect a transaction fee on all international credit-card purchases.

→ Holders of credit and debit cards can buy colones in some banks, though you can expect to pay a high transaction fee.

→ Cards are widely accepted at midrange and top-end hotels, as well as at top-end restaurants and some travel agencies.

→ All car-rental agencies require drivers to have a credit card.

Exchanging Money

All banks will exchange US dollars, and some will exchange euros and British pounds; other currencies are more difficult. Most banks have excruciatingly long lines, especially at the state-run institutions (Banco Nacional, Banco de Costa Rica, Banco Popular), though they don't charge commission on cash exchanges. Private banks (Banex, Banco Interfin, Scotiabank) tend to be faster. Make sure the bills you want to exchange are in good condition or they may be refused.

Taxes

Travelers will notice a 13% sales tax at hotels and restaurants, although many smaller budget and midrange businesses waive the tax (shhh) if you pay in cash.

Tipping

It is customary to tip the bellhop/porter (US$1 to US$5 per service) and the housekeeper (US$1 to US$2 per day) in top-end hotels, less in budget places. On guided tours, tip the guide US$5 to US$15 per person per day. Tip the tour driver about half of what you tip the guide. Naturally, tips depend

upon quality of service. Taxi drivers are not normally tipped, unless some special service is provided. Top-end restaurants may add a 10% service charge to the bill. If not, you might leave a small tip to show your appreciation, but it is not required.

Traveler's Checks

With the popularity of ATMs and credit cards, traveler's checks are increasingly uncommon in Costa Rica. They can be exchanged at banks, typically only for US dollars or Costa Rican colones.

Opening Hours

Banks Hours are variable, but most are open at least from 9am to 4pm Monday to Friday.

Restaurants Usually open from 7am and serve dinner until 9pm, though upscale places may open only for dinner. In remote areas, even the small *sodas* (inexpensive eateries) might open only at specific meal times.

Government offices Typically open between 8am and 5pm Monday to Friday, but often closed between 11:30am and 1:30pm.

Shops Most are open from 8am to 6pm Monday to Saturday.

Sights and activities Unless otherwise stated, count on these to be open daily.

DOLLARS VERSUS COLONES

While colones are the official currency of Costa Rica, US dollars are virtually legal tender. Case in point: most ATMs in large towns and cities will dispense both currencies. However, it pays to know where and when you should be paying with each currency.

In Costa Rica you can use US dollars to pay for hotel rooms, midrange to top-end meals, admission fees for sights, tours, domestic flights, international buses, car hire, private shuttle buses and large-ticket purchase items. Local meals and drinks, domestic bus fares, taxis and small-ticket purchase items should be paid for in colones.

All of our listings have prices in US dollars.

Photography

➡ Always ask permission to take someone's photo.

➡ With the prominence of digital cameras, it is increasingly difficult to purchase high-quality film in Costa Rica.

➡ Most internet cafes can burn your digital pictures onto a CD, and cheap media is available for purchase in most large towns and cities.

Post

➡ Mailing smaller parcels (less than 2kg) internationally is quite reliable; for example, a 1kg package costs around US$16 to ship to North America and takes one to three weeks to arrive.

➡ EMS (Express Mail Service) courier service costs a bit more but includes tracking and is speedier.

Public Holidays

Días feriados (national holidays) are taken seriously in Costa Rica. Banks, public offices and many stores close.

During these times, public transport is tight and hotels are heavily booked. Many festivals coincide with public holidays.

New Year's Day January 1

Semana Santa (Holy Week; March or April) The Thursday and Friday before Easter Sunday is the official holiday, though most businesses shut down for the whole week. From Thursday to Sunday bars are closed and alcohol sales are prohibited; on Thursday and Friday buses stop running.

Día de Juan Santamaría (April 11) Honors the national hero who died fighting William Walker in 1856; major events are held in Alajuela, his hometown.

Labor Day May 1

Día de la Madre (Mother's Day; August 15) Coincides with the annual Catholic Feast of the Assumption.

Independence Day September 15

Día de la Raza (Columbus Day) October 12

Christmas Day (December 25) Christmas Eve is also an unofficial holiday.

Last week in December The week between Christmas and New Year is an unofficial holiday; businesses close and beach hotels are crowded.

Safe Travel

For the latest official reports on travel to Costa Rica, see the websites of the **US State Department** (www.travel.state.gov) or the **UK Foreign & Commonwealth Office** (www.fco.gov.uk).

Earthquakes & Volcanic Eruptions

Costa Rica lies on the edge of active tectonic plates, so it is decidedly earthquake-prone. Recent major quakes occurred in 1990 (7.1 on the Richter scale) and 1991 (7.4). Smaller quakes and tremors happen quite often (particularly on the Península de Nicoya) cracking roads and knocking down telephone lines. The volcanoes in Costa Rica are not really dangerous, though, as long as you stay on designated trails and don't try to peer into the crater of an active volcano. As a precaution, always check with park rangers before setting out in the vicinity of active volcanoes.

Hiking Hazards

Hikers setting out into the wilderness should be adequately prepared for their trips.

➡ Know your limits and don't set out to do a hike you can't reasonably complete.

➡ Carry plenty of water, even on very short trips.

➡ Carry maps, extra food and a compass.

➡ Let someone know where you are going, so they can narrow the search area in the event of an emergency.

➡ Be aware that Costa Rica's wildlife can pose a threat to hikers, particularly in Parque Nacional Corcovado.

Riptides

Each year Costa Rican waters see approximately 200 drownings, 90% of which are caused by riptides (strong currents that pull the swimmer out to sea). Many deaths in riptides are caused by panicked swimmers struggling to the point of exhaustion. If you are caught in a riptide, do not struggle. Simply float and let the tide carry you out beyond the breakers, after which the riptide will dissipate, then swim parallel to the beach and allow the surf to carry you back in.

Thefts & Muggings

The biggest danger that most travelers face is theft, primarily from pickpockets. There is a lot of petty crime in Costa Rica, so keep your wits about you at all times.

Shopping

Avoid purchasing animal products, including turtle shells, animal skulls and anything made with feathers, coral or shells. Wood products are also highly suspicious: make sure you know where the wood came from.

Coffee & Alcohol

➔ Coffee is the most popular souvenir, available pretty much everywhere. Find specialty beans in places like Café Milagro in Quepos, throughout the Central Valley and Valle de los Santos (Santa Maria de Dota, for example) and around San Vito.

➔ The most popular alcohol purchases are Ron Centenario, Café Rica (the coffee liqueur) and *guaro* (the local firewater). All are available at duty-free shops inside the airport, or in supermarkets and liquor stores in every town and city.

Handicrafts

➔ Tropical-hardwood items include salad bowls, plates, carving boards, jewelry boxes and a variety of carvings and ornaments. The most exquisite woodwork is available at Biesanz

---

Woodworks in Escazú. All of the wood here is grown on farms expressly for this purpose.

➔ Uniquely Costa Rican souvenirs are the colorfully painted replicas of *carretas* (traditional oxcarts) produced in Sarchí.

➔ Intricately carved and strikingly painted masks made by the Boruca people are found at Galería Namu in San José and in the village of Boruca.

Telephone

➔ Cellular service now covers most of the country and nearly all of the country that is accessible to tourists.

➔ Public phones are found all over Costa Rica, and chip or Colibrí phone cards are available in 1000-, 2000- and 3000-colón denominations.

➔ Chip cards are inserted into the phone and scanned. Colibrí cards (more common) require you to dial a toll-free number (199) and enter an access code. Instructions are provided in English or Spanish.

➔ The cheapest international calls from Costa Rica are direct-dialed using a phone card. To make international calls, dial '00' followed by the country code and number.

➔ Pay phones cannot receive international calls.

➔ To call Costa Rica from abroad, use the country code (506) before the eight-digit number.

➔ Due to the increasing popularity of voice-over IP services such as Skype, and more reliable ethernet connections, traveling with a laptop and headset can be the cheapest way to call internationally.

Time

Costa Rica is six hours behind GMT, so Costa Rican time is equivalent to Central Time in North America. There is no daylight-saving time.

Toilets

➔ Public restrooms are rare, but most restaurants and cafes will let you use their facilities, sometimes for a small charge – never more than 500 colones.

➔ Bus terminals and other major public buildings usually have toilets, also at a charge.

➔ Don't flush your toilet paper. Costa Rican plumbing is often poor and has very low pressure.

➔ Dispose of toilet paper in the rubbish bin inside the bathroom.

Tourist Information

➔ The government-run tourism board, the **ICT** (☑in USA 800-343-6332; www. visitcostarica.com), has two offices in the capital.

➔ The ICT can provide you with free maps, a master bus schedule and information on road conditions in the hinterlands. English is spoken.

➔ Consult the ICT's English-language website for information.

➔ From the USA call the ICT's toll-free number for brochures and information.

Travelers with Disabilities

Independent travel in Costa Rica is difficult for anyone with mobility constraints. Although Costa Rica has an equal-opportunity law, the law applies only to new or newly remodeled businesses and is loosely enforced. Therefore, very few hotels and restaurants have features specifically suited to wheelchair use. Many don't have ramps, and room or bathroom doors are rarely wide enough to accommodate a wheelchair.

Outside the buildings, streets and sidewalks are potholed and poorly paved, making wheelchair use frustrating at best. Public buses don't have provisions to carry wheelchairs, and most national parks and outdoor tourist attractions don't have trails suited to wheelchair use. Notable exceptions include **Parque Nacional Volcán Poás** (☑2482-1226; admission US$10; ◷8am-3:30pm), **INBioparque** (☑2507-8107; www.inbioparque.com/en; Santo Domingo; adult/student/ child US$25/19/15, separate serpentarium admission adult/ child US$3/2; ◷9am-3pm Fri, to 4pm Sat & Sun; ▮) 🖉 and

the **Rainforest Aerial Tram** (☑2257-5961, in USA 1-866-759-8726; www.rainforest adventure.com; adult/student & child tram US$60/30, zip line US$50/35; ▮).

Visas

Passport-carrying nationals of the following countries are allowed 90 days' stay with no visa: Argentina, Australia, Canada, Chile, Iceland, Ireland, Israel, Japan, Mexico, New Zealand, Panama, South Africa, the USA and most western European countries.

Most others require a visa from a Costa Rican embassy or consulate.

For the latest info on visas, check the websites of the **ICT** (☑in USA 800-343-6332; www.visitcostarica.com) or the **Costa Rican embassy** (www.costarica-embassy.org) in Washington, DC.

Extensions

➔ Extending your stay beyond the authorized 30 or 90 days is time consuming; it's easier to leave the country for 72 hours and then re-enter.

➔ Extensions can be handled by the **migración** (immigration office; ☑2220-0355; ◷8am-4pm) in San José, opposite Channel 6, about 4km north of Parque La Sabana.

➔ Requirements for extensions change, so allow several working days.

Onward Tickets

Travelers officially need onward tickets before they are allowed to enter Costa Rica. This requirement is not often checked at the airport, but travelers arriving by land should anticipate the need to show an onward ticket.

If you're heading to Panama, Nicaragua or another Central or South American country from Costa Rica, you may need an onward or round-trip ticket before you will be allowed entry into

that country or even allowed to board the plane, if you're flying. A quick check with the appropriate embassy – easy to do via the internet – will tell you whether the country you're heading to has an onward-ticket requirement.

Volunteering

Costa Rica offers a huge number of volunteer opportunities. Word of mouth is a powerful influence on future volunteers, so a majority of programs in Costa Rica are very conscientious about pleasing their volunteers. Almost all placements require a commitment of two weeks or more.

English Teaching

Amerispan Study Abroad (www.amerispan.com) Offers a variety of educational travel programs in specialized areas.

Sustainable Horizon (www. sustainablehorizon.com) Arranges volunteering trips such as guest-teaching spots.

Forestry Management

Cloudbridge Nature Reserve (www.cloudbridge. org) Trail building, construction, tree planting and projects monitoring the recovery of the cloud forest are offered to volunteers, who pay for their own housing with a local family. Preference is given to biology students, but all enthusiastic volunteers can apply.

Tropical Science Center (www.cct.or.cr) This long-standing NGO offers volunteer placement at Reserva Biológica Bosque Nuboso Monteverde. Projects can include trail maintenance and conservation work.

Fundación Corcovado (www.corcovadofoundation.org) An impressive network of people and organizations committed to preserving Parque Nacional Corcovado.

Monteverde Institute (www.monteverde-institute.org) A nonprofit educational institute offering training in tropical biology, conservation and sustainable development.

Organic Farming

WWOOF Costa Rica (www.wwoofcostarica.org) This loose network of farms is part of the large international network of Willing Workers on Organic Farms (WWOOF). Placements are incredibly varied. WWOOF Mexico, Costa Rica, Guatemala and Belize have a joint $33 membership, which gives potential volunteers access to all placement listings.

Reserva Biológica Dúrika (www.durika.org) A sustainable community on an 8500-sq-km biological reserve.

Finca La Flor de Paraíso (www.la-flor.org) Offers programs in a variety of disciplines from animal husbandry to medicinal-herb cultivation.

Punta Mona (www.puntamona.org) An organic farm and retreat center that is centred on organic permaculture and sustainable living.

Rancho Margot (www.ranchomargot.com) This self-proclaimed life-skills university offers a natural education emphasizing organic farming and animal husbandry.

Wildlife Conservation

Earthwatch (www.earthwatch.org) This broadly recognized international volunteer organization works

in sea-turtle conservation in Costa Rica.

Sea Turtle Conservancy (www.conserveturtles.org) From March to October, this Puerto Limón organization hosts 'eco-volunteer adventures' working with sea turtles and birds.

Profelis (www.grafischer.com/profelis) A feline conservation program that takes care of confiscated wild cats, both big and small.

Women Travelers

Most female travelers experience little more than a *'mi amor'* ('my love') or an appreciative hiss from the local men. But, in general, Costa Rican men consider foreign women to have looser morals and to be easier conquests than Ticas (female Costa Ricans). Men will often make flirtatious comments to single women, particularly blondes, and women traveling together are not exempt. The best response is to do what Ticas do: ignore it completely. Women who firmly resist unwanted verbal advances from men are normally treated with respect

➡ In small highland towns, dress is usually conservative. Women rarely wear shorts, but belly-baring tops are all the rage. On the beach, skimpy bathing suits are OK,

but topless and nude bathing are not.

➡ Solo women travelers should avoid hitchhiking.

➡ Do not take unlicensed 'pirate' taxis (licensed taxis are red and have medallions) as there have been reports of assaults on women by unlicensed drivers.

➡ Birth-control pills are available at most pharmacies without a prescription.

Work

It is difficult for foreigners to find work in Costa Rica. The only foreigners legally employed in Costa Rica are those who work for their own businesses, possess skills not found in the country, or work for companies that have special agreements with the government.

Getting a bona fide job necessitates obtaining a work permit, which can be a time-consuming and difficult process. The most likely source of paid employment is as an English teacher at one of the language institutes, or in the hospitality industry in a hotel or resort. Naturalists or river guides may also be able to find work with either private lodges or adventure-travel operators, though you shouldn't expect to make more than survival wages.

Transportation

GETTING THERE & AWAY

Flights, cars and tours can be booked online at lonelyplanet.com/bookings.

Entering the Country

➜ Entering Costa Rica is mostly free of hassle, with the exception of some long queues at the airport.

➜ The vast majority of travelers enter the country by plane, and most international flights arrive at Aeropuerto Internacional Juan Santamaría, outside San José.

➜ Liberia is a growing destination for international flights; it is in the Guanacaste province and serves travelers heading to the Península de Nicoya.

➜ Overland border crossings are straightforward and

travelers can move freely between Panama to the south and Nicaragua to the north.

➜ Some foreign nationals will require a visa. Be aware that you cannot get a visa at the border. For more information on visas see the Directory (p516).

Passport

➜ Citizens of all nations are required to have a passport that is valid for at least six months beyond the dates of your trip.

➜ The law requires that you carry your passport at all times; if you're driving, you must have your passport handy, but otherwise the law is seldom enforced.

Onward Ticket

➜ Officially, travelers are required to have a ticket out of Costa Rica before they are allowed to enter. This is rarely and erratically enforced.

➜ Those arriving overland with no onward ticket can purchase one from international bus companies in Managua (Nicaragua) and Panama City (Panama).

Air

Airports & Airlines

➜ Costa Rica is well connected by air to other Central and South American countries, as well as the USA.

➜ International flights arrive at Aeropuerto Internacional Juan Santamaría, 17km northwest of San José, in the town of Alajuela.

➜ Aeropuerto Internacional Daniel Oduber Quirós in Liberia also receives international flights from the USA, the Americas and Canada. It serves a number of American and Canadian airlines and some charters from London.

CLIMATE CHANGE & TRAVEL

Every form of transport that relies on carbon-based fuel generates CO_2, the main cause of human-induced climate change. Modern travel is dependent on airplanes, which might use less fuel per kilometer per person than most cars but travel much greater distances. The altitude at which aircraft emit gases (including CO_2) and particles also contributes to their climate change impact. Many websites offer 'carbon calculators' that allow people to estimate the carbon emissions generated by their journey and, for those who wish to do so, to offset the impact of the greenhouse gases emitted with contributions to portfolios of climate-friendly initiatives throughout the world. Lonely Planet offsets the carbon footprint of all staff and author travel.

AIRLINES SERVING SAN JOSÉ

Over a dozen international airlines fly to/from Aeropuerto Internacional Juan Santamaría. Listed below are most of the airlines and the destinations to which they offer direct flights.

Aeroméxico (www.aeromexico.com) To Mexico City.

Air Canada (www.aircanada.com) To Toronto.

Air Transat (www.airtransat.com) To Montreal and Toronto.

American Airlines (www.aa.com) To Dallas, Miami and New York.

Avianca (www.avianca.com) To Managua (Nicaragua), Panama City, Bogotá (Colombia) and other Latin American destinations.

Condor (www.condor.com) To Germany via Santo Domingo (Dominican Republic).

COPA (www.copaair.com) To Panama City.

Delta (www.delta.com) To Atlanta, Denver, Los Angeles and New York.

Frontier (www.flyfrontier.com) To Denver.

Iberia (www.iberia.com) To Madrid.

Interjet (www.interjet.com) To Mexico City.

JetBlue (www.jetblue.com) To Fort Lauderdale and Orlando.

Nature Air (www.natureair.com) To Managua, and Bocas del Toro (Panama).

Spirit (www.spirit.com) To Fort Lauderdale.

United Airlines (www.united.com) To Houston and Newark.

US Airways (www.usairways.com) To Charlotte and Philadelphia.

➡ The national airline, Avianca (part of the Central American airline consortium Grupo TACA), flies to the USA and Latin America, including Cuba.

➡ The US Federal Aviation Administration has assessed Costa Rica's aviation authorities to be in compliance with international safety standards.

Tickets

➡ Airline fares are usually more expensive during the Costa Rican high season (from December through April).

➡ December and January are the most expensive months to travel.

Central & Latin America

➡ **American Airlines** (www. aa.com), **Delta** (www.delta. com), **United** (www.united. com) and **US Airways**

(www.usairways.com) have connections to Costa Rica from many Central and Latin American countries. Grupo TACA usually offers the most flights on these routes.

➡ **Nature Air** (www.natureair. com) now flies from Liberia to Granada (Nicaragua). Note that rates vary considerably according to season and availability.

➡ **Grupo TACA** offers daily direct flights to Caracas (Venezuela), Guatemala City (Guatemala) and San Salvador (El Salvador). TACA and **Mexicana** have daily flights to Mexico City, while both TACA and COPA have several flights a day to Panama City. Rates vary considerably according to season and availability.

Other Countries

➡ Flights from Houston, Miami or New York are most common.

➡ From Canada, most travelers to Costa Rica connect through US gateway cities, though Air Canada has direct flights from Toronto.

➡ From the UK, Costa Rica is served by **British Airways** and **Virgin**, typically with at least one stop.

➡ Most flights from the UK and Europe connect either in the USA or in Mexico City. Be aware that high-season fares may still apply during the northern summer, even though this is the beginning of the Costa Rican rainy season.

➡ From Australia and New Zealand, travel routes usually go through the USA or Mexico. Fares are highest in June and July, even though this is the beginning of the rainy season in Costa Rica.

DEPARTURE TAX

→ There is a US$29 departure tax on all international outbound flights, payable in dollars or colones.

→ At the Juan Santamaría and Liberia airports this tax can be paid in cash or by credit card; Banco de Costa Rica has an ATM by the departure-tax station. Note that credit-card payments are processed as cash advances, which often carry hefty fees.

→ Travelers will not be allowed through airport security without paying.

Land

Border Crossings

→ Costa Rica shares land borders with Nicaragua and Panama. There is no fee for travelers to enter Costa Rica; however, there have been several reports of towns recently adding their own entry/exit fees, usually US$1.

NICARAGUA

Situated on the Interamericana, **Sapoá–Peñas Blancas** is the most heavily trafficked border station between Nicaragua and Costa Rica (see p242 for more information).

→ This is the only official border between Nicaragua and Costa Rica that you can drive across.

→ Waiting times at this border can be several hours. Plan on at least an hour's wait.

→ **Tica Bus** (🖉 in Managua 222-6094, in Panama City 262 2084), **Nica Bus** (🖉 in Managua 228-1374) and **TransNica** (Map p68; 🖉 2223-4123; www.transnica.com; Calle 22 btwn Avs 3 & 5) all have daily buses that serve points north and south. Regular buses depart Peñas Blancas, on the Costa Rican side, for La Cruz, Liberia and San José.

→ Note that Peñas Blancas is only a border post, not a town, so there is nowhere to stay.

Very rarely used by travelers, the **San Carlos–Los Chiles** crossing must be done by boat (see p270 for more information).

PANAMA

Note that Panama is GMT minus five hours, one hour ahead of Costa Rica.

At the time of writing, entry to Panama required proof of US$500 (per person), proof of onward travel from Panama and two photocopies of your passport. Travelers have reported being turned away from Panamanian border crossings even with onward bus tickets, so our tip is to reserve an airline ticket online (for a flight originating in Panama), print the itinerary, and let the reservation expire without actually booking it.

The Carretera Interamericana (Pan-American Hwy) at **Paso Canoas** is by far the most frequently used entry and exit point with Panama, and is open 6am to 10pm Monday to Friday, and to 8pm on weekends.

→ The border crossing in either direction is generally straightforward, if slow.

→ Get an exit stamp from Costa Rica at the *migración* (immigration office) before entering Panama; do the same on the Panamanian side when entering Costa Rica.

→ There is no charge for entering Costa Rica. Entry to Panama costs US$1.

→ Northbound buses usually stop running at 6pm. Travelers without a private vehicle should arrive during the day.

→ Those with a private vehicle are likely to encounter long lines.

→ Tica Bus travels from Panama City to San José (US$42 to US$58, 15 hours) daily and crosses this border post. In David, Tracopa has one bus daily from the main terminal to San José (nine hours). In David you'll also find frequent buses to the border at Paso Canoas (US$2.50, 1½ hours) that leave every 10 minutes from 4am to 8pm.

Situated on the Caribbean coast, **Guabito–Sixaola** is a fairly tranquil and hassle-free border crossing (see p189 for more information).

→ If you are coming from Bocas del Toro, it's faster and cheaper to take the ferry to Changuinola (US$7, 45 minutes), from where you can take a quick taxi to the border or to the bus station (US$5). One daily bus travels between Changuinola and San José at 10am (US$15, eight hours). Otherwise, you can walk over the border and catch one of the hourly buses that go up the coast from Sixaola.

→ **Río Sereno–San Vito** is a rarely used crossing in the Cordillera de Talamanca. The border is open 8am to 4pm on the Costa Rican side and 9am to 5pm on the Panamanian side. The small village of Río Sereno on the Panamanian side has a hotel and a place to eat; there are no facilities on the Costa Rican side.

→ Regular buses depart Concepción and David in

Panama for Río Sereno. Local buses (four daily) and taxis go from the border to San Vito.

➡ For travelers departing Costa Rica, there is a US$7 exit tax, payable at the Coopealianza in Sabalito, or, if you have a digitally readable passport, at a **kiosk** (☎2784-0130; ◷8am-4pm) at the border crossing.

Bus

➡ If crossing a border by bus, note that international buses may cost slightly more than taking a local bus to the border, then another onward from the border, but they're worth it. These companies are familiar with border procedures and will tell you what's needed to cross efficiently.

➡ There will be no problems crossing borders provided your papers are in order. If you are on an international bus, you'll have to exit the bus and proceed through both border stations. Bus drivers will wait for everyone to be processed before heading on.

➡ If you choose to take local buses, it's advisable to get to border stations early in the day to allow time for waiting in line and processing. Note that onward buses tend to wind down by the afternoon.

➡ International buses go from San José to Changuinola (Bocas del Toro), David and Panama City in Panama; Guatemala City in Guatemala; Managua in Nicaragua; San Salvador in El Salvador; and Tegucigalpa in Honduras.

Car & Motorcycle

The cost of insurance, fuel and border permits makes a car journey significantly more expensive than buying an airline ticket. To enter Costa Rica by car, you'll need the following items:

➡ valid registration and proof of ownership

➡ valid driver's license or International Driving Permit

➡ valid license plates

➡ recent inspection certificate

➡ passport

➡ multiple photocopies of all these documents in case the originals get lost.

Before departing, check that the following elements are present and in working order:

➡ blinkers and head- and taillights

➡ spare tire

➡ jerry can for extra gas (petrol)

➡ well-stocked toolbox including parts, such as belts, that are harder to find in Central America

➡ emergency flares and roadside triangles.

Insurance from foreign countries isn't recognized in Costa Rica, so you'll have to buy a policy locally. At the border it will cost about US$15 a month. In addition, you'll probably have to pay a US$22 road tax to be allowed to drive in.

You are not allowed to sell the car in Costa Rica. If you need to leave the country without the car, it must be left in a customs warehouse in San José.

Sea

➡ Cruise ships stop in Costa Rican ports and enable passengers to make a quick foray into the country. Typically, ships dock at either the Pacific ports of Caldera, Quepos and Bahía Drake, or the Caribbean port of Puerto Limón.

➡ It is also possible to arrive in Costa Rica by private yacht.

GETTING AROUND

Air

Scheduled Flights

➡ Costa Rica's domestic airlines are **Nature Air** (☎2220-3054; www.natureair. com) and **Sansa** (☎2290-4100; www.flysansa.com). Sansa is linked with Grupo TACA.

➡ Both airlines fly small passenger planes, and you're allocated a baggage allowance of no more than 12kg.

➡ Space is limited and demand is high in the dry season, so reserve and pay for tickets in advance.

➡ In Costa Rica schedules change constantly and delays are frequent because of inclement weather. You should not arrange a domestic flight that makes a tight connection with an international flight back home.

➡ All domestic flights originate and terminate at San José. Destinations reached from San José include Bahía Drake, Barra del Colorado, Golfito, Liberia, Palmar Sur, Playa Nosara, Playa Sámara/Carrillo, Playa Tamarindo, Puerto Jiménez, Quepos, Tambor and Tortuguero.

Charters

➡ Travelers on a larger budget or in a larger party should consider chartering a private plane, which is by far the quickest way to travel around the country.

➡ It takes under 90 minutes to fly to most destinations, though weather conditions can significantly speed up or delay travel time.

➡ The two most reputable charters in the country are **Nature Air** (☎2220-3054; www.natureair.com) and **Alfa Romeo Aero Taxi** (www.

Domestic Air Routes

High-season scheduled flights with Sansa or Nature Air
— — — Some connecting flights with Sansa or Nature Air
• Some airports for light charter planes

Flights subject to change, especially in low season

alfaromeoair.com). Both can be booked directly through the company, a tour agency or some high-end accommodations.

➜ Luggage space on charters is extremely limited.

Bicycle

➜ With an increasingly large network of paved secondary roads and heightened awareness of cyclists, Costa Rica is emerging as one of Central America's most comfortable cycle-touring destinations.

➜ Mountain bikes and beach cruisers can be rented in towns with a significant tourist presence, for US$6 to US$15 per day. A few companies organize bike tours around Costa Rica.

Boat

➜ Ferries cross the Golfo de Nicoya, connecting the central Pacific coast with the southern tip of Península de Nicoya.

➜ The **Coonatramar Ferry** (☎2661-1069; www.coonatramar.com; adult/child/bicycle/motorcycle/car US$2/1/4/6/18) links the port of Puntarenas with Playa Naranjo four times daily. The **Ferry Naviera Tambor** (☎2661-2084; www.navieratambor.com; adult/child/bicycle/motorcycle/car US$1.65/1/4.50/7/23) travels between Puntarenas and Paquera every two hours, for a bus connection to Montezuma.

➜ On the Golfo Dulce a daily passenger ferry links Golfito with Puerto Jiménez on the Península de Osa, and a weekday water taxi travels to and from Playa Zancudo. On the other side of the Península de Osa, water taxis connect Bahía Drake with Sierpe.

➜ On the Caribbean coast there is a bus and boat service that runs several times a day, linking Cariari and Tortuguero, while another links Parismina and Siquirres.

➡ Boats ply the canals that run along the coast from Moín to Tortuguero, although no regular service exists. A daily water taxi connects Puerto Viejo de Sarapiquí with Trinidad on the Río San Juan. The San Juan is Nicaraguan territory, so take your passport. You can try to arrange boat transportation for Barra del Colorado in any of these towns.

Bus

Local Buses

➡ Local buses are a cheap and reliable way of getting around Costa Rica. The longest domestic journey out of San José costs less than US$20.

➡ San José is the transportation center for the country, though there is no central terminal. Bus offices are scattered around the city: some large bus companies have big terminals that sell tickets in advance, while others have little more than a stop – sometimes unmarked.

➡ Buses can be very crowded but don't usually pass up passengers on account of being too full. Note that there are no buses from Thursday to Saturday before Easter Sunday.

➡ There are two types of bus: *directo* and *colectivo*. The *directo* buses should go from one destination to the next with few stops; the *colectivos* make more stops and are very slow going.

➡ Trips longer than four hours usually include a rest stop as buses do not have toilets.

➡ Space is limited on board, so if you have to check luggage be watchful. Theft from overhead racks is rampant, though it's much less common than in other Central American countries.

➡ Bus schedules fluctuate wildly, so always confirm the time when you buy your ticket. If you are catching a bus that picks you up somewhere along a road, get to the roadside early.

➡ For information on departures from San José, pay a visit to the **Instituto Costarricense de Turismo** (ICT; Map p72; ☎2222-1090, in USA & Canada 866-267-8274; www.visitcostarica.com; Edificio de las Academias, Av Central btwn Calles 1 & 3; ☉9am-5pm Mon-Fri) office to pick up the reasonably up-to-date copy of the master schedule, which is also available online at www.visitcostarica.com.

Shuttle Buses

The tourist-van shuttle services (aka gringo buses) are an alternative to the standard intercity buses. Shuttles are provided by **Grayline** (☎2220-2126; www.graylinecostarica.com) and **Interbus** (☎2283-5573; www.interbusonline.com). Both companies run overland transportation from San José to the most popular destinations, as well as directly between other destinations (see the websites for the comprehensive list). These

services will pick you up at your hotel, and reservations can be made online, or through local travel agencies and hotel owners.

Car & Motorcycle

➡ Drivers in Costa Rica are required to have a valid driving license from their home country. Many places will also accept an International Driving Permit (IDP), issued by the automobile association in your country of origin. After 90 days, however, you will need to get a Costa Rican driver's license.

➡ Gasoline (petrol) and diesel are widely available, and 24-hour service stations are along the Interamericana. At the time of writing, fuel prices averaged US$1.25 per liter.

➡ In more remote areas, fuel will be more expensive and might be sold at the neighborhood *pulpería* (corner store).

➡ Spare parts may be hard to find, especially for vehicles with sophisticated electronics and emissions-control systems.

FLAT-TIRE SCAM

For years Aeropuerto Internacional Juan Santamaría has suffered from a scam involving sudden flat tires on rental cars. Many readers have reported similar incidents and it is commonly reported, but it continues to happen.

It goes like this: after you pick up a rental car and drive out of the city, the car gets a flat; as you pull over to fix it, the disabled vehicle is approached by a group of locals, ostensibly to help. There is inevitably some confusion with the changing of the tire, and in the commotion you are relieved of your wallet, luggage or other valuables.

This incident has happened enough times to suggest that travelers should be very wary – and aware – if somebody pulls over to help after they get a flat on a recently rented car. Keep your wallet and passport on your person whenever you get out of a car.

Hire & Insurance

➔ There are car-rental agencies in San José and in popular tourist destinations on the Pacific coast.

➔ All of the major international car-rental agencies have outlets in Costa Rica, though you can sometimes get better deals from local companies.

➔ Due to road conditions, it is necessary to invest in a 4WD unless travel is limited only to the Interamericana.

➔ Many agencies will insist on 4WD in the rainy season, when driving through rivers is a matter of course.

➔ To rent a car you need a valid driver's license, a major credit card and a passport. The minimum age for car rental is 21 years.

➔ Carefully inspect rented cars for minor damage and make sure that any damage is noted on the rental agreement. If your car breaks down, call the rental company. Don't attempt to get the car fixed yourself as most companies won't reimburse expenses without prior authorization.

➔ Prices vary considerably, but on average you can expect to pay over US$200 per week for a standard SUV, including *kilometraje libre* (unlimited mileage). Economy cars are much cheaper, as little as US$80 a week. The price of mandatory insurance makes this more expensive, often doubling the rate.

➔ Costa Rican insurance is mandatory, even if you have insurance at home. Expect to pay about US$15 to US$25 per day. Many rental companies won't rent you a car without it. The basic insurance that all drivers must buy is from a government monopoly, the Instituto Nacional de Seguros. This insurance does not cover your rental car at all, only damages to other people, their cars, or property. It is legal to drive only with this insurance, but it can be difficult to negotiate with a rental agency to allow you to drive away with only this minimum standard. Full insurance through the rental agency can be up to US$50 a day.

➔ The roads in Costa Rica are rough and rugged, meaning that minor accidents or car damage are common.

➔ Note that if you pay basic insurance with a gold or platinum credit card, the card company will usually take responsibility for damages to the car, in which case you can forgo the cost of the full insurance. Make sure you verify this with your credit-card company ahead of time.

➔ Most insurance policies do not cover damage caused by flooding or driving through a river, so be aware of the extent of your policy.

➔ Rental rates fluctuate wildly, so shop around. Some agencies offer discounts for extended rentals. Note that rental offices at the airport

DRIVING THROUGH RIVERS

Driving in Costa Rica will likely necessitate a river crossing at some point. Unfortunately, too many travelers have picked up their off-road skills from watching TV, and every season Ticos (residents of Costa Rica) get a good chuckle out of the number of dead vehicles they help wayward travelers fish out of waterways.

If you're driving through water, follow the rules below:

➔ **Only do this in a 4WD** Don't drive through a river in a car. (It may seem ridiculous to have to say this, but it's done all the time.) Getting out of a steep, gravel riverbed requires a 4WD. Besides, car engines flood very easily.

➔ **Check the depth of the water before driving through** To accommodate an average rental 4WD, the water should be no deeper than above the knee. In a sturdier vehicle (Toyota 4Runner or equivalent), water can be waist deep.

➔ **The water should be calm** If the river is gushing so that there are white crests on the water, do not try to cross. Not only will the force of the water flood the engine, it could sweep the car away.

➔ **Drive very, very slowly** The pressure of driving through a river too quickly will send the water right into the engine and will impair the electrical system. Keep steady pressure on the accelerator so that the tailpipe doesn't fill with water, but go slowly.

➔ **Err on the side of caution** Car-rental agencies in Costa Rica do not insure for water damage, so ruining a car in a river can come at an extremely high cost.

charge a 12% fee in addition to regular rates.

➡ Thieves can easily recognize rental cars. Never leave anything in sight in a parked car – nothing! – and remove all luggage from the trunk overnight. If possible, park the car in a guarded parking lot rather than on the street.

➡ Motorcycles (including Harleys) can be rented in San José and Escazú.

Road Conditions & Hazards

➡ The quality of roads varies from the quite smoothly paved Interamericana to the barely passable rural back roads. Any can suffer from landslides, sudden flooding and fog.

➡ Most roads are single lane and winding, lacking hard shoulders; others are dirt-and-mud affairs that climb mountains and traverse rivers.

➡ Drive defensively and expect a variety of obstructions in the roadway – from cyclists and pedestrians to broken-down cars and cattle. Unsigned speed bumps are placed on some stretches of road without warning

➡ Roads around major tourist areas are adequately marked; all others are not.

➡ Always ask about road conditions before setting out, especially in the rainy season – a number of roads become impassable during this time.

Road Rules

➡ There are speed limits of 100km/h or less on all primary roads and 60km/h or less on secondary roads.

➡ Traffic police use radar, and speed limits are enforced with speeding tickets.

USING TAXIS IN REMOTE AREAS

Taxis are considered a form of public transportation in remote areas. They can be hired by the hour, half-day or full day, or you can arrange a flat fee for a trip. Meters are not used on long trips, so arrange the fare ahead of time. Fares can fluctuate due to worse-than-expected road conditions and bad weather in tough-to-reach places.

The condition of taxis varies from basic sedans held together by rust to fully equipped 4WDs with air-con. In some cases, taxis are pick-up trucks with seats built into the back. Most towns will have at least one licensed taxi, but in some remote villages you may have to get rides from whomever is offering – ask at *pulperías* (corner stores).

➡ Tickets are issued to drivers operating vehicles without a seat belt.

➡ It's illegal to stop in an intersection or make a right turn on a red.

➡ At unmarked intersections, yield to the car on your right.

➡ Drive on the right. Passing is allowed only on the left.

➡ If you are issued with a ticket, you have to pay the fine at a bank; instructions are given on the ticket. If you are driving a rental car, the rental company may be able to arrange your payment for you – the amount of the fine should be on the ticket. A portion of the money from these fines goes to a children's charity.

➡ Police have no right to ask for money, and they shouldn't confiscate a car, unless the driver cannot produce a license and ownership papers, the car lacks license plates, the driver is drunk or the driver has been involved in an accident causing serious injury.

➡ If you are driving and see oncoming cars with headlights flashing, it often means that there is a road problem or a radar speed trap ahead. Slow down immediately.

Hitchhiking

Hitchhiking is never entirely safe in any country and Lonely Planet doesn't recommend it. Travelers who hitchhike should understand that they are taking a small but potentially serious risk. People who do hitchhike will be safer if they travel in pairs and let someone know where they are planning to go. Solo women should use even greater caution.

Hitchhiking in Costa Rica is unusual on main roads that have frequent buses. On minor rural roads, hitchhiking is more common. To get picked up, most locals wave down passing cars. If you get a ride, offer to pay when you arrive by saying '¿Cuánto le debo?' (How much do I owe you?). Your offer may be waved aside, or you may be asked to help with money for gas.

Local Transportation

Bus

Local buses operate chiefly in San José, Puntarenas, San Isidro de El General, Golfito and Puerto Limón, connecting urban and suburban areas. Most local buses pick up passengers on the street and on main roads. For years, these buses were converted school buses imported from the USA, but they have slowly been upgraded and now include coaches.

Taxi

In San José taxis have meters, called *marías*. Note that it is illegal for a driver not to use the meter. Outside of San José, however, most taxis don't have meters and fares tend to be agreed upon in advance. Bargaining is quite acceptable.

In some towns there are *colectivos* (taxis that several passengers are able to share). Although *colectivos* are becoming increasingly difficult to find, the basic principle is that the driver charges a flat fee (usually about US$0.50) to take passengers from one end of town to the other. In rural areas, 4WDs are often used as taxis and are a popular means for surfers (and their boards) to travel from their accommodations to the break. Prices vary wildly depending on how touristy the area is, though generally speaking a 10-minute ride costs between US$5 and US$15.

Taxi drivers are not normally tipped unless they assist with your luggage or have provided an above-average service.

Language

Spanish pronunciation is easy, as most sounds have equivalents in English. Also, Spanish spelling is phonetically consistent, meaning that there's a clear and consistent relationship between what you see in writing and how it's pronounced. If you read our colored pronunciation guides as if they were English, you'll be understood. Note that kh is a throaty sound (like the 'ch' in the Scottish *loch*), v and b are like a soft English 'v' (between a 'v' and a 'b'), and r is strongly rolled. The stressed syllables are in italics in our pronunciation guides.

The polite form is used in this chapter; where both polite and informal options are given, they are indicated by the abbreviations 'pol' and 'inf'. Where necessary, both masculine and feminine forms of words are included, separated by a slash and with the masculine form first, eg *perdido/a* (m/f).

BASICS

Hello.	*Hola.*	o·la
Goodbye.	*Adiós.*	a·dyos
How are you?	*¿Cómo va?* (pol)	ko·mo va
	¿Cómo vas? (inf)	ko·mo vas
Fine, thanks.	*Bien, gracias.*	byen gra·syas
Excuse me.	*Con permiso.*	kon per·mee·so
Sorry.	*Perdón.*	per·don
Please.	*Por favor.*	por fa·vor

WANT MORE?

For in-depth language information and handy phrases, check out Lonely Planet's *Costa Rican Spanish Phrasebook*. You'll find it at **shop.lonelyplanet.com**, or you can buy Lonely Planet's iPhone phrasebooks at the Apple App Store.

Thank you.	*Gracias.*	gra·syas
You're welcome.	*Con mucho gusto.*	kon moo·cho goo·sto
Yes.	*Sí.*	see
No.	*No.*	no

My name is ...
Me llamo ...   me ya·mo ...

What's your name?
¿Cómo se llama Usted?   ko·mo se ya·ma oo·ste (pol)
¿Cómo te llamas?   ko·mo te ya·mas (inf)

Do you speak English?
¿Habla inglés?   a·bla een·gles (pol)
¿Hablas inglés?   a·blas een·gles (inf)

I don't understand.
Yo no entiendo.   yo no en·tyen·do

ACCOMMODATIONS

Do you have a ... room?	*Tiene una habitación ...?*	tye·ne oo·na a·bee·ta·syon ...
single	*sencilla*	sen·see·ya
double	*doble*	do·ble

How much is it per night/person?
¿Cuánto es por noche/persona?   kwan·to es por no·che/per·so·na

Is breakfast included?
¿Incluye el desayuno?   een·kloo·ye el de·sa·yoo·no

campsite	*área para acampar*	a·re·a pa·ra a·kam·par
hotel	*hotel*	o·tel
hostel	*hospedaje*	os·pe·da·khe
guesthouse	*casa de huéspedes*	ka·sa de wes·pe·des
youth hostel	*albergue juvenil*	al·ber·ge khoo·ve·neel

TIQUISMOS

These colloquialisms and slang terms (*tiquismos*) are frequently heard, and are for the most part used only in Costa Rica.

¡Adiós! – Hi! (used when passing a friend in the street, or anyone in remote rural areas; also means 'Farewell!' but only when leaving for a long time)

bomba – gas station

buena nota – OK/excellent (literally 'good note')

chapulines – a gang, usually of young thieves

chunche – thing (can refer to almost anything)

cien metros – one city block

¿Hay campo? – Is there space? (on a bus)

machita – blonde woman (slang)

mae – buddy (pronounced 'ma' as in 'mat' followed with a quick 'eh'; it's mainly used by boys and young men)

mi amor – my love (used as a familiar form of address by both men and women)

pulpería – corner grocery store

¡Pura vida! – Super! (literally 'pure life,' also an expression of approval or even a greeting)

sabanero – cowboy, especially one who hails from Guanacaste Province

salado – too bad; tough luck

soda – cafe or lunch counter

¡Tuanis! – Cool!

¡Upe! – Is anybody home? (used mainly in rural areas at people's homes, instead of knocking)

vos – you (singular and informal, same as *tú*)

air-con	*aire acondicionado*	ai·re a·kon·dee·syo·na·do
bathroom	*baño*	ba·nyo
bed	*cama*	ka·ma
window	*ventana*	ven·ta·na

DIRECTIONS

Where's ...?
¿Adónde está ...? — a·don·de es·ta ...

What's the address?
¿Cuál es la dirección? — kwal es la dee·rek·syon

Could you please write it down?
¿Podría escribirlo? — po·dree·a es·kree·beer·lo

Can you show me (on the map)?
¿Me puede enseñar (en el mapa)? — me pwe·de en·se·nyar (en el ma·pa)

at the corner	*en la esquina*	en la es·kee·na
at the traffic lights	*en el semáforo*	en el se·ma·fo·ro
behind ...	*detrás de ...*	de·tras de ...
far	*lejos*	le·khos
in front of ...	*en frente de ...*	en fren·te de ...
left	*a la izquierda*	a la ees·kyer·da
near	*cerca*	ser·ka
next to ...	*a la par de ...*	a la par de ...
opposite ...	*opuesto a ...*	o·pwes·to a ...
right	*a la derecha*	a la de·re·cha
straight ahead	*aquí directo*	a·kee dee·rek·to

EATING & DRINKING

Can I see the menu, please?
¿Puedo ver el menú, por favor? — pwe·do ver el me·noo por fa·vor

What would you recommend?
¿Qué me recomienda? — ke me re·ko·myen·da

Do you have vegetarian food?
¿Tienen comida vegetariana? — tye·nen ko·mee·da ve·khe·ta·rya·na

I don't eat (red meat).
No como (carne roja). — no ko·mo (kar·ne ro·kha)

That was delicious!
¡Estuvo delicioso! — es·too·vo de·lee·syo·so

Cheers!
¡Salud! — sa·lood

The bill, please.
La cuenta, por favor. — la kwen·ta por fa·vor

I'd like a table for ...	*Quisiera una mesa para ...*	kee·sye·ra oo·na me·sa pa·ra ...
(eight) o'clock	*las (ocho)*	las (o·cho)
(two) people	*(dos) personas*	(dos) per·so·nas

Key Words

appetisers	*aperitivos*	a·pe·ree·tee·vos
bar	*bar*	bar
bottle	*botella*	bo·te·ya
bowl	*plato hondo*	pla·to on·do
breakfast	*desayuno*	de·sa·yoo·no
cafe	*café*	ka·fe
(too) cold	*(muy) frío*	(mooy) free·o
dinner	*cena*	se·na

food	comida	ko·mee·da
fork	tenedor	te·ne·dor
glass	vaso	va·so
hot (warm)	caliente	kal·yen·te
knife	cuchillo	koo·chee·yo
lunch	almuerzo	al·mwer·so
main course	plato fuerte	pla·to fwer·te
market	mercado	mer·ka·do
menu	menú	me·noo
plate	plato	pla·to
restaurant	restaurante	res·tow·ran·te
spoon	cuchara	koo·cha·ra
supermarket	supermercado	soo·per·mer·ka·do
with/without	con/sin	kon/seen

Meat & Fish

beef	carne de vaca	kar·ne de va·ka
chicken	pollo	po·yo
duck	pato	pa·to
fish	pescado	pes·ka·do
lamb	cordero	kor·de·ro
pork	cerdo	ser·do
turkey	pavo	pa·vo
veal	ternera	ter·ne·ra

Fruit & Vegetables

apple	manzana	man·sa·na
apricot	albaricoque	al·ba·ree·ko·ke
asparagus	espárragos	es·pa·ra·gos
banana	banano	ba·na·no
bean	frijol	free·khol
cabbage	repollo	re·po·yo
carrot	zanahoria	sa·na·o·rya
cherry	cereza	se·re·sa
corn	maíz	ma·ees
cucumber	pepino	pe·pee·no
fruit	fruta	froo·ta
grapes	uvas	oo·vas
lemon	limón	lee·mon
lentils	lentejas	len·te·khas
lettuce	lechuga	le·choo·ga
mushroom	hongo	on·go
nuts	nueces	nwe·ses
onion	cebolla	se·bo·ya
orange	naranja	na·ran·kha
peach	melocotón	me·lo·ko·ton
pea	petipoa	pe·tee·po·a

pepper (bell)	pimentón	pee·men·ton
pineapple	piña	pee·nya
plum	ciruela	seer·we·la
potato	papa	pa·pa
pumpkin	calabaza	ka·la·ba·sa
spinach	espinaca	es·pee·na·ka
strawberry	fresa	fre·sa
tomato	tomate	to·ma·te
vegetable	vegetal	ve·khe·tal
watermelon	sandía	san·dee·a

Other

bread	pan	pan
butter	mantequilla	man·te·kee·ya
cheese	queso	ke·so
egg	huevo	we·vo
honey	miel	myel
jam	jalea	kha·le·a
oil	aceite	a·sey·te
pastry	pastel	pas·tel
pepper	pimienta	pee·myen·ta
rice	arroz	a·ros
salt	sal	sal
sugar	azúcar	a·soo·kar
vinegar	vinagre	vee·na·gre

Drinks

beer	cerveza	ser·ve·sa
coffee	café	ka·fe
(orange) juice	jugo (de naranja)	khoo·go (de na·ran·kha)
milk	leche	le·che
tea	té	te
(mineral) water	agua (mineral)	a·gwa (mee·ne·ral)
(red/white) wine	vino (tinto/ blanco)	vee·no (teen·to/ blan·ko)

SIGNS	
Abierto	Open
Cerrado	Closed
Entrada	Entrance
Hombres/Varones	Men
Mujeres/Damas	Women
Prohibido	Prohibited
Salida	Exit
Servicios/Baños	Toilets

EMERGENCIES

Help!	¡Socorro!	so·ko·ro
Go away!	¡Váyase!	va·ya·se

Call ...!	¡Llame a ...!	ya·me a ...
a doctor	un doctor	oon dok·tor
the police	la policía	la po·lee·see·a

I'm lost.
Estoy perdido/a.   es·toy per·dee·do/a (m/f)

I'm ill.
Estoy enfermo/a.   es·toy en·fer·mo/a (m/f)

It hurts here.
Me duele aquí.   me dwe·le a·kee

I'm allergic to (antibiotics).
Soy alérgico/a a   soy a·ler·khee·ko/a a
(los antibióticos).   (los an·tee·byo·tee·kos) (m/f)

Where are the toilets?
¿Dónde está el   don·de es·ta el
baño?   ba·nyo

SHOPPING & SERVICES

I'd like to buy ...
Quiero comprar ...   kye·ro kom·prar ...

I'm just looking.
Sólo estoy viendo.   so·lo es·toy vyen·do

Can I look at it?
¿Lo puedo ver?   lo pwe·do ver

How much is it?
¿Cuánto cuesta?   kwan·to kwes·ta

That's too expensive.
Está muy caro.   es·ta mooy ka·ro

Can you lower the price?
¿Podría bajarle   po·dree·a ba·khar·le
el precio?   el pre·syo

There's a mistake in the bill.
Hay un error   ai oon e·ror
en la cuenta.   en la kwen·ta

ATM	cajero automático	ka·khe·ro ow·to·ma·tee·ko
credit card	tarjeta de crédito	tar·khe·ta de kre·dee·to

QUESTION WORDS

How?	¿Cómo?	ko·mo
What?	¿Qué?	ke
When?	¿Cuándo?	kwan·do
Where?	¿Dónde?	don·de
Who?	¿Quién?	kyen
Why?	¿Por qué?	por ke

market	mercado	mer·ka·do
post office	correo	ko·re·o
tourist office	oficina de turismo	o·fee·see·na de too·rees·mo

TIME & DATES

What time is it?	¿Qué hora es?	ke o·ra es
It's (10) o'clock.	Son (las diez).	son (las dyes)
It's half past (one).	Es (la una) y media.	es (la oo·na) ee me·dya

morning	mañana	ma·nya·na
afternoon	tarde	tar·de
evening	noche	no·che
yesterday	ayer	a·yer
today	hoy	oy
tomorrow	mañana	ma·nya·na

Monday	lunes	loo·nes
Tuesday	martes	mar·tes
Wednesday	miércoles	myer·ko·les
Thursday	jueves	khwe·ves
Friday	viernes	vyer·nes
Saturday	sábado	sa·ba·do
Sunday	domingo	do·meen·go

January	enero	e·ne·ro
February	febrero	fe·bre·ro
March	marzo	mar·so
April	abril	a·breel
May	mayo	ma·yo
June	junio	khoon·yo
July	julio	khool·yo
August	agosto	a·gos·to
September	septiembre	sep·tyem·bre
October	octubre	ok·too·bre
November	noviembre	no·vyem·bre
December	diciembre	dee·syem·bre

TRANSPORTATION

boat	barco	bar·ko
bus	bús	boos
plane	avión	a·vyon
train	tren	tren

first	primero	pree·me·ro
last	último	ool·tee·mo
next	próximo	prok·see·mo

A ... ticket, please.	*Un pasaje de ..., por favor.*	oon pa·sa·khe de ... por fa·vor
1st-class	*primera clase*	pree·me·ra kla·se
2nd-class	*segunda clase*	se·goon·da kla·se
one-way	*ida*	ee·da
return	*ida y vuelta*	ee·da ee vwel·ta

I want to go to ...
Quisiera ir a ... kee·sye·ra eer a ...

Does it stop at ...?
¿Hace parada en ...? a·se pa·ra·da en ...

What stop is this?
¿Cuál es esta parada? kwal es es·ta pa·ra·da

What time does it arrive/leave?
¿A qué hora llega/ sale? a ke o·ra ye·ga/ sa·le

Please tell me when we get to ...
Por favor, avíseme cuando lleguemos a ... por fa·vor a·vee·se·me kwan·do ye·ge·mos a ...

I want to get off here.
Quiero bajarme aquí. kye·ro ba·khar·me a·kee

airport	*aeropuerto*	a·e·ro·pwer·to
aisle seat	*asiento de pasillo*	a·syen·to de pa·see·yo
bus stop	*parada de autobuses*	pa·ra·da de ow·to·boo·ses
cancelled	*cancelado*	kan·se·la·do
delayed	*atrasado*	a·tra·sa·do
platform	*plataforma*	pla·ta·for·ma
ticket office	*taquilla*	ta·kee·ya
timetable	*horario*	o·ra·ryo
train station	*estación de trenes*	es·ta·syon de tre·nes
window seat	*asiento junto a la ventana*	a·syen·to khoon·to a la ven·ta·na

I'd like to hire a ...	*Quiero alquilar ...*	kye·ro al·kee·lar ...
4WD	*un cuatro por cuatro*	oon kwa·tro por kwa·tro
bicycle	*una bicicleta*	oo·na bee·see·kle·ta
car	*un carro*	oon ka·ro
motorcycle	*una motocicleta*	oo·na mo·to· see·kle·ta

NUMBERS

1	*uno*	oo·no
2	*dos*	dos
3	*tres*	tres
4	*cuatro*	kwa·tro
5	*cinco*	seen·ko
6	*seis*	seys
7	*siete*	sye·te
8	*ocho*	o·cho
9	*nueve*	nwe·ve
10	*diez*	dyes
20	*veinte*	veyn·te
30	*treinta*	treyn·ta
40	*cuarenta*	kwa·ren·ta
50	*cincuenta*	seen·kwen·ta
60	*sesenta*	se·sen·ta
70	*setenta*	se·ten·ta
80	*ochenta*	o·chen·ta
90	*noventa*	no·ven·ta
100	*cien*	syen
1000	*mil*	meel

child seat	*asiento de seguridad para niños*	a·syen·to de se·goo·ree·da pa·ra nee·nyos
diesel	*diesel*	dee·sel
helmet	*casco*	kas·ko
mechanic	*mecánico*	me·ka·noo·ko
petrol/gas	*gasolina*	ga·so·lee·na
service station	*bomba*	bom·ba
truck	*camión*	ka·myon

Is this the road to ...?
¿Por aquí se va a ...? por a·kee se va a ...

(How long) Can I park here?
¿(Cuánto tiempo) Puedo parquear aquí? (kwan·to tyem·po) pwe·do par·ke·ar a·kee

The car has broken down (at ...).
El carro se varó en ... el ka·ro se va·ro en ...

I've had an accident.
Tuve un accidente. too·ve oon ak·see·den·te

I've run out of petrol.
Me quedé sin gasolina. me ke·de seen ga·so·lee·na

I have a flat tyre.
Se me estalló una llanta. se me es·ta·yo oo·na yan·ta

GLOSSARY

adiós – means 'goodbye' universally, but used as a greeting in rural Costa Rica

alquiler de automóviles – car rental

apartado – post-office box (abbreviated 'Apdo')

artesanía – handicrafts

ATH – *a toda hora* (open all hours); used to denote ATMs

automóvil – car

avenida – avenue

avión – airplane

bahía – bay

barrio – district or neighborhood

biblioteca – library

bomba – short, funny verse; also means 'gas station' and 'bomb'

bosque – forest

bosque nuboso – cloud forest

buena nota – excellent, OK; literally 'good note'

caballo – horse

cabaña – cabin; see also *cabina*

cabina – cabin; see also *cabaña*

cajero automático – ATM

calle – street

cama, cama matrimonial – bed, double bed

campesino – peasant, farmer or person who works in agriculture

carreta – colorfully painted wooden oxcart, now a form of folk art

carretera – road

casado – inexpensive set meal; also means 'married'

casita – cottage or apartment

catedral – cathedral

caverna – cave; see also *cueva*

cerro – mountain or hill

Chepe – affectionate nickname for José; also used when referring to San José

cine – cinema

ciudad – city

cocina – kitchen or cooking

colectivo – bus, minivan or car operating as shared taxi

colibrí – hummingbird

colina – hill

colón – Costa Rican unit of currency; plural *colones*

cordillera – mountain range

correo – mail service

Costarricense – Costa Rican; see also Tico/a

cruce – crossing

cruda – often used to describe a hangover; literally 'raw'

cueva – cave; see also *caverna*

culebra – snake; see also *serpiente*

Dios – God

directo – direct; refers to long-distance bus with few stops

edificio – building

estación – station, eg ranger station or bus station; also means 'season'

farmacia – pharmacy

fauna silvestre – wildlife

fiesta – party or festival

finca – farm or plantation

floresta – forest

frontera – border

fútbol – soccer (football)

garza – cattle egret

gasolina – gas (petrol)

gracias – thanks

gringo/a (m/f) – US or European visitor; can be affectionate or insulting, depending on the tone used

hacienda – rural estate

hielo – ice

ICT – Instituto Costarricense de Turismo; Costa Rica Tourism Board

iglesia – church

indígena – indigenous

Interamericana – Pan-American Hwy; the nearly continuous highway running from Alaska to Chile (it breaks at the Darién Gap between Panama and Colombia)

invierno – winter; the rainy season in Costa Rica

isla – island

jardín – garden

josefino/a (m/f) – resident of San José

lago – lake

lavandería – laundry facility, usually offering dry-cleaning services

librería – bookstore

llanura – tropical plain

machismo – an exaggerated sense of masculine pride

macho – literally 'male'; figuratively also 'masculine,' 'tough.' In Costa Rica macho/a (m/f) also means 'blonde.'

maría – local name for taxi meter

mercado – market

mercado central – central town market

Meseta Central – Central Valley or central plateau

mestizo/a (m/f) – person of mixed descent, usually Spanish and indigenous

metate – flat stone platform, used by Costa Rica's pre-Columbian populations to grind corn

migración – immigration

Minae – Ministerio de Ambiente y Energía; Ministry of Environment and Energy, in charge of the national park system

mirador – lookout point

mole – rich chocolate sauce

mono – monkey

mono tití – squirrel monkey

motocicleta – motorcycle

muelle – dock

museo – museum

niño – child

normal – refers to long-distance bus with many stops

obeah – sorcery rituals of African origin

ola(s) – wave(s)

OTS – Organization for Tropical Studies

pájaro – bird

palapa – shelter with a thatched, palm-leaf roof and open sides

palenque indigenous settlement

páramo – habitat with by highland shrub and tussock grass

parque – park

parque central – central town square or plaza

parque nacional – national park

perezoso – sloth

perico – mealy parrot

playa – beach

posada – country-style inn or guesthouse

puente – bridge

puerto – port

pulpería – corner grocery store

punta – point

pura vida – super; literally 'pure life'

quebrada – stream

rana – frog or toad

rancho – small house or house-like building

río – river

sabanero – cowboy from Guanacaste

selva – jungle

Semana Santa the Christian Holy Week that precedes Easter

sendero – trail or path

serpiente – snake

Sinac – Sistema Nacional de Areas de Conservación; National System of Conservation Areas

supermercado – supermarket

telenovela – Spanish-language soap opera

Tico/a (m/f) – Costa Rican; see also *Costarricense*

tienda – store

tiquismos – typical Costa Rican expressions or slang

tortuga – turtle

valle – valley

verano – summer; the dry season in Costa Rica

volcán – volcano

zoológico – zoo

Food Glossary

a la plancha – grilled or pan-fried

agua – water

agua de sapo – literally 'toad water', a lemonade made with fresh ginger and brown sugar

agua dulce – sugarcane juice

aguacate – avocado

almuerzo – lunch

almuerzo ejecutivo – literally 'executive lunch'; a more expensive version of a set meal or casado

arroz – rice

batido – fruit shake made with milk or water

bocas – small savory dishes served in bars; tapas

café – coffee

camaron – shrimp

carambola – starfruit

cas – a type of tart guava

casado – inexpensive set meal; also means 'married'

cena – dinner

cerveza – beer; also known as birra

ceviche – seafood marinated in lemon or lime juice, garlic and seasonings

chan – drink made from chia seeds

chuleta – pork chop

comida típica – typical local food

desayuno – breakfast

dorado – mahi-mahi

empanada – savory turnover stuffed with meat or cheese

ensalada – salad

frito – fried

gallo pinto – stir-fry of rice and beans

guanabana – soursop or cherimoya

guaro – local firewater made from sugarcane

leche – milk

linaza – drink made from flaxseeds

lomito – fillet; tenderloin

macrobiótica – health-food store

maracuya – passionfruit

mariscos – seafood

melón – cantaloupe

mora – blackberry

natilla – sour cream

olla de carne – beef stew

palmito – heart of palm

pargo – red snapper

pan – bread

pan tostada – toast

panadería – bakery

pastelería – pastry shop

patacones – twice-fried green plantains

patí – Caribbean version of empanada

pescado – fish

piña – pineapple

pipa – young green coconut; harvested for refreshing coconut water

plátanos maduros – ripe plantain cut in slices lengthwise and baked or broiled with butter, brown sugar and cinnamon

pollo – chicken

queso – cheese

resbladera – sweet barley and rice drink

ron – rum

rondón – seafood gumbo

Salsa Lizano – Costa Rican version of Worcestershire sauce; a key ingredient in gallo pinto

sandía – watermelon

soda – informal lunch counter or inexpensive eatery

tamarindo – fruit of the tamarind tree

tapa de dulce – brown sugar

vino – wine

Behind the Scenes

SEND US YOUR FEEDBACK

We love to hear from travelers – your comments keep us on our toes and help make our books better. Our well-traveled team reads every word on what you loved or loathed about this book. Although we cannot reply individually to postal submissions, we always guarantee that your feedback goes straight to the appropriate authors, in time for the next edition. Each person who sends us information is thanked in the next edition – the most useful submissions are rewarded with a selection of digital PDF chapters.

Visit **lonelyplanet.com/contact** to submit your updates and suggestions or to ask for help. Our award-winning website also features inspirational travel stories, news and discussions.

Note: We may edit, reproduce and incorporate your comments in Lonely Planet products such as guidebooks, websites and digital products, so let us know if you don't want your comments reproduced or your name acknowledged. For a copy of our privacy policy visit lonelyplanet.com/privacy.

OUR READERS

Many thanks to the travelers who used the last edition and wrote to us with helpful hints, useful advice and interesting anecdotes:
Cayla Damick, Dan Allen, David Wingo, Donna Harshman, Duncan Smith, Enrico Mezzato, Fanny Wiedmer, Frances Pordes, Jennifer Covington, Juliette Giannesini, Jurgen van de Vijver, Luise Winkler, Nan Oomes, Paola Brighenti, Paul de lange, Sarah Hatherell, Sonia Rodrigue, Stefano Mezzato and Ville Ekman

AUTHOR THANKS

Wendy Yanagihara

I wish to acknowledge some amazing staff at Lonely Planet with whom I've had the pleasure of working, who have since departed, and who are greatly missed. Catherine, Kathleen and Bruce laid the groundwork for this book. Special thanks in Costa Rica go to Corey, Chapu, Bob, Monique and Marcel, Kathleen, rangers Herold and Roger, Yolanda and Manuel. *Abrazos* to Chris for traveling all the way from the Middle East to Central America, and to my superstar support system in Carp.

Gregor Clark

Muchísimas gracias to the countless people who shared their knowledge, especially Daryl and Lydia in Tortuguero, Sara and Toine in Orosi, Lis in Turrialba, José and David at La Danta Salvaje, Jürgen at Selva Bananito, Fernando vand Sarah in Punta Mona, and Andrés and Brian in San José. *Besos y abrazos* to Meigan and Dr Bwinkle, for adventuring with me from the Caribbean to the volcano-tops, and to Gaen, who always makes coming home the best part of the trip.

Mara Vorhees

Thanks to Catherine Craddock for many years of leadership and cooperation on Central America titles – you will be missed! I am so grateful to my parents for their patient hearts and adventurous spirits. And thank you to my boys, all three of them, for coming along on this amazing journey.

ACKNOWLEDGMENTS

Climate map data adapted from Peel MC, Finlayson BL & McMahon TA (2007) 'Updated World Map of the Köppen-Geiger Climate Classification', Hydrology and Earth System Sciences, 11, 1633¬44.

Cover photograph: Baby three-toed sloth, Mark Kostich/Getty ©

THIS BOOK

This 11th edition of Lonely Planet's Costa Rica guidebook was researched and written by Wendy Yanagihara, Gregor Clark and Mara Vorhees. The previous edition was researched and written by Nate Cavalieri, Adam Skolnick and Wendy Yanagihara.

This guidebook was commissioned in Lonely Planet's Oakland office, and produced by the following:

Commissioning Editors
Catherine Craddock-Carrillo, Kathleen Munnelly

Managing Editor Bruce Evans

Coordinating Editor Sarah Bailey

Product Editor Kate Mathews

Senior Cartographer Mark Griffiths

Book Designer Mazzy Prinsep

Senior Editor Karyn Noble

Assisting Editors Nigel Chin, Charlotte Orr, Gabrielle Stefanos, Ross Taylor

Assisting Cartographers Corey Hutchison, Valentina Kremenchutskaya

Assisting Book Designer Virginia Moreno

Cover Researcher Naomi Parker

Language Content Branislava Vladisavljevic

Thanks to Ljubomir Ceranic, Brendan Dempsey, Elizabeth Jones, Catherine Naghten, Claire Naylor, Martine Power, Eleanor Simpson, Ron Tjoeka, Tracy Whitmey, Amanda Williamson

Index

Map Pages **000**
Photo Pages **000**

Map Legend

Sights

- Beach
- Bird Sanctuary
- Buddhist
- Castle/Palace
- Christian
- Confucian
- Hindu
- Islamic
- Jain
- Jewish
- Monument
- Museum/Gallery/Historic Building
- Ruin
- Sento Hot Baths/Onsen
- Shinto
- Sikh
- Taoist
- Winery/Vineyard
- Zoo/Wildlife Sanctuary
- Other Sight

Activities, Courses & Tours

- Bodysurfing
- Diving
- Canoeing/Kayaking
- Course/Tour
- Skiing
- Snorkeling
- Surfing
- Swimming/Pool
- Walking
- Windsurfing
- Other Activity

Sleeping

- Sleeping
- Camping

Eating

- Eating

Drinking & Nightlife

- Drinking & Nightlife
- Cafe

Entertainment

- Entertainment

Shopping

- Shopping

Information

- Bank
- Embassy/Consulate
- Hospital/Medical
- Internet
- Police
- Post Office
- Telephone
- Toilet
- Tourist Information
- Other Information

Geographic

- Beach
- Hut/Shelter
- Lighthouse
- Lookout
- Mountain/Volcano
- Oasis
- Park
- Pass
- Picnic Area
- Waterfall

Population

- Capital (National)
- Capital (State/Province)
- City/Large Town
- Town/Village

Transport

- Airport
- Border crossing
- Bus
- Cable car/Funicular
- Cycling
- Ferry
- Metro station
- Monorail
- Parking
- Petrol station
- Subway/Subte station
- Taxi
- Train station/Railway
- Tram
- Underground station
- Other Transport

Routes

- Tollway
- Freeway
- Primary
- Secondary
- Tertiary
- Lane
- Unsealed road
- Road under construction
- Plaza/Mall
- Steps
- Tunnel
- Pedestrian overpass
- Walking Tour
- Walking Tour detour
- Path/Walking Trail

Boundaries

- International
- State/Province
- Disputed
- Regional/Suburb
- Marine Park
- Cliff
- Wall

Hydrography

- River, Creek
- Intermittent River
- Canal
- Water
- Dry/Salt/Intermittent Lake
- Reef

Areas

- Airport/Runway
- Beach/Desert
- Cemetery (Christian)
- Cemetery (Other)
- Glacier
- Mudflat
- Park/Forest
- Sight (Building)
- Sportsground
- Swamp/Mangrove

Note: Not all symbols displayed above appear on the maps in this book

OUR STORY

A beat-up old car, a few dollars in the pocket and a sense of adventure. In 1972 that's all Tony and Maureen Wheeler needed for the trip of a lifetime – across Europe and Asia overland to Australia. It took several months, and at the end – broke but inspired – they sat at their kitchen table writing and stapling together their first travel guide, *Across Asia on the Cheap*. Within a week they'd sold 1500 copies. Lonely Planet was born.

Today, Lonely Planet has offices in Franklin, London, Melbourne, Oakland, Beijing and Delhi, with more than 600 staff and writers. We share Tony's belief that 'a great guidebook should do three things: inform, educate and amuse'.

OUR WRITERS

Wendy Yanagihara

Coordinating author, Central Pacific Coast, Southern Costa Rica & Península de Osa Wendy Yanagihara first ventured to Costa Rica in 1996 and couldn't wait to get back...until she was distracted by Southeast Asia. Ten years later, she went on her first research trip to the land of *pura vida* and has been covering it since. She has explored Costa Rica from border to border and coast to coast as well as contributing to over 20 guides for Lonely Planet, including *Japan*, *Vietnam*, *Mexico* and *Grand Canyon National Park*. As it tends to do, Costa Rica has helped transform her into a budding birder, better sloth-spotter, still-terrible surfer (who sticks to the bunny breaks) and improviser of California-style *gallo pinto*.

Gregor Clark

San José, Central Valley & Highlands, Caribbean Coast On his first Costa Rican adventure in 1997, Gregor made a beeline for Corcovado National Park, where he so thoroughly enjoyed hiking and camping that he returned with his fiancée (now wife) the next year. Highlights of researching this guide included discovering off-the-beaten track destinations such as La Danta Salvaje and Volcan Turrialba Lodge with his nature-loving family, and seeing his first quetzal in the company of daughter Meigan Quetzal Clark. Gregor contributes regularly to Lonely Planet's Latin American and European guides.

Read more about Gregor at:
lonelyplanet.com/thorntree/profiles/gregorclark

Mara Vorhees

Northwestern Costa Rica, Arenal & Northern Lowlands, Península de Nicoya In 18 years of travel to Costa Rica, Mara has spotted 156 species of birds, all four New-World monkeys, anteaters, sloths and tapirs, a kinkajou and a jaguarundi. None of it, she attests, is quite as wild as her four-year-old twins, who accompanied her while hiking, swimming, rafting, birding and horseback-riding around Costa Rica. Mara has written many guidebooks for Lonely Planet, including *Central America on a Shoestring* and *Belize*. When not spying on sloths, she lives in Somerville, Massachusetts with her husband, two kiddies and two kitties. Follow her adventures online at www.havetwinswilltravel.com.

Published by Lonely Planet Publications Pty Ltd
ABN 36 005 607 983
11th edition – October 2014
ISBN 978 1 74220 889 3
© Lonely Planet 2014   Photographs © as indicated 2014
10 9 8 7 6 5 4 3 2 1
Printed in China

Although the authors and Lonely Planet have taken all reasonable care in preparing this book, we make no warranty about the accuracy or completeness of its content and, to the maximum extent permitted, disclaim all liability arising from its use.